READINGS IN THE HISTORY OF WESTERN CIVILIZATION

THOMAS P. NEILL received his M.A. in History from the University of Notre Dame in 1939 and his Ph.D. in History from St. Louis University in 1943. He is at present Professor of History at St. Louis University. Dr. Neill is the author of *Weapons for Peace* (1945), *Makers of the Modern Mind* (1949), *They Lived the Faith: Great Lay Leaders of Modern Times* (1951), and *The Rise and Decline of Liberalism* (1954). He was selected by the National Catholic Educational Association to deliver the Gabriel Richard Lecture in 1951, which was published under the title *Religion and Culture* (1952); recently completed a text on National Problems for the Doubleday Catholic Textbook Series; co-authored, with Dr. Raymond Schmandt, *History of the Catholic Church* (1957), and edited the first volume of *Readings in the History of Western Civilization* (1957). Dr. Neill is a frequent contributor to periodicals and scholarly journals and is a well-known book reviewer.

THE COLLEGE READINGS SERIES, No. 4

Readings in the History of Western Civilization

Selected with Introduction and Commentary

by THOMAS P. NEILL, Ph.D.
The Department of History
Saint Louis University

VOLUME TWO

THE NEWMAN PRESS • WESTMINSTER, MARYLAND

1958

The editor and publisher acknowledge with thanks permission to reprint copyrighted material from Arnold J. Toynbee's *A Study of History,* 10 Vols. (New York: Oxford University Press, 1935, 1939, 1954) in essay 29 of the present work.

Nihil obstat: Edward A. Cerny, S.S., D.D.
Censor Librorum

Imprimatur: Francis P. Keough, D.D.
Archbishop of Baltimore
March 13, 1958

The *nihil obstat* and *imprimatur* are official declarations that a book or pamphlet is free of doctrinal and moral error. No implication is contained therein that those who have granted the *nihil obstat* and *imprimatur* agree with the opinions expressed.

Library of Congress Catalog Card Number: 57-11824
Printed in the United States of America

Preface

This is the second volume of readings designed for the introductory college course in the history of Western Civilization. The first volume treated subjects normally found in the first semester of the course, that is, until about 1648. The topics treated in this volume are usually covered in the second semester of the Western Civilization course. The following selections are not designed to cover the subject matter of the course systematically. They do not replace the textbook. They aim rather to supplement the textbook by analyzing certain subjects that, the editor believes, are inadequately or improperly treated in many widely used textbooks.

The purpose of the following readings, then, is 1) to supplement the text on certain topics that seem important for understanding the history of Western Civilization and the Catholic Church's role in it; and 2) to present scholarly but readable analyses of subjects that are frequently misunderstood by people outside the Church. The authors of the selections are professionally competent scholars accepted by their fellows as good historians. Most of them are Catholics who have achieved a reputation in the history profession; a few are non-Catholics who write with penetrating comprehension of the Church's position on their subject. The immediate purpose of this collection of readings is not apologetic. It is rather to present historical truth to the student and thus enable him to achieve the end of the study of history: the apprehension and comprehension of the past in as full and accurate a measure as possible.

History is called a "social science." This means that its subject matter is man and that it tries to deal with him in scientific rather than rhetorical fashion. Certain norms have been accepted by historians for the ascertaining and verifying of past data, and these norms are scientific in the loose sense of the term. But the putting together of past data to reconstruct past happenings involves personal judgment on the part of the historian which is not and cannot be scientific. For this reason the historian's personal beliefs of a theological, philosophical, and sociological nature play a considerable part in his interpretation of the past. Despite protestations to the contrary by some historians, they all have some idea of the "meaning of history," if only to insist that it has no meaning, and their idea on the meaning of history, their "philosophy of history," enters into the way they explain the past to their students and their readers.

The editor of the present volume believes that many past events can be ascertained with moral certainty, but that the meaning of history is found not in history itself but in the mind of God, which has been partly revealed to man. He also believes that Western Civilization is unique because of the Christianity which has been its principal religion and has done so much to mold its institutions, form its thought, influence its manners, and even prepare the way for such accomplishments as the scientific and technological revolutions. Finally, he believes that man is a free, responsible moral agent, possessed of a rational intelligence which makes him potentially the master of creation. Man's freedom is conditioned by many economic, geographic and other factors, but these conditioning factors do not destroy man's freedom and his ultimate responsibility for his moral acts.

A student is well advised to know the presuppositions his author accepts or, to use the current phrase, "the frame of reference" in which he interprets the past. On the facts of history historians seldom disagree. But on the meaning of the facts, on the reconstruction of the past from the facts, there is frequent disagreement. Each student is obliged to be his own final judge on these matters of interpretations—as all good teachers insist—but first he must consider what expert historians have said, and he must understand why these historians have interpreted past happenings as they have. The following readings are designed to help the student arrive at intelligent, considered judgments on certain controversial subjects within the compass of the history of Western Civilization.

THOMAS P. NEILL

Saint Louis University
SAINT LOUIS, MISSOURI

Contents

Introduction

The Catholic Church has played an anomalous role in modern history. What was originally a revolutionary body has been essentially conservative, on the defensive since the sixteenth century. We can see how anomalous is such a role by considering the Church's twofold message to mankind. Her first message is the good tidings of life everlasting for those who will give up this world. This is primary: the renunciation of the things of this world. But there is a second message—for Christians to go into the world in order to reform it, to eradicate sin and injustice, to build anew so that God's will be done on earth as it is in Heaven.

This second message spells revolution, a turning over of the old institutions, a radical reform of society so as to eliminate every kind of evil. And from the beginning the Church played this revolutionary role in history. Her divine Founder was executed because He was revolutionary, and her early leaders were hunted down as subversive elements in the Roman Empire. Nor did the Church give up her revolutionary role when she became the established Church of the Empire. Throughout the Middle Ages she fostered every kind of intellectual advance. Under her auspices the universities were established, great advances were made in philosophy and theology, daring questions were asked and answered. To put the matter in modern terms, the Church fostered progress, change and advancement throughout the greater part of her history. Pursuing her primary mission, she endeavored to eliminate sin from society and make the city of man resemble the kingdom of God. But at the same time she fostered education, the gaining of new knowledge and the refinement of the old, the cultivation of men's minds and manners, the improvement of tools and techniques.

Throughout modern history, on the other hand, the Church has assumed a conservative role. She has been on the defensive because changes have been initiated by her enemies and they have frequently been directed against her. Thus, through force of circumstances, the Church found herself on the defensive in modern times, the guardian of the *status quo*. And frequently enough Catholics, who came to identify change with the Church's enemies, were driven into the uncomfortable position of opposing new things simply because they were novel and of defending the old simply because they were established. Such a siege mentality is not defendable, of course, but it is understandable and perhaps even excusable in the light of its development.

New religious doctrines were directed against the Church in the sixteenth century. Her authority was repudiated in favor of the private interpretation of God's revelation. Two centuries later deists rejected Christ, and in the last two centuries the very idea of God has been denied by "progressive" agnostics and atheists. Naturally, then, the Church condemned these "new" forms of thought. Naturally too it has condemned the new secularized religions which seek to take the place of Christianity—Socialism, Communism, Nationalism, Fascism, and the others, each with its own god and each demanding the total allegiance of its adherents.

Modern history can be looked at as a long process of secularization, or the withdrawing from God and His representative functions and properties which properly belong to Him, and turning them over to secular institutions. Secularization of thought has proceeded through the centuries until in contemporary times religion has been squeezed into a little corner of man's life or pushed out altogether. This process the Church has consistently opposed, and because the new mode of thought in each generation was a further step in secularization the Church took on the garb of conservatism. All too many Christians tried to prevent further change instead of insisting on a truly radical, Christian revolution.

The process of secularization has also worked out in social, economic, and political life. The French Revolution introduced "new" ideas of liberty and equality, of democracy and nationalism, but at the same time it confiscated Church property, provided for the election of bishops and priests, subjected the Church to government control, and finally abolished it in favor of a worship of Reason. Most people tend to see things in terms of black and white, and it was therefore natural for Catholics to condemn the French Revolution *en bloc* and to oppose the institutions which were born of that revolution. Thus Catholics generally found themselves instinctively opposing the developments of the nineteenth century and defending as good the Old Regime of the eighteenth century, a regime in which the Church had been subjected to the state and made to serve the sovereign's will.

The new way of life developed by the industrial revolution was a more subtle but an equally pernicious attack on Christianity. For it weakened the family, destroyed the independence of the worker, exploited women and children, reduced the human person to a unit of labor which could be reckoned solely in terms of cash. These developments the Church had to condemn. Time was required to sift out the evils of industrialism in order to condemn them without at the same time opposing progress itself. Meanwhile, solutions to the evils of industrialism were quickly proposed by Socialists, Communists, and others whose programs were even more directly anti-Christian than the society they hoped to replace. Again, the Church was caught on the defensive in having to condemn these "new" developments of the nineteenth and twentieth centuries.

It is easy for us to see, then, how Catholics became suspicious of change and how they tended toward conservatism. Each change in modern times seemed to take Western man farther from God and from

His Church. Only when we take a long view of history do we realize that the Church is not opposed to progress or to change itself. This becomes evident when we look at the Church's early history, or when we observe the developments which have taken place since Pius XII became Pope in 1939. In many of his allocutions and encyclicals the Pope has insisted that the Church be in the forefront intellectually, that Catholics take a lead in directing the course of history so that mankind progresses in a right direction. Moreover, his papacy has been a period of adaptation of the Church to contemporary society. Without changing in doctrinal or moral essentials, the Church adapts its organization and its cult to changing conditions. Moreover, it approves heartily of improvements in technique which make life easier for mankind and can bring to all men the material goods and the leisure which are necessary for living a truly human life. The Church, then, has no desire to stop the clock of history or stay the wheels of progress.

The following readings have been selected to clarify certain misunderstandings that can arise either as to the Church's role in modern history or as to the attitude of Catholics toward various developments which somehow impinge on their beliefs or their way of life. The first two selections deal with a double problem that has led historians to much soul-searching in the last decade: the epistemological problem of whether historians can arrive at objective truth, and the moral problem of whether a Catholic historian's faith hampers his freedom as an historian. The next three selections treat of problems that have persisted throughout modern history: the Index, the attitude of the Church toward science, and the rights that the Church insists upon as a divinely founded institution.

Selections 6 through 15 are on subjects that have been misunderstood or neglected by many historians. Only recently has Baroque culture been appreciated as something more than a decadent post-Renaissance culture; Dr. Hohl's article suggests that it is intimately connected with the Catholic Reformation. Similarly, the Puritan aspect of the French Revolution is generally neglected by historians in favor of more obvious developments; Father Stansell's article is a cautious, careful corrective for this neglect. Other selections in this group handle such topics as the suppression of the Jesuits, the *Kulturkampf,* and the basic reasons why the Church claimed a right in the nineteenth century to speak on economic and social matters.

Selections 16 through 23 are designed to give the student a better understanding of various "isms" which have developed in modern history. Each of these "isms" means different things to different people, and the student is apt to find that the words confuse him rather than help him understand past developments. The selected articles attempt to delimit, describe, and—where possible—to define the meaning of each "ism." The next six selections are on recent or contemporary subjects which have doctrinal or moral implications which the Catholic student and historian cannot ignore. The tremendous impact of Freud on literature and art, as well as psychiatry and psychology, makes it necessary for the student of Western Civilization to understand what Freud did and what parts of his theory have been accepted by later scholars as true. The moral implications of the Welfare State, again, are a complicated problem that can be solved only in their historical setting.

The final selection deals with the most recently formulated philosophy of history, that of Arnold J. Toynbee, whose *Study of History* is an outstanding intellectual achievement of our generation. Although we do not agree with all Toynbee's conclusions, we believe him deserving of serious attention because his work—written against Karl Marx, Oswald Spengler, and secularist historians—puts God back into history, makes history a dialogue between the Creator and His creatures, and sees man as that marvellous and mysterious creature made to the image and likeness of God. It is fitting to conclude this collection of readings in the history of Western Civilization with an analysis of Toynbee's *Study* because it is natural for the student to ask, when he has finished plowing through the facts of the past, what is the meaning of history? This is the question men have asked through the ages. Toynbee's *Study* is an attempt to answer that question.

READINGS IN THE HISTORY OF WESTERN CIVILIZATION

1

THE FAITH OF AN HISTORIAN *

Until less than two centuries ago history was considered a narrative art, a form of literature in which the narrator tried to tell as true a story as he could of man's past. Early in the nineteenth century the school of "scientific history" developed. Techniques of research improved, and a vast body of knowledge about the past was accumulated, classified, and published. Until the beginning of the twentieth century, historians believed that by imitating the techniques and adopting the norms of the natural sciences they could make history truly a science. Therefore, they believed, they could have the same certainty about a past event as the chemist has of a reaction he observes in the test tube.

A natural reaction set in against these extreme claims, and, as usual, the reaction went to the other extreme of asserting that we cannot have certain knowledge of any past fact or past event. Such historians as Carl Becker and Charles Beard insisted that the historian "creates the fact" by investing it with a meaning, a significance, a causality, and an influence which are entirely subjective. Thus every man must become his own historian, for the past differs with each viewer.

Meanwhile the great body of historians have done their work without bothering much about these extreme theories. They know the past exists objectively, and they know that there are ways and means of finding out what happened and, to some extent, how it happened. Most historians are men of common sense who realize that their personal biases and religious beliefs influence their interpretation of the past, and they try to guard against their personal bias. But they have never believed it is impossible to make some kind of contact with the past through records and documents that have been left for us to study and evaluate.

The following selection is an "act of faith" delivered by one of America's foremost historians as his presidential address to the American Historical Society. This act of faith is the working belief of most men and women who write or teach history. It acknowledges the limits under which historians work, but it insists that the past is not unknowable.

* Samuel Eliot Morison, "The Faith of an Historian," *The American Historical Review*, LVI, No. 2 (January, 1951). Reprinted by permission.

To you, fellow members, who have honored me by election to your presidency this year, I feel that I owe a sort of *apologia pro vita mea,* a statement of the beliefs and principles that have guided my teaching and writing during the thirty-eight years since my first article was published in the *American Historical Review.* I have nothing revolutionary or even novel to offer. Very early in my professional career I observed a certain frustration in a historian whom I greatly admired, Henry Adams, who had spent much time and thought searching for a "law of history." So I have cultivated the vast garden of human experience which is history, without troubling myself overmuch about laws, essential first causes, or how it is all coming out. My creed or confession is probably no different from that of the great majority of practicing historians in the Western world.

The late Charles A. Beard, certainly one of the most beloved and by all odds the most provocative of my predecessors, described all writing of history as "an act of faith." With that I agree, although after reading some of his books I suspect that Beard's "act of faith" was a literal translation of the Spanish *auto-da-fé.* Every historian with professional standards speaks or writes what he believes to be true. But he must also have faith in the receptiveness of his audience. If a lecturer, he wishes to be heard; if a writer, to be read. He always hopes for a public beyond that of the long-suffering wife.

This legitimate desire of the historian to interest, to instruct, and to please, is at once a leading motive for his labors, a challenge to present his work in artistic form, and a danger to his professional integrity. It tempts him to deviate from the truth in order to satisfy school committees on whom he depends for "adoptions"; or the prejudices of reviewers and the emotions of the public to whom he looks for circulation. Historians of repute have sold their skill for a mess of royalties; and I hope we do not envy them. Most writers of pseudo-history, however, are gifted amateurs seeking to bolster some pet theory with carefully screened facts, or people trained in journalism or some similar calling in which the story's the thing. If it accords with the facts, fine; if not, so much the worse for the facts.

No person without an inherent loyalty to truth, a high degree of intellectual honesty, and a sense of balance, can be a great or even a good historian. Truth about the past is the essence of history and historical biography, the thing that distinguishes them from every other branch of literature. Everyone agrees to that; but when we come to define truth, dissension starts.

For my part, I stand firm on the oft-quoted sentence of Leopold von Ranke, which we American historians remember when we have forgotten all the rest of our German. "The present investigation," said Ranke in the preface to his first volume, published in 1824, "will simply explain the event exactly as it happened." Ranke was far from being the first to say that. He picked up the phrase, I imagine, from Wilhelm von

Humboldt, who, in an address to the Prussian Academy three years earlier, declared the proper function of history to be "the exposition of what has happened." Some 2200 years earlier, Thucydides wrote, "The absence of romance in my history will, I fear, detract somewhat from its interest. But if he who desires to have before his eyes a true picture of the events which have happened, and of the like events which may be expected to happen hereafter . . . shall pronounce what I have written to be useful, then I shall be satisfied."

One might add quotation to quotation, merely to show that for almost 2500 years, in the Hebraic-Hellenic-Christian civilization that we inherit, truth has been recognized as the essence of history. In other words, the historian must be intellectually honest. Sublimating his own views of what ought to have been or should be, he must apply himself to ascertaining what really happened. Of course his own sense of values will enter into his selection and arrangement of facts. It goes without saying that complete, "scientific" objectivity is unattainable by the historian. His "choice of facts to be recorded, his distribution of emphasis among them, his sense of their significance and relative proportion, must be governed by his philosophy of life." No historian of my generation has ever pretended otherwise. Certain mid-nineteenth century historians fancied that they could be as objectively scientific about the multitudinous, unrefractory materials of human history as a physiologist should be (but seldom is) in describing muscular reactions. But none of these, from Ranke down, if pressed, would have denied that their philosophy of life influenced, if it did not dictate, their selection, emphasis, and arrangement.

So much has been written in recent years about these limitations on "scientific" objectivity as to obscure the plain, outstanding principle that the historian's basic task is one of presenting a corpus of ascertained fact. That is the hardest thing to get across to students today, especially to those who have been to the so-called progressive schools. Somewhere along the assembly-line of their education, these students have had inserted in them a bolt called "points of view," secured with a nut called "trends," and they imagine that the historian's problem is simply to compare points of view and describe trends. It is not. The fundamental question is "What actually happened, and why?"

It matters little what "method" the young historian follows, if he acquires the necessary tools of research, a sense of balance, and an overriding urge to get at the truth. Courses on historical methodology are not worth the time that they take up. I shall never give one myself, and I have observed that many of my colleagues who do give such courses refrain from exemplifying their methods by writing anything. It is much more fun to pick to pieces the works of their contemporaries who do write. Historical methodology, as I see it, is a product of common sense applied to circumstances. If the period be one of which few *monumenta* have survived, the historian must use his imagination to bring the disjointed fragments into some logical pattern, as paleontologists reconstruct a prehistoric monster out of a bone or two. If the era be a recent one for which there are mountains of facts, the historian may sink a few experimental tunnels and examine what they bring up; or he may laboriously try to pan out the "color" from the dirt, or may employ a corps of miners to do the preliminary sifting for him. In any case, his judgment and set of values, acting alone or through his assistants, determine not only what is gold and what is dross but the design of the history which he creates out of the metal. The historian decides what is significant, and what is not.

Significant for what, you ask? Significant for understanding that stretch or segment of the past which he is examining. The historian's professional duty is primarily to illuminate the past for his hearers or readers; only secondarily and derivatively should he be concerned with influencing the future. He must frankly look backward, with frequent glances over his shoulder at the world in which he lives, and perhaps a prayer for the future world in which he hopes his descendants may live out their lives in peace. But, you will ask, whence cometh the light with which he illuminates the past? The Light of the World, as reflected by the Church? The red light of dialectical materialism? Or merely the klieg lights of modern publicity? And will not the light vary from age to age? Surely, Governor William Bradford's bayberry candle cast a different light from Governor Thomas Hutchinson's whale-oil lamp; Prescott's student lamp and Parkman's gaslight differ from the 1950 model fluorescent bulbs under which most of us work. No historian can be free, or indeed ought to be free, of the best light that his own day and age affords, because he is writing of the past but not for the past; he is writing for the public of today and tomorrow, and his contemporaries ask very different questions of historians from those that his grandfather's generation asked.

Intellectual honesty is the quality that the public in free countries always has expected of historians; much more than that it does not expect, nor often get. Any child knows that history can only be a reduced representation of reality, but it must be a true one, not distorted by queer lenses. Commodore Richard W. Bates and another officer at the Naval War College, with parttime assistance of a third, spent two years on an intensive, blow-by-blow study of the battle of Savo Island, which lasted exactly 42 minutes in the graveyard watch on August 9, 1942, and they have just produced a 400-page monograph on it. They have honestly tried to find out exactly what happened and why, sparing nobody, praising few, although shocked to the core at the faulty tactics that their search revealed. Skilled, honest, and laborious though he was, Commodore Bates, for want of records sunk or lost, for lack of knowledge of what individual sailors, Japanese and American, out of the some ten thousand engaged, thought, felt, and did, could produce only an approximation of what happened on that tragic night. Like the best professional historians he took no short cuts, tested all *a priori* generalizations by ascertainable facts, and hesitated not to scrap his charts and shape a new course whenever new soundings revealed uncharted reefs. His Savo Island monograph is a fine example of intellectual honesty, because it was motivated by an earnest desire to "explain the event exactly as it happened." Gustaaf J. Renier rightly observes that "intellectual honesty is even more important for the historian than for the scientist, for, unlike the scientist, the historian cannot submit his conclusions to the test of experiment. He knows that his work may go unchecked for generations, and that he is therefore put on his honor."

As one aspect of intellectual honesty, the historian should feel a sense of responsibility to his public. The same contingencies of time and space that force a statesman or soldier to make decisions, impel the historian, though with less urgency, to make up his mind. His decisions will not, as the statesman's may, throw his country into a bloody war or a shameful capitulation; they will not, like the soldier's, win or lose a campaign; but they may well enter into the stream of history and vitally affect the future. Would the American Union have been preserved if Bancroft had not so vividly portrayed the struggle to achieve union? Would Napoleon III have made the fatal cast of dice in 1870 if French historians had not glorified Napoleon I? Would the English people have clung to their liberties through good and evil fortune if Hume, Lingard, and Mommsen had gained their ear, instead of Green, Macaulay, and Trevelyan? A mad or obstinate people may not hear the voice of a historian. The Greeks did not listen to Isocrates, who warned them with even greater authority than the Delphic Sybil, that, if they went on as they had gone on, their civilization would be torn asunder and they would be subjected to an alien domination. But the historian who knows, or thinks he knows, an unmistakable lesson of the past, has the right and the duty to point it out, even though it counteract his own beliefs or social theories.

Now some of you are doubtless thinking, Morison is skating on thin ice; if he doesn't look out, he will crash through into the bottomless pit where the spirits of James Harvey Robinson and Charles A. Beard are ready to embrace him as one of theirs! So, without further ado, I shall pay my disrespects to what Robinson called "The New History," and what Beard called "Written History as an Act of Faith."

Beard, in his confession of faith, sets up a straw Ranke who pretended to reproduce past "actuality" *in toto,* and in a syllogism that makes one gasp for breath, goes on to assert that, since no historian can escape his personal limitations or transcend those of space and time, he must so select and arrange the facts of history as to influence the present or future in the direction that he considers socially desirable. The historian's value in the long run will "depend upon the length and correctness of his forecast." Beard's personal guess was that American history was moving forward to a collectivist democracy, which he defined as "a worker's republic" without poverty or luxury, "a beautiful country . . . labor requited and carried on in conditions conducive to virtue." In other words, the Fabian dream that his English friends shared at the turn of the century.

While Beard's end was constant, his means, and so his "frame of reference" changed with the times. His first famous book, *An Economic Interpretation of the Constitution* (1913) was written apparently to break down that excessive respect for the Federal Constitutional which he believed to be the main legal block to social justice. The book had an immense success, promptly becoming the Progressives' Bible. Through it, Beard probably contributed more than any other writer, except Henry L. Mencken, to the scornful attitude of intellectuals toward American institutions, that followed World War I. But in course of time Beard came to believe that he had made a mistake; that if the millennial "worker's republic" was to be attained, the isolationists must come in first, like Kerensky before Lenin. This is evident in his *Basic History of the United States* (1944) and transparently clear in *The Enduring Federalist* (1948). In that, his penultimate work, the *Federalist* papers, which with few exceptions, he had formerly dismissed as rationalizations of the money-grabbers, become one of the greatest political treatises of all time, expressing deep political and moral truths. Thus Beard came full circle. His 1913 book was received with greatest acclaim in the camp of Eugene Debs; his 1948 book evoked the wild enthusiasm of the Hearst press and the Chicago *Tribune*.

Throughout this evolution from left to right, Beard always detested war. Hence his writings were slanted to show that the military side of history was insignificant or a mere reflection of economic forces. In his *Rise of American Civilization* (1927) he led a procession of historians who, caught in the disillusion that followed World War I, ignored wars, belittled wars, taught that no war was necessary and no war did any good, even to the victor. All these antiwar historians were sincere, and few of them were doctrinaire pacifists, as their actions in the last few years prove; nevertheless, their zeal against war did nothing to preserve peace. It only rendered the generation of youth which came to maturity around 1940 spiritually unprepared for the war they had to fight. One may share Beard's destestation for war—most Americans do—but one must admit that few of the things Americans value most, such as independence, liberty, union, or westward expansion, could have been won or secured unless men had been willing to fight for them. Nor may the social historian ignore the part that war and violence have played in American society. Think of the colonial train bands, the expeditions to Cartagena and Louisburg, Indian wars and western desperadoes, crack militia companies doing fancy drills in gaudy uniforms, soldiers' land bounties and veterans' assaults on the United States Treasury, the curious American craving for military titles, and the romantic militarism of Richard Harding Davis. Even Beard's fixed belief that war retarded the worker's millennium was a mere hypothesis; future historians may well find that the two world wars that Beard hated, and the Roosevelt administrations that he despised, did more for collective bargaining and for the worker's well-being and security than any previous half-century of peace.

Of course we historians were not altogether to blame for American spiritual unpreparedness for World War II. Pacifism, disillusion, and a disregard for settled values were rampant in literature, on murals and the screen, and over the air. But historians bear the greater blame, for they are the ones who should have pointed out that war does accomplish something, that war is better than servitude, that war has been an unescapable aspect of the human story. Any American historian could subscribe to the sentiment that Isocrates expressed for his native Athens: "To our forefathers let honor be rendered no less for their hazardous enterprises than for their other good deeds; for not slight, nor few, nor obscure, but many, great and terrible were the battles that they sustained, some for their own land, some for the freedom of others."

I wish that every young historian might read Beard's final book, *President Roosevelt and the Coming of the War* (1948), as an example of what happens when a historian consciously writes to shape the future instead of to illuminate the past; of a man becoming the victim or the prisoner of his "frame of reference." Without misstating many facts or garbling quotations, as the vulgar distorters of history do, Beard by ingenious arrangement and selection, ruthless rejection of attendant circumstances, and a liberal use in innuendo, compiled a powerful brief for the thesis that Franklin D. Roosevelt was the aggressor against Germany and Japan; that he wanted American entry into the war for his own purposes, planned and plotted for it and maneuvered Japan into striking Pearl Harbor in order to gain these sordid ends. If this be the New History, give me the old! But there is nothing new about it; to go back no farther, we can find the same sort of thing, not so well done to be sure, in *Mr. Madison's War* (1812) by John Lowell, and *A View of the Conduct of the Executive in the Foreign Affairs of the United States* (1797) by James Monroe. Beard used the facts of history—"actualities" he calls them—as Romain Rolland said politicians always use them: "History furnishes to politics all the arguments that it needs, for the chosen cause." I submit that this sort of thing is not history in the accepted, traditional sense of the word; but, at best, a sort of imprecatory preaching.

So, contrary to Beard who urges you to adopt a conscious "frame of reference" or form of Utopia as a basis for the selection and arrangement of facts, I say that every historian should be wary of his preconceptions, and be just as critical of them, skeptical of them, as of the writings of his predecessors.

Skepticism is an important historical tool. It is the starting point of all revision of hitherto accepted history. As Alfred Sidgwick says, "Our skepticism . . . consists of a recognition of the defects of knowledge only in the hope of helping knowledge forward. Among its leading principles are these: that doubt is always lawful but not always expedient; that human fallibility is only worth remembering for the sake of discovering and correcting actual errors; and that beliefs may be unquestioned without being unquestionable. So far from using the notion that man is fallible as an excuse for despair, or for tendering the advice that nothing should ever be believed, we use it as a justification of the effort to improve our knowledge little by little for ever."

Skepticism is properly a two-edged sword in the hands of the historian; and if one edge of the two is keener than the other, it should be turned against oneself. Every honest historian has, time and again, rejected the theory or "frame" with which he started his research, and has built another to suit the facts that he plows up.

"Frame of reference" history is of course the only kind that historians are allowed to write under a dictatorship, but they are not allowed to construct the frame. George Orwell's *Nineteen Eighty-Four* gives us a glance into the future. In that totalitarian England of his imagination—so horribly like certain regimes of today that it makes one shudder—the government keeps a corps of writers constantly at work writing new histories to replace the old, at every new turn of its policy. National figures associated with liberalism or democracy are either smeared, or, like Trotsky under the present Red regime, ignored as though they had never been.

Enough of what I do not believe. The positive task for the honest historian, I do believe, is to illuminate the past. He will inevitably try to answer some of the questions that contemporary society asks of the past, such as the causes of and prevention of war, the working of democracy under different sets of conditions and by various peoples, and the part that personality, climate, and environment play in determining events. But these considerations should be secondary in the historian's mind. After his main object of describing events "simply as they happened," his principal task is to understand the motives and to point out mistakes as well as achievements by persons and movements, even by those that he loves. In a word, he must preserve balance.

This principle of balance or proportion—what the French mean by *mesure*—is, I believe, the most valuable quality for a historian, after intellectual honesty. *Mesure* means, for instance, that you should not relate diplomatic history in a vacuum, confining your narrative to the exchange of notes, but try to discover the forces of economics, public opinion, and the like behind the foreign offices. *Mesure* means that in describing the humanitarian movement in the United States a century ago, you must at least refer to similar movements in other countries, which influenced ours. *Mesure* means that you can no longer write political history without considering social forces, or social history without describing political acts and conditions that translate aspirations into deeds, or naval history without touching on concomitant efforts of the ground and air forces. *Mesure* means that you should not write the history of an industry from the management point of view without considering labor; or a history of a labor union without considering the capitalist side. There is no royal road for a young historian to acquire a sense of balance, although a becoming humility toward his fellow workers, and skepticism directed toward himself as toward them, will be of assistance. It may be that a sense of balance and proportion is innate rather than acquired; possibly it may be patiently inculcated by a teacher who has it. That I do not pretend to know. But I do predict that no unbalanced history can live long; that in due time it will be a mere curiosity like those nasty antipapist and anti-Protestant tracts of the seventeenth century, which serve only to illustrate the partisan passions of the times.

Those partisan passions may not be ignored. Since the life of man, at least in his great moments, is emotional, prejudiced, and passionate, the historian should try to express some of the emotion, the prejudice, and the passion in his prose; and he must, through his imagination, enter to some extent into those feelings in order to portray them with sympathetic warmth or appropriate indignation. He will have no difficulty in doing this if he approach his subject with verve and enthusiasm. Unless it be the dull pedantry of the average doctoral dissertation in history, there is no quality more repugnant to readers than a chilly impartiality. Yet enthusiasm is no excuse for the historian going off balance. He should remind the reader that outcomes were neither inevitable nor foreordained, but subject to a thousand changes and chances. And if he records the passions of past times, he must appease them as well by showing how the "pointers with pride" were too complacent, and the "viewers with alarm" were too nervous; how every winning cause had elements of evil, and every losing cause had some kernel of good. He should be wary of numbers and statistics and not fall into the common fallacy that "mostest" is more important than "fustest," that the big battalions or the big production figures inevitably make the decisions.

A historian owes respect to tradition and to folk memory; for "History is corrected and purified tradition, enlarged and analyzed memory." Rosenstock-Huessy, in an address before this Association in 1934 from which this dictum is quoted, warned our profession that we were losing our hold on the public through wanton and unnecessary flouting of tradition. He meant not only the "debunkers" but the historians who embraced dialectical materialism as an easy explanation of past reality—which saved them a great deal of painful thought. One result was the mass murder of historical characters. Personality ceased to be important if statesmen were puppets of economic and social forces; hence in many works written in the 1920's and 1930's, there are no great men or leading characters, only automata whose speeches, ideas, or aspirations are mentioned merely to give the historian an opportunity to sneer or smear. Dialectical materialism will admit no highmindedness, no virtue, no nobility of character—unless on the part of a revolutionist. It made a great appeal to young scholars, as perhaps was natural during those two woeful decades, 1920-1940; yet none the less unfortunate. For the "debunkers" and dialectical materialists, by robbing the people of their heroes, by insulting their folk memory of great figures whom they admired, repelled men of good will from written history and turned other men, including many not of good will, to communism.

Dialectical materialists who did not go communist are now rather lonely. The age of "debunking" has passed; even Woodward, who coined the term, is dead; a new generation both here and in Europe is sounding and elucidating national and sectional traditions. But much harm was done, and little good. So, although it is less cogent today than fifteen years ago, I wish to repeat Rosenstock-Huessy's warning—historians, deal gently with your people's traditions! If you feel the urge to pull something apart, try your hand on a myth rather than a tradition. Some historical myths, like the Magna Carta one, were very useful in their day. Others, like Jamestown log cabins, Marcus Whitman's journey, or the exclusively Celtic composition of the Notre Dame football team, are harmless. But still others, like the Cavalier myth of Virginia, the forged letters of Washington and Franklin, the myth that the Pilgrim Fathers invented democracy and free enterprise, and the old "perfidious Albion" myth which still has currency, cater to regional *hubris* or racial prejudices, and need deflation.

Too rigid specialization is almost as bad for a historian's mind, and for his ultimate reputation, as too early an indulgence in broad generalization and synthesis. Everyone should, I believe, study something general or national in scope and something special or local; should do research on a remote period and on a contemporary period, and work on more than one type of history. The national field teaches you what to look for in local history; whilst intensive cultivation of grass-roots—or, as in my case, coral reefs and mudflats—teaches you things that you cannot see in the broad national view. Local history as a sideline also serves to integrate a historian with his community, to make him a valued and respected member of it, instead of "just another professor."

Contemporary history offers many pitfalls, and poses more and different problems than eras long past; as I know very well, after jumping from 1492 to 1942. There is an advantage in writing about admirals like Columbus who cannot answer back! Yet, my recent venture into contemporary naval history has been rich in experience, and has taught me much. For one thing, I no longer have the reverence for documents that I once had, or the distrust for oral sources that I was once taught. Military documents vary in value as their writers know the truth and try honestly to tell what really happened; one should not get along without them, but one must check them, not only against the enemy's documents but by the oral testimony of participants, provided always it be fresh; for "the strongest memory is weaker than the palest ink."

Participation in naval actions has taught me a greater tolerance of the mistakes of naval commanders than I could have entertained if I had fought the war in Washington. One has to experience the noise and confusion of battle to appreciate how difficult it is for the responsible commander to estimate a fluid situation correctly, and to make the right decision under pressure. And, although Tolstoy exaggerated the role of chance and denied the role of intellect in warfare, both are present. A sailor's opportunity for fame, or even for survival, often depends on a fortunate shot, or on a decision that was wrong in view of what he did know, yet right in view of the factors that he could not grasp. The planner of operations, in modern war, is just as important as the men who execute the plans; military planning calls for intellectual qualities of the highest order.

Fashions in history are constantly changing. Back in the 1930's few publishers would take a source book on American history. Since 1945 a spate of "liberty documents" and the like are competing for adoptions, and for the tedium of required readers. There is now a seller's market in early Americana—colonial history, folklore, early westerns, and the like—and I wish that more of our members would take advantage of it instead of letting journalists and novelists rake in the cash. There is a decided change of attitude toward our past, a friendly, almost affectionate attitude, as contrasted with the cynical, almost hateful one of young intellectuals twenty-five years ago. At that time Kenneth Murdock and I were voices crying in the wilderness against the common notion of the grim Puritan painted by J. Truslow Adams and other popular historians of the day: the steeple-hatted, long-faced Puritan living in a log cabin and planning a witch-hunt or a *battue* of Quakers as a holiday diversion. That picture has given way to one of the jolly Puritan sitting in a little frame house furnished with early American furniture, silverware and pewter, one arm around a pretty Priscilla and the other reaching for a jug of hard cider. Twenty years ago it was difficult to get any hearing for our denial that English colonists in general and Puritans in particular were hostile to the arts; now we have to discourage students from comparing a tavern-sign portrait of George II to a Romney, or going into ecstasies over the beautiful "functionalism" of a seventeenth century Connecticut hog-yoke.

Fifty years ago, it was difficult to find any general history of the United States that did not present the Federalist-Whig-Republican point of view, or express a very dim view of all Democratic leaders except Cleveland. This fashion has completely changed; it would be equally difficult today to find a good general history of the United States that did not follow the Jefferson-Jackson-F. D. Roosevelt line. That, I confess, is my own approach. I was converted to it, forty years ago, by doing my first piece of intensive research on New England Federalism, and discovering that the "wise and good and rich" whom Fisher Ames thought should rule the nation, were stupid, narrow-minded, and local in their outlook compared with the Republicans. I still believe that the Jeffersonian "line" is the one that the main stream of United States "actuality" has followed, just as British "actuality" is best explained by historians who write in the Whig-Liberal-Labour tradition. But I also believe that there has been altogether too much of it, and that the present situation is unbalanced and unhealthy, tending to create a sort of neo-liberal stereotype. We need a United States history written from a sanely conservative point of view, like Keith Feiling's recent *History of English.* But we do not want nostalgic histories that merely invoke an impossible return to the policies and conditions of some past era. For, as every classicist knows, the Stoic doctrine of recurrence impelled the political scientists and statesmen of Rome "to seek solutions for the ever more complex problems of Roman civilization by abortive effort to rejuvenate the virtues, and to reenact the policies, of the past." Frustration and failure will attend any American historian who tries to do that; but fame and success await one who will make a fresh distillation of our entire history, with the conservative tradition acting as the leaven.

Social history exhibits a similar uninventiveness, for it seems very difficult for social historians to describe anything but improvements, as they move on from decade to decade. But the main ill of American social historians is indigestion. You cannot include everything from wonder-working providences to badly working plumbing; better leave the one to Edward Johnson and the other to the Quennells. Social history puts a greater strain on literary expression and the sense of balance than any other kind. Hitherto the novelists have been very much better at writing it than the historians. We need to improve our human perception as well as our literary style if we expect to be the teachers of social history that, for instance, Marcel Proust was and Conrad Richter is. Historians notably lack the talent at description which novelists have developed to a high degree; Prescott had it, of course, and Parkman; but you can count on the fingers of one hand the American historians now writing who can describe a scene, an event, or a natural setting in such a way that the reader can see it. (The reason is largely that the writer cannot see it himself; he sits in a library and writes instead of going about by whatever means of transportation is available, and finding out for himself what historic sites look like today.) Then, too, some social historians forget that history is a story that moves; they divorce their subject altogether from the main stream of political history, giving it no context and no time. In the Western countries, political and constitutional history must always be the skeleton on which any other kind of history is hung; and if you are concerned over the decay of liberty, you should be also concerned lest political and constitutional history fall into desuetude. The American historian of architecture, education, labor, medicine, or any other social subject, should have a sense of chronology and not apply to 1850 the standards of 1950, or ignore the context and attendant circumstances of ideas, principles, and events that he may consider abominable.

Although the present conception of history as the sum total of all aspects of human activity has vastly complicated and increased the burdens of the general historian, he must accept the challenge. He should welcome, and must do his best to read and grasp, the flood of monographs that the presses are issuing on social-history subjects. He must do his best to apply to history the principles that the sociologists are painfully (and usually in horrible English) working out in human relations. He must admit that there is a vast amount to do in the social history of any Western country, with the whole of Asia opening up new fields to Western historians.

Although the magnitude of work before you younger historians, and the conditions under which you may have to perform it, are appalling, you are nevertheless to be envied. For the world has revolved to one of those "seasons, in human affairs," in the words of William Ellery Channing 120 years ago, "of inward and outward revolution, when new depths seem to be broken up in the soul, when new wants are unfolded in multitudes, and a new and undefined good is thirsted for." The times are your challenge; what will be your response? The historical profession will have little use for timid pedants, whose ambition goes no farther than to get a firm footing on one of the lower steps of the academic escalator, proceeding painlessly from one professorial grade to another until overtaken by death and oblivion. It wants men and women of courage as well as of honesty and balance. A historical career can be a great adventure, and not in ideas alone; witness the lives of Bolton and Trevelyan, men who write history that sings to the heart while it informs the understanding. A historian's life may be filled with conflict, not only the relatively clean fighting of armed forces but the dirty fighting of political campaigns and congressional investigations. We want more bold and positive characters to enter the profession.

Finally, a bit of advice nineteen centuries old, which St. Paul offered to all the faithful of Ephesus, but which seems particularly applicable to historians: "Henceforth walk not as Gentiles walk, in the vanity of their mind, having the understanding darkened, being alienated from the life of God through the ignorance that is in them, because of the blindness of their heart." Seek guidance from the Author of all lights, of all history, "and be renewed in the spirit of your mind." Or, as St. Thomas Aquinas put it, in his noble prayer for a scholar, "Grant me sharpness in understanding, sagacity in interpretation, facility in learning, and abundant grace in expression."

With honesty of purpose, balance, a respect for tradition, courage, and, above all, a philosophy of life, any young person who embraces the historical profession will find it rich in rewards and durable in satisfaction.

Such is the substance of my faith; and if I were to sum up my credo in a single word, it would be that proud motto of Fustel de Coulanges, *Quaero*—I seek to learn.

2

THE FREEDOM OF THE CATHOLIC HISTORIAN *

There is a popular feeling among many non-Catholics—and among many pious Catholics as well—that the Catholic historian cannot pursue his task freely. Non-Catholics often believe that the Catholic is committed to certain articles of faith and that he must reject historical facts which deny these articles; pietistic Catholics believe the Catholic should suppress information that seems derogatory to the Church, to long accepted ideas about the saints, or in any way admits defects in Church institutions or personnel. This popular feeling is less common than in the past, but it still persists in some quarters.

Pope Leo XIII and Pope Pius XII have both insisted that the Catholic historian has the duty to find and publish the truth, for the truth is ultimately one, and there cannot be contradiction between historical fact and revealed truth. In the following selection Father Aubert discusses apparent *difficulties facing the Catholic historian who would practice his craft freely. He shows that any contradiction between historical and religious truth must be apparent, that it is resolved on further study when the historical "truth" is found not to have been correct, or when the religious "truth" is not a matter of faith but of religious opinion.*

Father Aubert's selection deals with the freedom of the professional historian to find the truth and to publish his findings. Here, we see, his faith does not interfere with his freedom in any way. The popular presentation of historical truth is another matter, however, and here the virtue of prudence might dictate withholding certain information until immature minds are ready to receive it without scandal. This principle applies to the teaching of history rather than to research, and it is equally valid with other kinds of information which are to be taught to young people only when they have matured sufficiently.

* Roger Aubert, "The Freedom of the Catholic Historian," *Truth and Freedom,* by Louis de Raeymaeker and Other Professors of the University of Louvain ("Duquesne Studies," Philosophical Series: 5 [New York: The Ad Press, Ltd., 1954]), pp. 79-89.

Indirectly corraborating Father Aubert's thesis is the excellent work in history done by Catholics in Europe and in this country, men who could not have achieved such eminence in their profession if they were not free. The study of history, moreover, has led such outstanding historians as Carlton J. H. Hayes and Henry S. Lucas into the Church.

Introduction

JUST AS there are not two kinds of mathematics, one Catholic and the other non-Catholic, so also are there no two kinds of history, one Catholic and the other not Catholic. There is, or at least there ought to be, only one kind of history—*true* history, which is the same for all.

However, history is not concerned with abstractions, but with concrete human problems, notably problems having reference to man as a religious being and to the religious past of mankind, and therefore the conscience of the Catholic historian may ask certain questions. Is he free to let himself be guided solely by the tried principles of the historical method? Should he not rather take into account in his work also other principles, inspired by his religious opinions, which in certain cases could prevent him from coming to conclusions that are in line with the correct application of the historical method or which could oblige him to modify or mitigate certain conclusions? In other words, to what extent is the Catholic historian able to pursue his scientific research in complete freedom in spite of his adherence to a dogmatic Creed and his affiliation with the Church? In the following pages we should like to offer some considerations concerning this problem.

1. *The Catholic Historian and the Revealed Faith*

The Catholic Historian Remains Free in His Research. The story is told of a monk working in a storehouse of archives who one day declared, so the story goes, that if he were to discover any document prejudicial to the Catholic Church he would not hesitate to destroy it and thus forestall its use as an argument against his Faith. That is an extreme and rather rare case. More common, however, is another less spectacular way of violating the requirements of the strict historical method in the name of so-called exigencies of Faith. Certain historians think that they are obliged or at least authorized to make a choice among existing documents or to give a biased interpretation of them in order to present a reconstruction of the past which is in conformity with their religious ideas or useful for the glory of their Church. They believe that they must put history at the service of theological theses, just as others make history serve political, economical or social theses and therefore, to use the words of a great historian, they pass up with truly unbelievable lightheadedness or audacity documents contrary to their views, without even seeming to notice them, to concentrate all their attention on others which are favorable to them and exaggerate these beyond all measure.

Such a way of acting, whether it be done deliberately or not, proceeds, no doubt, from a good intention, but this does not make it less acceptable. We may repeat here with Fr. Lagrange, a Catholic scholar, who was criticized sometimes during his lifetime but before whom all now bow in respectful admiration, "Not to deviate from dogma is not synonymous with an untimely zeal in favor of it." Did not His Holiness Pope Pius XII himself recently affirm that the best way to serve the Church efficiently and to dissipate the prejudices against her is "tranquil research, without animosity or bias, by which nowadays more than in former times the facts of the past are reconstructed"? The Catholic historian has the right to investigate the facts and to bring them to light in all their objectivity. Those who would be tempted to see a lack of Faith or devotion to the Church in this concern to present the facts always as they really have been and not as one would sometimes like them to have been, can easily be answered by the Catholic historian with an appeal to authority by invoking the order given by Leo XIII to historians in the brief announcing the opening of the Vatican Archives:

> Let them keep in mind above all that the first law of history is not to dare say anything which is not true; the second, not to be afraid of saying anything that is true. Moreover, let the historian not give reason to be suspected of either flattery or animosity.

The Golden Rule of the Historian. Ne quid falsi dicere audeat, let him not dare to say anything false, and, what at first sight is much bolder, *ne quid veri non audeat,* let him not be afraid of saying anything that is true. This double golden rule of the Catholic historian, or any historian for that matter, presents and imposes itself as the only reasonable rule if one takes the trouble of only a little reflection.

There are not two truths, one religious and the other scientific. It is one of the glories of St. Thomas Aquinas that he took up the defense of this position of good sense against the Averroists. Whatever is an established scientific truth is *truth pure and simple.* It imposes itself as much upon the Catholic as well as upon the non-Catholic and cannot be incompatible with religious truth, i.e., with the data of Faith, if we admit that this religious truth is also truth. Consequently, the Catholic historian does not have to fear that the certain conclusions he reaches by means of tested scientific procedures can be in contradiction with what he is bound to admit as a believer.

On the other hand, it is important to be on guard against two kinds of confusion. The first consists in the confusion of scientifically established truths with more or less justified hypotheses. The second is to confuse the data of Faith with opinions which are more or less traditional in the

Church. It is perfectly possible for an historical hypothesis to be opposed to a truth of Faith or for a scientifically established historical conclusion to run counter to a pious tradition.

What are we to think about the conflicts which in such cases arise in the conscience of the Catholic historian? To what extent does he remain free to solve them in accordance with the requirements of the scientific method?

Conflict Between Faith and Historical Hypothesis. The scarcity of documents or the difficulties of interpretation very often prevent the historian from reaching conclusions that are *certain*. In such cases, he must restrict himself to the formulation of an hypothesis which is supported by more or less tenuous clues. By definition, these hypotheses have only a relative value. As experience shows, subsequent research will often oblige the historian, more perhaps than other scholars, to abandon hypotheses which seem quite close to the truth. A good many of today's historical hypotheses which some would like to see treated as proved truths will be tomorrow's historical errors. Should it surprise us, therefore, that historical hypotheses may be opposed to one or other religious truth? A number of historians in the past, for instance, thought it possible to conclude from the texts of ancient Christian literature that Saint Peter had never gone to Rome and that therefore the claim of the Popes to be the successors of the Head of the Apostolic College was baseless. This conclusion clearly contradicted one of the dogmas believed by Catholics. Subsequently, however, the position of these historians has been shown to be less solid than they thought. New works, among which we may name those of the Protestant Lietzman and, quite recently, those of the Protestant Cullman, have shown the fragility of a conclusion which was really only an hypothesis.

What will be the reaction of the Catholic historian when he is faced with an hypothesis which seems contradictory to that which he admits as a believer? Our answer is that he will only have to remember that an hypothesis . . . is only an hypothesis and therefore, from a scientific viewpoint, does not deserve more than a doubtful assent. He will, moreover, remember that one of the elements which must dispose him to admit or reject an hypothesis is the so-called criterion of probability, i.e., the conformity of the hypothesis with the general view taken by the historian of an historical period or of a complex of problems. The refusal of the Catholic historian to rally behind an hypothesis that goes against the truth which he as a believer admits is no more antiscientific than the refusal of the unbelieving historian who is faced with an hypothesis which he considers to be in contradiction with his rationalistic or materialistic philosophy. For both of them it is true that non-historical factors have made them more sensitive and more attentive to the absence of convincing values in the proposed arguments and consequently also to the purely *hypothetical* nature of a position to which at first sight one or other clue seemed to point. As a result, they rightly consider themselves justified in refusing their assent to an hypothesis which they judge to be "improbable." However, it would be antiscientific if in the absence of convincing arguments one would present as an alleged conclusion of history the particular hypothesis which fits best into the framework of a particular philosophical or religious conviction.

Accordingly, there is a possibility of conflict, though only apparently so, between a truth of Faith and a so-called historical truth, which upon examination shows itself to be merely a conjecture without a sufficient basis. We may recall here Renan's famous characterization of history as "that little conjectural science."

Conflict Between Historical Truth and Religious Opinion. There is also a possibility of conflicts between solidly established historical affirmations and traditional religious opinions which subsequently are shown not to be entirely in agreement with the truth.

The pronouncements which either the solemn or the ordinary Magisterium of the Church presents as objects of Faith must be considered by the faithful as irrevocable expressions of the truth. The same, however, cannot be affirmed of all doctrines which at one time or the other were current in the Church. No serious theologian, for example, would still dream of imposing upon the faithful the adherence to each and every affirmation contained in the famous Bull *Unam Sanctam* of Boniface VIII, which is one of the most pronounced expressions of medieval theocratic ideas. Accordingly, there is nothing impossible about the assertion that certain well-established historical facts are contrary to this or that particular theological thesis which was not expressed in sufficiently precise terms but enjoyed a certain vogue for some time in the past. For example, before the Vatican Council had clearly and precisely expressed the exact conditions which must be fulfilled before the Pope can be said to enjoy the gift of infallibility, a number of theologians were inclined to admit that the Pope was infallible whenever he made a public statement in matters of Faith or morals. For those who held this view the discovery of the more than ambiguous attitude of the Popes Vigilius and Honorius in the monophysitic and monothelitic controversies of the sixth and seventh centuries was bound to raise a grave problem of conscience. More than one of them was tempted to do violence to the texts in order to avoid having to admit that a Pope could have expressed himself in such an erroneous way as to lay himself open to the charge of heresy. For these theologians, such an admission seemed to be incompatible with their Catholic Faith. The difficulty, however, disappeared as soon as it was realized that the Catholic Faith is more specific than they thought and that the facts established by a sincere application of the principles of the historical method were incompatible only with a theological thesis that is not expressed with sufficient precision. It makes one happy to see these points, which sometimes are lost sight of, recalled by theologians as eminent and classical as, for instance, Mausbach:

> Many public statements of the Popes are not *ex cathedra* pronouncements, in spite of their religious character and their solemnity. . . . It is important to

make clear-cut distinctions in this matter. These distinctions are necessary in themselves, but also because they serve to rectify the exaggerations of certain adventurous theologians who, because of their insufficient knowledge of the facts in the history of the Church, seem to extend Papal infallibility to all measures taken by the Pontifical Power, even to those which belong to his pastoral function, without considering that in doing so they do more harm than good to the glory of the Church and the Papacy.

2. *The Catholic Historian and Human Weaknesses in the Church*

The foregoing considerations may be briefly summed up as follows. The Catholic historian who admits, on the one hand, that man's intelligence is capable of attaining the truth and who considers, on the other, the dogmas revealed by God as the expression of truth, is *a priori* certain that there can be no real contradiction between these dogmas to which he adheres by Faith and clearly established historical truth. Therefore, it is in all freedom of mind that he will pursue historical truth in conformity with the requirements of the historical method as it has been slowly perfected by generations of workers. If an apparent contradiction should arise, he will know that the explanation must be sought *either* in the purely hypothetical character of an historical position which he has somewhat hastily accepted as an established truth *or* in the fact that a given religious opinion does not really belong to the deposit of Faith, as at first he believed.

A fortiori therefore, the Catholic historian will feel himself free to apply the principles of the historical method in all sincerity when there is question of facts which have no direct connection with dogmatic truths but imply only practical judgments in matters of sanctity, morality or prudence.

The "Theandric" Nature of the Church. It may happen that the history of the past will show deplorable and even criminal attitudes of certain ecclesiastics, such as the immoral conduct of numerous bishops and some Popes at the time of the Renaissance or the indifference of Catholic circles with respect to the social question in the course of the nineteenth century. Why should the Catholic historian feel embarrassed by such discoveries? They constitute a problem only for those who have a false idea of the true nature of the Church founded by Christ. One of the points on which modern theological studies have been most insistent with respect to the Church is a fact which some call the "theandric character" of the Church and others the "law of incarnation," which forms part of the Church's foundation. We mean the fact that the Church, in imitation of Christ, is a reality both divine and human, really divine but also really human, composed of men who retain their human personality, and directed in the name of Christ by men who act with human virtues and faults. It is not surprising, therefore, if there is room in the Church, and even in the Hierarchy, for error and even sin. Leo XIII acknowledged this fact and expressed it in a pithy formula when he cried out against those who want to argue against the Church from the less prudent and less irreproachable actions they discover in the history of the Head of the Church. The great Pope simply drew attention to the fact that "to avoid all occurrences of this nature is more than can be accomplished by human nature," *plus difficultatis habet quam quod hominum natura patiatur.* It would be falling into a new kind of "monophysitic" error if we were to forget that in founding the Church God intended to respect human nature. Among others, Karl Adam has lately explained this idea in a beautiful article, "Faith," in which he develops the following idea:

Like Christ Himself, His Church is not an invisible spiritual community, but an incarnation of the divine in the domain of the terrestrial and the human. Her supernatural essence likewise reveals itself to us in the *condition of a slave.* Her *exinanitio* is even incomparably more profound and extensive than the dispossession of Christ and His revealed Word, especially because the Church is not the Word Incarnate Itself, but His mystical body.

Human Saints. What is true of the Holy Church of God herself, whose human face shows wrinkles which the historians has the right and the duty to point out, is all the more true of each Christian in particular, not excluding those select few who are the Saints. In former times, historians who wanted to apply the principles of the historical method to the study of the lives of the saints were often decried as "dethroners of saints." Nowadays it is readily admitted that they did a good job by separating the chaff from the wheat and removing pseudo-saints who in certain ages had been objects of an unenlightened popular devotion, but who were really nothing but the results of confusions if not of "pious" fraud. However, while there is a general agreement that those saints who had never existed should be removed, sometimes regret is expressed when historians are seen to reduce the miracles and virtues of the saints of former ages to a level less marvelous than the one to which the ancient hagiographers had accustomed us. Above all, some people are indignant when these historians dare to affirm that all the actions of the saints were not always saintly and begin to point out their defects and faults. Are not such people forgetting that the Kingdom of God is composed of men and that God has not miraculously changed these men but left them their personality and their freedom while offering them the gift of His grace? If one wanted to be naughty, one could denounce in these indignant censors an unconscious form of Hegelianism. First they conceive an *a priori* and abstract idea of holiness and then they want to reconstruct reality, against anything and everything, in conformity with this idea of holiness, instead of humbly bowing down to reality and thus learning their lesson from God and discovering His real intentions. How right is the historian P. Delhaye when, drawing attention to an idiosyncrasy of St. Bernard, he remarks:

If by chance it becomes evident that a famous man has shown some weakness or that a saint was not quite free from defects, one should keep in mind that history as it is written under the guidance of Providence is still more beautiful than the somewhat censored and biased dreams which we would like to substitute for it.

History as it is written under the guidance of divine Providence is more beautiful, not only because it is the only true history, but also because it is far more encouraging to us. Before the "artificial" saints of hagiographic legends—and it was not only in the Middle Ages that such legends flourished!—who were heroes from their most tender infancy we may perhaps be moved to admiration, but we also lose all hope of ever being able to imitate them. They give the impression of belonging to another world which is not ours, and therefore we hardly think of crying out with St. Augustine: "*Quod isti et istae, cur non ego?*" Why should I be unable to do what these men and women have done? But we recover our courage when we see that these saints were men like us, weak and unstable like us, but men with the help of God's grace were able to conquer their nature. Who would claim for instance that P. Debognie takes a jewel from the crown of a saint when, following the research of M. Grandchamps, he restores to us a St. Vincent de Paul who needed to be "converted" after a clerical youth dominated by an impatient ambition which did not recoil before improper means and lying declarations? Is it not rather true that he exalts the saint's courage and generosity which succeeded in overcoming his natural inclinations, while at the same time he gives glory to the marvels of God's grace, which was able to bring about this change and to make this youthful "pusher" a model of self denial?

Honesty With Respect to the Opponents of the Church. Enlightened by a healthy theology of the Church, the Catholic historian shall not be afraid to point out the faults of simple Christians, Churchmen and even the Heads of the Church. Loyal adherence to the Church does not restrict his freedom on this point. Likewise, he will not be afraid to show, when the occasion calls for it, the good qualities of the opponents of the Church and the virtues of heretics. Here again, only a false theology can give him the impression that his freedom as an historian is limited. The belief that the Catholic Church is the only true Church, the only Church which corresponds entirely to what Christ wanted, does not imply the denial of all grace to those outside the Church. As Fr. Sertillanges expressed it, "God is a generous sower. He sows the seed widely enough to allow some grass to grow up even outside His own field." Hearing Christ praise the woman of Canaan and remark that He found more faith in some pagans than in Israel, the Catholic historian, in his turn, feels free to recognize all the gifts of God, even outside the boundaries of the Church, and he does not hold himself obliged to write history from a "confessional" or partial point of view. As Diogenes demonstrated motion by walking, so Catholic historians furnish concrete proof of the freedom with which they can treat such delicate questions by writing works whose objectivity is highly appreciated outside their own Church.

One has only to think, for example, of the master's thesis, presented at Louvain and written by the Franciscan Maximin Piette under the direction of Canon De Meyer, about the Wesleyan reaction in the Protestant evolution, which was hailed by one of the principal leaders of the Methodist Church as the best study of the founder of Methodism.

3. *The Catholic Historian and Concessions to Expediency*

One more difficulty remains to be considered. Even if it is admitted that there is no real opposition between the Faith of the Catholic historian and the certain results of his research and that therefore his scientific freedom is never jeopardized by his Faith, nevertheless must it not be admitted that this freedom may find itself restricted sometimes by the necessity to make concessions to expediency? Does he not have to throw a veil of modesty over certain weaknesses and present in a favorable light certain events and attitudes which in reality were less honorable and less pure?

Of course, religious authorities have the right to complain about the procedure of certain Catholic historians who seem to have no other concern than to parade the weaknesses and miseries of the Church in order to incite Catholics to loud admissions of guilt. Those who under the pretext of objectivity fall into this eccentricity do not realize that, by isolating and displaying the unfavorable elements, they are just as unfaithful to the requirements of the true historical method as the apologetic historians who present the history of the Church in an idealized light which does not harmonize with reality. However, the excesses of these hyper-critics do not justify the viewpoint of those whom I have just called apologetic historians. Though it is true that these apologists are moved by the desire to serve a cherished cause, they should recall that, in the words of Péguy, the good God does not need our lies. Neither does the Church.

One could dwell long upon the danger there is, from a tactical point of view, in proceeding as these apologists do. Other historians, hostile to the Church, may undertake the study of the same subject and readily show that these apologists knowingly presented a partly biased picture and deformed the facts. Then it would be child's play to discredit in a more general way the whole work done by Catholics in historical questions and consequently to undermine the confidence of the faithful in the scientific foundation of their traditional positions.

However, rather than insist upon utilitarian considerations, I would like to draw attention to the fact that the procedure of these blundering apologists springs from a lack of Faith. They do not dare to accept the Church as God wants her, both *divine* and *human,* glorious and weak. I would like to add glorious partly because of her very weakness, for more than once this weakness should have brought about her destruction. Accordingly, it is precisely this weakness which shows to anyone who knows how to look at history that God is with her and permits her to overcome internal crises which would be fatal to any other purely human society.

Conclusion

As should be clear from the preceding considerations, it would be easy to conclude paradoxically that it is the very Faith itself of the historian which permits him to speak freely about the history of his Church. However, let us be more modest and limit ourselves to the conclusion that, no matter in what respect the matter be considered, the Catholic historian does not have to feel hampered by his religious convictions; that these convictions do not cloud his free outlook upon history; and that just as much as any other historian he has the right to study the religious past of mankind in the light of the principles and method proper to his branch of science.

3

THE ROMAN CATHOLIC CHURCH *

A considerable amount of bias against the Church in modern history arises from a misunderstanding of her nature and mission. Individual critics naturally identify the Church itself with members of the hierarchy and other "official" spokesmen they know or read. The result is that they frequently believe the Church is a "member-hungry" or a "power-hungry" organization that is anxious, like a political party, to enlist everyone within her ranks so as to control public policy in all countries.

In the following selection Father John Courtney Murray tries to clear up these misconceptions by indicating first of all that the Church is the Mystical Body of Christ whose essential nature will always remain a mystery to mortal man. But what the Church wants on this earth is transparently clear to anyone who understands her purpose and reads her message. The primary desire of the Church, the author points out, is that her members renounce the world to gain eternal life. This is the pearl of great price, and when it is forgotten or thrown aside the Church loses its very meaning.

The Church has a secondary demand, Father Murray points out, and

* John Courtney Murray, S. J., "The Roman Catholic Church," *Annals of the American Academy of Political and Social Science* (March, 1948), pp. 36-42. Reprinted by permission.

at first sight it seems paradoxical. For at the very time that the Church asks her children to renounce the world for life eternal, she insists that they immerse themselves in the world to make it a society in which justice and charity prevail, in which human dignity is respected, and in which men may live a truly Christian life. This secondary message is important for two principal reasons. First, the Church must oppose injustice and every form of sin, for this is her enemy. She is therefore interested in influencing the institutions and the leaders of this world. Second, she is interested in all men developing their natural as well as their supernatural faculties, both for the glory of God and for the welfare of each individual Christian. Therefore, paradoxically, the Church preaches life eternal, but she cannot remain aloof from worldly affairs when matters of truth or of morality are concerned.

RELATIVELY few people today ask what the Catholic Church *is,* but a great many seem to be asking what the Catholic Church *wants.* Especially, what does it want in the temporal order of human society; what place does it want for itself in relation to the structures of the social order; what part does it want to play in the process of their reconstruction?

The two questions are, of course, intimately related; the answer to the second depends on the answer to the first. However, to answer the first question would be impossible in the space at my disposal—impossible, in a sense, in any amount of space. Her children know that the Catholic Church is a mystery in the strict theological sense of the word. Her existence is not ultimately explainable in terms of human design and action; her total "idea" is not discoverable by sheer philosophical and historical research. The existence of the Church hangs on a sovereignly free divine choice, whereby God *gave* to men this particular form for their religious life; and the "idea" of the Church—what she intimately is—is possessed, as a secret, by God alone. When the Catholic says: "I believe . . . in the one, holy, catholic and apostolic Church," he has indeed evidence in the order of philosophical truth and historical fact sufficient to let him know with certainty that his act of faith is reasonable, he can explain *why* he believes the Church to be what it is. However, the Church itself, the thing-out-there, which his act of faith touches, transcends the power of his reason to comprehend, and much more the resources of his rhetoric to explain; he cannot adequately explain what the Church, in which he believes, is.

Obviously, if the Church were simply a social and juridical union, into which men had gathered themselves for their own reasons, and the structure of which they themselves had determined, one could quite adequately understand and explain what it is. One can, for instance, explain what the Catholic Association for International Peace is; one can, that is, explain the common idea and end, the common will and purpose that bind its members together into unity. And when one has explained the principle of a society's unity, one has explained what the society is. But precisely in this regard the Church escapes the comprehension of man. It is her unity that is her mystery. It is not explained by any human agreement among men to hold in common certain ideas, obey certain rules and officers, and work together towards some common ideal, as is the case with various voluntary associations. Nor is it explained by the profound exigencies for community living that are radicated in the social nature of man, as is the case with the natural institutions of the family and the state. The Church's principle of unity, which makes her what she is, is found neither in the will of man nor in his nature; it is a supernatural principle. Briefly, it is the Holy Spirit Himself, as given to the Church, dwelling in her as in His temple, and by His presence and action making her the Body of Christ, whose members are united, not merely by a bond of love or by the juridical bond of law, but by the mystical bond of a common sharing in the one Holy Spirit. As the classic formula has it, the Holy Spirit is the "soul" of the Church, the hidden source of her life and unity, her very "is-ness." Pius XII put the matter this way:

Although the juridical elements, on which the order of the Church also rests, have their origin in her divine constitution as given by Christ and themselves contribute to the attainment of her celestial end, nevertheless, what lifts the Christian society to a level that transcends the whole order of nature is the Spirit of our Redeemer—the Spirit who, as the source of all graces, gifts and charisms, is forever filling the Church in her inmost being, and energizing within her. To give an analogy: as the structure of our mortal body is, indeed, a marvelous work of the Creator that, nevertheless, falls short of the lofty dignity of our mind and soul, so the social structure of the Christian community, though it proclaims the wisdom of its divine Architect, is something of an essentially lower order in comparison with the spiritual gifts whereby it is endowed with life, and with their divine source (the Spirit).

There is, therefore, a mystery in what the Catholic Church is. Towards acquiring some manner of intelligence of it, by exploring its content and dimensions, a whole theolgy of the Mystical Body has been developed in Catholic sources; but it cannot even be outlined here.

The answer to the second question—what the Catholic Church wants—involves no mystery; no part of it is hidden in the mind of God, much less in the secret councils of the hierarchy. And since it is the question more frequently asked (whoever seriously asks what the Catholic Church is has somehow already reached the answer in his heart) I shall take it up here; not, indeed, with the thought of giving a complete answer—the subject is too large—but rather of offering an introduction to the answer.

Perhaps one could most successfully approach the answer by considering the two things that the pastors of the Church are in these days insistently saying to the laity. On the one hand, the laity are being taught that their Christian faith is a value in itself, to be lived for its own sake, independently of any repercussions it may have in the temporal order; on the other hand, they are being taught that their faith is also a value in the temporal order, and must have repercussions there, for the sake of the temporal order. They are being urged to seek simply and solely the kingdom of God in the heavens, and they are being urged to collaborate toward a Christian civilization on earth. It is impressed on them that it profits a man nothing to gain the whole world, if he lose his own soul; and it is likewise impressed on them that they must gain the whole world on peril of losing their souls. Their religious life is being given two orientations—towards God and His eternal city, and towards earth and the city of man. They are enjoined to work out their own salvation, keeping themselves immaculate from the world; and they are enjoined to immerse themselves in the world and work at its salvation. These sets of injunctions are seemingly opposed; but their principle of synthesis is in the nature of Christian faith itself. And it is this synthesis of values in their faith that is the cardinal contemporary lesson of the Church to her children.

The first part of the lesson has the primacy of importance. The basic tenet of the Catholic Faith is, of course, the Incarnation—the fact of the Word-made-flesh. The Word was God, the only-begotten God, the Son; He became man, born of a virgin, one of us; he suffered, died and rose again. And these resounding facts have one central significance—they have lifted the goal of human hopes. Not only is there now forgiveness of sins, but what the Gospels call "eternal life" is now given to man as his destiny; and it is put within his reach in that God through Christ has promised him the Holy Spirit, the "energy of the Most High," as an indwelling power, to heal his nature and lift his life to a new level and carry him through to his appointed end.

This hope of eternal life was a new thing. Aristotle's highest thought had set before man, as his sole possible end, a terrestrial beatitude—the felicity and peace of a virtuous life in the ordered human city. For the rest, man might, indeed, dream of playing the immortal, but his real horizons of hope were bounded by earth and time. In later ages, human reason, not without clarifications from Christianity, would teach that man was entitled by his spiritual nature to hope for a life beyond time, and a beatitude consisting in the possession of God through the possession of His creation, in whose myriad manifestations the soul, freed from the limitations of the body and sense, would know and love Him as in His images and in the effects of His power. No mean hope, this; but one infinitely inferior to the Christian hope, which is based not solely on a philosophy of human nature but on the fact of the Resurrection of Christ. The eternal life now put within the reach of man by the Word-made-flesh is the possession of God as He is in Himself, in a vision face to face, without the distorting, darkening "glass" of creatures interposed. Made son of God and co-heir of Christ by Baptism, the Christian is destined to possess the heritage proper to Christ, the Son—to know and love the Father as the Son knows and loves Him, to be in God "as thou, Father, art in me, and I in thee" (John 17:21).

This eternal life, this union with the Father through Christ in the Spirit, is the "pearl" and the "treasure" (Matt. 13:44-46). And such is its value that a man must sell all he has to purchase it. Compared with it, all the values of earth and time pale into shadows. The world is well lost, if this eternal life be gained. Beside it all other hopes lose their hold upon the heart. And if this hope be frustrated in the end, through man's negligence and sin, it does not matter what else he has achieved; he has lost everything, in that he himself, in his inmost self, is "lost."

This doctrine of the treasure and the pearl is necessarily in the foreground of the Church's preaching. In a sense, she has nothing else to announce than this, the basic "good news"; she would cease to be herself were she to teach or enjoin anything not related to it. The highest thing, then, that she has to say about her faith is that it is "the beginning of eternal life," and, as such, an end and value in itself, not to be perverted by subordination to any other end, even the end of peace and justice and love here on earth.

This is the primary doctrine of the Church. What perhaps gets emphasis in the America of our day is its austerity—an emphasis needed because the seductions of secularism, with its doctrine of the primacy of this-worldly material values, are so strong. Against them, the Church insists that the pearl is not purchased save at the price of all a man has; eternal life is not won by those who have their hearts set on this world and on the things—even the beautiful things—of time; the destiny of man is achieved only by the full discipline of unworldliness and other-worldliness. To this full discipline, to this "selling of all," the Church urges her children. And to help them bear it, she counsels their participation in all the great movements that are stirring her contemporary life, in answer to the challenge of secularism—the Biblical movement, the theological movement, the liturgical movement. The theme of the Bible, of theology and of the liturgy is simply "eternal life." Diligent study of them will, therefore, so quicken the beckoning of this destiny, the "joy of the Lord," as to fortify Christians against the appeal of other invitations; it will make their Christian hope so triumphant in their hearts that they will heed St. John's injunction: "Love not the world and what the world has to offer" (I John 2:15).

This, then, is the first thing that the Church is saying today. There is need to recall it here; otherwise it is impossible to see in perspective what the Church wants in the temporal order. Moreover, the message itself, although ancient, is precisely sharpened to the needs of the time. It is needed not only against secularism, but a more subtle temptation. So many, so grave and so urgent are the problems of the temporal order that there is the temptation, felt principally by noble souls, wholly to immerse oneself in them, to the oblivion of "the one thing necessary." There is the temptation to identify the kingdom of God with a just social order, and then to seek first the justice of the latter, thinking that all else will be ours as well. There is the temptation to make the Christian Faith itself simply a means to an earthly end—social change and progress toward an ideal of human brotherhood. All this would be to make the leaven simply part of the dough. And against all these temptations the doctrine of the pearl needs emphasis.

On the other hand, this doctrine, which teaches detachment from the world, cannot be made the pretext for disengagement from the world's problems. And here we come to the second major emphasis in the Church's teaching today. Pius XI reserved some of his scathing denunciations for what he called "social modernism." It is the appearance in the Christian camp of the 19th-century liberal thesis with regard to Church and State, that derived from Kant and was condemmed in the Syllabus. It maintained that "religion has nothing to do with politics," with the order and institutions of the earthly city; that religion is a "purely private matter"; that social, political and economic processes are immune from regulation by the heteronomous norms of religion and ethics. The Christian "social modernist" would maintain that his faith should have its sole flowering in personal piety; that he must keep his own hands clean by refusing to grapple with the grimy machinery of society. (One remembers Péguy: "Kantianism has clean hands; but it has no hands.")

This "social modernism" is an error on many counts; I shall signalize but two. The first is based on the fact that the regeneration of baptism, though it makes a man a "new creature" endowed with a new life, does not transfer him into a new world. He must live his new life in this old world; as a man and as a citizen he is involved in its institutions, and the life of the new man in him is conditioned by them. They can favor its growth or help to kill it; they can assist him to his destiny or turn him aside from it. Moreover, he has power over them, as they over him. All the institutions of this world are imperfect, unstable, capable of transformation, subject to free human action. Consequently, both by reason of their relation to his destiny and by reason of his relation to them, the Christian has the responsibility to see to the creation of conditions that will be favorable to his movement towards eternal life.

These favorable conditions are not, indeed, indispensably necessary; the Christian life can be lived to perfection in the inhuman conditions of a concentration camp. But it is so lived only by heroes; and the run of men are not heroic. The ordinary man needs the support of an environment whose institutions are shaped by the forces of justice and charity; otherwise he will fail to be ordinarily just and ordinarily charitable. Here, then, is the point of insertion of the Church's will with regard to the social order. Institutions that violate justice and charity are a manner of institutionalized sin, and a force for personal sin. And sin is the Church's enemy—her only enemy, but everywhere her enemy, whether in the city as such or in the individaul. Hence she enters the city as such—the political, social, or economic order—*ratione peccati,* by reason of the sin there found.

Much could be said about the historical development and exercise of this mission of the Church in the temporal order *ratione peccati.* My concern here is simply to point out the contemporary application—the insistence on the responsibility and duty of such action by every single Christian. To say that the Church has a mission in the temporal order is not to defend what is called "clericalism." It is simply to say that the virtualities of Christian faith are not exhausted by personal piety; they demand an attack on organized injustice in all its forms; they demand positive action to establish and secure such institutions in the temporal order as will be favorable to the growth of the seed of eternal life planted in baptism.

Against this reason for Christian concern with the temporal order it might be argued that it is "interested," it reveals no concern for the human as such, it regards the city and its good order as simply a means to a higher end. The objection does not, of course, destroy the validity of the reason, but it does bid us look beyond it for another.

This second reason is based on the fact, first, that human life is essentially a relationship between persons and, second, that the perfection of this relationship is precisely the end and purpose of the social order, with all its varied institutions. Society is a rational process, and its rationality consists essentially in its progress—never rectilinear, always interrupted by regressions—towards an ideal of human community structured after the demands of social justice and the equality of man, and informed by the spirit of social charity and the solidarity of all men. Moreover, this rational process and its ideal goal are the object of a divine will. God wills not only the eternal salvation of man, but his perfection here on earth as man—the perfection of his intellect, the perfection of his power over the material world and its energies (including atomic), the perfection of his social living. These things are ends and values in themselves, and not simply means. In the Christian scheme they are, indeed, only intermediate ends, being proper to earth and time; but nonetheless they are ends, and the very nature of man makes them desirable.

My point is that Christian faith here enters to affirm and support and then enlarge these human desires for the "secular" end of perfect human community—domestic, national, international. Obviously, Christian faith asserts its own supernatural ideal of human unity. It asserts, too, that this ideal will never be achieved on earth; it will always be blocked by the disorganizing action of Satan, by the divisiveness of sin, by the never completely healed disorder in the nature of man that makes him strangely tend to chaos. However, though Christian faith sanctions no myth about the city of God as realizable on earth, it allies itself strongly with the human hope for unity in the city of man. And for no mere sentimental reason. The Greek Fathers taught that the process of realizing mankind's "given" unity made a new beginning, on a plane higher than nature, in the fact of the Incarnation: in asserting His oneness with man, Christ asserted the oneness of all men in Him. Moreover, He died, as St. John says, that He might "gather into one God's scattered children" (John 11:52); and when He had risen, He sent from Heaven His own Spirit to accomplish the fulfillment of the prayer in which He had summed up the redemptive significance of His mission, that "all may be one" (John 17:21).

There is, then, in the Gospel an obsession with the idea of human unity, a passion for it. Initially, it is the passion for the unity of the Church, that has consequently turned so fiercely—at times too fiercely, we may think—on the error or disobedience or schism which would divide it. But the resonances of this passion are necessarily felt also in the earthly city—again at times too strongly, as when the political unity of the city was confused with the religious unity of the Church, and the latter was promoted and defended by means proper to the defense of the former. But this was an accident of historical circumstances, an aberration induced by the exigencies of a particular phase in political development. What permanently remains, as an exigence of Christian faith itself, is the enlistment of the energies of faith in the perfecting of the city's own unity, under new and due respect for the city's presently achieved autonomy.

The Church does not and cannot want her own unity, much less the structures that preserve it, to be reflected in the earthly city; the point has recently been emphatically made by Pius XII in a series of discourses to the Roman Rota, begun in 1945. The Church does, however, want the city to have its own proper unity—its own juridical structure wherein the equal rights and freedoms of citizens will be safeguarded, and its own spirit of civic friendship whereby the high values of human living together will be ensured. And to this end she is urging her children, as citizens, to employ the mystique of unity that is inherent in their faith. There is no more effective weapon against the divisive factors within the city: misunderstanding, jealousies, dissensions between classes, clashes of opposed egoisms, the conflict between ambitions for power—all the many forms that hostility and hate can take.

I suppose, then, that what the Church ultimately wants in the temporal order is to see there reflected, in civic friendship, the spirit of charity that is the primary expression of her faith. She wants this for the sake of the city, as essential to its good; she wants it, too, as the necessary expression of her own faith. Here is the point of synthesis of the twin values in faith—its value for eternal life and its value for temporal life. Love of the city's common good, with the faith in goodness that it implies, is itself an inchoative form of the love of the true God who is Goodness itself; this is so, whatever the strenously agnostic secularist may say. And if this be so, how shall Christian faith in Christ, the Son of God and one-time citizen of earth, not be the dynamic principle of a great love of the city's common good?

Obviously, the love of God and neighbor is no substitute for political maturity, or for the high technical competence required in organizing the economic life of man. The Church never said it was. What she says is that without the mystique of charity the technique of politics and economics will not be able to do more than tinker with the social machine; it cannot make it run. Again, charity is no substitute for social justice; it does not itself regulate the relations between men as possessors—that is the proper work of justice. But unless the relations between men as persons are regulated—and this is the proper function of charity—their relations as possessors will always be snarled. There is no society, national or international, without civic friendship as its soul. And since the time when political liberalism went beyond its premises and committed the course of society to purely secular dynamics, nothing has happened to convince an intelligent man that society can be ensouled by civic friendship unless civic friendship itself have, as its own soul, the virtue of charity that springs from Christian faith.

I have, therefore, dealt rather in general with two things that the Church wants in the temporal order. She wants her children, who are in the temporal order, to seek solely the pearl of great price that is not formed in the shell of time, and the hidden treasure that is not found in the fields of earth. Paradoxically, they are to render their greatest service to the world by not serving the world; for only one who sells all he has on earth leaves the earth itself enriched by the bargain. And it has been well said that there are just enough saints in the world to keep it from flying completely apart. The Church wants this situation to continue.

Secondly, at the same time that the Church recalls her children from absorption in the temporal order, she demands their engagement in it, for two main reasons. We have not here a lasting city, but while the city does last, it must be made a city of justice and friendship—on the one hand, for the value that its order has in freeing man for the pursuit of his eternal destiny; and on the other hand for the value that its order has in itself, as a realization, always imperfect indeed, of a rational ideal of human unity.

It may be said that this statement of what the Church wants in the temporal order is very general, and somewhat eschatological. Well, I was only writing a preface. And, as a matter of fact, to a statement of what anyone at all wants in time, would not the best preface, perhaps, be a sketch of his eschatology?

4

THE ROMAN INDEX OF PROHIBITED BOOKS *

The principle of the Index, or the Church's right to deny its members the reading of certain books, will be criticized by very few people in the modern world. Some few believe that absolute license is advisable, but most Americans understand that some kinds of reading are harmful and should be restricted. Nearly everyone, for example, agrees that local communities should take proper steps to keep obscene picture books away from young children.

The Roman Index was begun by the Church in the sixteenth century to protect Catholics from exposure to doctrinal error. The author of the following selection traces the development of the Index, showing how it has become less and less severe as times have changed. The Index was originally considered a temporary device to save the faithful from heretical works until such time as the new heresies would die out. It was prepared for Catholic countries where most of the literate people were clergymen and where a very small proportion of the population could read.

American students and scholars encounter little difficulty with the Index. They are required to obtain permission through the proper channels, usually the diocesan chancery office, to read the required work. If the reading of a given work is necessary for one's work as a scholar or a student, permission is readily given. Difficulty arises with those works that are not included by name but fall into one of the general categories of forbidden reading. Few students can judge whether any work falls into one of these categories. One is therefore well advised, if his conscience is not clear on the matter, to consult with a competent priest, such as the Newman Club chaplain, to find whether he must obtain permission to read any particular work.

* Humphrey J. T. Johnson, "The Roman Index of Prohibited Books," *Downside Review* (Spring, 1955), pp. 160-173. Reprinted by permission.

"THE ROMANS burnt the books of the Jews, of the Christians, and the Philosophers; the Jews burnt the books of the Christians and the Pagans; and the Christians burnt the books of the Pagans and the Jews." So writes the elder Disraeli in his essay on the "Destruction of Books" and we cannot feel sure that the philosophers, both ancient and modern, would not have done the same had it been in their power to do so. The tradition that the Alexandrian library was used as fuel to heat the baths because the Caliph Omar held that all profitable knowledge was contained in the Koran is rejected by modern historians. It is now agreed that when Omar's general 'Amr occupied the city the great assemblages of books which had been brought together by the Ptolemies had already suffered heavily in earlier troubles. If, however, the story of Omar's vandalism be a late fiction we are assured by the author of *Curiosities of Literature* that much of the ancient poetry of the Persians perished in consequence of an edict of the Mohammedan ruler of Khorassan, who declared that those of his faith had no use for any book save that of the Arabian prophet. But a day came when the tables were turned and on the capture of Granada it is said that several thousand copies of the Koran perished in the flames under the direction of the Inquisitors and even that of the great Cardinal Ximenez himself, fearful lest their survival would prove an occasion of backsliding to the new converts.

In the Apostolic Constitution *Officiorum ac Munerum* by which the Index was reformed, Leo XIII started with the burning of magical books as a result of St. Paul's preaching at Ephesus (Acts xix, 19) and sketched the history of the Church's attitude towards pernicious literature before the invention of printing. Her condemnations were primarily theological in scope at this epoch and only in the second place concerned the diffusion of dangerous writings. The warfare against books, revived in our own day by the demand for the destruction of works by National Socialists or by Communists was inspired, partially at least, by the belief held by all parties that a tradition deemed pernicious would languish if preserved only through oral transmission.

With the multiplication of books consequent on the invention of the printing-press the bonfire lost some, at least, of its efficacy and needed to be supplemented by other methods. The exact date of the discovery of printing is unknown but in 1740 some learned men in Germany celebrated its tercentenary and 1440 may be regarded, so far as there is one, as its traditional date. Paul II (1464-71), if less of a humanist than Nicholas V, yet welcomed the introduction of printing into Italy. But before the century was out the Popes had become alive to the fact that the new art could assist the spread of what was harmful as well as of what was good. Sixtus IV issued instructions to the Archbishops of the Rhineland with regard to the use of the press, while a Bull of Alexander VI required previous ecclesiastical censorship for all books printed there, a provision made universal by the fifth Lateran Council in 1515. This pope also directed that harmful writings already in circulation should be suppressed, to expedite which printers and others were to notify books in their possession, to the Archbishops, their vicars and *officiales* under pain of excommunication incurred *latae sententiae.*

Secular rulers felt themselves menaced from the same quarter and in 1535 Francis I prohibited the unauthorized printing of books under penalty of death. To the Sorbonne was accorded the right of deciding what should be printed. In England the Crown assumed the right of censorship after the Reformation, but it never issued what might be called an Index, though certain books were ordered to be burnt by a common hangman. The first Index properly so-called seems to have been that printed at Louvain in 1546 by order of Charles V for use in Spain and the Spanish Netherlands. The Spanish Index was not the only non-Roman one but it was the most famous. It included the Roman Index but contained certain additions of its own. In 1558 Philip II enjoined the punishments of confiscation and death against anyone who should sell or keep in his possession a book prohibited by the Index. "The contest with Protestantism in Spain under such auspices was short," says Ticknor (*History of Spanish Literature* [1863] i, 422, 423). The Spanish Index at one time occupied 1,200 pages. The last edition was published in 1790. A supplement published in 1805 includes Burke's *Reflections on the French Revolution* (Ticknor iii, 366). It was not however till 1892 that the Holy Office forbade the issue of new editions of the Spanish Index in the following enactment,

> *'Standum unice Indici romano librorum prohibitorum ejusque regulis, et prohibendas esse novas Indicis Hispani editiones.'* (Boudinhon, *La Nouvelle Législation de l'Index,* 2nd ed. [1925], p. 218).

The celebrated Roman *Index Librorum Prohibitorum* is a work but little known to Catholics in this country [England], so little known in fact that Mgr. R. A. Knox is able to assure Arnold Lunn that though he is ever poking about libraries only once in his life did he see a copy of it (*Difficulties,* 1952 ed., 202). Most Catholics of my acquaintance could not, I suspect, mention off-hand six of the 5,000 entries it contains. I doubt whether there is a canonist in England who could pass with credit an examination in its contents. We seem to have no serious study of the Roman Index by an English Catholic. Indeed the work of the Anglican controversialist, Joseph Mendham, entitled the *Literary Policy of the Church of Rome* and dedicated to Sir Robert Inglis, the anti-Newmanite Member for Oxford University, would appear to be the most which has been done in this direction. It is however marred by a singular acrimony of tone. Yet much of the material for a serious work is provided in Lord Acton's magnificent collection of editions of the Index at Cambridge.

The first of the long series was promulgated by Paul IV. It was of such severity as to alarm scholars and booksellers who felt deprived by it either of indispensable means of pursuing their studies or threatened with loss of livelihood. This Index distinguished three classes of books: (i) those written by authors who had erred *ex professo,* the whole of whose works were forbidden, even if they contained nothing against the Faith, such a measure being known as a condemnation *in odium auctoris;* (ii) books by authors of whose writings only certain ones were forbidden; (iii) books containing pernicious doctrines written by authors who were for the most part anonymous. Paul IV's Index included the *De Monarchia* of Dante, Boccaccio's *Decamerone* and Lorenzo Valla's work on the Donation of Constantine. England is represented by Henry VIII, Cranmer, Tyndale, John Astoe, John 'Hoperus' (Hooper) and John Oldencastle. Other forbidden writings include unauthorized versions of the Bible, the Talmud with commentaries on it and magical works. Needful though an Index may have been, Paul IV's was so severe that not even Pastor defends it. The Sorbonne and the Spanish Inquisition ignored it, though the Spanish authorities co-operated with the Roman Inquisitors in burning copies of the Talmud at Cremona (Pastor, *History of the Popes,* xiv, 276-80).

Pius IV issued a somewhat milder Index known as the "Tridentine" one. It was promulgated in 1564 and prefixed to it are the ten rules for the interpretation of the Index which though slightly altering their form disappeared only in recent times. Books by propagators of heresy, "heresiarchs," as they were called, were condemned as before. Among them were Luther, Calvin, Zwingli and two lesser known Reformers, Kaspar Schwenfeld and Balthasar Huebmaier (Pacimontanus). Books by other heretics not treating of religious matters were allowed. The ninth rule prohibited writings on "geomancy, aeromancy, pyromancy, onomancy, chiromancy and necromancy," as well as those treating of sorceries, auguries, auspices and magical incantations or making predictions of the future. But books written in aid of navigation, agriculture and medicine were to be permitted. In 1570 Pius V founded the Sacred Congregation of the Index which existed till 1918 when the censorship of books was transferred to the Holy Office by the *motu proprio* of Benedict XV, *Alloquentes proxime.* An attempt to build up an *Index Expurgatorius* for books which needed correction came to nothing, but traces of it remain in the formula *donec corrigatur* inserted after some entries in later editions of the Index.

No more than a cursory glance at those which appeared in the sixteenth and seventeenth centuries is needed to show that the quarters from which danger was most apprehended in addition to Lutheranism (as Protestantism was then called), were Judaism and Sorcery. The "observations" prefixed to the Index contain not only one on the Talmud, but one also on the "Magazor," a manual of Jewish ritual which was not allowed to circulate in any language except Hebrew. An "observation" concerned with Jean Bodin's *Démonomanie* disappeared only in the time of Benedict XIV. In the edition of 1664, promulgated by Alexander VII, the old division of writings into three classes is dropped and an alphabetical order definitely adopted. This is said to have been done not merely for purposes of convenience, but because a belief had grown up that reading books in the first class constituted a graver sin than reading those in the other classes. A curious entry in this edition is one ordering the deletion of some words in the Breviary lessons for the feast of St. Catherine of Siena.

In the following century Benedict XIV promulgated new rules for the censorship of books in the Apostolic Constitution, *Sollicita ac provida,* and gave to the Index legislation the shape it retained down to the reforms of Leo XIII. A perusal of Benedict XIV's *Index Librorum Prohibitorum* is instructive. The edition of 1744 before the condemnation of Voltaire is already a work of ample proportions, containing with a supplement 639 pages. Of greater interest is the edition produced towards the end of the pontificate after the condemnation of the Encyclopaedists and reprinted in 1770. Among English writers whose works are prohibited wholly or in part are Henry VIII and James I, Stephen Gardiner, John Knox, Tyndale, Lancelot Andrews, Francis Bacon, Joseph Bingham (author of *Antiquities of the Christian Church*), Gilbert and Thomas Burnet, Cudworth, Lord Herbert of Cherbury, Hobbes, Locke, Swift (*Tale of a Tub*), Tillotson, Woolston, Sherlock, Selden, Hume, Camden, Richardson and Ephraim Chambers, editor of the *Cyclopaedia.* But what may strike us as the most curious entry in the whole volume is *Paradise Lost,* smitten by censure on its translation into Italian by Paolo Brolli in 1732. France is represented by Montaigne, Bayle, Descartes, Malebranche, Fénelon, Voltaire and Rousseau, as well as by lesser known writers and by pastoral letters of various Bishops, including one of Cardinal de Noailles. Dante, Boccaccio and Guicciardini are still among condemned Italian writers, while Holland is represented by Grotius, Germany by Puffendorf and Sweden by Swedenborg. A more general condemnation of the literature of the Enlightenment was made by Pius IV in 1778 by which works seeking to overthrow the foundations of religion are condemned en bloc. Catholics and Protestants were now to a limited extent able to make common cause and the Jesuit apologist for the Index, Father F. A. Zaccaria, can quote the "pseudo-Bishop" of London, Edmund Gibson, on the harm done by bad books (*Storia polemica dei proibizioni di libri* 1777, 243, 269).

Permission to read heretical literature had of course to be granted from the beginning to meet the controversial exigencies of the hour, but they were not granted too readily; for the law assumed that the great majority of men were weak and could not be relied upon to resist the blandishments of heresy if it were presented in an attractive guise. Paul V felt anxiety at the number of permissions which were being granted and for a time they were revoked altogether under Gregory XV. But at the beginning of the nineteenth century they could occasionally at least be obtained by laymen and Chateaubriand related that, when he was ambassador in Rome, if he wanted to read a prohibited book he would on remission of a very small sum of money to an ecclesiastical official for his trouble, receive a written permission to read it, with the proviso however that he might only do so if his conscience allowed. Permissions to read and keep prohibited literature were, as was natural, most readily accorded to Bishops.

But from the time of Gregory XVI to that of Leo XIII there existed a short list of authors whose writings were considered so dangerous that reservation with regard to them was made in the quinquennial faculties granted to the local Ordinaries. The authors forbidden to members of the Hierarchy included only one Englishman, Jeremy Bentham; four of his works are condemned by name in the Index catalogue. The others include five Frenchmen: Charles-François Dupuis (1742-1809) and Constantin-François Volney (1757-1820), *savants;* Charles-Antoine Guillaume Pigault-le-Brun (1753-1835), novelist; Jacques-Antoine Dulaure (1755-1835), archaeologist and historian, and Pierre Jean-Baptiste Chaussard (1766-1823), man of letters. The works of the first four were forbidden to Bishops without special mention of any one of them. Chaussard's book *Fêtes et courtisanes de la Grèce* was expressly forbidden by name. It is described in the "Nouvelle Biographie Universelle" as an *ouvrage assez superficiel et souvent licencieux.* The author was an ex-ecclesiastic who during the Revolution had mounted the pulpit of Saint-Germain-l'Auxerrois and preached the doctrine of theophilanthropy. The other authors forbidden in the *facultates quinquennales* were M. Reghellini, Louis-Joseph-Antoine de Potter (1786-1859) and Giambattista Casti (1724-1803). Reghellini was a native of Chios. His principal book *Examen du Mosaïsme et du Christianisme,* a work of three volumes, was published at Paris in 1834 and condemned two years later. De Potter was a historian of "enlightened" views who played a part in the Belgian Revolution of 1830. He was the author of a life of Scipione di Ricci, the Jansenist Bishop of Prato-Pistoia, whose papers had been entrusted to de Potter by the Bishop's family. The last of the authors forbidden to Bishops, Giambattista Casti, was a cleric who became a writer of opéra bouffe. He travelled about Europe enjoying at one time the patronage of Joseph II and Catherine II. At the age of 78 he wrote an indecent poem of twenty-six cantos *Gli Animali Parlanti,* a skit on the antediluvian world. The works of these authors, Bishops might neither read nor give permission to others to do so. In the case of other forbidden writers, permission to read them might be conceded to trustworthy priests but not, it would seem, to the laity. The regulations of the Index do not appear to have contemplated a society in which the ablest Catholic apologists might be laymen.

But when the nineteenth century was well advanced, not even the warmest apologist on behalf of the Index could deny that it had failed to realize the hopes placed in it by the Popes of the Counter-Reformation.

Protestantism had shown itself to be no merely transitory phenomenon but something which had come to stay, and now Free Thought was doing likewise. Rules drawn up for the conditions of the sixteenth century when books and readers were relatively few could not without grave inconvenience be applied to those prevailing in the nineteenth. When the Index was instituted learning meant familiarity with the writers of antiquity. By the nineteenth century a new European literature had come into being, much of it falling under one or other of the prohibitions contained in the Index legislation but acquaintance with which was indispensable for entrance into cultured society. The congregations of the Holy Office and of the Index could moreover no longer count on the co-operation of the civil power. Voltaire's writings were first burnt and then tolerated. Then came the freedom of the press with all the advantages and disadvantages it brought in its train. Benjamin Constant's plea, in his treatise *De la liberté des brochures, des pamphlets et des journaux,* that a free journalist writing in Paris would show greater responsibility than one writing clandestinely in exile at Amsterdam or Geneva, helped to bring about a change in the French law and before the end of the nineteenth century all Europe except Russia had a "free press." When the State disinterested itself in what its subjects read and wrote, there were many who came to look upon ecclesiastical censorship and prohibition of books as anachronistic. Yet upon the vast majority of Catholics they did not in all probability weigh heavily. In countries like Italy and Spain the reading even of the higher ecclesiastics seems to have been restricted. Stendhal says of Cardinal Somaglia, Secretary of State to Leo XII, that he hardly dared to open a book lest he should find heresy in it, and that this represented an attitude which was not uncommon among the clergy of his day. Allowing for the necessary element of exaggeration in such statements, they nevertheless convey to us something of the impression created by the clergy on the lay mind.

But if in Southern Europe few Catholics felt the Index as an oppression, further north in France, Belgium and Germany restlessness began to manifest itself. Demands for a reform of the Index or even for its total abolition began to make themselves heard. When one such was made to Gregory XVI on the ground that there were now so many good books as to render it unnecessary, he is said to have replied that the abolition of the Index would be as sensible as the removal of restrictions on the sale of poisons, on the ground that antidotes could be purchased in the same shop. Lord Acton, than whom few men could have known more about the Index, was a severe critic of it. He charged it with being obstructive to scholarship.

One of the great instruments for preventing historical scrutiny [he wrote] was the Index of Prohibited Books, which was accordingly directed, not against falsehood only, but against certain departments of truth. Through it an effort was made to keep the knowledge of ecclesiastical history from the faithful and to give currency to a fabulous and fictitious picture of the progress and action of the Church. The means would have been found quite inadequate to the end, if it had not been for the fact, that while society was absorbed by controversy, knowledge was only valued as it served a controversial purpose.

("Conflicts with Rome," *Home and Foreign Review,* iv [1864], 676.) As the Vatican Council drew near, pleas were heard from the Bishops of France and Germany for a revision of the Index legislation, on the ground that much of it was now obsolete. The Bishops of the latter country stressed the anxiety caused thereby to penitents and confessors alike. When the Council met, a note of irony was heard. It was said that if the reading of books was forbidden, no less must it be forbidden to hear them read aloud. There was general agreement that the situation was unsatisfactory and the Council had the laudable intention of undertaking a reform of the Index. This was found to be impracticable and nothing had been done when Pius IX died, except a reduction in the number of classes of books for the reading and keeping of which excommunication *latae sententiae* was incurred. It was limited by the Constitution *Apostolicae Sedis* of 12th October 1869, to books of apostates, of heretics defending heresy and those condemned by apostolic letter. This excommunication was reserved to the Holy See *speciali modo.*

Leo XIII set himself to the task of revision, but at the outset he was confronted with a dilemma. Should reforms be in the direction of mitigation or of greater severity? If the aim of the Index was to prevent the Faithful from meeting with sympathetic presentations of the heretical point of view, then not only must the reading of books be curtailed, but a vast amount of periodical literature must be proscribed as well. To-day even this would be totally insufficient; for heresy may be heard in the theatre, at the cinema, on the radio. It may be heard in the factory, the office or the club. To achieve the aims of the Popes of the Counter-Reformation, it would be almost necessary to forbid Catholics to discuss religion with non-Catholics. If on the other hand a deepening of intellectual life among Catholics was needed, a reform in the way of mitigation was called for, unless of course, dispensations were issued on so lavish a scale as to render the law nugatory. The Leonine reform was embodied in the Apostolic Constitution *Officiorum ac Munerum* which appeared on 25th January 1897. It was followed in 1900 by a new Index, in which several well-known names such as *Paradise Lost* and *De Monarchia* are no longer to be met. The new legislation permitted the reading of books by non-Catholics, even though they treated of religious topics, provided that they contained nothing against the Catholic Faith. But if its tendency was to render the ancient rules "un peu plus douces," they were substantially unchanged. Moreover, a whole class of literature hitherto ignored by it now fell under the laws of the Index.

In 1832 the minds of the Swiss Bishops had been exercised as to whether the laity could be prudently permitted to read newspapers which had not previously been submitted to episcopal censorship. Rome had replied that the Faithful should have recourse to their confessors for the solution of this matter. Leo XIII included periodical literature within the scope of the Index legislation and approximated the rules governing it to those regulating the reading of books. Hair-splitting discussions now arose among the canonists touching the properties of *diaria, folia* and *libelli periodici*.

The Leonine reforms left substantially unaltered the laws regulating the reading and keeping of prohibited books and those who had counselled far-reaching changes had been unable to make their voices heard. One such was the erudite canonist, Mgr. Auguste Boudinhon, who advocated the introduction of a new principle under which books should be classified according to the degree of danger they were apprehended to possess, while the grounds of this danger were to be stated. Boudinhon further critized the Index for its failure to make more appeal to the conscience of the individual and its excessive severity towards Catholic authors who had exhibited certain tendencies rather than been convicted of definite errors. "It is abundantly evident that the Index is unsatisfactory," he concluded (s.v. Index, Hasting's *Encyclopaedia of Religion and Ethics*). This conclusion was widely held. "That the rules of the Index need further adaptation to the times," wrote Mr. Wilfrid Ward, "I have never heard denied, and the highest authority has recently admitted, that many of its provisions have become obsolete." ("Liberalism and Intransigeance," *Nineteenth Century Review* [June 1900], p. 970.)

In the intervening half-century some changes have been introduced into the form of the Index. In the edition of Pius XI (1922) the *pars prior* contains the pertinent provisions of the *Codex Juris Canonici*. In that of Pius XII (1948) the old division of the Index into a *pars prior* and *pars posterior* disappears and the catalogue of condemned works is preceded only by extracts from the Codex (canons 1395-1405), which themselves reproduced in substance the decrees of the Council of Trent with the modifications introduced by Leo XIII. The most important of these canons is 1399 which enumerates the eleven classes of books prohibited *ipso jure*. In the catalogue of condemned writings the penalty of excommunication reserved *speciali modo* to the Holy See is said to be incurred only in the case of books condemned by apostolic letter, which are marked with a cross in recent editions of the Index.

Opposition to the Roman Index began at an early date. The Sorbonne and the Spanish Inquisition ignored that of Paul IV, while Philip II objected to the Tridentine one on the ground that it omitted books which had been placed on the Spanish Index. Coming to a more recent period, we find the French Provincial Council of Toulouse in 1850 and that of Rheims in 1857 omitting all mention of the Index. They added it later, however, on the demand of the Roman Congregation charged with the revision of their acts. Mgr. Knox believes that in the period following the Reformation, English Catholics had a genuine grievance against the Index, but he feels able to assure Arnold Lunn that he need not fear to become a Catholic on account of it. "But I think it is fairly clear," he writes, "that it [the Index] does not give much trouble to the laity nowadays." (*Difficulties*, p. 202.) Mgr. Knox is strangely silent about the clergy. A similar conclusion has been reached by one occupying a very different standpoint from his. In a polemical work, *Roman Catholicism and Freedom,* the Non-conformist divine, Dr. C. J. Cadoux, argues that time spent in attacking the Index is wasted since the provisions are so mildly interpreted in this country. In the early nineteenth century the situation was not very different. When his antagonist, Robert Southey, told Charles Butler that he (Southey) would soon be on the *Index Expurgatorius* and that then Catholics would not be allowed to read him, Butler was overcome with indignation.

> How little is the Doctor acquainted with the state of those whom it pleases him to revile? Few of them know of the existence of the *Index Expurgatorius*; scarcely any know whether the Doctor's book will be named in it. If this should be the case, it will no more prevent them from reading it than the mention of Milton, Locke, Hume, Robertson and a hundred others on the Index prevents Catholics from reading their writings. Dr. Lingard [he continues] justly observes that the authority of the Index was always very confined, and in many countries never acknowledged.

Of even greater interest are the remarks of Archbishop Murray who, giving evidence before a Select Committee of the House of Commons on the State of Ireland on 17th May 1825, said, "the *Index Expurgatorius* has no authority whatever in Ireland; it has never been received in these countries and I doubt very much whether there are ten people in Ireland who have ever seen it." (Phelan and O'Sullivan, *Digest of the Evidence taken before the Select Committee of both Houses of Parliament to inquire into the State of Ireland,* 1824, 1825, Part I, p. 232.) The confusion between the *Index Expurgatorius* and the *Index Librorum Prohibitorum,* understandable in a layman like Butler, is strange in an Archbishop of Dublin.

As the nineteenth century advanced, the question which presented itself most urgently was not a juridical one concerned with the scope of the authority of the Tridentine Index, but a human problem. Could the degree of intellectual culture needed to enable Catholics to hold their own be achieved by one whose reading was confined to such works as the canons permitted? If not, how was a remedy to be sought? Newman could not escape the fact that the liberal education, which he so much desired for those English Catholics who were capable of receiving it, called for something wider. In 1850 we find him writing to Rome to ascertain how far the Tridentine legislation was to be considered operative in England. The reply which he received must have been highly gratifying to him. In a letter to Mgr. Talbot, at that time his friend, written on 23rd October, he says, "I have lately had good advice from Rome that one may act as if the rule about prohibited books had not been promulgated in England." ("Some Newman Letters" in the *Venerabile,* October 1938, p. 43.) Manning, however much he may have disagreed with Newman on other topics, seems to have shared his sentiments over this one, and to have contented himself with telling his clergy that they should not read heretical books without good reason for doing so.

The situation admittedly changed when Leo XIII declared that the new Index legislation foreshadowed in the Constitution *Officiorum ac Munerum* applied universally and, on 23rd May 1898, the Congregation of the Index gave the reply *Affirmative* to the *dubium 'Utrum dicta Constitutio vim obligatoriam habeat etiam pro regionibus britannici idiomatis quas tacita dispensatione frui quidam arbitrantur?'* No one could have expected a different answer, but Boudinhon reminds us that the Bull does not expressly mention the abrogation of existing customs, and thinks that special circumstances may exist in countries the majority of whose inhabitants are Protestants. The answer of the Congregation of the Index concerned the English-speaking countries. A milder one envisaging, it seems, England only, was given by Propaganda, to whom Cardinal Vaughan and the English Bishops had had recourse for guidance on the appearance of the Leonine Constitution. It is somewhat complicated, but Boudinhon interprets it as indicating that the *status quo* might remain in this country unchanged. This interpretation is favoured by the fact that in its joint pastoral on "Liberal Catholicism" issued by the Hierarchy in the last week of the century, though indiscriminate and unregulated reading was reproved, no direct reference to the Leonine legislation was made. This situation seems to have survived the promulgation of the *Codex Juris Canonici*. For when it came into force, though the attention of the Faithful was drawn to the new provisions touching fasting, abstinence, and marriage, no English Catholic considered himself debarred from reading a book or a newspaper which he could have conscientiously read before.

It is difficult now to conceive of the laws of the Index fully operating in any society except one controlled by ecclesiastics either directly or indirectly. In the absence of such a condition a knowledge of Canon law which few laymen possess seems to be postulated in every layman who can read. The layman must know that when a name of a book disappears from the Index he is not, as he might innocently suppose, allowed to read it. For a friendly moral theologian will tell him that as likely as not it belongs to a class of literature condemned en bloc, its withdrawal from the catalogue signifying no more than that it is not a work to whose danger the Church at present wishes to call special attention. A graver difficulty, facing confessor and penitent alike, lies in the extreme difficulty which most often occurs of determining whether a given book falls within one of the numerous catagories of prohibited literature. This is especially so in the case of many biographical, historical and scientific works. What, moreover, may be considered "dangerous" varies from century to century and between class and class. A book may be "dangerous" to one who reads little which would be innocous to one who reads much. If the faith of one young man is endangered through reading a particular book, more harm may be done to another by forbidding him to read it, than the reading of the book itself would do. For in the latter case he may conclude that the "priests" are seeking to bolster up their own shaky position by stifling truth. To some, and probably they are not a few, fantastic, unscholarly or uncharitable Catholic works do more harm than the writings of unbelievers. Newman said that he knew of no work which would so readily make him an infidel as Faber's book, *The Blessed Sacrament.* Discussions, therefore, among theologians as to whether the reading of three, four or five octavo pages of a forbidden book is needed to constitute a mortal sin are apt in our time to seem unhelpful.

Summing up the position as it existed in the early years of the present century, Boudinhon says that while the legislation of Leo XIII "resulted in the better observance of the rules for the publication of books" it did not apparently "modify the practice as regards the reading of prohibited books." His final conclusion is that "the tendency of the practice among Catholics at large is to reduce these condemnations to the proportions of the moral law."

5

THE CHURCH AND SCIENCE *

The conflict between religion and science puzzles men with a philosophic mind. Their resolution of the problem is pat and simple. "Truth is one," they say, "and religion and science are interested in two aspects of the truth. Their subject matter is different, their methodologies are different, they operate in different fields. If each stays in its proper field and each is free from error, then religion and science will support each other rather than conflict." This pat resolution of the apparent *conflict between religion and science is correct for* pure *religion and* pure *science, but it does not explain how* apparent *conflict has appeared very real, and how many scientists and theologians are suspicious of each other and inclined even to be hostile toward each other.*

In the following selection one of England's most prominent scientists, who was a convert to the Catholic faith, analyzes these difficulties and shows that they are largely psychological. Theologians in the past fre-

* F. Sherwood Taylor, *Man and Matter* (New York: McMullen Books, Inc., 1951), pp. 181-203. Reprinted by permission of Pearn, Pollinger & Higham, Ltd.

quently treated the Bible as though it were a source book of scientific information, which, of course, it is not. This caused them to make some manifestly absurd statements in the area of the natural sciences. But more recently the vogue of science has popularly attached an unquestioned infallibility to the scientific method and to scientists personally. The scientists' pronouncement on a religious doctrine was given greater credence than the theologian's—and there were many scientists, like Thomas Huxley or Ernst Haeckel, who spoke about God with the same assurance their fellows used in speaking about the atomic table.

Good scientists and good theologians agree with the philosopher that truth cannot contradict truth and that conflict between scientific truth and religious truth can only be apparent. They suspend judgment and go on investigating, secure in the knowledge that one or the other "truths" will turn out to be an erroneous hypothesis or a religious opinion that is widely taken to be truth rather than opinion. It is necessary that the scientist and the theologian respect each other, acknowledge that both fields are legitimate quests for the truth, and that ultimately apparent conflicts between the two are resolved without loss to the Truth itself.

THE selection of such a subject at once indicates that there is a problem connected with the relationships of the Church and science. There certainly has been and still is such a problem: whether there need have been or need be is quite another matter. In what sense are we to use the words "church" and "science"? The Church is a body of persons, a community united by a common faith and holding as true certain well-defined beliefs. Science is a method of making and ordering well-tested observations concerning the physical world, and, if we accept these definitions, the difficulty of the relation between the Church and science could only be that the beliefs of the Church lead us to affirm what science leads us to deny, or vice versa. But in fact there is more in the words Church and science than I have indicated. They are words which, in common speech, both now and in the past, have meant several different things. Both of them do, or at least may, include (1) a body of knowledge and so-called laws, (2) a method of considering the objects of perception, (3) a view of the world that varies from a working hypothesis to profound conviction: and in fact there is and has been conflict in all three of these aspects.

Let us first consider the question from the aspect of knowledge.

As we all know, the Holy Scriptures and the traditions of the Church enunciate certain propositions which appear, *prima facie,* to be matters of historical fact, e.g., that the human race has sprung from a single pair:

that Joshua caused the sun to stand still; that Esther succeeded Vashti as Queen of Persia, that Jesus was born at Bethlehem when Herod was king. . . . Science also claims to give opinions concerning such matters. Thus palaeontology or biology might adduce facts which could be interpreted as evidence against the origin of the human race from a single pair: a modern astronomer would probably express the strongest views concerning the sudden arrest of the earth in its rotation: archaelogists might find documents which enumerated the queens of Ahasuerus but made no mention of Esther, and a papyrus might be unearthed from the sands of Egypt giving an account of Our Lord's life very different from the accounts given by the evangelists.

In any of these events we would be faced with a conflict of testimony, and we should require to include the new evidence and our former belief in a scheme in which they would not be in conflict. To quote words which were used by Galileo, "From the Divine Word the Sacred Scripture and Nature did both alike proceed"—and so they cannot truly disagree. This is a fundamental proposition to which we must assent: but it is not correct to say that, except very indirectly, "From the Divine Word Sherwood Taylor's interpretation of Scripture and H. G. Well's account of Nature did both alike proceed," and there is the field of conflict.

Men very often disagree about matters of fact and their interpretation. Scientists differ among themselves on many such matters; and this although, nay because, they would be the first to acknowledge that there can be only one scientific truth about a natural phenomenon. So in the case of an apparent conflict between science and religion, a Christian philosopher has a clear duty; namely, to do as other men do in similar cases—that is, to investigate the matter further without alarm or misgiving, and if he cannot resolve the contradiction, to suspend judgment. He must very carefully inquire into the Scripture with a view to discovering the intention of the sacred writers, if this has not already been defined by an infallible authority, and endeavour to find out how far their assertions can be read as scientific fact and how far they are accommodated to the minds of those through whom they were written and to whom they were addressed—how far they are parables intended to be true in ethics but poetical in fact. On the other hand he must also inquire into the historical or scientific evidence which appears to conflict with the Scriptures, asking himself whether it be approximate or accurate; guess-work or measurement; observation, inference, or speculation. There is in consequence an enormous field for the exercise of judgment in any case of apparent conflict of science and religious doctrine. Every case must be faced, and we are neither entitled to refuse to consider any of the words of Scripture, nor any scientific evidence which appears to be worthy of consideration.

As I have already said, it is common knowledge that controversy between scientific men and churchmen has been bitter during many periods of the Church's history. My intention is to survey the general history of these difficulties, with a view to discovering how the problems in question have been so mishandled as to give rise to bitter controversy.

Since both are of the nature of truth, it is clear that pure accurate science and pure religion cannot conflict in the sense of being unable to co-exist in the same mind at the same time; and it would appear that all cases of such conflict are due to one party importing into their science or religion something which does not logically flow from the legitimate data.

The Christian has to make, with God's help, an act of faith in accepting Christian doctrine. God, who is Himself Divine Knowledge, has shown something of Himself by His actions towards men and these actions have been recorded in Holy Scripture. Man exercising his natural reason may be led to think that the Holy Scriptures are true, but reason cannot prove this irrefutably nor can the Holy Scriptures afford evidence of their truth, until they are believed to be the word of God. God gives to man the power of faith whereby he accepts that record of God's manifestations to man as a true record. Thus the Christian knows the truth of religion, while the non-Christian regards it as mere hypothesis depending on the credibility of the Scriptures. Yet, for all his knowledge of their truth, the Christian cannot certainly know the full and precise content of those Scriptures, which are not expressed in the language of science and philosophy but in that of symbolism and metaphor. Some articles of faith he can deduce with certainty from his Bible, but in many matters he cannot be sure how literally the sacred words are to be understood. So we have, in fact, two different standards of truth:

1. The truth adhered to by faith, which is accepted through that faith as absolutely true.
2. The results arrived at by reason, which are never truth, but only probable opinion, because the data they start from are never absolutely certain, but which are adequate practical guides in scientific matters and have demonstrated themselves by the production of the modern world with its wonders—and horrors—of science.

   So, on the one hand, rationalists have been saying for centuries that the Christians are believing in histories without any compelling evidence to support them, while on the other hand Christians have been saying that the conclusions of science are only provisional, and anyway have nothing to do with the important matters of human life.

Let us go right back to A.D. 300, to Lactantius who has been held up to derision as an obscurantist and flat-earther. Lactantius recognised perfectly clearly and correctly that natural philosophy is opinion, whereas what has been revealed to the Christian is true knowledge. He is not a sceptic, for he said: "Where then is wisdom? That you should neither think that you know everything, which is an attribute of God; nor that you know nothing, which is an attribute of a beast. For there is a middle path of knowledge conjoined and tempered with awareness of ignorance." He very justly pointed out that such theories as the atomic hypothesis of Democritus and the existence of the Antipodes are inferences which go beyond what is certified by observation, but he did not appreciate the strength of the arguments which, even in antiquity, had been advanced for them, and so has come to be known as a flat-earther, and a byword of the rationalist; all of which is unjust, for he only maintained that we had no certain, i.e., observational, knowledge that the underpart of the earth was like the part known to us. We have counterparts of Lactantius today, Christians who are quick to cavil at individual pieces of scientific evidence without appreciating their part in the whole. Thus we have those who discover faults in individual pieces of evidence, for, let us say, the theory of evolution, without realizing that these do not appreciably diminish or neutralize the force of the multiple convergent indications and analogies that confirm it.

In the next century, near A.D. 400, the question was advanced almost, if not wholly, to its modern state by one who was a philosopher and as much a man of science as any of his time, in addition to being the greatest of theologians—I mean St. Augustine, Bishop of Hippo. As one versed in Greek philosophy before his conversion, he understood the difficulties that faced the educated man of his time when confronted with the apparent difficulties of the Holy Scriptures. It is evident that even at an early period difficulties were felt by the pagans in accepting accounts of miracles, and these difficulties were essentially the same as the scientist of today feels: the difficulty of believing that something had occurred contrary to the common experience of men. Thus St. Augustine, writing concerning the book of Jonah, says, "This sort of question is mocked at by the pagans with great amusement" while Theophylactus remarks, on the same question, that "the matter seems to those that hear it to be beyond all belief, especially to those who come to the story from the schools of the Greeks and from philosophic teachings."

St. Augustine's masterly handling of the difficulties that arise from the interpretation of the Scripture is best seen in his commentary on Genesis. He sees quite clearly, that there cannot be any conflict between what is intended by the Scriptures and what is really demonstrated as true science. Speaking of the philosophers and scientists of his time he says, "Whatever they can demonstrate truly concerning the nature of things, that we can show is not contrary to our [sacred] writing. And whatever they may advance or even demonstrate by some means as contrary to our writings [that is, to the Catholic faith] we will without doubting prove to be most false. . . ." Furthermore, he tells us, if we cannot resolve such a contradiction we are to suspend judgment, not doubting either the Holy Scripture or the results of human observation and reasoning, but believing that it is possible, given sufficient knowledge and understanding, to reconcile the apparent contradiction.

This admirable doctrine has, alas, received little adherence, for the one thing that men will not do, is to suspend judgment and keep quiet.

So in all the difficulties that have arisen between science and the Church we find the writers on each side asserting with extreme positiveness views which were not in fact by any means proven.

After the time of St. Augustine there were five or six centuries during which the knowledge and practice of science was negligible, but in the twelfth to fourteenth centuries a new phenomenon appeared in the West, namely the assimilation by the Church of pagan learning, including philosophy and science. What seemed important to the men of the time was to establish a complete Christian philosophy of the universe; the materials of this were the Scriptures, the traditions of the Church and the writings of the Fathers, on the one hand; their own observations and those recorded in the works of the Greek philosophers, notably Aristotle, on the other. Aristotle's logic, psychology, ethics and metaphysics were of the first importance for this task; his works contain a great deal of science, which enters intimately into his philosophy. Thus his views of God are intimately linked with his view of the nature of the Cosmos, and hence with his quite erroneous views about motion and the vacuum. So much of the work of Aristotle was obviously true and so far in advance of the knowledge of the age that there was little disposition to carry out critical experiments to examine the foundations of his science. St. Thomas and his fellows were, in fact, inclined to build rather than to pull down.

The result was the magnificent structure of Thomistic philosophy and theology in which was embedded and entangled an inferior system of astronomy and some very false physics and physiology. This science can be detached from Thomistic works without affecting them in any essential, but the fact remains that as a part of its doctrine, were included certain false or at least inadequate scientific theories.

This was almost inevitable. Once Vesalius, Paracelsus, Galileo, had taught us to be critical, it became easy to examine the foundations of natural knowledge, but in the thirteenth century, the discipline of observation and experiment was scarcely existent. There were men who might have arrived at it. St. Albert (Albertus Magnus) was one who could report accurately on birds and beasts and insects, and distinguish what he had been told from what he had seen. Robert Grosseteste and Roger Bacon realized that scientific assertions should be verified by observation, but the standard method of the age was to gain knowledge from books of authority—and whose authority, outside the sacred writings came near to that of Aristotle?

Thus it was that the thirteenth century, which welcomed science together with the rest of Greek learning, did not know how to pursue it, and made the capital error of importing into Catholic teaching, if not into formally defined dogma, information about nature which they had not checked and which was in fact largely incorrect. Accordingly, to those whose most sacred and cherished knowledge was expressed in terms of Aristotle's philosophy, any attack on Aristotelian science seemed to be at least a dangerous threat to religion. There were, of course, many acute persons in the Church who saw quite clearly that it was not possible that matters of physical fact should ultimately conflict with the defined truths of the Christian faith. But, in the sixteenth and seventeenth centuries the greatest part of the hierarchy was both unlearned in natural science and very conservative about innovation, and consequently we find the Church fighting a losing battle for Aristotelian science.

When Copernicus published his great work in 1543—a work which was plainly contrary to Aristotelian science and to the generally accepted plan of the universe—little or no opposition was roused, for the book was a highly technical one and not widely read: consequently the threat to Aristotle was not as yet serious. Copernicus had set up a daring hypothesis, but scarcely anyone believed that what he said was intended to be taken as literally true. Copernicans became commoner at the end of the sixteenth century. Digges, Gilbert, Bruno, Kepler, Galileo may be named among them. Digges and Gilbert suffered nothing in this country, always notable for its tolerance of, or indifference to, scientific opinions. Kepler was at one time threatened by the Protestant theological faculty at Tubingen—and had to take refuge, but under royal patronage remained comparatively undisturbed. Bruno's fate we know well enough, but it seems quite impossible to regard him as having suffered for his Copernican opinions. The records of Bruno's trial are very imperfect. We know that these opinions were mentioned in the schedule of accusations against him, but play a very inconsiderable part compared with the many grave charges of heresy, which we must suppose to have been the grounds for his condemnation: for if the Copernican system had been regarded as heretical and action had been taken against Bruno on this count, it would not have been necessary in 1616, more than twenty years after, to inquire of the Holy Office whether it were heretical or not.

The case of Galileo appears to be the only one which has turned on the supposedly heretical character of scientific opinions. It has been scandalously misreported, and if the Catholic historians have been inclined to minimise the unwisdom or injustice of the Church, the Protestants and the Rationalists have gigantically exaggerated it. The story is a long one if it is properly told. The essence of it is that Galileo made certain astronomical discoveries that led him to assert the Copernican view as fact and not only as theory; that he was unwise enough, when attacked, to propound his views on the interpretation of Scripture; and that in 1616 the essentials of the Copernican system were declared by the Holy Office to be rash, unsound, and in part heretical. Galileo was ordered not to hold, teach or defend those opinions. After some years he published a work which purported to attack the Copernican views, but was, in fact, a strong defence of them. He was summoned before the Inquisition on the charge of disobeying the order of 1616 and made to recant his opinions: for the rest of his life he was confined to his house, but otherwise had full liberty.

So brief an account cannot possibly give the complex and disputed facts of the case; but here we may look, not at the intrigues, counter intrigues and personalities, but rather at the ultimate question, namely, how there came about this unhappy situation that has caused so much scandal. No one has any doubt now that the Copernican system was not heretical: where was the mistake? We do not know what happened in the deliberations of the consultors of the Holy Office, but the case advanced against Galileo by his adversaries was based on:

1. The alleged inconsistency of the Copernican hypothesis with certain texts of Scripture.
2. The unanimous opinion of the Fathers of the Church as to the geocentric meaning of the above texts.

In the first respect we can only say that the consultors acted very strangely and in a manner far removed from St. Augustine's counsels. They presumably did not dare to question Aristotle's false principles of physics because they seemed to be much involved in the theological arguments of the time; and they saw, quite correctly, that if these principles were accepted, the Copernican view could be disproved and must be false. Furthermore they clearly did not believe that there had been a true demonstration of the Copernican view—as indeed there had not, for many of Galileo's arguments were unsound and at best astronomy could do no more than render it probable. At this period the principle of the scientific method had not been fully established, and it is not surprising that both parties failed to draw that distinction between theory and fact which would have solved the problem. Certainly the consultors acted very unwisely in accepting Aristotle's physics so fully as to be convinced that a true demonstration of a heliocentric system would never be given, and Newton's *Principia,* seventy years later, came as near to such a demonstration as is possible for science. The consultors, in fact, panicked and decided a question of astronomical fact with the aid of a few slender texts of Scripture, which were capable of other interpretations, no doubt because they had too much respect for Aristotle's scientific teachings, which seemed to them to be indissolubly united to Catholic doctrine—a union which had only come into being because of the uncritical methods of thirteenth century science and philosophy.

The second point which seems to have influenced the consultors, was the universal agreement of the Fathers in the geocentric opinion. All, of course, did interpret these texts geocentrically, because that was the natural assumption in the times they lived in; for there was then no need to try to accommodate the Holy Scriptures to the half-forgotten eccentricity of Aristarchus of Samos and a few others, who had asserted that the earth rotated and revolved about the sun.

The Church did in fact soon recede from its anti-Copernican views and within some twenty years or so was permitting the teaching of Copernican astronomy. And the lesson was learnt, great circumspection having been used about speaking in too dogmatic a manner about any of the numerous difficulties that came up in the nineteenth century, the chief of which is the problem of the origin of man.

Many of us feel at times that we should like to be told exactly what the Church would have us believe or teach about Evolution; but how much wiser is the leaving of this and other such questions without comment, pending a more advanced state of scientific knowledge. The view of St. Augustine, that the deposit of faith is true and potentially reconcilable with correctly observed scientific fact is the sound one; and, in accordance with it, each of us can examine the works of the evolutionists of his age and say, "This is observation of such a degree of reliability: this is sound deduction: this is mere conjecture." Likewise he can examine the book of Genesis and consider the weight that has to be given to the various interpreters and to the responses of the Biblical commission concerning it (which themselves leave no little room for interpretation). Then he may form his synthesis—or leave his problem unresolved, and state the difficulties, and the correct attitude of suspense to be adopted. Nothing is worse than an attitude of fear or a lack of candour, both of which confess a weakness of faith.

But the problem of apparent conflict of the sacred writings and science must always be with us, fresh facts to be incorporated in our view of the world. We must not therefore think of finally settling the problem, but be continually prepared to try to understand the new difficulties that science brings and must bring to us, and by understanding them to learn new truths about the nature of the World and the Word.

We have here discussed the formal aspect of the conflict of the Church and Science, the actual conflicts and the manner in which they were resolved. Yet before the conflict can arise, men must find difficulty in believing what the Church asserts: so we must look not only at the actual resolution of difficulties, but at the reasons why they have arisen.

It is easy to see then that there is no formal contradiction between Christian doctrine and the observations of science, but it is even easier to see that science has been the principal factor in making men unready to believe many of the Christian doctrines, and it is of the first importance that we should find out how this has come about.

We have first to note a psychological factor. The examination of the truth of Christian evidences is not simply an interesting historical exercise, because the acceptance of the truth of the doctrines that flow from those evidences commits the inquirer to a certain way of life. You can scarcely believe in the miracles of Christ without believing Him to be God, or at least God-like, nor can you believe Him to be God without believing His teaching and His statements about eternal rewards and punishments to be true. Thus those who wish to live a life incompatible with Christianity have a bias towards unbelief: those who delight in the Christian way of living have a corresponding will to believe. I have been told that on the rare occasions when a Catholic priest announces that he has lost his faith, the first question asked is "What is her name?"—the story, I think, applies to every one of us. Furthermore the Christian doctrine has had, in the past at least, deep childhood associations reaching back into the life of the unconscious, and it has therefore been correspondingly difficult to consider the question with that impartiality and lack of emotion appropriate to a scientific or historical question.

But setting aside these influences of will upon belief, important as they are for evil or good, a question which can be practically discussed is why the growth of science has made the men of the twentieth century find the evidences and doctrines of Christianity less credible than did their thirteenth-century ancestors.

The essence of the answer to this problem is the growth of a way of thinking about the world in which the spiritual has no part. What did the man of the thirteenth century visualize when he thought of the universe? First and last he thought of God. God had created the world. He had created it for a purpose, namely, for the service of man, who was to serve God, who loved God and was, by God's grace and his own efforts to correspond to it, ultimately destined to make up the number of the company of Heaven. The earth was the scene of this grand plan. Small though it was known to be, it was a unique body; it was the only place where there was coming to be or passing away; it was the geometrical centre of the Universe, set in the middle of that vast sphere at whose periphery was Heaven. God transmitted his power to the intelligences that governed the starry spheres and their influence penetrated, informed and operated everything upon earth. The scientific scheme considered apart from God simply did not make sense. Every change on earth was indirectly the work of God, and was the copy of a part of the plan of the Universe, which was an idea in His mind. How could there be any difficulty in believing that any change, however contrary to experience, could be brought about by his Will, which was the cause of all that existed? What more easy to conceive than that God, the ultimate source of all forms (of all that makes things what they are) should superadd the form of wine to that of water? The difficulty was rather to conceive that God should have been united to so petty a thing as man, than to believe that a person at once man and God could fail to do aught that he might will. The essence of law was its existence in the mind of God; could that law which men saw in nature bind the author of nature? Nor is any of this scheme incredible today except the Ptolemaic astronomy and the astrological and other incorrect scientific notions in terms of which it happened to be expressed.

What happened to change men's views concerning these things?

First came the break-up of the scientific system in which it was phrased. After the acceptance of the Copernican system there was reason to suppose that the earth was not the unique centre of the universe. After Galileo, the celestial spheres were generally discredited and the planets thought to be mere other earths, not the sublime abodes of celestial intelligences: gradually there spread the idea that the universe was infinite in extent and the earth a spatially insignificant portion of it. From the late eighteenth century the duration of the earth was no longer considered to be but five days more than that of human history—less than 6,000 years—but to have extended vastly longer than that short span. The old picture of the universe built by God for man to serve Him therein lost its fine simplicity. Yet even that picture faded but slowly; Milton, a highly enlightened man, was still hesitating between the Copernican and Ptolemaic theories when he wrote *Paradise Lost,* and in places where science flourished less the ancient beliefs were even longer preserved.

But meanwhile there grew up in the seventeenth century quite another way of considering the world—the way of natural science. Its method was to observe and catalogue the phenomena accessible to our senses, with or without instrumental aid, and to discover their regularities and form a theory of how they worked. This way of considering things excluded the notion of purpose. It considered what happened, not what it happened for. The significant aspect of the world for the men of the Middle Ages was that God made it for man to use according to God's will: just how the things in the world were related to each other and what was their internal mechanism, if any, interested them little, if at all.

The new way of thinking, on the other hand, set out to give an account of phenomena in terms of one bit of matter pushing against another. Those terms proved to be insufficient and other concepts, such as force, were introduced, but essentially the modern scientific view of the world is a view which, in the limit, reduces everything to ultimate particles and quanta of radiation interacting in accordance with unvarying rules. This view of the world is, in part at least, true: that is to say that its predictions are fulfilled: eclipses take place to the second, the atomic bomb exploded as the calculations predicted. On the truth of scientific statements is founded the whole gigantic industrial system of today with its myriad machines and contrivances and new kinds of matter.

Is it surprising, then, that when men are torn between so many different opinions in religion and philosophy, they should greatly esteem this new way of thinking which is guaranteed by results? Is it surprising that they should seek to apply this method so fruitful of results in the physical sphere to every part of man's activity? It is not: indeed it was inevitable.

The position today is that man has accepted the fundamental entities of science as the standard means of constructing an explanation, and the scientific method of observation, leading to the discovery of laws, as the standard means of finding out the truth. But they have gone further. Many people, including some with no scientific training, have withdrawn their belief from all entities that do not enter into science. That they do not act rationally in so doing, I hope to show, but first let us consider the consequences.

The adoption of this way of thinking leads first to the minimising and then to the disappearance of religion. The process begins with the evidence. Science never adopts testimony as evidence if it can have any other, and indeed scarcely rates it as evidence without corroboration by direct observation. *Nullius in verba,* "On the word of no man" is the motto of the Royal Society. Thus the written evidences of Christianity, judged by the standards of science, are weak. Moreover, the miraculous events narrated therein cannot be envisaged as changes of the kind that science chronicles (that is their whole point)—so they do not fit into the scientific scheme. Thus the change of water into wine would involve the creation of matter or change of one kind of matter into another kind without perceptible simultaneous energy changes: such an event cannot be reconciled with what we have experienced concerning changes in matter—e.g., we have reason to suppose it to be impossible in the natural order. No deviation from the regularities that science chronicles fits into the scientific scheme, so, for those who adopt the criteria applied to scientific evidence, God is progressively reduced to a spectator. Sometimes it is improper to suppose that God would interfere with the order he has created: are we to set that order above the Creator of it? Are we to deny that such an interposition or alteration is not a part of a yet higher order? Furthermore, why do we suppose that the order that science observes is the order that God created, for is it not certain that finite man could perceive but an aspect of the whole order that is known by the infinite God? To think otherwise is to set science above God. This position has, I think, already been reached by many who bear the name of Christian. Be this as it may, the effect of this minimising of the supernatural is to make us believe that God is active only in the human mind, which has been but little studied by science. But the scientific world-picture still prevails in this region, even if science itself, does not: the subjective life of the mind is commonly envisaged as the product of the objective mechanism of the brain, this in turn as the working of chemical and physical processes, which follow our supposed unalterable law. How in fact does science consider man? It fits him into the sciences. It considers his physics and chemistry—fits him into the world of the non-living: it considers his comparative anatomy, his place in the world of organisms—fits him into the world of the non-intelligent: it only then begins to consider his actions and that from an external point of view; but it can never consider man as he knows himself, as an experiencing, living, choosing, free agent in a world of the stuff of thought. That is just what man is and what science can never see him to be. Thus the final result of adopting the scientific world-picture is to see all things as a physically determined piece of mechanism and to have to suppose our sensations of choice to be illusory. God, then, appears an unobservable, which for science, is non-existent.

Why, then, is this position not the invariable attitude of the scientist and the philosophers? Simply because the assumption that all things can be explained in terms of the fundamental entities of science is an assumption—a hypothesis, which we are not compelled to adopt.

We have in fact two sets of observations from which to draw our conclusions about the world. One set consists of scientific observations, data of the external senses so chosen as to be wholly comprehensible to every person and therefore purified of all that pertains to the individual. These impersonal, objective, indicative statements are material from which to build up a view of the world that is true for its impersonal objective aspects. That is science.

The other set of observations are precisely opposite, and are the experiences of the individual, the world of imagination, emotion, will, creativeness. This world is known by each of us, for and about himself, much more intimately and certainly than we know any of the facts of science. I may be deluded in supposing I am seeing a star but I cannot be deluded in saying "I have the sensation of a point of light." To give less reality to the subjective life of the spirit than to the conclusions of science is in the literal sense preposterous.

Now science cannot in fact give any account of this world of the personal, if for no other reason than that science deals with classes, and I, as far as I am I and not you or he, am therefore outside its range. There are, of course, other reasons: thus science can deal with that which can be described so as to be clearly understood, which the intimate workings of the mind cannot, and it deals with determinate regularities, whereas we know our minds to operate by deliberate choice. Let it be enough then that here is a field outside the ambit of science, and that it is precisely in this field that the principal work of God upon man is done. But if there is in the mind of man—and *a fortiori* in other minds if such exist—a set of realities which are not comprehended in terms of the fundamental entities of science, then nothing that science can say denies the possibility of this set of realities influencing matter, and all or any of the matters asserted by Christian doctrine being true. What is impossible in the scientific order—that is to say, impossible by the operation of matter and energy unaffected by the mind—may be readily possible if mind or some being of a spiritual nature be applied thereto.

For that reason I am utterly opposed to the minimising attitude in Christian doctrine. I do not pretend to know what in the Scripture is related as allegory and what as fact. I think that the story of Jonah and the Whale is a parable, an oriental mode of imparting instruction: but not only do I suppose that God could have caused the whale to swallow Jonah, but I suppose He could have caused Jonah to swallow the whale. I suppose all the miracles related of Our Lord to be literally true; I suppose miracles to have been worked through the intercession of the saints, and to be worked, e.g., at Lourdes, today. The only question to be asked about a miracle is "Did it happen?" not "Could it happen?"

To think of God as operating only through physical laws of science is to assimilate Him to a machine: I think we find the nearest earthly analogy to Him in our own minds. I think that the evidence for the power of the human mind to transcend the scientific laws deduced from non-living matter is very strong and that not only God, but we ourselves, under God, can make things happen that are not to be described in the order of science. The conditions for such action are described in the Gospel, namely faith and confidence—but whether these things are done by God at our asking or whether we do them, or whether there is any distinction at all in this sphere, I do not pretend to know. I feel quite certain, however, that there never was an age of less faith than the present and that no age is less likely therefore to see miracles—if we may go by what we read in the Gospels. Yet the evidence is there, I am confident, for those who seek it, even today.

Thus the influence of science on Christian doctrine has been in the direction of a progressive minimising of all that is not a matter of daily experience. The miraculous element that does not relate to the articles of the Apostle's creed is the first to be explained away as interpolation, accretion or the result of natural causes. Next comes the Virgin Birth and the Ascension, next the Resurrection. After that the Divinity of Christ is understood in various reduced senses, then God comes to be regarded as "the Divine"—an ideal and not a Person, which stage is scarcely to be distinguished from atheism.

It seems to me that if we are Christians, followers of Christ, we cannot possibly pursue this dreary descent. If one thing is clear from Christ's teaching and life it is the importance of precisely the element that science has been influential in making incredible. His ministry is shown to us as a succession of miracles. Angels minister to Him: the devil tempts Him: He casts out devils, speaking to them as persons. Men are to believe, if for no other reason, "for the works' sake." The human qualities commended by Him are "belief" and "faith"—not reasoning and weighing of probabilities. He "cannot" do miracles among those who lack faith—evidently a certain cooperation is required. Those who say he casts out devils by the aid of devils—so I read the context—commit the unforgivable sin against the Holy Ghost: and I believe that those who attribute these wonderful works to natural causes come very near to committing that sin by cutting themselves off from the recognition of the work of the Holy Spirit.

To consider Christ merely as an ethical teacher, as do those whom the scientific world-view has led to reject the miraculous, is to rob his teaching of authority. We are not bound to accept Christian ethics only because they are God-given ethics, and Christ himself regarded the wonderful works He did as guaranteeing His divine origin.

So take a good look at this idol of the sciencific world-view and reject it. Recognize that it is merely the result of considering all our experience as analogous to the natural phenomena that science studies. Recognize the primary and paramount character of your knowledge of your subjective life, and control of the body by that life. Do not let yourself be taken in by the marvels of science: the least gutter-urchin's mind is infintely more marvellous than the vast paraphernalia of the atomic bomb. Do not reject anything miraculous simply because it is miraculous. Believe the words of Christ that a man with faith as a grain of mustard seed can move mountains. Move in fact into an entirely different world, the world of the spirit, the true place of man which no other earthly creature can approach, and following Our Lord's counsel, take little or no account of the material world, which has so fatally enmeshed us. That is to my mind the essence of Christian doctrine, and that is what the misapplication of science has so seriously assailed.

6

BAROQUE CULTURE *

Each age in the history of a civilization develops its peculiar form of art, music, and literature. The culture so developed expresses the ideals, the aspirations, and the standards of judgment accepted by the age. It reveals what men thought was good and what they condemned as bad. Historians are therefore obliged to study the fine arts, the literature, the scientific thought, the architecture, and even the music of the past so as to understand what moved men's minds and inspired them to heroic deeds.

As the latter half of the seventeenth century and the eighteenth century is known as the Classical Age, and the first half of the nineteenth century is the Age of Romanticism, so the last part of the sixteenth and first half of the seventeenth centuries is the Age of the Baroque. The art forms of this cultural period show the important part that religion still played in the average educated man's life. There are two extremes which the historian must avoid when he studies the culture of an age: 1) he must be wary of reading too much meaning into symbolic forms; and 2) he must be careful not to criticize art and literature of one age according to his own standards or those of another period. Thus to judge baroque art and music by twentieth century standards is as wrong as to condemn football because it is not good ballet.

In the following selection Dr. Hohl surveys the most important cultural aspects of the Baroque Age, puts them in their historical setting, and interprets their meaning according to their own zeitgeist, *or spirit of their times. The student should understand the place of the Baroque*

[1] From Dr. Clarence L. Hohl, Jr., and Rev. Lowrie L. Daly, S.J., *Rebirth, Revolt, and Reform: Europe 1250-1648* (New York: Rinehart & Company, Inc., n.d.). Reprinted by permission.

in the development of Western Civilization, for it made significant contributions to that development which must be understood for a proper appreciation of the succeeding cultures.

But good architects preserve the most excellent forms of the orders. The painters and the sculptors, selecting the most elegant natural beauties perfect the Idea, and their works go forward and become superior to nature; this. . . is the ultimate excellence of these arts. Here is born the admiration and the awe of men towards statues and images, here is the reward and honor of artists. . . who all arose above human forms and aroused admiration with the Ideas and their works. So one can indeed then call this Idea perfection of nature, miracle of art, foresight of the intellect, example of the mind, light of fancy, rising Sun that from the East inspires the statue of Memnon, fire that warms into life the image of Prometheus. . . . But because the Idea of eloquence falls as far below the Idea of painting as sight is more potent than words, I here lack for speech and am hushed. . . .

—Giovanni Pietro Bellori (1615-1696)

THE LAST half century has witnessed a renaissance in Baroque studies which has resulted in a re-evaluation of the significance of that cultural epoch known as the Baroque. Chronologically, the Baroque period may be dated from the end of the sixteenth century to the beginning of the eighteenth century, the poles marking the termination of the High Renaissance and the beginning of the classical era. The term "baroque" was originally, and in some quarters, still is a term of derision, but serious students of the arts agree that the Baroque epoch represents an important and distinct episode in the history of man's culture. There is a school of thought which, because of its anti-Catholic bias, has linked "degenerate" Catholic thinking with "degenerate" Baroque art. Such an attitude fails to understand that the Baroque is as significant as the art of the Middle Ages or that of the Renaissance, or for that matter modern Impressionism and Cubism.

The word "baroque" has several origins but two are generally agreed upon: the Spanish word, *borocco,* which meant an odd-shaped pearl, or the scholastic definition *baroco,* which suggested a perverse and complicated form of logic implying the intricate, and/or eccentric: characteristic of the degeneration in scholastic philosophy. In the twentieth century, something baroque has implied the eccentric, the bizarre or the perverse; but these terms are used by the uninformed and the uneducated.

The Baroque represented a departure from the classical and time-honoured forms of both the Renaissance and the ancient world. Therefore, sympathizers with the Classical epoch held the seventeenth century up for ridicule and derision as a perversion of the great artistic styles of the Classical age. These critics were unaware of the artistic import of the Baroque and failed to comprehend its tremendous significance. The individual freedom which the Baroque epoch permitted corresponds to the freedom which modern artists enjoy today. Indeed, there is a definite connection between the so-called modernism in the arts and the Baroque era. A thorough analysis of the works of say, an El Greco, and Claude Monet, will bear definite witness to this statement.

Baroque art has been labeled "Jesuit art" or art of the Catholic Reformation. Both terms are partially true, but the Baroque is not simply understood or defined as the Jesuit style any more than it may be referred to simply as Catholic Reformation art. There is undoubtedly a connection between the Jesuits and the Baroque, and they certainly employed it in their churches, but investigation would seem to indicate that the connection between the Baroque and the Jesuits was at best casual rather than causal. Thus, Martin Haney in his *Jesuits in History* correctly observes,

> In the revival of Catholic art which succeeded upon the victories of the Farnese, the Jesuits participated especially in the erection of several [*sic*] fine churches. The fact that here as elsewhere most of the Jesuit churches were erected in the Baroque style has led to the misnomer of the "Jesuit" style of architecture and to the fiction of the Jesuits deliberately using Baroque as part of the Catholic propaganda. The frequent use of Baroque in Jesuit churches was merely coincidental, since most of these edifices were built when that style was enjoying wide popularity. That the fathers of the Society had no exclusive predilection for Baroque, is proven by the beautiful Gothic churches erected by them at Münster, Coblenz and Molsheim.[1]

Similarly, the label of the Baroque as exclusively a Catholic style of art needs serious qualification. The Council of Trent made specific references to the fine arts and laid down certain conditions which were to be followed in their use. Thus in the twenty-fifth session of Trent, December 3, 4, 1693, the Council issued its decree on Sacred Art which read in part,

> . . . let the bishops diligently teach that by means of the stories of the mysteries of our redemption portrayed in paintings and other representations the people are instructed and confirmed in the articles of faith, which ought to be borne in mind and constantly reflected upon; also that great profit is derived from all holy images, not only because the people are thereby reminded of the benefits and gifts bestowed on them by Christ, but also because through the saints the miracles of God and salutary examples are set before the eyes of the faithful, so that they may give God thanks for those things, may fashion their own life and conduct in imitation of the saints and be moved to adore and love God and cultivate piety. . . .

[1] Compare this statement with that of Emile Mâle in his *L'Art reliqieux après le Concile de Trente* who notes, "In the painting of the Counter-Reformation under close surveillance of the theologians (Jesuits), who assigned the artists their subjects, and, in considerable measure prescribed the treatment, lie incarnate the religious life of the age, its attributes and its themes. Everywhere in Italian churches one sees depicted the new devotions—the angels, who float rosily among the clouds of Jesuit frescoes; the Holy Family, St. Joseph, etc.—devotions particularly dear to the cloister."

Such a statement is hardly sufficient justification to equate the decrees with the Baroque. In some ways, the era of the Catholic Reformation merely coincided with the era of the Baroque and the connection was in many cases accidental. The art of the Catholic Reformation was designed to teach, instruct, inspire and uplift the spirits of the faithful. The Baroque was admirably suited to just such purposes and therefore it was a convenient instrument in the liturgical arts. But the Catholic Church has never dictated artistic styles and one of the best examples of such a statement is the continually changing nature of Catholic art and architecture—as any study of say, twentieth-century Catholic art would verify.

It is the fundamental thesis of this discussion that the Baroque era merely coincided with the age of the Catholic Reformation and the birth of the Society of Jesus.[2] That both institutions used the Baroque goes without saying, but that the Baroque was deliberately or specifically fostered or created by the Jesuits and the Catholic Reformation is not accepted without the preceeding qualifications. Now that some of the important premises have been established it would be well to look more thoroughly at the Baroque.

The age of the Baroque is mainly confined to the seventeenth century and a word about that remarkable one hundred years is necessary. Historians, with justification, have labelled it the age of absolutism in politics, and the age of genius in things intellectual. It was a century which saw the great constitutional struggle in England culminate in the triumph of parliament over king. Continental Europe stood in awe at the regal splendor and grandeur of the Sun King, Louis XIV, who used his talents and his nation's energies in senseless wars and found time to foster that masterpiece of French Baroque-Classicism, Versailles.

Elsewhere in Europe, Spain and the Holy Roman Empire had shrunk to mere shadows of their former greatness, to become the pawns and the battlegrounds of their more ambitious neighbors. Protestant Europe, Russia, Prussia and Sweden were arising to make their presence felt in the family of nations. The Ottoman Empire remained a constant menace to plague the peoples and nations of eastern Europe. The seventeenth century was an age of almost constant warfare highlighted by the disastrous Thirty Years' War and the almost incessant wars of the Sun King. It was an age which saw the beginning of the overseas struggle between the colonial powers and the consolidation of the French and Eng-

[2] This is not to say that the religious element was not a dominant element in the Baroque, and we agree with E.I. Watkin's statement in his *Catholic Art and Culture* that "Baroque art had a predilection for symbolism of light. A dissolved aureole invests the painted figures of saints. A heaven of light opens to the dying eyes of the martyr. . . . The halo is often a sun, for as a token that holiness is a communication of Divine Light. . . . Gilt rays frame pictures and altar pieces. . . . Without this light symbolism, Baroque religious art would not have sufficiently expressed the Infinite Deity. . . . With the Catholic faith, Baroque religion moves to and fro between its two poles, pure Godhead Incarnate in Its creation; between God and God made man."

lish empires. Warfare was perfected and became an important adjunct of a nation's policy.

Intellectually, the Age of Genius saw important developments. This was the century of Francis Bacon, whose *Novum Organum* popularized the new method of inductive reasoning. His fellow countryman, Robert Boyle, elevated the science of chemistry in *The Sceptical Chemist,* while William Harvey discussed the theory of the circulation of blood, and William Gilbert propounded the theory of magnetism. Overshadowing all was Sir Isaac Newton, whose *Mathematical Principles of Natural Philosophy* not only discussed the laws of light and gravity, but elevated the physical sciences to a plateau from which they have not fallen.

The triumph of Newtonian science was paralleled by the triumph of rationalism in philosophy, as expressed in the writings of René Descartes, whose *Discourse on Method* set the stage for that philosophical system which continues to dominate the secular mind. Rationalism, as it subsequently developed, implied the supreme ability of the mind to comprehend the mysteries of life, and what the mind could not understand was rejected as mere superstition. All human knowledge became subjected to the yardstick of reason which, with science, became the twin pillars upon which man sought to build his new world.

Finally, the seventeenth century was to witness important contributions in the realm of political science. The general trend of the age was in the direction of absolutism, and most political writers supported that view. King James I of England gave important impetus to the trend in his *Trew Law of Free Monarchies,* in which he sought to prove the validity of the unlimited monarch based upon his theories of divine right. Bishop Bossuet in France similarly strove to justify the unlimited sovereign for his master, Louis XIV. Thomas Hobbes' *Leviathian* and William Harrington's *Oceana* also pleaded for the all-powerful state as a solution to the chronic chaos and civil wars of the Middle Ages and the Reformation era.

Voices were raised in protest against the absolute state, but they remained in the minority. John Milton pleaded for freedom of speech in the *Areopagitica* and sought to justify the execution of King Charles I in his *Eikonoklastes.* John Locke justified the glorious revolution in the *Treatises on Civil Government* and advanced a comprehensive plan of governmental responsibility to the aristocracy known as the social contract.

The Age of Genius thus extended the range of man's world and opened new vistas for every man. It was an exhilarating century, marked by intellectual unrest. It was a precocious age, boldly charting new courses and attacking old standards of truth and knowledge. This exuberance and brashness is nowhere better seen than in the fine arts of the Baroque, although it must be remembered that these aforementioned characteristics applied to all aspects of the seventeenth century.

The twentieth century has witnessed an ever-increasing interest in the

Baroque era, and credit for this interest must be given to two Germans who were pathfinders in the study of the Baroque. In 1908, Alois Rigel published his *Die Entstehung der Barockkunst in Rom* and in the same year Heinrich Wölfflin published his *Renaissance und Barock* followed seven years later by his *Principles of Art History* (the first American edition of which did not appear until 1932). Rigel was concerned with Baroque architecture and Wölfflin with Baroque painting, but the general effect of their works was to stir interest in and an appreciation of the Baroque.[3] Today, virtually all studies of the Baroque continue to rely quite heavily upon the early work of these two men.

In attempting to delimit and contrast cultural styles, art historians seek to discover and point out those characteristics which differentiate one cultural period from another. Such techniques are valuable and necessary, but it is important to remember that the charactertistics are somewhat arbitrary and are not always unanimously accepted. Moreover, every artist who falls within the chronological limits of a cultural epoch does not necessarily have all the characteristics which mark the era under consideration. Indeed, some artists may not have any of the charateristics, others one or two, and still others all of them. Also every artistic creation does not necessarily have all the commonalities of the era, and the student should be cautioned against trying too hard to make an artist or his work "fit" the pre-established patterns. Because a work of art does not coincide completely with the characteristics, it is not to be rejected as not belonging to the particular cultural phase under study. And finally, artistic works at the beginning and the end of a cultural cycle generally contain elements which were part of the previous or succeeding periods.

Cultural changes generally take place as a reaction to preceeding periods and in the main come into being after the previous epoch has reached a point of perfection. Thus, Michelangelo is a fitting climax to the Italian Renaissance and those who followed him in the same view could only imitate his techniques. As a result, Roman art degenerated slightly for a short period after Michelangelo's death but the center of Italian art soon shifted to Venice and the Mannerist school of Titian, Tintoretto, Caravaggio and others. The Mannerist school represents the artistic transition from the High Renaissance to the Baroque, and is an important phase in man's cultural development. The discussion here, however, is limited to the Baroque.

In his *Principles*, Wölfflin lays down what he considers the basic charac-

[3] The literature on the Baroque is now immense, but the student will profit by a serious reading of anyone of the following: Manfred Bukhofzer, *Music in the Baroque Era* (1947); Wylie Sypher, *Four Stages of Renaissance Style* (1955); Gilbert Highet, *The Classical Tradition* (1949); Denis Mahon, *Studies in Seicento Art and Theory* (1947); Janos Scholz, *Baroque and Romantic Stage Design* (1950); Arthus McComb, *The Baroque Painters of Italy* (1934); T. H. Fokker, *Roman Baroque Art* (1938); S. Sitwell, *Southern Baroque Art* (1931; *German Baroque Art* (1927); Martin Briggs, *Baroque Architecture* (1914); Emil Kaufman, *Architecture in the Age of Reason* (1955).

teristics of the Baroque era, which we accept with certain qualifications. He was concerned primarily with painting, secondarily with architecture and sculpture, and rarely with music or literature. His principles were designed to contrast the Baroque with the classical era of the Renaissance, but again the contrasts are not always as marked as Wölfflin would lead us to believe. Nevertheless, any serious examination of the Baroque must rely heavily upon Heinrich Wölfflin.

The first of Wölfflin's contrasts is between the linear technique of the classical era and the painterly (*malerisch*) technique of the Baroque. The former emphasizes outlines, contours and details, whereas the painterly of the Baroque usually blurs the outlines, contours and details. The linear sharply differentiates the objects depicted, while the painterly merges them deeply into one whole unit. As Wölfflin observes,

> When Dürer or Cranach places a nude as a light object on a dark ground, the elements remain radically distinct: background is background, figure is figure, and the Venus or Eve we see before us produces the effect of a white silhouette on a dark foil. Conversely, if a nude in Rembrandt stands out on a dark ground, the light of the body seems as it were to emanate from the darkness of the picture space: it is as if everything were of the same stuff. . . .

Similarly, a comparison of Botticelli and Rembrandt would vividly depict the contrast between the Classical (linear) and the Baroque (painterly).

The second of Wölfflin's contrasts is the plane versus the recessional. The plane technique depicts things as if they were almost two dimensional. Even objects which appear in the background are depicted in a stratified plane and, as Sypher remarks, they "hold the surface" and do not give a real illusion of depth. An examination of Sandro Botticelli's *Birth of Vensus* (only a color reproduction should be studied in any of these references) will give the viewer a good example of the plane style. On the other hand, the recessional de-emphasizes the plane to the degree that it depicts its objects in depth and by effectively using illusions and foreshortenings suggests truer perspective and representation. A study of Tintoretto's *Adam and Eve*, or perhaps El Greco's *View of Toledo*, will further enhance the student's understanding of the recessional style.

The third contrast between Classic and Baroque forms is the closed versus the open technique. A closed composition is one which is self-contained and does not lead the viewer to imagine or seek for material beyond the range of the composition. The closed technique stressed a geometric balance and this is usually to be noted in the balance between the vertical and horizontal dimensions of the picture. The open composition is one which, as the name suggests, appears limitless and seems to flow beyond the composition itself. There is not the obvious symmetry of the Classic. The open forms seem at first glance to be out of balance; although there is a balance, it is not the same kind as the Classic. It would be well for the student to compare Leonardo da Vinci's *Last Supper* with Tintoretto's composition of the same name to note the contrast between the closed and open forms.

The fourth difference between the Classic and the Baroque, as discussed by Wölfflin, is the contrast between multiplicity and unity, or technically, multiple unity and unified unity. In a multiple composition the individual details are rather easily distinguished and maintain their identity while nonetheless fitting geometrically and harmoniously within the composition as a whole. But the details are very important for themselves as well as for the over-all picture. In contrast, unity means that the details are subordinated to the total picture and their importance exists more for the whole than for themselves. Baroque culture tends to emphasize a dominant theme or idea and that technique necessarily submerges the details to the whole. As Wölfflin describes it,

> A head by Rubens is not better, seen as a whole, than a head by Dürer or Massys, but that independent working out of the separate parts is abolished which, in the latter case, makes the total form appear as a (relative) multiplicity. The *Seicentisti* envisage a definite main motive, to which they subordinate everything else. No longer do the separate elements of the organism, conditioning each other and holding each other in harmony, take effect in the picture, but out of the whole, reduced to an unified stream individual forms arise as the absolute dominants, yet in such a way that even these dominant forms signify for the eye nothing separable, nothing that could be isolated.

The student will observe these contrasts by comparing Leonardo's *Last Supper* with that of Tiepolo, or perhaps by comparing a landscape by Dürer or Pieter Brueghel with one by Rubens or Rembrandt. These variances can only be noted by a concentrated study of the art objects themselves.

The last of the Baroque characteristics which Wölfflin discusses is that of clearness and unclearness or absolute clearness versus relative clearness. It should be noted at this point that many of these points bear important similarities and in some ways are variations or fuller explanations of one another. For example, a Classical style almost always contains the plane and closed techniques, and they serve to amplify the technique for the viewer. Thus this last category is very similar to the first, but with certain exceptions: in the absolute clearness the colors, light, and design, while possessing intrinsic values, actually serve to outline the forms of the individual objects in the picture; in the relative clearness technique of the Baroque the shading and colors have their own value and are not used merely to define objects or forms. Consequently, the artistic technique of treating light and dark areas with varying degrees of shading, known technically as chiaroscuro, is perfected in the Baroque. The Baroque artist deliberately sought to surround his objects with these shadings and in many cases gave the illusion that his subject was mounted in space. Rembrandt, who was probably the greatest Baroque master of chiaroscuro, perfectly demonstrates this technique in his *Supper at Emmanus* and in *The Night Watch*—the latter often adjudged the greatest Baroque painting. In Spain, where the mystical strain remained strong in the *seicento*, one may examine with profit the excellent paintings of Velásquez and Zurbarán to see what Wölfflin means by relative clearness.

The foregoing, then, is a brief summary of the artistic techniques of the Baroque as contrasted with the Classical epoch. Every work of art created in the Baroque does not necessarily possess all of these elements, just as every work of art by an individual Baroque artist does not contain all the same elements or even use the same techniques. The student should therefore be wary of assuming that all Baroque works may be simply categorized and catalogued according to the Wölfflin method. Intelligence and individual judgment, trained of course, play a major role in the study of any artistic work. And now other aspects of the Baroque may be discussed.

The Baroque is noted for its inclination towards movement and unrestrained emotion. At first glance these outward appearances suggest a complete disunity and disorganization, but a closer scrutiny will reveal that there is both organization and unity in the Baroque. Certainly the *Seicento* with its stress upon science and reason influenced the fine arts. There is by no means agreement on the relative merits of the Baroque and indeed there is not complete agreement upon what is meant by the Baroque. This is partially due to its early rejection as a degeneration of the Renaissance, and as a style which was produced by the craftsman rather than by the creative artist. The stresses, movements, grandeur and tremendous sweep of the Baroque were often considered vulgar and cheap; thus the sculptures of Giovanni Bernini, such as *St. Teresa in Ecstasy* in Sancta Maria della Vittoria in Rome, once dismissed as emotional craftsmanship, are now accepted as brilliant pieces of sculpture. Similarly, Bernini's Tomb of Pope Alexander VII in St. Peter's and his bust of Louis XIV are now considered excellent examples of art and Baroque sculpture.

This concept of emotion and movement deserves still further consideration since it is so important in the Baroque. Even a cursory glance at the work of Rubens' *The Abduction of the Daughters of Leucippus, The Kermesse*, or *The Judgment of Paris*, will clearly indicate both emotion and movement. The pictures seem to move, the figures appear as though they will take a step any moment and the faces seem ready to speak. The scenes are dramatic, intense and vivid. Similarly, a comparison of the Madonnas of the Renaissance, with their classic composures and their classical features, are in marked contrast with the Baroque Madonnas. Murillo, whose Madonnas are probably the most famous and most reproduced in the world, had them soaring through space, or about to take a step into space. The Baroque Madonna is surrounded by cherubs, angels and clouds, and everything seems about to move.

Only the Baroque could have produced the magnificent fountains which were so characteristic of the age and which even today identify many famous landmarks. The fountains of the Villa d'Este of Italy, the episcopal fountains of Salzburg, the magnificent fountains of Bavaria all reflect the Baroque love of movement. Modern Rome, with its famous Trevi fountains so dear to all tourists, and its hundreds of other fountains were products of the Baroque. Water appears from unexpected sources, spouts forth, and cascades over the statuary in a deliberate attempt to depict movement. The Baroque fountains strive to combine the natural effects of water with carved figures and to make both appear to tremble and shake. In this the Baroque artist was supremely successful.

It was a natural development, then, that music should be deeply affected by this concept of movement, and the opera was a logical outgrowth of the Baroque. The opera permitted the music and the performers to depict the full range of human emotions and actions. Whether the opera developed from the oratorios of St. Philip Neri, who sought to teach the faith through musical dramatizations, or whether Count Bardi's musical dramatizations for the marriage of Henry IV of France and Maria de Medici at Florence in 1600 originated opera, is for our purposes unimportant. The opera developed in the Baroque age and the performance of Claudio Monteverdi's *Orfeo* in 1607 at Mantua is considered a musical landmark. Venice built the world's first opera house thirty years later and by the eighteenth century hundreds of similar institutions had sprung up all over Europe. Italy adopted the opera as particularly its own, and in general has continued to dominate it through modern history.

Once the opera was established it spread to all parts of the world, and composers strove to amplify and expand its possibilities. Thus, the *Seicento* saw the development of the ballet, whose story is told by the music and by the actions of the dancers without the benefit of vocal explanations. Certainly no better example of the Baroque love of movement exists than in the ballet, whose father was probably Jean Baptiste Lully, court musician to Louis XIV.

Musical instruments naturally were amplified and expanded during the Baroque. Once again the emphasis is upon movement and individual expression. The organ, first brought into its own by Giovanni Frescobaldi, organist for St. Peter's in Rome, and perfected by Dietrich Buxtehude of the Mariankirche of Lübeck, became all-important in church music. The violin, pioneered by Nicolo Amati and perfected by Guarnieri and Stradivari, permitted a wide range of individual musical expression. The solo and concerto assumed major roles in music. Keyboard instruments were improved and expanded to meet the acoustical requirements of large opera houses and music halls. The professional conductor emerged, and no longer was he necessarily the composer of the work being performed.

The composers of baroque music began with the Italian John Peter Aloysius Sante, more commonly known as Palestrina from the town of his birth, and culminated in the great works of Johann Sebastian Bach. In between the Italians produced such renowned figures as Vivaldi, Scarlatti, and Torelli. England made halting beginnings with the writings of

Henry Purcell, but English opera had to await the coming of Handel. In France, Lully continued to dominate French music, and despite the creation of a French Academy of Music in Paris in 1669, French Baroque music did not measure up to German and Italian standards. In Germany, the initial emphasis in musical composition was upon church music and choral singing. Heinrich Schütz composed volumes of sacred music, while at Munich Johann Kerll produced the first German operas, though the center of the Baroque opera in Germany soon shifted northward to Hamburg. Everywhere in Europe music was accepted as a logical means of fulfilling the demands of the age.

The elements of the Baroque in literature are more difficult to discern, and the subject is still relatively unexplored. There is probably more disagreement about the Baroque in literature than in any other aspect of this subject. Movement in the visual arts is at times more readily discernible than in poems, novels, or other forms of written expression. Similarly, musical compositions permit the human ear to note violent contrasts and sweeping movement. But literature is a different problem.

There is no agreement among scholars to any prevailing theme in Baroque literature, but in general it strove to express man's great power and talents. It is characterized by the violent conflict between paganism and spiritualism. As with all other aspects of the Baroque, the secular competes with the sacred and man's free will permits him the choice of salvation or damnation. The Council of Trent exerted tremendous influence upon literature and in Catholic countries the dominant themes deal with Jesus, St. Teresa, the Crucifixion and other religious subjects. In Protestant nations the themes are less specific but express similar ideas.

Baroque literature is marked by extremes in ornamentation, a sweeping range of material and glittering quality. Again, the literature of the era appears disunified but in reality it is distinctly unified. The writer systematizes his works in the interests of order and imagination. Authors revealed in movement, in colorful and violent contrasts, and in employing exclamatory nouns and descriptive adjectives, as any reading of Milton's *Paradise Lost* or the poems of John Donne will amply demonstrate.

Metaphors such as, "blood drops like rubies," "tears like pearls," "flames and fountains," recur time and again. The motifs of tears, wounds, flaming hearts are characteristic of both the literature and other visual arts. Writers sought out new metaphors, antithesis and hyperbole, all in the interest of movement, tension, force and intensity. The theater, so convenient a vehicle for all these ideas, reached new heights in the extravagant comedies of Molière, the heroic tragedies of Racine and Corneille. The plays of the Spanish writers such as Góngora, de Vega and Calderón satisfied the native desire for mystical drama and expression. And certainly Miguel Cervantes' *Don Quixote* could only have been produced in an atmosphere of the Baroque tempered with the Spanish tradition.

Other forms of literature gave expression to the Baroque elements. Satire was an important weapon of the period, and the writings of Boileau, Swift and Dryden gave vent to polite but biting passages. Edward Gibbon's style in his *Decline and Fall of the Roman Empire,* along with Henry Fielding's *Tom Jones* demonstrate the range and depth of prose in the Baroque age, as does the oratory of Bishop Bossuet. The age produced the technique of characterization of individuals and types; for example, John Donne's famous passage, "No man is an island, entire of itself; every man is part of a continent, a part of the main," vividly expresses both idea and characterization. Similarly, Jonathan Swift writes, "Open a few mouths which are now closed, and close many more which are now open; curb the petulancy of the young, and correct the positiveness of the old, rouse the stupid, and damp the pert."

The Baroque knew no national boundaries, but it centered in Italy, southern Germany, Austria and Spain. These four regions best personify the Baroque; but it was most universally developed in all the fine arts in the first three mentioned countries. French and English historians have tended to deny the existence of the Baroque element in their countries, assigning the term classical to French culture of this age and preferring the term Renaissance for England. Thus, most Frenchmen will refer to Versailles as an example of French classical architecture, and Englishmen to St. Paul's Cathedral in London as Renaissance. Nonetheless, both Versailles and St. Paul's contain elements of the Baroque in their construction and design. Mansart and Leprun in France, Inigo Jones, Sir Christopher Wren and Vanbrugh in England contributed to the Baroque in their nations cultural development—as subsequent studies will someday demonstrate.

Rome however is the center of Baroque architecture, and indeed modern Rome is essentially the product of the seventeenth century. The theories of the Baroque in architecture were formulated by Giacomo Barocchio, commonly called Vignola, the architect of the Gesù in Rome, and Andrea Palladio whose treatise set the principles of the style. The Gesù of Rome is indeed considered the fountainhead which set the example for hundreds of churches throughout the world, and as such, deserves special attention.

The façade of the Gesù is divided into five parts, but the division does not destroy its unity, rather its emphasizes the oneness of the exterior. The exterior is somber and quite in contrast with the interior. Massive scrolls which sweep down the center of the façade are supported by four pairs of pilasters which are in turn supported by four common plinths. A central window occupies the space between the center pilasters. The interior of the Gesù, which is typically Baroque in its brilliance, sought to capture and hold the attention of the faithful and to draw their attention to the central altar. Light and color play on the ornate decorations and sculpture. The church consists of a short nave, the central portion is in the form of a Greek cross, and has a semi-circular apse. Light is permitted through a central dome which rises over the crossing of the larger side areas and the apse. The ceiling of the Gesù is noted for its illusionism in which the figures seem about to move or leap out into space. The effect is both moving and at times overwhelming, and a man worshipping in the Gesù cannot but stand in awe at the architectural grandeur dedicated to himself and his God.

While Rome is resplendent in its Baroque churches, and a listing of all Baroque architecture would degenerate into a mere catalogue of buildings, certain others need mention. Among the most famous, of course, is St. Peter's Basilica, a crowning masterpiece of both the Baroque and the Roman Catholic Church. St. Peter's, the world's largest and most magnificent church, is the product of many architectural eras. It is an excellent example for the study of changing cultural predilections.[4] Begun in the reign of Julius II (1503-12), it was not fully completed for almost two centuries, and during that time it witnessed the impact of the Renaissance, Mannerism, and Baroque styles. St. Peter's famous dome, designed by Michelangelo, crowns the edifice, although Maderna's façade has reduced the powerful effect of Michelangelo's masterful creation.

The proportions of this basilica stagger the imagination. It has room for 100,000 people, covers, with adjacent buildings, six acres, and is 700 feet long. There are five aisles, forty-four altars, and the distance from the floor to the interior of the dome measures 404 feet. The crowning aspect of the interior is the *baldacchino* of Bernini, which covers the main altar and rises to a height of ten stories. Maderna's façade is 377 feet long and 148 feet high, and is surrounded by statues four stories high. St. Peter's is deep in historic tradition, including the chair which St. Peter purportedly used, and the famous *Pietà* of Michelangelo, completed when this artistic genius was only 24.

Outside St. Peter's is the famous piazza of Bernini which set the pattern for so many of Europe's famous squares. As one looks down the Via della Consiliazione, the eye is drawn to the square and to St. Peter's. The obelisk, erected over the legendary site of St. Peter's martyrdom, is flanked by Maderna's fountains which are four stories high. On either side the colonnade appears as two gigantic arms reaching out to draw the faithful to the home of Catholicism. The colonnade contains 284 columns, 88 pillars and 140 statues of saints and popes. Truly, indeed, did Rome make itself the center of Baroque architecture.[5]

In other parts of Rome many buildings and churches were erected in

4 Among those who worked on St. Peter's were Bramante, Michelangelo, Maderna, Bernini and Fontana. Erected on the legendary site of St. Peter's tomb, the Basilica was dedicated in 1506 and was finally consecrated in 1626.

5 Jacques Maritain in *Art and Scholasticism* remarks of the Baroque, "If beauty delights the mind, it is because beauty is essentially a certain excellence or perfection in the proportion of things to the mind. Hence the three conditions assigned to it by St. Thomas; integrity, because the mind likes being; proportion, because the mind likes order and unity; and lastly and above all brightness or clarity, because the mind likes light and intelligence."

the style of the Baroque. Among them are the Santa Agnese and the Santa Maria in Campitelli by Carlo Rainaldi, the San Carlo alle Quattro Fontane and Santa Ivo della Sapienza of Borromini, the Santa Maria della Pace of Pietro da Cortona. In secular planning there is the Piazza Barberini of Bernini, the Piazza di Spagna (Spanish Steps) of Alessandro Specchi and Villa Torlonia of Rainaldi. These few examples are merely designed to indicate how the Baroque transformed Rome into a magnificent city.

Outside of Rome the Baroque affected the sacred and secular architecture of all of Italy. In Milan the San Gregorio (now destroyed) and the Palazzo Carignano reflected the Baroque influence. In Naples, the work of Giacomo Serporta transformed the architecture of that city, and in Lecce, Santa Croce indicates the impact of the Baroque. Venice, the queen of the Adriatic, has more than its share of Baroque buildings, but among the most famous is Santa Maria della Salute, dedicated in 1631.

Elsewhere in Europe the Baroque made rapid progress, but perhaps nowhere more effectively than in southern Germany and Austria. The Baroque love of symmetry and design was reflected in the new art of city planning and towns such as London, Florence, Copenhagen, Bern, Darmstadt and Versailles attested to this organization. The science of landscape came into its own and the formal gardens of the *Seicento* were created to remodel the setting for the architectural creation of a particular area. Sweeping staircases swirled upward to lead the eye and the human to the great chambers and halls. The epitome of this artistic creation is to be seen in the formal gardens of Lenôtre at Versailles, where the sculptured trees and shrubs, the systematically organized arrangement of the garden reflected the Baroque love of planning and geometry. Blenheim Castle, outside London, similarly is an English concession to the age of the Baroque.

In southern Germany and Austria, there developed what might be referred to as Alpine Baroque, and nowhere, except perhaps in Rome, does the Baroque element so dominate a nation's architecture. There were many Baroque artists in the Alpine region, but among the most important are Johann Berkhardt, Fischer von Erlach, Lukas von Hildebrandt, Killian Dientzenhofer, J. B. Neumann and J. M. Fischer. The last two named copied much from Rome, but the others strove for inventiveness with amazing results. Under the influence of all these men the face of southern Germany and Austria was transformed. Munich, Prague, Salzburg, Vienna, Karlsrue, Mannheim, Potsdam, Dresden, Würzburg all felt their influence.

Alpine Baroque emphasized the decorative element, and used light and shadows to stress this aspect of the style. The artists strove to achieve a central significance, which used movement and rhythm to strengthen the central themes. Individual parts were subordinated to the whole, and the totality of the particular object became paramount. Colors aided by natural light dance before the eye and sway the human emotions. There is a grandeur of style and magnificence rarely achieved in previous or subsequent cultural eras.

Fischer von Erlach is a monumental figure in the Baroque age. His first creation, the University Church in Salzburg, has helped to make that city one of the seven most beautiful towns in the world. The church bears a striking resemblance, in technique at least, to the work of Bernini on St. Peter's. The central altar is rayed and clouded in the manner of Bernini. The most famous of Erlach's works however is the Karlskirch in Vienna. Begun in 1715, it was completed in 1737 and is the most striking example of the Baroque in Austria. There is a certain element of the classical in the entrance, of the Gothic in the design and of the Baroque in overall planning. Erlach laid plans for the Hofburg but his death in 1723 prevented its completion, although his plans were carried out by his son, Josef Emmanuel.

Among the great achievements of the Alpine Baroque is the famous Belvedere, the summer palace for Prince Eugene of Savoy. Begun by Erlach, it was completed by von Hildebrandt and remains to the present a monumental achievement of both men. The palace appears surrounded by water, and its elaborate interior contains the most famous staircases in Germany. One passes over water to the entrance, and the three immense doorways, each caped by a balcony, cause the individual to pause momentarily. The interior is heavily laden with ornamentation and decoration. The effect is dazzling and striking—a monument to Austrian art.

The Czernin Palace in Prague, designed by Francesco Caratti and completed in 1682, helped to make that city a focal point of the Baroque. Dientzenhofer, however, made the greatest impact in Prague. His Kinsky Palace and the palace for Count Nostitz are remarkable examples of the Baroque, and the Clementinium, which Sitwell calls a Jesuit Kremlin, stands out in the mind of the observer as a tribute to the architect and to the age.

J. B. Neumann constructed the famous Residenz at Würzburg for the Schönborn family and it reflects a strong Italian influence. Its most important room, the Kaisersasl, where the Emperors held receptions on visits to Frankfort, is an excellent example of the Baroque influence in interior design. The last of the important German architects of the age was Fischer, whose church interiors are indeed remarkable. His Benedictine Abbey at Ottobeuren is a masterful example of Baroque creation. These men and their works are but representative examples of the influence and success of Baroque architecture. The selections and names could be listed indefinitely, but these will serve as examples for the beginner and perhaps a source for further study.

It is not possible to leave the Alpine Baroque without making reference to a few other outstanding examples. Munich, the capital city of Bavaria, is the center of Baroque works and needs special mention. Michaelskirche, the Augustinerkirche, the Heiiggeistkirche, the Johann Nepomuk-

Kirche, the Residenz, Schloss Nymphenburg—the names could go on indefinitely—are all or rather were good examples of the Baroque. They served to make Munich the artistic and cultural center of southern Germany and of the Baroque. World War II took its toll of some of these fine buildings.

In a similar vein the great Abbey of Melk, the Austrian town of Linz, which boasts three Baroque churches in one single block, the town of Innsbruck, the Cistercian monastery at Stams, the Landhaus in Klagenfurt, are all further examples of triumphant Baroque. The Germans strove to create masterpieces befitting their faith and themselves. They succeeded admirably, and today these monuments remain as testimony to man's creative ingenuity in an age of creative genius.

This brief discussion of the Baroque has no more than scratched the surface of a very intriguing and difficult problem. Its purpose has been to introduce the student to the important cultural epoch known as the Baroque and to point out to him its certain characteristics, influences and tendencies. It has been the thesis of this essay that the Baroque deserves more attention and better treatment at the hands of historians. The Baroque is no longer a term of derision or opprobrium, and its values in man's long cultural development are now recognized. The range, scope and sweep of the Baroque has been skeletonized in this discussion, but its impact upon the fine arts has it is hoped been demonstrated.

7

THE SUPPRESSION OF THE JESUITS IN 1773 *

The nadir of Church history in modern times was reached at the end of the eighteenth century when, some diplomatists believed, no more popes would be elected and the Catholic Church would disappear as an organized institution. One of the biggest steps in this decline of the Church in the eighteenth century was the dissolution of the Jesuits in 1773. (They were re-established by the papacy early in the nineteenth century.)

In their active defense of Roman supremacy over the Church universal, in their missionary, educational, and political activity, the Jesuits had made many enemies within the Church. They had fought Jansenism as a heresy within the Church, and they had earned the implacable hatred of surviving Jansenists in the eighteenth century. By preaching Roman

* Ludwig Pastor, *The History of the Popes,* translated by F. I. Antrobus, R. F. Kerr, & E. Graf (London: Routledge & Kegan Paul, Ltd., 1891), Vol. 36, pp. 371-383; Vol. 38, pp. 135-142, 283-292. Reprinted by permission.

supremacy they had earned the hatred of Gallicans. Their effective opposition to the secularist thought of the Enlightenment had earned them the enmity of such publicists as Voltaire, men who had influence in the courts of Europe. Thus by mid-century the Jesuits had enemies whose numbers were legion.

The Society of Jesus was first suppressed by royal edict in Portugal, and then in similar fashion in Spain. Both Iberian governments persuaded the French Bourbons to secure the suppression of the Jesuits in France, where they were strongly entrenched. It was not until a suit arose against the Society over a bankruptcy proceeding that an opportunity was offered to the judicial class in France to secure the suppression of the order. The Bourbon governments of France, Spain, and Naples then exerted all pressure possible on the papacy to obtain the complete and universal suppression of the order. Clement XIII refused to succumb to this overwhelming pressure, but his successor, Clement XIV, suppressed the Society of Jesus in 1773, not for abuses and faults within the order, but for what he considered the peace and welfare of the Church.

The following selections on this subject are from the outstanding work on the History of the Popes *by Ludwig von Pastor. The first selection deals with the general causes of the Jesuits' suppression; the second deals with the pressure brought on Clement XIV and with his suppression of the Society in 1773. Pastor is generally recognized as the outstanding authority on papal history in modern times.*

THE EXPULSION of the Jesuits from Portugal was the signal for a general outburst of animosity against them. They were ejected from France, Spain, and the Spanish dependencies, and pressure from Spain led to their suspension by the Pope.

The ultimate object of the campaign waged against the Jesuits in the eighteenth century was not the Society itself but the Papacy. The only reason why the attack was directed almost exclusively against the Society was because it was regarded as the bastion whose destruction would facilitate the combat with the enemy-in-chief.

The Papacy was detested at that time for a threefold reason. To the unbelievers of the eighteenth century it was the principal stronghold of Christianity. The Encyclopedists had little fear of Protestantism but a very considerable fear of the Catholic Church, with its firm and definite doctrine, its strict organization, and the self-sacrifice shown by its adherents. And as the Catholic Church is founded entirely on the Holy See, the Holy See becomes the object of a mortal hatred. Another cause of the enmity was Gallicanism, whose ideas had spread into Spain and Italy. According to the Gallicans, the Pope enjoys some honorary rights as honorary president of the Church, but fundamentally he is only a Bishop like any other. Any additional claim on his part is mere presumption, and it is for princes to restrict him to his original sphere of rights and duties. The third motive for implacable hatred was the conception that the Church, and consequently the Papacy in particular, was an obstacle to material progress in trade and industry. It was seen how Protestant England had become a world power and how Protestant Prussia had won a place for itself among the European powers, while the Catholic countries of the South were dwindling more and more in power, prestige, and wealth. Wherefore Pombal, and others with him, came to the conclusion that the Church, before all else, must be destroyed or at least kept within the narrowest possible bounds if they were to keep pace with the countries of Northern Europe. This conception was erroneous. Pombal did not transform his Portuguese into Britons and Prussians by oppressing the Church; on the contrary it was precisely through adopting this policy that Spain barred her own way to progress. Catholic France sank into squalor and dissension only because her monarchs refused to be guided by Catholic principles; and Austria's inability to summon enough strength to protect Silesia against little Prussia was due to other causes than ecclesiastical conditions. However, whatever the truth of the situation, appearances were against the Catholics, and the Pope had to suffer for them.

The reason why the Company of Jesus was regarded as the bodyguard of the Papacy is easily understood. The education of youth was largely in its hands, while its learning was a stout bulwark against Encyclopedism and it still influenced the upper classes. In its teaching it was a stronghold of "ultramontane principles," even in Gallican France, and still more so elsewhere. All the other religious Orders of any size in France had paid tribute to Gallicanism; the Jesuits had offered the most resistance, and their repeated promises, made after Damiens' attempted regicide, to teach the four Gallican articles was but a stain on their honour. In any case it was now too late for them to redeem their promises, and everyone knew that they had not been made from a desire to uphold Gallicanism but as a desperate attempt to save themselves from destruction.

In their proclamations to the world the statesmen of the eighteenth century did not openly state the reasons for their intention to destroy the Company of Jesus. There was always talk of removing the abuses which had crept into the Society, but for which there was no evidence, in the utterances made by the Popes or the Bishops who remained loyal to the Church. From time to time the Voltairians glibly posed as the reformers whose object was to lead the degenerate sons back to the ways of SS. Ignatius and Francis Xavier. In letters not intended for the public eye they spoke a different language. Tanucci especially spoke out most clearly in this respect and his word had all the more weight since his influence was decisive in Madrid, and it was he who continually exhorted the enemies of the Society to renew their attack upon it. He it was who urged on the king of Spain, and it was Spain that brought about the final suspension of the Society. And the attack was soon extended against the other religious Congregations.

Although the first impetus towards this result was given by Portugal, the Jesuit position was not seriously threatened until France took the field as an ally. It was on French soil especially that the pamphlets with which Pombal sought to excite public opinion against the Jesuits enjoyed a wide circulation and approval, which was fatal for the Company of Jesus, for France set the tone for all Europe and had long been the focus of hostility against religion in general and the Jesuits in particular.

Nowhere perhaps was Loyola's institution more liked by the people or more influential, even in the highest circles, than in the country where it had taken its rise. But here, too, in certain quarters, there was a determined hostility. In the heart of the Parlements an anti-Jesuit spirit had arisen even in the founder's lifetime; it was inherited by succeeding generations, so that it became a matter of *esprit de corps* in the legal body to oppose the Company of Jesus, and the cleavage was widened still more by the fact that the Parlements were the chief centres of Gallicanism and Jansenism. The hostility of the Parlement was particularly dangerous because it had won popular favour by opposing the intolerable burden of taxation, which itself was the inevitable consequence of unsuccessful wars and the extravagance of the Court. Furthermore, among the adherents of Jansenism were many members of the lower ranks of the clergy and of the religious Orders who were invariably not merely opponents but enemies of the Jesuits.

Even worse was the enmity of the Encyclopedists. Inspired by English "enlightenment," the *Philosophes* at first waged war only on intolerance, the lust of the hierarchy for power, the imposition of dogmas on the faithful, and so forth, but finally they rejected all positive Christianity and all revealed religion. "So long as there are rogues and fools in the world," wrote Voltaire, "there will always be religion. There can be no question but that ours is the most ridiculous, absurd, and bloodthirsty that ever infected this earth." Frederick II of Prussia, he went on, would render an everlasting service to humanity by destroying this superstition. The hotbed and stronghold of superstition, wrote Frederick to Voltaire, much to the latter's satisfaction, were the monasteries; once these lairs of fanaticism had been destroyed, their main task was ended. To "enlightened" eyes the most pernicious of all religious societies, "the chief bulwark of ultramontane principles," was the Company of Jesus, whose schools would have to be destroyed before the new spirit could reign supreme. Without openly attacking the Jesuits themselves, the *Philosophes* watched with evident satisfaction the battle waged so effectively against them by others, hoping that with the overthrow of the bulwark the way would be cleared for the destruction of the Church itself. In the correspondence between D'Alembert and Voltaire this hatred of the Jesuits and the hopes which they held of the Society's downfall are expressed without concealment.

> So far as I am concerned [wrote D'Alembert in 1762] I see everything in the rosiest colours at the moment. I can see the Jansenists here dying a peaceful death next year, after having brought about the ruin of the Jesuits by a violent death this year. I see the coming of tolerance, the recall of the Protestants, the marriage of priests, the abolition of confession, and the unobtrusive extirpation of fanaticism.

In 1761, he thought, "The time is probably approaching when philosophy will take its revenge on the Jesuits." On hearing that Voltaire still retained some sympathy with the Jesuits, his former teachers, he wrote to him in 1762, "Believe me, you must put away this human weakness. Let the Jansenist rabble rid us of the Jesuit rabble and don't stop these spiders eating each other up." Voltaire, for his part, wrote to the Marquis Villevieille, regarding the expulsion of the Jesuits from Spain (1767), "With my brave knight I rejoice at the expulsion of the Jesuits. . . . If only we could root out all the monks, who are no better than these ruffians of Loyola's!"

All this notwithstanding, the enemies of the Jesuits, numerous though they were, would hardly have won the day had they not had influential patrons in Court and Government circles. That the Duc de Choiseul played a part in the downfall of the Jesuits in France is much disputed, being as firmly maintained as hotly denied. An actual agreement between the Minister and the Parlement may be impossible to prove, but the opinion was widespread among his contemporaries that he was playing a double game, posing officially as the saviour of the Jesuits, while tacitly encouraging and favouring the Parlements, if not actually goading them on.

Choiseul, the creature and admirer of Madame de Pompadour, had no religious convictions; outwardly he was a Catholic, inwardly he was much in sympathy with the contemporary philosophy of enlightenment. He had been praised when ambassador in Rome by the Cardinal Secretary of State Archinto for having combined the service of his King with that of religion, the Church, and the Holy See, but even early in his career he was considered by the Curia to be an enemy of the Jesuits and to hold an unfavourable opinion of Rome. The Curia fully understood his reluctance to irritate the Parlements by harsh measures at a time when an unsuccessful war was being waged, since the Court and the Government were financially dependent on them, but it was realized also that the more these bodies were feared the stronger they grew. When the Cardinal Secretary of State Torrigiani voiced his suspicion that the Paris Parlement had secret supporters at Court, the nuncio Pamfili agreed but thought that the chief reason of its growing power lay rather in its popularity and, above all, in the feeble attitude of the Court. The King, he wrote, could not bring himself to take any energetic step for fear lest the Parlement cease to function and thus deprive the Government of the funds necessary for the continuation of the war. A year later the nuncio was taking it for granted that "various powerful personages at Court" had contributed more to the Jesuit disaster than the power of the Parlements. It appears from Tanucci's correspondence that also among the enemies of the Society it was commonly thought that the Court or the Ministry was aiding the Parlements only to bring about the downfall of the Jesuits. Within the Society itself it was believed that there was good reason to suppose that there were secret enemies at Court but it was also realized that these were only subsidiary causes and that the chief reason for the persecution was religion itself and the Society's attachment to the Holy See.

Louis XV himself was not inimically inclined towards the Jesuits; in fact, like the rest of his family, he had always appointed one of them as his confessor, although for many years he had never given him the opportunity of exercising his chief function. But in the Jesuit affair as in all others he was unable to throw off his habitual indolence, and even on the occasions when he was stirred to action by the feeling that his personal dignity had been affronted, the steps he took were usually belated and half-hearted and they accelerated rather than checked the Society's ruin. Moreover, although endowed with many other gifts, he was not sufficiently self-confident to make himself independent of the opinions proffered by his leading Ministers. And once he was subject to the influence of men who owed their positions to Madame de Pompadour, there was little hope of his intervening with any real effect on behalf of the religious who had refused to adapt the moral law to suit the King's favourite. The goodwill of a monarch who was despised for his excesses and failures and hated for his oppressive taxation was more of a liability than an asset to the Jesuits, as it gave the public an excuse for holding them partly responsible for the unpopular governmental measures.

The storm that was to break over the French Jesuits was heralded by many portents. Year after year Cardinal Noailles of Paris had persisted in the suspension of the Jesuits in his diocese. The condemnation of the books by Pichon and Berruyer and the *Bibliothèque Janséniste,* though technically justified, had a truly disastrous effect on the critical situation in France. The unfavourable decision of the censors was hailed triumphantly as a victory for Jansenism. Displaying the greatest indignation and absurdly exaggerating the importance of the whole affair, the Parlements had the books condemned again through the agency of their sympathisers in the Sorbonne and the episcopacy.

The anti-Jesuit attitude of the Parlements was evinced even more clearly on the occasion of Damiens' attempted murder of Louis XV on January 5th, 1757. The rumour was deliberately spread that until his marriage nineteen years previously the culprit had been a servant in a Jesuit college. Nothing was said of his having had a similar occupation in the homes of members of the Parlement or, according to his admission made under torture, of his having heard and read much that had incited him against princes. Although there was no mention in the charge of any Jesuit being involved, the mob was so infuriated that several actual or presumed Jesuits were assaulted. Attempts were made by means of pamphlets, partly produced in secret printing presses, to excite animosity against the Jesuits, as though they had been the moral instigators of the crime by their teachings on tyrannicide. The moral theologies of Busenbaum and Lacroix were condemned by the Parlement of Toulouse, and the threatened condemnation of these works by the Parlement of Paris was forestalled only by the Jesuits declaring that they had had no part in their production and that they abhorred the passages on regicide. They even went further, undertaking to teach the complete independence of secular princes and the four Gallican articles of 1682. The threatening storm was thus temporarily averted, but at the cost of the Society's principles.

The storm-clouds, however, continued to gather more thickly than ever and partisanship increased to fever-heat. The anti-Jesuits in France not only kept up a lively correspondence with their Portuguese allies, but also distributed their pamphlets far and wide. Isolated sentences from sermons, personal opinions on matters of conscience, even schoolboys' exercises, were cited for the purpose of making the Jesuits hated by the people and suspected by the Government and the Court. The severest measures were taken against the "culprits," whereby the unsoundness of the evidence had very often to be concealed by the unmeasured phraseology of the sentences.

In any case, the language of this prologue was only too clear; in addition, the adversaries of the Jesuits expressed their aims quite unconcealedly. The Jansenist church-journal *Nouvelles ecclésiastiques* openly demanded the expulsion of the Jesuits from France. While one pamphlet attempted to produce evidence that the Jesuits had done more harm to the Church than Luther or Calvin, another published the motives by which both spiritual and temporal authorities were bound in conscience to suppress the Society. An opportunity of bringing the final goal within sight was soon to be offered by the commercial transactions in which Jesuit Lavalette had involved himself on the island of Martinique.

* * * *

As in the case with Portugal, Clement XIV, as soon as he was elected, strove to obtain peace with Spain, France, and Naples by showing them the utmost goodwill. Here, however, he was faced with far more serious obstacles, the three closely united Bourbon Courts being determined to make a settlement dependent on the granting of very great demands. According to the ultimatum drawn up by Choiseul while the conclave was still in progress, the new Pope was to be compelled, by force if necessary, to make the following concessions: (1) Satisfaction for the duke of Parma; (2) the surrender of Benevento and Pontecorvo to Naples, which, in return, was to waive its claim to Castro and Ronciglione; (3) the surrender of Avignon and Venaissin to France in return for a monetary compensation; (4) the total abolition of the Jesuit Order.

With regard to the last point it was long thought that Cardinal Ganganelli had given a definite promise during the conclave and that his election had resulted from it. The authentic history of Ganganelli's elevation to the Papacy, however, shows that those who imputed to him a simoniacal transaction were doing him a grievous injustice. It has been proved, on the contrary, that the Cardinal refused to enter into any such pact and that there is no question of his having given a formal promise before his election. It is equally certain, however, that the ambiguous position towards the Jesuit question which he had adopted as a Cardinal was maintained by him in the conclave.

Inexperienced in the ways of the world, the Cardinal did not realize what a lever this attitude of his was giving to the enemies of the Jesuits; now that he was Pope they could exert pressure on him. If the utterances he had made, they calculated, were a true reflection of his inward conviction, he must, now that he had acquired the power, as Head of the Church, to suppress the Society, put them into execution. At first, however, this calculation showed no sign of coming true, though there was some evidence to indicate that Clement XIV was moved by anti-Jesuit feelings. When the Generals of the religious Orders presented themselves, as usual, to do homage to the new Pope, they were all received with affection except the Jesuit General Ricci, who was given an icy welcome by Clement XIV. When Ricci commended his Order to the Pope, the latter said not a word in reply but straightway imparted his blessing, which, of course, was the sign of dismissal. No less interest was aroused by the Pope's retention of the office of *ponens* for the process of beatification of the anti-Jesuit Palafox, which was so eagerly espoused by Charles III. Clement told the Spanish ambassador Azpuru that he would take a particular interest in the matter on account of his veneration of Bishop Palafox and his regard for the king's desire. As for the suppression of the Jesuit Order, Azpuru obtained no very clear statement from the Pope, it is true, but he thought that there were grounds for hoping that his king's wish in this matter, too, would receive favourable attention, seeing that the Pope himself had told him that he would remove the obstacles. The French ambassador Aubeterre was assured by Clement XIV at an audience on May 31st, 1769, that he would arrange everything to the satisfaction of the House of Bourbon; as for the Jesuits, he must be given a little time, as he could not do everything at once; but he could assure him that the Courts would have cause to be satisfied.

Like Aubeterre, Azpuru, at another audience on June 3rd, made no official request for the suppression of the Jesuits but merely stressed his king's great interest in the matter, arising from "Catholic zeal for the good of the Church," he being her obedient son and protector. Azpuru received the same answer as Aubeterre; he also learnt at this time that the Pope had spoken disapprovingly to Cardinal Orsini and the Maltese envoy of the Jesuits' attitude during the pontificate of Clement XIII. On June 15th Azpuru reported to Madrid that not a day passed without the Pope's showing signs of his goodwill regarding the suppression, so that there could be no doubt about it. In the audience he had granted him the day before he had spoken in exactly the same way as on June 3rd and he had asked confidentially for information about the property of the Spanish Jesuits in Rome. The Secretary of the Propaganda, Marefoschi, was collecting in the archives all the documents relating to the Jesuits, and Palafox's process was to be accelerated. Azpuru concluded: "I have no doubt that the Pope will satisfy our king in everything." Tanucci's friend, the Neapolitan agent Centomani, gave it as his opinion on June 20th, 1769, that the suppression of the hated Order was imminent or at any rate was no longer remote.

This conception was erroneous if only because the Bourbon envoys had still refrained from taking any official step. This was certainly not due to any lack of zeal, for it is hard to say who nursed the greatest hatred of Loyola's Order—Tanucci in Naples, Choiseul in Paris, or Charles III in Madrid. The same feelings animated the envoys in Rome, the main topic of whose reports was now the "extincion de los Jesuitas." Azpuru was determined to do everything in his power to bring this about, as he considered that the destruction of the Order was necessary for the good of Christianity. The same view was held by Cardinal Orsini, who had once been a supporter of the Order when the Courts had been more favourably disposed towards it. Cardinal Bernis, too, who succeeded Aubeterre as the French ambassador on June 27th, 1769, was filled with the conviction that now that the main branch of the tree had been lopped off, the axe must be laid to the trunk, for this was demanded by the political situation and the peace of the Catholic States and the Holy See. The underlying reason for the eagerness shown by the Bourbon statesmen was undoubtedly the fact that nothing short of the complete destruction of the Jesuit Order could sanction the forcible measures they had taken in their respective countries.

But despite the unanimity regarding their goal, the means of attaining it were far from clear. Charles III was of the opinion that the new Pope should be dealt with as firmly as Clement XIII had been, seeing that he was compromised both by his attitude when he was a Cardinal and by his election, which appeared to be the work of the Bourbons. This view was shared by Azpuru and Aubeterre. But Cardinal Bernis, the experienced diplomat, considered it more advisable to work for their desired object by gentle methods than by blustering and forceful ones. This immediately earned for him the mistrust of the Spanish king, who was burning with desire to see the Jesuit Order completely annihilated. The partisanship left behind by Loyola's disciples, even in the countries from which they had been driven out, he wrote to Louis XV on June 7th,

1769, was undoubtedly harmful both to religion and to national tranquillity. He considered the appointment of a Cardinal as ambassador endangered the attainment of their common goal to such an extent that Choiseul had some difficulty in setting his mind at rest on the score of Bernis' reliability. Inevitably the view held by the Spanish king affected the relations between Azpuru and Bernis. Even before the Cardinal had taken up his post as ambassador, a serious disagreement arose between them on account of Bernis' unwillingness to put the suppression of the Jesuits before all other demands. Soon their differences grew so many that Azpuru wrote complaining to Madrid that Bernis was trying to postpone the settlement of the Jesuit question as long as possible. This was correct inasmuch as the Cardinal wanted to obtain the extinction of the Order by gradually crippling it, without using force and provoking a stir. The complaints made by Madrid to Paris about Bernis' attitude were so frequent that Choiseul had to defend his ambassador every week.

Madrid was firmly convinced that Bernis was a friend of the Jesuits. Charles III accused the Cardinal of falsely asserting that he, the king, was trying to conduct the affair by indirect and secret methods. Everything was in the balance, he averred, because the Cardinal was not following the instructions of his Court. This charge was quite unfounded, for actually Bernis had no instructions, Versailles not being in so feverish a hurry as Madrid. Choiseul was primarily concerned with the acquisition of Avignon and he feared, not without cause, that Clement XIV wanted to combine the two affairs. On June 19th, 1769, the Spanish ambassador in Paris, De Fuentes, was instructed to see to it that strict orders were sent through Choiseul to Bernis to work for the suppression with energy and in conjunction with the other Bourbon envoys.

Choiseul took umbrage at the suspicion of the Madrid Cabinet and he disapproved of their haste.

Our feelings about the Jesuits [he wrote to Bernis on July 4th, 1769] are no less sincere than those of the Courts of Madrid and Naples, and nothing could be more unjust than to try to sow suspicion about our alleged lukewarmness. We have no other desire than to speak and act in conjunction with these two Powers and we shall never refuse to march along with them, step by step. I also notice with regret that our attitude towards their Ministers is far more open and sincere than theirs towards us. However, for prudence sake, we must overlook this and continue to strive as effectively as we possibly can after our worthy object by methods that are gentle, honourable, and creditable to the three Crowns. The way in which the Pope has already expressed his opinion of the Jesuits on various occasions is enough to set our minds at rest, both as regards the issue and his definite wish to be given time to fulfill the demands of the three rulers. The mere fact that he is inclined in this direction entitles him to consideration. Cardinal Solis and Azpuru agree with Your Eminence in this and they would be contradicting themselves were they to complain of a delay the necessity and propriety of which they appeared to acknowledge. But if Azpuru were to make Your Eminence the proposal which has already been submitted to

Aubeterre, namely that you should hand the Pope a copy of the memorandum made for Clement XIII on the general and complete suppression of the Jesuits, there is nothing against Your Eminence taking this step.

I am entirely of your opinion; in the handling of the matter in question gentleness and firmness must be used simultaneously with skill and intelligence. Success is often delayed by trying to rush things; the only result is to weary and upset the persons who have the say in the matter, and instead of progressing one loses ground. Your Eminence's wise power of discretion is a certain security for your conduct and it is much to be desired that the envoys of Spain and Naples should imitate you in this respect.

This instruction did not reach Rome till July 9th, 1769. On the 5th Bernis had reported from there to Choiseul that two days previously he had had a conversation with Cardinal Orsini and another with Azpuru, with the object of bringing some order and agreement into the proceeding which was occupying the attention of the three Courts. Azpuru had assured him that he would show "the same willingness to follow my advice" as he would Aubeterre's; he had shown him a dispatch which prescribed this line of action. If, as was expected, Cardinal Solis was not entrusted with the affairs of Spain, he, Bernis, would command the greatest influence in all matters of common interest to the three Courts. The Portuguese envoy had spoken in the same sense. He could also reckon on Cardinal Orsini, who, it was true, had the bad habit of reporting to Tanucci the most trivial details that were brought to his attention and of laying too great weight on whatever came to his ears from any quarter.

Bernis reported further that he, Orsini, and Azpuru had had a talk with Almada, who seemed to see the necessity of conducting the affair with great circumspection and absolute secrecy. "We will consult together as to how to find various excuses for seeing the Pope alone. The simplest way, in my opinion, would be to make it appear that the affairs of Parma, Benevento, and Avignon were the subjects of our conversation with the Pope." On July 13th, 1769, Bernis reported on a talk he had had with the General of the Augustinians, a Spaniard who had been let into the secrets of the Madrid Cabinet. This enemy of the Jesuits was also convinced that the matter of the suppression must be handled with extreme care and in the greatest secrecy and that it must not be allowed to pass through several persons' hands. The General thought that the carelessness and incompetence of the Portuguese envoy Almada, the imprudent vivacity of Cardinal Orsini, and the limited knowledge possessed by Azpuru resulted in his, Bernis', being badly supported. The General had also called his attention to the presence of Jesuit emissaries among his entourage. In the further course of the conversation the Cardinal managed to shake the General's belief that secret negotiations were being carried on between the Pope and the Spanish Court through the medium of Manuel de Roda and Charles III's confessor.

At the first session of the Congregation on August 9th, 1773 the Pope had announced that the suppression would take place on the 16th. This time there was no more delay. On the evening of the appointed day the secretary of the Congregation of Cardinals, Macedonio, an intimate of Moñino's, accompanied by soldiers and police officers, presented himself at the professed house "al Gesù" and announced to the General Ricci and his Assistants the Brief by which the Order of St. Ignatius was dissolved.

Ricci, a gentle and peace-loving character, had never thought of using any other defence against the growing storm than prayer and still more prayer. With his "almost naïve sense of justice" he could not imagine his Order being suppressed by the Pope, especially as he had formed a very good opinion of Clement XIV, even at the time of his election. Even after Clement had struck some very severe blows at him personally as well as at his Order, it seemed to him incredible, as Cordara explains,

that the Vicar of Christ will burden his conscience with so blatant an injustice as the destruction of a society which has deserved well of the Holy See and the whole Church, and this without a court of inquiry and without revealing the charges that have been raised. Surely the Pope agrees—and to think otherwise is impossible—that before an accused person can be condemned his guilt must be evident and that he must be given the opportunity of proving his innocence? All this is demanded by natural justice, which no monarch and no Pope can violate, and failing which any finding of a court of justice would be null and void. And is it also to be believed that a Vicar of Christ would contradict what was said by his predecessor eight years ago in the Bull *Apostolicum,* in which two hundred Bishops concurred? In this Bull the Pope approved of our Institute and took it under his protection, he praised the members of this Society, and stated that it was persecuted only by heretics, unbelievers, and free-thinkers, that it was only they who desired its destruction and for no other reason than because this Order had defended the rights of the Holy See so vigorously and had opposed the errors of the time. Was the present Pope to contradict this because he has not the apostolic courage to oppose the libertines and infidels? And is it to be believed that the Head of the Catholic Church, an enlightened theologian, like the present Pope, will suddenly tear this great breach throughout the whole of Christendom by depriving it at a single blow of so many instructors of Christian youth in almost every Catholic city, of so many spiritual advisers, of so many heralds of the divine message in the pulpit, in the oratories, in the retreat houses, and by drying up the source of so many missionaries to the heretics, infidels, and savages? In this year alone they have converted a thousand Arians and other heretics in Transylvania. Is it not an outrageous injustice to a Vicar of Christ even to think him capable of creating such havoc in Catholic Christendom and of helping the enemies of the Church of Rome to gain such a triumph?

On July 31st, the feast of the founder of the Order, Ricci had written to Cordara,

To-day, with God's help, we have celebrated the Feast of our holy father

Ignatius with less pomp and ceremony but with the unusually large participation of the people. It was said that this would be the last time, but St. Peter was freed from his chains just as Herod was about to bring him forth to the people for execution.

No wonder that on reading the Brief Ricci was amazed; but he retained full control of himself and when asked, on the Pope's orders, if he accepted the Brief, he replied that whatever the Pope decided must be sacred to everyone; it did not need his concurrence.

At the same hour the Brief of suppression was made known to the Rectors of all the other colleges and houses of the Jesuits in Rome by prelates accompanied by armed escorts, and at the same time the archives, account offices, and sacristies of the Jesuits were sealed up by notaries. The Jesuits were forbidden to perform any ecclesiastical functions or to leave their houses until further notice. On August 17th the General Ricci was taken to the English College.

The Brief of suppression, dated July 21st, which was not posted up in the usual places and of which it was impossible to obtain a printed copy in Rome as late as August 18th, opens with the following considerations:

> Our Lord and Redeemer (*Dominus ac Redemptor*) Jesus Christ who was preannounced and revealed as the Prince of Peace, committed his office of atonement to the care of the Apostles and conveyed to them the power of the word, so that they, as emissaries of Christ, who is the God of peace and love, not of dissension, might proclaim this peace to the whole world and that all begot in Christ might form one body and one soul. Thus it is above all the duty of the Pope, who administers Christ's office of atonement, to secure the peace of the Church and in this cause to sacrifice even those things which are personally dear to him. Assuredly the religious Orders are the best means of ensuring the welfare of the Church, but if an order ceases to fulfil the mission entrusted to it, the Pope must revive it, reform it, or dissolve it.

This preface is followed by the body of the Brief composed of three main parts: the first two are of a historical character intended to provide the grounds for the last one, which contains the actual enactments and the provisions made for their execution.

The first part, then, is a survey of the actions taken by the Popes in regard to the reform or extinction of religious Orders. To effect this purpose Clement XIV goes back to the time of Innocent III and then cites in chronological order the suppression of the Templars in 1312, of the Humiliati, of the Reformed Conventuals in 1626, the Order of SS. Ambrose and Barnabas *ad Nemus* in 1643, then the reform of the Poor Servants of the Mother of God of the Pious Schools in 1645, the suppression of the Order of St. Basil of Armenia in 1650, of the Priests of the Buon Gesù in 1651, of the Canons of St. George in Alga in Venice, of the Hieronymites of Fiesole, and of the Jesuati of St. John Colombino —these last three in 1668. On all these occasions the Pope had not adopted any regular judicial procedure, which would only have provoked further dissension, but had acted on his own authority "according to the dictates of prudence," decreeing the suppression at a single stroke without leave of appeal or defence. With the same care (these words introduce the second part of the Brief), he too, Clement XIV, has informed himself about the origin, existence, and present state of the Society of Jesus.

At this point the Brief refers at length to the history of this Order, sketching it in broad strokes and treating it in a highly one-sided manner. Everything good and favourable which should certainly have been said about the Order has been carefully passed over in silence, whereas the shady side has been proportionately accentuated. The assertion is made and an attempt made to prove it by evidence that

> at the very birth of this Society there germinated manifold seeds of dissension and jealousy, and that not merely within itself but also against other Orders, against the secular priesthood, against academies, universities, public schools, and even against the princes in whose States the Jesuits had been received.

Thus it is, the Brief proceeds to relate, that steps against the Order have been taken in Rome by individual princes from the earliest times. The inquiry undertaken by Sixtus V at the urgent request of Philip II of Spain unfortunately had to be left unfinished owing to his death. In spite of all the subsequent Papal decrees and privileges the accusations and disputes increased. The prohibition against Jesuits taking part in State affairs was of no more avail than the most recent confirmation of the Order—extorted rather than petitioned—by the Pope's predecessor, Clement XIII. Those princes "whose piety and magnanimity towards the Society of Jesus, inherited from their forefathers, is universally renowned" have indeed decreed the expulsion of the Society's members from their lands to preserve the unity of the Church, but for the sake of the lasting pacification of the whole Church they have insisted on the general suppression of the Order.

And so in the last part of the Brief Clement XIV disposes of the Society in the following manner: "Since it can no longer bring forth the abundant fruits or be of the usefulness for which it was founded," also because "it is hardly, if at all, possible to restore a true and lasting peace to the Church as long as it remain in existence," and finally for other reasons "suggested to Us by the principles of prudence and which We retain concealed in Our breast" after mature deliberation, with certain knowledge, and in the fulness of Our apostolic power, we dissolve, suppress, extinguish, and abolish the said Society."

The various executive instructions which follow correspond entirely with the eighteen points of the draft which the Pope accepted from Moñino's hands on September 6th, 1772. The novices were to be released, the members of the Order who had taken simple but not solemn vows were to choose another occupation within a year, those who had taken solemn vows to leave their houses and either enter another Order or place themselves under the direction of a Bishop as secular clerics; only when the first of these two alternatives was impossible might they reside in their houses as secular clerics until the premises were finally used for charitable purposes. Next come instructions concerning the hearing of confessions and preaching by the ex-Jesuits, with episcopal license, their exclusion from schools and missions, their release from the vow of poverty, whereby they had been forbidden to accept benefices and Mass stipends, also the revocation of all the privileges and liberties which had been granted to them. Finally any attempt to lodge an appeal which would have a delaying effect, or to defend the Order by word or writing, was forbidden. The princes were asked to issue the necessary laws for the Brief, and the faithful were admonished to preserve peace and concord.

This Brief of July 21st, 1773, represented the most obvious victory of "enlightenment" and royal absolutism over the Church and its head, and for this reason, naturally enough, the most diverse judgments have been upon it. In the camp of the "enlighteners" and in the Bourbon Courts it was received with sheer joy, while the enemies of the Society praised it to the skies. A calmer and more sober judgment was reserved for recent times.

Of the Pope's authority to suppress the Order there can be no doubt, whether the measure was justified, that is to say whether the motivation which was imposed on the Pope was sound enough and whether he personally was convinced of its justice, is another question. That the text of the Brief itself was conclusive evidence against the Society of Jesus must be firmly contested, for the signature on the document which was practically appended under duress is of no value for establishing the truth. The decisive step had already been taken by Clement XIV on November 29th, 1772, when he gave his word to the King of Spain. All former statements might have been considered as private expressions of opinion having no binding force, but this was in answer to an official request. Previously it might have been possible for him to utter a *non possumus* (which he never had the strength to do), but from that moment onwards his hands were tied. If any fact can be established by documentary evidence it is that the Pope was subjected to enormous moral pressure.

This, of course, does not answer the question, to what extent the Order was responsible for its fate and whether the mischief it caused really called for its reform or suppression. This is not the place to speak of the great services rendered by the disciples of St. Ignatius in the cause of the Catholic restoration and the missions. On the other hand, that there were many instances of individual failings cannot be denied: pronounced exclusiveness, for instance, and interference in political matters. There may well have been other discrepancies, such as those of a financial nature in the various houses, though these were of a purely local and personal character. But the Pope did not dissolve the Order on account of its immorality or its false doctrines or its relaxed discipline, but solely to preserve the peace of the Church. It was tragic that precisely those princes who had gained most power, both internally and externally, through the work of the Jesuits and the Catholic restoration should have been misled by evil counsellors to use that power to wreck the Society. But that it aroused so much hostility among the "enlightened" was due, not to its lapses and failings, which might occur in any human undertaking, but to the realization that this was the strongest bulwark of the Roman Church and that it had to be destroyed.

There still remains to be considered Clement XIV's personal attitude towards the Society of Jesus. The complaint was often raised by those who were in frequent contact with him that no one knew what the Pope really thought about the Order. In this respect his actions were no true guide. If he was convinced of the Jesuits' guilt and was sincerely opposed to them he would hardly have resisted for three years. If he thought them innocent he should have taken the part of the persecuted and harassed Order in a more energetic fashion. Cordara, who knew the Pope well and consistently tried to justify his conduct, was of the opinion that at first Clement was a friend of the Jesuits. When he was promoted to Cardinal, he says, Clement XIII called him as "Jesuit in Franciscan clothing." But in order to gain the Papacy Ganganelli thought it expedient to throw in his lot with the other side and he entered the conclave as an enemy of the Order. His behaviour there confirmed his adherents in their belief that as Pope he would certainly and quickly decree the suppression, but what actually happened was very different.

Was it that as Pope he felt a heavier responsibility in the matter than as an ambitious Cardinal? However that may be, he took care not to let his temporizing attitude, which became more and more suspicious as the affair approached its climax, appear too noticeable, and in his efforts to convince the importunate Bourbons of his zeal he overstretched himself. He still hoped to escape from the net that he himself had woven, but beginning with trifling concessions he allowed himself to be driven from one weakness to another, and the crowning tragedy was that the few counsellors to whom he lent an ear had been corrupted. He hesitated long before inflicting this deep wound on the Church; but there was no other way left. Why was it too that he dealt only with the princes, never with the dignitaries of the Church, never with the Bishops? Why too in a matter so important for the Church did he allow the decision to rest with the temporal powers? And even after the Brief had been issued and he thought that it could not be revoked, Clement XIV still continued his enigmatic attitude, showing remarkably little interest in the fate of the victims.

8

THE CATHOLIC CHURCH IN REVOLUTIONARY FRANCE *

The Church of the Old Regime in France was an established Church over which the government had a large measure of control. When dissatisfaction with the Old Regime grew strong, as it did in the last half of the eighteenth century, the Church as well as the government became the object of reform proposals. The Church in France had grown effete in these years. It was not guilty of extreme abuses, as in the sixteenth century, but it was guilty of complacency and inertia. The best minds of the age, by and large, were found among the Church's enemies rather than in her ranks.

When the Estates General became the National Assembly in June of 1789, therefore, it was natural for the constitution-making body to turn its attention to ecclesiastical reform. The need for money led the assembly to confiscate Church property, and this measure, in turn, necessitated measures providing for the upkeep of the Church in France. The Civil Constitution of the Clergy divided the country into those who remained loyal to the Roman Catholic Church and those who accepted the new Constitutional Church. In effect, two Frances were created by this measure—a division which persisted through the nineteenth century and into the twentieth.

Napoleon realized that a majority of Frenchmen remained loyal to the Roman Church and that in the last years of the eighteenth century a religious revival had grown strong in France. He therefore proposed to end the schism by negotiating a concordat with the papacy, for above all else Napoleon was anxious to rule over a united country. The Concordat of 1801 served as the basis for Church-State relations in France until it was abrogated by the French government in 1905. But the chasm between the two Frances was too wide and deep for even Napoleon to bridge. Loyalty to Catholicism in most Frenchmen's minds was identified with a rejection of the Revolution, an attachment to the monarchy, and a desire to restore the greater part of the Old Regime. Some Catholics did

* Douglas Woodruff, "The French Revolution and Beyond," *Church and State* (Papers Read at the Summer School of Catholic Studies, Cambridge, England, July 27th to August 6th, 1935 [London: Burns, Oates & Washbourne, Ltd., 1936]), pp. 133-158. Reprinted by permission.

not accept this "package deal," of course, but they were few and they were held suspect by the others. To understand French history in the nineteenth century, then, one must understand the fate of the Church during the French Revolution.

FRANCE in the eighteenth century was much the greatest country in Europe. All kings, great and small, from the King of Spain to the smallest German prince, looked to Versailles as to the supreme example of a thoroughly organized monarchy. Culturally, all eyes were equally turned to France, and French language and letters set the tone. The first enthusiasts for the ideas of '89 and '93 might well refuse to consider national frontiers, and might consider that their mission was to the whole of mankind, for they had grown up in a world in which the old French culture passed easily across the jigsaw of frontiers which made up the Old Europe.

The prestige of the French Government was the more effective because there was a great similarity in the political structure everywhere. The first lively newspapers of Camille Desmoulins carried in their title, in which France and the Low Countries were grouped together, a recognition that the same opposition between the inherited structure of society and reforming zeal was manifest in the dominions of the Empire as in those of Louis XVI.

It accordingly resulted that the particular history of conflict between the Revolution and the Church became much more than an episode in French history. The debate which was precipitated, the discussions on the proper relationship of Church and State, had an influence throughout the greater part of Europe, and on the model of the Concordat with which Napoleon concluded the struggle in France many lesser concordats were to be framed. The French Revolution takes its place in history as a European movement, not only on account of the magnitude of the disturbance, but on account of the universal nature of the questions which it focused, and the solutions it attempted.

It was thus doubly unfortunate for Catholicism in Europe that the Church in France had peculiar weaknesses at the close of the eighteenth century. The violence of the Revolution, a natural sense of the dramatic in historians, the deep penitence of Catholic writers in the last century, the justification of the Revolution by other writers, all tended to throw into relief the dark spots of the eighteenth-century Church. It seemed reasonable to suppose that luxury and avarice had gone to great lengths, because the fate of the Church proved so violent and so filled with blood. Fortunately no part of modern history has been sifted and re-sifted with more minute care by successive generations of French scholars, and we are able to-day to appreciate the state of the Church in the decades just previous to 1789. It can now be seen that the weakness and corruptions, in the strict sense of the word, while real and important, were not the immediate and obvious ones of over-rich and haughty prelates, separated by a wide gulf from their own lower clergy, and representing in their persons one of the worst abuses of the days of privilege without responsibility. The truth is less simple.

There were in France, in 1789, some one hundred and thirty-five archbishops and bishops. In proportion to the population of the faithful this was exactly the same ratio as exists in England to-day between the Catholic hierarchy and the Catholic population, for France then was a country of 24,000,000 people. In the pre-railway era, a bishop's range of action was not very large, but the number of sees, though defensible, was not the result of policy but the inheritance of history. It bore witness to the way France had grown up by the coming together of different provinces and local centres. The dioceses were exceedingly uneven in size and wealth. For centuries now the King had appointed the bishops, and the more valuable sees were greatly sought after by members of the great families. In the list of the hundred and thirty may be found most of the great territorial names, but it is a great mistake to let the shadow of the Cardinal de Rohan, of Diamond Necklace notoriety, of Talleyrand, and Loménie de Brienne fill the imagination. Rohan had in Strassburg the most valuable see in France with an income of nearly half a million francs a year. Talleyrand and Loménie, because they play a large part in the first two years of the Revolution, have tended to stand for examples of the old episcopate. They must be considered side by side with de Beaumont, Archbishop of Paris from 1746 to 1781, and his successor Juigny who held the see till the Concordat. Paris had only become an archbishopric in the previous century, it was far from being the premier see, but it was inevitably a post of great importance, whose holder bore the brunt of the perennial struggles with the lawyers of the Parlement. Neither de Beaumont nor Juigny gave any handle to charges of luxury or negligence. It was not till Napoleon I that any elaborate furniture was placed in the official residence in Paris, and both bishops maintained a steady stream of disinterested charity, even at the expense of the personal appointments of their lives. In the very severe winter '88-9, Juigny borrowed 400,000 frs. in order to be able to distribute more relief. He was surprised to be signalled out for the stones and abuse of the mobs in the autumn of '89, and when he turned and asked a woman in the crowd if she was among those who were breaking the windows of his carriage, she replied, "Yes, indeed. They gave me the stone and six francs, so I put the francs in my pocket and threw the stone." If Juigny was signalled out for organized opprobrium, he suffered because his see was the heart of revolutionary violence, not because he was representative of abuses. Louis XVI made his appointments with some conscientiousness. He refused for a long time to make any large provision for Talleyrand, and it was characteristic that even when he yielded, against his better judgment, it was to meet the dying wish of Talleyrand's father. There were standards for bishops, and by thirty-five Talleyrand had made it plain that he did not reach them.

If few of the bishops were witty atheists like Loménie or Talleyrand at that time, a number were worldly, and more were unspiritual, but by and large, the eighteenth-century episcopate in France could hold up its mitred head without shame. So, too, with the regulars. There were a thousand abbeys in France, some of them with vast incomes. The monks, for three-quarters of the abbeys were for men, had shrunk in numbers, and most houses did not reach double figures and had permanent trouble to find novices. But the monks kept up the rule, and where they had large resources they dispensed large charity. They had shrunk to being but a small proportion of the total number of French men and women living under religious vows. Of these there were in all some sixty thousand, more than half of them women, belonging to congregations founded mainly in and for the towns, and long after the great centuries of feudal endowment. It was from these religious that the martyrs and victims of the Terror were to come. The great abuse lay in the control of the property of the old foundations. By the system of holding abbeys *in commendam* most of the revenues were deflected towards a titular abbot, and the wealth of the most historic abbeys in France went mainly to swell the already adequate incomes of the greater archbishops, of leading nobles, or of members of the royal house and its connections. Thus Cluny belonged to de la Rochefoucauld, Bishop of Beauvais, St. Vaast at Arras to Rohan of Strassburg, St. Ouen and the great Carolingian abbey of Corbie to Loménie de Brienne. Henry Stuart, Cardinal York held two such French abbeys. It may be mentioned in passing that these tidbits were commonly enjoyed by Cardinals at Rome, and the system tended to take the edge off any Roman zeal for a reform of the system established by the French kings. The system extended to cover the canonries, the prebends' stalls, and other offices connected with cathedrals and wealthy city churches. The place to obtain the more valuable of these offices was Versailles, but in each centre there was a vested interest in maintaining the system. The city clergy, recruited from the higher *bourgeoisie,* lived on the lower slopes of a ladder of preferment which might lead able and fortunate men to archbishoprics. These clergy came from families outside the feudal order and critical of it. They were largely sympathetic to literary and philosophic unbelief, and to the new concentration of interest on practical and social reform. Many of them were members of the Masonic lodges and laughed at their stricter brethren who spoke of Freemasonry as naturally allied with scepticism. The canons at Mons, Benedictines, and even Carmelites at Besançon, thought no harm of being active Masons. The class from which a clergy is recruited will naturally colour its professional outlook. The country clergy came mainly from the homes of farmers, the people who suffered most from the exemptions enjoyed by the wealthier landowners from the main taxes. The country clergy, some 50,000 strong, were very poor. Where they were the rectors and drew directly the tithes and the rents of parish lands, they might have incomes of £30 to £60 a year, but where they were vicars or curates and some intermediary took the tithes and paid them a salary, this salary was definitely fixed at 500 francs or £20 a year. They had some ways of supplementing this meagre sum by farming on their own, but in their economic interest they were one with the people whom they served. They held the key position in their villages, for they were the channels for all sorts of secular announcements. On Sunday after the Epistle and Gospel and Church notices, they read out notices from the Government, and they had definite duties in aid of the police, like reading out the descriptions of wanted persons. It naturally followed that while their level of education varied greatly in different parts of France, their situation made them take an interest in public questions. At every turn they saw things that called for remedy: it might be the low standard of medical and obstetric skill, or the absence of scientific agricultural instruction. They were turned to for information, and their names are often found as subscribing to the Encyclopædia from their small means. One place in Perigord has yielded a list of forty subscribers to the Encyclopædia, twenty-four of whom are *curés*. This is an exceptional thing to find, but it illustrates the great point of sympathetic contact which bound together Diderot and his friends and the mass of the lower clergy, a burning desire for the practical application of knowledge for the relief of man's estate. The Encyclopædia, one of the practical ideas borrowed from England at a time when intelligent Frenchmen found a great deal to copy in English methods and the English approach, contained masses of technical information, mingled with the tendentious propagation of scepticism. The philosophic attack grew up on the flank of the Church while the Jansenists still held the centre of the controversial stage. When successive assemblies of the clergy from 1762 onwards put on record their alarm at the spread of infidelity, they had in their ranks no good apologists, and could only vote large sums to re-edit the works of Fénelon and Bossuet, and to provide pensions to encourage writers to come forward.

The Church when the States-General assembled in May of '89 was accordingly inviting attack on the side of privilege, while being itself sympathetic to the reforming movement. Whether it was those of the upper clergy, from Court circles downwards, who shared the positive temper of the philosophers, and who laughed with them at superstitions, or the clergy of the towns who came from the heart of the class whose energies were most necessary for France, and who suffered most from the lop-sidedness of the existing fiscal arrangements, or the country clergy, the representative of agriculture at a time when it found new hope in the application of knowledge to the most traditional and customary of callings; the clergy, as one of the three estates who made up the States-General, arrived riddled with sympathy and even enthusiasm for projects of far-reaching reform.

But the States-General had been called because France was in grave financial straits. Whatever its members might think or plan in the larger sphere of constitution-making, they could not neglect their immediate duty of devising some means for meeting the deficit. When they surveyed the field, the wealth of the Church stood out, suggesting an immediate solution. In the first critical days of the States-General the attitude of the clergy was decisive. It began when a number of the lower clergy, parish priests, at first three, and then nine, joined the Third Estate and thus gave colour to the decisive claim of the Commons that it represented the nation. When the Comte D'Artois, the future Charles X, thought to prevent these unauthorized meetings of the Third Estate by reserving for his games the tennis-court where they met, it was the parish priest of a Versailles church who provided his church as a meeting-hall for the deputies. Here, while the first of the nobles were joining the Commons, the aged Archbishop of Vienne suddenly appeared with a hundred and forty-eight clergy to join the assembly. The action of the clergy turned the scales, and Louis XVI had to recognize that he was faced, not with three orders who might be played off one against the other, but with a single Assembly.

Nevertheless, among the major actions of the Assembly were far-reaching attacks upon the Church. The Assembly made itself the sovereign legislative power, and as such claimed not only to speak for the nation, but to incarnate the national will. At the beginning of 1790 the attack developed. "You sit discussing things," cried Mirabeau, the chief figure in the Assembly, "and all the time bankruptcy is at your doors." All the obvious expedients had been exhausted, two attempted loans had come to nothing, the Banque d'Escompte, which was already owed 155 million, was not inclined to lend any more, and no security could be found on which to build a national bank. The clergy might have anticipated matters by coming forward in the first enthusiasm of the summer with voluntary offerings similar in principle though necessarily much larger in amount than the grants they were in the habit of making to the King, and might have saved the rest of their property by the sacrifice of a large part. They might have arranged to guarantee a loan, but they did not do these things because they were not alarmed. The very men who might have taken such an initiative, the leaders in the debates, were naturally the men whose own sympathy with the principles of '89 was the most ardent, and who could not believe in the possible enmity of men for whom they themselves entertained such friendly feelings. But as early as October the figure of Talleyrand, symbolical of the inner weakness of the Church, rose and proposed that the property of the Church should be placed at the disposal of the State. The clergy had in fact already resigned their tithes, worth 80 million francs a year, and the Church property now in question was worth less than this. To give it up meant for the clergy to place themselves in economic dependence on the State. This property had been bequeathed or given with conditions attached, and to particular bodies doing particular work. In confiscating it, the State would make itself the heir to the responsibilities, educational and charitable, that were attached. The motive, of providing for the deficit, which weighed most with Mirabeau was supported by other motives; in particular it jarred on the political philosophy of the disciples of Rousseau to recognize any other corporate wills than that of the whole people. It was not politic, said the anti-clerical Le Chapellier, to allow large bodies of men to hold property. But the fateful measure was passed by a narrow majority, 368 to 346, with three hundred abstentions. The State Treasury found itself the richer by 3 billion francs, but it also had to make provision for the livelihood of the priests, and the confiscation led directly to the Civil Constitution of the Clergy. A budget of public worship was drawn up, but the clergy were alienated, and denounced from their pulpits the whole proceeding. It was an operation which even so anti-clerical a person as Condorcet declared to have been performed without equity and without prudence, and it was followed by the dissolution of the religious orders.

Camus, who had once been the lawyer to the clergy as Talleyrand had been their agent-general, was representative of the new point of view when he declared "the Church is part of the State. We are a convention, we have power to change our religion." It is significant that Camus was a Jansenist, bitter, as too were many of the men in the Assembly with Calvinistic blood, in his desire to see the Church firmly under the heel of the State, that the oppression which the Jansenists had suffered might be avenged. In the same month a rising in Avignon against the pope began a definite breach with the Court of Rome. There were scattered among the members of the Assembly, atheists, Protestants, Jansenists, filled with much hatred of the papcy, and this inherited feeling really dictated the form of the new constitution for the Church. "The Assembly," writes Madelin, "which fancied itself so modern was led into its worst mistakes by a coalition of hatreds centuries old."

The capital error consisted in invading the sphere of spiritual authority. Because it considered itself as representing the nation the Assembly thought itself omni-competent. It was not satisfied with redrawing the ecclesiastical map of France, with dividing into neat compartments, of roughly the same size, dioceses and parishes which exhibited the utmost profusion of disparity. It was led away by its enthusiasm for democracy into arranging for the election of bishops and priests. It envisaged the Church as organized from below, and it ignored the pope altogether. The clergy themselves, impregnated with the Gallican spirit, showed little enthusiasm for the pope, and were half-hearted in resistance to a course of action which only carried to a logical conclusion that practice of ignoring Rome as far as possible, which had been the clergy's own policy for so long. What they objected to was that these far-reaching changes should be made, not by any assembly of the clergy, but by a predominantly lay gathering. Just as they had opposed confiscation, so bishops and clergy opposed from their pulpits the new constitution, and when they proved to be rather dangerous critics of the work of an Assembly whose members had little experience and were by no means sure of themselves, the reprisal took the form of the legal imposition of oaths. A refusal to take the oath, accepting the Constitution, was to be the equivalent of resignation. The King, in great affliction of spirit and mental doubt, refused in the end to sanction either the Constitution or the oath, as long as the pope refused his approval, and Pius VI had a memorial of ninety-three French bishops against the Constitution, and said that were he to approve it, in the face of such memorial, he would justly incur the reproach of over-riding the liberties of the Gallican Church. When the day came for taking the oath, most of the clergy refused it, and two-thirds of the priest-deputies, men who were obviously keen for the cause of reform, gave this lead to the rest of their brethren. Many of those who consented withdrew their consent as soon as they learned that the pope had definitely condemned the Constitution. Only four bishops, led by Talleyrand and Loménie de Brienne, took the oath, but all the other bishops were declared deposed by the Assembly. Their successors were elected, and Talleyrand, helped by two other bishops, of Lydda and Babylon, who had joined the original four, consecrated the new episcopate. From the moment when the pope formally condemned the Civil Constitution as schismatic, Louis XVI found himself fatally estranged from the work of the Assembly, and an impassable gulf had appeared. It was the tragedy of the two years that followed that this religious question, which need not have been raised at all, in fact emerged to embitter this struggle between the Court and the men of '89. The non-juring clergy became increasingly identified with the extreme monarchists. In Brittany, the religious motive brought fuel to the rising against the new order, and everywhere, to be Catholic and ranged in opposition against the religious provisions decreed by the Assembly, was to be *prima facie* the enemy of the Assembly and in favour of the foreign invader who dominated the horizon from the end of 1791.

The Civil Constitution never came effectively into force. The non-juring clergy continued to reside and to exercise their priestly offices, and they alone were recognized by the faithful. The official Church was a schismatic minority, its priests and bishops were without friends in any quarter. Those who had created them did not believe in them, and those on whom they had been imposed refused to recognize them. It was to protect its own clergy that the new legislative assembly began to persecute the old clergy, on the grounds that they were accomplices of the *émigrés*. By the end of 1791 it was the law that priests must take the oath on pain of being treated as suspected rebels liable to arrest and imprisonment. The war fever, when it flared up in the spring of 1792 in answer to the invasion of the Austrian and Prussian armies, turned everywhere upon the clergy and the Catholic laity as persons probably in secret sympathy with the foreign invader. The September massacres planned by the Commune of Paris to establish its power, the cold-blooded slaughter of all those arrested and held in prison under suspicion, were aimed particularly, in the words of the decree, against "all priests or suspected persons in prisons in Paris, Orleans and elsewhere." The actual murderers who went round the prisons of Paris on that fateful 2nd of September were not a numerous army; what was so sinister was that for three days no one sought to interfere with their butchery while they murdered between one and two thousand people, of whom the clergy formed the largest element. The Assembly, the Mayor of Paris, the executive council, any of the three centres of governing authority could have stopped the massacres; that they did not do so is some measure of the hatred which was felt, particularly against the order of the clergy.

In the spring of '93, the penalty of imprisonment was changed to death, and in the following month it was extended to cover all members of religious orders as well as seculars. These measures were in some sort the answer to the rising in Brittany, but in the main, they were part of the Terror, the system of summary court-martial, arising directly out of the state of invasion. It was not to be supposed that the constitutional Church would escape now that the Christian religion was so generally identified with the cause of monarchy and the foreign invader. At first the legislative assembly contented itself with small changes, with legalizing, for example, the marriages of priests and bishops, and with removing from the keeping of the Church the registers of marriage. But in the course of 1793 the plans for getting rid of the constitutional clergy altogether made rapid progress. To such men as Fouché any church was an unnecessary stone of offence. The Paris Commune was allowed to abolish worship, and its example was followed by the rest of France. On November 7, 1793, Gobel, the constitutional bishop of Paris, with many of his clergy, formally apostatized in the presence of the Assembly, and three days later the Feast of Reason was celebrated in Notre Dame, when an actress impersonating the Goddess of Reason sat on the High Altar, and was adored by the mob. Robespierre, whose own religious views were sufficiently unorthodox for a pupil of the Jesuits, objected to the crude atheism of the Paris Commune; he swept away the worship of Reason and brought in the worship of the Supreme Being. On June 8, 1794, he himself officiated at the Feast of the Supreme Being, wearing a sky-blue coat, and carrying a bouquet of flowers and wheat-ears in his hand! "If there had been no God," said Robespierre, "we should have been obliged to invent him! The idea of a great being who watches over oppressed innocence and punishes triumphant crime is a thoroughly popular one." Rousseau had held that the atheist was necessarily anti-social and deserving of death, and Robespierre's associate, the crippled Couthon, in announcing the Festival of the Supreme Being, declared: "Pure souls felt recognition and adoration of a superior intelligence to be a real need." The Mayor of Paris declared that God would show His gratitude for this formal recognition of His existence by giving France abundant harvests, and the wheat-ears which Robespiere carried had reference to this hope.

The Feast of the Supreme Being was the high-water mark of Robespierre's ascendancy. The prominent personal part which he took in the ceremonies, his long sermon, and the way he let himself be enveloped in the incense which was burned to the Supreme Being, hastened the estrangement of his followers, and led directly to the conspiracy of the atheists like Fouché who had not forgiven Robespierre's destruction of their creed and friends. To save themselves, they resolved to strike. Fouché was president of the Jacobin club, and to the club he said, in Robespierre's presence: "Brutus rendered worthy homage to the Supreme Being when he buried a dagger in a tyrant's heart. Learn to follow his example."

A few weeks later, the conspiracy against Robespierre destroyed him, a reaction set in against the orgies of mutual suspicion, denunciation and bloodshed, and France settled down to the milder days of the Directorate. But the Directorate was headed by men of ingrained hostility to religion. The executions ceased, but the priest, whether constitutional or nonjuring, remained an outcast, the representative of ideas which had no place amidst the licentiousness and secularism of the new Republican State. The salaries of the constitutional clergy were abolished. "The French Republic," ran the decree, "no longer pays expenses or salary for any form of religion." This disestablishment put all religions on an equal footing, and prepared the ground for the introduction of a measure of toleration. In February, 1795, Boissy D'Anglas made a great speech whose line of argument was that Christianity was a superstition, destined to disappear before the religion of Socrates, Marcus Aurelius and Cicero, but that persecution was not the best way to hasten its dissolution. That would come from the spread of enlightenment. "The best way," he said, "of slaying the Church is to grant it a disdainful toleration." The reasoning made an instant appeal, and a law was at once passed, declaring the exercise of every form of religion to be legal, subject to police supervision, it being understood that the Republic would pay no salaries and provide no buildings. In the Provinces this law outran public opinion. Faithful believers were harried because they were the only people left to harry after the emigrations and the guillotine had between them removed the other enemies of the Revolution. To hasten the final disappearance of Christian belief the Convention thought it must do something positive as well. The seven-day week, and so the Christian Sunday, was abolished, and ten-day periods in honour of the decimal system made the new calendar. Every tenth day, the Decadi, there were to be civic festivals "for the solemnizing of the pure worship which is celebrated under the open sky," a phrase which is a foretaste of the people afterwards to be called Blue Domers. But the Decadi was never a success. The only thing to do at these festivals was to utter generalities in praise of the Republic, or to engage in abstract symbolism like the presentation of a rose to Innocence. So while the Convention approved of the Decadi system, it refused to make attendance compulsory. Meanwhile any deported priest who returned to France was liable to the death penalty. As the Convention had encouraged Decadists, so did it encourage the last attempt at a new religion, the sect of the Theophilanthropists, whose leader, Lareveillère-Lépeaux, was one of the five Directors.

It was the sect of the Theophilanthropists which gave occasion for one of Talleyrand's more memorable sayings when Lareveillère complained that the meetings were badly attended and wondered what could be done to make the new religion more of a success. "Nothing is easier," said Talleyrand. "you should get yourself crucified, and rise again the third day." But the France of the Directory had little enthusiasm for any religion. Madame de Staël, who was bitterly anti-Catholic, thought that only Protestantism could destroy the Church. Others thought that persecution should be renewed, and the first victories of Napoleon in 1796 gave hope that the pope himself could now be made to suffer as the French bishops and priests had been made to suffer. When the art treasures and the money of the Holy See were seized and sent to France, the Directorate threatened that the temporal power of the pope would be entirely abolished unless the condemnations of the Civil Constitution of the Clergy were withdrawn. It was over these proposals that Napoleon first gave an inkling of his own line of policy. As the general in command in Italy whose victories made possible the Directorate's haughty attitude, he was able to moderate the demands of the Government in Paris. He quietly dropped the ultimatums about the Civil Constitution, which was indeed, in 1796, of no real interest.

The elections of 1797 strengthened the conservative element in the Government, and some of the more severe of the penal laws still in force, such as those of deporting priests for refusing to swear submission to the Republic, were repealed. The brief flare-up of the old Jacobin fever which goes by the name of the 18th Fructidor led to an outburst of persecution, but it was persecution based on no new idea or fact, but a final exasperated fit of rage on the part of the most anti-religious elements in the country. The Decadi feasts were made compulsory, many priests were deported—and deportation to the French colonies went by the ominous name of the Dry Guillotine—and the pope himself was brought captive from Rome in February, 1798, and died a prisoner at Valence, in 1799. Brittany again rose in revolt, and the illtimed outburst of persecution undoubtedly prepared the way for Napoleon's *coup d'état,* because all the people in France who had welcomed the gradual extension of a spirit of toleration were filled with despair at seeing the Terror return again.

In spite of the 18th Fructidor, the nation began to return to the practice of its ancient faith. Each year from 1796 onwards larger numbers attended the churches. Even the constitutional Church, under the temperate leadership of the Abbé Gregoire, made progress and purged itself of its less worthy members. But this progress took place under continual pinpricks and exhibitions of petty spite on the part of the Directorate, foreshadowing the small-minded malevolence of later French administrations. Bishops and priests were moreover in the direst poverty. But with all handicaps progress went on, there were services in more than 32,000 parishes as early as 1796, and in the next year, at a National Gallican Council, real efforts were made to end the schism, and many of the constitutional clergy were prepared to recognize the pope as head of the Church.

Napoleon boasted afterwards that it was he who had re-established the altars in France, but in fact the altars were re-established before he had seized power. He had been given unmistakable signs that, by and large, a tolerant settlement of religion would be exceedingly popular throughout France.

At the time when he became First Consul, Napoleon had long outlived his earlier enthusiasm for the teachings of Rousseau about the natural perfectibility of man. Himself deficient in faith, he regarded religion as a main bulwark of society, following the reasoning to which Robespierre had given powerful expression six years before. It was not only that government as government needed religion in the people, but that the new regime of Bonaparte needed to ground itself on the widest possible basis. "You will discover," he said, "what a great party I shall make for myself from the priests." Between the alternatives of reviving the constitutional Church, of adopting Protestantism, or of coming to an accomodation with the pope, the advantages for the third course, from the statesman's point of view, were quite decisive.

Insofar as it had any religion the French nation was Catholic. The constitutional Church had no authority in reason or history, it was the mushroom creation of ten years before. The Protestants had always been a minority, and their doctrines were not spreading and could not be imposed. The Frenchmen who revolted from the Church—and they were numerous in every generation—became, as they still become, complete unbelievers.

Having taken the resolution to re-establish Catholicism, Napoleon was concerned to drive the hardest bargain he could. In the summer of 1800, in an interview with Cardinal Martiniana, he gave the first outlines of a Concordat. The new pope, Pius VII, heard the news with joy, but it was a long and often strained negotiation which preceded the settlement. Napoleon was determined to keep the Church under strict control, he wanted to keep the authority which the civil constitution had arrogated to the State while securing the approval of the pope. The pope wished to return to the arrangements of the *ancien régime,* which, after all, had given the temporal ruler in France an authority in practice unfettered over appointments. Napoleon recognized that it was a crowning stroke of good fortune that the pope existed and enjoyed in the minds of all Catholics full authority to enter into new arrangements with the Government. "If the pope had not existed," said Napoleon, adapting Robespierre's words, "it would have been necessary to create him for the occasion." Only the pope could compel the old bishops, already embittered by years of exile, to abdicate. No one could have negotiated with them had they been the supreme authorities in the Church.

Napoleon began with five demands: (1) the resignation of all existing bishops; (2) the renunciation of all claim to the Church property which had been seized in 1790: (3) fewer sees in the future; (4) the French Government to choose the bishops; and (5) the clergy to take an oath of loyalty to the new Government of France. Drafts and counter-drafts were put forward, and Talleyrand, the Foreign Minister, who hated, as highly dangerous to his own position as a renegade bishop, any reconciliation between the Government and the Church, did all he could to make the negotiations miscarry. The pope did not like to consent to the wholesale dismissal, at the dictation of the civil power, of bishops who had done no sort of wrong. In particular the Court of Rome found very irksome Napoleon's insistence that everything must be done without delay. The Court of Rome was accustomed to delay, and liked it for its own sake. It was necessary for Napoleon to carry matters with rather a high hand in order to appease the indignation of the army and of the old republicans intensely jealous for the dignity of France, and only prepared to tolerate a Concordat if it was imposed or seemed to be imposed by the State. In intellectual circles the whole idea of a restoration of religion was ridiculed, but already the publication of Chateaubriand's *Génie du Christianisme* was being announced in the journals. This book, the herald of the new Romanticism, did not appear till the year after the Concordat, but its immense success showed that it fell on congenial soil. But official France was in the main intensely anti-clerical. Fouché and Talleyrand, if rather extreme instances from their personal histories, were more representative of the feeling of Prefects and the other officials who had actually to deal with Church questions than was Napoleon. The existence of this hostile element was useful to Napoleon in putting pressure on Pius VII to hasten matters forward, and it was in the end Napoleon's insistence on an immediate decision that swept away the last hesitations at Rome about the refusal of the new French Government formally to declare itself Catholic. Napoleon's phrase that the Catholic religion was the religion of the great majority of Frenchmen had to stand instead of a declaration that Catholicism was the State religion.

There were further difficulties when Napoleon insisted that members of the constitutional Church should be included among the new appointments, and when some of the *émigré* bishops, indeed the majority of those who were in safe refuge in England or Germany, firmly refused, to the number of thirty-eight, to resign at the pope's request. The pope was compelled to issue a Bull suppressing all the hundred and thirty-five sees of monarchical France, thus deposing the incumbents. The pope gave way about appointing a number of constitutional bishops on condition that they made an act of submission to him and repudiated their former schism. Napoleon said the acceptance of the Concordat must count as such a repudiation, and in fact insisted on nominating ten constitutional bishops. On Easter Day *Te Deum* was sung in Notre Dame, Napoleon being present, to celebrate a double achievement, peace with England and peace with the Church. No sooner was the Concordat signed than Napoleon issued the organic articles which seemed to churchmen to take away all that the Concordat had granted. In the new France there were sixty sees filled with new men appointed by the Government. The pope enjoyed a veto and no more; and the new men were tied down by the articles to extreme dependence on the man who had chosen them.

In short, under the Concordat the bishops enjoyed more authority in their dioceses than they had ever enjoyed before. A clean sweep had been made and they started afresh with all the privileges of religious orders or parish priests or laymen abolished. Bishops were supreme over their clergy, but they paid for this by much greater dependence on the Government. The First Consul reserved the right to examine them on their religious doctrines, and to refer the result to the Minister of Public Worship. They had to swear not only to be loyal to the Government, but to inform it of any disloyalty that came to their notice. They had to reside in their dioceses, and get leave of absence to go away, and they could not keep up any state. No one could be ordained priest who had not three hundred francs a year and who was not twenty-five years old. The bishop became in effect a sort of prefect side by side with the Departmental Prefect, and the appointments were in fact made with a view to placing in each district the man who would be most effective in obtaining support for the new regime. Because the lower clergy had taken so much part in bringing about political changes in 1789, Napoleon, the heir to their work, was determined that they should enjoy no political influence in the future. They were placed absolutely under their bishops, and their bishops were held strictly responsible to the Government for what they said and did. If the bishops were thus fortified against their priests, they were also fortified against their own superior, the pope. The Concordat itself had been, inevitably, a great ultramontane gesture, and the assertion of sweeping papal authority, but for the future the power of the pope was to be carefully limited. The old Gallican doctrines were to be taught in the seminaries, and no act of the Holy See and no papal legate could be received in France without the authorization of the Government. The religious orders, as being particularly difficult to control, found no place in the new Church until Napoleon made certain exceptions for teaching and charitable orders of a kind the Government approved.

But the Catholic instinct was right in hailing the Concordat, with all its limitations, as a great gain for religion and the Church. It closed the schism, it gave to orthodoxy a definite field, it secured it the material means for worship and teaching. Through all the violent subsequent quarrels between the Emperor and the Holy See the underlying structure of the Concordat remained. Certain parts of it, notably the new supremacy of the episcopate inside the Church, remained as permanent features through the nineteenth and twentieth centuries.

In surveying this story of twelve crowded years it is easy to see in the successive attitudes taken up by the statesmen of France a foreshadowing of the anti-clericalism of the next hundred years along the whole gamut of irreligious feeling. At first the offence of the clergy was their wealth. Their reluctance to make a complete surrender of property, most of which was held for definite sacred purposes, then raised the whole question of the authority of the State. The members of the Constituent Assembly found their justification in over-riding the will of the King in their claim to personify the nation. They could not envisage bounds to their authority, and it was fatal for them to do so. But the particular form which the hostility of unbelieving men took was not dictated by any sense of the outraged majesty of the sovereign State; it was part of the bitter fight for life in which the ideas of the Revolution were so soon involved. When the danger of conquest and defeat had died away from 1795 onwards, a small minority sought to continue the persecution, because the Church stood in the way of the educating mission of the State. The Decadists and the Theophilanthropists wished to mould the minds and hearts of Frenchmen, and to sweep away the Church because it stood in their way. Napoleon inherited their desire, but he profited by their miserable ill-success, and saw in Catholicism the very thing which his administration, the heir to the revolutionary tradition, could not supply. It was not necessary to conciliate the old nobility, although he took care that they should be prominently represented among his officials, if only the Church could be brought into line, with its age-old hold in every village in France, to support the new ruler.

Napoleon was the most realistic, and so the most successful of the statesmen who from Mirabeau's time onwards had sought to found a new basis for the religion of France, but Napoleon was also the heir, if not to the political unwisdom, yet to the doctrinal error of his predecessors. It is the characteristic error of political men to make of the Church no more than the bulwark of civil authority just because it is indeed a bulwark. No subsequent survey of the French episcopate can blur the conclusion that in fact the system of Government appointment produced, save exceptionally, a mediocre type. The very arrangements which made everything depend on the force of character and intellect of the episcopate also worked to keep the level of vigour and intellect low, and to produce a succession of safe men and blameless nonentities. From the statesman's point of view the result was intended and achieved, but in playing for safety against the possibility of the Church lifting its head too high, the State needlessly and wrongly crippled the spiritual life of its people. If bishops are to control everything in their dioceses, they must be recruited themselves with proportionate care. The fecund history of the Church in France in the nineteenth century found the bishops, although almost invariably picked as safe Gallican men, turning to the Holy See as the only safe guarantee of their independence.

9

THE PURITAN SPIRIT IN THE FRENCH REVOLUTION *

Until recent decades one of the most important abiding factors in modern history has been the Puritan spirit. As the author of the following selection tells us, "Puritan" is understood here not in the restricted sense of referring to a religious sect in seventeenth-century England, but rather in the general sense of an attitude toward life and toward one's fellowmen.

Throughout all of recorded history there have been Puritans in this general sense of the term, men who have been severe toward their fellows, demanding of themselves, censorious in their judgments, inflexibly rigid in their morality. But it was not until the time of Calvin that Puritanism was given a solid theological basis, and for that reason the term is usually associated with Calvin and his followers. There is justification in this association, for Puritanism is strongest among Presbyterians, Dutch Reformed, Huguenots, and other Calvinistic sects. But Puritanism is not confined to these religions. It rubbed off, as it were, to a greater or less degree on all Europeans. Catholics living among Protestants adopted many Puritan attitudes and practices, and in some countries, notably France and Belgium, they adopted doctrines to support these beliefs.

In the following selection Father Stansell shows that the Puritan spirit played a considerable—and a frequently overlooked—role in the French Revolution. Its role can be shown statistically, as the author does, by singling out the Jansenists and Huguenots. It turns out that they had influence disproportionate to their numbers in France. The role of Puritanism can also be shown by an investigation of the institutions established and the objectives proposed by revolutionary leaders. Here again these is striking similarity to the ideals of Puritanism as stated by Calvin's followers.

* Harold L. Stansell, "The Puritan Spirit in the French Revolution," *The Historical Bulletin,* XXX (November, 1951), 3-20. Reprinted by permission.

The history of Puritanism is a fascinating and intriguing study, but in many respects not a very satisfying one. Familiarity with the works of those who have given much of their time to the study of the Puritan way of life leads one to the conviction that a clear and thorough understanding of Puritanism is attained, if at all, only with great difficulty. The more one analyzes the history of Puritanism, the more one appreciates the difficulty of being able to start from a simple and universally acceptable definition, for the simple reason that the meaning of the word Puritan becomes ever more elusive, its application ever broader. William Haller realized this after his research into the rise of Puritanism and felt constrained to conclude that there were Puritans before the name was invented and that there probably will continue to be Puritans long after it has ceased to be a common epithet. This is a conclusion with which Marshall M. Knappen concurred when he wrote that "the beginning of Puritanism may be traced back to the Middle Ages, and we have yet to see its end."

Nevertheless, anyone who wishes to delve into history in an effort to expose certain traces of the Puritan spirit in some histrocial development must endeavor, in spite of the difficulties, to ascertain just what the Puritan spirit was. Investigation reveals that the term Puritan is used in various ways, which for the purposes of this study may be reduced to two. First, the word Puritan denotes a way of life which has certain basic characteristics and which has a rather broad application; secondly, the word is used in a more restricted sense to denote a specified group of men in a definite period of history. When the word Puritan is used in this latter sense it refers to that group of men in the Church of England who organized in the time of Queen Elizabeth with the purpose of carrying out the Protestant Reformation to its logical conclusion. Obviously, this understanding of the term Puritan has no place in the present investigation. In its broader sense the word Puritan is used to denote a religious movement which was essentially Calvinistic; one which had as its foundation the basic virtues of sobriety, righteousness, and godliness; and which from some inner necessity drove its adherents to endeavor to establish the holy community here on earth.

However, it must be remembered that although John Calvin and his early disciples were preoccupied with the role which God as the absolute arbiter and governor of all things played in all things pertaining to creation, animate and inanimate, the Puritans of a later day under the influence of the Deists tended to abandon Calvin's religious teaching while closely adhering to his moral precepts. This development was described by Chesterton with characteristic succinctness when he wrote, "In most cases the Puritans lost their religion and retained their morality; a deplorable state of things for anybody."

The Puritans who abandoned Calvin's God but kept his morality developed certain common characteristics which can be found even among those who became preoccupied with the affairs of this world.

These characteristics can conveniently be summed up under three heads. First, in the realm of ecclesiastical affairs, the Puritan maintained that it was imperative that he should lead a return to the simplicity of the Church in Apostolic times; secondly, in those things that pertain to good morals, the Puritan must actively engage in a crusade to transform corrupt society and see to it that all men lead virtuous lives; finally, the Puritan must set up the holy community so that the "elect" might possess the land, even when the "elect" meant only the simon pure patriot. In those societies, then, where the Puritan managed to make his influence felt we see in the words of Tawney, a

> picture grave to sternness, yet not untouched with a sober exaltation—an earnest, zealous, godly generation, scorning delights, punctual in labor, constant in prayer, thrifty and striving, filled with a decent pride in themselves and their calling, assured that strenuous toil is acceptable to Heaven . . .

Such, in very brief summary, is a picture of the Puritan way of life. The purpose of this study is to endeavor to ascertain whether or not these characteristics of what, for practical purposes, may be called the Puritan spirit, can be found in the unfolding of the French Revolution. The task at first sight is a difficult one, for, as Crane Brinton points out, the average foreigner is inclined to look upon the French as a people who are at all times and places thoroughly Rabelaisian. Nevertheless, even a superficial review of the history of France from the Protestant Revolt to the French Revolution will reveal the existence of certain men who bore more than a tinge of Puritanism; men whose influence was not inconsiderable even on the eve of the Revolution.

The men referred to are, obviously, the Huguenots and the Jansenists. The former managed to hold themselves together in spite of the ill-advised revocation of the Edict of Nantes, and on the eve of the Revolution numbered, according to the best available figures, about 500,000. The number of the Jansenists in France in 1789 cannot be given with any degree of accuracy because the Jansenists never admitted that they were outside the Catholic Church; as one writer puts it, "they neither accepted their exclusion, nor renounced the authority of the Church that had condemned them." But however much the Jansenists protested that they were true sons of the Church, it cannot be denied that they had much in common with those followers of John Calvin who were known in France as the Huguenots. For example, Bernard Groethuysen in his study of Jansenism emphasizes the fact that the Jansenists stood for a reform which would emulate the simplicity of the early Church when he calls attention to the influence of the Jansenists on the lower clergy: "The Jansenists, longing for a pure Christianity aloof from all secular concessions, persisted and continued to inspire the lower clergy with a desire to reform the Church." The existence of the Jansenist view of life must be kept in mind in the present study because some of the members of the Oratory of Divine Love were influenced by the teaching of the

Jansenists, and it was the Oratorians who were given charge of a number of the Jesuit colleges after the suppression of the Society of Jesus in France in 1762.

There can be little doubt, then, that there were men in pre-revolutionary France who were imbued with the Puritan spirit; men who manifested the same sternness in their attitude to life as the most devoted follower of John Calvin; men who made the same insistence on external virtues, who had the same austere and uncompromising attitude toward those who did not agree with their view of life; men who had the same absolute sureness of being right which made forebearance with the faults and weaknesses of others an impossibility. The Puritans moreover, of all lands and times, were insistent on industry, thrift, and frugality. Besides, professing a doctrine which made salvation depend solely on an eternal decree of God, and removing all belief in the possibility of working for an eternal reward, the Puritan's interest in time became entirely intra-mundane and he bent every effort toward making the world safe for the "elect" by building the heavenly city on this earth. The question remains, can one legitimately maintain that there were vestiges of this Puritan spirit in the French Revolution?

If there is any validity in the premise that the basic characteristics of the Puritan spirit can be reduced to three, namely, reform in ecclesiastical organization to achieve greater simplicity; the crusade to improve the morals of all by legislating people into leading virtuous lives; and, the effort to establish the holy community, then, it will be legitimate to conclude that there were traces of the Puritan spirit in the French Revolution.

In the first place, with reference to the question of ecclesiastical reform, there was a determined effort on the part of a group of headstrong men to bring about a reform not only in the morals of the clergy, especially those of the higher clergy, but also to introduce changes which would make for greater simplicity in the organization of the Catholic Church in France. It is true that there was not an overt attack on the hierarchical organization of the Church; but it is none the less true that the proposed reorganization of the Church in France so struck at the foundations of the hierarchy that the charge of attempting to introduce Presbyterianism was openly made from the floor of the Assembly. As early as August 20, 1789, the members of the National Assembly provided for the formation of an Ecclesiastical Committee. To this Committee was entrusted the task of providing for the expenses of public worship after a decree of November 2, which declared that all Church property was at the disposal of the nation.

The Ecclesiastical Committee was composed of fifteen members; the more vocal of these members being magistrates or lawyers of the *parlements;* men who were learned in Canon Law, and who were known for their Gallicanism and Jansenism. The Bishop of Clermont, the first president of the committee, insisted on proceeding cautiously, too cautiously for some of the members who succeeded in forcing him to yield the chairmanship to the well-known Jansenist, Jean-Baptiste Treilhard. But even Treilhard was not able to direct the activities of the committee as he would wish, and a deadlock ensued. At the suggestion of the new chairman the Assembly doubled the number of members on the Committee; the deadlock was broken and the Civil Constitution of the Clergy was reported out of the Committee. This took place late in May, 1790.

The Civil Constitution of the Clergy was divided into four parts. The first part was concerned with the reorganization of the dioceses in France; it stipulated that a diocese should be coterminous with a *department,* and ordered that all dioceses above the number of eighty-three were to be abolished. The second part provided for the election of bishops and pastors by all qualified voters, Catholics and non-Catholics. The third part arranged the wage scale for the salaries which the state was to pay the clergy. Finally, the last part set down rules pertaining to the residence of bishops.

The debate on the Civil Constitution of the Clergy became bitter, and the Jansenists led by Treilhard and Camus, had to work hard to keep their handiwork from being destroyed. It is true that a recent study of the non-parliamentary origins of the Civil Constitution of the Clergy has established the conclusion that the decree was the work of men whose chief concern was a victory for *étatisme* rather than the work of those whose chief concern was a vindication of the Jansenists, the regeneration of the Church, and the achievement of a quasi-Presbyterianism. Nevertheless, it is still difficult to gainsay the fact that it was the Jansenists, Camus and Treilhard, who fought so persistently, and successfully, for the constitution, as well as the fact that the charge of Presbyterianism was openly levelled at the proponents of the constitution.

A perusal of the debates on the constitution will reveal evidence of a spirit which was kindred to the Puritan spirit. For example, Treilhard, speaking before the Assembly on May 30, pleaded for the suppression of benefices and collegiate churches (*collegiales*), on the grounds that they were useless, so full of abuse, and so dangerous for religion. The arguments used to support the new constitution for the Church in France remind one of the vigorous denunciations of the Puritans of other times and places. It was the same Treilhard who in the course of the debate insisted that the proposed changes were useful and that they would establish foundations which were designed to bring about good reforms and assure the faithful ministers of great integrity and of great virtue.

Armand-Gaston Camus so ably and censoriously supported his co-religionist, Treilhard, that Aulard was moved to comment that in his (Camus') eyes the National Assembly "was a council, and a Jansenist council at that." Camus vigorously defended the provisions regulating the election of bishops and *curés* and appealed to that favorite authority of John Calvin, Saint Augustine, to support his contention that elections to ecclesiastical offices were accepted as the proper mode of attaining those offices in the primitive Church. In the course of his defense, Camus, in denouncing the bishops for declaring that they were waiting for the sanction of the Sovereign Pontiff, added, "as if there was any other such than Jesus Christ its founder." His meaning was not lost on his hearers, and there were demands from the right that Camus declare what religion he professed.

As the debate raged on, the Jansenists found allies who came to their support. Usefulness became the focal point of much that was said, and who will deny that the Puritan was greatly concerned over those practices in the Catholic Church which seemed to serve no useful purpose in the religious life of man. On May 31, 1790, it was Maximilien Robespierre who rose to support the arguments of the members of the Ecclesiastical Committee. In Robespierre's opinion, priests had their place in the social order as true magistrates who were destined for the maintenance and service of the cult. Usefulness is the maxim according to which it should be decided whether benefices, cathedrals, collegiate churches, along with the *curés* as well as the bishops, can exist in any society; consequently, if these are not demanded by the public needs, they must be done away with.

The inevitable consequences of the new proposals regulating the ecclesiastical constitution in France were not lost on some members of the right. Speaking on May 31, 1790, Leclerc, a *curé,* took a firm stand against the proposed decree on the grounds that it advocated Presbyterianism, when he said, "We boldly condemn a doctrine which leads to Presbyterianism, and if we find it impossible to place ourselves in opposition to it, on the day of judgment the bishops will have the right to ask us to render an account of our cowardice." This accusation was not lost on Treilhard; it drove him out into the open and he attacked the hierarchical organization of the Church by arguing that the fact that Saint Peter presided over the Council of Jerusalem did not give him jurisdiction over the other bishops. This outburst was met by Jean-Jacques d'Espremenil who remarked that the Assembly had been transformed into a council, and a schismatic and Presbyterian one at that. When a fellow Jansenist of Treilhard's, Emmanual Marie Freteau, took issue with d'Espremenil, he was met with the caustic remark that he, d'Espremenil, was astonished that a man as well instructed as Freteau was ignorant of the fact that the *curés* render an account of their conduct to the bishops, and the bishops, in their turn, render an account of their conduct to the provincial councils, and, d'Espremenil added, when you give simple priests jurisdiction over the bishops, you establish real (*véritable*) Presbyterianism.

The proponents of the Civil Constitution of the Clergy protested their loyalty and devotion to the Catholic Church, but they were forced in the heat of debate to manifest their true sentiments. The *curé* Leclerc saw through their protestations and did not hesitate to lay bare their true aim when he pointed out that the members of the Ecclesiastical Committee proposed only suppression and destruction. Leclerc called the attention of the Assembly to the fact that houses of religion no longer existed, and that bishoprics and archbishoprics, collegiate churches and cathedrals were menaced with proscription, and, this, he concluded, was taking place in a country which made profession of the Catholic religion.

In dealing with ecclesiastical affairs, then, some members of the National Assembly gave evidence of certain manifestations of a Puritan spirit—such manifestations as the demand for a return to the simplicity of the primitive Church; making the profession of ecclesiastical offices depend upon election by the people; suppression of religious orders and solemn vows; and, finally, by giving evidence of the conviction that by instituting a reorganization of the Church, reform of morals would be assured. Treilhard himself sounded the keynote of the campaign when he told the deputies that the proposed changes of the Civil Constitution would lead to good reforms, and would assure to the faithful ministers of the highest integrity and virtue. In so doing, he laid himself open to the charge which Chesterton levelled at all Puritans, namely, they lost their religion but retained their morality.

Because of limits of space it is impossible to enter into a discussion of that second basic characteristic of the Puritan spirit, namely, the crusade to improve the morals of all men by legislating them into leading virtuous lives. However, mention should be made of the fact that the members of the National Convention, under the leadership of the Jacobins, made definite efforts to carry on a moral crusade for the regeneration of France. In doing so they gave evidence of a spirit which was akin to the Puritan spirit which was manifested by efforts to improve the morals of Frenchmen by legislation. In the course of the moral crusade great emphasis was placed by the Jacobins on the surveillance of all citizens. Though much that was said on this subject concerned patriotism and the necessity for citizens constantly to be on the alert for subversive activities against the Republic, it became clear in time that the watchfulness was to be extended over moral conduct of others because the Jacobin was convinced that morality was a norm by which patroitism could be judged. The attitude of the Jacobins to anything approaching slothfulness, as well as their penchant for abolishing holidays, and legislating in matters concerning prostitution, the theatre, and begging, gives clear evidence of a spirit which could easily have been recognized in all of the Puritan commonwealths.

Over and above the intensive moral crusade, the aim of which was the reformation of the social and moral habits of men, there was, in all societies in which manifestations of the Puritan spirit are to be found, a determined effort to set up the holy community. This is the third, and in many ways the most important, of the basic characteristics of the Puritan spirit. Recent investigation into the history of Puritanism has induced one author to formulate the following working definition of Puritanism in its social and political aspects: "Puritanism means a determined and varied effort to erect the holy community and to meet, with different degrees of compromise and adjustment, the problem of its conflict with the world." The same investigator after an analysis of the motivation of a certain Puritan faction, the Millenarians, arrived at the conclusion that these Puritans repudiated, or at least were indifferent to, the democratic ideas of agreement, of representative institutions, and of safeguards for the rights of the individuals; and, consequently, boldly put their feet on the road which leads not to the democratic state but to junta and dictatorship.

The basis for this development in the Puritan concept of government can easily be found in the writings of John Calvin. As Calvin saw things, God willed that society be governed in such a way that the "elect" would be guaranteed a safe conduct through the trials of life. Consequently, Calvin undertook to show that magistrates, that is, those men who held the power of governing in civil society, were men appointed by God, men who were also constituted by Him the ministers of divine justice. As such, they were also constituted "the protectors and vindicators of the public innocence, modesty, probity, and tranquillity, whose sole object it ought to be to promote the common peace and security of all." Furthermore, these magistrates, in the words of another Puritan divine, Richard Baxter, must be vigilant against the enemies that sow the seed of sedition among men, and must supply every vacant place with godly, valiant men, while weeding out the ungodly and seditious. With these directives of the spokesmen of the Puritans in mind we propose to investigate the history of the attempt to establish the Republic of Virtue in France in 1794, to see whether there is any similarity between the planned ideal society of a group of French revolutionaries and that of the Puritans of the sixteenth and seventeenth centuries.

The efforts of the Jacobins to establish the Republic of Virtue were accelerated when they gained control of the Revolutionary Tribunal and the Committee of Public Safety by their *coup d'état* on June 2, 1793. Only then did they feel that they were finally in a position to prosecute their aims in earnest. Much has been written in defense of the program of the Jacobins on the grounds that the policy which they followed was made necessary by the war which France was waging against nearly the whole of Europe. Much can be said for this contention and those who live in the twentieth century know well how a nation can gird itself for war and subordinate all other activities to one primary objective. But it is doubtful that the summary actions of the government of a nation at war can justify the waging of a vigorous campaign for the improvement of the morals of the people under the pretext that the nation needs virtuous men to win its battles.

The Jacobins lost little time in their efforts to improve the military situation. On August 23, 1793, the *levée en masse* was ordered. By September the English and Austrian forces were stopped in the north, and the Alsatian frontier was secured by the French army. By December the

English were forced to yield Toulon to the Republican army. The price of these victories, however, was high as far as the liberties of Frenchmen were concerned. In September the Convention passed the Law of Suspects and in doing so put a very effective weapon of terrorism in the hands of the Committee of Public Safety. The Law of Suspects stipulated that not only those who showed themselves sympathetic to the royalist cause should be considered suspects, but also those who could not justify their means of existence or who failed in the performance of their civic duties. The implications of this law were far reaching, for, once the true patriot was defined as a virtuous citizen, the way was prepared for the denunciation of all those who looked with the slightest favor on the enjoyment of the good things of this life. This Law of Suspects, especially when it was enforced by Jacobins who maintained their pristine fervor, went far toward verifying in France what Tawney has written of Calvin's Geneva, namely, it was a city of glass in which every household lived its life under the supervision of a spiritual police.

The effort to establish the Republic of Virtue did not reach its climax until the leaders of the Jacobins made sure of their control of the Committee of Public Safety. It was not until September, 1793, that it was obvious that sufficient control had been won. Late in that month, Robespierre, the spokesman for the Jacobins on the Committee of Public Safety, lectured the Convention on the necessity of strong measures in order to preserve the republic. Once the Convention succumbed to the censorious preaching of Robespierre the initiative passed to a determined group of men who capitalized on their chance and perfected the machinery of the Terror by pushing through the decrees of October 10, and December 4, 1793. The decree of October 10, declared among other things, that the government was revolutionary, that is, super-constitutional, until the peace, and placed the provisional executive council, the ministers of the government, the generals, and the *corps constitués* under the surveillance of the Committee of Public Safety which was to render an account to the Convention every eight days. The decree of December 4 strengthened that of October and provided specified punishments for every infraction of the law, every betrayal of one's trust, every abuse of authority committed by a police official or by any other principal or subordinate agent of the government in the civil military administration.

These two decrees considered in themselves do not necessarily imply that their authors were determined to set up a holy community. They could be, and have been defended on the grounds that they were necessary for a nation at war. However, it is a fact that just when the machinery of the Terror was being perfected, the French armies were beginning their triumphant advance against the enemy on all fronts. Brinton called attention to this fact when he pointed out that during the bitterest months of the Terror the French armies were fighting on foreign soil.

There seems to be need, then, for additional explanations of the insistence by the members of the Committee of Public Safety on a strong centralized government. One possible explanation can be found in the speeches which Maximilien Robespierre made shortly after the decree of December 4 was passed by the Convention. Robespierre, an acknowledged leader of the Jacobins, gave evidence that he was preoccupied with an ideal, an ideal which envisaged a France purged of all corrupt men and their practices while virtue reigned supreme. In the eyes of Robespierre every true citizen of the Republic must be a virtuous man; but if a man is corrupt in morals, it was a sign that he was an enemy of the republic and a friend of those who wished to promote counter-revolution. Many of the things which Robespierre said remind one of the ideal of the Puritans who longed for the day when the "elect" would realize their destiny in the City of God on earth.

The more one studies Robespierre in his speeches and his declared determination to make France virtuous by force of terror, the more one is inclined to agree with those historians who have concluded that Robespierre was a Puritan, albeit a secular Puritan. Limits of space make it impossible to summarize the evidence which has led historians to this conclusion; however, it will be very helpful to refer to one of the conclusions of a man who has given much of his time and effort to the study of the life of the lawyer from Arras. James Mathew Thompson has remarked that Puritanism means more than moral preaching and strictness in one's private life; it often means also untiring effort in making others conform to a virtuous way of life, an effort which sometimes culminates, as it did in Robespierre, in the ruthless shedding of blood, because the Puritan is often a "conscientious inquisitor, torturing the body that he might save the soul."

With a self-righteousness that reminds one of the "elect" of the Puritan Commonwealths, Robespierre looked upon the enemies of France and their abettors as the reprobate from whom no good could be expected. He divided men sharply into two classes, and gave the ominous warning that those who did not conform to the code established by the "elect," which in this case were the patriots, would be punished; and in practice, this punishment meant that the corrupt were to be liquidated.

Two examples of Robespierre in action before the Convention must suffice to demonstrate the fact that he was preoccupied with the ideal of establishing the reign of virtue in France and exterminating all those who refused to reform their lives and become virtuous citizens of the Republic. On December 25, 1793, in an effort to forestall the increasing uneasiness of some members of the Convention, Robespierre insisted that revolutionary government must be maintained against the attacks of those who advocated moderation as well as those who proposed excess. In defense of his program Robespierre insisted that the reign of virtue had not yet been accomplished, and virtue is the measure of success in building the Republic. In his eyes the true defenders of the republic are virtuous men, and those who oppose it in any way are corrupt. True republicans boast of virtues that are simple, modest, poor, often ignorant, sometimes gross, while the enemies of the republic manifest vices which are surrounded by all wealth, ornamented with the charms of voluptuousness and with all the enticements of perfidy. In concluding the speaker asked the Convention to authorize the Committee of Public Safety to devise changes which would tend to render the action of justice equitable, still more propitious to innocence, and at the same time, more inevitable for crime and intrigue.

Encouraged by the reaction of the members of the Convention to the promise to rid France of corrupt enemies, Robespierre outlined his campaign in more detail. As yet, the republic was not prosecuting its enemies with sufficient vigor. In the speech of February 5, 1794, the spokesman for the Committee of Public Safety insisted that it was necessary to remake France by a complete reformation of her citizens; this reformation would be effected by restoring morality to a place of prime importance. Inspired by his own dream of a triumphant and virtuous France, Robespierre insisted that all the virtues and miracles of the republic must be substituted for all the vices and puerilities of the monarchy. The inspiration that was Robespierre's in this February speech is remarkable. Time and time again, he reiterated the principles of his ideal republic, a republic in which virtue was to be the touchstone. Here in rather free translation are the speaker's own words:

> Hence all that tends to arouse love of country, to purify morals, elevate souls, to direct the passions of the human heart toward the public interest, ought to be adoped or established by you; all that tends to concentrate them in the abjection of the personal *ego,* to reawaken the taste for little things and contempt for great things, ought to be rejected or repressed by you. In the system of the French Revolution, that which is immoral is bad policy, that which corrupts is against the Revolution. Weakness, vices, prejudices, are the way of royalty. Dragged along too often by the weight of our ancient habits, as well as by the insensible tendency of human weakness toward false ideas and cowardly sentiments, we must rather defend ourselves from the excess of weakness than from the excess of energy. Perhaps the greatest pitfall that we must avoid is not the fervor of zeal but rather the lassitude of the good and the fear of our own courage.

As the speaker pictured France to himself he saw that there was still too much corruption, too much ambition to profit from the great upheaval of the Revolution, too little interest in the effort to establish the reign of virtue. Such a France was an intolerable place for virtuous men, and something must be done to rid the country of the corrupt and the indifferent. As Robespierre expounded his theory of the Terror, he must have been moved, though unconsciously, by that *dictum* of the Puritan divine, Richard Baxter, who had said that holiness must have the principal honor and encouragement, and a great difference must be made between the precious and the vile. In the eyes of the spokesman for the

Committee of Public Safety the government had not yet proved itself worthy of true virtuous Frenchmen; to be able to do so, the members of the government must be given even more power. Why? The reason was set forth in unequivocal terms by the speaker when he said that in time of revolution the source of strength and energy in popular government is both virtue and terror; and, he continued, "virtue, without which intimidation is harmful; intimidation, without which virtue is powerless" ; then the speaker concluded with these ominous words, "intimidation is nothing but prompt, severe, inflexible justice; therefore, it is an emanation of virtue. . . ."

It is impossible to attempt here a complete analysis of Robespierre's ideas. But from what has been discussed it should seem clear that there are certain similarities between Robespierre's ideas and those of the Puritans. For example, the Incorruptible agreed with the Puritans in dividing mankind into two groups; for the Puritan the division was between the "elect" and the reprobate; for Robespierre it was the virtuous citizen and the corrupt agent of counter-revolution; there was no room in either system for the indifferent. The Incorruptible agreed, too, with that principle set down by Calvin that magistrates are constituted the protectors and vindicators of the public innocence, modesty, probity, and tranquillity. The Terror, in practice, was not only aimed at aristocrats and manifest traitors; it was also directed against those who endangered the morals of the young men of France. In bringing such people to justice, the terrorists were guided by the same principle which had been enunciated by John Calvin, namely, "to avenge the afflictions of the righteous at the command of God, is neither to hurt nor to destroy." Baxter had expounded essentially the same principle when he insisted that the security of the nation required that the militia be in honest, faithful, obedient, and valiant hands, which can be assured by supplying every vacant place with godly, valiant men, and weeding out the ungodly and seditious. Robespierre's essential agreement with these conclusions was summed up in his own words, "to punish the oppressors of mankind is mercy; to pardon them is barbarity."

Since we have considered the attempt on the part of the Jacobins to establish the Republic of Virtue to be similar to the attempt of the Puritans to set up the holy community, it will help to call attention to a rather recent analysis of this Puritan phase of activity. Ralph Barton Perry evidently was struck by the effort of the Puritans to maintain the holy community at all costs. In developing his ideas Perry, without intending it, presents an excellent description of what was going on in France from September, 1793, to July, 1794. If one conjures up the picture of Robespierre and his cohorts working for the establishment of the Republic of Virtue he will agree that the following description of the Puritan attempt to establish the holy community fits perfectly as a description of what was taking place in France when the Jacobins were trying to make that country virtuous by means of terror. Perry writes:

It is necessary that the remnant of the faithful should lash itself into fury, and then keep itself and the community at large at a high pitch of crusading enthusiasm by perpetual excitation, and by periodically sounding a tocsin of alarm—*even imagining or creating dangers where they do not exist* [emphasis supplied]—in order to stimulate a mentality of war. It is necessary to suppress dissent with a methodical violence proportional to its extent, so that prosecution becomes persecution. In order to nip opposition in the bud, it is necessary to employ constant vigilance; in other words, a secret police, which creates a pervasive condition of mutual distrust. The party itself must by recurrent "purges" keep its purity uncorrupted, lest the salt lose its savor. And in proportion as this effort is successful, what is the result? The state is not a means of giving effect to a genuine agreement or sober consciousness of community interest, but an oligarchy in which a ruling class derives a specious appearance of general support from an admixture of hysteria with sullen conformity.

What transpired in France during the months from February to July, 1794, is well known to every student of the Revolution. March and April witnessed the destruction of the factions, the Hébertists and the Dantonists, not only because they threatened the political control of the simon-pure Jacobins, but because, in the words of Robespierre's confrere, Louis Antoine de Saint-Just, "it is time to make war on unchecked corruption, to make a duty of economy, of modesty, of civic virtues, and to annihilate the enemies of the people who flatter the vices and passions of corrupt men in order to create parties. . . ." With the removal of the Dantonists the tempo of the Terror was accelerated until the number of executions for both April and May were higher than those for any preceding month except December of 1793, and January, 1794. It is true that a statistical study of the incidence of the Terror yields little evidence that men were executed for those crimes which Robespierre abhorred. However, it is very interesting to note that the study of the incidence of the Terror led its author to the conclusion that the Terror is better understood in the light of the psychology of the minority that governed France, a minority which held the very dangerous belief that it was possible to create, by means of political changes, a terrestrial paradise.

It is true that there is a basic difference between the faith of the Puritans and that of those men who endeavored to build the Republic of Virtue. The Puritan's faith was one founded on the Bible, especially the Old Testament; that of the French revolutionary was founded on rationalism and the dream of an all-powerful France in which all citizens would be virtuous. The Puritan seems to have endeavored to build his holy community with the idea that it would be a stepping-stone to the eternal bliss to which he had been chosen; while the revolutionary of 1794 was content with the rather vague belief that he would have fulfilled his destiny if he did all in his power to help bring about the reign of virtue in a regenerated France.

A study of this nature must necessarily leave many questions unanswered. Yet, it seems fair to conclude that the study of the way of life and the habit of mind of the men who for a time controlled the destinies of the French Revolution at its height shows a great deal of resemblance to the Puritans who went before them. There is the same sharp distinction of mankind into two completely separate classes. For the revolutionary the true patriot is as much one of the "elect" as Calvin himself; the principal difference being that Calvin's "elect" were sure of heaven, whereas, the true patriot was sure of his heavenly city in a victorious and virtuous France. Those who opposed the builders of the Republic of Virtue were considered just as obstinate and perverse as the reprobate at whom the Puritan railed—the reprobate who was to be made to conform to the Puritan code of conduct or be exiled and in some cases exterminated.

In both the ideal France, which was the dream of the revolutionary, and the Puritan's City of God there was the same everlasting insistence on virtuous living; the virtues insisted on were the same in both societies, namely, reverence—for God and magistrates in the one society, for the fatherland and magistrates in the other—chastity, sobriety, frugality, industry, and honesty. The true patriot, like the Puritan, could not waste his substance in enjoying leisure and the good things of life; he must ever be alert to do all in his power to better his own condition and that of his country. The tirelessness, the austerity, the lack of humor and anything resembling gentleness is evident on every page of the history of the Committee of Public Safety while its members were busy building the Republic of Virtue. It is true that the morality which these men preached was a morality divorced from religion, but for that very reason it was the more austere. The picture which Robespierre presented of the ideal republican is much the same as the picture of the true disciple of Calvin in Geneva.

10

PIUS IX AND THE NINETEENTH CENTURY*

Pope Pius IX, whose pontificate (1846-1878) is the longest in the history of the Church, has been misunderstood and more unjustly treated than most historical figures, because he stood against the forces of the nineteenth century and was therefore condemned by liberal historians as "reactionary." In recent years, however, historians have come to study his pontificate more sympathetically and understandingly. The best work on Pius IX to appear in English is E. E. Y. Hales' Pio Nono, *from which the following selections have been taken.*

* E. E. Y. Hales, *Pio Nono, Creator of the Modern Papacy* (New York: P. J. Kenedy & Sons, 1954), pp. 57-72, 255-262. Reprinted by permission.

Pius IX was a "liberal" when he was elected in 1846. His liberal reforms are described in the first selection from Hales' study, and they are seen to be abreast of the most progressive and liberal thought of the time. Unfortunately, the climate on continental Europe in 1846-1848 was such that no middle ground was possible between arch-conservatism and a full-blown secularistic liberalism. The pope soon found that he had unloosed a revolutionary flood that threatened to destroy him, the traditional Christian way of life, and the very freedoms he prized.

The second selection from Pio Nono *deals with the much misunderstood "Syllabus of Errors," a catalogue of eighty propositions attached to the encyclical* Quanta Cura *and dispatched to the bishops in 1864. The Syllabus was supposed to be read by bishops and pastors alone, and it referred to previous encyclicals and papal allocutions with which it presumed the clergy were familiar. In this way it was to serve as a catalogue or index of propositions which the pope had already condemned. When the Syllabus stands as an independent document, it seems to condemn technical progress, democracy, and other advances of the nineteenth century. But when the original document to which each proposition refers is consulted, as Hales shows with the eightieth proposition, it is seen that the pope is condemning a particular version of progress or of democracy.*

THE AMNESTY it was that took the world by storm. Placarded on the walls of Rome, on the hot summer evening of July 17th, 1846, it spelt release for more than a thousand captives and return from exile for hundreds more.

Pio Nono had worked on it with a committee of six cardinals, Lambruschini and Bernetti (the ex-Secretaries of State), Macchi and Mattei (two more conservatives), and Amat and Gizzi, who were two liberal friends. But his right-hand man was the secretary, the very liberal Corboli-Bussi; and outside the committee he was encouraged by his sometime tutor in theology, the Abate Graziosi.

There was opposition to the project—and not without reason. It was bound to lead, as Metternich foresaw, to the return of incorrigible revolutionaries who would foment trouble; the promise of good behaviour required from them was of small value—Mazzini's agents, men like Galletti, who was soon to lead the revolution, returned now, with promises and tears of gratitude that were very soon forgotten. Mostly they were Romagnuols, or from Umbria or the Marches. Very few were Romans; the Romans, even under Gregory XVI, had remained, for the most part, enthusiastically loyal; almost all the later revolutionary leaders inside the city came from elsewhere, though some, like Ciceruacchio, belonged to the Trastevere slum across the Tiber.

If the Pope must make a gesture, thought Metternich, let him grant a pardon. An amnesty of this sort, liberating, or bringing home from exile hundreds of revolutionaries seemed to suggest a change of outlook, almost an acceptance of pernicious principles. "God never grants amnesties," Metternich observed, "God pardons." As usual, Metternich was right; the world did not take the amnesty as a sign of mercy, it took it as a sign of political change of heart. That was why it made so great an impression in Europe, and why it started off the whole movement of reforms in the states of Italy which led to the constitutions of 1848, and to revolution.

The amnesty was no flash in the pan. Pio Nono, appointing the liberal Gizzi as his Secretary of State, went straight ahead in the path of reform, maintaining the lead in Italy until the spring of 1848.

The range of these reforms was wide. The first, which followed closely upon the amnesty, was the commission on railways. Pius had never been sympathetic with Gregory's mistrust of railways. He set up a commission as early as August 22nd, and received its report on November 7th. Four lines were projected, one from Rome to the Neapolitan frontier, one to Anzio, one up to Civita Vecchia, and one right across the Apennines into Umbria. A gold medal was offered as a prize to the person who could find the best route for this last line across the mountains. The work was to be undertaken by private companies. Unfortunately the revolution had occurred before it was seriously started.

While these plans were being laid, others were being prepared to provide gas lighting in the streets. There was to be established a distillery for gas outside the town, to contribute "not only to the beauty and splendour of the streets but also to the safety of the citizens." To some this was to symbolise, rather literally, the break with the obscurantism of the Gregorian régime.

Then there was to be an Agricultural Institute. Agricultural Institutes were all the rage at that time in Italy, stimulated by the visit of Cobden to Florence, and the enlightenment of the Georgofils society in that city. The Institute was not merely to study practical problems, like cattle breeding, in the light of new scientific knowledge, but to give advice to agriculturists, of the kind county agricultural committees have given more recently in England. It was also to educate the rural unemployed and even to start rural infant schools. It was to be a private affair, with the chance of earning a government grant later on. Pius was very keen about it, as he was about the holding of scientific congresses in the Papal States—another new enthusiasm, particularly in Piedmont. He was genuinely interested in his reforms, especially those that concerned education; he was always dropping in to inspect the convent schools and he was liable even to visit a night school.

It would be superfluous to list all his reforms of this kind. At the end of '46 he introduced a measure of tariff reform, mainly to tidy up the complicated customs dues; he eased the lot of the Jews, excusing them from the tiresome obligation of listening to a Christian sermon once a week and inviting them to share in the Papal charities. He simplified the complicated system of criminal courts, and even undertook a general reform of the criminal code. He ordered the regular inspection of prisons (which he visited himself) and endeavoured to establish a general system of *habeas corpus*. In all this he was playing the part of the benevolent despot, but playing it à la nineteenth-century. More was necessary if he was going to be an up-to-date liberal monarch, and he knew it. Some measure of freedom would have to be conceded. His first step in this direction was his press law of March 15th, 1847, which established a free press, subject to a council of five censors, four of whom were to be laymen. From this new freedom arose the plethora of newspapers, estimated at the beginning of 1848 at nearly a hundred in Rome alone, and destined in the new circumstances of that year to become, with the newly formed clubs, the chief agency in bringing about the Pope's own downfall.

But the big issue was a reform of the government. The main complaint was that it was exclusively in the hands of ecclesiastics. It is, perhaps, not altogether surprising that it should have been since "clerks" (a high proportion of the so-called clergy were only in minor orders) formed the larger part of the educated population. All the same, critics like d'Azeglio or Farini, who were educated men of advanced but constructive opinions, were always urging the introduction of the lay element into the government and it was a point which the French liked to make in the advice on governmental matters that they were never slow to proffer. The Roman populace had been taught to think that their grievances would be remedied if the government were no longer ecclesiastical; so that when the first of Pius' major governmental reforms, that by which he formed a Council of Ministers in June, 1847, made no provision for lay Ministers of State, there was a chilly silence on the part of the Romans, deliberately staged to contrast with the habitual demonstrations of enthusiasm. It need hardly be said that the idea of laymen in the government was not one which it was likely that the College of Cardinals or the Curia would welcome with much enthusiasm, and it is very natural that Pius decided to tackle first problems of administrative and economic reform of which the object was to do something practical and to do it as soon as might be.

A start was, however, made towards introducing laymen into the government as early as April, 1847, when the Pope invited lay representatives from the provinces to confer with him on the form which some sort of Consultative Assembly at Rome might take (this produced, on April 22nd, the popular demonstration of thanks which Ozanam witnessed). By October 14th his plans were ready, and, with the warmest demonstrations of enthusiasm yet witnessed, Rome greeted the news that there was to be a *Consulta* to assist in the work of government. It was to consist of twenty-four councillors, elected by indirect vote from the state as a whole, beginning in the communes. No member had to be a cleric, but the president was to be a Cardinal nominated by the Pope. There was a property qualification for members. As its name implies, it was only consultative. But it had the right to discuss all matters of state before they went to the Council of Ministers, and to make suggestions. When coupled with the new freedom of the press this right meant that the people had been put into the picture in the matter of government, even though they might have little legal power. And two other governmental changes, carried out at about the same time, should be considered with the *Consulta.* One was a municipal government for the city of Rome, with a deliberative council of 100 members; these members were nominated in the first instance by the Pope, but recruitment was to be by co-option and only four were to be clerics. To this body a very large part of what had hitherto been done by the Papal government was transferred. And the other was a reorganisation of the Council of Ministers, so that by *motu-proprio* of December 29th, 1847, it became a committee of the nine heads of departments. The most important minister, the Secretary of State, who was responsible for foreign affairs, was to be a cardinal. Otherwise the ministers might be laymen.

Such were the constitutional reforms of the new liberal Pope. They represent what Pio Nono was prepared to concede as being reasonable, and even desirable, in order to bring his state into harmony with enlightened and moderate liberal opinion in his day, while at the same time ensuring that the last word rested with him and that he could not be pushed, against his will, into doing what he did not approve. The peculiar importance of this last point, in the case of the Papal State, arose from the dual role of the Pope as a temporal Prince and as Head of the Church. In theory these two functions might be distinguished, but in practice the distinction never proved to be possible. Later on, in 1848, when Pius had been driven by popular pressure and by the revolutionary hurricane in Europe into sanctioning a number of steps which gave him the greatest misgiving, an attempt was to be made by various men, notably Terenzio Mamiani, to separate the spiritual and the temporal power—to set up, for instance, two distinct ministries of foreign affairs, one for the temporal power and one for the spiritual power. But so long as the Pope remained in ultimate possession of both powers such a distinction could not work. He could not, for instance, bless his spiritual children in Catholic Austria, and at the same time declare war upon them as ruler of the Papal State. He could not denounce the civil marriage laws or the dissolution of the monasteries, in Piedmont or in Switzerland, and yet be obliged, at the instance of a lay minister or assembly, to agree to such measures in his own state. His dual role made it impossible for the Pope to become a constitutional monarch in the sense of possessing a limited sovereignty, a power which was subject to the will of an elective assembly. That was the position into which he was going later to be forced by the constitution which was imposed upon him in March, 1848. It proved to be an untenable position. He could, indeed, veto what he refused to approve, but that only brought government to a standstill and an angry crowd into the streets.

But we are here concerned with what was happening in 1847, not with the upheavals of 1848. Pio Nono knew that with the granting of his *Consulta,* in October 1847, he had gone as far as he could rightly go, and he made his position abundantly clear. When the new body met for the first time, on November 15th, under the presidency of Cardinal Antonelli (there was only one other cleric on it) he took the opportunity, in thanking them for their address of loyalty, to reiterate that their functions were purely consultative:

> Greatly deceived is anyone who thinks that his duties are different from these; greatly deceived is anyone who sees in the Consulta thus set up some Utopia of his own, and the seeds of an institution incompatible with the pontifical supremacy.

This, then, was Pio Nono's limit. It is worth noting that it seems to have been a further limit than any of the cardinals had contemplated. Even Gizzi, regarded as the liberal candidate for the Papacy in '46, and now Secretary of State, resigned his office rather than go on supporting such changes. But before he did this, he issued, on June 22nd, '47, a formal *Notificazione*—of course approved, and possibly written by Pius—in which he warned the people that the reforms must not be misunderstood, and in particular must not be interpreted as meaning that the Pope was hostile to Austria.

> His Holiness has not been able to see without serious distress of mind that some restless spirits would take advantage of the present conditions to set forth and cause to prevail doctrines and thoughts entirely contrary to his maxims; and to push on or set up claims entirely opposed to the calm and peaceful disposition and the sublime character of one who is Vicar of Jesus Christ, Minister of the God of Peace, and Father of all Catholics alike—whatever be the part of the world to which they belong; or, similarly, to excite in the populations, by writing and by speech, desires and hopes of reform beyond the limits above stated.

Gizzi had issued his warning in June, '47. In July he resigned.

The leading liberal amongst the cardinals was finding the new Pope's changes altogether too sweeping; the immediate cause of his resignation was the granting of a Civic Guard.

All over Italy there was an agitation going on for the formation of these "Home Guards." The idea was to form a volunteer force which could be used either to restore order (which was the purpose that the "moderates," alarmed by the revolutionaries, had in mind) or else to train men to fight the Austrians (which was what the revolutionaries had in mind). In June, '47, following some mild disturbances in Rome, the moderates were successful in persuading Pius to allow the formation of such a guard within the city. They were confident that they could officer it themselves, and keep it under their own control; but Gizzi saw the danger quite clearly. Putting arms into the hands of the people meant, in the long run, putting power into their hands, or into the hands of whatever revolutionary leaders might succeed in gaining their ear. Profoundly aware that this was the beginning of revolution, he held unofficial and highly confidential conversations with Metternich's ambassador at Rome, Count Lützow, to see whether, in the event of serious disturbance, Austrian help would be forthcoming. Lützow was evasive. Gizzi resigned, and Pius replaced him with Cardinal Gabriele Ferretti, who was then serving as Legate at Pesaro, on the border of the Romagna. Gizzi had probably been more realistic than Pius, but he had shown that the more liberal Cardinal had, in fact, been elected Pope.

What Pio Nono only came to realise—to his horror—during the winter of '47-'48 was that, to Italians, and to the revolutionary liberals everywhere, the significant thing about his régime at Rome was not the sensible reforms themselves but the fact that he was carrying them out. There was no middle party in Italy, anyhow as yet; there were only "the tradition" and "the revolution," and the Pope seemed to have sided with the latter. The result was that every demonstration, every insurrectionary outbreak put his name upon its banner, so that busts of him were being carried in honoured procession, in places as distant as Sicily or Milan, by crowds that were demonstrating against the Bourbons, or against the Austrians, or against any rulers whatsoever. And in the same way, those, like the Mazzinians or the Carbonari, who were interested in promoting general revolution, and whose headquarters were at Paris or at London, saw in what was happening at Rome merely the opportunity to grind their own axes. Their policy was to secure control of the newly formed political clubs there, and to turn men's minds towards gaining effective leadership in the whole peninsula and particularly towards driving the Austrians out of Lombardy-Venetia, because it was from Milan and Venice that Metternich was able to exert his decisive influence in maintaining the rulers in the other Italian capitals.

Lambruschini had few illusions about the true state of things, but Lambruschini no longer held power. There was, however, one man who was in a position to act, and who understood.

Metternich's experience and understanding of Europe were unique. There was now nobody else left, if we except the Duke of Wellington, who had had to grapple with the revolution, incarnate in Napoleon. As he had been the architect in chief of the 1815 settlement of Europe, so, of all men, he understood the menace to that settlement which lurked, implicit, in every liberal revolution. He was perfectly aware that a storm was being whipped up by the spiritual children of Rousseau, and especially by Mazzini, that was likely to engulf everything; and he was equally aware that the new Pope had an inadequate appreciation of the gravity of the danger. How, indeed, should Pio Nono have appreciated it when, apart from a one-year mission to Chile, as a very young man, he had not been outside Italy, and had scarcely been outside the Papal State?

In these circumstances Metternich had felt it his duty to educate the new Pope. He had started as early as the first month after his election, writing to Lützow, at Rome: ". . . I think it my duty to submit to him some impressions which are the product of the advance of my mind and of my long experience of public affairs." He went on to recommend that there should only be one Secretary of State, in supreme charge, at home and abroad—Pio Nono agreed about this—then to discourage amnesties, in the terms already discussed, then to discourage concessions in general:

A concession always presupposes, if it is concerned with a moral question, an act renouncing a *right,* and, if it is concerned with something material, renunciation of a *property* . . . Are such concessions at the free disposition of the reigning Sovereign?

Metternich's teaching had some success with the Secretary of State, Gizzi; in the Pope he roused little but resentment. But when Pius put arms into the hands of his citizens by granting them the Civic Guard, and Gizzi resigned, then it seemed to the Austrians that the time had come for more than good advice. Already, in November, '46, Metternich had nipped revolution in the bud in Poland, by occupying Cracow. The time had come to make a move in Italy.

The first step was not taken by Metternich personally, but on the initiative of the veteran Austrian commander in Lombardy, Radetsky, now eighty years of age, but destined, in the following two years, to achieve victory in two more campaigns. He decided to reinforce, with some ostentation, the garrison which Austria maintained, by the Vienna treaties, in the citadel of Ferrara, in the Romagna. His men were marched in on July 17th, 1847, the day when all Italian cities were celebrating the anniversary of the amnesty. Nor did he give any warning to the Papal Legate at the city, Cardinal Ciacchi, that he would be needing billets for his soldiers. All the same, he was acting within his rights.

But Pio Nono was thoroughly roused. Anticipating the move, he had instructed Cardinal Ciacchi not to find billets in the town for the Austrians, and to report any move on their part at once to Rome. Ciacchi had obeyed, and the new Secretary of State, Ferretti, had made a formal complaint to Lützow. What particularly impressed Lützow was the personal resentment of Pius over the matter; the Pope regarded it as a deliberate and insolent affront, and even as a hostile act.

On August 6th, the Austrian commander in charge of the operation, Count Auersperg, informed Cardinal Ciachi that, on account of popular demonstrations against his troops, he would be obliged to extend his occupation to other strategic parts of the city, as well as the citadel; his aim seems chiefly to have been to protect his men from insult. The upshot of this was no less than an appeal by the Pope to Europe, addressed by the Secretary of State, but written by Pius. Lützow was astonished. He told Metternich the Pope was merely yielding to popular pressure. But there is no reason to suppose this. Pius knew the Romagna, knew the Austrian itch to interfere there, remembered his own conversations at Imola with

Count Pasolini. There seems little doubt that he shared with his subjects a strong Italian *amour-propre,* and that he was genuinely angered by what he considered were clumsy and arrogant Germanic moves. But further, he was always, at every stage of his pontificate, insistent upon maintaining the independence of the Papal State, and the integrity of his sovereignty within it.

Nevertheless, on August 13th Auersperg proceeded to the full occupation; whereupon Pius' Secretary of State threatened first to break off diplomatic relations, then, if necessary, to excommunicate the Austrians; after that he might appeal to the Italians to drive them out.

At this point in his career Pius IX stood poised between the Revolution and the Tradition. He was the idol of Italy, fantastically popular, the one man for whom, at a word, the country would have risen. Any crowd, in any town or village, shouted *viva Pio Nono,* whatever the object it had in view. The "Hymn to Pius" was chanted through the streets. He was the Patriot-Pope—the *Papa Angelica.* Even Mazzini, who for years had ridiculed the "Effete Papacy" and the "Moribund Church," yielded at last to the popular passion, recognising in Pius the one man who might, at that moment, save Italy. On September 8th, from London, he addressed an Open Letter to him.

Mazzini's Open Letter to Pio Nono was clearly sincere in the sense that he believed the Pope to be a good man, believed him capable of achieving a great deal for Italy, and would have been glad to see him initiate a national revolution. That does not mean either that he accepted, for himself, the Pope's religious faith, or that he did not intend, after making use of Pius, to direct the revolution, through his own party, into the channels he wanted; nor does it protect him from theological absurdities, not to say impertinencies.

There is no man [he writes] I will not say in Italy but in Europe more powerful than you. You have, therefore, most blessed father, immense duties; God measures them in accordance with the means which he gives to his creatures. Europe is in a tremendous crisis of doubts and of desires. Through the passage of time, aggravated by your predecessors and the exalted hierarchy of the Church, beliefs are dead; catholicism is lost in despotism: protestantism is losing itself in anarchy. Look around you: you will find superstitious men or hypocrites, but not believers. Intellect wanders in the void. . . . Do not deceive yourself, most holy father: this is the state of Europe. But humanity cannot live without heaven. The social idea is none other than a consequence of the religious idea. We shall therefore have, sooner or later, religion and heaven.

We shall have them not from the kings and from the privileged classes whose very position shuts out love, the spirit of all religions, but from the people. The spirit of God descends upon the many, gathered together in His name. The people has suffered for centuries upon the cross; and God will bless it with a faith.

This is almost pure Lamennais. It is the *Paroles d'un Croyant* once again. But what is the Pope to do?

. . . To fulfil the mission which God entrusts to you two things are necessary: to believe, and to unify Italy. Without the first you will fall by the wayside, abandoned by God and by men; without the second you will not have that lever with which, alone, you can achieve great, holy, and enduring things.

No doubt Mazzini, optimist as he was, hardly hoped to convert the Pope from Catholicism to his own religion of the Nation and Humanity; but whatever interpretation we put upon his publishing the letter it is immensely significant. Even if, as is often supposed, he wanted to show Pio Nono up as no true prophet of the New Italy, it is remarkable that he should have thought it necessary to point out the distinction between the Pope's faith and the peculiar brand of pantheism of which he himself was the leading prophet. It implied that others, too, were failing to make that distinction.

Pio Nono found that his bold stand against Metternich over the Ferrara affair had had the most lamentable results. Everywhere it had fanned the flames of Italian ardour, everywhere the cry was now "out with the barbarians!" and he was hailed throughout Italy as the national leader. It was appalling. He had no intention of merging the Papal State in a unified Italy controlled by Mazzini. Nor had he any idea of aggression against the Austrians, who were his faithful Catholic children. To turn them out of his own state, if they trespassed at Ferrara, was one thing; but to wage aggressive war against them in their legal dominions, or to encourage others to do so, was quite another, and altogether incompatible with his spiritual position.

The quarrel with Metternich over Ferrara was protracted, but in the end it was Metternich who gave way; the Austrians retired again into the citadel on December 16th, 1847. It was a diplomatic victory for the Pope, which meant that again he appeared in the light of the Champion of Italy.

Thus once more did he store up for himself inevitable future embarrassment.

One cannot be surprised that Metternich raised his eyebrows at the political naïveté of the new ruler of Rome. In October he had written sadly to the Austrian Ambassador Apponyi at Paris:

Each day the Pope shows himself more lacking in any practical sense. Born and brought up in a *liberal* family, he has been formed in a bad school; a good priest, he has never turned his mind towards matters of government. Warm of heart and weak of intellect, he has allowed himself to be taken and ensnared, since assuming the tiara, in a net from which he no longer knows how to disentangle himself, and if matters follow their natural course, he will be driven out of Rome.

This was accurate prophecy. So was his letter in December to his agent, Ficquelmont, at Milan. After lamenting the influence of Gioberti, Balbo, d'Azeglio, and their French prototypes, he says that, looking back over the past few years, he could:

. . . write the history of the conspiracy which has ended by giving birth to *Pio*

Nono. The spectre has assumed a body in the visible Head of the Church . . . [but] A *liberal* Pope is not a possibility. A Gregory VII could become the master of the world. a Pius IX cannot become that. He can destroy, but he cannot build. What the Pope has already destroyed by his liberalism is his own temporal power; what he is unable to destroy is his spiritual power; it is that power which will cancel the harm done by his worthless counsellors. But to what dangerous conflicts have not these men exposed the man and the cause they wanted to serve!

As the fateful year 1848 opened Metternich foretold what would happen:

. . . many realities will have lifted from them the veils with which they are still covered . . . The veil is liberalism; it will disappear in Italy, as in every other country, before radicalism in action.

And a final warning—the radicals would not stop at unsetting the State:

. . . the starting-point, to seize upon, of the social movement which today covers the world, is to be found in the reformation of the sixteenth century, in that immense catastrophe, religious, political, and moral which has divided Europe into governments and countries catholic and protestant. From the reformation in the sixteenth century to the social upheaval it was only a step, and it is the same to-day from reform of the government to reform of the Catholic Church.

But by the end of 1847 Pio Nono, too, was beginning to see a little more clearly what lay behind the dangerous elements that were being stirred up in Europe. At the end of November '47 had come to Rome the news of the crushing of the seven Catholic cantons of Switzerland—the *Sonderbund*—in a quick civil war, by the Protestant Federal Diet, supported by the majority of the cantons. In Europe this sharp struggle, long foreshadowed, was widely appreciated for what it was, namely the crushing, by the majority, of the Catholic liberties of the minority; its result was the expulsion of the Jesuits, the closing of other religious houses, and interference with the free working of the Church in Switzerland. Metternich had tried to prevent it, in conjunction with France; but Guizot, though pressed by Lacordaire, Montalembert, and their friends, had not felt sure enough of French support to join with him, and the Swiss liberals had therefore defied the Austrian chancellor. The revolutionaries in Rome applauded the victory of the anti-Catholics in Switzerland, and proceeded to demonstrate against the Jesuits, to the pain and grief of Pius. They were making it very clear to him that liberal revolution might not prove compatible with freedom for the Church.

There was another discovery that Pio Nono was making about this time which compelled him to consider more carefully what a big national disturbance, and particularly any rising against the Austrians might bring: he had discovered that the Piedmontese government of King Charles Albert was not interested in his own Giobertian idea of linking the Italian states together into some sort of federation. This could only mean that the Turin government had plans for expanding the territories and influence of the House of Savoy in northern Italy, which must, inevitably, upset the balance of the Italian states and involve some sort of Piedmontese hegemony, which would be fatal to the Papal State. Pius had started, in August '47, by proposing a customs union, imitating the policy of the German states which had already formed the *zollverein*. He found the Grand-Duke of Tuscany enthusiastic, but Turin very awkward. By November '47 he had secured a basis for discussion, but nothing concrete. What the negotiations had shown was that, behind the matters under discussion, there lay a real difference of outlook: Pius was working for the peaceful evolution of an Italian federation, Charles Albert was biding his time for the moment when he could make war on the Austrians and unite northern Italy under himself. For this war he would evidently want, in due course, a Papal blessing and a military alliance; but Pius was not prepared to give either.

The new year, 1848, was only twelve days old when the first revolution of that year of revolutions broke out in Sicily. The grievances of the island were mainly local, and the revolutionaries were more concerned with freeing Sicily than with freeing Italy, but the extreme boldness of the Sicilians, and the surprising success of their movement when it spread to the Neapolitan mainland, where it foreshadowed Garibaldi's success eleven years later, quickened the excitement and ambition which had been whetted by the Austrian hesitation in face of Pio Nono at Ferrara. More and more widely Pio Nono found his name being used as the symbol of revolution and a war of liberation against Austria.

Filled with foreboding by the behaviour of the Mazzinians, by the revolution at Naples, by the designs of Piedmont, and convinced that the independence of the Papal State might soon be in danger, Pius put something of his own Italian political philosophy into words, in his *Motu Proprio* of February 10th, '48. It was really a last despairing attempt to arrest the course of events, though it was interpreted very differently. The argument which Pius sought to impress upon Italians was that their true security, in a turbulent world, consisted in the very existence, in their midst, of the Papal State.

> For Us especially—for Us as Head and Supreme Pontiff of the most holy Catholic religion—if We were unjustly assailed, is it possible that we should not find for our own defence innumerable sons who would support the centre of Catholic Unity as though it were their Father's house? A great gift from heaven is this: one of the many gifts which He has bestowed on Italy; that a bare three million of our subjects possess two hundred million brothers of every nation and every tongue. In times very different from these, when the whole Roman world was disordered, this fact remained the salvation of Rome. Owing to it, the ruin of Italy was never complete. And this will always be her protection so long as the Apostolic See stands in her midst.
>
> Therefore, O Lord God, bless Italy and preserve for her this most precious gift of all—the faith! . . .

His meaning was clear enough; yet such are the perversities of politics, such the delusions of enthusiasts (egged on, undoubtedly, by interested parties) that they took up the cry "O Lord God, bless Italy" as being the Papal blessing upon their dream of an Italy freed and united from the Alps to the Mediterranean, the dream of Mazzini, and the anti-Austrian war party. It was as though Pius had already launched a crusade. He could no longer exercise any control over opinion; he had been cast by the enthusiasts for the role of Peter the Hermit, and his words were interpreted to fit the part. All that remained for him, and he was not going to flinch from it, was to refuse, as sovereign, to take the expected actions.

When the crowd came, as usual, to the Quirinal, the day after the *Motu Proprio,* to congratulate him, and to thank him for blessing Italy, he was found, for the first time on such an occasion, to be very sad. He seemed to be ill.

It was the day after this that the news came of Ferdinand's granting a constitution at Naples; a week later it was reported that the Grand-Duke had granted one at Florence. On February 24th the Paris revolution broke out, and Louis Philippe was fleeing to England. On March 5th Charles Albert gave way and granted a constitution at Turin. Finally, on March 13th, there came the revolution at Vienna itself with Metternich, too, in flight. But before the arrival of that dramatic news even the College of Cardinals had become convinced that Europe's most progressive sovereign could hardly, overnight, become the most retrograde; the granting of a constitution by Pius, which occurred on March 15th, had, indeed, become inevitable.

The details of the Roman constitution of 1848 are not of very great interest. There was a standard pattern of limited monarchy generally available to European liberals at this time, the prototype being that of 1830 in France, the constitution under which Louis Philippe had ruled and which, ironically enough, at this moment of its adoption in the Italian and German states, was being abandoned in France. The Roman version was drawn up by a commission of the Sacred College, which was careful to see that the rights of the Church and of the Cardinals were not endangered. The two Councils, a High Council and a Council of Deputies, which were created, were incompetent to discuss religious matters, which included education, and moral (not political) censorship, and all bills which they passed had to be submitted first to the Sacred College, to be pronounced upon, and then sent to the Pope, who either approved or vetoed. The Pope could thus be sure of not being constitutionally compelled to agree to measures of which he disapproved, but stalemate was made likely enough by the fact that any civil administrative or political law, including the imposition of taxes, had to be voted by the Councils. There was thus a real division of power, a situation entirely different from that which existed under the régime of the merely advisory *Consulta,* which the Pope had previously established. Ministers had to command a majority in the Councils. The Council of Deputies was elected, by indirect vote, on a property qualification; the Higher Council was nominated by the Pope, on the advice of his government and the Sacred College.

Of more constructive consequence than the new legislature thus set up were some of the "fundamental rights" acknowledged by the new constitution, and notably the independence of the courts, with irremovability of judges; equality before the law, with abolition of special tribunals and commissions extraordinary; freedom from arrest without cause shown; abolition of exemption of any corporate body from state taxation; state guarantee of the public debt; abolition of political press censorship. Some of these, and notably the legal reforms, had already been introduced by Pius, and were, indeed, dear to his heart.

The constitution was not going to last long because an absolute impasse between Pius and the Chambers on the issue of war or peace was to cause a revolution the following November. But a contributory cause of that revolution was the bourgeois character of the Councils themselves. The Mazzinians were working for "God and the People," not for God and the propertied classes, and by autumn of '48 the clubs in Rome had superseded the Councils as the real seat of power—a repetition of what happened in Paris in 1793, with the rise of the Jacobin club.

The Roman populace duly demonstrated in front of the Quirinal in gratitude for the constitution. But the news that came in from abroad continued to be even more exciting. The rejoicings for the constitution were still continuing when the much more heady news of the flight of Metternich arrived. This was, of course, the most important news of all. If there were revolution at Vienna it was obvious that Italy's opportunity had come. Moreover the maintenance of the established order in the Italian states was personally identified with Metternich and his policy. A new and presumably liberal government in Vienna was expected to be sympathetic with the liberals in Italy. But first Radetzky and his troops must be driven from Lombardy.

* * * *

The Syllabus of Errors and the Encyclical *Quanta Cura* which accompanied it are formidable documents, sweeping in their denunciations, and harsh in tone; they were profoundly upsetting to many within the Church and to others outside who were friendly disposed to her. They gave most satisfaction to the more authoritarian party within and to the more ardently hostile without. To the former they seemed to give official justification; to the latter they seemed so completely unreasonable and absurd as to spell the doom of the Papacy.

They were therefore documents of some consequence, in one sense of even greater consequence than the two dogmas defined in Pio Nono's pontificate, the Immaculate Conception and Papal Infallibility, because those definitions only made dogmatic what the Church as a whole believed, whereas the Encyclical and the Syllabus plunged—though not with dogmatic force—into the most controversial problems of thought and politics.

So wide were their implications and repercussions that it is wise, before considering them, to recollect within what limits and having what immediate purposes Rome issued them. The immediate purpose of the Encyclical was to announce a Jubilee, during the following year, 1865, when a plenary indulgence might be gained. It is not long, and, while it runs over much of the same ground as the Syllabus, and condemns most of the same ideas and teaching, it does so in terms which, though indignant, are measured and conventional in form; had it been issued by itself it would probably have attracted little more attention than that small measure which it is usual for Encyclicals to meet, and would have taken its place along with others issued by Pio Nono or with Gregory XVI's *Mirari vos,* which had condemned, in 1832, the principles of Lamennais' *Avenir*.

But the Syllabus was another matter. It was sent out together with the Encyclical, though it was not signed by the Pope, and the only clue to his personal responsibility for its issue is that given by Antonelli in his short introduction:

> Our Holy Father, Pius IX, Sovereign Pontiff, being profoundly anxious for the salvation of souls and of sound doctrine, has never ceased from the commencement of his pontificate to proscribe and condemn the chief errors and false doctrines of our most unhappy age, by his published Encyclicals, and Consistorial Allocutions and other Apostolic Letters. But as it may happen that all the Pontifical acts do not reach each one of the ordinaries, the same Sovereign Pontiff has willed that a Syllabus of the same errors should be compiled, to be sent to all the Bishops of the Catholic world, in order that these Bishops may have before their eyes all the errors and pernicious doctrines which he has reprobated and condemned.
>
> He has consequently charged me to take care that this Syllabus, having been printed, should be sent to your [Eminence] on this occasion. . . .

The Syllabus is headed: "A Syllabus, containing the principal errors of our times, which are noted in the Consistorial Allocutions, in the Encyclicals, and in other Apostolic Letters of our most Holy Lord, Pope Pius IX." It is, in fact, as Newman called it, an *index raisonné,* drawn up by the Pope's orders and conveyed to the Bishops, through his Minister of State; and its real value lies in its references, i.e. in the Allocutions, etc., to which, in each case, the reader is referred. Read straight through, as though it were an independent document in its own right, it is as irritating and as indigestible as any summarised index of condemnations read consecutively must necessarily be.

Strictly speaking neither the press, nor the public, nor governments were concerned with it, because it was a technical document, requiring theological knowledge for its interpretation, addressed to Bishops, with a view to giving them guidance upon certain matters, for use at their discretion in teaching the faithful. But Antonelli was realist enough to know very well that it would be publicised, and would raise a storm. He had been told as much by those in a position to know, and notably by Dupanloup. He may not have foreseen that in France and in Italy the governments would go so far as to allow the press to publish and to comment (with inevitable ignorance) upon the text, while not allowing the Bishops equal freedom to expound and explain the propositions, which they alone could do authoritatively; but he knew it would not be ignored, if only because for at least four years there had been much talk of the Pope's intention of issuing a document which would condemn the errors of the century. Europe was, in fact, waiting for it.

The responsibility for publication rests with Pio Nono, even though he seems to have concerned himself very little with the precise form in which the condemnation was issued. He had considered various drafts, similarly concerned with condemning "errors of the times." There was one by Veuillot, which he liked, and which later formed the basis of the journalist's pamphlet *l'Illusion Libérale*. There was another by Mgr. Gerbet, the Bishop of Perpignan. He seems to have been dissuaded by Dupanloup from publishing either of these. He eventually decided in favour of a collection to be made from his own pronouncements, but publication was delayed because Antonelli was very anxious not to offend Napoleon, who believed in, and whose government rested upon, several of the censured propositions, and whose attitude and behaviour were, indeed, one of the objects of the Pope's attack. But the Convention of September, between Paris and Turin, ended in 1864 the long doubt about Napoleon's intentions, finally convincing Rome that the "new Saint Louis" had merely served to eliminate the power of Austria in her defence and then to hand her over to the tender mercies of the anti-clerical forces of the *risorgimento*. In these circumstances, persuasion at Paris having become useless, Antonelli's objections to the issue of a condemnation lost their force.

The Syllabus catalogues 80 propositions which were being taught in one place or another, in Pio Nono's lifetime, and which had been adjudged by him to be erroneous. The first 7 concern Pantheism, Naturalism, and absolute Rationalism. 8 to 14 concern "Moderate Rationalism." 15 to 18 concern Indifferentism and Latitudinarianism, and it is immediately following these that a paragraph is included condemning Socialism, Communism, Secret Societies, Bible Societies, Clerical-Liberal Societies. 19 to 38 concern the Church and her Rights. 39 to 55 concern Civil Society, considered in itself and in its relations to the Church. 56 to 64 concern Natural and Christian ethics. 65 to 74 concern Christian Matrimony. 75 and 76 concern "the Roman Pontiff's civil princedom." 77 to 80 are "errors which have reference to the Liberalism of the day."

Of all the condemned propositions, it was number 80 which caused the most stir. It reads as follows: "The Roman Pontiff can and should reconcile and harmonise himself with progress, with liberalism, and with recent civilisation." Like all the other propositions it is stigmatised as an error, and the Allocution from which the condemnation is drawn is that *Jamdudum Cernimus* of March 18th, 1861, with which, as we have seen, the Pope concluded all idea that he would treat with Cavour about the

Temporal Power, or about the setting up of a new relationship between Church and State. Coming at the end of the series, and seeming, in some sort, to sum up the whole, it appeared, in England, or Belgium, or France, to be an anathema hurled at the most cherished ideals of the nineteenth century. Actually, as reference to the Encyclical from which it is drawn shows, it was the Piedmontese government's idea of what constituted progress and civilisation with which the Pope was declining to come to terms. Similarly, the Clerical-Liberal societies which are condemned under proposition 18 are found to be those groups of dissident clergy, in Piedmont, who were opposed to the attitude of Rome about the Siccardi Laws, or the closure of the monasteries, or the Temporal Power, and which were fostered and supported by the government at Turin—they are not, as was widely supposed, Montalembert and his distinguished friends in France. Error number 45, which asserts that entire control of schools, including the appointment of teachers, belongs as of right to the Civil Authority, is condemned in accordance with an Allocution of November 1st, 1850, which stigmatised the Piedmontese education law. Error number 60, which declared that "Authority is none other than the sum of the material forces," is condemned in accordance with an Allocution of June 9th, 1862, which, while it is a lofty exaltation of the spiritual over the material, and of Right over Force, has obvious reference to the Piedmontese seizure of territory in Italy and to the subsequent justification of that seizure by the holding of plebiscites; it does not condemn plebiscites, but it does imply that plebiscites are not to be regarded as the sole source of legitimate authority. Error number 62, the assertion that "It is necessary to proclaim and observe the principle of non-intervention," is condemned in accordance with an Allocation of September 28th, 1860, which was wholly concerned with the situation created by the invasion of Umbria and the Marches. Errors 75 and 76 specifically concern the Temporal Power.

These are examples of errors denounced in the Syllabus which had specific reference to Italy. But in a wider sense most of the Syllabus was prompted by the Italian situation. Pio Nono was witnessing, in Italy, the practical results, as he saw it, of atheist, rationalist, pantheist, or protestant propaganda, of secret societies, of indifferentism, of a wrong view of the relations between the Church and the State. In a sense it was almost all a *cri-de-cœur* against the Turin government and its religious and political works; but it was a *cri-de-cœur,* too, against Mazzini. Mazzini at Rome was not forgotten; and Mazzini, in the wake of Garibaldi, was still, behind the Piedmontese, a likely enough heir to the leadership of that United Italy which he had been the first to preach. Nobody had taught about progress, or liberalism, or recent civilisation, with greater eloquence or sincerity, or interpreted those concepts in a less Catholic sense than the sometime Triumvir and prophet of the new religion of God and the People.

Piedmont, and Mazzini. When to these are added the fanatical extravagances of Garibaldi, who was now talking of the Papacy as the "Cancer of Italy," and all the other iconoclastic elements in the *risorgimento,* together with the not negligible progress of protestantism, especially in Piedmont and Tuscany, and the increased prestige and influence of Italian Freemasonry, it will be recognised how naturally the publication of the Syllabus followed upon the Pope's view of the state of affairs amongst Italians.

But it is equally natural that Europeans as a whole did not interpret the Syllabus as though they were Italians. Every Italian knew that "Progress, Liberalism, and Recent Civilisation" meant the closure of the convents and monasteries, and the imposition of secular education. It meant railways, too, of course, and street-lighting by gas, and all those improvements which so interested men like Pasolini, Minghetti, or Cavour; but Italians were not likely to put such matters in the forefront of their thinking; in their context in controversy the terms stood for secularism and anti-clericalism. In England, however, Progress and Recent Civilisation meant primarily the Great Exhibition of 1851, while Liberalism meant conservatives like Peel or Mr. Gladstone who had very few counterparts in Italy. The French interpretation of the phrases was more analogous to the Italian, meaning, to most men, the "Principles of 1789," or just "the Revolution." But in America the words stood, of course, for all that was held most sacred. The question inevitably poses itself whether words capable of such various interpretation, and drawn from an encyclical specifically reprimanding the overrunning of Umbria and the Marches, should have been used as the conclusion to a Syllabus sent to Bishops at Birmingham and New York.

The hierarchies of most western countries found themselves embarrassed in their relations with their governments and with public opinion as a consequence of the Syllabus. That might well be a small matter; but to meet a situation in which "the majority of Catholics were stupified" was a big one, and particularly big in December, 1864, because some of the greatest leaders of Catholic thought in Europe, and notably Montalembert, had recently been engaged in urging politico-religious concepts of a kind that were specifically reprobated in the Syllabus. With much of the Syllabus, of course, there was no quarrel on the part of Catholics or of other Christians. Thus it condemned propositions such as the denial of the Divinity of Christ, or the validity of Atheism, which any Christian teacher would condemn. But it also condemned certain propositions which were not only generally held outside the Catholic Church but were also widely held within it, and the most controversial of these related to the concept of Toleration. Thus the Syllabus condemned the propositions that: "in our age it is no longer expedient that the Catholic Religion should be regarded as the sole religion of the State to the exclusion of all others" (No. 77); that "The Church has not the power to employ force nor any temporal power direct or indirect" (No. 24); and that everybody should be free "to give public utterance, in every possible shape, by every possible channel, to all his notions whatsoever," an attitude which was held to lead to "corruption of manners and minds" and to the "pest of indifferentism" (No. 79). These condemnations were generally taken to mean that religious toleration and freedom of speech were condemned.

The answer of the Church to those who criticised the Pope's teaching on toleration and the explanation given to the bewildered faithful were supplied by Dupanloup in his pamphlet *The September Convention and the Encyclical of December 8*. The indefatigable Bishop of Orleans received the thanks of no less than 630 Bishops for this pamphlet, as well as the approval of the Pope. Dupanloup's line of argument at once brought to light the background against which any series of pontifical statements of principle must be seen, namely that the Pope was talking in terms of absolute and eternal principle, or of "the perfect society," not of what at a given time in any given country might be either expedient or even just. Her enemies were laying down principles which they conceived and claimed were of universal and eternal validity; the Church was denying that they had such validity. Thus, in condemning the claims of the Rationalists, she was denying the absolute supremacy of Reason, without Faith, not the validity of Reason as such, or as the ally of Faith; and in condemning the claim to absolute freedom of belief, worship, speech, and press, she was saying that she could not contemplate, as the ultimate ideal, a society which held false beliefs, or tolerated propaganda against the sacraments or other essentials of Catholic practice, or which taught such errors in speech or print. The "true society" would not do these things, and it was therefore erroneous to teach their acceptance as an ultimate ideal. Further, she was saying that in some Catholic countries it would be wrong, even at that day, to disestablish Catholicism and to permit other Churches (this condemnation comes from an Encyclical concerned with Spain); while in others it might be wrong to try to hold on to the privileges of establishment. Throughout Dupanloup's pamphlet runs the distinction between the *thèse* (the ideal of the true society) and the *antithèse* (what is possible or just in the existing state of society). Her opponents were talking in terms of absolutes; so the Church had to make clear what were the true absolutes, or at least must deny those that were false. The great mistake was to suppose that when she condemned a proposition on the absolute plane there might not, yet, be much relative good in it, and that some measure of its practice might not often be healthy and beneficial. And when the absolute claims of a proposition were denied it by no means followed that the contrary proposition was always valid—thus it was erroneous to say that the Catholic Church should everywhere be disestablished, but it was not true to say that she should always be an Established Church.

This relativism was valid argument, even if to those who looked upon the Church only as one amongst competing "interests" it seemed like opportunism. Nor was the criticism that Dupanloup was "watering down the Syllabus" a fair one; he was arguing in strict accord with the implied thought of the Church; and if the lay press considered him specious he was entitled to reply that the Syllabus had not been addressed to them but presupposed an audience familiar with the terms of theological argument.

11

THE ROMAN QUESTION *

The seizure of Rome by Italian troops in 1870 created the Roman Question, which remained one of the world's serious diplomatic problems until it was finally settled in 1929. There was much misunderstanding about the papacy's stand on the question, except among experts in international law, who knew that the pope had to have some territory over which he was sovereign so that he would not be chaplain to any king or under any government. Apparently the solution of giving the pope a few acres of Rome did not occur to either the popes or the Italian government until the twentieth century. It seemed rather that the problem was insoluble: Rome must belong either to the popes or to Italy, and neither power could be itself without the city.

The Italian government tried to settle the problem with a Law of Guarantees which, on the surface, seemed a generous solution. Pope Pius IX refused to accept the law, however, because it was a unilateral solution of a problem that, he insisted, could legally be settled only by bilateral action. On this principle the papacy could not give ground, because to accept a unilateral solution would be to put the popes under Italian jurisdiction. On the matter of how much territory the pope would need for his sovereignty, however, the popes came to realize that they would not need the entire city of Rome.

Until the time of St. Pius X, no solution seemed possible. The Italian government passed many bitterly anti-clerical laws and frequently insulted the pope publicly. Pius IX and Leo XIII answered by prohibiting Catholics from participating in national Italian politics, an action which made it easier for the radical forces to have their way in Italian political

* Wilfrid Parsons, S.J., *The Pope and Italy* (New York: The America Press, 1929), pp. 27-41, 64-71. Reprinted by permission.

life. St. Pius X, however, withdrew these prohibitions, and on several occasions he suggested that there were no essential reasons why the Roman Question could not be settled. Much preliminary work was done early in the twentieth century, but it remained for Mussolini and Pope XI, both men of energetic and determined action, to settle the problem in bilateral fashion in the famous Lateran Treaty of 1929.

THE END came when France, in the throes of the Franco-Prussian War, had to withdraw her defending troops from Rome. On September 20, 1870, a breach was made in the Roman walls near the Porta Pia, a formal show of resistance was made by the Papal troops—mostly volunteers from France—Rome was occupied by the King, and Italian unity was achieved, in fact if not by right. The Papacy had weathered a score of frightful storms from every quarter; waves of barbarian hordes, and of armies from Spain, France and Germany, had dashed over its walls and each time had receded, leaving it in undiminished independence. It fell at last before the Italian people, leaving Rome the object of two apparently unassailable but contradictory rights: the right of United Italy to its own capital, and the immemorial right of the Papacy to its own possession, which had come to it as an historical inevitability and a logical necessity.

Thus arose the Roman Question. It was at its very bottom a conflict of principles, not a squabble for land. This is well put by Carrère, a French writer, in his interesting work, *The Pope*.

What answer must we give to the two questions already asked: Was Italy right? Was the Papacy right? To both these questions the only answer is, yes.

I. Yes, Italy, a very ancient people going back more than a thousand years before Christianity, having in the nineteenth century once regained consciousness of her real nationality and fundamental unity, had a right to try to reunite under the control of a single Government all the regions forming that living entity which is called a nation, and consequently could not renounce Rome, that essential city, the very center of her territory and history.

II. Yes, the Papacy whose historical role has been visible and uninterrupted for nineteen centuries, and which for eleven centuries has exercised power in Rome and its neighboring territory for the greater good of the governed population, and with the unanimous consent of all European nations; the Papacy to which Rome was assigned by its founder; and which could never separate from it, had the right to claim this domain which it considered indispensable to its dependants and to the free exercise of its spiritual power.

The conflict of these two rights, both equally irrefutable, constitutes, properly speaking, the *Roman Question*.

It is precisely because they are both irrefutable that this question has been so burning and so ceaselessly renewed. For if one of the two rights invoked by the two parties could have been denied, diminished, or even disputed, sooner or later one of the two theories would have ousted the other.

On the one side, then, there was the absolute spiritual necessity for the Papacy to be the territorial subject of no earthly power, and the consequent necessity that it exist on a territory belonging to no State; on the other side, there was the natural desire of the Italians to make Rome the capital of their new State and a certain logic in the choice of that city for this purpose.

On the one side, there was the inseparable link of the Pope to Rome, as his episcopal city; on the other, there was the reluctance of the Italians to choose another capital, for Rome is central and the traditional head of Italy. It was impossible for either to depart, yet it seemed that both could not remain as friends.

This tragic situation was well seen by the non-Catholic Ernest Lavisse. He writes:

> Since Charlemagne deposited on the tomb of St. Peter the "title of donation," eleven centuries have rolled by. But eleven centuries do not count in the immutability of the Church. . . . Italy has become a world Power. But she is not entirely at home as are the other nations. Between the Alps and the capes of Sicily the soil is not all Italian; at the center there is a palace surrounded by a garden. It is the domain of St. Peter. Here the King of Italy entereth not. . . . And in the meantime the Apostle does not cease to protest and to lament. The plaint of the immortal old man sounds like a never-stopping funeral bell tolling over the capital, Rome. Its sound disquiets and irritates kings and ministers. What is the use of being at Rome, if there is still at Rome a Roman Question?

It is not surprising that until the recent very simple solution it was thought by most people that the Question was insoluble.

An attempt was, indeed, made to solve the Question soon after it arose. Spurred by worldwide condemnation of their course, and by the moderates in their own ranks, who suffered from an acute conflict of conscience, the triumphant party passed the so-called Law of Guarantees, on May 13, 1871.

This law has been freely admitted by ecclesiastical authorities to have been a masterpiece of legislation. Its terms were in striking contrast to the restrictive and intolerant terms of the national Constitution, though it is rarely remembered that this latter document (Art. I) made the Catholic the official State religion of Italy. By the Law of Guarantees, the sacredness of the person of the Sovereign Pontiff was safeguarded; royal honors were to be accorded him in all of Italy; the Vatican property was declared extra-territorial; he was allowed unhindered access to the outer world and his relations with it were to be facilitated; and an annuity of 3,225,000 lire ($622,425) was settled on him for expenses. The law was in many ways extremely wise, even generous, though it allowed much previous oppressive anti-clerical legislation to remain on the statute books.

Yet Pope Pius IX refused it, and every Pope since him has continued to do so. Pius IX did so two days after it was passed, in the Encyclical of May 15, 1871. His first protest was in the Encyclical of November 1,

1870. Leo XIII lost no time after his election, but protested on April 21, 1878, in the Encyclical "Inscrutabili." Pius X, in a *motu proprio* of December 18, 1903, referred to his "intolerable position"; Benedict XV, in the Encyclical "Pacem," May 23, 1920, reiterated the protestations; and Pius XI, in his first Encyclical "Ubi Arcano," December 23, 1922, said:

> The true guarantees of liberty . . . which Divine Providence . . . has conferred upon the sovereignty of the Vicar of Christ here below, which for centuries have fitted in so marvelously with the Divine designs in order to protect the liberty of the Roman Pontiff, and for which neither has Divine Providence itself manifested, nor human ingenuity as yet discovered, any substitute . . . these guarantees We declare have been and are still being violated. Whence it is that there has been created a certain abnormal condition of affairs which has greviously troubled and up to the present hour continues to trouble the conscience of the Catholics of Italy and of the entire world.
>
> We, therefore . . . protest against such a condition of affairs in defense of the rights and of the dignity of the Apostolic See, not because We are moved by any vain earthly ambition of which We should be ashamed, but out of a sense of Our duty to the dictates of conscience itself.

Because of their refusal the Popes have had to remain "Prisoners" in the Vatican, prisoners not by physical force but by the force of reason; to have left the Vatican was to accept the Law of Guarantees, and that was an impossibility. The "Question," as it began to be called, was not thus to be solved. And yet that law in its terms uncannily resembles the actual treaty recently signed.

Why did they refuse it? That can be answered in few words: precisely becaue it was a law, and not a treaty. All these years the Popes have stood ready to accept most of the terms of the Law of Guarantees if they came in treaty form, but not if they were merely a law.

The reason for that position is now clear. The law created only an internal, not an international, situation. It was a unilateral, not a bilateral, document. It was a grant of certain things from the Italian parliament, not a recognition of sovereignty. It was a piece of legislation, changeable by any legislature. No territory was acknowledged in which the Pope was sovereign, for the Vatican palace and grounds were declared an extra-territorial, but not an independent, piece of land. Sovereignty was, therefore, implicitly denied; the instrument of sovereignty, namely, free territory, was not acknowledged, and to have accepted it was to renounce his sovereignty, which no Pope was at liberty to do by virtue of his supreme spiritual mission of the universal care of the souls committed to him by the Chief Shepherd.

In a word, the Law of Guarantees was refused precisely because it was an act of a legislature, passed on a subject of Italy, not a contractual instrument between Italy and a co-equal sovereign. The Pope was in the unfortunate position of remaining in the Vatican a virtual prisoner, for to go out was implicitly to accept the Law of Guarantees.

But by the refusal of the Popes an entirely novel situation was created for the Papacy. I said above that there were only three means by which an independent sovereignty could be safeguarded: possession of sufficient force to repel invasion, an international agreement to protect it, or at least an acknowledged free, juridical status before international law. Here was the Pope possessing none of these, and yet remaining a sovereign.

The explanation of the anomaly is that a fourth mode of national existence had come into being, that of *protest.* For by protest, and not by any other means, did the Popes protect their precious sovereignty for fifty-nine years. That they did protect it, is evidenced by the fact that in the year 1928, twenty-seven countries had full-fledged diplomatic representatives, ambassadors or ministers plenipotentiary, at the court of the Holy See. Since the Pope could not be called a plenary subject of international law, the lawyers invented a new and exclusive term for his status: they denominated him a subject *sui generis* of international law, and as such he was entitled to entertain diplomatic relations.

It is clear that such a situation was highly anomalous and by its very nature impermanent. Protest has by itself this character, that the longer it is repeated the weaker it grows. Moreover, a certain tolerance grew up gradually between the Holy See and the Quirinal, and this in itself constituted an extreme danger to independence, for acquiescence in the situation might easily lead to sanctioning it. The Church could not renounce its principles, for they were based on its spiritual mission. And yet year by year it became more difficult to explain them and defend them, since the Papacy seemed very well off as it was. It was long ago decided in Vatican circles that the first favorable opportunity should be taken of coming to an agreement with an Italian Government.

The Pope's position, so far from being satisfactory, as many well-intentioned persons imagined, was actually becoming dangerous. A recent writer, Msgr. Filippo Bernardini, of the Catholic University, and a nephew of Cardinal Gasparri, explains this fact:

> The necessity of a solution of the Roman Question, for the Holy See and for Italy, had become more and more apparent every day. The witnesses of the historical events of 1870 have passed away, and the new generation, leaving aside the ideas of a half-hearted tolerance, have gradually become used to the existing state of affairs. Under the inevitable pressure of historical events, and especially of the World War, a new national spirit has arisen. The conception of an Italy, united under Rome as its capital, has been generally accepted as an established fact, the many advantages of which are too evident to be disregarded.
>
> This new viewpoint, common to the clergy and people, has already suggested a *modus vivendi* in the relations of the Church and the State, which, avoiding, as far as possible, all useless contentions, would permit a sufficiently peaceful existence. This acquiescence in existing conditions has been very dangerous to the principles which the Catholic Church could not renounce, and which, nevertheless, year by year, were becoming more inexplicable to the Catholics of Italy and of the entire world, notwithstanding the repeated and explicit declarations of

the Popes. Hence, the necessity, on the part of the Holy See, of finding an early solution for this so-called Roman Question.

Granted the original proposition that sovereignty is necessary to preserve the Pope's spiritual prerogatives, this position is unassailable.

The opportunity to make it valid in act was long in coming. It must be admitted that sectarian prejudice and hatred kept Italy from making peace with the Pope. Freemasonry was in the saddle, and to Freemasonry, Catholicism was *l'infâme,* to be crushed out of existence. Never, in all the long years from 1870 to the World War, was there a Government in Italy willing, if it was able, to come to terms with the Holy See. Moreover, Italian Masonry practically did the bidding even in internal affairs of a foreign ministry, that of France, and it was never the policy of France to allow Italy to grow strong as it undoubtedly would if it managed to heal the cancer of dissension that was eating it from within.

But the World War brought an entirely new shuffle of affairs. For the first time it might be said that Italy became truly conscious of unity, for before that it had, as Nitti once said, been still a mere collection of localities, mutually hating or despising one another. That local spirit was burned out in the fires of war, and Italy emerged a nation in very truth. Nobody recognized this more quickly than the Papacy.

This new spirit of unity was not long in bringing about its inevitable reaction, impatience with the mediocrity of Italy's parliamentary rulers since 1870 and with the inefficiency and corruption that followed in their train. Fascism was foreordained to rule Italy from then on. Mussolini saw his chance and the "March on Rome" took its place in history as the last act in a bloodless revolution, or rather a revolution that shed all its blood in a social civil war before it performed its first political act. The revolution would have happened even had there been no Mussolini. It might have been a Bolshevist revolution.

One of the first things that Mussolini saw was the necessity of settling the religious question. He firmly held the Catholic contention that religion is the prime factor in that moral education of a people to which he himself was so passionately devoted and also the most important element in political unification and tranquil stability. For five years, however, he tried in vain to win the support of this element for his ideal of unity, for every attempt to do so was wrecked by the repeated protests of the Sovereign Pontiff, and his constant reminders not to overlook the fundamental aspect of the Roman Question. Hence, from this position where both the Pope and the Government recognized the necessity of a solution, it was not long before a new step was taken, that of sitting down behind a table and talking terms. In October, 1926, the fateful conferences began.

The implications of the Treaty are vast and complicated. The most startling, so important that it really deserves the much-abused name of historical, is one, strangely enough, that almost escaped the notice of commentators. It is nothing more nor less than that the Popes, after holding it in fact or by right for fifteen hundred years, have irrevocably and freely abdicated their immemorial right to the city of Rome. Greater far in its meaning than the loss of Temporal Power in 1870, and worthy to be classed with the original gift in 754, is this fact. Papal Rome! The blood that has been shed for it, the memories that cluster around it, the precious treasures that it contains, have been handed over to the Italian people for their undisputed possession. It will be long, perhaps, before we are able to realize what that means.

The second consequence of the Treaty, hardly less important, and almost as little noticed, is that the unity of Italy, a process begun in 1848, is at last a fact. Up to February 11, its very capital was held under protest from its former owner, who still persisted in calling its loss a robbery. The Papal States were occupied by a foreign prince and the rightful sovereign had never recognized his occupation as legitimate. Now by a deliberate contract, his legitimate possession is established, his title to Rome as his capital has a cloud on it no longer, and the Italian people are freed from the incubus of a divided allegiance which weighed so heavily on it, and poisoned much of its social and political life.

The third fact that is most worthy of notice in the settlement is the tininess of the new Papal State. It is this, more than anything else that makes clear the declaration of the Pope that his motive in seeking temporal sovereignty was spiritual and nothing else. Leo XIII, in his vivacious way, had long ago settled this point forever:

> Men dare to state [he said in an allocution to Cardinal Alimonda and some Italian priests] that the vindication of the Pope's rights is dictated by a spirit of ambition and worldly grandeur . . . Our aim scales far loftier heights than that, it is the very cause of our liberty and independence that we espouse.

It is a paradox of the situation that in order to enjoy spiritual independence and sovereignty, it was necessary that the Pope be a temporal sovereign. It is clear that to be really free to exercise his religious mission, so that the members of the Church all over the world should clearly apprehend that freedom, the Pope must be the subject of no earthly sovereign. It is equally clear now to those who are not members of the Church that possession of territory for itself was not what was sought, since the Pope was content with little more than he has actually possessed since 1870! This, as Count dalla Torre says so finely, is "that least strip of material territory from which the spiritual cannot prescind here on earth."

Finally, it must be noticed that by the treaty a really clever guarantee has been given the Popes that they will continue to enjoy their independence, no matter what changes take place in the government of Italy. The only justifying pretext for the taking of Rome was the political necessity of Italians owning their own natural capital. It was claimed that the

Pope stood in the way of a just aspiration of the Italian people and as doing this he must be sacrificed. This pretext is forever removed. What the Pope will hold in actual land, he has already held with Italy's unity unimpaired; his territory is a menace to nobody, and no reasonable pretext will ever be forged to take it away from him. Only pure malice will ever be able to justify Italy again dethroning the Pope, and that will bring upon it the reprobation of the whole world.

It remains to brush away some of the misconceptions that have grown up since the treaty was signed.

The first of these has to do with the position of Catholics throughout the world, those, that is, who are not actually residents in the Vatican and its grounds. There has arisen the grotesque notion that these 300,000,000 people have by a stroke of the pen lost their own citizenship and acquired a new one in the 160 acres owned by the Pope, or at least had forced on them a dual allegiance, that to their own country and that to the Pope.

Such a charge is material for popular controversy, but not for reasonable men. Nothing whatever has happened except to those who actually will be registered as habitual residents in the Vatican. For all others the Pope will remain in the same position he has always occupied; he is their supreme spiritual superior and nothing else. Nothing that he could not do to them before can he do now. Their relations with him were of a spiritual nature and they are unchanged. This fact is almost too clear to devote the space to it, were it not for the fact that it has actually been questioned by those who have not clearly apprehended what really did happen by the Treaty.

The settlement has also been attacked on the grounds that union of Church and State is an obsolete doctrine, relegated by all modern peoples to forgotten limboes. Apart from the fact that the time element does not enter into the truth of a doctrine, a common fallacy, this also is based on a misconception. If it means anything at all, it means that Mussolini and Cardinal Gasparri, in signing the treaty, committed a wrong. A wrong against what? Against other peoples who do not practise union of Church and State? Hardly. It is none of their business. Against an abstract opinion, held by some people, though not by all? But in political theory nobody is at liberty to prescribe to a sovereign nation what form of government it shall adopt for itself, or agree to in another. The very people who utter that objection are those who are most outspoken against our interferences in the nations of Latin America. Even to object to monarchy in another country in the name of liberty is a denial of liberty.

But is there not something especially heinous in the head of a Church enjoying the rights of a sovereign king? If there were, we should have to take up the cudgels against the King of England, who has been head of a church for 400 years. One becomes suspicious that the objection has dwindled down to objecting only to the head of the Catholic Church receiving royal honors, even though it has been made clear a thousand times that these same honors exist merely for the purpose of protecting his spiritual independence, as a practical necessity for a universal religion in a world divided into nations.

The last fallacy of any importance that needs to be pointed out is that the Pope by this new act acquires an international importance which will cause him to interfere in the purely temporal affairs of the world and make him a menace to free peoples. This charge was uttered before the actual treaty was published. Now that it has seen the light, there is no longer any justice in making it. For by Article twenty-four the following is agreed:

> The Holy See, in relation to the sovereignty due to it also in the international sphere, declares that it wishes to remain and will remain extraneous to all temporal disputes between States and to international congresses held for such objects, unless the contending parties make concordant appeal to its peaceful mission; at the same time reserving the right to exercise its moral and spiritual power (*la sua potestà morale e spirituale*). In consequence of this, the territory of Vatican City will be considered neutral and inviolable territory.

12

BISMARCK'S *KULTURKAMPF* *

When the German empire was created in 1871, Chancellor Otto von Bismarck set about consolidating the loosely joined states which composed it. He unified such physical things as the railway and telegraph systems, and he tried to bring about uniformity of mind and spirit as well. He was anxious to Germanize Poles and Danes who lived in the empire and to "free" German Catholics from dependence on a "foreign" pontiff.

Bismark's attempt to nationalize the Catholic Church in the empire is known as the Kulturkampf. *It consists of a series of laws passed through the 'seventies in Prussia and copied in most of the other German states. These laws attempted to control the education, the appointment, and the preaching of Catholic priests. The* Kulturkampf *was opposed by the Catholic Center Party which, under the astute leadership of Ludwig Windhorst, grew stronger with each election through the 'seventies. Within a few years Bismark realized that his attack on the Church was a failure, but it was not until the election of Pope Leo XIII in 1878 that*

* Reuben Parsons, D.D., "The Bismarkian So-Called 'War for Civilization,'" *Studies in Church History,* Vol. VI (New York: Frederick Pustet & Co., 1901), pp. 12-19, 38-44. Reprinted by permission.

he found it possible to retract the laws against the Church with good grace.

Several events combined to induce Bismarck to bring about the end of the Kulturkampf. *First of all, Socialism had grown strong during the years of the* Kulturkampf, *and socialists made two attempts on the emperor's life. Bismarck needed the cooperation of the Center Party to curb Socialism, and the Center leaders made repeal of the* Kulturkampf *the price of such cooperation. Secondly, more and more Germans had come to feel that the attack on the Church was a shameful and an unnecessary thing. Finally, in 1878 the diplomatic Leo XIII succeeded Pius IX. Leo made it easy for Bismarck to repeal the laws against the Church without losing face. The German Catholics who led the Center Party receive chief credit for the failure of the* Kulturkampf, *however, because of their stubborn and well disciplined resistance to Bismarck's leadership after he began his attack on the Church. In the following selection, the author describes in detail the laws that made up the* Kulturkampf *and the measures that repealed it.*

THE FIRST information concerning the hostile intentions of the Prussian Government in their regard was conveyed to the Catholics by a sequence of articles in the *Gazette of the Cross,* a journal which was practically owned by Bismarck; and very soon, that is, during the first months of 1871, all the subsidized press—those journals which now came to be known as the "reptile press"—began to ring the changes on the impudent lies of the chancellor. The world was informed that, having vanquished "her external enemies," Germany had now determined to conquer "her internal foes"; namely, the Ultra-montanes who, by their acceptance of the decrees of the Vatican Council, had "caused a lamentable division in the Catholic Church, and were thus endangering the peace of the empire." It was not the intention of His Majesty, the world was assured, to disturb the "real Catholics" (so the chancellor styled the handful of Döllingerites); the enemy was that "Jesuitism" which had become insupportable since the declaration of Papal Infallibility. The first attack on the Catholics, or on *Jesuitism,* as the lying Minister described it, was the suppression of the Catholic Department in the Ministry of Worship on July 8, 1871—a measure which was equivalent to a declaration that thereafter the government would pay no attention to any grievances which the Catholics might suffer. The next blow was directed against a dogma of Catholic faith, and against ecclesiastical jurisdiction. A priest named Wolmann, professor of religion in the Catholic College of Braunsberg, having persisted in rejecting the Vatican decrees, his ordinary, the bishop of Ermland, had excommunicated him. In spite of the protests of the parents of the students, the Minister of Worship threatened with expulsion all the lads who would not take their lessons in the Catholic faith from an excommunicated man. The third enterprise was directed against "the abuses of the pulpit." A law was proposed in the German Reichstag by the Bavarian Minister, Lutz, an avowed patron of the "Old Catholics," according to which imprisonment for perhaps two years was to be the punishment of any priest who, in a church or elsewhere, in a sermon or in any kind of speech, should "disturb public tranquillity." This law, sacrificing to "Borrussianism" the liberty and honor of all the German clergy, was rushed through the Reichstag on Nov. 28. In Feb., 1872, the same Reichstag was asked to consider a law which would deprive the clergy of their right of surveillance over primary schools; the law was passed, and the consequences were terrible. In some places, the new government inspectors forbade the children to use the "superstitious" salutation, "Praised be Jesus Christ!" universally given by German Catholics where we are satisfied with a "How d'y do?" In many districts the crucifixes and holy pictures were thrown out of the schools, and were replaced by portraits of their Sacred Majesties, the emperor and empress. In nearly all schools the little pupils were taught that the Biblical stories with which their Catholic teachers had loaded their memories, were mere fables. Some inspectors gave to young girls themes for composition which were more "patriotic" than moral; thus, a favorite subject was: " What are the sentiments which ought to agitate the heart of a young woman, when she sees an officer of hussars?" From the middle of May until the end of June, the imperial government occupied itself with measures for the expulsion of all Jesuits and their "affiliated orders" from the empire. The impudence of the design was so patent, however, that it became necessary to show that the governmental action was caused by the "pressure of public opinion." On Sept. 22, 1871, the "Old Catholics" had proclaimed, in their Congress of Munich, that the good of the State demanded the expulsion of the Jesuits. "It is notorious," said the Döllingerites in the sixth article of their programme, "that the said Society of Jesus is the cause of the dissensions at present troubling the Catholic Church. This Society uses its powerful influence in order to propagate in the hierarchy, among the clergy, and among the people, tendencies which are contrary to civilization, dangerous to the State, and anti-national. It preaches a false morality, and it strives for power. Therefore we are of opinion that peace, happiness, and unity in the Church, as well as amicable relations between the Church and civil society, are impossible, if an end is not put to the baneful proceedings of this Society." It was to this declaration of a few excommunicated recalcitrants that Bismarck pointed, when he asserted that even among Catholics, "public opinion" called for the banishment of the Jesuits. That the same action was demanded by "public opinion" among Protestants, was said to be evident from the fact that a representative body of Protestants, who had met at Darmstadt eight days after the "Old Catholic" pronouncement, had adopted a resolution condemning the Jesuits in the strongest terms. In the parliamentary debates to which this "public opinion" gave rise, it was evident that the ministerial orators were attacking the Catholic Church, although the Jesuits alone were mentioned; one of these declaimers, Windthorst of Berlin (never to be confounded with his uncle, Windthorst of Meppen), in a moment of passion, exclaimed: "There is no other way. *'Ecrasez l'infâme!'* " By a vote of 181 against 63, the German parliament banished from the empire "the Society of Jesus, as well as all the orders or congregations affiliated to it." In vain the Catholics of Westphalia and of the Rhenish Provinces appealed for relief to the much-vaunted justice of the emperor; the "pious and loyal" William I refused to receive their deputation, and on July 4, 1872, he signed the infamous decree. The reader will note that this ordinance was framed so as to affect not only the Society of Jesus, but also "all the orders or congregations affiliated to it." This provision accentuated the malice of the chancellor and his worshippers. There never have been, and are not now, any orders or congregations in "affiliation" with the Jesuits; the sole connection between the sons of Loyola and the members of any other society is that which must subsist among all the children of the Church. But Bismarck chose to affect the crass ignorance which is frequently found among Protestants, as they unwittingly compliment the celebrated Society by an application of the term "Jesuit" to every uncompromising Catholic; and the event proved that when the chancellor proclaimed the same punishment for the Jesuits and their "affiliated orders or congregations," he prepared the way for the banishment, at his convenience, of any religious who might incur his displeasure.

The incidents which we have just narrated were mere preludes to the "War for Civilization" on which the German enemies of the Church had already resolved, and which was solemnly declared in May, 1873, by the promulgation of those enactments which have rendered the name of Falk infamous, but which are often designated as the "May Laws." Some time before Bismarck entered on his greatest enterprise, Friedeberg, a professor of law in the University of Leipsic, who was afterward made a privy-councillor to Falk, had published a work entitled *The German Empire and the Catholic Church,* in which he had detailed, with an effrontery which was almost Satanic, a plan for the complete extirpation of Catholicism in Germany, for the greater glory of Prussia, and of free thought. Friedeberg disagreed with the doctrinarians who thought that the power of Catholicism could be diminished by a separation of Church and State. On the contrary, said Friedeberg, such a separation would be of great profit to the Church, since in our day Catholicism is in perfect accord with the people. Were the Church of Rome, he added, as free from governmental surveillance in Prussia as she is in the United States of America, her power in Prussia would be more than doubled. Again, observed the professor, Protestantism in Prussia would suffer greatly, if

Church and State were separated; indeed, without the aid of the State, Protestantism would perish in Prussia. Let the State continue, therefore, to aid its most valuable ally in its struggle with Catholicism. Finally, insisted Friedeberg, a separation of Church and State in Germany would injure the "Old Catholics," the men whom Prussia had encouraged to revolt with her promises of pecuniary and other aid. Then Friedeberg thus resumed his plan: "We have indicated our reasons for not wishing, at the present for a separation of Church and State; and we have also pointed out the path on which the State should enter. If, as we think, the Church must one day be cut away from the social body, we should begin now to prepare for that operation, so that it will injure or weaken the State as little as possible. In the meantime, let us put a ligature on the artery through which runs the blood of the Church—that artery which communicates to the Church the strength and life of the State. We should isolate the ecclesiastical limb gradually, accustoming the State to do without it, so that when the amputation is finally made, the loss of the limb will not be perceived. There will not be much blood lost, and the wound will cicatrize quickly." Such was the plan adopted by Bismarck; the Church was to be cut away from the social body; but the operation was to be performed so dexterously that the patient should not screech too fearfully, and the State should not receive too serious a shock. Had the Catholic Church been an institution of the State, like Prussian Evangelical Protestantism with the sovereign for its supreme pontiff, then Friedeberg, Bismarck, and Falk would have been numbered among the "great men" of the world. Very little study of the "May Laws" is required for the conclusion that they were well designed for the accomplishment of the intention of Friedeberg—"to asphyxiate the Church, and to dry up her vital source." The first of these laws, enacted by the Diet of Berlin on May 11, 1873, concerned the education of the clergy, and the nomination to ecclesiastical offices. It ordered that no person could exercise ecclesiastical functions in Prussia, unless he was a German, unless he had been educated according to the terms of the law, and unless he was perfectly acceptable to the government. The education of all prospective priests was to be conducted by the State. The aspirant was to take his bachelor's degree in a government *gymnasium;* during three years he was to study what the State designated as theology in a German University; and an examination by officers of the State was to finally pronounce on his fitness for the priesthood. Every ecclesiastical educational establishment was to be subject, at all hours and in every matter, to governmental surveillance. No nomination to a parish or to any care of souls could be made by a bishop without the approbation of the civil authority. The second law, enacted on May 12, concerned ecclesiastical discipline; and its spirit was that of the preceding ordinance. The Roman Pontiff could have no voice in any matter concerning discipline in any diocese or parish of Prussia; for all disciplinary ecclesiastical matters were declared to pertain exclusively to German ecclesiastical authority, exercised with the permission of the government. And the last appeal in all cases of ecclesiastical discipline was to be made to a royal tribunal, sitting in Berlin; this court was to dismiss bishops and priests, as though they were so many sub-prefects of the State. The third law, enacted on May 13, prohibited any ecclesiastical censure of any act commanded by the State. All public excommunication was absolutely forbidden. The fourth law, enacted on May 14, ordered that when any person wished to change his religion, he should signify that desire to the Minister of Public Worship, who would charge him one *marck* for a permissive license. Our limited space forbids citations from the protests issued by the Prussian bishops against these laws, or from the many eloquent speeches condemning them which were pronounced in the Prussian parliament by Mallinckrodt, Windthorst (of Meppen), and other valiant members of the Centre. The efforts of these champions were of no avail; the united forces of Protestantism, Freemasonry, "Borrussianism," Judaism, and "German intelligence," had decided "to crush the infamous one," even though their weapons constituted a serious danger for public liberty. In a cynical discourse which was worthy of his school, Wirchow, one of the most prominent representatives of materialistic "German science," admitted quite cheerfully that the May Laws were "arbitrary in the extreme, and dangerous to liberty"; but, he added: "Since we need not fear that the Centre will soon attain power, and since these arbitrary laws injure the Catholic Church alone, we ought to adopt them." This admission that the May Laws would injure "the Catholic Church alone" is very significant; for the reader must know that those ordinances ostensibly affected the Protestants as well as the Catholics. Falk had announced, however, that the enactments had been made to apply to Protestants "for the sake of symmetry"; that is, that the government wished to present the appearance of impartiality, knowing full well that the Protestants of Prussia had been accustomed so long to State-slavery, that it was a matter of small consequence to them when they were loaded with a few more chains. And two other facts must be considered. Nothing in the Falk Laws affected the conscience of a Protestant, even of a sincere one; and even though the sectarian conscience had been affected, it would have regarded as too heavy no sacrifice which might purchase the degradation of the Catholic Church. Some curious persons asked Falk why it was that the Jews were not included among those affected by his Laws; the reply was that "the government did not perceive any practical necessity" of including the children of Abraham. Had he dared, the Minister would have assigned the true reason for the Jewish exemption—the plethoric purses of the Jewish magnates, without whose aid the power even of Bismarck would have vanished into thin air.

We need not insult the intelligence of the reader by any lengthy disquisition on the absurd lie uttered by Bismarck, when he termed his war on Catholicism a "War for Civilization." Even a tyro in the study of history knows that in the combat against truth and virtue, error and sin never wage war under their own names; that from the time of Lucifer's rebellion down to the exploits of the Commune of Paris, evil has always clothed itself in the mantle of enlightenment and progress. Even "German science," in which Bismarck was an adept, is forced to admit that to the Catholic Church alone is due the fact that the modern Germans are not now barbarians; and that to the Catholic Church alone did the original Prussians—a Slavic, not a German tribe—owe their liberation from the degrading idolatry to which they had been victims for centuries after the other European barbarians had become civilized under the shadow of the Cross. And truly phenomenal impudence was requisite for the assertion that a state of war existed between parties, only one of whom was armed, and with the weapons of confiscations, imprisonment, and exile, while the resistance of the other consisted only of fidelity to God's law, and of invincible patience under persecution. Some publicists have qualified the phrase "War for Civilization" as a convenient euphemism; but that which it meant was a downright lie. "In the entire course of this affair," observes Msgr. Janiszewski, "the government and the pseudo-liberal party cared nothing for law, truth, or justice; they thought of nothing but the attainment of their object. The means could be of any nature, since it was the Catholic Church that was to suffer. At different periods, different passions and vices have dominated other passions and vices; the inheritance of our time is *falsehood*. It was on falsehood that the plan of the war of Prussia against Austria (1866), and that of the war against France (1870), were based; it was falsehood that characterized the entire conspiracy against the Church. Falsehood, systematically developed and abundantly rewarded, took possession of the press, and not a ray of truth was allowed to reach the people. The German language itself was travestied. Such words as 'culture,' 'instruction,' 'civilization,' 'liberty,' 'science,' 'Liberalism,' 'Ultramontanism,' 'progress,' and other expressions which often seduce simple minds, received, in this chaos, meanings which sound reason and logic never dreamed of attributing to them." It was but natural that such should be the course of a party which brazenly avowed that it despised mere principles. Thus that most "intelligent" Progressist, Wirchow, when told in the parliament that the May Laws violated the Prussian Constitution, brutally retorted: "I care not to bother my brains in an effort to save mere principles, since the government now abandons such things in order to act in accordance with the desires of its party." Mere truth was a matter of no value to the "man of blood and iron" who affected to scorn everything that savored of the Middle Ages; to the Minister who dared, on June 16, 1873, to inform the Reichstag that he "wished to be excused from listening to any more talk about the pretended rights of the people—mere reminiscences of days long vanished, and which merit no other designation than that of declamatory phrases."

From what we have said concerning the May Laws, the reader will readily understand that any concession on the part of the Holy See was impossible; and that since the German chancellor refused to abandon any of his arrogant and absurd pretensions, the "War for Civilization" seemed destined to last until the disintegrating forces of Socialism would have destroyed the power which knew not how to avail itself of its sole means of salvation. But an unexpected circumstance showed both parties to the struggle that peace might not be far distant. On May 13, 1878, a Socialistic workman, one Hoedel or Lehmann, made an attempt on the life of William I. The aim of the miscreant was not true; but the shock produced a deep impression on the mind of the monarch, and he remarked to the author of the May Laws that probably the contemplated crime was due to the fact that the people had been robbed of their religion. A few weeks afterward, on June 2, another Socialist, a certain Dr. Nobiling, made a second attack on the emperor-king, wounding him seriously in the face and arm, and forcing him to relinquish the reins of government, for a time, to the crown-prince. The second danger augmented the imperial disgust with the "War for Civilization"; and the feeling became predominant, when, on the occasion of the inauguration of the *Germania* monument at Niederwald on the Rhine, it was discovered that a mine had been prepared for the destruction of the entire imperial family. If we add to these facts the revelation made at the recent elections, that Berlin alone counted 56,133 resolute partisans of Liebnecht and Bebel, we will comprehend the significance of the many invitations which Bismarck extended to Msgr. Marsella, the papal nuncio at Munich, to visit Berlin. The Holy See was certainly gratified by this advance on the part of him who had said that he "would never go to Canossa"; but the dignity of the nuncio forbade a journey to the Prussian capital under the circumstances then subsisting. The chancellor then suggested Kissingen, a neutral place, for the desired interview; he was accustomed to repair thither annually for the sake of the waters, and the prelate might like to try the "cure," and at the same time to have a little talk about matters which interested both Rome and Germany. The nuncio found it convenient to visit Kissingen, and several interviews were held by the two diplomats. But saving the fact that the ice was broken, nothing came of these meetings; for while Bismarck offered to send an ambassador to the Vatican, he insisted on a recognition of the May Laws by the Pontiff. Shortly after this tentative attempt at reconciliation, negotiations were resumed at Vienna between Msgr. Jacobini, papal nuncio at the Austrian court, and Count Hubner, acting for the chancellor. Msgr. Jacobini was one of the most conciliatory of men; and Hubner became convinced that if the prelate and his master were to meet, the latter would obtain his desires. Gastein, in the duchy of Salzbourg, was selected for another trial of Bismarckian cajolery or intimidation; but the conciliatory Jacobini informed the chancellor that the Holy See would never recognize the May Laws. Not until 1880 did Bismarck resume his approach toward Canossa. Then he introduced in the Landtag his first modification of the May Laws. While retaining the power of maintaining or abolishing, at its own good pleasure, the royal commissaries whom it had charged with the duty of administrating the temporalities of dioceses, the government renounced its usurpation of the right to depose ecclesiastics; and in 1881 it recognized, without forcing them to take the obnoxious oath of absolutely universal obedience, vicars-general for the dioceses of Paderborn, Osnabruck, and Breslau. Bismarck even recognized the Pope's appointment of Msgr. Kopp to the see of Fulda, and that of Msgr. Korum to the see of Treves. However, the new bishops, disposed as they were to yield to the chancellor in all reasonable matters, found themselves so trammelled that Windthorst styled them *"bishops in vinculis."* Such was the condition of ecclesiastical affairs when Windthorst forced the hand of the government by his proposition to grant freedom to the Catholic clergy "in everything concerning the Sacrifice of the Mass and the administration of the Sacraments." This installment of justice having been rejected by two thirds of the deputies, and the same fate having befallen a proposition to restore their olden "donations" to the clergy, Bennigsen, the leader of the National Liberals, declared that all such projects were very inopportune, since "Rome was then very nearly vanquished. Let us have but one or two years of patience, and we will gather the fruits of our excellent policy, for we will have conquered the Pope." But the elections of 1882 showed that the Liberal leader had erred; the Centrists gained several seats, and Rome manifested no signs of yielding to the governmental pretensions. Another step toward Canossa was taken on May 31, 1883, when it was decreed that a deposed bishop might be "pardoned" by the emperor, and might then resume the administration of his diocese; that the Minister of Worship might dispense candidates for ecclesiastical offices from "legal formalities"; that ecclesiastical students should not be obliged to undergo those State examinations which had been proclaimed as the best guarantees against superstition and fanaticism. This enactment was certainly a great relief to the harried clergy; but not one of the deposed bishops was "pardoned" by William I until after the visit of the crown-prince (the future Frederick III) to Leo XIII, when that "favor" was accorded only to the bishops of Limbourg and Munster. It is evident that Bismarck, realizing that the more severe features of his "War for Civilization" should disappear, still trusted to be able to save the principles for which he had contended; those principles would be abandoned only when the May Laws would be abrogated. This truth was so evident to Windthorst, the leader of the Centre, that when Msgr. Galimberti, then nuncio at Vienna, advised him to use his influence with his party in favor of a less vigorous opposition to the chancellor, His Little Excellency, as the Catholics affectionately termed their chief champion, replied: "I shall accede to your request most willingly; but not before the May Laws have been formally withdrawn. They do indeed swear to us that these laws will no longer be applied; but while that assurance may suffice for today, who will answer for tomorrow? The freedom of us Catholics is a right. Can we abandon it to the caprice of a Minister?" And here let it be noted that this refusal of the Centre to hearken to the recommendation of Msgr. Galimberti, who was known to have merely echoed the views of Pope Leo XIII, was an excellent refutation of that falsehood which the school of Bismarck had so assiduously circulated in justification of its persecution of the Catholics; namely, that the Roman Pontiff held in his hands the political opinions and the votes of the German Catholics. And the firmness of Windthorst was rewarded when, by suggesting the pontifical arbitration in the affair of the Caroline Islands, the chancellor showed that he was willing to advance a little further on the road to Canossa. The proceedings connected with this arbitration afforded to Bismarck an opportunity of treating directly with the Holy See; and the first consequence of the *rapprochement* was the governmental consent to the filling of the then vacant sees of Cologne and Fribourg. It was then that Cardinal Ledochowski, yielding to the wishes of the Pontiff, resigned a diocese to which he could scarcely hope to return; and the provost of Koenigsberg, Dinder, was made archbishop of Posen. Then Msgr. Kopp, bishop of Fulda, was called to a seat in the Upper House of Prussia; and although the traditions of the German Church seemed to forbid such a course, the prelate thought that circumstances dictated his acceptance of the position. Bismarck had confidence in Msgr. Kopp; but his object in ranging him among the peers was to obtain a means of treating with the Centre without any intervention of his own personality. On May 21, 1886, another modification to the May Laws was decreed. The State renounced its examination of clerical students, re-establishing the theological schools as they had been before 1873, but requiring their superiors to furnish to the Minister of Public Worship their statutes and the names of their professors. The Pope was recognized as the superior judge in ecclesiastical affairs; and the royal court which had sat in Berlin since 1873, for the purpose of deciding those affairs, was suppressed, thus exhibiting no longer the anomaly of a Protestant tribunal finding or imprisoning Catholic priests who had refused absolution to persons who were unworthy, or who had celebrated Mass or attended the dying without governmental permission. Finally, the elections of Feb., 1887, convinced Bismarck that the power of the Centre was growing instead of diminishing, and he determined to make such further modifications of the obnoxious laws as he deemed apt to conciliate a party, whose aid he sadly needed. These modifications were presented in five Articles; and when they were examined by Windthorst in the name of the Centre, the perspicacious leader decided as follows: The first Article ought to be rejected, he contended, because although it allowed the existence of diocesan seminaries, it gave to the State a very badly defined right of surveillance over the teaching in those institutions —an indefiniteness which bade fair to invite trouble of various kinds. The second Article, treating of the right of Veto, should be partly amended, said Windthorst, and partly rejected; it was condemnable as an entirety. The third Article, acknowledging the disciplinary authority of the Church, was welcomed by the great Centrist. The fourth Article, recognizing the right of the Church to inflict canonical punishment on her subjects when they violated her laws, was of course approved. The fifth Article, which permitted the return of certain religious orders or congregations, and excluded others, was sternly criticized. The eminent jurisconsult said: "Among the demands which Catholics will never cease to make, is that for the freedom of the religious orders and congregations. We shall say nothing here concerning the Society of Jesus, and the orders which are alleged to be affiliated to it; their return must be considered by the Reichstag, for it was a law of the empire that crushed them. But we must declare at once that there are two objections to the law which is now proposed. The first objection arises from the fact that permission to return is granted solely to the orders or congregations which are either devoted to the care of souls, or are given to offices of charity, or lead a contemplative life." Then the government is reminded of the moral, enconomical, and material losses which have been entailed upon the Catholic populations by the expulsion of the teaching orders. The second objection to Article V is derived from the state of utter dependency on the government in which the restored orders will be, if the law is passed. Windthorst concluded his report with this declaration: "It is indubitable that this project cannot be regarded as a final revision of the existing politico-ecclesiastical legislation; and until such revision is effected, it will be futile to talk about a durable peace between the Church and the State." The arguments of its leader convinced the entire Centre; but it soon transpired that Pope Leo had written to the archbishop of Cologne, manifesting a willingness to be content, for the present, with the governmental concessions. Then the Centre yielded, not deeming it good policy to be more exigent than the Roman Pontiff in matters concerning which he was certainly the better judge. The new law was enacted and thenceforth the State exercised its "right" of Veto on the appointment of a pastor, only so far as the title of pastor was involved. The government merely insisted that the bishops should appoint to pastorships no priests who already labored under civil condemnation. The ordinaries were to be no longer obliged to fill vacancies within a stated period of time; and if a pastor were condemned to prison, the pastorship was not to be regarded as *ipso facto* vacant, as the May Laws had prescribed. Disciplinary measures were no longer to be notified to the governors of the provinces. The Law of May 20, 1874, concerning the administration of vacant dioceses, was cancelled. Toleration was to be extended to religious orders which were devoted to the contemplative life, to exercises of Christian charity, or to the education of young girls. With these final modifications, the "War for Civilization" practically terminated; as its instigator and conductor avowed, nothing of his scheme remained, save "ruins and rubbish." Bismarck had arrived at Canossa.

13

THE MEANING OF THE FRENCH LAIC LAWS *

The Kulturkampf *was not unique to Germany. Similar sets of laws were enacted against the Church, under other names, in the other countries of Europe. In Italy a series of laws restricted the Church after 1871 and sought to destroy her as an influence in Italian life. Similarly, a series of laws under the French Third Republic was devised to destroy the Church as an organized body in French life. These laws, known as the* lois laïques, *were passed from the end of the nineteenth century until 1907, and, had it not been for the coming of the First World War, might have temporarily erased Catholicism in France.*

The background of the lois laïques *goes back to the French Revolution and the Civil Constitution of the Clergy, which turned most Catholics against the Revolution and led them to support the monarchy and the Church-State relations of the Old Regime. One can say that two Frances emerged from the French Revolution. Republican France endorsed the Revolution and its accomplishments. It was anti-clerical, anti-monarchical, and to a large extent anti-religious. Monarchical France rejected the Revolution and its accomplishments. It advocated a return to the monarchy and, in a general way, to the arrangements of the Old Regime. Monarchical France was clerical and religious, although in a strange way, because Catholicism was valued as an essential part of a monarchical regime.*

The Third Republic was established after the Franco-Prussian War, when the three monarchical groups could not agree on a common candidate. At first the Republican leaders were mildly anti-religious, but a series of events—such as the Boulangist episode and the Dreyfus Affair—and the imprudent role played in these events by intransigent Catholics led to more extreme attacks on religion by the radical Republicans. Their work is summed up in the following selection by Professor Evelyn M. Acomb, the outstanding American authority on the subject.

* Evelyn M. Acomb, *The French Laic Laws (1879-1889)* (New York: Columbia University Press, 1941), pp. 249-260. Reprinted by permission.

From the foregoing study it should be evident that no one factor was responsible for the enactment of the laic laws. The position of the Church in 1876 was such as to make it vulnerable to attack. Its growing ultramontanism and increasing influence in education, philanthropy, the army, and politics during the years of monarchist coalitions aroused alarm among the advocates of an all-powerful national state. Republicans coveted the positions held by the secular and regular clergy. The status of the Church under the Concordat and Organic Articles was ill-defined, for, in the course of the nineteenth century, certain provisions of those measures had become dead letters, especially those of a Gallican character. The Church had obtained additional concessions, such as the right of the pope to give prior consent to the appointment of bishops by the government, the exemption of the clergy from military service, and the monopoly of funerals. Some of the terminology of the Concordat was ambiguous and some of its omissions, especially that of any reference to the religious orders, were used by the radicals for their own advantage. Within the Church itself there were signs of weakness. The number of candidates for the priesthood was rapidly falling off, and the clergy was less highly educated than it had been. Catholics offered few constructive proposals for reform and were divided by their political, doctrinal, and social views. The aristocratic outlook of their leaders alienated the working classes.

The sympathy expressed by many members of the Church for the monarchist cause antagonized the republicans, whose position was insecure while the pretenders lived. The foolish attempt of Marshal MacMahon to dismiss a government supported by a majority in the Chamber brought retaliation upon the Church, which was accused of encouraging this move. The promulgation of the *Syllabus of Errors* in 1864 and the Declaration of Papal Infallibility in 1871 seemed to deny the very principles upon which the republic was founded.

By 1879 the republicans were in control of both chambers, where the Extreme Left and the Republican Union held one-third of the republican seats. The Extreme Left openly asked for separation of Church and state, suppression of the religious orders, and the secularization of Church property. It also demanded decentralization and greater liberty for all but the Church. Clemenceau, Madier de Montjau, and Naquet were leaders of this group. The Republican Union, headed by Gambetta and containing such active men as Spuller, Waldeck-Rousseau, and Paul Bert, was somewhat less radical in its anti-clericalism, preferring restriction of the privileges of the Church through strict execution of the Concordat. The Left, led by Jules Ferry, wished to respect the Concordat but gradually secularize French institutions. Both Gambetta and Ferry at heart looked forward to eventual separation of Church and state, but they deemed it impossible of fulfillment until the public mind had been sufficiently influenced by modern philosophies and until the wealth and authority of the Church had been brought under control. The Left

Center wavered in its religious attitude between the Right and Left. A group of liberal conservatives, including such men as Jules Simon, Laboulaye, Dufaure, Étienne Lamy, and Bardoux, was opposed to the laic laws as a violation of those principles of freedom of conscience, freedom of instruction, and freedom of association for which the republican party had long stood. The Bonapartists, whether they were followers of Jerôme or of Victor, opposed the anti-clerical legislation and wished to maintain the Concordat, although they were more willing to abstain from voting or occasionally join the Left than the Legitimists or Orleanists, who were unwavering in their opposition.

The attack upon the Church would not have been so generally supported if the ground had not been prepared by the anti-clerical philosophies then popular. Most influential of all were the ideas of Auguste Comte, as revised by his disciple, Littré. The assertion that scientific knowledge alone was valid, that mankind could gradually attain perfection through the intellectual and moral development of the masses, that woman was destined to be the moral guardian of the family, and that the state should be separate from the Church contradicted fundamental conceptions of Catholicism and inspired the laic laws. The views of Comte and Littré on education, the position of the priesthood, the signficance of the French Revolution, the function of the industrialists and workers, centralized government, and civil liberties also underlay the legislation.

The Deism or "Spiritualism" popular in the University retained only two cardinal tenets of the Christian faith: belief in God and the immortality of the soul. Materialism rejected the supernatural completely, and the Personalism of Renouvier opposed the Church's restraint upon the autonomy of the individual. Free-thinkers agitated for freer expression. Readers of Kant, Condorcet, Quinet, and Proudhon declared that education should be laic and include instruction in the principles of morality. They found in Condorcet equal education for girls and courses in patriotism and in Spencer an enthusiasm for science. Liberal Protestantism, the religion of a conquering race, was popular in France because of its emphasis upon democratic practices and moral principles, subservience to the national state, and belief in scientific education and freedom of examination. It was similar to "free thought" in its content and method and was regarded as a likely substitute for Catholicism among the common people. Subscribers to these philosophies and freethinkers resented the privileged position of the established churches under a republic based upon freedom of worship and equality of rights.

The demand for reform of the French school system, which had been revived during the last years of the Second Empire, encouraged discussion of the relative merits of state and religious schools and facilitated the anti-clerical attack upon Catholic schools. Education in the latter was denounced for its preoccupation with memory work and the classics and neglect of science and "modern" ideas. Members of the religious orders were declared ill-prepared to teach. It was said that instruction would benefit by the creation of a real competition between public and private schools. Although both educational systems were obviously in need of improvement, the private schols were discriminated against in the endeavor to strengthen the schools of the state.

Anti-clericalism was an expedient policy for the Opportunists to pursue for several reasons. It was useful as a weapon against the monarchists, who were united in their loyalty to the Church. It also served to retain the allegiance of the radicals, through whose aid Gambetta had risen to power, whose voice was loudly heard in the Chamber, and who were in the majority in the municipal council of Paris. It was substituted for abrogation of the Concordat and social reforms which must be postponed until the conservative *bourgeoisie* and peasantry had been won over to the republic through a peaceful and profitable régime. Since France was still weak from the crushing blow of 1871, Gambetta, although he did not relinquish the hope of revenge, endeavored to remain at peace until the country was re-armed and the republic secure. Anti-clericalism assured peaceful relations with Italy, which feared that France might champion the claims of the Pope to temporal power. It promoted friendship with Germany, which had carried on its own *Kulturkampf* and believed that an anti-clerical, conservative republic in France would be weak at home and abroad. And it was a policy with which England, Austria, and Russia were sympathetic. The republicans cleverly substituted it for *revanche* in political campaigns and contrived to fasten upon the monarchists the stigma of inciting neighboring countries to war. They were abetted by Bismarck, who used his influence to persuade the French electorate that an ultramontane, monarchial régime would endanger the cordial relations between France and Germany.

Republican, Jacobin nationalism contributed to the anti-clerical movement through the propagation of its ideals. The thirst for revenge led to an imitation of Prussian education, military methods, and science. The traditions and principles of the French Revolution filled the minds of the republican statesmen and inspired the legislation which they enacted. Freedom of conscience was used to justify the secularization of the school, the courts, the army, cemeteries, funerals, marriages, and holidays. Equality and fraternity were invoked to defend free, compulsory, and lay primary education and universal military service. Belief in the authority of force, derived from Comte and from the success of Prussian militarism, led to the exaltation of ideals far removed from those of the Christian Church. The national army was to be not only an instrument of defense, but also a source of patriotic inspiration. The more radical republicans even believed that some day faith in the fatherland might replace the supernatural and divisive dogmas of Catholicism.

Republican, Jacobin nationalism was hostile to the Church, whose privileges it regarded as derogatory to the sovereignty of the national state and as inimical to freedom of conscience. To civil society it attributed mankind's achievement of freedom of conscience and thought, and accused the Church of antipathy to free investigation, scientific discoveries, and social reform. It declared that an organization with a foreign head could not be patriotic and that religious sects prevented the fulfillment of a sense of national fraternity. It denounced religious orders as unpatriotic, violators of the law and of individual liberty, and sponsors of provincialism. It asserted that the state should be the supreme dispenser of instruction in civics and morality to its future citizens, that it should have the right to inspect and even suppress rival institutions, and that it alone should have the power to confer advanced degrees. The state should direct theological education, since it was the guardian of Science. The Church should watch over dogma, but in case of conflict, the temporal power should be supreme. The state was neutral in doctrine, but it might teach an "independent morality" in the public schools, based upon that which underlay all forms of thought. This morality might be divorced from both philosophy and religion or it might be deistic in principle. The state was also to assume charitable responsibilities.

Various agencies propagated these Jacobin ideals: assemblies of teachers, the army, the press, the Educational League, and the Freemasons. The clubs of the League carried on an active propaganda in behalf of free, compulsory, and lay primary education, freedom of association, and civic and military education. Many prominent deputies and senators were members of the League and promoted its objectives in the chambers. The organization was anti-clerical in sympathy, although its founder, Jean Macé, was a deist and denied that it was irreligious. The Freemasonry of the period, which was republican, positivistic, and anti-clerical, stirred up sentiment for the laic laws through pamphlets, lectures, and meetings. Many members of the chambers and government were Masons. Although the society theoretically did not engage in politics, individual members or lodges probably used every opportunity to further its ends.

Once in power, the republicans became increasingly intolerant of internal dissent. Their experiences during the war and Commune, their conceptions of state sovereignty, and the peril of their own position led them to adopt ruthless tactics. They discriminated against private institutions, failed to provide for freedom of instruction and freedom of association, and sometimes violated the conscience of Catholics. The danger that the "neutral" school would become a center for the propagation of the doctrines of those in power was great. Not only the Right, but men of the Left and Left Center, philosophers, writers, and clergymen protested against these policies.

The concurrence of all these forces and motives resulted in the introduction and enactment of a series of anti-clerical measures from 1876 to 1889 which foreshadowed the eventual separation of Church and state and postponed consideration of constructive social legislation. The state alone was given the right to confer higher degrees, and Catholic faculties were denied the title of university. Freedom of instruction was thus violated, and the provision regarding degrees was made retroactive. Bishops and those susceptible to religious influences were excluded from the Higher Council of Public Education, which was composed henceforth of representatives of education, the great majority of whom were from public schools and elected by their colleagues. This council had jurisdiction over the curriculum, administration, and discipline of public schools and rights of inspection and discipline over private schools. In matters affecting the latter, it was thus judge in its own cause. The academic councils were now composed of elected representatives of the schools and municipal councils, as well as government appointees, and dealt with the administration, discipline, and budgets of public schools. If disciplinary or disputed matters in connection with private education were discussed, two members of such schools, appointed by the minister, entered the council. The Faculties of Catholic Theology were finally abolished in 1884, while the Protestant Faculties were fostered.

Secondary schools for girls were created, in which religious education was optional and given within the school, outside class hours, and in which instruction in morals was compulsory. An attempt to require principals of private secondary schools to have a certificate of pedagogical aptitude given by a state jury and teachers in those schools to have the baccalaureate or *licence* failed, despite the support of Ferry and Bert. These qualifications were higher than those demanded of public school instructors. Likewise a bill to require that the last three years of study for the baccalaureate be passed in state schools was never adopted.

The reforms in primary education were much more extensive. Every department was required to have a normal school for men and one for women, to prepare teachers to replace the members of religious orders. Every teacher in both public and private schools was forced to possess a teaching certificate; or, in other words, the letter of obedience, by which nuns had been permitted to teach, was abolished. Free, compulsory, and lay primary education was established, with instruction in civics and morals a compulsory part of the curriculum. The content of these subjects was so nebulous that politics might well be introduced into the schools. Religious education and religious teachers were excluded from the public schools. The departmental council, composed largely of state officials, was given the power to forbid the opening of private schools and to discipline their teachers. Instructors were still to be appointed by the prefect, a political appointee. Some deputies even proposed the organization of a public school of political science, which would teach only doctrines acceptable to the state.

The religious orders were attacked directly or indirectly by this legislation. By decree the government expelled the Jesuits and required other unauthorized orders to seek government approval within a short period. Unauthorized orders for men were dealt with severely, but those for women were tolerated. This action was taken by executive order after the

Senate had refused to confirm it, and redress in the courts was denied the orders. The chambers refused to give freedom of association to the religious orders but gave it to workingmen. Religious orders were no longer exempt from service in the army, and ecclesiastical students of state churches were required to serve one year. The property of the orders, which was generally devoted to charitable purposes, was doubly taxed in an effort to check the development of mortmain. Members of religious orders were excluded from public schools and branded as unpatriotic or even criminal. Attempts to suppress the orders completely or confiscate their property never became law.

Chaplains were permitted to carry on their work only in garrisons of at least 2,000 men, three miles from churches. Every Frenchman was forced to spend in time of peace three years in the national army, unless he was a teacher serving ten years in public education in France or abroad, a student for a higher degree, or an ecclesiastical student, in which case he must serve one year. In time of war all must serve the fatherland, although ecclesiastical students were placed in the health division.

Divorce was finally re-established after an interlude of sixty-eight years. The cemetery was declared open to men of all faiths on equal terms, although this was contrary to Catholic dogma. Civil funerals were encouraged, and a priest who insisted upon religious burial after a deathbed confession might incur heavy penalties. The *curé* was no longer to be an *ex-officio* member of administrative committees for hospitals and benevolent bureaux, and he was no longer eligible to sit on the municipal council, which had supervision of the budget of vestries. Property owned by the commune but used by the Church, outside the terms of the Concordat, might be returned to the commune, if its council so desired. The Panthéon was secularized and restored as a burial place for patriots by executive decree. Labor was legalized on Sundays, except for officials, the law courts, and children in industry. This was an economic hardship to Catholics and a social one for the workingman. An attempt to suppress the use of the oath and religious emblems in the courtroom failed. Public prayers for the work of the chambers were abolished as a symbol of the laicization of the state. Outrages to public and religious morality and to a state religion in the press were declared no longer punishable.

The radicals attacked the Concordat itself in budget discussions and bills, and asked for the recall of the ambassador to the Vatican, but in vain. Likewise bills to strengthen the independence of the lesser clergy, to curb the power of the bishop, and to penalize the clergy for political activity failed. But an opinion of the Council of State approved the government's suppression or suspension of the salary of the clergy.

The intolerant nature of much of the anti-clerical legislation of this period should not, however, obscure the outstanding contributions which the republicans made in the direction of personal freedom and enlightenment. The enactment of a divorce law did not injure the conscience of Catholics and freed the non-Catholic from a bond in which he might not believe. Separation of Church and state by gradual processes and respect for the position of the free-thinker were in accordance with the principle of freedom of conscience. The establishment of secondary schools for girls and of free, compulsory, and lay primary education diffused culture more widely and strengthened democracy. The requirement of uniformly high qualifications for teachers and the revision of the curriculum to include scientific subjects and civics improved the quality and content of instruction.

A study of the laic legislation of the 1880's has a wider significance than is at first apparent. It is more than a tedious analysis of conditions and laws in a brief decade long since forgotten by all but the professional historian. It is an illustration of the fact that subservience to the ideal of a highly centralized national state may produce intolerance, violation of civil liberties, and suppression of the rights of autonomous groups within the state. These evils, it should be noted, may exist in a democratic republic, governed by men who once extolled individual liberties. Private educational institutions and associations differing in doctrine from those of the controlling régime are especially vulnerable to attack. The danger to religion of any political affiliation is likewise demonstrated by the history of the Church in this period.

The laic laws of the 1880's are also significant as a prelude to a more intense struggle between the anti-clerical and religious forces which took place between 1899 and 1907. After Cardinal Lavigerie's plea for reconciliation with the republic at Algiers in 1891, there was a period of *Ralliement,* during which more moderate Catholics cooperated with the government in the hope that the laic legislation might be repealed peacefully. The Dreyfus crisis, however, interrupted this truce, for many Catholics joined the anti-revisionist forces and brought down upon the Church the vengeance of the radicals. Under the Waldeck-Rousseau ministry all religious orders were required to be authorized and regulated by the government in 1901. The Combes ministry interpreted this law strictly and dissolved many of the orders. In 1904 every member of a religious association, authorized or unauthorized, was forbidden to teach in either public or private schools after ten years. Finally in 1905 Church and state were separated, although the provisions regarding the supervision of churches were not agreed upon until 1907.

After the World War the question of diplomatic relations with the papacy, the retention of the Concordat in Alsace-Lorraine, and tolerance of the religious orders continued to be issues in French political life. The Vichy government has repealed the legislation of 1901 and 1904 in regard to the religious orders and has declared that primary education should contain courses in morals and civics and should stress in the teaching of history the continuity of French effort under all régimes. It has decreed the suppression of the primary normal schools by October,

1941, and the division of secondary education into classical and modern studies. It has required all educational associations to join a national federation, whose president and council are named by the government, and has abolished secret societies. The motto of France will henceforth be "Country, Family, Work." Conversations have been inaugurated with representatives of the papacy in regard to a concordat.

These laic campaigns have continued the division within the French nation which has existed since the French Revolution, that of "the two Frances." In peace this hostility has wasted energy in recrimination and has diverted attention from pressing social questions. In war it has indirectly weakened the unity and powers of resistance of the French people, as has been vividly disclosed in the events of 1939-40. It will be recalled that Gambetta once wrote:

> It is an inexorable law of politics that peoples incapable of destroying domestic tyrannies are powerless to maintain their national integrity. . . . To resist this always conscious invasion of the races of the North, which have achieved science, discipline, courage, order, the feeling of primacy, one only knows how to make scholars with the methods of seventeenth century Jesuits. . . . These are signs which foretell decadence, and if old France has not a violent crisis soon, the end of the century will consecrate its fall.

Yet the anti-clerical policies which he and his followers pursued became a "domestic tyranny" and perpetuated a schism which contributed to the collapse of France. Mutual tolerance and fulfillment of the revolutionary ideals of liberty, equality, and fraternity might have preserved the Third French Republic.

14

CATHOLICISM, EVOLUTION AND DARWINISM *

When Darwin's Origin of Species *appeared in 1859, it seemed to give scientific verification to the theory of evolution. For Darwin's book was imposing in size and in its appeal to scientific evidence. What Darwin had done was to offer the principle of natural selection as a means to account for the survival of the fittest and, he argued, the origin of new species. Although Darwin did not use the word "evolution" in the* Origin of Species, *his name was soon identified with evolution.*

The reaction of scientists was far from unanimous in favor of Darwin's theory of natural selection. Some believed that he put too much

* Joseph Husslein, S.J., *Evolution and Social Progress* (New York: P. J. Kenedy & Sons, 1920), pp. 72-82, 95-103. Reprinted by permission.

emphasis on this factor to the detriment of others, such as use and disuse. Others believed that his assumptions about the inheritance of acquired characteristics were incorrect. And still others believed that he was essentially correct in all his observations and the deductions he made from them.

The reaction of religious leaders was not unanimously against Darwin. Fundamentalists had to reject Darwin's conclusions about evolution or else give up their religion. But intelligent Catholics saw nothing in the Origin of Species *to cause them alarm. They were free to admit man's evolution from inferior animals, they knew, as long as they insisted that at some point in the evolutionary process God intervened to create the soul—and therefore man. Many Catholics, like people of the other Christian faiths, denounced Darwin unreservedly and continued to insist on the special creation by God of each species.*

Darwin's theories of struggle for survival and of natural selection were applied to all fields of thought—to economics, politics, and sociology, to philosophy, of course, and to international warfare. This application of Darwinian principles outside biology was dangerous and sometimes vicious. It seemed to justify and make natural unlimited competition among business men, between nations and races, among all living things—and the rule was that the fittest survived. In time Darwin's influence in the biological sciences was limited by other biologists' discoveries, but in the field of "social Darwinism" his influence was extensive into the mid-twentieth century, something he never dreamed of and something he would hasten to repudiate if he were alive.

UPON comparing the scientific proofs for the probability of the theory of evolution, we find that they grow the more numerous and weighty, the smaller the circle of forms under consideration; but become weaker and weaker if we include a greater number of forms, such as are comprised in a class or in a sub-kingdom. There is in fact no evidence whatever for the common descent of all plants and animals from a single primitive organism. Hence the greater number of botanists and zoologists regard a polygenetic evolution [*i.e.*, from various primitive organisms] as much more acceptable than a monogentic [from a single form]." Such is the accurate and scientific summary of our evolutionary knowledge as presented in the article on "Evolution," in the *Catholic Encyclopedia*. It agrees with what has already been stated. How little reason, consequently, there can possibly be for dogmatism on this subject is now apparent. But the briefest outline of the history of evolutionary doctrine will make this even more evident.

Evolution is an ancient theory. Its modern renaissance, with which alone we are here concerned, was due in the first place to Lamarck, just half a century before the first edition of Darwin's *Origin of Species* was published. Jean Lamarck appeared before the world in 1809 with his *Philosophie Zoologique,* in which he ascribed the evolution of species to the use or disuse of the various organs. His doctrine essentially implied the possibility of the transmission of acquired properties by the individual to his descendants. Darwin, fifty years later, was not to disregard this theory, but merely assigned greater importance to his own specific doctrine of natural selection. Hardly another fifty years elapsed and Darwin's fading star was to be again outshone by the reappearance of the Lamarckian comet, under a new form and under the new name of Neo-Lamarckianism. Sir Bertram Windle offers a very apposite illustration of the difference between Lamarck's and Darwin's theories in the case of the giraffe as explained according to their respective views:

> The giraffe is provided with an extraordinary long neck and very tall forelegs. These he acquired, according to Lamarck's view, by constantly stretching after the foliage of trees, on which he feeds, and by ever reaching after higher and yet higher boughs. According to the Darwinian view certain giraffes were by reason of causes inherent in the embryo provided with somewhat longer necks than their fellows. In time of stress these giraffes could get food where others could not. Hence they survived, and their progeny, also long-necked, gave rise to animals with still further development in the same direction.

Neo-Lamarckians hold that new habits will produce new organs. Thus, rejecting Darwin's doctrine of selection as applied to this same interesting specimen at sight of which the clown protested there was no such creature, Cunningham asks how the horns of the giraffe could have been produced by this method, and then suggests his own neo-Lamarckian explanation: "What then caused such excrescences to appear in the ancestors of the horned ruminants? Butting with the forehead would produce them, and no other cause can be suggested that would." But enough said, though we may mention here with that Darwinian champion, August Weismann, that there is no evidence that acquired characteristics are ever transmitted. So we leave these contending evolutionists to their own struggle, like two stags with inter-locked antlers.

The theory of Lamarck was championed in the lists by the two St. Hilaires, Étienne and Isidore Geoffroy. A series of sharp conflicts between these early evolutionists and the great scientist Cuvier now took place, the latter stanchly defending the permanence of species. The struggle, in which the members of the French Academy participated, ended in the complete discomfiture of the upholders of evolution and the triumph of Cuvier's opinions. Lamarck himself died in poverty and neglect. Such was the first act of this modern drama.

With the appearance of the *Origin of Species* the curtain rose again, but this time upon a new conflict. Its central figure was Charles Darwin.

Not now about evolution only did the battle royal develop, but largely about the theory of "natural selection," which alone constitutes Darwinism, in the proper sense of that much-misused word. It is Darwin's main original contribution to science. But before the close of the nineteenth century that doctrine, too, had already met with serious reverses.

There was no question indeed of abandoning the theory of evolution, whose existence is entirely independent of the acceptance or rejection of Darwinism, but merely of gradually relegating to a very subordinate position the doctrine of natural selection, particularly in its extreme acceptation. The followers of Darwin, in their turn, rapidly fell away from his standard, though his name was wildly used as a battle-cry for evolutionary doctrines with which he never had the slightest sympathy. We have heard Bebel, like countless Socialists and atheists of every class, using "Darwinism" as synonymous with materialistic evolution. Typical of the changed attitude towards real Darwinism, at this time, was the change that took place in the mind of Huxley himself: "The farther he went," wrote T. B. Crozier, "the farther he departed from his early belief in natural selection as the principal factor in the evolution of species."

Darwin held that in the so-called struggle for existence some species could more readily maintain themselves than others. Their favorable characteristics were then accentuated through constant transmission in successive generations. The less capable varieties succumbed.

Under a momentary spell of enthusiasm this theory was extended to almost every department of science and became a commonplace of literature. Materialistically interpreted, it postulated no plan governing this natural selection. And yet the necessity of such plan, even in his own hypothesis, constantly reasserted itself in Darwin's mind. The theory of sexual selection was added merely as a particular phase of his general doctrine.

All that need here be said of the principle enunciated by Darwin is that it was wholly inadequate for the purpose of explaining either the "origin of species" or the "descent of man." At the best it might account for the elimination of the unfit. But it could cast no ray of light upon the only vital problem in question: the origin of specifically new qualities not possessed before. Thus no process of elimination can account for the formation of a new organ, much less, according to the theory of ultra-Darwinists, for the appearance of so wonderful an apparatus as the human eye or ear, or the marvelous and inexplicable power of reproduction, where it is presumed that these faculties had not existed before. Darwin himself denied that natural selection could be the *cause* of variations. It can therefore be at most a very secondary factor, accounting to a certain degree for the further accidental perfection of organs, already existing within a given species, but cannot possibly explain the origin of the species itself.

To Darwin's credit it must here be said that he refused to go the length of his militantly materialistic followers, and even freely confessed in his *Descent of Man* the need of accepting a preordination according to a previous design. Logically this could mean nothing less than the acceptance of a Creator, as Lyell pointed out to him on March 11, 1863: "I think the old 'Creation' is almost as much required as ever."

Although in a familiar passage we find Darwin, by a strange confusion of mind, rejecting the "argument from design," yet in the book just referred to he clearly recognizes his error, when he thus seeks to defend himself against the charge that his doctrine is irreligious:

> I am aware that the conclusions arrived at in this work will be denounced by some as highly irreligious; but he who denounces them is bound to show why it is more irreligious to explain the origin of man as a distinct species by the descent from some lower form, through the laws of variation and natural selection, than to explain the birth of the individual through the laws of ordinary reproduction. *The birth both of the species and of the individual are equally parts of that grand sequence of events, which our minds refuse to accept as the result of blind chance.* The understanding revolts at such a conclusion, whether or not we are able to believe that every slight variation of structure, the union of each pair in marriage, the dissemination of each seed, and other such events have all been ordained for some special purpose.

What we are to think of the origin of man, both from a Scriptural and scientific point of view—the two being in perfect accord—we shall fully make clear. For the rest, Darwin, with his complete lack of knowledge in religious matters, which he quite frankly confesses, found a childish difficulty in accepting the idea of a Divine Providence carried into all the details of a supposed evolutionary process, though he does not here reject that possibility. A grasp of what is implied in the almightiness and omnipresence of God could readily have solved his difficulty, but he admits that he gave no thought to these questions so that his ignorance of such matters was often naïve, to say the least, as when he asked if his own nose was designed! To which Dr. Thomas Dwight replies:

> A foolish speech by the way, and quite unworthy of him. As well ask whether the rings spreading over the water from a falling stone are designed. They are formed in accordance with certain physical laws. They vary with the size of the stone, and the height from which it descends. They vary also with the depth of the water, with its condition, whether it be at rest or flowing, and whether it be a calm or windy day. In the same way the shape of a person's features depends first on the laws of generation, modified by those of heredity and probably by others of which we know next to nothing, such as the influence of surroundings. Moreover, many circumstances during childhood, such as health, climate, mode of life, must be counted. *Design,* it seems to me, *is implied by the very fact of the establishment of those laws.*

Yet Darwin obviously admits, in the passage quoted above, the need of what Lyell calls "the old 'Creation,'" though explained in a new way, and is forced also to accept, as the only alternative to an impossible blind chance, the truth of Lord Kelvin's words that: "science positively affirms creative and directive power," in as far as the denial of this would lead to what Darwin realized to be a preposterous assumption against which "the understanding revolts."

We do not, of course, accept his conclusions regarding the origin of man, but that is another chapter. Nor is there any desire here to explain away the agnosticism of Darwin, which grew at the same time that he also lost his appreciation for art and beauty. So much we gather from his self-confessions. Yet to him, as to so many others who have never possessed the light of faith, the universe simply remained an insoluble mystery, if we are to trust his own words. He does not deny, but merely confesses his utter inability to decide upon a question to which he had never given the necessary consideration. Writing to Fordyce, in 1879, he says of this subject:

> What my own views may be is a question of no consequence to anyone but myself. But, as you ask, I may state that my judgment often fluctuates. In my own extreme fluctuations I have never been an atheist in the sense of denying the existence of God.

Nothing, therefore, could be more untrue and more unhistorical than to confuse Darwinism with materialistic evolution whose first tenet is the utterly false statement that evolution has disproved the existence of a Creator. No such foolish arrogance ever asserted itself in the mind of Darwin. Quite correctly he says, when this question of religion is absurdly forced upon him for judgment, as if his position as a scientist could possibly render him an authority in such matters: "I feel in some degree unwilling to express myself publicly on religious subjects as I do not feel that I have thought deeply enough to justify such publicity."

His attention, like that of many another scientist, has been restricted to purely material facts. However accurate these studies may have been, his deductions from them, even in the purely natural order, were not necessarily reliable, and at times were decidedly unwarranted upon the evidence he had gathered. But his labors could not furnish him with the slightest reason for dogmatizing upon religious matters. Would that all scientists, under similar conditions, have confined themselves to the confession made by him when he wrote: "I cannot pretend to throw the least light on such abstruse problems." But again, it did not follow that because he himself failed to attain to an unshaken certainty regarding the existence of God, owing, we may presume, to his own want of effort and proper disposition, that therefore "the mystery of the beginning of all things is insoluble to us." It is insoluble merely to unaided science. Yet the intellect of Darwin, no more than that of any other normal human being, could be permanently blinded to the great truth of a Creator. Never in fact, even to its latest edition, did he eliminate from his best-known work, *The Origin of Species,* those concluding words:

> There is grandeur in this view of life, with its several powers having been originally breathed by the Creator into a few forms or into one; and that, while

this planet has gone cycling on according to fixed law of gravity, from so simple a beginning endless forms most beautiful and most wonderful have been and are being evolved.

Men like Wallace, Huxley, Asa Gray and Spencer greatly helped to popularize the Darwinian theory in the English-speaking world. Haeckel, as we have seen, carried it to such extremes that already in 1868 Darwin wrote to him: "Your boldness makes me sometimes tremble." And good reason Darwin had for his apprehensions. The atheistic theory of the universe, according to which the entire order, beauty and glory of the existing world has arisen out of primal chaos through the accidental survival of the fittest, should be called Haeckelianism and not Darwinism. It was never Darwin's purpose to use his speculations as an attack upon religion, though they might readily lend themselves to this purpose.

* * * *

"We declare that every wise thought and every useful discovery, where-ever it may come from, should be gladly and gratefully welcomed." These words of Pope Leo XIII will sufficiently define the attitude of Catholics towards evolution. The Church is eager as any scientist can ever possibly be for the truth, but, as was already stated, she desires the whole truth and nothing but the truth.

There is no fact that science can demonstrate, "wherever it may come from," in the words of the Pontiff, or whatever it may be, that will not be "gladly and gratefully welcomed" by her and accounted as gain. Let it be clearly understood that there is no limit and no exception to this statement. No true child of hers is the Catholic scientist who harbors in his heart even the faintest suspicion that any discovery of science could ever contradict the Word of God. Least of all, however, is the Church ever to be startled by the word, "Evolution." Hear what the blind Jesuit orator, Father Robert Kane, has eloquently to say upon this subject:

Evolution? It is an old story told by old men, long ago.

Fourteen centuries ago, all the principles of evolution that are not irrational were taught by the great St. Augustine. He held that all things at first existed only as *Semina rerum* (the seeds of what was to be), that was at first in things only the potency of what, under the action and reaction of strong or slow forces, they should become; that during days which were epochs of unmeasured duration and of cumulative result, the Moulder of the world worked merely through natural elements and uniform laws, until the universe crystallized into order. He held indeed, as all who are not materialists must hold, that man's spiritual soul was not made of mere mud nor begotten of a monkey, but was created by the immediate power of God. Since Augustine, this theory has been commonly accepted as a probable hypothesis by Christian theologians.

There is as much wonder in an acorn as in an oak. In that bewildering world of interlocked atoms or rebounding vortices, of subtle gas or seething vapor, of dizzy whirl or aeonic change, of molten mass or adamantine ice, of eddying unison or of titanic clash, there was the potency, the germ of all that is or shall be.

Now we look upon the branching forth of that strange power which then was in the seed. But to go no further than an acorn for ultimate explanation of an oak, is to stop short upon the threshold of thought. To account for the oak, the acorn, and the universe, by the virtue of some primitive cell which held within it the potency of all worth and the energy of all power, which, yet, had no cause, no reason other than itself, is to change science into superstition, and to learn history from the *Arabian Nights*.

Is that facing the issue squarely? And of the great patristic writer of the Church above referred to, Father Wasmann says:

Even to St. Augustine it seemed a more exalted conception, and one more in keeping with the omnipotence and wisdom of an infinite Creator, to believe that God created matter by one act of creation, and then allowed the whole universe to develop automatically by means of the laws which He imposed upon the nature of matter.

God does not interfere directly with the natural order when He can work by natural causes: this is a fundamental principle in the Christian account of nature, and was enunciated by the great theologian, Suarez, whilst St. Thomas Aquinas plainly suggested it long before, when he regarded it as a testimony of the greatness of God's power, that His providence accomplishes its aims in nature not directly but by means of created causes.

It is therefore an old theory within the Church that the act of Creation took place at once, and that what followed was but an evolution according to the laws that God had given. Since a separate Creation, we have said, is philosophically required for the origin of life, it is supposed in this theory that the seed or seeds of life were virtually present *in semine* "in germ" and all living things were later evolved, under God's Providence, from the seeds thus created originally. The days of Creation are then explained as merely "marks of progression or indefinite periods." Father Hull thus interprets St. Augustine's hypothesis:

He says that while the original act of Creation was direct and simultaneous, the subsequent formation was gradual and progressive. He tells us distinctly that animals and plants were produced, not as they appear now, but virtually and in germ, and that the Creator gave to the earth the power of evolving from itself, by the operation of natural laws, the various forms of animal or vegetable life. His treatment of the subject, in fact, reads like the anticipation of a modern scientific treatise. His view did not "necessitate perpetual search for manifestations of miraculous powers and perpetual catastrophies" but a search "for the institution of laws of nature rather than interference with them."

St. Thomas Aquinas, in the thirteenth century, commenting on St. Augustine, declares that "in the institution of nature we do not look for miracles but for the laws of nature." He gives preference to the view of St. Augustine as against that of St. Basil, saying that "while the latter is more conformable to the text, the former is more reasonable, and better adapted to defend the Sacred Scriptures against attacks of unbelievers." As regards the apparent division of the creation-process into several parts, and the picture of God issuing successive edicts to bring successive events about, St. Augustine has some very wise words on the folly of trying to take all the statements of Genesis literally, and says:

"Although the creation is presented to us as though it took place in regular (*i.e.*, separate) sequence, yet it really took place at once." On this St. Thomas remarks: "And so Moses, since he was instructing an uneducated people about the work of Creation, divided up into parts what really took place at once."

Father Bernard J. Otten, in his learned work on the history of dogmas, writes of what these authors describe as the Augustine theory of evolution that: "Although the *rationes seminales* were implanted in matter at the beginning of time, nevertheless the actual production of finally complete beings is according to him [St. Augustine] the work of God, and not of matter alone." It is thus at all events distinct from all forms of materialistic evolution. In illustration the following quotation is offered from the writings of the Saint:

> The earth is then said to produce the herb and the tree casually—*i.e., it received the power to produce them. For in it were now made, as in the roots of time, those things which were afterwards to be produced in the course of time.* God afterwards planted Paradise, and brought forth of this earth all manner of trees fair to behold and pleasant to eat of. But we must not suppose that He added any new species (*creatura*) which He had not previously made, and which was needed to complete the perfection of which it is said that they were good. No, for all the species of plants and trees had been produced in the first creation (*conditione*), from which God rested, thenceforth moving and administering, as time went on, those same things, which He had formed. Not only did He then plant Paradise, but even now all things that are produced. For who else creates them now, but He who worketh until now? For he creates them now from things that already exist; then, when they had no existence whatever, and when that day (the first) was made.

It is very interesting to note in this connection how the Batesonian theory, described as Mendelism to the *n*th power, recalls the Augustinian view, surprised as its author may be to hear this mentioned. Every new evolution, according to him, was contained in the original organism. Variations are merely the result of removing something that prevented certain hidden characteristics from freely manifesting themselves. A reviewer of Professor Adami's *The Lecture on Life,* a medical contribution to the study of evolution, thus writes of Bateson's thesis in the Dublin *Review:*

> The theory logically necessitates the incredible view that the original microscopic sphere of protoplasm, which evolutionists postulate as the beginning of life, must have contained all the properties of all living things and therefore, must have been the most remarkably endowed organism ever existing. He says that "the potentiality was there, not the determinants." The last word being used, of course, in the Weismannian sense. We agree with him but would like to remind him that the sentence is almost a literal translation of St. Augustine's "*nihilominus potentialiter, quorum numerus tempus postea visibiliter explicaret.*" A short reflection may prevent the author from further jibes at medieval schoolmen.

It will suffice finally to quote upon our subject the statement of a foremost Catholic lay exponent in the scientific field whose labors have been of notable service to both science and Faith, and who in his own person shows the perfect harmony that exists between them.

To me, at least, it seems [Sir Bertram Windle says] as if the language of Peter Lombard and of St. Thomas Aquinas in commenting on St. Augustine, makes it clear that the teaching of the greatest and most influential Doctor in the history of the Church is quite consonant with any reasonable theory of evolution—*nay, it is broad and comprehensive enough to provide not only for whatever limited degree of evolution is yet fairly established, but even for anything that has even a remote probability of being proven in the future.* Nor am I deterred from coming to that conclusion by the very obvious criticism that the Saint did not state the doctrine with the clearness with which it is now laid down, a thing which no reasonable being would expect him to have done.

More need not be said. Catholic evolutionists, in brief, hold as probable the theory that the organic world has assumed its present form, "not in consequence of God's constant interference with the natural order, but as a result of the action of those laws which He Himself has implanted upon nature." In the question of the origin of species, there would thus be as many or as few *natural* species as there were primitive forms created, and the creation of these first organisms, so far as we may assume it, would not necessarily be out of nothing, but out of pre-existent matter, until we would finally come back to original creation in the strict sense of the word, such as reason postulates. Matter cannot be self-existent, philosophy teaches, nor can life be educed from dead matter. Here therefore at least two strictly understood creative acts are required by reason itself, as also in the creation of the rational soul of man.

The natural (*i.e.,* distinctly created) species would then be differentiated, by the process of evolution, into more or less systematic species, whose extent it is left to natural science to determine. "Eventually many hundreds of thousands of systematic species may unite to form one single line, one natural species." All this is understood to be pure, but perfectly legitimate, hypothesis, and by species are not understood *species metaphysicæ,* or logic; but *species physicæ,* or natural philosophy. Whatever therefore may be each one's private opinion—since it would be rash to speak of certainty on either side—every believing Jew or Christian can heartily subscribe to Wasmann's conclusion that whatever the fate of evolution may be, the Christian cosmogony remains as firmly established as ever.

Surely there is no need of trembling for the Rock on which Christ built His Church. True science will ever prove the strongest natural defense of religion. It is the breakwater on which every wave of false theory must eventually be dashed to foam and idle spray.

15

THE POPES AND SOCIAL REFORM *

Statesmen and businessmen occasionally complain that the Church has no business "meddling" in economic, political, or social affairs, that it should confine itself to "purely spiritual" matters and let secular organizations take care of social affairs. Such a complaint might be valid if social matters could be separated from moral and doctrinal considerations. The Church has no interest and no right to speak on purely technical matters, such as the most efficient way to organize an assembly line in a modern industrial plant. But it has a duty to speak when moral principles are involved and when man's dignity and rights are at stake. If organizing an assembly line in some way, for example, were to make exorbitant physical demands on some of the employees or violate their human dignity, then the Church would have the right to condemn such working conditions.

Christian social teaching was part of the framework of Western culture in medieval and early modern times. But the industrial organization of society in the nineteenth century was based on purely economic considerations. In effect, economics and sociology were divorced from morality and from religion. In the following selection Father Joseph N. Moody explains how under Pope Leo XIII the Church began to formulate a body of social teaching adapted to modern conditions. He explains how the popes limit themselves to stating general principles applicable to all countries, how they do not undertake to study technical problems, but how they are interested in the human, moral aspects of all social problems.

THE PONTIFICATE of Leo XIII marked the beginning of an official effort to restate the traditional social teaching of the Catholic Church in the context of modern industrialism. The social encyclicals did not initiate the movement. In large part they were the consequence of pioneering by social-minded lay and clerical Catholics in many of the countries affected by the new conditions. But with Leo's reign, the movement "captured" the Papacy in the way that the eleventh century

* Joseph N. Moody, ed., *Church and Society: Catholic Social and Political Thought & Movements 1789-1950* (New York: Arts, Inc., 1953), pp. 49-62. Reprinted by permission.

Reform had "captured" Leo IX or the Reform of the sixteenth century had Paul III. In 1878, the See of Peter was occupied by a man who was familiar with the broad social currents of the age and who was personally sympathetic to the needs of the industrial proletariat. From this time on, social issues were to receive major papal attention.

The materials for a Catholic social doctrine were already at hand. The Gospels inherently contained the outlines of a program, for Christ had given the religious and ethical foundations of human relations. The early Church Fathers, conscious of their social environment, had applied Christian principles, often with startling vigor, against the social abuses of their age. The Scholastic philosophers had systematized this teaching in the light of Medieval economic conditions. What was needed was not a search for principles but a new or fresh application of these principles to the radically different conditions of the nineteenth century.

As Archbishop of Perugia, Leo had been interested in the material well-being of his flock. In his pastoral letter of 1877, he had written of the "colossal abuses perpetrated against the poor and the weak" and had called for legislation to correct the "inhuman traffic" of children in factories. Upon becoming Pope, he took a special interest in the international meetings of social Catholics at Fribourg under the chairmanship of Msgr. Mermillod. Leo encouraged their investigations and, in his encyclicals, drew heavily on their conclusions.

To evaluate the work of Leo and his successors in this field, the following points must be considered:

1. The Popes have sought merely to formulate the moral directives that should govern economic life. They have claimed no competence in the purely technical aspects of production and distribution. But they have argued that religious authorities are justified in intervening in economic matters, not only because these matters profoundly affect human beings and are therefore subject to moral law, but also because the objectives of economics are themselves matters of moral concern. For instance, whereas no Pope would deem it within his competence or prerogative to write a text on military tactics, he would feel perfectly justified in writing or speaking on the ends for which a war might be fought, on the conditions of a just war, and on the treatment to be accorded prisoners and civilians.

2. The Popes have spoken for a world-wide audience; hence, they have confined themselves to general directives, leaving it to their followers in each country to apply the ethical norms to precise conditions.

3. The encyclicals carefully avoid the extreme positions of outright individualism or outright collectivism. Such an intermediate position is necessarily less amenable to exact formulation than the absolute asseverations of the simplifiers.

The social encyclicals build their ethical structure upon these basic assumptions:

1. Man is necessarily a social being. He is not sufficient unto himself

but needs his fellowmen in order to realize fully his powers and aspirations. This need to live in society adds a new dimension to man's rights and duties as an individual. Since man's social need is rooted in his nature, it must be attributed to the will of his Creator.

2. Man is the center of the universe, the greatest act of God's creation. Because he is a creature of God, possessed of a spiritual nature with reason and free will, destined for eternal life with God, every man has a sublime innate dignity that raises him above all creation. Thus, it is man who is, who must be the measure of all economic activity. No social arrangement is valid which denies man's essential worth. "The origin and the primary scope of social life is the conservation, development, and perfection of the human person. . . ." The major objective of all economic life is to provide a proper atmosphere for the fulfillment of man's capabilities.

3. Since man is sacred, he radically possesses "God-granted" rights. These are not conferred by society, nor are they the consequence of law and custom. They do not depend on the state or on the will of the community. They do not flow from expediency and social utility though these may strengthen man's claim to their possession. Human rights are inherent, inalienable. But they do not exist apart from duties, for duties and rights are correlative: each right implies a corresponding duty to recognize a right in others.

Human rights are not all on the same level: the primary ones are those most intimately connected with man's nature. Pius XI listed these in *Divini Redemptoris:*

> In consequence, man has been endowed by God with many and varied prerogatives: the right to life, to bodily integrity, to the necessary means of existence; the right to tend toward his ultimate goal in the path marked out for him by God; the right of association and the right to possess and use property . . .

Of these, the most sacred of all is the right to life. It necessarily implies the right to the possession of economic goods. This is not satisfied by mere subsistence that would not give title to a truly human condition of life. Human dignity demands opportunity for leisure in order that man may develop his intellectual and spiritual faculties. Also, man has a right to a family, for without family life his fundamental needs could not be satisfied.

4. The primary objective of a social order is justice, which may be defined as a recognition of such rights and duties of the human person as will result in each receiving his due. The concept of justice is essentially moral, and it can be secured only where moral values are recognized. Inherent in the idea of justice is the acceptance of the fundamental equality of the human person.

On the basis of these ethical principles, the Popes proceed to reject two common approaches to the social problem:

1. That of extreme individualism, as formulated by the Economic

Liberals. They declare it inadequate because it ignores the moral factor in human relations. Nor can its principle of competition be accepted as the sole regulator of the economic system. Competition has its place and is "certainly useful provided it is kept within certain limits, but it clearly cannot direct economic life—a truth which the outcome of the application in practice of the tenets of this evil individualistic spirit has more than sufficiently demonstrated." Among the undesirable consequences of unbridled competition are the failure to recognize man's need for security, the neglect of his human personality, waste, duplication, and the artificial stimulation of wants. Perhaps most serious is its final consequence: the consolidation of economic power in the hands of a few.

This concentration of power and might, the characteristic mark, as it were, of contemporary economic life, is the fruit that the unlimited freedom of struggle among competitors has of its own nature produced, and which lets only the strongest survive; and this is often the same as saying, those who fight the most violently, those who give least heed to their conscience. This accumulation of might and power generates in turn three kinds of conflict: first, there is the struggle for economic supremacy itself; then, there is the bitter fight to gain supremacy over the state in order to use in economic struggles its resources and authority; finally, there is the conflict between states themselves, not only because countries employ their power and shape their policies to promote every economic advantage of their citizens, but also because they seek to decide political controversies that arise among nations through the use of their economic supremacy and strength.

2. That of collectivism. Leo XIII censured materialistic Socialism as unjust and dangerous to the freedom of the human person. Pius XI, reaffirming the condemnation, notes that Socialism has split into two bitterly hostile sections. One of these, Communism, "has undergone almost the same change as the capitalistic economic system." It preaches class war, aims at violent revolution, and is absolutely indifferent to human rights. Its entire philosophy is repugnant to Christian teaching.

The other section, which has kept the name Socialism, is surely more moderate. It not only professes the rejection of violence, but modifies and tempers to some degree, if it does not reject entirely, the class struggle and the abolition of private ownership. One might say that, terrified by its own principles and by the conclusions drawn therefrom by Communism, Socialism inclines toward, and in a certain measure approaches, the truth which denied that its demands at times come very near those that Christian reformers of society justly insist upon . . . it can even come to the point that imperceptibly these ideas of the more moderate Socialism will no longer differ from the desires and demands of those who are striving to remould human society on the basis of Christian principles.

But insofar as it has retained its initial materialistic philosophy, it is still in error.

Having rejected these alternatives, the Popes set forth these constructive points as guides to the solution of the social question:

I. *Reform of morals.* Since the social question is not merely economic it cannot be improved without moral reform. Men will be self-centered or God-centered. Only if they discover a principle outside themselves will they recognize the objectives of justice and charity. If men are to live together, they must practice virtue: they must cultivate moderation and benevolence, and restrain excessive desire for wealth, insatiable greed, and a thirst for pleasure. Many have lost all sense of conscience in the grim battle for economic advantage. Individualism encourages greed, and corruption is inevitable. As a consequence, men are often wretched amid abundance. Happiness does not depend on material possessions.

Catholics are not exempted from these strictures. Some

are almost completely unmindful of that sublime law of justice and charity that binds us not only to render to everyone what is his but to succor brothers in need as Christ, the Lord Himself; and, what is worse, out of greed for gain do not scruple to exploit the workers. Even more, there are men who abuse religion itself, and under its name try to hide their unjust exactions in order to protect themselves from the manifestly just demands of the workers. The conduct of such We shall never cease to censure gravely.

True religion is still a necessary ingredient of the social order. Man's freedom rests on an assertion of his spirituality; so do his rights and his dignity. Man cannot recapture the necessary reverence for work without religious motivation. Nor is there any truth in the charge that Christians are so preoccupied with the next world that they have no concern for this. On the contrary, everything material takes on a new importance, for it is by use of the material that man gains eternal life. "A convinced Christian witnesses the needs and miseries of his brothers."

II. *Self-help through organization.* A constant theme in the social encyclicals is the right of labor to organize to protect its interests and to fulfill its needs. Leo XIII called this "a right of nature" which the state cannot deny. As a consequence of the right to associate freely, workers have the right "to adopt the organization and the rules which they judge most appropriate to achieve their purpose." Only through organization can the individual worker protect himself from entrenched power—and he has the greatest need of this protection.

The basis of this prerogative is the principle that the worker has the right to those things consonant with his human dignity. By individual effort, he cannot present his views effectively or marshal power to win attention. Even though his material interests be secure, he still needs his union as a coordinating and representative body; indeed, if the class-war mentality is to be replaced by cooperation, workers must have organization.

Certain conclusions follow from the oft-repeated affirmation of the natural right of workers to organize. On the principle that all rights have correlative duties, it is clear that employers must recognize duly constituted labor unions. Moreover, it is equally evident that these unions have the right to strike for valid ends and with lawful means. As the Australian Hierarchy declared:

> Under modern conditions, the right to organize in trade unions and the right to strike, under certain defined conditions, are inseparable. It would be futile to urge the formation of trade unions if the Church did not realize this recognition of the right to strike as a last resort, and when other measures of achieving social justice have failed.

Finally, it may be argued that workers have an obligation to organize. Without this first step, there can be no further institutional reform; just conditions in an industrial unit do not depend entirely on the good will of an individual employer but on the ensemble of economic conditions in the industry, which conditions cannot be assured without industry-wide labor organization.

Not only has the industrial worker the right to organize, but, according to the papal encyclicals, all other groups are equally urged to do so. Employers, farmers, clerical and civil service personnel, even professional people have need of organization. Only if all classes have appropriate social units will it be possible to proceed to that radical transformation of society the Popes propose.

The encyclicals recognize the reality of class conflict. Pius XI terms it "the deadly internal struggle that is rending the family of mankind" and "a conflict between hostile classes." But such a condition is not desirable. The State and every good citizen should work to the abatement of the class struggle. Harmonious cooperation must be developed among various social groups. This is not Utopian: industrial production has been a unifying as well as a divisive force, and the modern urbanized community is much more closely integrated than the pre-industrial agricultural societies. Besides, basic social improvement depends on higher levels of production, and these cannot be achieved in an atmosphere of conflict.

As one can see, the Popes sketch the ideal toward which industrial society must move:

> The time has come to repudiate empty phrases, and to attempt to organize the forces of the people on a new basis; to raise them above the distinction between employers and would-be workers, and to realize that higher unity which is a bond between all those who cooperate in production, formed by their solidarity in the duty of working together for the common good and filling together the needs of the community. If this solidarity is extended to all branches of production, if it becomes the foundation for a better economic system, it will lead the working classes to obtain honestly their share of responsibility in the direction of the national economy . . .

The realization of this ideal demands the acceptance of the Industrial Council Plan. This is neither a rigid blueprint nor a magic nostrum but an institutional reform that would encourage a new attitude in industrial relations and promote the intelligent cooperation of capital and labor. The basis of the Plan is the association of trade unions and managerial bodies on all levels: plant, industry, the whole economy; local, regional, national, and international. These bodies of employers and employees would determine wages and industrial conditions; control prices and profits; plan the quality, quantity, and distribution of the product; fix the qualifications for workers; arrange pensions, insurance plans, and other social benefits; associate the workers in production in order that their experience might be utilized to improve methods; and, on the highest levels, discuss general policy for the development of industry, technological changes, and access to raw materials.

In presenting this Plan as the ultimate objective of social reform, the Popes are anxious to avoid two misconceptions:

1. That the organization of industry would eliminate competition. Obviously, this factor would no longer be supreme, as it certainly is not in fact in our contemporary society; but it would not disappear. Cooperation in fixing the rules of the game does not destroy competition in sports; nor would it in business.

2. More importantly, that the Plan would be tantamount to governmental direction of the economy. Precisely because of the perversions of Fascism, Pius XI, when discussing the Plan in *Quadragesimo Anno,* used the word "free" five times in a single paragraph. The very purpose of this free association of autonomous groupings would be to protect them from giant power, either political or economic, and to encourage free activity without dependence on the impersonal State. These groups are not to be *organs of the State,* nor are their representatives to be chosen by the political power. The essence of the Plan is its voluntary character. Hence, the Popes expect it to be achieved only by evolution. The State would have only the general, regulatory power that it exercises over all private and semi-private associations.

III. *Wider ownership of productive property.* The encyclicals approach this broad question from the viewpoint of the dignity of human labor. They explicitly reject the Liberal Economists' definition of labor as a commodity. "No one should be ashamed because he makes his living by toil," for labor has been sanctified by the example of Christ and is an important contributor to virtuous living. These ends, however, cannot be secured if workers are subjected to conditions which belie their human dignity. Workers must not be treated as slaves or regarded as engaged in shameful activity.

> It is inhuman to use men as things of gain and to put no more value on them than they are worth in muscle or energy. . . . Likewise, more work is not to be imposed than strength can endure, nor that kind of work which is unsuited to a worker's age or sex.

Since men are morally equal and intrinsically valuable, they shall not be prevented, because of exhausting hours of work and inhuman conditions, from making their just contribution to society. And in justice they must be granted a living wage. Leo XIII struck a fundamental and often casually ignored truth when he wrote:

> . . . it is incontestable that the wealth of nations arises from no other source than from the labor of workers. Equity therefore commands that public authority show proper concern for the worker so that from what he contributes to the common good, he may receive what may enable him . . . to live his life without hardship.

All wage contracts that take advantage of a worker's need by paying him less than is sufficient for his decent support are immoral. To be sure, mere payment of a subsistence wage is not enough. Since man has the right to family life, he must receive a wage adequate for the support of wife and children in decent comfort. Finally, he cannot be denied the opportunity to acquire a modest fortune and "so make suitable provision through public or private insurance for old age, and for periods of illness and unemployment."

Certain consequences follow from this principle of the living wage:

1. It justifies the workers' right to unions and collective bargaining.
2. It implies that women should get equal pay for equal work, both in justice and by way of preventing the depression of wage standards.
3. Payment of a living wage is due "in strict justice" ; consequently, employers who are able to pay it and do not are bound to restitution.
4. The standard of a living wage is not absolute but relative to the resources and economic situation in a given country; still, it can never fall below a basic minimum.
5. Because most industrial workers depend on their wage, work is a right to which man is justly entitled. Property owners have a duty to provide work and, where they cannot, the State must intervene.
6. Failure to provide a living, family wage often ends, deplorably enough, in the practice of engaging child and female labor in industrial establishments.

> To abuse the years of childhood and the limited strength of women is grossly wrong. Mothers, concentrating on household duties, should work primarily in the home or in its immediate vicinity. It is an intolerable abuse, to be abolished at all costs, for mothers, on account of the fathers' low wage to be forced to engage in gainful occupations outside the home to the neglect of their proper cares and duties, especially the training of children. Every effort must therefore be made that fathers of families receive a wage large enough to meet ordinary family needs adequately . . .

7. A just wage, for all of that, is not the final goal of the workers' participation in the fruits of industry.

> We consider it more advisable, however, in the present condition of modern society that, as far as is possible, the work contract be somewhat modified by a partnership contract, as is already being done in various ways and with no small advantage to owners and workers. Workers and other employees thus become sharers in ownership and management or participate in some fashion in the profits received.

8. Work, like ownership, has a social as well as individual character, which can never be ignored.

These considerations on the dignity of labor and the right to a just wage are necessary to appreciate the doctrine of property that appears in the social encyclicals. In large part, the doctrine is based on St. Thomas: property is desirable and natural to man in the present order of human society, and is productive of the best social results. His arguments for private property are largely utilitarian, laying particular emphasis on its value as a preservative of human freedom. But as regards its use: "Man ought to possess external things, not as his own, but as common, so that, to wit, he is ready to communicate to them in need."

This distinction of St. Thomas between the individual and social aspects of private property is preserved in the encyclicals. The Popes assert the right of private property in order that "individuals may provide for themselves and their families," but stress also the social obligations that are inherent in its possession.

Private property is not an absolute right, but is a "right circumscribed by the necessities of social living." While abuses do not destroy the right, they have led men to question it, for some "so interpret and use the relationships of private property that they succeed—even better than their adversaries—in overturning this very institution, so natural and indispensable to human life, and especially to the family."

The ownership of private property involves duties. Men are only the stewards of the goods which God has given. Property is a trust, and superflous wealth must be devoted to charity or used to promote new opportunities for employment. The social aspects of property become more prominent when there is question of productive property. All property, especially the latter type, must be regulated in the interest of the common good though not to the point of collectivization. The owners of property have also responsibilities toward the State, and taxation should be imposed progressively according to ability to pay.

The Popes always insist that property be extended to include the largest possible number as owners. The aim, therefore, should

. . . not (be) to abolish private property, which is the foundation of family stability, but to work for its extension as the reward of the conscientious toil of every working man and woman. . .

The Church is opposed to the accumulation of these goods in the hands of a relatively small and exceedingly rich group, while vast masses of people are condemned to a pauperism and an economic condition unworthy of human beings. The immense multitude of non-owning workers on the one hand, and the enormous riches of certain very wealthy men on the other, establish an unanswerable argument that the riches which are so abundantly produced in our age of "industrialism," as it is called, are not rightly distributed and equitably made available to the various classes of people. Therefore, with all our strength and effort we must strive that at least in the future, the abundant fruits of production will accrue equitably to those who are rich and will be distributed in ample sufficiency among the workers . . . that they may increase their property by thrift . . . and have assurance that, when their lives are ended, they will provide in some measure for those they leave after them.

IV. *Sound social legislation.* The welfare concept, so much a matter of present controversy, is advocated in the papal encyclicals. The philosophical basis, again, is the value of the human person. The State has the right and duty to interfere in the economic process when the welfare of the whole society is at stake or where the rights of an individual or of a group are threatened. Especially must legislation "prevent the worker, who is or will be a father of a family, from being condemned to an economic dependence and slavery which is irreconcilable with his rights as a person."

Quadragesimo Anno praised the progress that had been made in this field of social legislation during the forty years before it. It reiterated the position of Leo XIII that

> government must not be a mere guardian of law and good order, but rather must put forth effort that "through the entire scheme of laws and institutions . . . both public and individual well-being may develop spontaneously out of the very structure and administration of the State." Just freedom of action must, of course, be left both to individuals and to families, yet only on condition that the common good be preserved and wrong to any individual be abolished. The function of the rulers of the State, moreover, is to watch over the community and its parts; but in protecting private individuals in their rights chief consideration ought to be given to the weak and the poor.

The State must regulate private property in the common interest; it thus furnishes a service to owners and strengthens property rights by preventing intolerable evils. It should not succumb to the evil of individualism but recall that one of its primary functions is to benefit the condition of the workers. On this basis, the Popes approve a wide range of welfare legislation.

One caution is introduced: the State ought to allow subordinate groups to handle matters of lesser importance and should confine itself to "directing, watching, urging, restraining, as occasion requires and necessity demands." This is the principle of "subsidiarity," so frequently referred to in papal documents. "The State should be the coordinator and supreme guardian, encouraging private groups where possible and intervening only where necessary to correct abuses."

This principle is applied to the problem of nationalization. Complete nationalization is unequivocally condemned. But where there is danger of excessive individual concentration of economic power, nationalization is approved:

> For certain kinds of property, it is rightly contended, ought to be reserved to the State, since they carry with them a dominating power so great that they cannot without danger to the general welfare be entrusted to private individuals.

But in general, public control is preferable to public ownership; likewise, limited public ownership on the model of the TVA is more desirable than the absorption by the State of a whole segment of the economy.

V. *Organization of international economic life.* The economic relations among nations should aim at such a harmony and cooperation as should be the goal of the classes within the national economy. Nations are historic facts, but they should not ignore the larger truth that

the human race is bound together by reciprocal ties, moral and juridical, into a great commonwealth directed to the good of all nations and ruled by special laws which protect its unity and promote its prosperity. Now no one can fail to see how the claim to absolute autonomy for the State stands in open opposition to this natural law that is inherent in man—nay, denies it utterly—and therefore, leaves the stability of international relations at the mercy of the will of rulers, while it destroys the possibility of true union and fruitful collaboration directed to the general good.

As leaders of a supranational religious community, the Popes had little tolerance of the economic nationalism that played such a large role in the history of this century. They consistently pleaded that "all nations have a right to live and seek prosperity." They opposed "the egoism which tends to hoard economic resources and materials destined for the use of all, to such an extent that the nations less favored by nature are not permitted access to them." Evidences of a disposition on the part of possessing nations to share their riches were warmly praised. But much remains to be done:

In international trade relations, let all means be sedulously employed for the removal of those artificial barriers to economic life which are the effects of distrust and hatred. All must remember that the peoples of the earth form one family in God.

Barriers to emigration are equally deplored. The favorable distribution of men over the surface of the earth "which God created and prepared for the use of all" is both a human and economic boon. Emigration will be a real asset to the recipient country if it will give the newcomers a plot of land. Thus,

the thickly inhabited areas will be relieved and their peoples will receive new friends in foreign countries; and the states which receive the emigrants will acquire industrious citizens. In this way, the nations which give and those which receive will both contribute to the increased welfare of man and the progress of human culture.

In all international matters the principle is the same:

Since the various nations largely depend on one another in economic matters and need one another's help, they should strive with a united purpose and effort to promote by wisely conceived pacts and institutions a prosperous and happy international cooperation in economic life.

* * * *

The social encyclicals concentrate on the moral aspects of the social problem. As the summary given above indicates, the term "moral" stresses the human factors in economics. Religion is necessarily involved. Men must be human beings before they can be Christians, and it is difficult to preach virtue if the foundations of human living are destroyed.

The Popes, while stressing the importance of moral and religious remedies, do not claim that these are sufficient. We might compare their analysis to the distinction that should be made today between Soviet imperialism and Communism. The former can be met primarily by military means although the moral factor is an element in military strength. The latter cannot be repelled by arms but must be fought by intellectual and spiritual weapons, as well as by social reform. In economic questions, problems of unemployment and production are largely technical; but the overall purpose of economic activity and of factors such as distribution have important moral aspects. It is to these that the Popes have directed their attention.

Finally, the Popes do not intend the encyclicals to remain essays in ethical elucidation. The documents are studded with demands that Catholics translate these principles into concrete action. The clergy are particularly urged to interest themselves in social matters, to study them scientifically, and to work for the economic betterment of their flocks. To them was addressed the command: "Go to the workingman, especially where he is poor; and, in general, go to the poor."

> If you truly love the laborer (and you must love him because his conditions of life approach nearer to those of the Divine Master), you must assist him materially and religiously: materially, bringing about in his favor the practice not only of commutative justice but also of social justice, that is, all those provisions which aim at relieving the condition of the proletarian; and then religiously, giving him again the religious comforts without which he will struggle in a materialism that brutalizes him and degrades him.

The laity too must engage: "The first and immediate apostles to the workers ought to be workers; the apostles to those who follow industry and trade ought to be from among themselves." A constant theme is that Catholic Action must be a social apostolate and work for the betterment of economic conditions. In this effort, the Catholic press can play a prominent role.

16

THE MEANING OF SECULARISM *

The history of Western civilization in modern times could be written around the theme of the secularization of Western man's thought and action. Secularism means pushing God out of man's life and transferring various functions from religious to secular authority. The Renaissance and the Protestant Revolt, with which modern history begins, were essentially secularistic movements. The Deism of the seventeenth and eighteenth centuries denied Providence and restricted God to a single act of creation, after which He had to withdraw so that man could run his own world. The French Revolution was a gigantic act of secularization in which Church property was confiscated, religious functions were assumed by the state, and la Patrie *was divinized.*

In the following brief selection the American bishops show how Christian freedoms are logically impossible in a world that ignores God and denies the distinction between the spiritual and the political. For if God is denied, all things are rendered unto Caesar. Secularism is the breeding ground of totalitarian regimes, for it removes the most effective brake on political power. Moreover, it robs human life of its meaning, its depth and richness when it denies eternal considerations and their effect on daily life. Secularism deadens literature and the fine arts by denying man that mysterious character which comes from his having been made to the image of the Creator, being the free lord of the universe and still a mere creature. Secularism, it can be said, robs life of its romance and its high adventure by making it a pedestrian, dull, day-to-day, birth-to-death existence without any meaning above the physical.

An awareness of how secularism has worked its way progressively into Western man's life will enable the student to understand the significance of a great many historical events that might otherwise be lost upon him. He will see, for example, how national anthems, patriotic processions national holidays are all secularized versions of what were originally

* Statement by the Hierarchy of the United States (issued through the administrative board) on November 14, 1947. Published by the National Catholic Welfare Council, Washington 5, D.C. Reprinted by permission.

religious observances. And he will see how many functions performed by the modern state were once taken care of by religious authorities. He will then understand what the bishops mean when they say that most of our modern difficulties stem from secularism.

NO MAN can disregard God—and play a man's part in God's world. Unfortunately, however, there are many men—and their number is daily increasing—who in practice live their lives without recognizing that this is God's world. For the most part they do not deny God. On formal occasions they may even mention His name. Not all of them would subscribe to the statement that all moral values derive from merely human conventions. But they fail to bring an awareness of their responsibility to God into their thought and action as individuals and members of society.

This, in essence, is what we mean by secularism. It is a view of life that limits itself not to the material in exclusion of the spiritual, but to the human here and now in exclusion of man's relation to God here and hereafter. Secularism, or the practical exclusion of God from human thinking and living, is at the root of the world's travail today. It was the fertile soil in which such social monstrosities as Fascism, Nazism, and Communism could germinate and grow. It is doing more than anything else to blight our heritage of Christian culture, which integrates the various aspects of human life and renders to God the things that are God's. Throught the centuries, Christian culture has struggled with man's inborn inclination to evil. The ideals of Christianity have never been fully realized—just as the ideals of our Declaration of Independence and of our Constitution have never been fully realized in American political life. But for that reason these ideals can neither be ignored nor discarded. Without doubt, Christians have often failed to meet their responsibilities and by their transgressions have permitted ugly growths to mar the institutions of their culture. But wherever, despite their lapses, they have held steadfastly to their Christian ideals, the way to effective reform and progress has been kept open. The remedy for the shortcomings and sins of Christian peoples is surely not to substitute secularism for godliness, human vagaries for divine truth, man-made expedients for a God-given standard of right and wrong. This is God's world and if we are to play a man's part in it, we must first get down on our knees and with humble hearts acknowledge God's place in His world. This, secularism does not do.

Secularism, in its impact on the individual, blinds him to his responsibility to God. All the rights, all the freedoms of man derive originally from the fact that he is a human person, created by God after His own image and likeness. In this sense he is "endowed by his Creator with certain inalienable Rights." Neither reason nor history offers any other solid ground for man's inalienable rights. It is as God's creature that man generally and most effectively recognizes a personal responsibility to seek his own moral perfection. Only a keen awareness of personal responsibility to God develops in a man's soul the saving sense of sin. Without a deep-felt conviction of what sin is, human law and human conventions can never lead man to virtue. If in the privacy of his personal life the individual does not acknowledge accountability to God for his thought and his action, he lacks the only foundation for stable moral values. Secularism does away with accountability to God as a practical consideration in the life of man and thus takes from him the sense of personal guilt of sin before God. It takes account of no law above man-made law. Expediency, decency, and propriety are, in its code, the norms of human behavior. It blurs, if it does not blot out, the ennobling and inspiring picture of man which the Christian Gospel paints. In divine revelation, man is the son of God as well as God's creature. Holiness is his vocation, and life's highest values have to do with things of the soul. "For what does it profit a man, if he gain the whole world, but suffer the loss of his own soul? Or what will a man give in exchange for his soul?" Secularism may quote these words of Christ, but never in their full Christian sense. For that very reason secularism blights the noblest aspirations in man which Christianity has implanted and fostered. Unfortunately, many who still profess to be Christians are touched by this blight. The greatest moral catastrophe of our age is the growing number of Christians who lack a sense of sin because a personal responsibility to God is not a moving force in their lives. They live in God's world, quite unmindful of Him as their Creator and Redeemer. The vague consciousness of God which they may retain is impotent as a motive in daily conduct. The moral regeneration which is recognized as absolutely necessary for the building of a better world must begin by bringing the individual back to God and to an awareness of his responsibility to God. This, secularism, of its very nature, cannot do.

Secularism has wrought havoc in the family. Even the pagans saw something sacred in marriage and the family. In Christian doctrine its holiness is so sublime that it is likened to the Mystical Union of Christ and His Church. Secularism has debased the marriage contract by robbing it of its relation to God and, therefore, of its sacred character. It has set the will and convenience of husband and wife in the place that Christian thought gives to the will of God and the good of society.

A secularized pseudo science has popularized practices which violate nature itself and rob human procreation of its dignity and nobility. Thus, selfish pursuit of pleasure is substituted for salutary self-discipline in family life.

Secularism has completely undermined the stability of the family as a divine institution and has given our country the greatest divorce problem in the Western world. In taking God out of family life, it has deprived society's basic educational institution of its most powerful means in molding the soul of the child. Public authority and the press are constantly emphasizing our grave problem of juvenile delinquency. On all sides is heard the cry that something be done about the problem. Our profound conviction is that nothing much will ever be done about it unless we go to the root of the evil and learn the havoc that secularism has wrought in the family. In vain shall we spend public moneys in vast amounts for educational and recreational activities if we do not give more thought to the divinely ordained stability of the family and the sanctity of the home.

God planned the human family and gave it its basic constitution. When secularism discards that plan and constitution it lacerates the whole social fabric. Artificial family planning on the basis of contraceptive immorality, cynical disregard of the noble purposes of sex, a sixtyfold increase in our divorce rate during the past century, and widespread failure of the family to discharge its educational functions are terrible evils which secularism has brought to our country. What hope is there of any effective remedy unless men bring God back into family life and respect the laws He has made for this fundamental unit of human society?

In no field of social activity has secularism done more harm than in education. In our own country secularists have been quick to exploit for their own purposes the public policy adopted a century ago of banning the formal teaching of religion from the curriculum of our common schools. With a growing number of thoughtful Americans, we see in this policy a hasty and shortsighted solution of the very difficult educational problem that confronts public authority in a nation of divided religious allegiance. But it should ever be kept in mind that the original proponents of the policy did not intend to minimize the importance of religion in the training of youth. Erroneously, however, secularists take this policy, adopted as a practical expedient in difficult circumstances, and make it the starting point in their philosophy of education. They positively exclude God from the school. Among them are some who smile indulgently at the mention of the name of God and express wonder that inherited illusions last so long. Others are content with keeping God closeted in the inner chambers of private life.

In the rearing of children and the forming of youth, omission is as effective as positive statement. A philosophy of education which omits God, necessarily draws a plan of life in which God either has no place or is a strictly private concern of men. There is a great difference between a practical arrangement which leaves the formal teaching of religion to the family and to the Church, and the educational theory of the secularist, who advisedly and avowedly excludes religion from his program of education. The first, reluctantly tolerated under certain conditions as a practical measure of public policy, may actually serve to emphasize the need of religious instruction and training, and to encourage public school administrators to co-operate with home and Church in making it possible. The other strikes at the very core of our Christian culture and in practice envisions men who have no sense of their personal and social responsibility to God. Secularism breaks with our historical American tradition. When parents build and maintain schools in which their children are trained in the religion of their fathers, they are acting in the full spirit of that tradition. Secularists would invade the rights of parents, and invest the State with supreme powers in the field of education; they refuse to recognize the God-given place that parents have in the education of their children. God is an inescapable fact, and one cannot make a safe plan for life in disregard of inescapable facts. Our youth problems would not be so grave if the place of God in life were emphasized in the rearing of children. There would be less danger for the future of our democratic institutions if secularism were not so deeply intrenched in much of our thinking on education.

Economic problems loom large in the social unrest and confusion of our times. Research students of varying shades of opinion are seeking the formula for a sound program of economic reform. Their common objective is a beneficent social order that will establish reasonable prosperity, provide families with an adequate income, and safeguard the public welfare. The Christian view of social order rejects the postulate of inexorable economic laws which fix recurring cycles of prosperity and depression. It lays the blame for instability in our social structure on human failure rather than on blind and incontrollable economic forces. It faces the plain fact that there is something gravely wrong in our economic life and sees in secularism, with its disregard of God and God's law, a potent factor in creating the moral atmosphere which has favored the growth of this evil. Pointedly, indeed, has an eminent modern economist called attention to the fact that "in one hundred and fifty years economic laws were developed and postulated as iron necessities in a world apart from Christian obligation and sentiment." He adds: "The early nineteenth century was full of economic doctrine and practice which, grounded in its own necessity and immutability, crossed the dictates of Christian feeling and teaching with only a limited sense of incongruity and still less of indignation."

God created man and made him brother to his fellow man. He gave man the earth and all its resources to be used and developed for the good of all. Thus, work of whatever sort is a social function, and personal profit is not the sole purpose of economic activity. In the Christian tradition, the individual has the right to reasonable compensation for his work, the right to acquire private property, and the right to a reasonable income from productive invested capital. Secularism takes God out of economic thinking and thereby minimizes the dignity of the human person endowed by God with inalienable rights and made responsible to Him for corresponding individual and social duties. Thus, to the detriment of man and society, the divinely established balance in economic relations is lost.

In Christian thought the work of man is not a commodity to be bought and sold, and economic enterprise is an important social function in which owner, manager, and workman co-operate for the common good. When disregard of his responsibility to God makes the owner forget his stewardship and the social function of private property, there comes that irrational economic individualism which brings misery to millions. Helpless workers are exploited; cutthroat competition and antisocial marketing practices follow. When men in labor organizations lose the right social perspective, which a sense of responsibility to God gives, they are prone to seek merely the victory of their own group, in disregard of personal and property rights. The Christian view of economic life supports the demand for organization of management, labor, agriculture, and professions under government encouragement but not control, in joint effort to avoid social conflict and to promote co-operation for the common good. In default of this free co-operation, public authority is finally invoked to maintain a measure of economic order, but it frequently exceeds the just limits of its power to direct economic activity to the common good. In the extreme case, where Marxian Communism takes over government, it abolishes private ownership and sets up a totalitarian State capitalism, which is even more intolerable than the grave evils it pretends to cure. Surely it ought to be plain today that there is no remedy for our economic evils in a return either to nineteenth-century individualism or to experiments in Marxianism. If we abandon secularism and do our economic thinking in the light of Christian truth, we can hopefully work for economic collaboration in the spirit of genuine democracy. Let us be on our guard against all who, in exiling God from the factory and the market place, destroy the solid foundation of brotherhood in ownership, in management, and in work.

In the international community there can be only one real bond of sane common action—the natural law which calls to God, its Author, and derives from Him its sanctions. There is objective right and objective wrong in international life. It is true that positive human law which comes from treaties and international conventions is necessary, but even these covenants must be in accord with God-given natural law. What may seem to be expedient for a nation cannot be tolerated if it contravenes God's law of right and wrong. In the international community that law has been flouted more openly, more widely, and more disastrously in our day than ever before in the Christian centuries. Shocking crimes against weak nations are being perpetrated in the name of national security. Millions of men in many nations are in the thralldom of political slavery. Religion is persecuted because it stands for freedom under God. The most fundamental human rights are violated with utter ruthlessness in a calculated, systematic degradation of man by blind and despotic leaders. Details of the sad and sickening story seep through the wall of censorship which encloses police States. Men long for peace and order, but the world stands on the brink of chaos. It is significant that godless forces have brought it there. Nazism and Fascism and Japanese militarism lie buried in the debris of some of the fairest cities of the world they vowed to rule or to ruin. Atheistic Communism, for a time thrown into alliance with democratic nations through Nazi aggression against Russia, stands out plainly today as the force which, through violence and chicanery, is obstructing the establishment of a right juridical order in the international community. That is plain for all to see. But thoughtful men perceive as well that secularism, which over the years has sapped the divinely laid foundations of the moral law, bears a heavy burden of responsibility for the plight of the world today.

Secularism which exiles God from human life clears the way for the acceptance of godless subversive ideologies—just as religion, which keeps God in human life, has been the one outstanding opponent of totalitarian tyranny. Religion has been its first victim; for tyrants persecute what they fear. Thus secularism, as the solvent of practical religious influence in the everyday life of men and nations, is not indeed the most patent, but in a very true sense the most insidious hindrance to world reconstruction within the strong framework of God's natural law. There would be more hope for a just and lasting peace if the leaders of the nations were really convinced that secularism which disregards God, as well as militant atheism which utterly denies Him, offer no sound basis for stable international agreements for enduring respect for human rights or for freedom under law.

In the dark days ahead we dare not follow the secularist philosophy. We must be true to our historic Christian culture. If all who believe in God would make that belief practical in their workaday lives, if they would see to it that their children are definitely imbued with that belief and trained in the observance of God's way of life, if they would look across the real differences which unfortunately divide them, to the common danger that threatens, if they would steadfastly refuse to let a common enemy capitalize on those differences to the detriment of social unity, we might begin to see a way out of the chaos that impends. Secularism holds out no valid promise of better things for our country or for the world. During our own lives it has been the bridge between a decaying devotion to Christian culture and the revolutionary forces which have brought on what is perhaps the gravest crisis in all history. The tragic evil is not that our Christian culture is no longer capable of producing peace and reasonable prosperity, but that we are allowing secularism to divorce Christian truth from life. The fact of God and the fact of the responsibility of men and nations to God for their actions are supreme realities, calling insistently for recognition in a truly realistic ordering of life in the individual, in the family, in the school, in economic activity, and in the international community.

17

TOWARD A DEFINITION OF LIBERALISM *

The loose use of words like "Liberalism" creates confusion in history writing and leads the student into making incorrect judgments on historical events. The body of thought called "Liberalism" a century ago, for example, was quite similar to the thought now labelled "Conservatism" in this country. A century ago Liberals wanted to confine the government to a purely negative role in society. They insisted on the benefits of unlimited private enterprise, free bargaining for wages and prices, and the freest reign possible to individual initiative. Today, however, Liberals advocate a large role for the government in economic and social matters, and they want individual enterprise closely regulated by the state.

Much confusion would be avoided if the word were dropped from our vocabulary. But it will go on being used. In the following selection the author suggests that the student would do well to find out what "Liberalism" stands for at each period in history. The body of doctrine called "Liberalism" differs according to 1) the established powers and authorities of the time; 2) the intellectual and cultural tradition of a nation; and 3) the general "climate of opinion" in which it is formulated. Thus Liberalism tends to be anti-clerical in countries where an established church has considerable authority over social, political, and economic matters. It tends to be deductive, abstract, and absolute in countries like France with a strong rationalistic tradition. And it tends to be chiefly economic, temporizing, and somewhat amorphous in a country like England.

The following selection attempts to suggest the various meanings Liberalism has had in the century and a half it has been in Western man's vocabulary, to classify the various kinds of Liberalism, and to indicate how they differ from each other and how they still have something in common.

* Thomas P. Neill, *The Rise and Decline of Liberalism* (Milwaukee: The Bruce Publishing Company, 1953), pp. 3-32. Reprinted by permission.

Max Lerner has written that Liberalism is "perhaps the most disputed term of our generation." Writers and speakers who disagree vehemently with Lerner and with each other on the meaning of Liberalism and on the worth of its program do at least subscribe to this statement. Such opposite-minded persons as John T. Flynn and Norman Thomas, for example, are in accord on this one point. "No word has been subjected to more bizarre uses than the word 'Liberalism,'" according to the former, and, according to the latter, "No word, not even Christianity or socialism, is used to cover a greater or more contradictory variety of thought and action than Liberalism."

"Liberty" is a beautiful word in any language. Its connotations have always been appealing, noble, high-minded. It is hard to find philosophers who inveigh against it, and even harder to find politicians who advocate its suppression—except perhaps as a temporary thing and for what they claim is a greater good. The adjective "liberal" imputes loftiness of view, concern with things of the spirit, a respect for human decency. "Illiberal," on the other hand, is a word of ugly connotation. It implies smallness of soul, pettiness of outlook, selfishness of nature. Everyone, then, wants to be considered liberal in this sense. The noun "Liberal," however, does not have so universally acceptable a meaning. Early in 1949 the New York *Herald Tribune* asked its readers to write their own simple and concise definitions of the term "Liberal." Definitions ran the gamut from "one who wants someone else to support him, to think for him . . . to protect him from those who would impose on him responsibilities," to one who "acts as though he believes that man is made in the image of God and that the nurture, development and release of that God-likeness are his first duty and only wholly worthy employment." Although some considered the term degrading, still the great majority defined it as a term of honor. The editors of the *Herald Tribune* found, however, that the replies were "generally vague" and that Liberalism "has ceased to be either a concrete program of action or a consistent body of doctrine."

One would expect philosophers to have more precise ideas on the meaning of the term. But when the American Philosophical Association held a symposium on "The Crisis of Liberalism" in 1935, the only thing apparent was that the philosophers did not agree on the meaning of their topic. In one address Professor Jordan of Butler University condemned "The False Principle of Liberalism." He was followed by a professor who spoke glowingly in favor of contemporary Liberalism—and there was nothing on which the two disagreed. Obviously they were talking about different things to which they attached the same name. So it went throughout the program. Each speaker had his own peculiar concept of Liberalism; there was no meeting of philosophical minds.

Even worse, the word is used in contrary and in contradictory senses. Herbert Hoover wrote an encomium to Liberalism when he believed that the New Deal threatened our basic liberties, and in this book he said many fine things about the Christian tradition and the worth of the human person. But his "Liberalism" was better described, even in 1934, as "Conservatism." About the same time the Marxist quarterly *Science and Society* was using the term to cover Popular Front activity and Marxian doctrine. The great Italian authority on the history of Liberalism, Guido Ruggiero, wrote for the *Encyclopedia of the Social Sciences* that "its primary postulate, the spiritual freedom of mankind, not only repudiates naturalistic or deterministic interpretations of human action but posits a free individual conscious of his capacity for unfettered development and self-expression." Nevertheless the term has been more frequently associated in America with the naturalist philosophers, centering around John Dewey, than with any other group. Liberalism in America has often meant a denial of any spiritual quality in man.

Liberalism is a term, then, which means different things to different people. The average American believes it stands for a decent, humane attitude toward social questions. Thus Harold Stearns defined it some years ago as "a whole philosophy of life. It is scientific, curious, experimental. It is willing to face opposite views; it welcomes them. It tries to base its beliefs on genuine historical background. It believes in the validity of the cultural claims of life. It is urbane, good-natured, nonpartisan, detached." And in 1947 Dorothy Thompson described it this way:

> Liberalism is, to me, the noblest of all political philosophies and ways of life. . . . It is the political philosophy of the free, who would have all men free; of the strong, who would have all men strong; of the reasonable, who appeal to reason; of the fearless, who have faith in man. . . . Liberalism is the philosophy of faith, hope and love, the eternal catalysts of social tensions. It is an optimistic, affirmative attitude toward life and society; the defender of man as a separate and precious person, in a harmonious society.

Any right-minded person would approve such attitudes and "philosophies" as described by Stearns and Miss Thompson. Certainly no one could condemn them. Nevertheless another author entitled his book on this subject *El Liberalismo es Pecado*—"Liberalism Is a Sin"—and the English translation of that book asserts that "Liberalism is a greater sin than blasphemy, theft, adultery, homicide, or any other violation of the law of God, save in such case as where one acts in good faith, in ignorance or thoughtlessly." Whether the reader believes in sin or not, he cannot help despising the thing described as Liberalism in this study by Sarda y Salvany. Obviously the Spanish doctor and the American journalist are writing about two different things.

It might be well to recall at this point that the word "Liberalism" is an abstraction, a generalization from concrete data that are supposed to have something in common. Moreover, it is an abstraction with a highly emotional content, a "loaded" word today like communism or democracy or euthanasia. The replies to the *Herald Tribune*'s appeal for definitions revealed more emotion than reason in the writers' thinking about Liberalism. The definition of a Liberal as "an indolent farmer who believes that the government should pay him for the things he does not raise" betrays pent-up feeling rather than objective thinking. Not as much rational reflection as strong emotion is behind the assertion that "a Liberal is generous, hospitable, considerate, charitable, and tolerant."

Now an abstraction like this creates difficulties for the historian. He is concerned with ideas as they are held by concrete persons at given times and places in history. He must be careful not to read his own or his age's understanding of a word back into the minds of men using the same word three or four generations ago. Thus it would be a mistake to read the rather decent meaning given Liberalism in the twentieth century by Herbert Hoover or Dorothy Thompson into the nineteenth-century Liberalism of Herbert Spencer or Harriet Martineau. If the historian were to do this he would fall into the trap of nominalism and tell the story of labels instead of analyzing the wine in the bottles. He must also be careful not to transfer the contents of the term from one country to another. *Liberalismo* in Spain, where the term seems to have been first used, did not mean exactly the same thing as *Liberalisme* in France, and it meant something quite different when it found its way into the English vocabulary as *Liberalism* within a few years.

Despite these difficulties the historian finds the study of the history of this bundle of attitudes and doctrines known as Liberalism a profitable pursuit, for it was an all-pervading idea which, when understood, throws considerable light on how men's minds worked in the past, and it reveals how the working of their minds affected the society in which they lived—as well as today's society which we have inherited from our predecessors. This is particularly true of Liberalism because, as Harold Laski has put it, "Liberalism has been, in the last four centuries, the outstanding doctrine of Western Civilization." Certainly it dominated the nineteenth century, and it has been, with democracy and communism, a most important current in our own age. An understanding of Liberalism and a knowledge of its history are therefore contributory to our knowledge not only of the past but also of the issues which press for solution today.

Our aim in this introduction is to pin down the slippery term "Liberalism" and to see whether some delineation is possible of what, from the above definitions, seems to be an amorphous entity. The word was apparently first used in 1811 in Spain to indicate the proponents of the constitution adopted the following year and modeled after the French Constitution of 1791. Opposed to this group were champions of the monarchy and the Catholic religion of the old regime. So the new Liberalism naturally took on a strong anticlerical flavor, made stronger still by the Spanish temperament and sharpened by clashes between the two parties. Consequently, as one neutral authority has put it, "Liberalism was anti-clericalism." It was doctrinaire, as only the Spanish can be doctrinaire, arbitrary, and, paradoxically, quite illiberal.

As the use of the term spread to Italy, then England and France, its meaning varied according to the problems at issue in each country, according to the traditions and tempers of the intellectual class of each nation, and according to the stand of the opposition. Thus in England Liberalism was at once associated with a long tradition of specific liberties. It set itself up against the Radicals—who were somewhat outside the English tradition and were closely akin to doctrinaire Liberals in Spain or France—and against the Conservatives, who were much more liberal than their continental counterparts. So, as we shall see later, the English variety of Liberalism started off as a congeries of rather moderate doctrines. Its aim was not revolutionary, as were the Spanish and Italian brands of Liberalism, nor conservative, as was the French brand of 1815, but rather moderately reformist. Liberalism in England meant a bundle of concrete liberties, whereas on the continent the term soon came to mean a doctrinaire political and social philosophy arrived at deductively from certain assumptions about the nature of man and society.

There is no single road, therefore, along which one can trace the history of Liberalism. Almost from the beginning the paths run in all directions at once and, to continue the simile, we are confronted with an area rather than a line. Our problem in this introduction is to observe the concrete manifestations of Liberalism wherever we find it in the nineteenth century, and to generalize from these various specific instances to the essential elements found in them all. Let us proceed by attempting (1) to eliminate those things which are associated with Liberalism only occasionally but which are popularly thought today to be essential to it, (2) to enumerate those attitudes and ideas with which it is most frequently associated, and (3) to arrive at some kind of provisional definition or at least description of the elements constant in all manifestations of Liberalism in the nineteenth century. This will involve our touching on many points of Liberal belief of the nineteenth century without analyzing them critically or describing them fully. Such random "sampling" is necessary for arriving at a definition—it is not meant to prejudice the fuller study which will follow this introductory chapter.

First of all, Liberalism is not a creed or a set of beliefs which remain essentially unchanged throughout the century. The Liberal attitude toward "the masses," for example, underwent a complete reversal within a century. Voltaire, often described as the greatest Liberal of the eighteenth century, had nothing but contempt for his inferiors. "The laborer and the artisan," he advised, "must be cut down to necessaries, if they are to work," and they must be kept uneducated by those like himself who owned property. The modern Liberal, on the other hand, sees his task as "insistence that the great mass of plain people shall be permitted to develop their natural capacities and to attain better living conditions directly and by their own devices." Modern Liberals have rather consistently believed that the most sacred of their duties has been to provide free education for all.

Liberals of the early and mid-nineteenth century, as we shall see in a later chapter, were smugly content that poverty was a decree of the all-wise Providence who had decided that the poor would always be with us. "In all civilized communities," Macaulay asserted in 1829, "there is a small minority of rich men, and a great majority of poor men." And from this observation he concluded that poor men must not be allowed to vote, for they would use the ballot as a weapon for plundering the wealthy. That is why he considered Dickens' *Hard Times* "sullen socialism." Herbert Spencer, like Thomas Malthus before him, tried to show in 1850 that poverty was caused by "natural laws" and that "the process must be undergone and the suffering must be endured. No power on earth, no cunningly-devised laws of statesmen, no world-rectifying schemes of the humane, no communist panaceas, no reforms that men ever did broach or ever will broach, can diminish them one jot."

By the end of the century, however, the program of Liberalism included such measures as old-age pensions, minimum wages, unemployment insurances, and even school lunches for poor children, because Liberals had decided that the suffering of poverty need not be endured. Thus W. Lyon Blease wrote in 1913 that "no one who seriously believes that it is the duty of society to secure freedom of growth to every one of its members can doubt that it is the duty to mitigate, so far as it is able, those consequences of poverty which no degree of thrift, enterprise, or fortitude can avert." And young Winston Churchill—the same Churchill who is today leader of the Conservative party and who has not noticeably changed his principles—who was then called "the best expression of the philosophy of the new Liberalism," claimed:

> it is our duty to use the strength and the resources of the State to arrest the ghastly waste, not merely of human happiness, but of national health and strength, which follows when a working man's home, which has taken him years to get together, is broken up and scattered through a long spell of unemployment, or when, through the death, the sickness, or the invalidity of the breadwinner, the frail boat in which the fortunes of the family are embarked founders, and the women and children are left to struggle helplessly on the dark waters of a friendless world.

This Liberalism of the early twentieth century is the "sentimentalist heresy" which the Liberal Herbert Spencer damned as "spurious philanthropy" in 1850.

A final example of a complete reversal in Liberalism's creed is the view typical Liberals held of the role of the State. Herbert Spencer, who has been called "the philosophic exponent of the nineteenth century Liberalism," wanted the State to do nothing—literally—except protect its citizens. In his opinion even such things as sewer systems and highways should be handled as profit-making adventures by private companies. Spencer narrowly limited even the State's role as protector of its citizens. It was apparently to restrain only physical violence against property and persons, for Spencer would not let it protect people from incompetent druggists or quack doctors. He admitted that incompetent druggists and fake healers killed many people every year, but still he believed that to forbid them to operate "is directly to violate the moral law. Men's rights are infringed by these, as much as by all other, trade-interferences." We shall see how Liberals of the next generation went to the opposite extreme, all the way to a modified socialism. In 1909, J. A. Hobson wrote:

> Liberalism is now formally committed to a task which certainly involves a new conception of the State in its relation to the individual life and to private enterprise. . . . For the first time in the history of English Liberalism (its leaders advocate measures) which have the common result of increasing the powers and resources of the State for the improvement of the material and moral condition of the people.

It is useless, therefore, to try to find an unchanging doctrine which can be labeled Liberalism. Not only does the content of its creed change through the course of history, but within a generation it has frequently adopted beliefs which flatly contradict those which the older Liberals still consider essential articles of faith. It is not uncommon, as a matter of fact, to find that two Liberals, both considered perfect exponents of the creed at the time, differ on important specific measures. Macaulay argued, rather reasonably, that "the ignorance of the common people makes the property, the limbs, the lives of all classes insecure," and that "the education of the common people is a most effectual means of securing our persons and our property." He concluded, therefore, that the government should exercise its police power through the school. Teachers will keep the people submissive more effectively, and more economically than will the police. Spencer, on the other hand, insisted that education was purely a private matter, and for the government to undertake it was a manifest injustice to the taxpayers. As late as 1891 one of Spencer's associates asserted that education was a form of State socialism whereby "you take your education out of your neighbor's earnings."

As we shall see later in this chapter, there are some attitudes and even some ideas common to all manifestations of Liberalism in the nineteenth century, but it is obvious that there is no formula of faith which can be labeled Liberalism at all times and all places. It is, indeed, of the very nature of Liberalism to have no set creed, no formula of faith to which all true Liberals must adhere.

Contrary to the generally held identification of Liberalism and democracy, historically they have not been the same thing. As we shall see later, the two movements were deadly enemies in the early part of the nineteenth century. They tended to merge in the last quarter of the century, and then to part company again in our own day when Liberalism became involved in class alignments. Macaulay thought that universal manhood suffrage was "incompatible not with this or that form of government, but with all forms of government, and . . . it is consequently incompatible with civilization." He would not even allow the Chartists to present their case in a petition to Parliament in 1842 because one of their demands was for universal manhood suffrage. Better known to Americans, of course, is Hamilton's warning about "the poison of democracy" and the general fear of popular rule felt by almost all the Founding Fathers, who were certainly eighteenth-century Liberals. The best known Liberals of England and France, men like Gladstone and Guizot, Constant and Lord Russell, all opposed democracy as we understand the term today.

Nor is Liberalism a theory of liberty. If words mean anything at all, then Liberals must believe in liberty. They all do, but there is no agreement among them on the meaning of the term. Nevertheless, Liberals did tend, with almost infinite variation, to take two general stands as regards the nature of freedom. The first tendency historically was to regard liberty as a negative thing. Thus it was understood by Liberals for more than three centuries. As late as 1884 Herbert Spencer wrote with nostalgia of "the days when Liberals were rightly so called, and when the definition was—'one who advocates greater freedom from restraint, especially in political institutions.' "

Liberty to Spencer and those he described as true Liberals means freedom from political, ecclesiastical, social, and economic control. The battle of freedom for them was the long struggle of removing these external limitations on one's liberty of movement, both intellectual and physical. It meant the removal of one obstacle after another through modern history. Some were religious or quasi-religious: the power of Church doctrine, the authority of a providential personal God, the hold of the past's dead hand. Other obstacles were social, the so-called "cake of custom" at which Liberals consistently chipped away. The most immediate obstacles were political: the many limitations imposed in the past by the State in its attempt to promote the dynastic interest of the ruler. The aim of Liberalism throughout most of modern history was the removal of these external restraints. Its freedoms were conceived in terms of this struggle.

But in the latter half of the century, as we shall see in the course of our study, liberty came to take on another meaning. Instead of freedom *from* something, Liberals began to talk about freedom *for* something. The aim was to convert the negative theory of liberty into a positive concept, because, as Ruggiero has shown, when the negative freedom was obtained it became a meaningless thing in itself. More than anyone else, Thomas Hill Green transferred to the Anglo-American tradition the positive concept of liberty which German philosophers had worked out in the early nineteenth century.

When we speak of freedom as something to be so highly prized, (he said) we mean a positive power or capacity of doing or enjoying something worth doing or enjoying. . . . Freedom in all the forms of doing what one will with one's own, is valuable only as a means to an end. That end is what I call freedom in the positive sense: in other words, the liberation of the powers of all men equally for contribution to a common good.

On the basis of this positive idea of freedom, Liberalism reversed itself on the role of the State in social life and came to hold all over again for political control and direction of individual activities. Thus Brotherston could define it in 1934 as "the process no longer of leaving the individual free but of making him free by rightly conceiving and instituting the political, economic, educational, and social order which alone will fulfill the nature of man." Liberalism which a century before had denounced Rousseau's idea of "forcing men to be free" was coming around to accepting it. And today, we know, at least one school of Liberalism has gone totalitarian.

So although Liberalism is always somehow concerned with freedom, it has not held a consistent theory of liberty. Liberals today admit this. Most of them go on to describe Liberalism as a concept of life that has always been humane and benevolent at the core. Thus Morris Cohen tells us that he "would suggest that Liberalism means a pride in human achievement, a faith in human effort, a conviction that the proper function of government is to remove the restraints upon human activity." Dorothy Thompson, to cite just one other example from among many, looks on Liberalism as "a kind of spirit and a sort of behavior, the basis of which is an enormous respect for personality. It is, therefore, above everything else human and humane." But this has not always been so. We shall see that the great proponents of Liberalism in the past century can hardly be considered humanitarian or humane. Conservatives and utopian socialists were the humanitarians of the time; it was they who pushed factory laws and poor relief against Liberal opposition. Ironically, as regards the modern concepts of Liberalism, Liberals like Malthus and Spencer condemned the conservatives for this very sense of social responsibility and for their concern with the poor. "It is best," wrote Spencer, "to let the foolish man suffer the penalty of his foolishness. . . . To others as well as to himself will his case be a warning." Nor is Spencer unique. He is instead typical of his age's Liberalism. Historically Liberalism has been tough-minded, even callous, in its attitude toward the great mass of human beings.

Nor is it correct to equate Liberalism with tolerance and with a sympathetic understanding of every point of view, as is so often done by our contemporaries. Morris Cohen voices a popular belief when he tells us that one of Liberalism's two key doctrines is "belief in toleration," and Max Eastman claims that "to be liberal is to be able to enter with one's imagination into any point-of-view that is proposed," that tolerance is the second great principle of Liberalism. Such descriptions apply to many Liberals today. But we shall see that most Liberals were doctrinaire and tyrannical about their very Liberalism. Even today many Liberals are like those described by Eugene Lyons as "notoriously illiberal, intellectually parsimonious and emotionally conservative in anything affecting their favorite preconceptions and misconceptions." Tolerance has not been a monopoly of either Liberalism or Conservatism.

It is incorrect, therefore, to equate Liberalism with any of the above points of doctrine or attitudes, with democracy or tolerance or liberty or benevolence. Some Liberals, at one time or another, have held one or another of these things. But other Liberals have held the contrary. On the other hand, it is equally far from the truth to believe that "Liberalism is a sin," or that it is a "satanic social solvent," as Cardinal Billot wrote early in this century—unless, of course, one accepts the restricted definition he gives the term. Liberalism through the nineteenth century did many fine things, which Cardinal Billot thoroughly approved, such as reforming penal laws or providing care for the insane and the crippled. These things, he would answer, are not what he means by Liberalism. But they are included in the meaning of the term by many others.

It is obvious from what we have seen so far that Liberalism changes its shape and its content from generation to generation. Let us see if we can observe any constant tendencies that inhere in the subject through its variations. This will help us disengage the essential core of Liberalism from the accidental features with which it is associated from time to time.

1. First and foremost, whether as a creed or a program of action, Liberalism has been rather closely associated with the middle class, the *bourgeoisie* of western Europe. This is not to accept, without considerable modification, the thesis ably propounded by Harold Laski that "Liberalism came as a new ideology to fit the needs of a new (bourgeois) world." Laski interprets the movement in a now outmoded Marxist fashion, and thus he sees Liberalism simply as "a by-product of the effort of the middle class to win its place in the sun." This is a typical Marxist oversimplification of a complex set of interrelationships between things material and things spiritual. But the fact remains that Liberalism is closely connected with the *bourgeoisie*, at least down until our own century.

2. Liberalism and capitalism are therefore closely interlocked systems of thought, for both are more or less middle-class doctrines, one applying to all facets of life, the other more specifically to the economic problem of producing and marketing wealth. Through the first part of the century, when the middle class was fighting to remove traditional restrictions on its economic and political freedom, the two doctrines can be identified. Later on, after the bourgeoisie came to power, they tended toward conservative rather than Liberal thought—but capitalism remained a sacred economic doctrine in their minds. Liberalism thus diverged from capitalism as it was identified with reformist movements that were often anticapitalistic.

3. Like the middle class, Liberalism has had an affinity for certain brands of Protestantism. This connection is not absolute or necessary.

But Liberalism worked in close logical compatibility with the various nonestablished religions, just as it was logically hostile to Catholicism and Anglicanism and orthodox Lutheranism where these were the established religions. The outstanding Liberal thinkers of France were Protestant, like Guizot and Constant, or they were Catholics who were held suspect by their coreligionists, like Montalembert and Ozanam. The outstanding Liberal thinkers of England were nonconformist in religion, men like Bright and Mill and Cobden. Gladstone later observed that nonconformity was the backbone of English Liberalism, and when the Liberal party was trying to redefine its program and revivify its membership after World War I, Professor Gilbert Murray insisted in his keynote address: "We are politically the descendants of the Puritans." In his analysis of the connection between nonconformity and Liberalism in all European countries, Ruggiero concludes that the similarity of economic and religious position naturally provoked a similar reaction in the two fields and lodged in the same group of minds. "The dissenting sects were free communities animated by a Calvinistic spirit whose very existence depended upon individual initiative, propaganda, and competition."

4. Throughout the nineteenth century, we shall see in a later chapter, Liberalism consistently showed strong respect for property rights. Someone has observed, with about as much truth as wit, that the Liberal's nerve center was his wallet. Liberal legislation of the nineteenth century was certainly much more tender in its regard for property rights than human rights. We in America are aware how the Fourteenth Amendment was abused in that respect. Far worse was the exploitation of children and women in western Europe, an exploitation justified by Liberalism as a necessary extension of the mill owner's property rights. Religious groups inveighed against this inhuman disregard of human life; Marxists analyzed it as the ratiocination of property ownership; conservatives and humanitarians condemned Liberals as lacking any sense of social responsibility. But through all these attacks Liberals held fast to an inordinate respect for property rights because they believed those rights were the basis of their civilization. Laski does not therefore overstate the case when he asserts that "the idea of Liberalism is historically connected, in an inescapable way, with the ownership of property." Liberalism has historically had a highly sensitive property nerve, although in our own day this is no longer true.

5. These constant elements we have so far seen in Liberalism are all connected in one way or another with the middle class. There is still another element of Liberalism that is found most commonly among the bourgeoisie—but the connection here is much looser and more elusive. It is a matter of intellectual temper. As a form of social thought Liberalism has been empirical, scientific, mundane, and more or less skeptical-minded. The Liberal has always been a restless sort of person, discontent with the world as he finds it and with the commonly accepted authority. He has therefore tended naturally to the experimental ap-

proach to social problems, to the trial-and-error system whereby he sets himself up as judge of the merits or the truth of a proposition. One of Liberalism's modern champions says that it "is eternally probing, revising, and building ampler systems." The Liberal mind—if we may speak of such a thing—grew up in the age of developing science, hostile to the philosophical or theological approach to life's problems, sympathetic to the method which proved so fruitful in the physical sciences. This was a heritage which we shall find Liberalism maintaining throughout the nineteenth century.

In his recent work on *Liberalism and the Challenge of Fascism*, Professor Schapiro asserts that "the scientific approach to social problems, as seen in the social sciences, was distinctively liberal. It was the very antithesis of the revelation of truth through supernatural intervention. Nothing was so distinctive of the liberal temper as its aversion to dogmatism in any and all forms." Such assertions could be made only by a contemporary Liberal, for the best scientists today admit that science itself contains subjective, non-scientific assumptions at the core and that much of its method is "intuitional" or "dogmatic." But the fact remains that Liberals followed a method which was considered objective and scientific. They applied the norms of physical science to social studies—and thereby, as we shall see, they forged the weapons of their own destruction. But in those methods the Liberal put full faith. Thus Stephen Spender—who has progressed from Liberalism to Communism, logically, he believes—has written that Liberalism "is the product of a scientific and progressive age: when the age ceases to be objective, scientific and progressive, then Liberalism will be defeated."

6. Another constant note in nineteenth-century Liberalism is its full trust in the goodness and the rationality of the individual. Both the rationalist tradition from the eighteenth century and the romanticism of the early nineteenth century put a full, naive faith in man's inherent goodness. Ignoring the lessons of history, both rationalist and sentimentalist denied what Christians referred to as an inclination to evil and a confusion of the intellect. Such evil as existed they explained away in terms of archaic institutions and bad laws. Reform these, the Liberals believed, and the naturally good man would no longer be made evil by his bad environment. Today we wonder how the same persons who claimed they were objective and realistic in their approach to social problems could hold so naive a view of human nature. Their psychology, as we shall see later, was a mechanistic thing which has long since been discredited. It fit in nicely with the other pieces of their theory, however, and it enabled them to concentrate fiercely on legal institutional reform with full assurance that they could create a perfect society by refurbishing the social order. By locating evil in institutions and asserting man's innate goodness they seemed to put their El Dorado within the reach of the next generation—always the next generation.

7. Faith in man's goodness referred not only to his will but also to

his intellect. Liberalism is in the rationalist rather than the romantic tradition; its adherents take very literally the Aristotelian definition of man as a rational animal. This is a logical item of Liberal belief—and it is necessary, for the Liberal must put faith in man's ability to be guided by the light of reason. He "has faith in the individual," as Stearns has put it, "faith that he can be persuaded by rational means to beliefs compatible with the social good." The early English Liberals looked on man as a human calculating machine that mechanically and undeviatingly followed the rationale of self-interest. Later Liberals took a less extereme, less naive view of the working of the human mind, but they continued to believe that man is essentially rational.

This has always been a "central idea" of Liberalism, as George Sabine has expressed it.

> Throughout its history (he was written) Liberalism has been, first and foremost, a belief in the supreme social value of intelligence. . . . They (the Liberals) were actuated by a profound moral conviction that intelligence is the core of personality, the distinctively human faculty in man, and the part of him that could not be limited without crippling all his powers. Liberalism was built upon the moral postulate that men have a right to be convinced, to understand and evaluate the demands that are laid on them, and if possible to consent to them.

The psychological advances of the twentieth century, especially behaviorism and now probing into the unconscious and formerly neglected realms of the mind, have made it difficult for Liberals to maintain the old faith in man's full rationality. But through the nineteenth century and down pretty much to our own generation, the faith remained intact.

8. Another more or less constant element of Liberalism has been its faith in progress. The fact of material progress became increasingly evident as the nineteenth century unfolded its technological revolution. Liberalism proceeded from the fact of material progress to build a theory of inevitable progress in all fields, moral and material, toward an ever better, ultimately perfect world. "Progress" was associated in their minds with an advancing limitation of authority and a cumulative increase in the stock of individual freedoms. With some, like Herbert Spencer, "progress" was a law of nature that had its way whether men willed it or not. "Progress is not an accident but a necessity." It entailed suffering, which was justified by the better world to which it was ever giving birth. "It seems," Spencer wrote in his *Principles of Sociology*, "that in the course of social progress, parts, more or less large, of each society, are sacrificed for the benefit of society as a whole. . . . Men are used up for the benefit of posterity; and so long as they go on multiplying in excess of the means of subsistence, there appears no remedy."

Down until our own day Liberals heroically—sometimes myopically and almost obstinately—maintained their faith that man is constantly progressing toward a better world. They are not certain of the road to their better world as Christians are of the path to the kingdom of God.

But their faith is no less eschatological. Apparently the goal is partly realized in the going. Joy is taken in the journey. Morris Cohen puts this item of faith well when he writes: "Liberalism . . . regards life as an adventure in which we must take in new situations, in which there is no guarantee that the new will always be the good or the true, in which progress is a precarious achievement rather than an inevitability." This willingness for change, whatever it might bring, has been part of the Liberal's faith because of his dissatisfaction with the existing situation. That is why his negative thought has always been sharp and incisive, his positive program shifting and nebulous. There is a humorous but apt description of a Liberal being a man who "very earnestly disbelieves in almost everything that anybody else believes, and he has a very lively sustaining faith in he doesn't know what." The aptness of such a description is revealed by Roger Baldwin's pride in the fact that "Liberals don't know where they are going but are on their way."

9. Because of their faith in progress and their dissatisfaction with the existing order of things Liberals have always inclined toward favoring change of any kind. They have therefore naturally predisposed themselves toward reform measures, temperance leagues, and better government campaigns. "Liberalism turned away from the ideal of the medieval saint," Schairo says, "and proclaimed the modern ideal of the reformer." Liberal ministries in English history have been reform government, like Gladstone's great reform ministry of 1868-1874, which set about with burning moral earnestness to reform the pubs, the army, the civil service, all the way down to the bodies and the very minds of the people. Liberal movements in American history have likewise been reform movements, such as all the great reforms—abolitionism, feminism, the extension of education, the organization of labor—which originated in the liberal decade of the 1830's.

Throughout modern history, then, and especially throughout the nineteenth century with which we are concerned in this book, Liberalism has been associated with the middle class. It has therefore taken on typical bourgeois characteristics. It has found its strongest expression in dissenter ranks; it has stressed the rationality and the inherent goodness of man; it has adopted an empirical, scientific approach to social problems. It has held property sacred, but at the same time it has favored change in the name of progress and has therefore backed reform movements in church, state, and social custom.

Little toward clarifying the meaning of Liberalism has been accomplished by the descriptions of Liberalism so far offered, and the discussion of which features are only occasionally and which are constantly associated with the term. But these definitions and descriptions have suggested that Liberalism is used today in two main senses. This has been the basic cause of confusion on what the term means. It has divided men who agree basically on almost everything into *pro* and *contra* camps relative to Liberalism. For the term means something essentially different to the two groups, and its meaning is the result of historical associations. Thus we find Americans with a Latin background using the term in a more specific, limited sense than those with an Anglo-Saxon heritage or no recent European heritage at all. Catholics, again, because of their struggles against certain kinds of antireligious and anticlerical Liberalisms in the Latin countries, tend to use the word in a derogatory sense.

It therefore seems proper and useful to distinguish between ecumenical Liberalism and sectarian. The former refers to that Liberalism which is identified with generosity of spirit or liberality of mind, the latter to a precisely defined and rigidly held body of doctrine, a secular religion. The former is a generally accepted thing; the latter is reserved to relatively few. Many of the descriptions of liberalism we have so far given obviously refer to the ecumenical kind, especially the definitions of contemporaries like Dorothy Thompson, and Herbert Hoover. This certainly is the liberalism Brotherston referred to as "one of those long-continued historical movements which have arisen from primal demands of human life. . . . Reflection soon reveals that Liberalism is the sum total of all movements in the history of man which have had their rise in the normal urgency of the human spirit. It has covered the whole field of life, practical and theoretic." It is the ecumenical brand that Ogden Mills had in mind when he asserted that "our American social philosophy can be expressed in the single term—liberalism." This is the type that John H. Hallowell, one of America's leading authorities on Liberalism, has in mind when he writes that "in the United States . . . practically everyone calls himself liberal and embodies in the term all that is congenial to his particular way of thinking."

Other descriptions we have employed obviously refer to sectarian Liberalism. This is the type Eugene Lyons had in mind when he wrote that Liberals "are notoriously illiberal," and that "Liberalism had become just another orthodoxy." Sarda y Salvany and Cardinal Billot were referring to the sectarian kind of Liberalism when they condemned the doctrine as sinful and satanic. Historically the term "Liberalism" has generally been used to refer to a sectarian doctrine rather than a certain attitude. It is still so used in most of Europe and in South America. But in England and especially in this country the ecumenical meaning has come in our time to be more generally accepted. The result is the confusion we referred to above, the sort of confusion of tongues that causes a scholar like Hallowell to say that Liberalism "should be more precisely defined than it is today or else it should be abandoned."

There is little likelihood that the term will be abandoned. The most we can hope for is an approach to greater precision by distinguishing various types of Liberalism. The ecumenical kind is at most a temper or a spirit or a habit of mind, a disposition or an attitude toward the problems of life. It is so defined by almost all Americans and Englishmen using the term nowadays. On this point there is general agreement. Professor Ramsay Muir described ecumenical liberalism well in these words:

Liberalism is a habit of mind, a point of view, a way of looking at things, rather than a fixed and unchanging body of doctrine. Like all creeds it is a spirit not a formula. It gets expression from time to time in formulae and programmes of policy, but these are always and necessarily determined by the circumstances of the time in which they are framed; they can, therefore, have no permanent validity; they need to be continually revised and recast, or they become mere shackles on the spirit which they try to express.

In similar fashion Blease defined it as "not a policy, but a habit of mind," Cohen called it "an attitude rather than a set of dogmas," and Miss Thompson, as we have seen, considered it "a kind of spirit and a sort of behavior."

Liberals of this ecumenical school include at least half the human race. In America they number many more than half. Robert Bendiner went so far as to estimate in the *Nation:* "Out of some 140,000,000 people in the United States, at least 139,500,000 are liberals, to hear them tell it, 'liberal' having become a rough synonym for virtuous, decent, humane, and kind to animals. . . . Any American would sooner drop dead than proclaim himself a reactionary." We can dismiss this type of liberalism as being too general for profitable discussion—unless we were to attempt a full cultural and political history of modern times. Our concern is instead with the more definite body of doctrine which is sectarian Liberalism. In the following pages we shall therefore discuss something that has no direct reference to Dorothy Thompson or the Tennessee Valley Authority or adult education in the Great Books.

Our discussion is instead about the sectarian Liberalism of the nineteenth century, or, more properly, the period between the surrender of Napoleon in 1815 and the beginning of World War I in 1914. Let us therefore see if we can begin to isolate this term by seeing what attitudes remain constant in it—for even sectarian Liberalism will be forced by its very nature to change its creed according to the circumstances with which it is confronted. In doing this we must remember that the two kinds of Liberalism are not always mutually exclusive. There will consequently seem to be in the next few pages a certain amount of repetition of matter already considered. This is inevitable, however, if we are to approach a definition of our subject matter.

In the first place, sectarian Liberalism has consistently opposed the establishment government. When its political battle is won and its program comes to be worked into the law of the land, as happened in England after 1832, in France after 1830, and in this country after the Civil War, its champions become conservative. They hold the same doctrines, to be sure, but they are given another label. Thus Guizot was a sectarian Liberal of the Restoration period (1815-1830), but under Louis Philippe's bourgeois monarchy of 1830-1848, wherein his program was fully accepted and he governed as premier, he became the enemy of all further change. So it was with those Whigs who accepted the Victorian compromise as a final settlement. As opponents of further change they became conservative, and the mantle of sectarian Liberalism fell on others who were dissatisfied with the settlement of 1832. The former Liberals do not easily surrender the name, and even today many use the term "Liberalism" to refer to the doctrines and policies of those who were in power in the middle of the nineteenth century. Hence the confusion. But the label of sectarian Liberal is properly attached to those who oppose the established order.

In the second place, and a corollary of the first point, sectarian Liberalism has consistently inveighed against authority of any kind. Between authority and Liberalism there has always been strong antipathy. They can make peace, as we shall see, only by one or the other denying its own nature. For the essence of sectarian Liberalism has consistently been a throwing-off of restraint, a cutting loose from what seems to oppress the individual. Liberalism therefore demands that the government surrender its power to the Liberals. Historically it has stood for resistance to absolute, arbitrary government, and it has fought the good fight for responsible parliamentary rule. It has stood for resistance to undue interference with industry and trade. It has stood for the rejection of authority in both Church and State, for a repudiation of tradition, custom, convention. And in the struggle it has championed bad causes as well as good; it has rejected much that was evil and some that was good.

It therefore follows, in the third place, that the tendency of sectarian Liberalism has been toward anticlericalism, and toward an anarchism which it never reached but always approached. Tom Paine considered government at best a necessary evil—but an evil nonetheless; and Adam Smith adopted what has become the typical Liberal attitude toward that "insidious and crafty animal vulgarly called the statesman or politician." The evil of government was to be reduced to the minimum, the Liberal always hoped, and long before Marx sectarian Liberals prophesied the eventual withering away of the State. Spencer put this idea pithily when he asserted that "the ultimate man will be one whose private requirements coincide with public ones." For the aim of progress is to reach that condition where "the individual is everything and the State nothing." In the same way, Liberalism has been hostile to religious authority. "The religious mind," Spencer has written, "is naturally repelled by Liberalism, which sets up humanity in place of God, the doctor or the psychologist in the place of the priest." Liberalism has tended to make the individual person absolute master and final judge of all things. It stands for the subjection to individual judgment of all claims—political, intellectual, and spiritual—and it therefore regards with hostility organized churches, party discipline, or philosophical systems.

Sectarian Liberalism is obviously bound to be forward-looking, always in favor of change from the existing order toward something new and, the Liberal feels sure, better. The doctrine of the sectarian Liberal therefore changes with each generation, unless the conservative element in a society is strongly enough entrenched in power to remain for successive generations. But though the Liberal's doctrine changes, his state of mind remains the same.

This state of mind, this attitude toward existing institutions is indeed the only constant element in sectarian Liberalism throughout its history. We shall see in later chapters that the sectarian Liberal of 1914 has essentially the same temper as his predecessor of 1815 or of 1865. The constant element even in sectarian Liberalism, then, is not a set of doctrines but a doctrinaire temper of mind. But it differs from ecumenical liberalism in having a definite fighting creed at each moment in history, in having a program and frequently an organization dedicated to putting that program into practice. It is the Liberal frame of mind, however, and not any consistent body of doctrine which justifies the use of the word "Liberalism" to describe certain groups of thinkers and actors in modern history.

As a final word of introduction to our subject, let us take an overview of the way sectarian Liberalism has evolved through the nineteenth century. In 1815 sectarian Liberals were excluded from power, except in France where they had a precarious, partial grip on the government which was threatened by reactionary groups gathering around the restored Bourbon king, Louis XVIII. These Liberals stemmed from the French Revolution on the continent and from the Industrial Revolution and its associated economic and political thought in England. (In America the case was quite different, because here was no "conservative" group entrenched in power. In many ways we started with a clean slate in America and for a while there was nothing to be "against" except perhaps sin or the memory of George III. As we shall see later, political parties soon formed, but not on the clear-cut issue of Conservatism versus Liberalism.)

Sectarian Liberals in this period before 1830 built up the doctrine of classical or integral liberalism, and with that program they came to power in England in 1832 and in France in 1830 and temporarily in other places in 1848. The period of classical Liberalism—called the Victorian compromise in England, the Bourgeois monarchy in France—lasted until about 1865. Within it, while the satisfied classical Liberals were growing conservative, there grew up a new sectarian Liberalism which held the same position and the same temper toward the classical Liberals that the latter had formerly held toward the restored order of 1815-1830. This new Liberalism of Gladstone and John Stuart Mill was democratic. Its program was the enfranchisement of all adult males and the extension of governmental protection over a severely restricted group of "legal infants," such as women and children working in the mines. In most other respects it did not differ from its predecessor type of Liberalism.

Democratic Liberalism was generally accepted by about 1885, and for the next thirty years it was in power in most of western Europe and in the United States—at least formally and on paper. But there had grown up in its midst a new sectarian Liberalism which urged a larger role upon the State, the positive role of guaranteeing minimum existence to all citizens and of protecting the people against the new tyrant of big business. Its opponents labeled this new brand of Liberalism "socialist." A better term would be "welfare Liberalism." It had won a number of victories in all European countries by the time World War I began in 1914, and there were many who believed that socialism of some kind or other would be generally realized at the end of the war.

Although this threefold division of doctrinaire sectarian Liberalism into classical or integral, democratic, and welfare is valid, we must remember that all classical Liberals did not conveniently die by 1865, or even by 1900. Some of them lived on, protesting the new movements and calling for a halt to the trend. Herbert Spencer, for example, was a classical Liberal, still writing in 1900; though no longer deserving the label "Liberal," he was still using it. So in our own generation Ogden Mills' *Liberalism Fights On* is an attack on the New Deal by a man who would have rightly been called Liberal in 1850 but not in 1936. The Liberals by this latter date were the New Dealers.

Thus we can see that a man who holds the same doctrine in old age that he accepted in his youth will unlikely remain a Liberal in the sectarian sense—at least he would not in the nineteenth and twentieth centuries. A man born in 1806, as John Stuart Mill was, who was a sectarian Liberal in 1830 would be a conservative by 1850 and a reactionary by 1875, unless he consistently discarded one set of beliefs in favor of another more advanced set. John Stuart Mill actually did this, so that he remained consistently, though not always as confidently and stridently, Liberal down until his death in 1873, when he was a qualified and moderate socialist.

Our purpose in the following chapters is to study the development of this sectarian Liberalism. From an understanding of its development several very practical advantages should result. First of all, such an understanding should do much toward clarifying our thought about the various kinds of Liberalism in western Europe and America today. It should enable us to separate the sectarian Liberal from the ecumenical, and in the process it should help us realize that it is often words rather than programs which divide us into supposedly opposed camps. Many persons have a bad reputation in liberal circles for condemning "Liberalism," because it is assumed that they are blind opponents of all forward-looking proposals to improve the lot of men here on earth. Professor Jordan of Butler University, for example, described Liberalism in 1936 as "this mongrel (which) is often a lovable and pious beast, and frequently knocks its brother's head off in the interest of brotherhood. . . . It may heal and bless with the one hand and murder and ravish with the other, and there is no way of knowing in advance which it shall be. Liberalism as a social and political and ethical attitude is a psychological monstrosity, and what is veridical in it is self-contradictory."

Strong words about Liberalism, these, and still words that would be accepted by most persons who call themselves liberal today if they knew what Professor Jordan meant by them. Because they do not, they pin the label of "reactionary" on him. All through the nineteenth century there were men who prized liberty highly, and yet in its name they condemned what we call sectarian Liberalism. There are many today who understand the word in the sectarian rather than the ecumenical sense, and they therefore look on all who call themselves "liberal" as their enemies—when they would indeed be friends if they knew what each other means by the term. It is unfortunate that the word has divided so many who should fight together against the common enemies of freedom instead of pinning labels and then throwing insults upon each other.

Our second reason for examining the history of sectarian Liberalism in the past century is to be able to plot the future course of freedom more knowingly. For such an examination should reveal to us the contributions made toward our contemporary civilization by the various forms of sectarian Liberalism, contributions which were sometimes salutary and sometimes harmful. It should also enable us to determine why the Liberal, who was such an enemy of the State in 1815, became a modified socialist by 1914. Various answers to this puzzle have been suggested, and each seems to contain its measure of truth. Laski and other Marxist critics consider Liberalism the creed of the bourgeoisie, and like Christianity it is supposed to disappear as the masses obtain control of the economic forces of production and of the State.

Others, modern Liberals like Ruggiero and Schapiro, suggest that Liberalism changed in nature as circumstances changed, but they insist that the real threat to Liberalism is a conspiracy among reactionaries and clerics, that it is in Fascism or some other anti-Liberal and authoritarian movement. All these authorities seem agreed that Liberalism changed its direction because of forces over which it had no control, such as the technological revolution or the perversity of clerical and agricultural elements that are inherently opposed to change.

There are still others who see in sectarian Liberalism an attitude of thought which leads to its own self-destruction. Thus Jordan sees subjectivity as its false principle, and Michael Polanyi claims that the "logic of liberty" leads inevitably to anarchism and consequent totalitarianism, a point which such Catholics as Juan Donoso Cortés, Louis Veuillot, and Orestes Brownson made a century ago. Shortly before World War II the Liberal English poet Stephen Spender, by then a Communist, wrote: "I do not doubt but that in the modern world communism—the classless, internationalist society—is the final goal of Liberalism."

It is a matter of no small import to us today to know whether totalitarian government—either the total State of Communism or that of any other coloring—comes logically from the principles of sectarian Liberalism, or whether the one is hostile to the other. Knowing this, we shall be in a better position to conduct the strategy of the battle for freedom—

a battle which every generation has had to carry on, but which seems more pressing and critical at some times than at others. Surely ours is a time when the issue is critical for the future of human freedom.

18

CAPITALISM *

It sometimes happens that two people who agree on basic principles will find themselves in complete disagreement about "capitalism." One will condemn it as essentially evil and the other will believe it inherently good. On examination, it turns out that the two have different ideas of what "capitalism" means. To the first it means the exploitation of labor, the denial of man's human dignity, the unjust enrichment of property owners. To the second it means the right to private ownership of productive property, freedom of occupation, a just reward for talent and for individual effort.

The following selection, by one of the country's outstanding Catholic economists, is helpful in getting behind the label of "capitalism" to the economic and social realities of a system of private enterprise, and thus showing that in many ways the concept "capitalism" has little relation to any concrete economic arrangement for the production of goods. Father Dempsey uses the historic approach to show how and when the word was first used, and then he describes the work of Sombart and Schumpeter, who have done more work on the subject than any other economic theorists. The revealing sub-title of Father Dempsey's original work is "But Don't Call It Capitalism."

IN THE quest for the content of a concept, a little nominalism is sometimes useful. If the concept has objective validity, determination of the time at which a term describing it emerged may be instructive. The method is a slippery one; it has its pitfalls and must be used judiciously, but it can be helpful and enlightening.

"Capital" as a fund of money or goods appears in the English language as early as 1611, with reappearances in 1630 and 1647. By the time of Adam Smith it seems to have been fairly current for what we

* Bernard W. Dempsey, S.J., "Capitalism," *Social Order,* IV (May, 1954), 199-208. Reprinted by permission.

now call working capital. By 1825, the content had sufficiently developed that McCullough could define capital as "the accumulation of the produce of previous labor, or as it is more commonly called capital or stock." The "capitalist" is the next term to materialize; in 1792 Arthur Young, the agricultural economist, in his *Travels in France,* speaks of "moneyed men or capitalists," but it is not until 1867 that we meet "the capitalist class."

"Capitalism" first appears, of all places, in Thackeray's novel, *The Newcomes,* in a passage of dubious economic reference. So not until 1877 in Douai's *Better Times* do we find capitalism in an unequivocal context, "This system of private capitalism is of comparatively recent origin," and we do not find the word again in English until the *Pall Mall Gazette* for September 11, 1884, speaks of a "loophole for capitalism to creep in upon primitive Christian economics." The *Communist Manifesto* and other Marxian writings use "capital" constantly in a sense where today the abstract "capitalism" would be found as, "by bourgeoisie is meant the class of modern capitalists" or "bourgeoisie, i.e. capital."

Sombart put the period of "full capitalism" as 1740-1914, perhaps in deference to Marx's statement in 1848 that the rule of the bourgeoisie was then "of scarce one hundred years." Certainly persons in the land universally regarded as the native habitat of capitalism, who were writing vigorous English about enclosures, guild restrictions, mercantilism, foreign trade, joint stock companies, etc., before and after 1740, were aware that important economic changes were taking place. What they did not seem to be aware of (if it was there to be perceived) was that these changes followed a simple social principle that, with the system resulting, could be adequately summarized in one word.

This negative nominal argument yields no positive conclusion beyond the fact that prior to Marxism, it was not obvious to anybody else that "capitalism" was a good name for either the motive force behind the changes or for the system (if it be a system) resulting from the changes.

Capital, as a fund of either money or goods, was acknowledged almost as far back as the English language is recognizable. This is scarcely surprising since capital, as an economic factor, exists to some degree even in the most primitive economy. Eskimos have their kayaks and American Indians, their bows and arrows, neither of which was designed for direct consumption but both of which had great value and produced a standard of living higher than would be possible without them. If we accept these crude, observed facts as examples of true capital—and we must—we may define it provisionally as "produced means of production."

Yet an Eskimo economy is not what is meant by capitalism. And at the opposite extreme, in a totally controlled communist economy, there is an enormous preoccupation with produced means of production. Until recent months, when the unrest revealed at Stalin's death gave the Russian consumer a small but much-needed break, no price was too high for an increase in capital. The brutal methods employed have produced an increase in Russia's capital, especially since military expansion requires the production of many goods of capital value apart from their military uses. Yet words lose all meaning if we apply to Soviet communism and Russian imperialism the term capitalism, though the production of capital has been perhaps their prime economic goal.

Though "produced means of production" is a sturdy working definition of capital, it is not without real difficulties and limitations. Conceivably a person in a near paradise could live wholly off the bounty of nature, but if he consumed all that he gathered he could never improve his state. Improvement comes when he "produces" more than he consumes and saves the rest. Saving therefore is a condition of capital formation, but the fulfillment of that condition results in nothing final. Useless things can be saved and no capital formation eventuate; things useful for consumption can be saved only to spoil if something further is not present to make them capital goods. Saving may be necessary to capital formation, but it is not in principle sufficient.

There are important cases where *additional* saving does not seem to be necessary to increase output. If our Eskimo with his kayak learns in some fashion that he catches twice as many fish by working in the morning rather than in the evening or going upstream instead of down, his output is doubled. The natural resources are the same; let us suppose the labor to be the same. Whence the increased output? Knowledge is capital of a sort. Or in a highly complex economy, let us suppose that a chemist, by merely changing the sequence in which the same operations are performed, eliminates costly waste or saves valuable time to the equivalent of a fifty per cent increase in output. The value of the capital goods involved will increase accordingly, but has "capital" increased?

When accumulation (the necessary condition of capital formation) takes place in the form of money, the process is complicated. Saving by the consumer now consists in restriction of consumption, refraining from the purchase of consumer goods and saving the money. In an efficient banking system, these sums will be lent at an appropriate rate of interest to borrowers who wish to buy materials for the production of capital goods. Money is borrowed, but materials are bought and sold. The effects, as Wicksell pointed out in a sweeping and brilliant insight, are different than if the goods were borrowed instead of bought and sold.

Under modern conditions of credit creation, even apart from crude monetary inflation, money becomes the only thing of value which has a negligible cost of production. When money, which has almost no cost of production, is increasing in supply and consumers are saving, while goods, which have a cost of production, are constant or decreasing in supply, then the fact that money is borrowed but goods are bought and sold can become an explosive source of tension in the price system. The supply of money can be increased in a short time; the supply of goods cannot. The borrowed, created money can send the price of goods to any level.

Under the crude inflation which, however disguised, has become common in the two world wars and their intervening depression, this same process can become even more interesting. Consumers can be doing little or no saving, spending all their increasing money incomes in a vain attempt to maintain their standard of living. The state meantime creates money to commandeer more and more materials for capital formation. Here no one is saving, but resources are nevertheless preempted from consumption, and capital is formed.

There is no attempt here to outline a positive theory of capital, but only an attempt to indicate the elusiveness of capital, considered strictly as an economic category. There can be no question of the reality or the weighty character of capital as an economic fact. Yet analysis reveals that it is as complex as it is weighty and as subtle as it is complex. These preliminaries are essential to a discussion of capitalism as a social system because capital as an economic factor must be a major element in capitalism as a social system. And if capital is not a simple concept, capitalism cannot be.

Werner Sombart is the economist who has devoted himself most exclusively and tenaciously to the study of modern capitalism. Since his problem was the description of a concrete society, his approach through genetic study of economic history, rather than abstract economic analysis, was defensible. Despite his notable labors and the assembly of many striking facts, his conclusions take us wholly out of the realm of economics. This is not necessarily a fatal objection: the economic situation at any time is not the product solely of the antecedent economic situation but of the *entire* antecedent situation. A change in educational policy in one generation, for example, may have notable economic effects in the next generation, though educational policy is not an economic datum in the first instance. Yet when Sombart reduces capitalism to a class society dominated by a "spirit" of acquisition, a "spirit" of competition and a "spirit" of rationality, it is hard to feel that anything very substantial has been uncovered.

The "rationality" is pure nineteenth-century positivist presumption that all men prior to the enlightenment were non-rational or irrational. Improvements in communication, including printing, made possible quicker as well as more accurate accounting of costs. But anyone who thinks that business rationality is distinctive of "modern" capitalism has never seen the rapid calculations of Middle Eastern merchants flourishing in their native air and has forgotten that chap (Luke 14, 28) who was the laughing stock of the neighborhood because "he did not first sit down and count the cost."

Mammon, or the spirit of acquisition, likewise cannot be regarded as an innovation of the nineteenth century. "The love of money is the root of all evil things," Paul warned Timothy, and if one agree that modern capitalism is an evil thing, the love of money may well be at the root of it. But it cannot be the distinguishing characteristic that sets capitalist society apart from all other systems.

Competition was different in the nineteenth century than it was before. The elder Toynbee indeed defined the so-called Industrial Revolution as nothing more or less than the market changes resultant upon the abolition of the market control exercised by the guilds. The competitive situation, heightened by improved transport and communication in both internal and foreign markets after the passing of the guilds, might indeed furnish grounds for calling the modern economic era the Competitive Society, but that need not be the same as capitalism—as any Stakhanovite can testify.

Acquisition, rationality and competition in modern economics differ (if at all) only in degree from the same influences in other societies. Without some criterion to specify the point at which this degree produces capitalism and the previous society ceases to be something other than capitalism, these qualities and any similarly undefined combination of indeterminate degrees of them cannot be regarded as a definition of capitalism.

Much the same is to be said of the "Protestant Ethic" analysis of Weber, Troeltsch and Tawney. The religious upheavals of the sixteenth century and their many later secondary movements produced social effects of commensurate consequence. In general, any social upheaval involves a redistribution of wealth, income and opportunity, even when it is not associated with anything so barefaced as the new politicians enriching themselves by appropriating monastic assets. Specifically in Northwestern Europe and in the British Isles, the religious revolutions, beside producing a "new rich," produced some unusual refugees. Families of wealth, education and worldly experience found themselves under pressure to move on or, if they stayed where they were, to vindicate their conduct and maintain or regain their standing. When "successful" people are hungry or feel called upon to make a fresh start and have the added motivation that what they are doing is done from adherence to radical religious principle, then things begin to move, things, for example, like the *Ark* and the *Dove* or the *Mayflower.*

No great acumen is required to explain the vigor of activity among certain groups of Protestant displaced persons. There was no more "rationality" in their actions than there is in the action of any man who is doing the best he can with high purpose: there was no more "vocation" than there is in the life of any Christian who says, "Thy will be done on earth as it is in heaven." That may be a great deal of vocation; but it was not new and it was not capitalistic. However, as we shall see, even if these elusive concepts could be shown to be valid, they might constitute a theory of the origin and social dynamics of modern industrial and commercial society, not a theory of capitalism.

We must deal with one author whose fundamental position is crystal clear. Though the early Marx preferred "capital" to "capitalism" to describe "bourgeois society," there can be no question that the vogue of both the word and the idea supposedly lying behind it are both *post* Marx and *propter* Marx; it is "a term, if not coined, at least given wide currency by Marx." Capitalism to Marx was simple; any system of social economy which tolerated private property was capitalistic and therefore evil. In this sense, the theory of the communists may be summed up in the single sentence: Abolition of private property. Since labor was the sole source of value, and labor did not get the whole value, labor was robbed or exploited. Because wherever private property existed, labor was thus being robbed, class conflict was perennial, inevitable. "Property in its present form is based on the antagonism of capital and wage labor." To explain the obvious progressive character of the society he was criticising Marx had recourse to some Hegelian metaphysics to propel his "scientific" socialism, so the abolition of bourgeois private property, exploitation and class struggle are harnessed to the materialistic interpretation of history to give it the tempo of a revolutionary movement and to provide its "stages" and inevitability.

In addressing himself to the dynamic character of the nineteenth century, its technical progress, its distribution of income, its energy and enterprise (especially overseas), its proneness to crisis, Marx was asking good questions, which Ricardo and Mill had ignored. But he gave wrong answers to the right questions, and capitalism emerges from the Marxist movement not as a clear and consistent analysis of an economic society but as a battle cry.

Capitalism to the Marxist is not an accurate picture of things as they are; it is the bloated caricature of a slimy monster to be crushed, even though its dimensions are not known with precision. Essentially it is a negative thing; it is what the Marxist is against. A military man may be concerned with detailed intelligence of his adversary; a social reformer need not be. All that is necessary for his purpose is to show that the adversary is bad. This Marx sought to do, and this is "the origin of modern capitalism."

Other writers, serious and competent economists not engaged in polemics, have sought to define capitalism in a genuinely objective way. The definitions of these students have much in common, and if capitalism can be defined or if capitalism is a good name for the thing actually defined, the work of one of these writers should provide us with the answer. Yet none of them has achieved wide acceptance, even though some of the authors are economists of considerable authority.

In a work described by von Nell-Breuning as "one of the few books on the subject that are of real value" Paul Jostock sets down the following as the essential notes of capitalism: 1. The system serves the purpose of gain by exchange; 2. production is regulated by the cooperation of two groups bound by contract, one of which possesses all necessary goods while the other possesses and contributes merely its personal labor; 3. the theoretical possibility that each of the two groups as an organizing factor engages the other and directs the course of production according to its own law is practically decided in favor of those possessing the capital.

The first item cannot be a distinguishing characteristic of modern capitalism since it is true of any economy except the far extremes of primitive direct appropriation or complete totalitarianism. The crux of the matter is in the second point: the existence of these two groups and the manner and terms of their co-existence. If these two groups are well defined; if the differences in income between the bottom of the owning group and the top of the working group are sharp, so that capital accumulation through saving by the working group is negligible; if these income differences are buttressed by social custom, by educational, cultural and other opportunities so that transit from the working group to the owning group is difficult and rare, these conditions differ from Marx's only in the ethical view of property, not in the practical view.

It is not enough that at any given moment a certain large number of people are working for wages under contract to others. The owning group must, as Jostock indicates, possess *all* necessary goods and the other must contribute *only* its labor. And if this arrangement is to merit the name of a system and is not merely a transient fact, these two groups must not only be well defined, so that only a negligible number of capitalists work and a negligible number of workers save, but the groups must remain well defined and remain so for some generations. Otherwise the statement merely says that at a given moment of time, you have such and such a distribution of wealth and income which is regarded as unsatisfactory but says nothing about how it got that way or why it is likely to stay that way.

In Europe and the British Isles where the inertia of feudal custom tends to consecrate any status and where the master-servant relationship between employer and employee keeps the latter in a menial state, something like this may well be true. But in the United States, it does not seem to be true, and if the United States is not capitalistic, where can capitalism be found? Perhaps in New England and New York may be found a few small dynasties. But America's most typical industry grew up under the personal touch of Ford, Durant and Chrysler. In merchandising, Sears, Roebuck and Marshall Field all served time as "drummers," and Woolworth failed twice before his idea took hold. Our second largest corporation, Bell Telephone, was founded by one of the few inventors with business ability and has now 1,265,000 stockholders of whom fifty per cent own ten shares or less and whose average holding is 28. Much of our electrical industry, as well as a long list of inventions, dates back to and enriched a former telegraph operator named Edison.

Two things are to be observed about such a list: 1. the examples are are drawn from very big business where capitalistic conditions should flourish if they do anywhere. Nothing is said about the large number of substantial businesses with annual sales of one to fifty million dollars whose founders are still alive. 2. Even the oldest of the persons named in the examples above lived and worked after Marx's theories were completed and widely circulated, when capitalism was supposed to be in its final crystallized form, with time the only additional ingredient necessary for it to shatter itself by its own internal stresses.

In the United States there are also about four million owner-operated farms of all sorts using about fifteen billion dollars worth of machinery, to say nothing of buildings and land. These owner-operators are largely outside any system by which an owning class contracts with a working class. Yet we can scarcely deny them an important role in giving tone to American society.

If a true proletariat, owning nothing, saving nothing, expecting nothing, were to settle to the bottom in any country, that country should be the United States. In addition to whatever "capitalism" is inherent in any industrial economy, the United States for decades admitted immigrants by the million and after 1924 by the half-million, and since 1937 (after a depression interlude) by the hundred thousands, not allowing for the recently authorized D.P. quotas. These immigrants were typically poor people with little education, not speaking the language of this country and many with European Marxist ideas, excellent raw material for a permanently submerged class. Between 1890 and 1910 the Pittsburgh steel area would have furnished all the data a Marxist needed to prove the imminence of the uprising of the proletariat. Today, some families then in a proletarian condition may still be so, but enough sons of the district have successfully played football for a university education (strictly a gentleman's prerogative) to obscure the class lines completely.

The labor union, the engine of the revolution, has not run on a Marxist schedule. The union itself is now big business, especially in the insurance field, supposedly one of the happiest hunting grounds for purest finance capitalism. The union executive now hires an extensive staff and lives and works much as the businessman. This is not a criticism of the union or the leader. Management of a large union today requires all the skills of the successful entrepreneur plus the common touch of the successful politician. When a union has found a man possessing that rare combination of qualities, it is only commonplace to take good care of him and give him all the help he needs.

When Harold Ickes called Wendell Willkie a "simple, barefoot Wall Street lawyer," he was making a smart political sally. He was also summarizing the reasons why Jostock's essentials of capitalism are not found in the U. S.

A current American writer of judicious temper, David McCord Wright, has insisted that in such discussions of a going economy we must be satisfied with *relative* notions of efficiency, productivity, success, equality. Marx could safely compare actual British industrial society with his ideal society. Adjustments in an ideal society are made more easily and less expensively than in a real one; a going economy should be appraised not against a philosopher's blueprint but against workable alternatives. Under these sensible conditions, Wright defines capitalism as any

> system in which on the *average* much the *greater* portion of economic life and particularly of net investment is carried on by private (i.e., non-government) units under conditions of active and *substantially* free competition and avowedly at least under the incentive of a hope for profit.

The important relative expressions here may be fully justified in describing a going society, but the question of degree in a definition is also important. Capitalism here depends on two ratios, private investment to government investment, and monopoly (government or private) to competition. At what values of these ratios does capitalism become something else? What the definition actually defines is non-socialism. If capitalism and socialism form a complete disjunction, then I can define capitalism by framing words to exclude socialism. But if they are not, if socialism is a definite thing but capitalism isn't, if non-socialism admits of degrees which would be of greatest economic significance to persons living under the system, then why not let us say, *these are the characteristics of the American economy which works thus and so.* There is no particular reason for calling it capitalism.

One of the strong points of Marx's approach to modern industrial society was his realization of its dynamic and fluctuating nature, so different from the equilibrium picture with no possibility of overproduction painted by the "classics" whom he despised.

> The bourgeoisie cannot exist without constantly revolutionizing the instruments of production and thereby the relations of production and with them the whole relations of society. . . . Constant revolutionizing of production, uninterrupted disturbance of all social conditions, everlasting uncertainty and agitation distinguish the bourgeois epoch from all earlier ones.

Here we have a genuine distinguishing mark of capitalism which might co-exist with private property and yield some intelligible interpretation of an era deserving the name capitalistic. Marx of course did not follow this lead except within the framework of his non-economic preconceptions. It is one of the places where he was asking the right questions.

Furnishing the right answer remained for the late Joseph A. Schumpeter, who stands supreme as a non-Marxian analyst of capitalism. He is one of the few writers who can take Marx's original economic insights and use them without in any way becoming infected. By

> our economic system, we mean an economic system characterized by private property (private initiative), by production for a market and by the phenomenon of credit, this phenomenon being the *differentia specifica* distinguishing the 'capitalist' system from other species historical or possible of the larger genus defined by the first two characteristics.

Schumpeter in his classic *Theory of Economic Development* traces out the circular flow of incomes in an unchanging economy. With the passage of time under the influence of competition all values are correctly imputed to their actual sources. In such an economy, interest as a distinct and independent economic share disappears. There is no source from which it can flow. No one can profitably borrow $100 and after twelve months pay back $105 and not lose money by the transaction. Contracts in the form of interest payments may still be written and may still be economic in spite of the money loss. But the payments are not interest; they are transfers of wages and rents. In an economy which has had time to adjust itself perfectly to an accepted way of doing things, the rate of interest moves to zero; there is no relation between man and nature, land and labor from which it can spring as an independent and stable economic share. Into this serene, pedestrian economy, Schumpeter introduces the entrepeneur with his cost-reducing innovation financed by created credits. We have now a source of true profits from the cost-reducing innovation, and the profits are a source from which interest can be paid. Borrowing is now not only economic but also profitable in money for the entrepeneur. This is the *differentia specifica* which defines modern capitalism.

Correct appraisal of Schumpeter's keen, illuminating analysis requires a correct perception of its relation to reality. In order to highlight the essentials, Schumpeter has stripped his argument down to a very abstract construction. Even in this abstract form, the picture is convincing, realistic and points the way to an understanding of much modern economic history. But as we approach actual economic life, alternative possibilities present themselves. Innovation and the entrepeneur have no essential connection with *created* credit. Entrepeneurs *could* borrow actual savings and still do business. Interest rates would be high, prices would be lower and perhaps less volatile, development would be less rapid, but crises would be fewer and milder and associated chiefly with abnormal events originating outside the economic system like drouths and war.

Because as a matter of fact, much sweeping innovation since the foundation of the Bank of England has been financed by created credit, Schumpeter was fully justified in the simplification and exaggeration involved in making created credit the *sole* means of financing innovation in his abstract construction. The memory of the "war millionaires" each conflict produces and the great acceleration of the rate of economic change under war-time inflation are all the facts we need to realize the legitimacy of his procedure.

There can be no question then of objecting either to Schumpeter's analysis or to his procedure. The question arises only as to whether this process deserves to be called capitalism. A system of 100 per cent reserve money or even a system of commercial banks for short-term credit with 100 per cent reserve with a system of equity banks for longer investment (provided the equity banks were mutual and the benefits of created credit would accrue *pro rata* to all savers) would eliminate the obvious inequities and most of the cyclical fluctuations from the present "capitalistic" system. Either maintained for long enough would correct the most undesirable features of present income distribution. The fruits of saving accruing to the real savers would diffuse the ownership of investment goods and completely obscure the "class" distinctions by making interest an important item of income for large numbers of people.

John Hicks raised the question as to whether the "capitalistic era" was not simply a vast secular boom based on the great population increase that has characterized the same period of time. Schumpeter's analysis indicates that increased population was supported by the increased output which in its turn was made possible by the acceleration of investment with the forced savings of created credit. But if it is as simple as that, if correction of one aspect of the monetary and banking system would remove our economy from the capitalistic group, why should we call the whole thing capitalistic?

Despite occasional strong statements as that of the Cardinals of France, September 8, 1949, that "the very essence of capitalism" is "the absolute value that it gives to property without reference to the common good or to the dignity of labor" and that there is in this "a materialism rejected by Christian teaching," the attitude of the Church is generally more guarded. Pius XI called attention to the fact that "Leo XIII's whole endeavor was to adjust this economic regime to the standards of true order. Whence it follows that the system itself is not to be condemned. And surely it is not vicious of its very nature." While the word "capitalism" may occasionally appear in Catholic writings of high authority, the expression "present economic regime" or "contemporary economic system" is much more commonly used.

This example could fruitfully be followed. We have seen the variety of meanings that have been assigned to the term, and we have seen that none of them is compelling even when combined with superior analysis, as in Schumpeter. We have seen the variety of causes that have been assigned for the origin or rise of this undefinable something and none of these is compelling.

The answer is that there is no such thing as capitalism. The word is incapable of scientific definition; it exists only in the Marxist dream world. It should be used "only with great reluctance since it is largely a creation of [the] socialist interpretation of economic history." "Capitalism is what Marxists are against" is the only definition that will cover all cases. The term is no more than a socialist dirty word for use in the rough-house of agitation. Only a very foolish general accepts battle on terrain of his adversary's choice. But defenders of "capitalism" do just that when they undertake the defense of "capitalism" on Marx's terms.

Under the influence of Marxist propaganda, we have become accustomed to calling the economic system which during the last hundred years has spread across the realm of European-American civilization and thence across the whole world, 'capitalism.' For a multiplicity of reasons, this is an unfortunate habit.

High on the list of this multiplicity of reasons must be placed the fact that such inadequate nomenclature is an obstacle to both action and thought. The social reformer who is taken in by the term and believes that by cutting the jugular vein of one dragon, all our economic ills will disappear, is going to be disappointed sooner or later when he finds out there is no dragon. More important, the student who believes there is one unique system to be studied is going to overlook important facts. Preoccupation with capitalism as an abstract concept has inhibited study (at least in Catholic circles) of institutions as they are. We have the institution of private property, a good thing but inadequately governed by social justice because that fertile notion has not been made operative. We have the institution of a market economy for goods and services, highly conditioned by monopoloid controls of both. Commutative justice is not always easy to observe in these markets even by him who is most anxious to do so. The institutions within the market are not organized with a built-in bent to make the promotion of the common good an easy thing while observing commutative justice. We have banking, monetary and fiscal institutions which facilitate the institutional usury by which the benefits of saving are swept to those who have not saved.

No matter where we are going we must start from where we are. These institutions should be studied as they are, and the relevant moral concepts must be studied as they can be applied to these institutions as they are. Enough good hard work on the economic and moral aspects of these problems can combine with recent technological progress to produce a really "good society." When that good society is achieved it really doesn't matter what it is called. But let's not call it capitalism.

19

SOCIALISM:
A. THE NATURE OF SOCIALISM *

Socialism is such a broad and loose term that in our times it has become almost devoid of meaning. A "socialist" measure is one which gives the government a larger role in economic and social life, and "Socialism"—if it means anything—means a system which turns over a great part of the means of production to government ownership and operation. People also speak of "modified Socialism," in which the government would compete with private enterprise, especially in such public utilities as

* Hilaire Belloc, "An Examination of Socialism" *Catholicism and Socialism* (Second Series [London: Catholic Truth Society, 1910]). Reprinted by permission.

electric power, irrigation projects, and municipally-owned transportation services.

But Socialism has had more specific meanings at various times in history. Early in the nineteenth century, during the Romantic age, various forms of "Utopian Socialism" were presented as correctives of the abuses that developed early in the industrial revolution. After 1848 Karl Marx developed a system of "scientific Socialism," in opposition both to industrial capitalism and to Utopian Socialism. Marx's system came to be known as "Communism," although we find authors referring to it simply as "Socialism" as late as 1900.

In England Socialism took on a less doctrinaire form than with Marx. The "Fabian Socialists" were mostly literary people like George Bernard Shaw who were interested in alleviating the miseries of the working class and in effecting a more equitable distribution of the wealth. The term "Fabian" refers to their tactics, which were not revolutionary. Their aim was to gain popular support by appealing to the workers with rational argument, and to have a modified form of Socialism adopted in England by parlimentary legislation.

One of the outstanding opponents of Socialism in the first decade of the twentieth century was Hilaire Belloc. Belloc was never trapped into defending the abuses of private enterprise, as some Catholics were, but instead he showed that Socialism replaced one set of evils with another, more radical set. Belloc was one of the first English writers to develop the thesis that personal freedoms are intimately connected with the private ownership of the means of production, and that when the state is the sole owner of productive property all citizens are reduced to potential slavery. The following selections are typical of the excellent polemical work of which Belloc was capable.

SOCIALISM is a political theory according to which people would be happier and better if the means of production—that is, the land of a country and its buildings, ships, machines, rails, &c.—belonged to the Government instead of belonging, as they now mainly do, to private citizens and private corporations.

That is the only exclusive meaning of Socialism. All the other wobbly ideas that have been tacked on to it by its enemies or its friends—that it is "atheistic," or that it involves sexual "immorality," that it is "progressive," that it is "Christian"—have nothing to do with the one proposition which alone distinguishes it from all other policies.

A Socialist State need be neither more democratic nor less democratic than the present state of affairs. A State in which all the means of production were owned by the Government might be under a despot or under an aristocracy, or it might be managed as a democracy. However it was managed it would be a Socialistic State if the means of production were owned and controlled by Government.

Socialism does not in its essence imply that nobody should own anything. There is no reason why a man in a Socialist State should not own a great quantity of things for his own private enjoyment. The only thing that would be denied to private ownership would be something commonly used or usable as a means of production; something which, when one part of the community owns it and the other part does not, permits the owning part to live upon the labour of the non-owning part. A man in a Socialistic State would be allowed to own ornaments and purely personal possessions such as pictures and furniture, watches, and even productive machines should they be used for his own enjoyment alone; but he would not be allowed a share, large or small, in a factory, or a railroad, or a commercial steamship, or a piece of land (to be used for profit), except that share which he might be said to own as a member of the community whose Government owned and controlled all these things.

Again, a State could be Socialistic and yet have very different degrees of enjoyment among its citizens. The Government might reward men according to merit, distributing very unequally the wealth produced by labour applied to the capital and land it owned. The Government might give large amounts of the good things to a few people whom it thought deserved them, and very little to the mass of mankind whom it might think so wicked as not to deserve them. It might make an unequal distribution by giving high rewards to the talented, the good organizers and the good managers, in order to secure efficiency of production, and very little to the general mass of labourers. It might act purely by caprice, giving large amounts to its favourites and small amounts to the rest of the community. It might (as many confusedly think that it *must*) distribute to each according to his need; it might make a rigidly equal distribution to each family in the community according to the age and number of its members. Whatever form the distribution took, whether there were great differences between the amounts distributed or exact equality in them, whether the distribution were determined by competition in talent or by caprice, or by the sense of human equality, the State would still be a Socialistic State if the means of production were owned and controlled by the Government.

This is the main point to seize; for it is in this, and in this alone, that Socialism differs from other political theories.

It is certain that, whatever may have happened in other parts of the world, our ancestors here in Western Europe never had anything of the kind. There was plenty of co-operative production in the Middle Ages; there was plenty of common land (as there still is) side by side with land privately owned. There existed for a short time a legal fiction, which still theoretically survives, that the land of the country ultimately belonged to the Crown; but in practice no Socialistic State can be discovered in the past history of men of our own blood. Many have thought to discover it, and guessed it to be present in certain ill-understood and very obscure primitive customs, but the evidence in favour of this kind of guesswork was never strong enough to convince a close critic of evidence, and, as research proceeds, gets weaker every day.

The proposal, then, which is the Socialist proposal, to convert all private property in the means of production—that is, in the factories, machines, land, houses, &c.—into Government property is a novel proposal. It is a proposal to do something quite new and as yet untried by men of our descent with our inherited traditions and instincts and ways of looking at things. Why has so revolutionary a proposal been made, and what arguments can be brought forward in its favour?

This revolutionary proposal has been made because the present state of society is in itself a novel one, suffering from evils new in the history of our country, and, for that matter, of the world; and the arguments in favour of it—the arguments, that is, by which it is attempted to prove that England would be a better and a happier country under Socialism, are many and strong. As things now are in England, a small proportion of the inhabitants of the country possess by far the greater part of the means of production. It is very difficult to obtain exact figures, and all general statements made in this connection must be received with caution. But I think the following general statement is not very wide of the mark, though, of course, it does not pretend to be rigidly accurate. I think one may say that less than two hundred families at the very most control one-quarter of our means of production. Another quarter is in the hands of perhaps two thousand families at the most. And the remaining half (unless we are to include properties so small that they hardly count as capital) cannot at the utmost be made to include as much as a sixteenth of the whole community. The rest consist of families working for a wage, and unlikely, save in exceptional individual instances, to be anything other than wage-earners, either now or in the future. Side by side with this concentration of ownership in few hands you have a highly competitive system of production under which security of employment is at its minimum. Thus a great and an increasing proportion of the population—so it is maintained— has no share in the permanent wealth of the country, and can only enjoy what it does on condition of continual labour for others who own that permanent wealth; while the workers, though not perhaps becoming actually poorer, are becoming relatively poorer compared with the owning classes, and with all this they are less and less secure of permanent employment as trade competition extends over a wider and wider area of the world's surface. A good crop of some product on the other side of the globe may suddenly throw out of employment any number of men employed here in the production of a similar article. The cessation of demand for something produced by us, but consumed by people whom we have never seen, in India or in China, may suddenly destroy the livelihood of a whole group of artisans in England. Every progress even, every new invention, tends to bring into the experience of some group of labouring men a period of insecurity at the best, and at the worst of acute distress. Meanwhile there is a constant tendency for property to amalgamate still further, there is a constant tendency for the big business to swallow up the small one, and it is the main Socialist argument that if we leave things as they are we shall end in a state of society where quite a small number of exceedingly rich men will control the destinies of all the rest of their fellows. It will, moreover (they say), be a state of society in which competition for employment will always maintain the average earnings of the labouring class at an exceedingly low level, and the power of enjoyment of the mass of the community will be miserably small compared with the power of enjoyment of the few owners who control it.

It is to avoid a consummation of this kind that Socialists propose the fundamental transformation of our social system, towards which transformation they are working with such enthusiasm and conviction.

Now let us look at another aspect of the matter, and consider certain consequences that would follow upon Socialism were it ever brought into being.

In the first place, no man in a Socialistic State would be what we now call *free*. This is a proposition very hotly denied by many Socialists, because they believe it to be an unfair and a misleading one; but no clear thinker can deny it, and by far the best arguments used in this connection by the clearest thinkers upon the Socialistic side are to the effect that, though the citizen in a Socialist State would not be "free" in the sense in which an old independent owner of land and capital used to be, he would be much *freer* than the mass of the population is to-day. Before returning to that, however, it is well to repeat the first and fundamental objection to the Socialist solution of our modern difficulties. No man under a Socialist State would be what *we* call *free*. He could not exercise his will as to where he should go, what he should consume, what he should do with his time, to what activities he should direct his energies.

There is a rather muddle-headed habit, but a common one, present not only in Socialist discussion but in most other political discussion, which may be briefly described as trying to have your cake and eat it too. Men like to believe that some ideal of theirs would have all the advantages inherent to itself, and also the advantages in contradiction with its very nature. All men love individual freedom—even such a remnant of it as the modern artisan may claim is very dear, and the threat of losing it is a serious one. It is, therefore, not surprising that those who see in Socialism the only remedy for the appalling evils which we suffer today try to reconcile that remedy with individual freedom. But consider for a moment how impossible such a reconciliation is. A man in a factory under a master may, if he choose, leave that factory and look for work elsewhere. If he prefer, for the sake of security, to remain in that one employment, he is in many things at the disposal of his master's will during the hours of his labour. He cannot go to the manager or to the master and say: "I don't like this job; I feel inclined for that other one. Be good enough to give it me." At least he can go and say it, and perhaps in certain cases if he shows large aptitude for the new job and is able to convince his master of it, or if he finds a special favour extended to him, that liberty of choice will be conceded; but it is obvious that it could not be universal. You could not have every employee in Mr. Jones's mill saying exactly what he would do and for how long he would do it, or choosing his job according to his private inclination. So far liberty is already largely restricted by the industrial system, and the rich man is far freer than the poor one. But now go a step further. Work is done, and the man goes out into the street. He thinks he will have a glass of beer; but all the public-houses in the neighborhood are owned by Mr. Jones just as much as the mill is, and Mr. Jones will or will not let him drink, according as he sees fit. He goes home, and, finding something not suitable to him in his present house, he decides to move into another which has caught his fancy, and which is more convenient to him for some reason. He finds, to his astonishment, that not only is Mr. Jones the owner of his present house, but of the other house too; and can deny him the faculty of exchanging his old residence for the new one. He thinks he will use part of his wages to get a pair of boots; but he can only get boots of the sort provided by Mr. Jones, and Mr. Jones can allow him to have a new pair, or not, just as he thinks fit. He will go to a music-hall. He finds that Mr. Jones owns that, too, and decides on his entertainment. Wherever he turns, all the things he desires to get, all the places in which he desires to move and to have his being, belong to the same man as owned the mill where his working hours were spent, and wherever he goes, no matter how far afield, this omnipotent being is everywhere the owner and controller, not, indeed, of his person, but of the food by which his person remains alive, and of the shelter by which he remains alive, and of every recreation or necessity relative to his being.

Now Mr. Jones is, under Socialist conditions, the Government; and to the loss of freedom which every man feels during those hours which he gives as a wage-earner to the capitalist who employs him must be added, under a Socialist system, a similar loss of freedom in all the other hours of his life. There is no way out of that truth.

To this criticism the Socialist has an answer. The answer is as follows:

I admit that the ownership of all the means of production by the Government would be a bad thing, if it were used despotically, as such ownership is now used by individual owners. But I would never tolerate a Socialist ideal unless that ideal included democratic management.

Note at this point that the two ideas of Government ownership and democracy have no connection. We have all of us met Socialists who were not in the least democratic, and it is perfectly easy to be a Socialist and a most rabid anti-democrat, especially if you are keener on people being made to do whatever you think is good for them than you are upon their being free to choose between good and evil. Still, it must be admitted that the desire for Socialism, springing as it nearly always does in hearts powerfully affected by the misery of the people, is usually associated with a democratic ideal of government; and most Socialists will say to you:

The man will not be free as regards the Government, but since he will, as a citizen, be the master of the Government, he will be really just as free as the most independent owner is to-day, and much more free than the ordinary wage-earner is to-day. He will be able to make or unmake the regulations which shall control his life.

The critic of Socialism at once replies that this will not be the case. A man voting as one of many thousands or millions is quite a different thing from a man enjoying elastic and immediate personal control every moment over his own actions. No one would be so insane as to say that the actions of a modern Government, on however democratic a base, are invariably consonant with the will of the great majority of its citizens. Most people would say that usually the actions of the Government were out of touch with the will of the great majority of the people. This, they would say, was true even of the very limited sphere of Government to-day, and of the very slow and imperfect action which it can take in quite a few matters. Those who believe this to be true even of Government as it is cannot believe that Socialism, no matter how democratic the political system with which it was combined, would give freedom of action even to the majority of citizens.

The critic of Socialism asks a further question: What about the minority? Either you must have a constitution where nothing can be done without an overwhelming majority, in which case you would be perpetually coming to a deadlock, or else you must work by ordinary majorities, in which case you would be perpetually creating hearty and intolerable discontent in large minorities opposed to you. Further, this system of majority voting, even if it worked, could only apply to the very large decisions of life. In all the innumerable minor details that make up our circumstances we should necessarily be in the hands of officials. I am not saying that would be a bad thing, or that it would be worse than the state of affairs that exists now for most of our citizens. I am only pointing out that this is an absolutely inevitable result of Socialism, and a result that cannot be avoided save by a process of confusion of thought: by trying to believe that a thing can both be and not be at the same time. Nor has any one ever been able to show how so clear and obvious a resultant of the Socialist system could possibly be avoided.

The next criticism offered to Socialism is of a more subtle and profound kind, but is none the less very real. As Socialism would destroy what we call freedom, so it would destroy what we call the satisfaction of the desire for property. Now here two very important arguments used by Socialists against their opponents must be immediately noted.

First, they say, under present conditions the vast mass of our fellow-citizens cannot satisfy that human desire for property in so far as it exists; their whole efforts are directed—and God knows under what an anxious strain of body and mind!—to satisfy the bare necessities of human appetite—the necessary food, and clothing, and house room. They would, under a Socialistic State, if it were democratically managed, own, not indeed any of the means of production, but far, far more of the enjoyable permanent possessions of life than they do to-day. This is perfectly true, and all that the critic of Socialism can set against it is a repetition of the undoubted truth just stated—namely, that under a Socialist State the desire for property which can now in theory be satisfied by all, and is in practice satisfied by some, would not be satisfied by any if private property in land and the means of production were abolished.

But even to this the Socialist has a second and a very strong reply. He can say:

> The desire for property does not exist very strongly in the case of land and of machinery. The desire to have these things is only a desire to be what is called 'rich'—that is, to be able to exchange the product of land and capital so owned against daily enjoyments. The desire is not for the things themselves, for the land itself, or for the machinery itself; and those things which a man really does desire to own, the things which are part of his permanent possessions, and with which he is constantly in contact, and out of which he obtains a permanent enjoyment because he is their owner, those things—his books, his furniture, his ornaments, his pictures, perhaps even a little plot of land (if he promises to produce nothing for sale with it)—he could possess under the Socialist State; and that everybody would have such personal possessions, whereas now very few do.

There is but one reply to this very powerful contention, which is that, as a fact, men do desire to own land and the means of production, and to own them absolutely, not only in order that they may be what is called "rich"—that is, that they may command passing enjoyments—but for the pleasure and consequences of owning the things themselves, and that for the following reasons:

First, that you cannot distinguish between the desire of ownership in a thing according to whether that thing is productive or not. It is true the interest which a man takes in a share of a business is not the same as the interest he takes in a particular instrument which he himself handles and uses. Still, it is a personal interest, and not a mere crude sense of superior opportunity for enjoyment. This is particularly the case with regard to land, which arouses the most powerful sentiment of affection and interest in the possessor, quite independently of whether it is cultivated for profit or not, and quite independently of the amount in which it is owned.

Secondly, this general desire to own is connected with certain human consequences which have nothing to do with whether the thing owned is capable of exploiting the labour of others or not. Of one of these human consequences, economic freedom, mention has been made above. Another well worth noting, and closely attached to it, is the preservation of personal honour. Where few own, the mass who do not own at all are under a perpetual necessity to abase themselves in a number of little details. That is why industrial societies fight so badly compared with societies of peasant proprietors. The mass of the population gets trained to the sacrifice of honour; it gets used to being ordered about by the capitalist, and partially loses its manhood. If there were but one capitalist, the State, this evil would certainly be exaggerated. Men might be better fed, better clothed, and materially much happier; they might be brighter in spirits, better companions, and healthier men all round, but they would necessarily have lost all power of expression for the sentiment known as personal honour; they would have one absolute master, all forms of personal seclusion from whom would be impossible. This, when it is in the midst of modern evils, appears a very small point; but those who have passed by compulsion from a higher to a lower standard of personal honour can testify how vital a point is that honour in the scheme of human happiness.

It must, however, finally be asked of the man who criticizes the Socialist proposal: "If you will not accept this positive and clear remedy for the intolerable conditions of modern industrial society, what alternative have you?"

It is as though a man suffering from a bad limb were to hesitate to have it amputated, and the surgeon were to say to him: "If you will not let me cut it off, what other course do you propose to pursue in order to be cured?"

This question is a strong and insistent one; it is the root question of the whole affair, and it requires reply; for any one who pretends that the present condition of society in England is tolerable, or has even the least chance of enduring, is of a mental calibre worthy rather of what is called "practical politics" than of serious and vital discussion. Let us see, then, what the answer is which the serious opponents of Socialism (not the politicians, for they do not count) make to its demand.

What they say is, that if you could make a society in which the greater part of citizens owned capital and land in small quantities, that society would be happy and secure. They say (as every one must) that such a subdivision is quite possible with regard to land; but they also believe it to be possible with regard to shares in industrial concerns. When they are told that a high division of this sort would necessarily and soon drift again into a congested state of ownership, with a few great captitalists on the one hand and a wretched proletariat upon the other, they answer that, as a matter of fact, in the past, when property was thus well divided, it did not drift into that condition, but that the highly divided state of property was kept secure for centuries by public opinion translating itself into laws and customs, by a method of guilds, of mutual societies, by an almost religious feeling of the obligation not to transgress certain limits of competition, &c. When they are told that a State in which property was highly divided would involve more personal responsibility and personal anxiety than would the Socialist State, they freely admit this, but they add that such responsibilities and anxieties are natural to freedom in any shape and are the price one must pay for it.

Consider carefully this alternative theory. It is valuable because—First, it is the only possible alternative; secondly, because it is one which has hardly entered into the consciousness of English people.

So few English people have ever owned anything during the last few generations that the idea of highly divided capital is not present as a social experience. It is hardly an historic memory. Nevertheless, it remains with English people, just as much as with any other Europeans, an instinctive ideal. And I repeat, between that ideal of highly divided capital and Socialist collectivism there is no possible third ideal; we must go one way or the other. Every reform, every little tinkering and futile Bill which people maunder through in the House of Commons necessarily tends one way or the other.

The whole contention of the future in Europe lies between these two theories. On the one hand you have the Socialist theory, the one remedy and the only remedy seriously discussed in the industrial societies which have ultimately grown out of the religious schism of the sixteenth century—that is, the industrial societies of North Germany, of the Northern United States, and especially of England and the lowlands of Scotland. On the other hand, you have the Catholic societies whose ultimate appetite is for a state of highly divided property, working in a complex and probably, at least, in a co-operative manner. That is certainly the way the Irish nation is going. The Irish people—unilke the aliens of the North—have steadily refused to turn themselves into a proletariat, whether in the modern industrial phase or in preparation for the final Socialistic phase. The Irish are determined to own. The same solution appeals to the great mass of the French people (with the exception of certain plague spots such as the mining and spinning districts of the North), and the interest of all our debates in the near future in Western or European society will lie, I think, in the victory of one or other of these two ideals—the Socialist ideal, in which the diseased industrial world will attempt to heal itself upon lines consonant with its existing nature; the ideal of widely-diffused ownership, in which the healthier and older world, which has survived outside the modern industrial system, proposes to build up its new life, until it can see its way to basing an intensive production upon highly divided individual property.

Which of the two systems will win no one can say. The Socialists, of course, do the most prophesying: but then they have grown out of that Biblical enthusiasm in religion and philosophy to which prophecy is native. But prophecy has always been worthless in human affairs, save where it regarded transcendental things.

B. THE CATHOLIC CHURCH AND SOCIALISM *

THE CATHOLIC CHURCH is throughout the world opposed to that modern theory of society which is called *Socialist*.

That is a plain fact which both parties to the quarrel recognize and which third parties, though they commonly explain it ill, recognize also.

It is further evident that, the nearer the Socialist theory comes to its moment of experiment, the larger the number of souls over which it obtains possession, the more definite and the more uncomprising does Catholic opposition to it become. But this native opposition between the Faith and Socialism is not one out of many phenomena connected with Socialism. It is the chief.

The movement of Socialism as it advances, discovers no other serious opponent besides the Catholic Church; and in a general survey of Europe I cannot but believe that the struggle between these two forces is the matter of our immediate future.

The arguments which Socialists are accustomed to meet in their own non-Catholic surroundings are either puerile or vicious; the demolition of such arguments is too facile a task to occupy an intelligent mind, and the Socialist by the very exercise of such a controversy against ineptitude grows to think there is no permanent obstacle to the propagation of his system—it is merely a question of time. Give him time to illuminate the darkened and to let it be exactly known what he desires, and all—or at least the vast unfortunate mass which make up the bulk and stuff of our modern industrial society—must agree with him.

In such a mood of ultimate intellectual security the Socialist comes across the Catholic Church and for the first time meets a barrier. He finds opposed to him an organism whose principle of life is opposed to his own, and an intelligence whose reasoning does not—as do the vulgar capitalist arguments to which he is so dreadfully accustomed—take for granted the very postulates of his own creed. He learns, the more he comes across this Catholic opposition, that he cannot lay to avarice, stupidity, or hypocrisy the resistance which this unusual organism offers to his propaganda. Even in this country, where less is known of the Catholic Church than in any other, he has an example. The Irish people deliberately chose to be peasant proprietors upon terms most onerous

* Hilaire Belloc, "The Catholic Church and Socialism," *Catholicism and Socialism* (Second Series [London: Catholic Truth Society, 1910]). Reprinted by permission.

and delayed, when they could immediately and on far more advantageous terms have become permanent tenants of the State. Such a political attitude in a whole people arrests a Socialist. He cannot lay it to the avarice of the rich: it is, on the contrary, the act of men who are among the poorest in Christendom. He cannot lay it to the moral influence of a wealthy class indoctrinating the rest of the community with the idea of property, for of all the nations of Europe the Irish are the least subject to oligarchy. He cannot but observe that a people completely democratic and occupied in redressing the most glaring example of the evil which he, the Socialist, combats, have determined to redress it upon the lines of private ownership and not of collectivism. The concentration of the means of production in few hands, the exploitation of the whole community by a few, had reached in Ireland after three hundred years of anti-Catholic administration, the very limits of human endurance. It was the worst case in Europe and the very field, a Socialist would think, for the immediate acceptance of collectivism; and yet private ownership, with its complexity, its perils and its anxieties, was deliberately chosen instead.

Again, the Socialist can but notice when he first comes across them that the Catholic priesthood and the men and women incorporated as Catholic Religious are the most resolute in their opposition to his campaign; and yet these are the only institutions in Europe to which poverty is, as it were, native: they are the only institutions which revive under poverty and are at their best and healthiest when they are least able to enjoy wealth; and, what is more, they are the only flourishing institutions in which the means of production are often held in a corporate manner.

There remains one facile explanation which, for a moment, the Socialist may accept. The Catholic resistance he may for a moment, when he first meets it, ascribe to stupidity. He may believe, as was universally believed in Oxford in my time (and, since the place is isolated, is probably still believed), that no intelligent and trained man sincerely holds the Faith, and that a true conviction of it is possible only to those in whom ignorance or lack of exercise have atrophied the powers of reason. I say the Socialist may imagine this for a moment, in his first shock of surprise at finding men so fixedly opposed to his conceptions, but his very activity in propaganda will soon change such a judgment. Socialists are at once the most sincere and the most actively curious of men. They seek out everywhere men of all kinds to convince them of justice: it is their occupation and their very breath; and in this process they will learn what all travelled and experienced men appreciate, that the spirit of the Church is not a spirit of intellectual supineness. The Catholic irony, the Catholic rhetoric, the Catholic rapidity of synthesis, the Catholic predilection for general ideas and for strict deduction therefrom, the Catholic passion for definition and precise thought—all these may spring from one erroneous attitude towards the Universe; but whatever that attitude is, more certainly (says the man with a wide experience of European life) it is not an attitude inimical to the exercise of thought. The Church heeds a continual vivacity of intellectual effort, which is discoverable both in history and in contemporary experience. It is alive with an intellectual activity which is perpetually supporting and extending a firm scheme of general philosophy and is perpetually applying it to the concrete and ever-changing details of society. Those countries which have preserved Catholic tradition may be and are blamed by their opponents for too great an attachment to abstract principles and to ideas: not for the opposite tendency which shirks the effort of thinking and codifying and takes refuge in mere experiment.

The Socialist, then, who comes at all frequently upon Catholic opposition to his creed, grows interested in that opposition as in something novel and challenging to him. After so many unworthy opponents he inclines to look at the Catholic view of economic society as an orthodox Victorian economist, tired of answering idiotic objections to Free Trade, might look at a society hitherto unknown to him and actually advancing to prosperity through Protection. To put it in few words, Catholic opposition nearly always—at least--makes a Socialist think. He recognizes that he has before him another world, another order of ideas from those which he has taken for granted in his opponents as in himself. Two societies and two vast organisms meet in this quarrel. The one will necessarily, and that in the near future, attempt to destroy the other; they cannot co-exist; it is of supreme importance to all of us to-day to grasp the nature of the division.

What is it in Catholicism which negatives the Socialist's solution? Here is modern industrial society, evil beyond expression, cruel, unjust, cowardly and horribly insecure. The Socialist comes forward with an obvious and simple remedy. Let private property in land and the means of production be abolished, and let the State control them: let all become workmen under the State, which shall have absolute economic control over the lives of all and preserve to all security and sufficiency. Why does the Church, to which this modern industrial society is loathsome, and which is combating it with all her might; why does the Church, which continually points to the abominations of our great cities as a proof of what men come to by abandoning her; why does the Church, whose every doctrine is offended and denied by this evil, reject the solution offered? It is because she perceives in a certain proportion and order the exercise of human faculties; and having grasped that arrangement she refuses to sacrifice the greater to the lesser, the primary to the secondary thing: she will not imperil what is fundamental in society for the sake of some accidental need, nor deny what is permanent for the convenience of passing conditions. In all the miseries and shipwrecks of the sexual relation she will not admit one exception to the institution of marriage. In all the corruption and injustice of political society she will not abandon the principle of a social order with its necessary authorities, subordinations, and sanctions.

And to-day in all the disease of economic society and amid all the horrors which the abuse of property has brought about, she will not deny the institution of property, which she discovers to be normal to man, a condition of his freedom in civic action, but much more a necessity of his being.

I will put my argument upon a purely temporal basis for the simple reason that upon any other basis it is not an argument at all. One cannot argue with a man save upon common premisses, and since those to whom this explanation is addressed would never admit the premiss of revelation or of Divine knowledge in the Church, no appeal can be made to it if one desires to explain to them what it is that the Church rejects in their attitude.

Put, then, in purely temporal terms, the Church is a supreme expert in men. Not only is she an expert in the nature of men, but she is from the necessity of her constitution, experience, and expectation of the future, an institution which only considers men in the absolute. The Church will never give a definition that shall apply to men under particular and ephemeral conditions alone, nor, conversely, will she ever accept as general or true a definition constructed only for peculiar and ephemeral conditions. She is concerned with man for ever and is here to preserve, even in mortal conditions, permanent and enduring things. For instance, to a man of the twelfth century resident in any agricultural part of Northern and Western Europe, it would have seemed the most monstrous of absurdities and the most wicked of doctrines that a man should not be under a lord; the whole of society was permeated with that idea, yet did not the Church at that time define the feudal relation? She continued to lay down only what is universally true and in the most universal terms that if civil society is to exist, there must be first a subordination to constituted authority, and secondly that such a subordination must repose upon a moral basis and have no sanction in mere force, and was, whether in the commander or the commanded, an end superior to both.

Now the Catholic Church, as an expert in men and as an expert whose peculiar character it is to refuse as general anything which does not cover the whole nature of man, rejects in Socialism its particular economic thesis—which is the distinguishing mark of it—but much more rejects, I mean more instinctively and with a more profound reaction, the consequences and connotations of that thesis.

The test thesis of Socialism is this—that man would be better and happier were the means of production in human society controlled by Government rather than by private persons or corporations. If the Socialist regards that as universally true, then he holds what may justly be called a Socialist creed, he holds a general theory true under all conditions and at all times, and that creed the Catholic Church rejects. She maintains (I am not speaking here of her Divine authority or of her claim to speak with the voice of Divine revelation, but only of her judgement upon the nature of men)—she maintains, I say, that human society is fulfilling the end of its being, is normal to itself, is therefore happier when its constituent families own and privately control material things, and she further maintains (just what, as we have seen, she did in the matter of civil authority) that this institution of ownership is not merely a civil accident unconnected with the destiny of the soul, nor a thing deliberately set up by man, as are so many of the institutions of a State, but a prior thing based, created with man himself, inseparable from him, and close in touch with the sense of right and wrong: ownership for a Catholic involves definite moral obligations, exterior to and superior to ownership. The owner may be a very bad man, the thing owned may be of very little use to him and of great use to another; it still remains *his*, and the evil of depriving him of it is an evil wrought against what the Church regards as a fundamental human conception without which humanity cannot repose nor enjoy the sense of justice satisfied.

Let no Socialist say at this point that so absolute a proposition as that which I have called the test Socialist thesis is not his; that some part of property is the means of production he will always admit: still less let him, in meeting a Catholic, indulge in a hoary fallacy and argue from the necessary influence of the State in economic affairs that Socialism is but an extension of an admitted principle. Every Catholic, from the nature of his creed, is possessed of the elements of philosophy, and every Catholic perceives that to the very existence of a system some definable principle is necessary. The principle of Socialism is that the means of production are morally the property not of individuals but of the State; that in the hands of individuals, however widely diffused, such property exploits the labour of others, and that such exploitation is wrong. No exceptions in practice destroy the validity of such a proposition; it is the prime conception which makes a Socialist what he is. The men who hold this doctrine fast, who see it clearly, and who attempt to act upon it and to convert others to it, are the true Socialists. They are numerous, and what is more, they are the core of the whole Socialist movement. It is their uncompromising dogma which gives it its vitality, for never could so vast a revolution be effected in human habit as Socialists in general pretend to effect, were there not ready to act for it men possessed of a definite and absolute creed.

For example, let us ask these men what they think of a community composed of, we will say, two farming families, each family to be the owner of its farm and each to employ the members of the other in certain forms of labour, which those members are especially skilled in. To the Catholic such a condition of society presents itself as absolutely just. Here is at once ownership, a fundamental human necessity, and yet no inequality, still less any grievance based upon the contrast between luxury above and want below.

Now, your true Socialist rejects a society of that kind. He says that even if the exact balance were struck, and even if the two owning families here supposed had precisely equal enjoyment of material things (a condition which, note you, the Socialist does not propose, for it is not equality of enjoyment that he is seeking, but the socialisation of the means of production, which he regards as morally exterior to the category of ownable things), even then he would disapprove of such a community; for though each member of it was exploiting the other equally, yet *exploitation was going on,* and exploitation of itself he conceives to be morally wrong. Note that it is this fundamental attitude which makes the Socialist more bitter against schemes for the dispersion of capital than he is against schemes for its accumulation in few hands. Capital held by many, still more capital held by all, each with a share that forbids him to be proletarian in the State, is the opposite and the contradiction of the Socialist ideal. It is, on the contrary, the consummation of the Catholic ideal, and it is curious to note how those of the chief nations of Europe which resisted the "Reformation" have, since that crisis, tended to the perpetual accumulation of small capital in many hands, while societies which succumbed to the storm have tended to the accumulation of capital in few hands, and to the turning of the mass of citizens into a proletariat economically unfree. Contrast Protestant and Catholic cantons of Switzerland, France and Ireland *v.* England, North Germany with South, &c., and this historical truth will be apparent.

The whole of this quarrel may be put in a nutshell thus: The Catholic Church does not admit that the possession of the means of production differs morally from the possession of objects which cannot be used or are not used as means of production.

Now there arises on this point a very interesting question which a man not a Socialist, but convinced that a temporary Socialist experiment is necessary if society is to be saved, may put with great force. All rules with regard to the nature of man are subject, says he, to the existence at least of mankind: and the rights, however fundamental, must give way before the supreme right of the citizen to live. For instance, shipwrecked sailors upon a raft at sea have a right to declare all food common property. The Catholic Church, with its doctrine of a certain minimum below which society may not compel a man to live, with its profound contempt for the results of wealth upon individual character, and with its acute perception of the order or ratio in which men supply their needs, is the first to perceive the necessity for exceptions to many of her own rules. And the questioner I am supposing may say to her this:

Since as a fact our society has got into this abnormally wicked condition in which a handful own the means of production and the mass are economically their slaves, will you not regard it as an exceptional time, and, under circumstances so abnormal and so vicious, promote the establishment, for a time at least, of the Socialist principle?

This was the position which an intimate friend of mine, a Protestant and a member of the Ministry (Mr. Masterman) took up in a debate at the New Reform Club some time ago. He said: Try collectivism, and of course it will turn into divided ownership; but you must have collectivism as a preliminary step.

To this question the Catholic Church again replies in the negative, and her reason for so replying is as follows: That the time in which we live, though historically considered it is most abnormal and vicious in its economical arrangements—perhaps in modern England worse than ever any society was before—yet is not fatally bound to these arrangements. Those arrangements are not fatal things which humanity must suffer; they are not due to external or natural forces which man is not responsible for: they are the direct results of a false philosophy and a vicious training of the mind. The Catholic Church replies to those who point out the monstrous inequalities into which industrial society has allowed itself to drift, that such inequalities have arisen through a myriad tiny agencies all of which have their root in the same false philosophy of life which is now attempting to remedy its own errors by the introduction of a remedy still reposing on the same false philosophy: the remedy of collectivism. It was precisely because men wanted to enjoy rather than to own, because they lost the sense of what is fundamental in man, that they promoted a machinery by which first the great landlord of the "Reformation" rising on the ruins of religion was economically dominant, next the merchant capitalist reached the head of affairs, until now more and more the mere gambler or the mere swindler enjoys supreme economic power in our diseased and moribund economic society. It was precisely because the old European sense of personal connection between the owner and the thing owned was repudiated and lost when the true conception of human life was repudiated and lost with the loss of the Faith, that these monstrous financial fortunes which are the very negation of property at last arose. And the Catholic Church can reply to those who oppose her in this matter, that though she rejects the short cut of collectivism, society can still remedy itself, slowly indeed but effectually, by the adoption of her system with its full consequences, conscious and subconscious, upon every human action and upon the framing of laws. She would further reply that the adoption of but one principle of hers, the sanctity of property, and its consequent diffusion with the corresponding suspicion and repression of all forms of acquisition which depend less upon production than upon violence or intrigue, would transform society. It is a remedy which every politician could apply who desired to see free men freely possessed as citizens of the means of production, which every voter if he were in earnest could apply, which every writer if he were in earnest could apply.

The Catholic Church, acutely conscious as she is of the abominations of the modern industrial and capitalistic system, sees that system to be dependent upon human wills and curable by their right ordering. She refuses to cure it at the expense of denying a fundamental principle of morality, the principle of private ownership, which applies quite as much to the means of production as to any type of material object.

I will not extend these remarks nor expand the slight scope of my paper by showing that the refusal of the Catholic Church to admit collectivism is not a merely negative, but rather a constructive attitude. Every Catholic knows instinctively, as it were, that the erection of society upon Catholic lines makes for the destruction of servitude in every form. Every Catholic knows that Catholic morality produced the European peasant out of the material of the Pagan slave, every Catholic knows that it is in Catholic societies that revolt against intolerable economic conditions has been most fruitful, and every Catholic further knows how impossible it would be and is to establish in a Catholic society the monstrous institution of industrial capitalism. In a word, a Catholic feels that a Catholic society dealing with modern methods of production would be a society admitting great differences in the properties possessed by and controlled by individuals, but that it would of its nature eliminate that type of citizen who is in possession of none of the means of production and is proletarian. The Catholic Church—I speak here continually of its historical and temporal action, not of its revealed doctrine—knows men so thoroughly that, while insisting upon equality in certain temporal rights and in all spiritual things, it does not insist upon equality in economic enjoyment, for the simple reason that what men primarily need in this province is not equality but sufficiency and security. The Catholic conscience is convinced that sufficiency and security are more permanently attached to a society or divided ownership with the responsibilities, the family organizations, the sense of inheritance, the mutual obligations which make it an organic and forbid it to be a mechanical thing, than they are attached to the deliberate action of a despotic government. Now, a Catholic, relying upon Catholic training in thought and morals, can go further. He can say that were you to establish collectivism it could not but ultimately result in some form, and probably a very evil form, of private ownership.

Personally I cannot but see the future in this light. A society in which the Church shall conquer will be a society in which a proletariat shall be as unthinkable as it was unthinkable in the Middle Ages. Such a society would, under modern conditions of production, end as a society of highly divided properties bound together by free co-operative organizations. On the other hand, a society in which one Socialist experiment after another takes its place in the scheme of laws will not end as the ideal collectivist society which those just, sincere, and ardent men whom I am here opposing propose. It is far more likely to end as a state in which a very small class of free owners shall control a very large servile class into which the mass of citizens shall have sunk.

This is the peril which I believe to lie before society, and especially before the non-Catholic societies of Northern and industrial Europe, with their subservience to Jewish finance and their inheritance of an anti-Catholic philosophy. Every step towards the artificial regulation of contract brings us nearer some such final solution; and a solution it will be, though I dread it. A society once established upon those lines would have forgotten how to rebel; the security and sufficiency of the servile class would be the price of their servility, and the sense of freedom, with its incalculable consequences on human character, will, for the bulk of our descendants, have disappeared. It is a peril inconceivable to either party in the great modern quarrel, but it is close at hand. The only alternative I can see to that peril is, even in the temporal and economic sphere, the action and effect of the Catholic Church upon citizenship.

20

COMMUNISM:
A. THE PHILOSOPHY OF COMMUNISM *

Marxian Communism is not properly understood unless it is analyzed as a philosophy, a theology, a way of life, as well as a body of economic doctrines. For Communism came upon the Western world in the nineteenth century as a faith demanding of its adherents complete and blind submission, as a faith with a creed, a code, and a cult from which one may not deviate unless he is willing to be branded a heretic.

Communism took hold of men's minds because of the religious vacuum that existed in the Western world in the late nineteenth and twentieth centuries. It made a strong protest appeal against the injustices of an unreformed capitalistic system, and it offered hope to a class condemned by the laws of classical economics to perpetual poverty. One did not have to be a worker to subscribe to Marxian Communism. Anyone without religious faith and with a strong sense of justice might easily fall victim to the appeal of Communism. Once the "mystery of the dialectic" was accepted, the Communist was immune from rational criticism of his faith.

In the following selection Bishop Fulton J. Sheen makes an excellent

* From *Communism and the Conscience of the West* by Fulton J. Sheen, copyright 1948. Used by special permission of the publishers, The Bobbs-Merrill Company, Inc.

critical analysis of the philosophy of Communism by dissecting it into its component parts and by putting it into simple language. The technique of reducing Marxian thought to logical, simple conclusions is the most effective way of showing its tyrannical domination of the intellect and its totalitarian grip on all human activity.

THOUGH communism has millions of followers, hangers-on and fellow travelers throughout the world, there are actually only a few outside the Communist leaders themselves who know anything about its philosophy. Many think that communism is just an economic theory in which production is for use rather than for profit; others believe it to be a defense of the worker and the disinherited, which indeed if it were, we would all be Communists. Others believe it is a form of collectivism opposed to the individualism of the Western world. Basically, communism is none of these things. Rather it is a complete philosophy of life, what the Germans called a *Weltanschauung,* an integral comprehension of the world, different from all other secular systems in that it seeks not only to dominate the periphery of life but to control man's inner life as well. Communism has a theory and a practice; it wishes to be not only a state but a church judging the consciences of men; it is a doctrine of salvation and as such claims the whole man, body and soul, and in this sense is totalitarian.

It has its origin in the brain of a German, Karl Marx, who on both his mother's and father's side, though his father was a lawyer, was descended from a long line of rabbis. He was born on the fifth of May in the year 1818 in the city of Treves, Germany. At the age of six, Karl Marx along with his family was baptized and became a member of one of the Christian sects, not for religious but for political and business reasons.

It is his philosophy rather than his life which interests us. The first stage in the development of his thought began when, at the age of 19, he enrolled at the University of Berlin to study law, but in his own words, "above all to wrestle with philosophy." At that particular time German universities were obliged to teach the philosophy of Hegel, who had died in 1831. Marx plunged into the almost unintelligible abstractions of Hegel, whose philosophy was known as dialectical idealism: *idealism,* because it was concerned with ideas, thoughts, spirits, mind, for the reality of the universe is not things but ideas; *dialectical,* because it described the method by which thoughts or ideas developed, namely by contradiction.

For Hegel there are no immutable truths or principles. Ideas are fluid and are arrived at by a debating or dialectical process, in which like a tennis ball they are batted back and forth over the net until a point is scored. First there is the *affirmation* of an idea, then its *negation* by another idea, and finally a *synthesis* of the two. Suppose the problem under discussion is the decoration of a room. One group says: let us do it in blue; another group argues against it in favor of green and finally out of the conflict of ideas there emerges a synthesis of opinion that it be done in red. This is indeed an oversimplified explanation of Hegel, so simple that if Hegel heard it he would turn over in his grave, but it is often the business of philosophers to complicate and obscure the simple things of life.

Marx was tremendously impressed with the dialectical side of Hegel which denied any truth is permanent, or any principle immutable. In the year 1841 Marx presented to the University of Jena a doctoral thesis, so dialectical in character that the second sentence contradicted the first and the third united the two. Then he started all over again. In the preface to this bizarre piece of writing, Marx wrote a summary of his thesis: "I hate all the gods."

A more elaborate presentation of the foundation of dialectical materialism necessitates a study of Hegel (1770-1831), who said that any element (idea, sentiment, human institution, emotion) has an essential tendency to beget the contrary, and as a result to transform itself into a new thing which *includes* and yet surpasses the first two antagonistic terms. This process with its three stages he called thesis, antithesis and synthesis, or position, opposition and composition. Every synthesis is a conquered or overcome contradiction. In the synthesis, the thesis and antithesis are said to be "*Aufgehoben*" that is, transposed, sublimated, transfigured. The dialectical law applies to any newly created synthesis, which in its turn as thesis begets a new antithesis and then becomes a new synthesis. Hegel thus makes contradiction the fundamental law of thought, "That which moves the world in general is contradiction and it is laughable to say that one cannot think contradiction."

Now begins the second stage in the development of Marx's philosophy. The very year Marx received his doctorate there appeared the most popular attack on religion that had been delivered in Germany up to that time. While other Germans like Strauss and Bauer were trying to destroy Christianity through historical criticism, Ludwig Feuerbach in his *Essence of Christianity* tried to destroy it by a full-fledged materialistic philosophy. Marx read the book and his enthusiasm is recorded as "unbounded." Feuerbach had killed the idealism of Hegel, which he never liked anyway, and he destroyed all religion by showing that it is an illusion projected by the brain of man. This pleased Marx tremendously. Feuerbach did this by denying thought, ideas, mind and spirit, and by affirming that matter is the basic reality. "Man is only what he eats."

Now that the gods were dethroned, Marx got what he thought was a brilliant idea. Wouldn't it be wonderful to take the dialectical method which Hegel applies to ideas, and apply it to matter and to history? Marx then summoned to the altar of his own construction the groom of dialectics which came from the house of Hegel and united it in marriage to the materialism of the house of Feuerbach and out of that union came the child dialectical materialism which Marx adopted as the philosophy of communism. Reality then became for Marx not spirit made manifest through moving matter as Hegel thought, but matter paramount, and moving spirit. All thought, all spiritual existence thus became merely a product of dialectical matter.

From now on Marx would see contradiction at the very heart of reality. There is no need of a God to explain matter, because matter itself is endowed with motion. It develops by shocks, oppositions, clashes, struggles, catastrophes. The whole universe is dialectical. *Reality is revolutionary.* Marx now took the position that knowledge is not speculative (spiritual) but practical (materialistic). We know the world only by living in it and undergoing what Marx called "revolutionary practice." Materialism of the Feuerbachian variety was corrected because it had two defects which Engels reveals through his *Anti-Dühring.* It took a too mechanistic view of the universe and it left no room for process. Marx and Engles "corrected" this mistake by applying the dialectics they took from Hegel to the materialism they took from Feuerbach and out of it came *Dialectical Materialism* or the *philosophy of communism.* From now on, not ideas would grow by contradiction but reality. Thesis, antithesis, synthesis would be descriptions not of the unfolding of spirit, but stages in revolution which would produce a Communist society.

That brings us to the next phase in the development of Marxist philosophy: the influence of French sociology. Marx had read and was tremendously impressed with a pamphlet written by Proudhon on the subject of property, in which Proudhon was trying to apply the dialectics of Hegel to economics. One night at the lodgings of the famous Russian revolutionist Bakunin, Marx met Proudhon and expounded to him the beauties of dialectics as applied to matter and also to politics with which he was concerned because of Hegel's emphasis on the state. Proudhon the Frenchman told Marx he was typically German, 'way up in the air with his abstractions and too little concerned with economics. The big problem, said Proudhon, is economic, not political, social, not Hegelian, and if he, Marx, wanted to keep his dialectics, he should apply it in some way to property. This Proudhon did by stumblingly suggesting that perhaps capital was the affirmative side of dialectics, which in turn begot its contradiction, which was labor. Somewhere there ought to be a synthesis which would involve changes of property. Where the Frenchman led, the German followed, and when Marx left the garret of Bakunin that night the complete philosophy of communism was born. Proudhon became the inspiration of the main cog in Marxist communism. Dialectical materialism applied to economics became *economic determinism* and applied to history became *historical materialism,* both of which are here discussed as a unit.

As Hegel used history as a method of investigation, so too would Marx, in the sense that history was now to be interpreted materially rather than ideally. What interested Marx was not the origin of historical phenomena, but rather their development and change; he was seeking for the dynamic of history. His system repudiates the idea that men freely make their own history. He has recourse to the myth that history is determined by inner laws which are proper to the economic development of mankind. Even granted that men have motives, Marx considers that there is a still more basic analysis to be made, namely, what factor in history determines men's motives. As Engels interpreted Marx's thought:

> We have seen that the many individual wills active in history for the most part produced results quite other than those they intended—often quite the opposite; their motives therefore in relation to the total result are likewise of only secondary significance. On the other hand, the further question arises: What driving forces in turn stand behind these motives? What are the historical causes which transformed themselves into these motives in the brains of the actors?

While Marx is willing to admit that there are certain factors such as religion and literature and great heroes who have influenced history, he nevertheless challenges the contention that these factors are basic. Starting with the assumption of Franklin that man "is a tool-producing animal," Marx says that it is at this point that man is distinguished from the animal; therefore, production must be the basic force in history.

When Marx speaks of production as being basic to man he does not refer merely to the technical process of making things. He includes this but also two other factors, namely, the material upon which man works and his own psychological and physical contribution. Marx is now prepared for the fundamental principles of his economic determinism, namely that the art, literature, morality, religion, law, in any given age are the results of the economic methods of production in use at any time. As Marx put it in the *Communist Manifesto:*

> In every historical epoch, the prevailing mode of economic production and exchange, and the social organization necessarily following from it, form the basis upon which it is built up, and from which alone can be explained, the political and intellectual history of that epoch.

If there is a system in existence which recognizes personal property rights there will be a system of morality to protect those rights such as the commandment: "Thou shalt not steal." Where there are no personal property rights there need be no such moral commandment because there would be such an abundance of prosperity that no one would ever want to steal.

Until, however, communism comes to pass, so long as there are private property relations prevailing in methods of production, there will necessarily be classes. One of these classes will own and the other class will work. In Marxist language one will be the exploiting class and the other the exploited class. History is full of this struggle of class conflict. As the *Communist Manifesto* puts it: "The history of all hitherto existing society is the history of class war." Class war is the essence of all history and all ideas are merely ideological forms in which men become conscious of this conflict and fight it out. Reading his theory of the primacy of economics into history, Marx presents history in three sequences. First came the feudal society which by its very nature gave rise to inner conflicts and resulted in the rise to dominance of the bourgeois and the advent of capitalism. In the final phase the exploited or the proletariat class will, through co-operation with the inner forces of history, overthrow the capitalist regime and create a new art and culture more glorious than ever before. Then there will no longer be class conflict but a classless community in a golden age. In the language of Hegel, capitalism (*thesis*) in its monstrous development of an owning and exploiting class engenders necessarily an improverished and oppressed class (*antithesis*). Between these two a class conflict necessarily arises. The synthesis will come when the workers destroy all property personally owned, and as workers form an ensemble of workers possessing property collectively.

But how will society undergo this basic revolutionary transformation? By a

> revolution in which the working class will use its political supremacy to wrest by degrees all capital from the bourgeoisie, to centralize all instruments of production in the hands of the state. . . . In the beginning this cannot be done except by means of despotic inroads on the rights of property.
>
> It may be taken for granted that bloody conflicts are coming. . . . The workers must aim at preventing the subsiding of the revolutionary excitement immediately after the victory. On the contrary, they must endeavor to maintain it as long as possible. Far from opposing so-called excesses, and making examples of hated individuals or public buildings to which hateful remembrances are attached, by sacrificing them to the popular rage, such examples must not only be tolerated, but their direction must ever be taken in hand. . . . The arming of the workers with rifles and ammunition must be carried out at once and steps be taken to prevent the rising of the army which would be directed against the workers. . . . If the small middle class propose to purchase the railways and the factories the workers must demand that such railways and factories, being the property of the reactionaries, shall be confiscated by the state without compensation. . . . The workers need not be misled by democratic platitudes about freedom. . . . Their battle cry must be 'the revolution in permanence.'

The ethics of communism are the natural sequence of its materialistic belief. The Communist theory of ethics is that all moral standards grow out of certain economic conditions. "All moral theories are the product in the last analysis of the economic stage which society has reached at that particular epoch." Morality as consonance with the Eternal Law of God reflected in conscience is denied, since it is not God but economics which makes morality. There would logically be a repudiation of both the Jewish belief in a Divine Law as expressed in the Ten Commandments and the Greek view of a Divine Order expressing itself in purpose and fixed behavior, once one translated Hegel's idea of a flux in the world of ideas to flux in the world of reality and history. Then there can no longer be any transcendent order, but only the historic process itself which moves by dialectical necessity to a classless society. If a man is a member of the Communist class he is predestined as was the Calvinist of old, except that his heaven will be the classless kingdom on earth. If however a man belongs to the "exploiting class," then he is historically doomed. There is a certitude of election in the perverted Pauline sense to those who are now not in Christ, but in Marx. All morality to Communists is therefore "class morality." When classes are done away with through revolutionary expropriation of those who own property, there will no longer be any need of what the Communist calls "bourgeois morality." As Lenin said: "We deny all morality taken from super-human or non-class conceptions. We say that this is a deception, a swindle, a befogging of the minds of the workers and peasants in the interests of the landlords and the capitalists."

Underneath Communist ethics is the principle "the end justifies the means." The needs of the revolution determine morality; hence whatever fosters the revolutionary overthrow of democracy and the violent dispossession of those who own property is a morally good act; whatever hinders the revolution, such as a refusal to take orders from the dictator, and the refusal to think the way you are supposed to think, is a morally bad act. As Lenin put it:

> We say that our morality is wholly subordinated to the interests of the class struggle of the workers. . . . We deduce our morality from the facts and the need of the class struggle of the proletariat. That is why we say that a morality taken from outside of human society does not exist for us, it is a fraud. For us morality is subordinated to the interests of the workers' class struggle.

The Communists find no ethical contradiction when, for example, they extend a friendly hand to religion one year and the next year persecute it; or when they ally themselves with democracy at one time, and the next time seek to overthrow it; or when they sign a treaty with Nazism and then fight against it. When conditions change, new techniques must be developed, but all are equally true and moral to the Communist as long as they further the revolution. But is there any limit to chicanery, duplicity and deviltry? Absolutely none! As Lenin said: "It is necessary . . . to use any ruse, cunning, unlawful method, evasion, concealment of the truth." Stalin added approvingly: "Dictatorship means nothing more nor less than the power which directly rests on violence, which is not limited by any laws or restricted by any absolute rules."

Because Communist ethics is based on a complete repudiation of a moral order under God, it does little good to complain against it that it leaves us no room for compassion, brotherly love and sympathy. As a matter of fact the Communist "saints" are "canonized" to just the extent that they suffer all things for the sake of their class morality. The Communist

> is damned always to do what is most repugnant to him: to become a slaughterer in order to abolish slaughtering, to sacrifice lambs in order that no lambs may be slaughtered, to whip people with knouts so that they may learn not to let themselves be whipped, to strip himself of every scruple in the name of higher scrupulousness, and to challenge the hatred of mankind because of his love of it—an abstract and geometric love.

The Communist idea of religion is difficult to determine, blurred and confused as it so often is by propaganda which, for tactical purposes only, declares itself in favor of religion. The truth on this subject is that communism and atheism are intrinsically related and that one cannot be a good Communist without being an atheist and every atheist is a potential Communist. Since the thought of Marx on the subject of religion was inspired principally by Feuerbach, it is necessary to examine the three works which had the most influence on Marx, *The Essence of Christianity* (1841), *Preliminary Thesis for the Reform of Philosophy* (1842) and *Fundamental Principles of the Philosophy of the Future* (1843).

As regards the origin of belief, Feuerbach contended it was psychological. A man who does not have a consciousness of his own supreme nature attributes the qualities which he lacks, such as goodness, disinterested love, to a being outside himself, and thus the idea of God is born. Every act of love of God is begotten of a want of self-love; the exaltation of the Divine is built on the ruins of the self-debasement. It is much better to love oneself rather than God, and to declare oneself divine rather than to empty oneself of divinity. Each man must make the choice between himself and God. "I deny God," means for me, "I deny the denial of myself," writes Feuerbach, as anthropology takes the place of theology. The idea of God according to Feuerbach is theoretically stupid and practically harmful since it is nothing else than a projection of imaginary ideals of a human nature not yet conscious of its divinity. Religion appears then as an *alienation* of human nature by which man is rendered a *stranger* to himself. By ceding to another that which is rightly one's own, there results a fission or dispossession which distorts the true nature of man.

It follows that human nature must be restored to itself. This is done first by identifying self with the attributes formerly attributed to Divinity. "Religion progresses as it suppresses relationship with God, and develops into a religion under a new form, a superior form, the cult of man." Secondly, human nature passes from a negative to a positive state by the deliberate edification of man, which is called "absolute humanism." From now on it is a question of destroying the ancient separation of heaven and earth, so that humanity can concentrate on its own soul, on all the forces of its heart and on the present. This concentration alone will produce a new life and new great characters and great actions. In place of immortal individuals, the new religion "demands men completely healthy of body and 'spirit.' " This religion he calls 'Anthropotheism' or religion conscious of itself.

The Christian religion is the name of man united with the name of God in the same name: the God-man; the name of man here being understood as an attribute of the Supreme Being. The new philosophy conforming to the truth makes the attribute the subject and the subject the attribute.

"The task of philosophy is not to know the infinite as finite, but the finite as the infinite, or better still to place not the finite into the infinite, but the infinite into the finite."

Engels in his *Ludwig Feuerbach* tells with what enthusiasm he and Marx became Feuerbachians, which is indeed confirmed by Marx himself. "You, theologians and speculative philosophers, let me give you some advice. . . . There is no other way to arrive at truth and liberty than by that which passes by Feuerbach. This torrent of fire is the purgatory of the present." Like Feuerbach, Marx insisted that to choose God was to sacrifice man. Using the language of Feuerbach he wrote: "Religion is the affirmation not of self-consciousness, but the consciousness alienated from self." In his *Critique of the Philosophy of Law of Hegel* Marx was true to his master in contending that "the criticism of religion is the first condition of all criticism. . . . Once the holy image which represents the aberration of man from himself has been unmasked the task of philosophy is to demask the aberration." "The great merit of Feuerbach is to have furnished the proof that philosophy is nothing but religion put into thought and developed by thought." "Feuerbach represents materialistic humanism in the order of thought, as communism represents it in the order of social action." Marx was an atheist before he was Communist, historically and logically. The instrinsic relation between the two he noted as follows: "Communism begins where atheism begins."

In Theses 6 and 7 on Feuerbach Marx corrects his master for ignoring the economic factor in belief. Marx too believed that religion is a compensation not for a want of divine consciousness in man himself, but for the privations of life. To express this idea he borrowed the phrase of Charles Kingsley and called religion "the opium of the people." Marx believed that when the proletariat takes over the forces of production, then there will disappear all need for religion which kept man in subjection. In another work he interprets Christianity as individual spirituality and as such makes it the parent of all forms of individualism such as liberalism and capitalism.

Under Feuerbachian inspiration Marx argues that man has been alienated from himself in two ways: by religion and private property. Religion alienates a man for himself by subordinating him to God; private property alienates a man from himself by subordinating him to an employer. It follows that if a man is ever to be restored to himself, both religion and private property must be destroyed. From this argument of Marx it is clear that any system which would socialize production but not persecute religion is only half Communistic and leaves man half enslaved. Engels energetically affirmed this intrinsic relation between atheism and communism by saying that the "internal putrefaction of all institutions has its foundation in religion." Marx in the same vein states that

the suppression of the alienation which reigns in the domain of production under the form of private property, *entails necessarily* the suppression of all those alienations which constitute or vitiate the diverse institutions and diverse human activities. The religious alienation as such operates in the domain of conscience in the *foro interno* of man, but economic alienation is that of life itself—its suppression embraces both sides.

Marx is concerned not merely with the suppression of religion, but with the installation of what Feuerbach called the "new humanism." Atheism for Marx is therefore not something *negative,* for he makes the distinction between "negative" atheism or the suppression of God, and "positive" atheism which is humanism. The purpose of persecution of religion is to restore man to himself. Thus from an entirely different point of view, the intrinsic relation of atheism and communism is once more forced upon us. "The criticism of religion has for its purpose . . . to *make man move about himself as his own sun.* . . . Religion is only the illusory sun which moves around man, so long as he does not move around himself."

"The criticism of religion ends in the doctrine that man is the Supreme Being for man." Marx furthermore distinguishes between theoretical and practical humanism in order to bring out the unbreakable bond between anti-God and anticapitalism philosophies, or between atheism and communism. *Theoretical humanism* is the giving to man by the suppression of religion consciousness that he is an absolute being and possesses the power to become the most perfect being possible. *Practical humanism* is the consequent realization of man's true nature as a social being in a socialist society devoid of private property. "Just as atheism which suppresses God is the beginning of the theoretical humanism, so Communism as the suppression of private property . . . is the beginning of practical humanism." This indissoluble bond between the two Marx reaffirms by a tribute to Feuerbach. "As Feuerbach represents in theory, so socialism, both French and English, represents in practice how materialism coincides with humanism."

A little noted aspect of Marxism is that its hatred of capitalism is based not on human dignity as the "pinks" would have it, but upon the *absolute divinity of man.*

Being radical means to take things by their root. The root for man is man himself. . . . The criticism of religion ends in the doctrine that *man is the supreme being for man* and in the *categorical imperative of* overthrowing all social relations in which man is degraded, subjected, abandoned, and despised.

Here Marx deduces negatively the destruction of capitalism, and positively communism, for atheistic humanism. In this passage at least Marxism is Communist because atheistic.

If it be objected from time to time that communism is not antireligious, it must be retorted that any concessions made to religion are for ulterior motives related to world revolution. As Lenin wrote: "Our program rests in its entirety on a *scientific* philosophy and notably on a materialistic philosophy. . . . Our propaganda therefore necessarily embraces atheism."

One ought not to confine the struggle against religion to an abstract ideological presentation; one ought to tie up the struggle to a concrete practical class movement which is capable of eliminating the social roots of religion. . . . It would be a great error to think that the apparent 'moderation' of Marxism to religion is to be explained by 'tactical' considerations, such as the desire *de ne pas effaroucher*. On the contrary, the political line of Marxism is tied up indissolubly with its philosophical basis.

But though communism denies God, it affirms another god—the Communist collectivity before which men must prostrate themselves, to whose new shrines, the factories, they must make their pilgrimages; to whose will, expressed by the dictator, they must make complete abandonment of self; before whose secret police, as the new priesthood with unholy orders, they must take their brew of propaganda, and though they have not an empty tomb to give them hope, they still have the cadaver of Lenin, periodically injected with embalming fluids, to give the appearance of life where there is only death and decay.

To the credit of Marx it must be said that he foresaw the inherent weakness of historical liberalism as few saw it while it was in its heyday. It may be said that only three others saw it as clearly, and they saw it from totally different angles: Pius IX, Dostoevski and Nietzsche. But though he was able to announce the crisis of capitalist society, he was unable to offer a solution, because he started with the basic assumption of capitalism itself, namely, the primacy of the economic. Communism to this extent is monopolistic capitalism with a fester.

The philosophy of dialectical materialism is nothing but a crazy quilt made up of patches of Hegel and Feuerbach sewed together to cover up the nakedness of its own ideas. One might just as well try to make a living organism out of the head of an ox, the body of a canary and the tail of an ichthyosaurus, as to take the split ends of Hegelian and Feuerbachian hairs and make them a living philosophy. What Marx failed to see was that Hegel in his philosophy was trying to secularize and prostitute and humanize the theological doctrine of Father, Son and Holy Ghost in thesis, antithesis and synthesis, as Marx himself later on would take another Christian doctrine, the Kingdom of God, and secularize it into a classless society where all men would be brothers without a Father. The dictionary has a stronger name for that kind of society.

The errors, such as his confusion of contradiction and opposites, are so obvious to a thinking mind that there is no need of refutation. Dialectical materialism was only a nineteenth-century form of animism. As the primitive peoples assumed that spirits inhabited the stones and flowers and thunder and the clouds, so Marx believed that thought and mind and reason inhabited matter, and that eventually he could pull them out as a magician pulls rabbits out of a hat. Once he assumes that matter is revolutionary, he goes to history to try to make it prove that his theory was right that all history is economically determined. But this was too unsound. First of all, if history is dialectical, why is it that history stops being dialectical when communism comes? Why should not communism beget its opposite, such as Trotskyism, and why should not both turn into something else, for instance, Fascism? Marx constantly confuses *cause* and *condition*. A window is a condition of light, not its cause. Economic methods of production do *condition* law, literature, art, philosophy, etc., but they do not *cause* or *create* them. Like most impractical men—and Marx was impractical, because he was supported most of his life by a rich friend—Marx isolates one factor from life, namely, the economic, and allows it to go to his head like wine on an empty stomach. If the economic method of production were "the real ultimate driving force of history" then why should it be necessary for man to add his revolutionary fervor? Why not just sit back and read the *Daily Worker* until it happens? But if man can add something to history or hasten the revolution with his emotions, then may not these emotions against capitalists be dismissed as by-products of economics?

Did not Lenin and Stalin have something to do with furthering the revolution? But if their consciousness has been economically determined, then why praise them for doing the inevitable? If change in production creates new ideologies what causes changes in production? Shall invention be ignored and is invention the triumph of mind over matter? Either men are *determined* by economics or they are *conditioned*. If they are only *conditioned*, then one must turn in his Marxian badge; if they are *determined* then they are not free, and if they are not free then why prattle about freedom? Marxists try to escape the dilemma by saying that "freedom is necessity"—which makes just as much sense as to say that blindness is eyesight.

Furthermore, to say, as communism does, that a moral code is necessary only to justify a capitalist method of production is nonsense, because the Christian moral code existed centuries before a capitalistic method of production came into being and therefore was not necessary to sustain it. Nor can it be alleged, as communism does, that the Christian moral code was always based on the defense of property, because the more one practices the Christian code the less one becomes attached to property. That is why there is the vow of poverty in strict religious communities, that, like their Master Who had not whereon to lay His Head, those who take the vow may be poor in spirit. If, as communism alleges, the Christian moral law is a class morality, why is it that it has produced saints in all classes from peasants to kings, and why is it that the greatest number of saints have come from what the Communists would call the proletariat class? If the Christian morality were ever intended to be a defense of a ruling class, then the Saviour would never have chosen His Apostles from fishermen, nor would the Church have canonized a John Bosco or a Little Flower.

There is not a single Russian idea in the whole philosophy of communism. It is bourgeois, Western, materialistic and capitalistic in its origin. It was a creature of its age and could never have arisen in the thirteenth or even the eighteenth century, because the influence of Christianity was still too strong in the world. Only when the organism of the Western world began to weaken could the germ infect it. If the intellectual origin of communism is Western, how did it ever get into Russia? Obviously through the dissemination of ideas by those who became the apostles of Marx. The concrete event through which it became effective in its final form happened during the First World War. Germany, anxious to save herself, felt that her cause would be helped if she could woo Russia away from the Allies. One way of doing this was to start a revolution in Russia. Accordingly, the German General staff tossed 31 revolutionists into a boxcar marked "Extraterritorial," and attached it to a train leaving indirectly for Russia. In this boxcar was Vladimir Ulyanov, better known as Lenin, who, on arriving in Petrograd, mounted an armored car and began preaching the revolution. As General Ludendorff, in justifying his position, said: "In having sent Lenin to Russia, our Government took upon itself a special responsibility, for, from a military point of view, his journey was justified. Russia had to fall." There was something fitting about Germany assisting in the birth of communism in Russia. Germany had already given birth to the idea of communism, so now it would give birth to its reality. Russia paid back its debt to Germany in 1939, when the ignominious treaty between the Nazis and the Communists was signed, which allowed the Nazis for two years to overrun Europe, and which proved that there was no radical opposition between Nazism and communism. On the occasion of signing the treaty, Molotov said: "Fascism is only a matter of taste, and our friendship has been sealed in blood." Unfortunately it turned out to be the blood of Poland.

So much is communism a secularization or a dedivinization of Christianity that it can be presented as an ersatz for Christian doctrines.

Trinity: Three Persons in one God: Father, Son and Holy Ghost.	*Matter:* Three processes in one theory: capital, labor and communism; thesis, antithesis and synthesis.

Messias: Christ the Son of the Living God, foretold by Jewish history.	*Revolutionary Proletariat:* Foretold by the history of economic methods of production.
Redemption from sin: Christ on the Cross nailed by the evil of men.	*The Revolution:* The exploiter on the cross nailed by the exploited.
Church: Mystical Body of Christ, governed by one visible head.	*The Mystical Community of Collectivity:* The dictatorship over the proletariat.
The Last Judgment: The separation of the good and the evil.	The violent expropriation of the property owners and the liquidation of the enemies.
Bible: Revealed Word of God.	*Das Kapital:* Revealed word of Marx.
Heresy: Deviation from Divinely revealed Truth.	Deviation from the apostolic teachings of Marx, Lenin, such as Trotskyites and Mensheviks.
Sacrifice: The condition of spiritual union with God.	Class Struggle and violence, the condition of a classless society.
Final Destiny: Kingdom of God in Heaven.	*Destiny:* Kingdom of Man on earth.
Sacraments: The Divinely ordained channels of communion with Divinity.	*Decorations:* The Order of Lenin, etc.

B. COMMUNISM IN ACTION: THE BOLSHEVIK PARTY *

Marx said almost nothing about how the revolution was to be accomplished and how the final goal of the classless society was to be achieved. Various interpretations arose on what "Marx really meant" in this respect. It can be said that these interpretations fell into four classes. Two were evolutionary, taking the position that the revolution could be achieved only when capitalism had reached its full development. One of the evolutionary schools believed that Communists should participate in democratic government until they became the majority and could remake the state legally and without bloodshed. The other evolutionary school maintained that Communists were not a "revolution-making" party be-

* Waldemar Gurian, *Bolshevism: Theory and Practice,* trans. by E. I. Watkin (London: Sheed & Ward, Inc., 1932), pp. 163-204. Reprinted by permission.

cause they must sit by until capitalism developed all its contradictions. Then the revolution would come.

The other two schools were revolutionary. One of them insisted on an immediate, violent revolution. When the fighting was over, they said, the Communists would undertake to build a new world. The other revolutionary school, led by Lenin, insisted that such unplanned revolution could never succeed. Lenin and his associates believed that the revolution must be conducted by a carefully selected, highly disciplined group who would be the "vanguard of the proletariat" and would act in their name. This is the program and the technique adopted by the Bolshevik Party.

The first Russian Revolution of 1917 occurred in March. The provisional government, under Prince Lvov and Alexander Kerensky, was not able to satisfy the Russian masses or to control public opinion. Meanwhile, the Bolsheviks shrewdly demanded "Peace, Bread, and Land," thus identifying their program with the desires of the people. Lenin and his followers set up the cry of "All power to the Soviets," and they were meanwhile obtaining control of the various Soviets of workers, soldiers, and sailors. Thus the Russian Revolution came under the monopolistic control of the Bolshevik Party in the last months of 1917. In the following selection one of the world's outstanding authorities on the subject analyzes the nature, the organization, and the techniques of the Bolshevik Party.

As our account has shown, the sovereign power which has determined the political triumph of Bolshevism, the state it has constructed, and its economic and social policy, the power from which there is no appeal, is the party. The Bolshevik party has unfettered control of the entire machinery of government; it wields the authority of the state; it is the master, and even the Soviets are its tools. The party settles the economic policy, and decides what measures must be adopted to transform society in accordance with its wishes. The Soviet Union as a political and social reality is inseparable from the party, for the party is the omnipotent power which controls, guides, and moulds it.

It is absolutely inconceivable that the party should one day be replaced in power by some other group or party. Such a change would be equivalent to the downfall of the entire system. The Bolshevik state is simply the dictatorship of the Bolshevik party exercised in the name of the proletariat. The party is, therefore, not a party comparable to those which exist in a constitutional monarchy or in a parliamentary democracy based on party government. It recognises no other party which could be admitted as a partner with equal rights to share its rule. The original coalition with the Left Social Revolutionaries was a purely strategical measure, ending in the exclusion and political annihilation of the group which had at first been recognised. The Bolshevik party recognises no opposition which might take its place; if the party no longer ruled, the entire constitution of the Soviet Union would be stultified, even though it is formally constructed on the basis of the Soviets and takes no account of the party. But the mere statement that the Bolshevik system of government is a party dictatorship does not take us very far. It throws no light on the distinctive structure of the party organization, or upon its outlook and methods. Only a study of the party from the historical and social standpoint gives meaning to the formal and juridical description of Bolshevism.

The early history of the Bolshevik group has been related already in the first and second parts of this work. The Bolshevik party is a group led by professional revolutionaries under a rigorous discipline, accepting revolutionary Marxism as their common platform. It deliberately renounces a vast membership, for it intends to be the van of the proletariat —not the entire army. Moulded by its experiences of illegal underground activity during the old regime, it regards itself as the nucleus for propaganda and agitation among the masses. That is to say, it does not wish to be an elite cut off from the masses; it wishes to function as their brain or, to use an official phrase, as their "advance-guard." Its authority, therefore rests on a union with the masses, constituted by a series of central bodies. It intends to be a party of action; not like other Socialist parties, a combination of different groups everlastingly at war among themselves. To maintain this unity—in official terminology, the *"monolitnostj"*—of the party, its members must accept a strict discipline; only by such discipline can it become the brain of the proletariat and leader of the masses, capable of guiding them to the goals which correspond to their genuine desire without pandering to their passing fancies. Lenin has explicitly insisted that the work of the party is to lead the masses, not to reflect their whims.

The party is at once the representative and educator of the masses. Its task is so to shape its policy as to know what at any particular time it can call upon the masses to accomplish in order to bring them nearer to the goal. It is never weary of emphasising its proletarian character, its union with the positive, working and productive classes of society.

The Bolshevik party is no debating society for intellectuals, but a party of political action and economic achievement. Its composition is intended to express the double fact that for the Bolshevik economics is the power which determines the whole of human life and that the masses are no longer subjects, but holders of the power of the state. The organisations formed by the party, its control over its members, its recruiting of new members, are means whereby the bond between the party and the masses and its select character are permanently maintained. Care is taken that the proletarian membership of the party should not diminish, but increase. Every election of the Soviets, every campaign of economic propaganda, is accompanied by recruiting for the party. The recruiting serves at once as propaganda and as a justification of the policy followed by the party, which is, of course, the policy of the Government. The public are informed that a large number of poor peasants and manual workers have asked to be enrolled in the party. They are also told that the action of class opponents, rich peasants protesting against the collectivisation of agriculture, anti-Semites appealing to the instincts of the ignorant, and clergy exploiting the religious prejudices of the people and attempting to excite them against the Soviet Government, has aroused the indignation of the best elements of the proletariat and decided them to become members of the party. Such facts surely prove what confidence the masses possess in the Bolshevik party. Even the so-called purgings (*Tchistka*) which have been regularly held in the party since 1920—their extent can be gauged from the fact that in 1921 no fewer than a third of its members were expelled—serve to maintain, at least as propaganda, this contact with the masses. These purgings, designed to rid the party of unacceptable members, help to weaken the impression among the masses that Bolshevik rule signifies the dictatorship of a party over themselves. It is constantly being pointed out that these purgings are not simply an instrument of internal party discipline. The masses of non-party workers must be interested in them and take an active part in them; their participation counteracts any tendency to independence which the subordinate bodies dependent on the party might otherwise display.

The development of the party into a strong group strictly disciplined for militant action, which, while laying particular stress on union with the masses, is determined not to lose the select character indispensable for leadership, is only intelligible to those who are acquainted with the most important stages of its inner history; they alone can understand the full extent of the powers at the disposal of the party for political action.

It would be an entire mistake to imagine that even its main features as it is today existed from its foundation. Lenin no doubt always emphasised the necessity of central groups of leaders wielding authority. He refused to open the party to camp-followers and sympathisers. This attitude resulted in its constitution as a group which, in spite of all attempts to unite it with other groups, never gave up its separate existence within the Socialist party. But the decisive importance of the party disputes was not yet evident, especially since Lenin's tactics achieved no great practical successes in the revolution of 1905-6, but rather seemed only the manifestation of an unpractical doctrinaire radicalism that engineered stupid insurrections, which by terrifying the middle class deprived the revolution of indispensable bourgeois support. This failure was followed immediately after the revolution by the outbreak of dissensions among Lenin's followers which seemed to prove that the founder of the party was a man completely out of touch with reality, the fanatical slave of a theory. For they were concerned with Lenin's defence of Marxian materialism against the alleged idealistic attempts of Bogdanov and his followers to rejuvenate the Socialist creed by an infusion of modern positivism, and with his protest against the so-called party school at Capri, of which Gorky was head. Lenin seemed wholly isolated, his following reduced to a handful of professional agitators in Russia. These fought the established Government with every weapon of underground warfare, from occasional confiscations—the forcible robbery of gold on its way to or from a bank—to replenish the party coffers, to setting up secret presses maintained in activity by dint of great sacrifices.

Nevertheless, the Bolsheviks who had remained faithful to Lenin succeeded in establishing a firm hold among the section of the proletariat which had been captured by Socialist propaganda. They certainly had a greater following than the Mensheviks, the heterogenous groups of Lenin's Marxian opponents. But it was only after the revolution of February 1917 that Lenin could develop his principles of organization; not until then was their decisive importance clearly revealed. In his hands the Bolshevik party was transformed into the only powerful and compact group under the new republican system. Party discipline could not, of course, be enforced, since the Bolsheviks were not yet in control of the state. There were dissensions among the party leaders, in which it was only his personal influence that enabled Lenin to carry his views. For example, his declaration of fundamental policy in April aroused keen opposition, as finally his plans for the October rising and his rejection of a Coalition Government embracing all the Socialist parties. Seizure of power by the Bolsheviks, with the control of the Government machine that it involved, led to a rigorous discipline. The discussions about the peace of Brest-Litovsk and the action taken on that occasion by the so-called Left Communists, who were dissatisfied with Lenin's cautious tactics, proved the danger of any relaxation of party discipline. Only if they acted as a unit and were able to place all the instruments of government, such as the army and civil service, under the control of their nominees could the Bolsheviks manage to maintain themselves in power. The civil war and the consequent construction of a new military machine strengthened party discipline still further; the members of the party were mobilised and despatched to defend the Government at any point where it was in danger.

The decisive importance of the fact that the central organs of the party had at their disposition members accustomed to obedience was now manifest. The possession and firm establishment of their governmental authority led to an ever-increasing insistence upon the observance of a strict party discipline. No longer, as in the past, would conflicts within the party merely involve unimportant secessions from its ranks; they would shatter the entire regime. The conclusion of the civil war could not bring with it the relaxation of party discipline; it could only involve its application in a thoroughgoing control of the political and economic machine. Occupation of the government and successful defence of its authority had naturally fostered the party's sense of mission. Its claims seemed to have been justified in practice. The party took energetically in hand the education and guidance of the masses.

As the tasks to be accomplished multiplied, the work of organisation became of primary importance. This is shown very clearly by a document drawn up in 1924 in the early days of NEP, which sets out in detail the party's plans for distributing its human material so as to make the most profitable use of its members. It is to his perception of the supreme importance of this work of organization that the general secretary, Stalin, owes his power. For a long time he took no part in the political decisions of his party, devoting himself entirely to its internal organization. He thus secured control of the party machine, and with it control of a political system which under the name of the dictatorship of the proletariat is in reality the dictatorship of the Bolshevik party.

Already towards the close of the civil war there had been revolts against the iron discipline of the party, and therefore against the dictatorship. They found typical expression in Schliapnikov's so-called workers' opposition, which sought to transfer political power to the entire body of the proletariat as represented by the trade unions and co-operative societies. This, of course, would have brought the dictatorship of the party to an end, since the unity of the holders of office would have been destroyed. The Bolshevik party would very shortly have met a fate similar to that of Kerensky's Provisional Government. Lenin, therefore, fought this workers' opposition and its watchword, "The Soviet against the Party," by every means in his power.

He did not shrink, it is true, from theoretical discussions of the most searching character, but he had no hesitation in employing forcible measures, such as imprisonment, against recalcitrant members of the party, for he was well aware that only by its united action, to be maintained by prescribing dictatorially the limits within which public discussions were permitted, could the existing Government be maintained. Nor was he prepared to allow the party to lose its character as a select body; for all its proletarian character, it must not become fused with the masses, but remain their vanguard. For the same reason, in 1920 he resisted Trotsky's attempts to make the trade unions state institutions, and thus forge a link between the party and the masses. For the trade unions and co-operative societies, although under Bolshevik control, were open to those who were not members of the party, and if they were made part of the government machine they could be no longer employed to sound the sentiments of the masses. In consequence of the party conflicts occasioned by this trade-union controversy Lenin demanded an even more vigorous suppression than heretofore of all attempts to form factions within the party. Besides the supervision of the entire political machine for which it was created, this repression was to be the special task of the Commission of Control, which was remodelled in 1921 at Lenin's proposal and given a place beside the Central Committee.

These measures, however, did not succeed in putting an end to dissensions within the party. After Lenin's illness, which as early as 1922 made regular active political work impossible for him, these were once more strongly in evidence. They were occasioned by attempts to set up what was called internal party democracy, which by allowing the younger members of the party to come to the front would have weakened the position of its executive organs. Trotsky made himself the champion of this party democracy, which protested against the rigidity that had overtaken the party. But even Trotsky was no match for the party machine, although the feeling of the rank and file was in his favour. The organising section of the Central Committee took effective action. It allotted posts in such a way as to isolate his supporters. Simultaneously it brought into play party purgings and receptions of new members. In particular the so-called Lenin levy (Prisyv), a wholesale enrolment of workers after the death of the founder of the party in 1924, played a decisive part in the struggle.

Throughout the period of internal feuds—at first a struggle of all the other leaders against Trotsky, later of the general secretary, Stalin, against a combination between Trotsky, Zinoviev and Kamenev which ended with the expulsion of the opposition in 1927—the leaders employed methods in complete harmony with Lenin's conception of the party. For Lenin had always placed its unity in the forefront as an instrument of warfare, insisting on the exclusion of all controversies that might jeopardise that unity and the repression of all factions that might cripple its activity, dear as such factions are to the Russian Socialist. With that end in view unity was maintained artifically, Stalin being thus ensured a compact and overwhelming majority in all the party organs and cells. Lenin's method, which had always given the Bolsheviks a decisive influence in the Soviets, was thus applied to the party itself. The opposition, banished from the public eye, could easily be expelled, as soon as it seemed expedient to do so; it was therefore faced with the alternative of renouncing all political activity or submitting to the leaders of the party.

It was an easy task to point out that the Opposition, in contrast to the masters of the party machine, were unable to maintain contact with the masses and express their will. For what other expression of that will could there be than the Bolshevik party? The Opposition could, therefore, be repressed by every weapon at the disposal of the leaders on the ground that it was attempting to set up against the party a second party to take its place. Expulsion was followed by a banishment, which, in the case of Trotsky, was followed by exile from the country. The majority of the Opposition leaders, however, from Zinoviev and Kamenev to Radek, submitted, and have since been employed by Stalin in subordinate positions; that the death penalty was never employed against them was simply a matter of expediency. Thus, although the Opposition appealed to the authority of Lenin in support of its distinctive views—an objection to an alleged excessive leniency towards the Kulaks; greater emphasis on propaganda for the world revolution, in the belief that it is impossible to contruct a Socialist system in a single country; the demand for a more intensive industrialisation; a different estimate of the revolution in China—there can be no doubt that these conflicts within the party imperilled Lenin's conception of it. Whether or no the intellectual superiority lay with Stalin; whether the means he employed against his opponents were or were not moral and humane, is beside the point. Judged from the Bolshevik standpoint, there can be no doubt that Stalin was justified in his employment of political weapons. At bottom the conflict was a struggle for the organisation of authority within the system, even if political arguments of superior practical weight could be produced in support of particular items in the Opposition programme. Moreover we must not forget the human background of the struggle, especially if we consider the particular questions at stake less important than the struggle for the control of the party organisation between the general secretary and leaders who relied on their personal popularity, for it has had a decisive influence on the development of the type of man that dominates the Bolshevik party, and thus determines its entire system of government. It has also determined the selection of the ruling classes affected by the Bolshevik party.

To understand this process of selection we must go back to the original types characteristic of the party when first founded. Two quite different groups must be distinguished and their general features described, if the future development of the party is to be intelligible. Both groups alike were inspired by an unquestioning faith in the political and social revolution which would be produced by the conditions obtaining under the Tsardom, a faith which, as a result of the Russian temperament, the Russian radicalism, and the special situation of the subject races, such as the Jews, Letts, and Georgians, went to the utmost extremes and assumed the most fanatical shape. But that common faith was expressed by the two types in an entirely different way. One type was the revolutionary theorist, a man of letters and an agitator, the other the practical revolutionary, the man for whom the revolution and Socialism represented his only chance of social advancement, the only education he would receive.

The revolutionary theorist and man of letters often springs from the intelligentsia. To this type belong many men and women of Jewish birth to whom the old regime denied sufficient opportunities. These revolutionary men of letters and intellectuals were disposed to make a romance of revolution. They loved revolutionary phraseology, employed ethical arguments for choice, were filled with violent indignation at the barbaric methods of the Tsardom and the inhumanity of its bureaucratic machine. Their ranks have produced many assassins, and it is typical of their mentality that the revolutionary is invested with the halo of romantic achievement. This type has no love for systematic agitation without any visible result, or for the work of practical organisation. Among the exiles it has played a prominent part. Interested in theory, it is self-opinionated, addicted to those interminable discussions which lead to party splits.

Lenin regarded and treated this type as the cancer of revolution. His demand for the information of a compact and strictly disciplined party was primarily directed against it. The exiles' chatter—exiles' "*Kloka*," to use the common Russian expression—was particularly odious to him. And he also rejected that revolutionary phrase-making, of which he thought Kerensky was the typical example in the post-revolutionary epoch, which was based on sentiment, not on a definite scientific doctrine. Hence, even before the revolution this intellectual literary type had proved unable to maintain a footing in the Bolshevik party, as was shown by Lenin's struggles with Bogdanov, Lunatcharsky and other armchair revolutionaries. They only make their way back into the party after the February revolution, when the so-called Meschrayonz, intellectuals belonging to no particular section of the Socialist movement, joined the Bolsheviks. Among their members were Trotsky, Joffe, the first Bolshevik ambassador to Berlin, and Lunatcharsky.

Besides the theorist and man of letters the movement produced the practical revolutionary. He has no desire to re-mediate and re-examine the principles of the party to which he has once given his allegiance. For him the all-important thing is practical work, agitation among the proletariat, the establishment of secret presses, the systematic recruiting of suitable members. For his narrow vision, in which he is inferior to the more plastic and sensitive literary type, he compensates by his greater energy and consistency, and more definite and unambigous position. To this type belong many who from earliest youth, almost from their school-days, have devoted themselves to the cause of revolution and can, therefore, even if students, scarcely be termed intellectuals. A frequent and characteristic example of this type is the man who has risen from the humblest origin and owes his advancement to his membership of the party.

The decisive importance of Lenin for the Russian revolution and the victory of Bolshevikism is due to the fact that he knew how to make use of both types for his cause. The radical aims and apparently extreme orientation of the organization he founded enabled him to obtain the adherence of those intellectuals whose support turns the scale at a crisis. On the other hand, his practical disposition, his insistence on the necessity of learning from experience and adapting oneself to actual life, attracted the practical revolutionaries to his standard. He was indispensable to the party because throughout his career he was successful in keeping the intellectuals and men of action united. On the one hand he preserved the party from the danger of intoxicating itself with revolutionary phraseology, high-sounding catchwords and unattainable dreams, and thereby losing sight of the practical policy demanded by the actual situation. On the other hand, he prevented it from becoming fossilised in an unintelligent bureaucratic routine, wholly absorbed in practical questions and admitting no exchange of views. Neither the revolutionary romantic nor the general secretary was permitted to take charge. To educate the party Lenin made use of its organisation and his dominant position in it, which rested on his personal influence, not on the official post he occupied or on any point of view he represented.

"Lenin the educator"–the description sums up the greater part of his activities after 1917. He utters his warnings against formalism, red tape, the infantile complaint from which the Left Communists suffered, owing to their capacity to learn from daily experience–a complaint typical of their philistine and tradesmanlike attitude to life, which fluctuated between cowardly panic and a hysterical enthusiasm which over-estimated the possible rate of development. He blames all attempts to carry particular views by adroit sectional manoeuvres rather than by convincing arguments and loyal co-operation with committees. He opposes venomous polemics within the party ranks. He is determined to make the party a training college for men and women who are at once revolutionary Marxians and men of action. It must be the school of the proletariat in which the new classes called to govern will be educated. They must learn to administer, organise, shape the industrial and economic system. The party must produce genuine experts to replace the old bureaucracy, which was without practical knowledge and consisted at best of skilled manipulators of the official machine, by the direct control and administration of the masses, that is of the social body as a whole.

But as a result of this insistence on practice combined with a fixed, if in some respects pliable, creed, distinctive principles of selection became operative in the party when Lenin's control had been withdrawn. The practical emphasis led to the restriction of free discussion, to the predominance of the practical type for whom the philosophy of the party had become a rigid, easily comprehensible body of doctrine which need only be sufficiently general in character to admit and justify all tactical manoeuvres. The secretary secured control of the party–a secretary who was, no doubt, also a remarkably skilfull intriguer and therefore able to adapt himself to practical exigencies; but a secretary, nevertheless, who had no new ideas, but organised and applied the old as the master's "most faithful disciple." There was no more room for differences of opinion. The conception of the party as a machine for applying compulsion triumphed over all attempts to make it a school of mutual education. The selection of members effected from this standpoint, the supersession of the intellectual by the so-called active corps of old Bolsheviks, the men who had organized and led the Bolshevik party in Russia under Lenin's instructions from exile in conjunction with representatives of the proletariat who joined the party after the revolution, was accomplished on the plea that it was an application of the principles that had guided Lenin's action: they had to foster the type which was adapted to carry out the daily work of Socialist construction.

There was no longer time for debating theories. There was no more use for the romantic heroes of revolution who had proved so invaluable during the stirring times of the civil war. Now the demands of theory were sufficiently met by the man who could draw up emphatic and simple resolutions suitable for purposes of propaganda, to justify the politics and tactical aims pursued at the moment by the party. What was now required before any other quality was capacity for work and organisation, the temper which aims at solid achievement, not momentary spectacular results. It was not the striking personality that was wanted now, but the man who could work in harness and did not, like Stan, the leader of the young Communist opposition, claim the right to test party instructions by his own experience of their operation.

That is to say, the completely unintellectual, but correspondingly more energetic practical revolutionary finally vanquished the romanticist and litterateur of revolution, who as a man of daring strokes and novelties was invaluable during the period of transition. The former type has determined the present character of the party. It has moulded it into a compact body which by every possible means, from peaceful propaganda to the application of force, seeks to build up the Socialist edifice, and carry out the Five-Year Plan. What matters the intellectual level? An exclusive practicality interested solely in questions of political and industrial organisation is now all-powerful. Theory is valued only by its utility for the economic and political work of every day.

This primitive attitude, this deliberate turning away from all independent thought, this exclusive concern with economic and political practice, determined as it is by a Marxian purpose and an ideology already fixed in a cut-and-dried formulation, gives the party today its unique efficiency as an instrument of action. It has no more leisure for speculation. Its entire existence is consecrated to work for the practical projects of Socialist construction, which demand its entire time. It may well be that this political and economic activity expresses a lust for power, but the coincidence of both invests the party with a passionate fanaticism. Beyond itself there is nothing; the economic society directed by party instructions is the sole reality.

Hence the de-intellectualisation of the party accomplished under Stalin's leadership has not weakened it in the very least; on the contrary it has only made it more efficient as an instrument of political power. The members now know what they have to do and are no longer confused by public dissensions among the leaders. Anyone who disagrees with the bureaucracy governing the party is disposed of as a traitor to the Socialist state. He is denounced either as a man who, like Trotsky's Left Opposition, befuddles himself with fine phrases, but in reality doubts the capacity of the proletariat to undertake in isolation the construction of a Socialist society in Russia, or as one who, like the members of the Right Opposition, is a defender of the Kulaks, or, like Bucharin, is without genuine understanding of Marxism, a man who has failed to grasp the dialectical foundations of Leninism. Whether the charges are or are not well founded is immaterial; the important point is to turn the publicity controlled by the party machine against its opponent. He is immediately ruined, as an enemy of the general line of policy on which the party has decided. He is worth spending time over only so far as the attack upon him is propaganda for the construction of Socialism, and his mistakes prove the justification of the official policy. His exclusion from publicity makes it possible to learn from him by making use of his criticisms without the knowledge of the public. In its struggle against the various oppositions the party has strengthened its position, proved its efficiency, and mastered its practical work. Characteristic of the normal type of party machine and at the same time by suitable propaganda it forces one to conform one's thought and to adapt one's language to the accepted phraseology. A man of this type has given a guarantee of practical success in industrial and political work. For the party machine cannot, of course, ever be idle. It must never cease thrusting society forward, reorganising and transforming the industrial and economic system.

How, then, is the party machine organised, controlled as it is today by men of action, unintellectual, but skilled tacticians endowed with a sense of economic realities and understanding how to manage the masses? Its foundations are the party cells which cover the entire territory of the Soviet Union. They are to be found in every locality, every important factory, every technical school, and every organisation, trade union, or cooperative society. They are responsible for maintaining the activity of the party on the right lines and carrying out the orders of the central authority. Public complaints are made against them and their officials, their "bureau," whenever attention is drawn to a failure—to some negligence in work, laziness, or refusal to carry out orders. The calls are combined into districts, which possess a special secretary. The secretaries are indeed elected, but the election is in reality a purely formal confirmation of the choice made by the Central Committee. All appointments are now made by the organising section of the Central Committee, which has come into prominence since the end of the civil war. Latterly the so-called instructors despatched by the Central Committee to each district to impart the necessary instructions and to control the organisations have acquired an ever-increasing importance. The central organs of government are the Central Committee and the so-called Commission of Control, set up to decide party disputes and remedy any abuses in the working of the party or state machine. Lenin hoped that it would act as a counterpoise to the Central Committee; but it has become a mere tool in the hands of the General Secretary. A new controlling body was set up at the opening of 1931 to see that the decisions of the central executive are carried out by the administrative machinery.

The Central Committee is divided into subordinate committees, among them the important Political Bureau, which has, however, lost some of its importance since Stalin's victory over the Right Opposition. Like the Commission of Control, the Central Committee is elected by the Party Assembly, which at present meets every two years. But this internal democracy is simply a blind for the public, since the Central Committee previously in office and the General Secretariat can determine the composition of the Assembly by making use of their right of expulsion from the party, their power to forbid public discussion altogether, or reduce it to a mere formality, and their choice of the party officials, who in turn can influence the composition of the party cells.

The party leaders control the appointment of the organs of Government, among them the Council of People's Commissars and the revolutionary Council of War, over which the Commissar for War presides. The Executive Committee of the Congress of Soviets and its *praesidium* are simply tools chosen and controlled by the leaders of the party. Every republic in the Federation possesses its own party, organised on the model of the Federation Party, but the Federation is as much a fiction in the party as in the Constitution of the state. Centralisation is secured in the party machine by the power of the Central authority to intervene directly. It is therefore impossible for an opposition condemned by the Federation Party to establish itself permanently in one of the national Communist parties. Nevertheless, difficulties have arisen with the national parties, particularly in the Ukraine and the Caucasus.

Contact between the party and the proletarian masses is sedulously maintained. It is regarded as most important to increase the labour membership, particularly "workers from the bench." The character of the party as the picked force of the proletariat is to be upheld and the self-respect of the members increased by purgings, expulsions, and apprenticeships whose length is measured by the social origin of the applicant for membership. Offences committed by members of the party which have been held worthy of prosecution are severely judged when they are of a nature calculated to injure its prestige. Efforts are persistently made to prevent the party morale falling below a determinate level.

Action is taken against a luxurious and ostentatious style of living. The income of members is limited, so that managers of factories, and engineers who belong to the party, receive a far lower pay than the bourgeois expert. The discussions on the question whether it is permissible for a member of the party to take winnings from state lotteries are typical of this attitude. As we should expect, the observance of the party code of ethics is often purely formal. A large proportion of the expulsions for regular drunkenness, inefficiency, abuse of official authority, and similar offences, are only carried out as a means of settling dissensions in the party ranks. The limitation upon monetary income is compensated for by numerous social and political privileges, by the opportunity of buying the necessaries of life at a cheaper rate, by favoured treatment at state institutions and in the allocation of dwellings.

Nevertheless, measures are taken to prevent the growth of a privileged and irresponsible class composed of party members, as is shown among other things by the prosecutions of Bolsheviks who have taken advantage of their position to seduce women.

The party is flanked by a number of auxiliary organisations. Among them we may reckon the Soviets, the "immediate organs of the proletarian dictatorship," whose election is always accompanied by the recruiting of new party members. Other auxiliary institutions are the co-operative societies, the trade unions and the Kolhoses, which, although not confined to Communists, are under Communist control, like all associations supported by the Government; for example, the League of the Godless, or the Proletarian Listeners-in. In April 1931 it was decided that only associations pursuing objects in harmony with those pursued by the state should be allowed to exist. The execution of this decree was to put an end to the possibility, hitherto existing in theory at least, of forming associations for purposes determined by individuals, in accordance with their founders' wishes; all associations were now to be openly transformed into auxiliaries of the ruling Communist party.

Of particular importance for the development of the party are the associations of youth, to which the authorities accordingly devote special attention. The so-called Pioneers are an institution for children up to about the age of fifteen or sixteen. It is a preparatory organization for the League of Communist Youth, the Komsomol. The Pioneers devote themselves particularly to influencing the older generation. They are encouraged to introduce the Bolshevik spirit into the family, without the least regard to parental authority or the respect due from children to parents—for the parents' commands must yield to the Bolshevik principles of the Pioneers. How far the destruction of parental authority has gone is shown by the fact that during Ramsin's trial for wrecking, the son of Syntin, one of his fellow accused, wrote to the papers demanding the infliction of the death penalty upon his own father. The Pioneers are taught to interest themselves in politics and economics. They must already participate actively in the self-criticism. Their organ, the *Pionerskaja Pravda,* publishes complaints of inadequate accommodation at school, counter-revolutionary teaching, and invitations to the Commissariat for Education to take part in the congresses.

The Komsomol, which contains youth up to the age of twenty or even twenty-five is the immediate preparation for the party. It is trained intensively for industrial and political work. To it is entrusted a leading part in the collectivisation of agriculture; from it squadrons are formed to carry out particularly urgent tasks; it supervises the execution of the Five-Year Plan, for example, by removing difficulties of transport or calling attention to defects of organisation; one of its most important functions is to serve as an auxiliary force for the Red Army; it encourages the military training of all its members, so that it may be regarded as actually a militia; during the civil war it took a particularly active part in the fighting.

Although its membership is not confined to members of the party, the Komsomol is closely connected with it. It possesses its own paper, but neither the league as a whole nor its central committee has a right to a policy of its own. The Komsomol is intended to constitute an active group of young people working in the interest and the control of the party, though attempts to replace it by junior sections of the party have been abandoned. It is designed to give the young men and women an illusion of independence, the sense of being engaged in important activities. Any attempts to exploit the Komsomol in opposition to the general policy of the party and win its support for an opposition are most vigorously repressed. All such attempts have hitherto completely failed, from Trotsky's in 1924 to the attempt of the so-called Right-Left Bloc under Syrzov-Lominadse in 1930, which sharply criticised the execution of the Five-Year Plan, complained of bureaucracy and the falsification of statistics, and demanded freedom of discussion within the party.

All who showed sympathy with the bloc, among them founders of the Komsomol, such as Tchaplin, were simply deposed and expelled from its ranks. They thus shared the fate which in 1926 befell the Leningrad leaders who refused to accept the decisions of the Communist Party Assembly. The Komsomol is not even permitted to be neutral in these disputes, for it must be an auxiliary force to help the party to carry out its plans—that and nothing more—and its activity must be satisfied by their execution. The Komsomol must provide the most active workers for the Five-Year Plan; there must be no time or opportunity for the individualism which presumes to discuss the orders of the party from the standpoint of the young generation and its outlook. Particular care is taken to protect the Komsomol from alleged anti-proletarian influences. These influences are, it is maintained, represented by the sons of once wealthy peasants, Government employees, and men of similar station, who often join the Komsomol for purely personal reasons; for example, to secure an opening in life, to be able to study. The class enemy within the Komsomol figures regularly in the Communist press. But we must not therefore conclude that there exists a permanent underground struggle between the rising generation and the ruling party. On the contrary, it is precisely upon youth that the Bolshevik usurpation of Russian public life has exerted the most potent influence. The young can hardly conceive of any other world; the Bolshevik ideology has become self-evident to them, and—what is even more important—their active bent is constantly finding new outlets in the innumerable tasks of industrial reconstruction.

A large number of technical schools and institutes serve the party, and minister to the desire of the members of Komsomol to make a career for themselves. Their number has been steadily increasing, since Stalin pronounced the slogan: "Turn out Communist experts." The training schools for future teachers and expert engineers are of particular importance, as also the Institute of Red Professors and the Communist Academy, whose function it is at present to control the entire intellectual life of Russia and appraise it by its relation to the practical work of the Five-Year Plan. The party is also closely linked with the Red Army. The entire youth of Russia and all her workers are to receive military training without distinction of sex. For it is essential to Bolshevik publicity and the justification of their forcible government to keep in the foreground the peril of a foreign intervention in the interest of the bourgeoisie. This imparts a military character to the whole of public life, for the achievements of the revolution must be secured by the military training of the workers. The Red Army is thus used as an educational institution and a training college for propagandists.

Particular stress is laid upon political education, *politgramotnostj*. This *politgramotnostj* consists in the knowledge of selections from the works of Marx, Lenin and Stalin, and the uncritical acceptance of the official ideology and phrases. With the aid of the Pioneers, the Komsomol, and all the educational institutions which are also intended for older people, the ruling party intends to form a new class to lead society. The old experts must be replaced by proletarian experts. That is why at every educational establishment such importance is attached to the class and party of those who attend them, and all who have grown up in an environment alien to Bolshevism are as far as possible excluded. How ruthless the procedure can be is shown by a letter published in the *Komsomolskaya Pravda,* demanding that the daughter of Ramsin, who was condemned for sabotage and wrecking, should be expelled from a technical institute, although she was not personally guilty of any offence. The destruction of the old educational institutions by submitting the professors to examination by the Communist students to test their modernity and their attitude to Marxism serves the same purpose of making the youthful proletariat, believed to be especially sympathetic with the party outlook, the leaders and experts of the future. Lenin's dictum that the dictatorship of the proletariat is at the same time its education, is thus being fulfilled. First the proletariat seizes the reins of power through its party; next it compels the intermediate class, the technically trained intelligentsia, to work for it; and finally it substitutes for these bourgeois experts an intelligentsia of proletarian origin and sentiments.

The Third International belongs equally with the Komsomol to the institutions for education and propaganda controlled by the Bolshevik party. In theory, no doubt, ever since its foundation by Lenin in 1919 it has occupied a position superior to that of the Russian Bolshevik party. But in reality it is, of course, dependent upon the one proletarian state in the world, not only for such external reasons as finance, the necessity of a country where agitators can find refuge, and the fact that Russia is the seat of its central organ, but because the existence of the proletarian state is of supreme importance for the world revolution. It therefore supports everything that serves the interests of that state and so becomes the political instrument of whatever group controls the Russian party. Attempts of the opposition to secure control of the party by the indirect route of the Third International are doomed to fail lamentably, since the parties of the International are dependent on the support of the Soviet Union, and therefore all opposition movements in the foreign sections of the Communist International are treated in the same way as the Russian.

Like the Russian party, the International is surrounded by a number of auxiliary organisations. These are the Communist International for Youth and the Revolutionary Central Union of Trade Unions—and Communist opposition to the Socialist control of the Freethinkers' International has led to the formation of a special Revolutionary Central Union of Freethinkers in which the Russian League of the Godless plays a decisive part. These organizations, among which we must also reckon the Red Helpers and the Association of Friends of the Soviet Union, recruit sympathisers who assist and pave the way for the activities of the Third International, protest against alleged calumniations of Soviet Russia and arrange, as, for example, the League of the Godless, correspondence between Russian and foreign proletarians which serves the purpose of propaganda, and gives information as to conditions in Bolshevik Russia. Their entire existence is bound up with the existence of the Bolshevik state in Russia, so that they may be regarded as centres of propaganda for the present Russia, the Soviet Union and the Bolshevik party in control of it. In short, the Third International is an agent of the Bolshevik party, since it makes preparations for the world revolution. Its propaganda aims at weakening the foes of the sole proletarian state, the Bolshevik dictatorship, and crippling the established order by undermining the discipline of the army, by combating the churches and by industrial espionage. It would obviously be impossible for a counter-organization to the Third International to carry on in the Soviet Union a campaign of religious or anti-Marxian propaganda; its activity would be regarded and condemned as counter-revolutionary and favourable to the threatened intervention of the capitalist powers.

Since the Third International does not form part of the machinery of government, the Government can officially disclaim responsibility for its action. This, however, is merely a legal quibble; only the Bolshevik party, not the Council of Peoples' Commissars nor the Executive Committee of Soviets, is represented in the Third International. When appeal is made to this legal fiction, the actual sovereignty of the Bolshevik party in Russia is conveniently passed over. In their dealings with the bourgeois world, by concealing the real situation, the Bolsheviks apply without the least scruple the very "fetishism of legal rights" against which Bolshevism contends. How unimportant the Council of People's Commissars really is in the Soviet Union today is shown by the fact that Stalin does not even trouble to belong to it. He is satisfied with his position as general secretary of the party. He is, it is true, a member of the Executive Committee of the Soviets, but he leaves the presidency of this "sovereign" body to Kalinin.

Our account of the structure, development, and organisation of the group which controls the Soviet Union will be completed by a sketch of particularly important and typical leaders of the party. We have often had occasion to speak of Lenin, who founded and led the party, and stamped upon it the character it possesses. Without him Bolshevism in its present form would be unthinkable. Although Trotsky and Stalin, whom he considered the most capable members of the Central Committee, have failed, in spite of his wishes, to work in harness, his example has nevertheless left its impression on every Bolshevik. All sections of the party invoke his authority, from Stalin to Trotsky, the leader of the Left opposition, and Bucharin and Rykov, the leaders of the Right section. If, however, his authority after death seems inpregnable, we must not imagine that in his lifetime he governed the party as an absolute dictator. He was continually obliged to meet more or less determined oppositions, from his return from exile to the discussions relative to the October rising, from the heated debates about the peace of Brest-Litovsk, in which he did not carry the day immediately, to the disputes about the trade unions and the new economic policy.

Lenin the educator—in this phrase we have already summed up his work in the party. His authority steadily grew, because in practice he nearly always proved right. Suchanov relates how Kamenev, after long doubts, was finally obliged to admit that "Lenin's political judgments have always proved correct." Radek was accustomed to say the same thing in his slovenly style when he spoke of "the old fellow's infallibility." Lenin's peculiarity consisted in the combination of a rigid and even doctrinaire creed with an extremely skilfull and pliant strategy and propaganda. He understood how to give his ideas a form in which they were intelligible to the masses. But, on the other hand, he could be extraordinarily reticent as to his own aims.

When on his return to Russia in 1917 he perceived that the time was not ripe for a public avowal of his disbelief in the sovereignty of the National Assembly and his hostility to the war he cleverly shaped his propaganda among the masses accordingly. He was prepared when necessary to submit to party discipline. In April 1917 he renounced his proposal to change the name of the party from Social Democratic to Communist, and in 1918 he yielded to the wish of the majority that the negotiations of Brest-Litovsk should be concluded, as Trotsky proposed, not by acceptance of the German conditions, but by the formula, "Neither war nor peace"—for he knew that he would get his own way in the end. Actually in 1918 the party changed its name as he desired, and it was found necessary to prevent the advance of the German army by accepting the conditions originally rejected, which were now, as Lenin had foreseen, made more severe.

It would therefore be a complete mistake to regard Lenin as a fanatic determined to carry his point immediately and expecting his proposals to be unconditionally accepted. On the contrary, he loved practical discussions. He did not wish to impose the acceptance of his point of view, but to get it accepted on its merits. The scraps of paper on which he jotted down brief questions, suggestions, and criticisms are famous. But this adaptability had its limits. Lenin was an educator and strategist only within the limits of an extremely definite doctrine. Marxism and his interpretation of Marxism he regarded as the self-evident foundation of his entire thought and action. He simply wished to gain experience and to learn. The strategy and adaptability were entirely a matter of method, and never led to any radical change of opinion. The very notion of a different belief, a departure from Marxism, was for Lenin wholly inconceivable.

Lenin's Marxism—this must be made clear from the outset if we are to understand his psychology—was marked by distinctive features. Its predominant characteristic was the will to political power. Lenin was not content to wait for the objectively inevitable Socialist development which Marx had predicted; he insisted on the importance of action and strict organisation for the Marxist party. For him the state, with its equipment of compulsion, must be the midwife of the Socialist society. He rejected all revolutionary phrase-making. He detested the Second International for its divorce between speech and action. He wanted to make his ideal a concrete reality; for it was self-evidently a force which drove the believer to undertake the alteration of society. On points of details he acknowledged himself in the dark. "It is far better to learn from revolutions than to write about them," is a remark which prefaced his "State and Revolution," published after his advent to power, but composed before it. "Learn and keep on learning," was his motto throughout his administration; "learn to govern, learn to select the right men and learn to handle them; never be satisfied with fine phrases and meaningless slogans." "Socialism is accountancy," he declared; he wished to turn out competent practical experts, not to surround himself with a following of ignorant revolutionary heroes.

This social and economic training must mould a particular class, and enable it to lead the new society, the proletariat. That the proletariat is the chosen class was as self-evident for the Marxist Lenin, as the right of his party to govern. Belief in the proletariat determined his entire political and economic projects. The new society cannot function smoothly in a day; its birth-pangs are a situation of direct need and stress; it does not come into being of itself; it is not born full grown—on this he was never weary of insisting. It may be that he often underestimated the difficulties of the transition period, especially at the beginning of his rule, but he was never blind to them, and as time went on he laid greater stress upon them. Did he therefore lose faith in the Socialist goal? Did his Marxian creed gradually become a pure matter of form, phraseology employed only to justify his personal power? For such a development there is not a shred of evidence. It was simply that his practical experience made him realise more clearly the need of experience and education. He himself learnt by the experiments he tried.

In this insistence on the unity of theory and practice, which made it possible to find a logical justification for every step he took, Lenin probably gave the clearest proof of his inhumanity. He was thoroughly inhuman in his belief in his creed, in the advent of the Socialist society, in the right of a particular party to hasten its advent by every means in its power, in the vocation of the proletariat to create the new society and therefore to govern during the period of transition. He was unfettered by any consideration of morality or humanity. He had no objection to compelling the bourgeoisie to cooperate with the Communists by wholesale shootings, and by degrading labour, such as the cleaning of latrines, and he regarded terrorism as a political weapon to be employed when expedient. Friendship, personal considerations and sympathies ceased to exist for him where the cause was concerned. In all this he showed himself proof against pity, but his harshness was inspired by an objective simplicity of purpose so complete that it lends it a human quality.

There are utterances which show an even naive trust in class instincts, stories of his everyday life which give proof of a genuine love for the masses. Personally he was completely selfless. Without a touch of conceit he regarded it as obvious on purely objective grounds that he and his party should govern as organs of the Socialist society. He appealed to no mission of any kind; simply to the cause. In the cause he merged himself completely, and this is the secret of his distinctive personality. His very passions were governed by the cause; it was not the individual bourgeois that he hated, but the bourgeoisie, not the individual Menshevik, but Menshevism. But his hatred was all the more intense and unrelenting, for as the agent of the great historical revolution which was to establish the reign of justice throughout the world it was his duty to use every means at his disposal to crush every opponent.

This absolute faith in Marxism was Lenin's most human trait, for in this he showed that his roots lay in the Russian tradition. He showed himself a typical Russian intellectual, the fanatic who regards his political and social beliefs as necessary for the salvation of mankind, the religion which will set up the kingdom of righteousness. Lenin did not become a different man when he exchanged a life of exile and privation for the government of Russia. His adaptability was fostered by the necessities of practical administration, nothing more. Hitherto his task had been to secure the orthodox creed and fashion a compact body of followers; now at length he had to put his theory into practice, a task for which until now party discussions and organisation had provided the sole opportunity. By this insistence on practice he distinguished himself from Russian intellectuals, and proved himself the one man who could link them up with the practical revolutionaries and combine both in the same group. By this excessive practicality he produced a commonplace, everyday, even philistine effect. He loved to appeal to sound common sense, to mock at eloquent declamations and rhetorical flights. To these characteristics he owed his effectiveness as a model for the masses. He was not only the teacher of the true faith, but also the man of action, of the daily task. It is under his influence that the Soviet Union has become a nursery for the practical man who has no turn for the speechifying and debating so dear to the Russian intellectual, for the man who is not lazy and averse from action, but one who prizes hard work, and whose sole interest is to master, organise and carry out efficiently the economic and industrial tasks with which he is faced. This was the type of man that Lenin praised and held up to admiration as the ideal Socialist. In the disciples, however, the type is expressed far more crudely than in the master. They lack the personal greatness and genius of Lenin, for whom the insistence on practical work had been a deliberate self-discipline, not the result of a contracted vision due to external causes, insufficient experience of life, or want of cultivation.

It is not altogether easy to discover from Lenin's biography the causes which determined this combination of a fanatical devotion to his cause with the employment of immoral and inhuman methods. His life is entirely devoid of striking or romantic episodes. As soon as he had completed his studies this son of an inspector of schools became a professional revolutionary and one of the first founders of Marxian associations among the labourers of Petersburg. After the usual banishment to Siberia he lived as an exile abroad. Only during the revolution of 1905-6 did he return secretly to Russia. His second return in 1917 was the prelude to the rising by which he seized power. During the years of exile he led the party formed in 1903 under his influence. He was indeed its only brain, since intellectuals could not long endure his dictation and intolerance. His bitterly envenomed polemics were as famous as his apparently unpractical radicalism. It was only after 1917 that he ceased to be regarded as a man of no practical importance, the head of a Marxian sect, and stood revealed as a political leader of genius. He was happily married, affectionate and human in his relations with his friends, very modest and opposed to revolutionary affectations of dress or behaviour. As president of the Council of People's Commissars he showed no appreciation of the new art championed by Lunatcharsky, the Commissar for Education. His favourite authors were Zola and Jack London. He would have made a good professor. Miliukov, the leader of the Cadets, tells us that Lenin gave him the impression of a scholar obstinately defending his thesis.

Two events may, however, be pointed out as possible explanations of the fanaticism and immorality of his political action. One is the execution of his elder brother for taking part in a conspiracy against Alexander

III. Lenin has told us what a powerful impression was made upon him by the attitude of his middle-class environment. His family was boycotted by all their neighbours, for nobody dared to risk unpleasantness or bring suspicion on himself. This behaviour determined Lenin's judgment of the bourgeoisie; it seemed to him a society of cowards who concealed their cruelty under fine phrases and high-flown oratory. This conviction of a real inhumanity behind humane pretences is operative in all Lenin's attacks on the bourgeoisie and their lackeys, the Mensheviks and Social Democrats: they do not really desire the freedom and justice to which they appeal; their appeal is but a screen for the reality, a brutal selfishness.

The second event is the disillusionment experienced at his first meeting with Plechanov, which occurred when Lenin first went abroad after his return from Siberia. Plechanov, the first important representative of Russian Marxism, was regarded by the youthful agitator and man of letters as a species of demigod. And now as soon as they met he was revealed as a conceited adventurer, unable to agree with his young visitor and his companion, the future Menshevik Potressov, about the paper they were to publish, dishonourable, a past master of crooked intrigues. Lenin's ideal world collapsed, as he confessed in letters written at the time. He saw the necessity for that objective inhuman attitude which later determined his entire position in the party struggles. And these struggles were in turn an earnest of the policy of hate and violence towards opponents which he pursued as ruler. Lenin recognised no other reality than the brutal world of hard political and economic fact through which the just society without classes must necessarily be achieved. To preach Marxism in opposition to all the idealisms which distract man from the sole realities, economics and society, became the purpose which dominated his life. And with him Marxism was no mere theory; it moulded his entire life and action. This passionate rejection of everything transcendental expressed his idealism, the fact being that for him Marxism was an absolute value, a religion.

Stalin, who is regarded today as Lenin's most faithful disciple, and like Lenin is the real leader of the Bolshevik party, is a man very unlike his master. He is a Georgian, whereas Lenin was a Great Russian, with, apparently, a strong Mongolian strain in his blood. No doubt Stalin has received a modicum of education, since he studied for the priesthood; but the Georgian seminary where was a student can hardly be regarded as a nursery of culture, and he left it very early, won over to the cause of revolution by Marxian tracts. Unlike Lenin, Stalin has never received a thorough intellectual training. He has been all the more active as a practical revolutionary and efficient organiser. He arranged the daring confiscations necessary for replenishing the Bolshevik party funds. Constantly banished to Siberia, he returned every time to foment new revolutionary agitation. He has never been an exile, has indeed only left Russia for brief visits abroad to attend party congresses. An essay on the question of nationalities published under his name is asserted by his opponents with a certain probability to have been written by Lenin. In the period immediately following the October revolution Stalin kept in the background. A few hesitations apart, he was on the whole a faithful follower of Lenin, without coming into any special prominence. As Commissar for the Nationalities he worked for the destruction of the Great Russian supremacy. As a member of the revolutionary Council of War he appears to have been to some extent an opponent of Trotsky. Whether the military services with which he is now credited were really so important as his panegyrists assert cannot be determined. His power increased when in 1921 he became general secretary of the party. He contrived first to get rid of Trotsky by combining with Zinoviev and Kamenev, only to overthrow later on, when his power was secure, the opposition formed by a union of Kamenev and Zinoviev with Trotsky. He continued the struggle against dangerous opponents by destroying the Right opposition of Bucharin and Rykov in 1929-30. Today his power as party leader is uncontested, and his authority openly recognised.

Unlike Lenin, he has no love for objective discussions. A clever strategist, now that his power has been secured he will admit no dangerous colleagues. Purely practical in his interests, he is responsible for no original ideas. He continues energetically Lenin's work of practical education, of economic and industrial organisation, making use of the official doctrine as a convenient framework. He is the most perfect example of the practical revolutionary of the period after the revolution, distinguished from such colleagues as Enukidse, Ordchonikidse and Bubnov only by his greater energy, ruthlessness and tactical skill. He is characteristic of the old Bolsheviks, whose intellectual limitations were lamented even by Lenin, but who under the influence of power and the self-confidence and self-satisfaction of a governing class have developed into good organisers and political strategists. In contrast to Lenin, who might have been a scholar, Stalin has no intellectual interests. Bolshevism is for him something completely self-evident, for his entire life has been formed by it. His skilful tactics and the diplomatic abilities which he displays in party discussions are combined with a rudeness which has not spared Lenin himself.

Stalin's rival in the party was Trotsky. A typical revolutionary litterateur devoted to display, he could not, like Stalin, be content with the simple possession of power. In the eyes of the old Bolsheviks he is the typical representative of a body of exiles which shrinks from the burdensome toil of daily work and organisation. Phrase-maker and revolutionary hero—such is the figure he cuts in these circles. The purity of his motives, unlike Lenin's, is very dubious; his vanity makes it difficult to decide whether he is really working for the cause or himself.

A man of wide interests, he loves to write on a host of different subjects. The Commissar for War has published studies in literary history. He is an inspiring orator, invaluable at a crisis, as was shown by the part he played after the October revolution. During the construction of the Red Army Lenin recognised his ability as an organiser, his power to electrify his environment. But he lacks the unity of purpose, the self-assured consistency for which Stalin is distinguished. He is more remarkable for brilliant inspirations than for steadiness. He cannot endure to cooperate with others—for instance to take part in a commission during the so-called trade-union strike. His probably unconscious over-estimate of his personal importance makes him undervalue the importance of the technical routine and organisation in which Stalin excels. Even his partisan, Eastman, calls attention to his failure to collect around him a body of faithful helpers.

He was therefore gradually isolated by Stalin, since, although he made several attempts to seize control of the party, he could not make up his mind to defy party discipline. His combination with other leaders whom Stalin has forced into the background, Kamenev, Zinoviev, Radek, Preobrachensky and Smilga, came too late. These eminent leaders could no longer reach the public—the party machine had been too powerful for them. After they had been disposed of by expulsion and banishment Stalin continued to isolate Trotsky. He was abandoned by Kamenev and Zinoviev first, then by all the other leaders of the opposition. Yet by his industrialisation and collectivisation Stalin actually carried out considerable portions of Trotsky's programme. An exile abroad, Trotsky has been ever since the ghost of former greatness, impotent for the present, at least so long as Stalin is able to maintain his control of the party organisation. But whether he would benefit even by Stalin's fall may be doubted. He has too many personal enemies and no body of reliable followers.

After Lenin, Stalin, and Trotsky, Dzerzhinsky, the first head of the Cheka and Ogpu—a position which he held for several years—deserves a special description. He was the idealistic and therefore the more ruthless revolutionary fanatic. His personal disinterestedness and honour are as incontestable as his unbounded cruelty, a cruelty purely objective and decided by motives of political expediency. He was an intellectual sprung from the Polish nobility—of the same origin as his successor Menchinsky, who gave himself unreservedly to the Bolshevik party and the revolution. He is perhaps the most striking example of the dehumanising effect of a social creed which makes absolute claims. Though in private life anything but a man of brutal violence, in the name of revolution he put thousands to death. The statement is frequently made that he was afflicted with a strain of insanity. Whether this is true it is hard to say; if so it certainly did not impair his powers of judgment and action. It was his revolutionary faith which made him so completely inhuman and capable of wholesale murder—the only name we can give to his execution of every political and social opponent, even potential.

The same tribute of personal disinterestedness cannot be given to Zinoviev and Kamenev. They are intellectuals of Jewish origin. As is shown by their opposition to the venture of the October rising and the struggle with the neo-Bolshevik Socialists, they gave their adhesion to the dictatorship only when it had succeeded. Both are marked by a lack of personal courage, as their attitude towards Trotsky has proved. Though at first they took Stalin's part against him, when they had been expelled from the government of the party they allied themselves against Stalin with the man they had so vigorously opposed. This, however, did not prevent their being the first to abandon him after his fall. From Suchanov's descriptions Kamenev seems to be a feeble man of average capacity and without strength of character, who lacks the courage to combat a determined opponent. Zinoviev's entire action is determined by the craving for personal power. It is characteristic that the slogan on which the contest was waged against them when they were at the head of the Leningrad and Moscow Soviets was: "No satraps in the party organisation."

The Commissar for Education, Lunatcharsky, whom we have often mentioned already, is a radical intellectual whose connection with Bolshevism is an accident out of keeping with his character. His removal from his post by Stalin is due to the present purely economic and practical orientation of the party. There is no more time for his aesthetic experiments, and the sympathies of the international bohemians on whom his enthusiasm for every artistic novelty and his bold schemes had made a great impression are no longer dispensable. Chicherin, for years Commissar for Foreign Affairs, is, like Ossinsky (Obolensky), a man of the old nobility who espoused Marxism under the influence of an enthusiasm kindled by the revolutionary intelligentsia. Like Krassin, he is one of the old Bolsheviks who in the days following the October revolution came to the front as specialists, and whose activities have little connection with the official philosophy.

The same is true of the members of the Right opposition, especially their leaders Tomsky and Rykov; both are definitely practical men, who would willingly abandon radical schemes. This explains why the trade unionist Tomsky was accused of Social Democratic revisionism and Rykov of favouring the Kulaks. Bucharin occupies a position by himself in the Right opposition. From a Left Communist he became the upholder of a greater leniency towards the peasants and a slower rate of industrialisation. Lenin had spoken of him as a man whom it was impossible to hate, in spite of his constant changes of opinion. He also regarded him as a man who, in spite of his knowledge of economics, did not really grasp the materialist dialectic which was the foundation of Marxism. Trotsky in his Memoirs describes him sarcastically as a man who must always cling to someone else's coat-tails. He is a typical Russian intellectual, who loves writing, and is addicted to logic-chopping, which, as Lenin's criticism observed, he dresses up in a complicated scientific terminology. For a time he was useful to Stalin as a publicist, but he has been completely excluded from political authority since the programme of radical industrialisation and collectivisation was set in hand. Radek, who since his abandonment of the opposition bloc is once more employed as a journalist and undertakes foreign propaganda, is the characteristic "international Bolshevik" as he is popularly conceived. Cynical, extremely clever, and a nihilist, he is the picture of the unchanging revolutionary agitator whose chief concern is to destroy the existing bourgeois world.

It would serve no purpose to describe individually the new men who have succeeded the Trotskys, Rykovs, Kamenevs and Zinovievs. They are marked by a complete lack of intellectual interests, and by the contrast they present to the revolutionary intellectual, as variously represented by Trotsky and Radek. Nor yet are they completely unselfish revolutionary fanatics like Dzerzhinsky. They bear stamped all over them the mark of their origin in the practical work of revolution, or in those circles of the proletariat which have been awakened by Bolshevism. They are far too uncritical to take the responsibility for any departure from Lenin's creed, which has proved so successful as the foundation of the new system. They regard Bolshevism as something self-evident, to which, moreover, they owe their careers. They are too prosaic to be influenced by literature or theories. Trotsky loathed them as bureaucrats, but they defeated him. They show no interest whatever in culture, apart from such things as technology and hygiene. They despise a liberal education because they care for nothing except political and economic power. Their fanaticism, such as it is, is simply the expression of a political and economic realism, without a trace of the idealism, the desire to help the people, which we can detect behind their realism in Lenin and certain of the old Bolshevik intellectuals who were not absorbed in the conduct of the party machine. Whether it is Vorochilov the Great Russian and the present Commissar for War, Chubar the Ukrainian, president of the Ukrainian Council of People's Commissars, or Ordchonikidse, the Georgian head of the Economic Council—whatever their individual differences, they belong to the same type. They are distinguished from Stalin only in degree. The time has gone by when under Lenin the Bolshevik party could be led by a body of men representative of altogether different types. Today the man of the everyday task, the practical organiser, is in the saddle; in the background are a few more or less ambitious self-seeking intellectuals, pocket editions of Zinoviev, like the present Foreign Commissar, Litvinov. For Bolshevism the period of original development is over. It is no accident that Stalin describes himself as Lenin's best and most faithful disciple. The rule of Lenin's successors is characterised by the type of leader who is now at the head of the party and occupies the important political and industrial positions.

21

THE NATURE OF FASCISM AND NATIONAL SOCIALISM *

Shortly after World War I, Mussolini's Fascist Party came to power in Italy, and in similar fashion Hitler's Nazi Party took over the government of Germany in 1933. The two movements had a good deal in common: both were reactions against "bourgeois materialistic capitalism," and both claimed that they sought to protect the Western world from the onslaught of Communism: both made a temporary alliance with religion and with the property-owners in their countries, and both ended up dominating religion and controlling the use of property. Finally, both were primarily programs of action that reduced all individuals to the totalitarian state, but both worked out a doctrine or a philosophy to justify their program of action.

In the following selection the author undertakes the difficult task of analyzing both Fascism and National Socialism in such a way as to indicate their similarities and their points of divergence. His analysis was made in 1936, when the Fascist and Nazi regimes had formulated their doctrines and had not yet pushed them to the logical conclusions that were to bring on the Second World War.

*Fascism and National Socialism are essentially two forms of modern paganism. The former divinizes the state and subjects all creatures to it; the latter divinizes race and denies man all rights except as a member of a given race. Both are totalitarian philosophies which attribute infallible intelligence to the Leader—*Il Duce *in Italy and* Der Feuhrer *in Germany —and deny the traditional Christian distinction between objective reality and the knowing subject. Both made a deceptive appeal to young people and to those who feared the godlessness of Communism, for both Fascism and National Socialism seemed to demand heroic and noble qualities of their adherents, and both claimed to be "spiritual" as against the degenerate materialism of a capitalistic society and its logical offspring of Communism. Finally, both Fascism and National Socialism, when once in power, proved as ruthless, as tyrannical, and as anti-Christian as the Communism from which they were "protecting" Europe.*

* From Michael T. Florinsky, *Fascism and National Socialism*, copyright 1936 by The Macmillan Company, and used with the permission of the publisher.

Fascism and National Socialism both claim to be much more than mere forms of government. "Like all sound political conceptions," writes Mussolini, "Fascism is action and it is thought. . . . Fascism is not only a law-giver and founder of institutions, it is also an educator and a promoter of spiritual life. It aims to refashion both the outward form of life and also its inward content—man, his character and his beliefs. To achieve this purpose it enforces discipline and uses authority. It enters into the soul and rules with undisputed sway. Therefore it has chosen as its emblem the lictor's rod, the symbol of unity, strength and justice." Hitler takes a no less solemn view of his movement. He declared that National Socialism is "a heroic doctrine which brings out the value of blood, race and personality as well as the eternal laws of natural selection (*Auslesegesetz*) and finds itself in an avowed and irreconcilable opposition to the philosophy of the pacifist international democracy and to its products (*Auswirkungen*)." Mussolini maintains, moreover, that the influence of Fascism is by no means limited to Italy. "Fascism, as an idea, a doctrine, a realization, is universal; it is Italian in its particular institutions, but it is universal in the spirit, nor could it be otherwise. The spirit is universal by reason of its nature."

It is hardly necessary to say that to an outsider the prophetic and the oracular in Mussolini and Hitler appear to be based on a very flimsy foundation. Their teachings, to begin with, are extremely loose and uncertain in some essential parts. This undoubtedly contributed in no small degree to the success of the Fascist and National Socialist movements: the less precise and definite the slogan and the program, the wider the appeal. It will be remembered that while the program of the National Socialist Party was declared in 1926 to be "unchangeable" it was officially explained that this applied only to the fundamental principles, and not to the methods by which the latter were to be put into practice; some of the principles were anything but clear and concrete. Even today they are open to innumerable interpretations. This is particularly true of the economic policies of National Socialism and, in a lesser degree, of Fascism. To be rigidly doctrinaire is, moreover, repugnant to the spirit of these movements. Mussolini maintains, for instance, that "Fascism should be revised, corrected, enlarged, developed." Under these conditions it is by no means easy to be sure that the views of even the leaders themselves expressed some time ago represent the opinion of the Party now.

No intellectual movement is entirely independent, and a number of influences have been suggested as having left their imprint upon the teachings of Fascism and National Socialism. Mussolini is said to owe much to Machiavelli, Schopenhauer, Nietzsche, Renan, Blanqui, George Sorel, William James, Bergson and Pareto. The antecedents of National Socialism have been traced to Luther, Kant, Hegel, Fichte, Friedrich List, de Gobineau, H. S. Chamberlain and, of course, to Mussolini himself. Many of these affiliations have been clearly established or even openly acknowledged. Nevertheless the combination of the various elements, none of them absolutely original, in the philosophy of Fascism and National Socialism, bears the distinct marks of their respective leaders and presents a system of thought which, if rather obscure, is fairly comprehensive.

It would seem that the vogue of the new cults arises in part from the already traditional and almost "ritualistic" terminology in which the writings of the Fascists and National Socialists are clothed. The written works and speeches of Mussolini and Hitler and of many of their followers have not lent themselves readily to interpretation in plain English. National Socialism has in particular distinguished itself by evolving a new vernacular which specializes in spinning endless and bizarre sentences, often to say very little indeed. A non-believer who attacks these verbose monuments of pagan theology certainly needs courage and perseverance.

One of the fundamental ideas of Fascism is the supremacy of the State. "Anti-individualistic, the Fascist conception of life," writes Mussolini, "stresses the importance of the State. It accepts the individual only in so far as his interests coincide with those of the State. And it stands for the conscience and the universal will of man as an historic entity. . . . The Fascist conception of the State is all-embracing. Beyond it no human or spiritual concepts can exist, much less have value." This principle is summarized in the well-known watchword: 'All in the State, nothing outside the State, nothing against the State.'"

The "totalitarian" State of Fascism is endorsed by the National Socialists. In either case it is accompanied by a violent denunciation of democracy in the struggle against which the two movements have fought relentlessly. *Mein Kampf* is full of invectives against parliamentarism and against democratic institutions in general; for they put their faith not in quality, but in numbers. "Democratic regimes," writes Mussolini, "may be described as those under which the people are, from time to time, deluded into the belief that they exercise sovereignty. . . . Democracy is a kingless regime infested by many kings who are sometimes more exclusive, more tyrannical, and destructive than one, even if he be a tyrant."

The totalitarian State is not simply an abstraction devised for the purpose of disguising the political dictatorship of Fascism and National Socialism. It is supposed to be the vehicle through which the higher conception of the Nation finds its external manifestation. The Nation is just as exacting as the totalitarian State. "The individual is nothing—*das Volk* is everything!" according to a statement by Hitler. And the German conception of *das Volk* comprises elements which are entirely alien to the Italian idea of the Nation. The Hitler conception of nationality is in theory deeply rooted in racial, biological and ethnographical concepts. It is based on the assumption of the superiority of the Nordic race, the purest representatives of which are believed to be the Germans. Hitler, Rosenberg, Goebbels, Streicher and the other leaders of the movement have devoted much space in their writings and speeches to the glorification of the Nordic virtues. The question of "blood" is in the forefront of the National Socialist program. The totalitarian State they are trying to build is to be based on the principle of race. It will be a national community of people of the same racial stock to the exclusion of all "non-Aryan" elements. "The science of the race is our German Gospel," Heinrich Himmler, the leader of the S.S. troops, declared in the summer of 1935 in a speech which was given much prominence in the German press. The scientific shallowness of this doctrine is so obvious that it hardly needs to be emphasized. Its application in practice presents insurmountable obstacles, since to arrive at any minute determination of the racial sources of the population of Central Europe, or of any other part of the world, is an entirely hopeless task. In Germany herself the racial policy of the National Socialist Government has been reduced for all practical purposes to a relentless and systematic persecution of the Jews and of all those who have any drop of Jewish blood in their veins. All members of the Party and of its affiliated agencies, all civil servants and the employees of many private concerns have been requested to prepare family trees going back several generations, and these are carefully scrutinized by learned "experts." The discovery, sometimes quite unexpected, of a grandmother or other ancestor whose Aryan origin was open to doubt has been the cause of the ruin of more than one promising career. The same principle, as will appear later, is now being enforced in the land policy of the National Socialist Government. Daily reminders of this strange obsession from which Germany is suffering today may be seen in the neat little folders bearing the legend "My Ancestors" which are displayed in the windows of practically every stationery store throughout the land. Some are in expensive leather bindings, but many are cheap little things which can be purchased for a few pfennigs. I was strongly urged to buy one by a friendly and enthusiastic salesman who was surprised and grieved by my firm refusal.

Mussolini, too, has spoken of the Nation in terms that have been interpreted by German writers as an endorsement of their racial theory. This interpretation is a distinct mistake. "The Italian Nation is an organism having aims, a life and means superior in power and duration to the single individual composing it," says the opening paragraph of the Italian Charter of Labor. "It is a moral, political and economic entity which finds its integral realization in the Fascist State." The Italian Nation as understood by the leader of Fascism, however, is something very different from the National Socialist conception of race. In an interview with Emil Ludwig, Mussolini declared that "race . . . is a feeling and not a reality: 95 per cent a feeling." And this sentence has since been reprinted in an official Italian publication under the Duce's own signature. The Italian conception of the Nation is, if not more scientific, at least far less objectionable than that of Hitler. It would seem to be a romantic idealization of the Roman tradition, of Rome as "a political conception, not a race but an animating spirit," to quote Professor Gioacchino Volpe. "Rome is our point of departure and our reference," wrote Mussolini, ". . . We dream of a Roman Italy, of an Italy wise and strong, disciplined and imperial. Much of the immortal spirit of Rome has been revived in Fascism. Roman are our lictor's rods, Roman is our fighting organization, Roman is our pride and our courage: *Civis romanus sum*. . . . The Romans were not only warriors but also formidable constructors who could defy and did defy time. In the war and in victory Italy was Roman for the first time in fifteen centuries." This theory of the Nation as a spiritual conception and not as a radical entity is a fundamental and significant difference between Fascism and National Socialism. Its practical consequence is the absence in Italy of any anti-Jewish movement. German anti-Semitism, of course, is not merely the creation of Adolf Hitler. It also has its historical and social roots. But the personal opinions of the supreme leader in a totalitarian State are of paramount importance, and no reasonable person could possibly doubt that the Chancellor and Fuhrer must bear the full burden of responsibility for the treatment to which the Jews have been subjected in the Reich.

Having proclaimed the supremacy of the Nation and of the State, and rejected democracy as a form of government, Fascism and National Socialism must inevitably repudiate the principle on which parliamentary government is based. "Fascism denies that the majority, by the simple fact that it is a majority, can direct human society," writes Mussolini, "it denies that numbers alone can govern by means of periodical consultations, and it affirms the immutable, beneficent and fruitful inequality of mankind, an inequality which can never permanently be turned into equality by the mere operation of a mechanical process such as universal suffrage." This idea, which is fully shared by the National Socialists, in itself leads the two movements toward the acceptance of that principle of hierarchy and leadership which implies, in the words of Hitler, "the absolute authority of the leaders over those below and their responsibility to those above." Parliamentary rule, which is represented as a squabble of selfish interests for power, is to give place to the rule by an elite bound by a strict discipline and embodying the highest aspirations of the Nation. Hitler extols this restoration of the "unity of the spirit and the will of the German people." Mussolini declares that he "who speaks of hierarchy says discipline."

Government by an elite is not in itself an objectionable principle. This is, I think, what democracy is striving to achieve through the machinery of general elections. That the procedure has not always been successful will be readily admitted. But what have Fascism and National Socialism to offer in place of the despised methods of democracy? To this all-important question they give no definite answer. In theory the leaders are, presumably, brought forth by the workings of the law of natural selection. In practice, however, as we know, this merely means the hegemony of the political party which has seized power and has ruthlessly stamped out all opposition. Ernest Raue, following in the footsteps of other German writers, rightly observes that in the last analysis the entire doctrine of Fascism and National Socialism must be traced to the will of their leaders. It is the will of the leaders, again, that determines who shall form that elite which will hold in its hands the destinies of the country. Raue's little book, which is a glorification of this and similar principles, not only won him the degree of Doctor of Social Sciences in the University of Berlin but has also had wide circulation.

It is, moreover, maintained by Italian and German writers that hierarchy and elite principles are by no means incompatible with "real" liberty. So long as the State and the Party are the representatives of the Nation and the mouthpieces of National interests the liberties of the citizen are fully safeguarded. "Far from crushing the individual," writes Mussolini, "the Fascist State multiplies his energies, just as in a regiment a soldier is not diminished but multiplied by the number of his fellow soldiers." The individual is free, it is claimed, so long as he has performed his duty to the State, and as duties to the State have an unquestioned priority, no conflict between the "real" interests of the individual and the interests of the State is possible. It is only through the State that the individual can achieve complete self-expression. "Freedom is not a right, it is a duty," writes Mussolini. "It is not a gift, it is a conquest. It is not equality, it is privilege. The concept of freedom changes with the passing of time. There is a freedom in time of peace which is not freedom in time of war. There is a freedom in times of prosperity which is not a freedom that can be tolerated in times of poverty." It is the protection offered to the individual by the State, which is the only real guarantee of his freedom. Hitler, too, declared that "one must not always speak of the rights; one must also speak of the duties" of the individual. This conception of the duty of the citizen to the State is given immense prominence in Germany today and the word *Pflicht* is one of the most abused words in the German language. The whole concept of hierarchy and of the obligations of the individual to the State have a distinctly militaristic flavor, which cannot but be pleasing to those who were brought up in the Prussian tradition. Mussolini is quoted by Dr. Goebbels as having declared that "Fascism is the Roman version of Prussianism (*romisches Preussentum*)" which is, broadly speaking, true so far as the principles underlying the two conceptions of the State are concerned. But the vast differences in the psychologies of the two countries have not been much diminished, I think, even by thirteen years of Fascist rule.

The subordination of the interests of the individual to those of the State or of the community plays a very prominent part in the theories of

Fascism and National Socialism. "Fascists . . . ," writes Mussolini, "think of life in terms of duty and struggle and conquest. They feel that life should be high and full, lived for oneself, but above all for others—for those who are at hand and those who are far distant, for our contemporaries, and for those who will come after us." The same idea is tersely expressed in the motto of the Program of the National Socialist Party: *"Gemeinnutz vor Eigennutz"*, "the interests of all before the interests of one." This is the corner stone of the concept of "national solidarity," of that *Gemeinschaft* which is one of the chief objectives of the totalitarian State. It has a strong appeal to the sentimental side of the German character and is used effectively. In his address opening the Winter Relief campaign of 1934, a campaign that was carried on under the slogan of "national solidarity," Hitler strongly stressed the fact that it was not enough to contribute to the campaign fund; the contribution should be made in such a manner as to mean a real sacrifice for the giver. "If the entire Nation realizes that the relief measures we are taking involve an actual sacrifice for everyone," he declared, "then these measures will serve not merely to relieve material needs but they will also achieve something far more important. They will make one realize that the national community (*Volksgemeinschaft*) is not a mere empty concept, but an actual living one."

National solidarity is also the denial of class struggle. Mussolini and Hitler both won their spurs in fighting the red menace. Nothing more natural for them, therefore, than to reject the Marxian interpretation of history. Here again, however, as in the case of their definitions of what is meant by the concept of the Nation, there is a significant difference in its interpretation by the two leaders. Mussolini had long been an ardent Socialist. When he was expelled from the Socialist Party in 1914 he declared that he would remain a Socialist even if he had lost his membership card. He has travelled far in the last twenty years and today he rejects the class struggle as the great moving power of human society. But he still believes that there is a conflict of interests between capital and labor. This conflict however is not irremediable, as is thought by the Marxian Socialists. On the contrary, the interests of the two parties can be reconciled and it is the duty of the totalitarian State to see to it that an amiable solution is brought about. This is exactly the purpose of the corporate organization that has been painstakingly built up in Italy since 1926. On the other hand, Hitler, the son of a modest government employee, had to work for a time as a manual laborer. He gives in *Mein Kampf* a vivid and unhappy picture of the conditions of life of the proletariat. In spite of this experience he held himself altogether aloof from the official Socialist *mots d'ordre*. National Socialism, therefore, not only rejects class struggle as a great historical force but also denies that there is any necessary conflict of interests between capital and labor. If such conflict existed under German capitalism it was merely the effect of the greed and stupidity of the ruling classes of the "Liberal-Marxist" State. Under the benign influence of the National Socialist regime, it is held, they must and will disappear.

The conception of national solidarity determines the attitude of Fascism and National Socialism toward economic problems. The course they have chosen is a middle one between capitalism and socialism. Article 7 of the Charter of Labor declares that "private interest in the sphere of production is the most effective and useful instrument in the interest of the nation." This also expresses the National Socialist view. The right of private property is thus maintained, but the exercise of this right is subject to the control of the state, which reserves the power to intervene at any moment and direct private initiative into the channels which it considers desirable. Sombart has stated that the economic organization of Fascism is "the highest synthesis of State power and authority compatible with the capitalist system." The argument is advanced that in the German totalitarian State the employer is no longer the "hereditary enemy of labor" but has been transformed into one of the "soldiers of the mighty Labor Front (*Arbeitsfront*) of the German people" and as such is doing his duty in the service of the nation. It will be shown in a later chapter to what extent this statement is justified by the changes that have actually taken place in the position of the employees. The general principles of the Fascist and National Socialist policy toward capital and labor are briefly set forth by Hitler in a speech delivered in March 1936. "The people do not live for economic organization (*Eirtschaft*) and economic organization does not exist for capital but capital is the servant of economic organization and economic organization is the servant of the people." This is a formula that is both broad and obscure. It is like a promise and a menace and it may prove to be both or neither.

Little need here be said about other important economic principles that appear in the program of the National Socialist Party; the expropriation of land without compensation for public purposes, the elimination of interest on agricultural debts and of speculation in land values, the nationalization of trusts, public ownership of department stores, profitsharing in the case of large concerns, and the abolition of the "slavery of interest." All these demands, of course, continue to form a theoretical part of the official program. And some of them, it will be seen, have not remained dead letters. The most puzzling of all is the question of the abolition of the "slavery of interest." The real meaning of this mysterious and ominous phrase is still a matter of conjecture. Interpretations range from the complete nationalization of all banks, the abolition of unearned income and the cancellation of all debts to the most innocuous explanations. It has been suggested, for instance, that the abolition of the "slavery of interest" really means that "every one should pay his debts and make no new ones"!

The socialist tendencies of Fascism and National Socialism have also found their expression in their attitude toward labor. Article 2 of the Italian Charter of Labor declares that "work in all its forms—intellectual, technical and manual—both organizing and executive, is a social duty." National Socialism enthusiastically accepts this principle and maintains that it is not only the duty of every citizen to work, but also his right. Hitler has stated that while every German was under obligation to contribute by his work to the general advancement of the Nation, it was, more than that, his right to demand that the government should provide him with the ways and means of finding a place and purpose for his labor. "Work and Bread" (*Arbeit und Brot*) has been one of the Nation's slogans, and it has been the moving power behind the Government's program of fighting unemployment. There has also been much talk about the dignity of labor. It has been extolled in glowing terms by Mussolini, Hitler and their lieutenants. Hitler's dictum, "Honor work and respect the worker" was treated as if it were a revelation. And the passages from *Mein Kampf* which proclaim that the happiness and contentment of the worker are conditions on which depend development and progress of business enterprise and the success of the employer himself were reproduced in innumerable articles and pamphlets, with comments which would seem to imply that no such thing could be possible under the Liberal-Marxist regime!

Considerable attention is also paid by Fascism and National Socialism to the situation of the tiller of the soil. It is deemed essential to improve the condition of the rural class and to promote farming not only for reasons of economic expediency—both Italy and Germany are striving hard to become self-sufficient in foodstuffs—but also as a matter of social policy. The totalitarian State thinks in terms of a balanced economy in which a certain ratio between the urban and the rural population will be maintained. The excessive industrialization of Germany in pre-war years is believed to be responsible for many of her present economic evils, for social unrest and the growth of Communism up to 1933. The movement back to the farm, it is argued, will restore the traditional balance of the German people; it will also contribute powerfully to the rejuvenation of the race by relieving the congestion of overcrowded urban tenements and will give further generations a better chance to grow and develop in the healthy surroundings of the countryside. "Blood and Land"—*Blut and Boden*—is another National Socialist watchword of far-reaching importance.

I have already pointed out that Fascism and National Socialism claim to be new philosophies, almost new religions. The heroic and idealistic part of their teachings therefore must not be disregarded. Their glorification of the State and the Nation leads them along the path of extreme militarism. Mussolini derives much of his inspiration from the martial heritage of ancient Rome. Hitler draws his from Germany's Teutonic forefathers and the Prussian Army. "Fascism . . . ," writes Mussolini, "believes neither in the possibility nor in the usefulness of perpetual peace. War alone brings to its highest tension all human energy and puts the stamp of nobility upon the people who have the courage to engage in it." Hitler has advanced very similar views. "No one can doubt that in the future the world will witness tremendous battles for the existence of mankind," he says in *Mein Kampf;* "in the long run only the passion for self-preservation can win a lasting victory. When confronted with it, so-called humanitarianism, that product of a mixture of stupidity, cowardice and superciliousness, will melt away like snow in the March sunshine. In everlasting battles mankind has achieved greatness—in everlasting peace it would be doomed to destruction." These ideas permeate the entire social and political structure of the two States. We have already seen that the Italian Fascist Party officially describes itself as a "civil Militia." The militarist spirit of the two movements is undoubtedly due to the fact that they are products of the aftermath of the war. Mussolini, it will be remembered, had been the leader of the "interventionists" both before and after the war. Hitler began his political career as a champion of that German army which, it was alleged, had been "stabbed in the back" by traitors behind the firing line. The bulk of the followers of Fascism and National Socialism in the early days were drawn from the men who were demobilized from the army. Even today a war record is the best introduction to Party officials and the best qualifications for a Party office.

According to Fascism and National Socialism war is not only the supreme test of the Nation but also the most sublime of experiences for the individual. National Socialist leaders have repeated over and over again that war is for the man what child-birth is for the woman. "Fascism believes . . . in holiness and in heroism," writes Mussolini, "that is to say in actions influenced by no economic motive, direct or indirect." And it rejects with contempt the materialistic concept of happiness. "Fascism denies the validity of the equation well-being = happiness which would reduce men to the level of animals, caring for one thing only—to be fat and well fed. It would degrade humanity to a purely physical existence." War occupies the very opposite end of the scale of values. It is in the supreme sacrifice of personal interest, comforts and life itself that the idea of national solidarity and of the supremacy of the Nation finds its highest expression. Contempt for purely material aims is preached today in Italy and Germany with remarkable candor and truly religious fervor. "Remember," said Mussolini in 1930, addressing the Young Fascists, "that Fascism does not promise you honors or rewards, but only duty and fighting." And these are the promises that raise the youthful Spartans of modern Italy to the highest pitch of enthusiasm. For Fascism, as well as National Socialism, is above all a heroic doctrine.

Assuming that the foregoing survey of the fundamental ideas of Fascism and National Socialism gives a sufficiently accurate summary of their teaching, it will be readily admitted that the new philosophy contains little to afford a rational explanation of the amazing success of the movements themselves either in Italy or in Germany. The claims of Mussolini and Hitler to foremost places among the spiritual leaders of mankind is not borne out in an examination of their contribution to human thought. The secret of their success therefore must be sought not in their philosophy, which contains little that is new and even less that is convincing, but rather in the historical, political, economic and social conditions of the post-war period which paved the way for their triumph. It was the appeal to the emotions and not to reason that made Fascism and National Socialism what they are today. Their ideology nevertheless is the daily bread of some 43 million Italians and 64 million Germans, and it is being disseminated with an energy and persistency that no other government, except perhaps that of Soviet Russia, has ever displayed before—and this with a technique greatly superior to that of the U.S.S.R. It would be a fascinating study to attempt to discover what the supporters of Mussolini and Hitler really think of the fundamentals of the regime they are helping to establish. I cannot claim to have made any such study which moreover, for obvious reasons, is not feasible. But during visits to Italy in 1935 and to Germany in 1934 and 1935 I made a practice of asking Italians and Germans whom I had a chance to meet to tell me what, in their opinion, represents the essence of the philosophy of their national government. Such casual conversation, needless to say, offers no real ground for broad generalizations. Nevertheless the answers I received proved to be interesting and sometimes illuminating.

There are obviously a large number of people in both Italy and Germany who are opposed to their present governments, and their criticism is no less unsparing, if more discreet, than that we are used to outside their frontiers. Discreet though it be, criticism of this kind is much more frequent and outspoken than the outsider usually imagines. In Italy, where Fascism has been at the helm for thirteen years, the ranks of the Party have inevitably absorbed certain elements whose attitude toward the regime is in certain cases lukewarm and in others even hostile. I have heard men wearing in their lapels the Fascist badge, which is compulsory for members of the Party, denounce Mussolini with a bitterness which no political emigre could possibly excel. And I was told that their membership in the Party was a necessity which made them feel ashamed of themselves.

The attitude of such people, whose personal tragedy cannot but inspire the deepest sympathy, may have no special value for the present discussion, since it is an attitude necessarily similar to that of the many critics of Fascism and National Socialism abroad. Moreover, what I was trying to get was some glimpse of the reasoning which makes the masses of the people rally to the lictor's rods and the swastika. It was therefore from men and women who were in one way or another associated with the respective regimes that I attempted to obtain my information. There is probably a considerable percentage among them who have bowed to necessity and are serving Fascism and National Socialism because

Fascism and National Socialism are now their masters, and because any sign of opposition might get them into the most serious trouble. But far the greatest number, I think, are supporting the regime because they have found in it certain elements which they can endorse. One of the advantages of political and social doctrine that partakes of many elements is that it offers opportunities to its followers to concentrate on certain phases only and to disregard altogether or at least thrust into the background those which they find particularly unpalatable.

The discussions I had with Italians over a bottle of *Chianti* in some backstreet *trattoria* or with Germans over a glass of *Würzburger* in a *Bierhalle* brought out very clearly the fundamental difference in the attitude of the two peoples. The Italians, as a rule, do not take the official doctrine of Fascism too seriously. Except for the learned and the academic who produce elaborate volumes on the theory of the Corporate State, they usually dismiss the subject with general comments on Mussolini's genius, the remarkable progress Italy has made under his rule, the improvement in public services and building activities, the progress of physical education or some kindred matter, which would seem to betray an interest in the concrete results obtained, rather than in the metaphysical aspects of Fascism.

Even high government officials in charge of the important policies of the regime frequently discuss Fascism's theoretical aspects in a manner which, while very witty and entertaining, is a better proof of their delightful sense of humor than of any blind bowing down to Fascist Truth. The young people, with whom the Duce is immensely popular, seem to be more interested in football and skiing than in the moral principles underlying the Charter of Labor. Who would blame them for that? The glorification of the regime in Mussolini's passionate rhetoric is not incompatible with a certain carefully measured degree of self-criticism. After thirteen years of its rule Fascism, I think, is willing to look upon itself in a manner that is not wholly uncritical. It is proud of what it considers to be its achievements, but it does not completely shut its eyes to its shortcomings. Freedom from dogmatism and a keen sense of humor have always been among the most attractive aspects of the Italian character. It is by no means certain that the Duce himself does not sympathize with this attitude. Did he not for years keep the movement from any dogmatic entanglement as a "free body of athletic men"?

The Germans take their National Socialist philosophy or *Weltanschauung* in much more serious vein. This may be due partly to the fact that Hitler's road to power was longer, his struggle more stubborn and partly to the fact that his tenure of office has been shorter than Mussolini's. But the real explanation is probably to be found in German character itself and that attitude toward life in which duty (*Pflicht*) in the sense of dogma sanctified by the proper authority plays so important a part. The *Weltanschauung* is duly canonized and is the subject of learned lectures in schools and universities and of innumerable discussions in the organizations of the Party and its various subsidiaries. Nevertheless it should not be thought that the intricacies of the National Socialist theology have already penetrated deeply into the mind of the rank and file. The usual answer to the question "What, in your opinion, is the essence of the *Weltanschauung?*" was that this was a very difficult thing to explain. Some of the members of the National Socialist Party displayed no more interest in its ideology than did many of the Italian Fascists in the ideology of Fascism. But even among those who had pondered over the writings of the National Socialist prophets or received the proper schooling in the teachings of Hitler, Goebbels, Rosenberg and Streicher there is a considerable divergence of view as to what constitutes the kernel of the new philosophy. One hears, of course, invariable references to the achievements of the regime, to the elimination of the Communist danger, the reduction of unemployment, the resumption by Germany of her place as a great military Power. The intense nationalism and the heroic aspect of National Socialism make a strong appeal to many, and at least on one occasion I was told that the "liberation" of Germany from the Jews was the real and the highest aim of the Hitler movement. This remark came from a magnificent-looking young man in a black S.S. uniform. Among the younger generation there is also a very definite tendency to dwell on the presumably unlimited possibilities for national betterment resulting from unified leadership and the creation of a "common will." My very definite impression from contacts with the local officials of the National Socialist Party is that many of them are sincerely and deeply engrossed in the work of social and economic rehabilitation in which the present Government is very active, and that to them this effort to improve the lot of the less fortunate members of the community represents the very essence of the *Weltanschauung*. I tried to argue, in answer, that there was no necessary connection between such commendable efforts and the theory of the race and National Socialist dictatorship in general. They would not listen to me, of course, and invariably replied that National Socialism is succeeding where democracy failed, which, historically, is probably not true.

The older generation, including some of the vast army of government officials, finds itself in a more difficult position since it has been brought up in ideas that are different in more than one respect from those of Germany's present rulers. These people, I think, try hard to restore their moral balance by concentrating on the nationalist parts of the Hitler philosophy, on the principle of national solidarity and the sacrifice of one's individual interests to those of the Nation. This is why one finds, neatly framed on the wall of so many German offices and homes, the following verses ascribed, wrongly I am told, to Fichte:

> Believe in the future of Germany;
> in your people's insurrection.
> Undismayed, believe;
> in spite of all that may befall.

With unwavering courage
act as though on you and on what you do
depends Germany's high destiny;
as though you alone were responsible
and the fate of the Fatherland in your hand.

22

WHAT IS NATIONALISM? *

Nationalism has been one of the most important and most moving of the modern secularized religions. Nationalism is distinguished from patriotism as hate is distinguished from love, for it is a perversion and an improper overintensification of a natural virtue. In 1938 Pope Pius XI declared that nationalism had become "by now a true form of apostasy," and Hilaire Belloc called it the last of the great heresies.

Nationalism is a term that is used loosely to mean different things. Some historians use it in a broad sense to refer to national feeling, patriotism, loyalty to king or country. But it has come to have a more precise meaning with such specialists as Carlton J. H. Hayes, whose selection is included below as the best single description of modern nationalism. With the Hayes school the term has an opprobrious meaning, as it did with Pius XI and Hilaire Belloc, for it means a divinization of nation, a worship of the national state which properly belongs to God alone.

In the following selection Professor Hayes shows the ingredients that are used to compose the product of nationalism: tradition, language, religion, all those things which set one people apart from others. He shows in this selection and elsewhere that nationalism is not a natural development, but that it has been artificially cultivated to weld people together, to gain their unthinking assent to every government policy, and to stifle all criticism as disloyal or subversive.

Nationalism played an important role in the nineteenth century in helping to bring about the unification of Italy and Germany, the establishment of such "national" states as Greece, Roumania, Serbia, and Belgium. Moreover, it was a major factor in promoting the First World

* From Carlton J. H. Hayes, *Essays on Nationalism,* copyright 1926 by The Macmillan Company, and used with the permission of the publisher.

War and in effecting the peace treaties which created a national Poland and broke up the multi-national Hapsburg Empire. It was a major factor, also, in the unrest of the non-European world, as nationalistic movements rocked China, India, Palestine, Egypt, and other areas formerly under European dominance. Thus in the twentieth century nationalism became a world-wide movement as it was directed against the European countries where it originated in the eighteenth and nineteenth centuries.

1

THE MOST significant emotional factor in public life today is nationalism. Of the current age it is the mark at once intense and universal.

Look you at the state of popular feeling in France in respect to Germany, or in Germany in respect of France; look you at the zeal of the Italians for the newer, greater Italy, at the enthusiasm of the Poles for a Poland restored and unified, at the determination of a Turkey for and by the Turks. Observe the outcome of the latest and greatest war in human annals: on one hand, the smashing of the non-national empires of the Tsars, the Hapsburgs, and the Sultans, and, on the other, the building of the sovereign independence and national unity of Czechoslovakia, of Estonia, of Finland, of Greece, of Latvia, of Lithuania, of Rumania, of Yugoslavia. Note the patriotic ardour of Englishmen in behalf of the British Empire and the no less nationalist reaction against it of Irishmen, East Indians, and Egyptians. Perceive in the United States the pursuit of a policy of national isolation, the heightening tariff, the increasing restrictions on foreign immigration, the picturesque activities of citizens in masks and nightgowns, the vogue of Americanism and Americanization.

Study the sentimental background of diplomatic intrigues, competitive armaments, and the economic rivalries, not only in general as abstract causes of hypothetical war, but specifically as concrete predisposing causes of the late World War and as definite motive forces in contemporary international tensions, exemplified most pertinently perhaps in the strains and stresses of Americo-Japanese relations. The background of all these things and of much else is nationalism. Hardly a cloud appears nowadays on the horizon of domestic politics, social action, and international affairs, which is without a lining of nationalism. This fact should at once be obvious, though some painful reflections may be required to determine whether the lining be of silver or of brass.

2

Peculiar difficulties confront the student who essays to deal with the impressive and vital phenomenon of nationalism. There has been, especially of late, a good deal of "popular" writing on various aspects of it, and several scholarly treatises have recently dealt with its history among particular peoples, but no profound systematic treatment of the whole subject—the nature and history of patriotism, nationality, and nationalism—exists in any language. To undertake such a treatment would be, of course, a gigantic task: one would have to know a vast amount of history, and history of ideas quite as much as of actions; further, since patriotism is a matter more of feeling than of thought, one would have to be trained in social psychology as well as in philosophy and history, and, finally, alas, before one could advance into the very heart of contemporary nationalism one would be forced to traverse the wide fields and devious paths of anthropology. Small wonder that publicists have bungled and professors have been afraid! Lacking scientific investigation and scholarly analysis, the phenomenon appears vague and intangible and mysterious. There is no agreement as to precisely what it is or as to whether it is good or bad, transitory or eternal.

Reluctance to deal adequately with nationalism is ascribable not only to the complexity of source-materials and the paucity of scientific treatments but also to the deep and powerful emotions with which the whole subject is charged. Nationalism touches all manner of current popular prejudices—personal, national, religious, and racial—and he who would expose the mainsprings of nationalist thought and action must guard particularly against his own emotional bias and at the same time face courageously the distrust and opposition of a large number of his fellows whose own manifold prejudices are enshrined in a collective herd-prejudice. It is almost inevitable that thoughtless persons—the bulk of mankind—should accuse the thoughtful national critic of being an "internationalist" or a "radical," an "anarchist" or a "bolshevist"; at least they will call him "unpatriotic." And what sane man likes to be called unpatriotic? The flushed faces of those who resent imputations upon contemporary forms of patriotism and the cold shivers which run up and down the spine of him who is denounced for making such imputations, are the most eloquent tributes to the strength and force of nationalist feeling. They are the most difficult hurdles in the course of the scholarly study of the phenomenon of nationalism.

A minor difficulty, but a troublesome one, must be dealt with at the outset of our study. I refer to the different and sometimes conflicting uses and connotations of the words "nation," "nationality," "nationalism," and "patriotism." Yet, if we are to comprehend and eventually to judge the phenomena which these words express, we must seek some mutual understanding of what they mean and how they are related one to another. We must endeavour to assign to them fairly precise definitions, no matter how tentative or arbitrary such definitions may be. We must speak the same language and employ the same terms in the same sense.

The word "nation" is tantalisingly ambiguous. It is an old word and has gathered much moss with the lapse of centuries. As derived from the

Latin "natio" it meant birth or race and signified a tribe or social grouping based on real or fancied community of blood and possessed presumably of unity of language. Later it was used in certain mediaeval universities to designate a division of students for voting purposes according to their place of birth. Edmund Spenser in the *Faery Queen* spoke of a "nation of birds"; Ben Jonson styled physicians "a subtile nation"; and Samuel Butler referred to lawyers as "too wise a nation to expose their trade to disputation." Since the seventeenth century "nation" has been employed by jurists and publicists to describe the population of a sovereign political state, regardless of any racial or linguistic unity, and this description still enjoys general sanction. Thus, not only the relatively homogeneous peoples of Denmark and Portugal are called nations, but the polyglot peoples of the Hapsburg Empire until the close of the last war were collectively called the Austrian or the Austro-Hungarian nation, and the bi-lingual Belgians and the tri-lingual Swiss are still called nations. In the United States a special usage obtains, for here the word is frequently applied to the whole body of the people coming under the jurisdiction of the federal government.

It was in part to atone for the abuse of the word "nation" that the word "nationality" was coined in the early part of the nineteenth century and speedily incorporated into most European languages. Thenceforth, while "nation" continued chiefly to denote the citizens of a sovereign political state, nationality was more exactly used in reference to a group of persons speaking the same language and observing the same customs. The jurists have done their best to corrupt the new word "nationality," just as they had corrupted the old word "nation"; they have utilised "nationality" to indicate citizenship. For example, they speak of a person of British nationality though thereby they may mean any subject of King George V, a subject mayhap who, in the non-legal sense, belongs to the Boer nationality of South Africa or to the French-Canadian nationality of North America.

In general, however, "nationality" is far less ambiguous than "nation" and is most commonly and can be most properly used to designate a group of people who speak either the same language or closely related dialects, who cherish common historical traditions, and who constitute or think they constitute a distinct cultural society. In this sense, a nationality may exist without political unity, that is, without an organised sovereign state of its own, and, vice versa, a political state may embrace several nationalities, though the tendency has been pronounced in modern times for every self-conscious nationality to aspire to political unity and independence. A nationality which is not politically independent and united is metaphorically styled an "oppressed" or "subject" or even "enslaved" nationality. A nationality, by acquiring political unity and sovereign independence, becomes a "nation," or, to avoid the use of the troublesome word "nation," establishes a "national state." A national state is always based on nationality, but a nationality may exist without a national state. A state is essentially political; a nationality is primarily cultural and only incidentally political.

The word "nationalism" appeared in European vocabularies about the same time as, or shortly after, the appearance of "nationality" and has acquired several shades of meaning. It stands in the first place for an actual historical process, that of establishing nationalities as political units, of building out of tribes and empires the modern institution of the national state. Secondly, the term indicates the theory, principle, or ideal implicit in the actual historical process. In this sense it signifies both an intensification of the consciousness of nationality and a political philosophy of the national state. Thirdly, it may mean, in such phrases as "Irish nationalism" or "Chinese nationalism," the activities of a particular political party, combining an historical process and a political theory; this meaning is clearer when the adjective "nationalist" is employed, for example, in speaking of the historical Irish Nationalist Party. A fourth and final use of "nationalism" is to denote a condition of mind among members of a nationality, perhaps already possessed of a national state, a condition of mind in which loyalty to the ideal or to the fact of one's national state is superior to all other loyalties and of which pride in one's nationality and belief in its intrinsic excellence and in its "mission" are integral parts. Though hereafter we shall give some consideration to nationalism as an historical process, we shall chiefly be concerned with nationalism as the condition of mind just indicated. For this is the nationalism which in the twentieth century is most in evidence. It is this nationalism which colours thought and conditions action in political, social, and cultural spheres, in our domestic politics and in our foreign relations.

3

Nationalism is a modern emotional fusion and exaggeration of two very old phenomena—nationality and patriotism. There always have been, so far as historians and anthropologists know, human entities that can properly be called nationalities. There has been from ancient times the love of country or native land, which is patriotism. But nationalism is a modern, almost a recent, phenomenon. This point is so impressive in itself and so fundamental to our study as to merit and require some detailed explanation.

Let us begin by considering the basis of nationality. We have already defined nationality as "a group of people who speak either the same language or closely related dialects, who cherish common historical traditions, and who constitute or think they constitute a distinct cultural society." But what is the historical and anthropological basis of such a grouping? What determines nationality in general and distinguishes one nationality from another?

Human nature, it has been suggested. In a certain sense this is perfectly true, for man is by nature gregarious and has always lived and labored and fought in groups, and nationalities are certainly human groups. But nationalities are not the only groupings in which man has fought, labored, and lived; outside of national limits man's gregariousness has repeatedly been exhibited in religious or economic groupings. It is no more an expression of human nature for citizens of France to display a distinguishing community of interest than for French and Polish Catholics, for Dutch and Scottish Protestants, for Rumanian and Galician Jews, for Russian and Italian Communists, or for American and German bankers.

It has been contended that geography makes nationality. The fact that Britain and Japan are islands separated from large continents and that the United States covers a large part of a continent widely distant from Eurasia has doubtless had something to do with the formation of the British, Japanese, and American nationalities. But geography alone will not explain why the British Isles are parcelled out among at least four nationalities, or why the Philippines are not Japanese, or why the Rio Grande rather than the Mississippi or the Rockies is the boundary between the American and Mexican nationalities. When we consider that some four nationalities—Portuguese, Castilian, Catalan, and Basque—coexist in the geographic unit known as the Iberian Peninsula, that the Polish and Magyar nationalities occupy parts (and only parts) of great plains, that the Greek nationality inhabits rocky coasts and islands, that Norwegian geography is similar in many significant aspects to Swedish, Yugoslav to Bulgarian, and even German to French, we must conclude that the idea of natural frontiers between nationalities is a myth.

A myth likewise is the notion, often advanced by uniformed or unreflective persons, that nationality is determined by race. While scientists are not at all agreed as to what precisely are the races of man, they are in complete agreement that every modern nationality consists of racial mixtures. Racially, modern Germans, Frenchmen, Englishmen, Irishmen, Russian, Italians—almost all Europeans, and the Jews as well—alike comprise mongrel descendants of long-heads and round-heads, blonds and brunets, tall persons and short, stout and slim. The mixture may vary in the relative strength of its component elements from one part of Europe to another, but the degree of racial variation does not change abruptly at national borders. Even the Japanese and Chinese, though marked off by certain physical characteristics from Europeans, afford clear evidence of racial admixture, and the peoples of India, who of late have been developing a consciousness of common nationality, are a veritable hodge-podge of racial strains. Purity of race, if it exists nowadays exists only among uncivilized tribesmen. Nationality actually cuts through and across race, though it must be confessed, in deference to racial propaganda, that an imaginary belief in blood relationship, that is, in race, has been an effective force in building and cementing nationalities.

Then there is the "soul of a people," the theory that every nationality has a group-mind with peculiar and constant mental qualities and endowments. Group-mind, in this sense, is a metaphysical concept, and we may be pardoned for wondering at the simple faith with which many recent writers, including some who deny or doubt the existence of the individual soul, have ascribed eternal fullfledged souls to the several nationalities. It is an obvious fact that in social customs nationalities do differ from one another: the English probably drink tea more commonly and inveterately than any other Europeans; the Germans are more addicted to especially tasty brands of beer; the Italians flavor their culture more pungently with garlic; and there are doubtless other and even greater national distinctions. Besides, it is a fact amply demonstrated by competent psychologists that human beings may behave in one way in a crowd and in another way when they are alone, in a certain manner when they are subjected to group-pressure and in a different manner when such pressure is removed, that, in other words, there is a group-mind which is a part of, but in its effects distinct from, individual minds. In this sense we may admit the existence of a "national mind," a psychological force which impels the members of a nationality-group toward some community of thought and action, but to dub this national mind a "soul" is literary license. As a matter of fact, the group-mind of a nationality is demonstrably fickle and inconstant. Most characteristics ascribed to a given nationality are found on investigation to belong to several nationalities, and what is characteristic of a particular nationality at a given time is not necessarily characteristic of it at other times. The Greeks of the age of Pericles doubtless reeked with garlic quite as much as the Italians of the nineteenth century. The Germans who fought Caesar had not yet associated great music and profound philosophy with the refinements of Pilsener or Culmbacher. The king who signed Magna Carta and the barons who drove him to it did not drink tea.

Much buncombe has been talked and written about national characters. From examples which are legion, note may profitably be taken of a quotation from an otherwise informing essay by Mr. Charles Roden Buxton: "Just as England contributes her sense for political liberty, France her intellectual honesty and lucidity, Germany her industry and discipline, Italy her aesthetic aptitude, so Finland has her advanced democracy, Poland her music and art, Bohemia religious independence, the Serbs their warm poetic temperament, the Greeks their subtlety and their passion for the past, the Bulgarians their plodding endurance and taciturn energy, the Armenians their passion for education and progress." The fallacies here are numerous and prodigious. It is implied, absurdly implied, that all Englishmen have a sense for political liberty and that only Englishmen are so endowed, that all Frenchmen are intellectually honest and clear-headed, that all Germans are industrious, that all Italians are artists or art-critics, that all Finns are ultimate democrats, that all Poles are musicians, that all Czechs are religious independents, etc. It is doubtful in some instances, as in that of the Czechs, whether the characteristic mentioned may be ascribed to any considerable section of the nationality. It is certain in every instance that the characteristic assigned to a nationality may be attributed with equal propriety to other nationalities, ancient as well as modern. Modern France is no more marked by intellectual honesty and lucidity than was ancient Italy; modern Italy possesses no greater aesthetic aptitude than Spain, France, southern Germany, or Japan; Finland has advanced along democratic highways no further than New Zealand, Switzerland, or Oregon; the thermometer of poetic feeling records no higher temperature in Serbia than in England, Ireland, Germany, and Arabia; Greek subtlety is outclassed by Armenian, and in passion for the past Greeks are surely equalled by Jews and Chinese; "plodding endurance and taciturn energy" have conventionally been ascribed less to Bulgarians than to Scots; and to anyone who gives a thought to the national traits of Americans, Japanese, Germans, or Australians it seems utterly ridiculous to hit upon the "passion for education and progress" as a peculiarity of Armenians.

It is but fair to Mr. Buxton to quote later and wiser words from his essay: "Peoples are not, in fact, to be distinguished from one another by a single mark, detaching itself from a background of pure similarity. It is the total combination of qualities, of historical events, of natural surroundings, which makes them what they are—conglomerations of various conflicting personalities and parties, touched nevertheless with some unifying character which makes even their very divisions distinctive." With much of this I for one am in agreement, but I would warn against rash imaginings and easy generalizations as to what precisely may be the "unifying character" of a nationality, and at the same time, I would reemphasize the point that national traits undergo radical alterations, often in a relatively brief time. Voltaire, writing in the first half of the eighteenth century, contrasted the English and the French: the English he thought to be changeable and revolutionary, beheading one king and exiling another, perpetually tinkering with government and religion, forever fermenting; the French he stigmatized as conservative and as being too fondly attached to the past and to the moss-covered traditions of divine-right monarchy and orthodox Christianity, stolid and stagnant. The late Mr. J. E. C. Bodley, writing at the end of the nineteenth century, again contrasted the English and the French: the English, to him, were a conservative, anti-revolutionary, and substantial people, among whom liberty slowly broadened out, with the emphasis on "slowly," whilst the French were fickle, volatile, and revolutionary, beheading one sovereign and expelling several others, fitfully experimenting with constitutions, and feverishly repudiating religious orthodoxy. Both Bodley and Voltaire possessed no little critical acumen, and the explanation of their widely divergent estimates must be sought in a change, within two centuries, in the "group-minds" of the French and English nationalities.

Summing up the objections against the concept of peculiar and constant "souls" in the several nationalities, Mr. Israel Zangwill has wittily remarked: "The Bulgarians anciently had a word *pravit,* meaning 'to say.' It now means 'to do.' They had a word *dumat,* 'to think.' It now means 'to speak.' Similar changes, as of Hamlets into Othellos, occur in the souls of every people. The Mongols turned from agriculture to militarism and back again. The Magyars were Oriental shepherds before they came prancing westwards as mounted archers. The Germans were once meek and musical; a native editor of Schiller's 'Robbers' opined that 'even the Germans' could produce great passions and characters. . . . The people of Magna Carta clamour daily for more bureaucracy. The heirs of Mazzini demand court-martialling of free-spoken Deputies. The oldest monarchy in the world has just turned into a Republic, and Bushido-bound Japan has acquired a National Debt."

The conclusion is forced upon us that the basis of nationality is not to be found in inherent mental or spiritual differences among human groups, or, for that matter, in racial heredity or physical environment. Nationality is an attribute of human culture and civilization, and the factors of zoology and botany are not applicable to it. The forms and behaviour of animals and plants are explicable in terms of environment and heredity, because animals and plants have no civilization. It is not that heredity and environment do not apply at all to man, but that they apply only indirectly and remotely to his civilization. This fundamental fact has often been overlooked, especially in modern times, because the biological sciences having achieved successful increases of knowledge and understanding, the temptation was great to borrow their method outright and apply it without serious modification to the human material (of the social sciences). This procedure simplified the situation, but yielded inadequate and illusory results. For a very long time the idea that man possessed and animals lacked a soul influenced people's thought to such a degree that they scarcely thought of human beings in terms of biological causality, of heredity and environment. Then when a reaction began to set in, less than two centuries ago, and it became more generally recognized that man was an animal, the pendulum swung to the other extreme and the tendency grew of seeing in him only the animal, the cultureless being, and of either ignoring his culture or thinking that it could be explained away by resolving it into the factors familiar from biology. The just and wise course lies between. The biological aspects of man must be interpreted in terms of biological causation, his cultural aspects in terms first of all of cultural causation.

Nationality is certainly an aspect of culture, and the causation of national groupings and national traits must be sought in the factors of the social and essentially humane sciences rather than in those of botany and zoology. The distinctive marks and qualities of Russian, Greek, German, Japanese, or any other nationality are no mere appanage of race or incident of geography; they are the creation of social circumstance and cultural tradition.

4

Among the cultural characteristics of nationality, language is, and always has been, preeminent. Anthropologists tell us that with primitive men tribal distinctions coincide with linguistic differences, and that the occurrence of two tribes with precisely the same speech is so rare that it may be regarded merely as a transient condition. With more highly civilized peoples, as historians can testify, the tendency is the same. The ancient Hebrew nationality had a distinctive language, and so did the Egyptian, the Punic, the Greek, the Latin, the American, the Japanese, etc. The formation of most modern nationalities has been historically dependent upon the development of particular languages. There was no such thing as the English nationality which we know until Anglo-Saxon had been fused with Norman French to produce the English language. There was no such thing as the French nationality until the Germanic Franks, mingling with the Latinized Gauls, had modified the Latin speech so far as to give rise to a new and different language called French. The rise and decline of nationalities and tribes have always been closely paralleled by the rise and decline of their respective languages, and both processes still go on together.

Language as a determining mark of nationality has been criticized by some writers, who usually cite in support of their contentions such facts as that Switzerland has three official languages and Belgium two, that the Canadians of Quebec speak French and the Basques and Bretons of France do not, that English is spoken in the United States and Welsh and Gaelic in parts of Great Britain. These citations might be multiplied but they would be of the same kind and equally beside the point. For the difficulty of the critics arises either from a confusion of nationalities with political entities or from a failure to perceive the fluid and dynamic nature of nationality.

No nationality is fixed and static. Just as in the middle ages the long survival of Norman French at the court of the English kings served to unite the fortunes of the English royal house with those of France and to militate against the development of a distinctively English nationality, so in modern times the use of the English language in the United States tends to link American thought and action with that of England and at the same time to obstruct the growth of an absolutely separate American nationality. Language is not the only mark of nationality, but if we will forget for the present the division of the world into sovereign political states we shall be in a better position to recognise that English-speaking peoples, wherever they may be, constitute a nationality in contradistinction to the French, the German, or the Chinese nationality. Within a given nationality differences of dialect may become in time so pronounced that, in conjunction with other separatist factors, they may exalt what have been, so-to-speak, mere "subnationalities" into true and distinct nationalities. Time alone will tell whether the American nationality is truly distinct from the English, and the French-Canadian from the French. The old Slav-speaking Prussian nationality long ago lost its language and was absorbed into the German nationality; as yet the languages of Welsh, Gael, Basque, and Breton survive and the nationalities which they severally represent have not been completely absorbed by the English or the French.

On the other hand, despite the artificial attempts to promote a sense of social solidarity, akin to nationality, among all the Swiss and among all the Belgians, the real fact remains that the citizens of Switzerland differ in social consciousness and in certain elements of culture according as their speech is French, Italian, or German, and that the Belgian Flemings differ similarly from the Belgian Walloons. During the World War the cleavage of Swiss sympathies along linguistic lines was patent, and of late Belgium has been torn by dissensions between Walloon and Flemish nationalities. From the recent disintegration of the Austro-Hungarian Monarchy into its several component nationalities, it may not be utterly fantastic to draw a lesson which may at some future time be applicable to Belgium and to Switzerland, and even to the British Empire. Just as Austria-Hungary was dissolved by the last World War into its constituent national elements, so in another world war the British Empire and other non-national states, such as Switzerland and Belgium, may be broken into several independent and mutally exclusive national states.

It is readily comprehensible why language should be an important, probably the chief, factor in forming and sustaining a nationality. Uniformity of language tends to promote like-mindedness, to provide an inclusive set of ideas as well as of words, and like-minded persons tend to develop group-consciousness, to experience a sense of common interest, to constitute a tribe or nationality. Members of such a group naturally regard persons who speak a strange and alien language as "unlike" or different from themselves and hence as inferior and not entitled to belong to themselves. The historical antitheses between Jew and Gentile and between Greek and Barbarian have analogies in all languages and among all peoples.

Language, too, is the medium in which is expressed the memory of successful achievement or distressing hardship shared in common, and thereby it acquires cementing value for a nationality. It is the bridge between the present and the past. In the words of Ossian, "It is the voice of years that are gone; they roll before me with all their deeds." And this brings us to the second distinguishing attribute of nationality—the cherishing of common historical traditions.

History is essentially human. To men, as to no other animals, have been vouchsafed a sense of time and an endowment of memory. Not only do human beings naturally recall certain outstanding events in their own lives and in those of their immediate family, but also, being gregarious, they preserve and embroider the recollection of past crises in the life of the linguistic group to which they belong. They are especially prone to celebrate the memory of the group's heroic figures and collective fighting prowess. Indeed, man's innate tendencies to hero-worship and group-combat, tendencies which doubtless are closely connected psychologically with his gregariousness, combine with his time-sense and his memory-endowment to fashion the traditions upon which nationality most conspicuously thrives.

In the crudest forms of nationality, the tribes of primitive men, a more or less official body of elders or priests or wise men or medicine men constitute the recognized custodians of the tribal experiences and legends, and elaborate ceremonies usually attend the initiation of youths into the "mysteries" of the past. With historic peoples it is similar. The sagas of the Norsemen, the vedas of the Hindus, the pentateuch and the chronicles of the Hebrews, the Homeric poems, the Virgilian hexameters, all the famed deeds of the brave men before Agamemnon, no less and no more than the heroes and battles cherished in memory and embellished in the telling by present-day peoples, have served to inspire linguistic groups with corporate consciousness and to render them true nationalities.

With the garnering of historic traditions appears the tendency to personify the group, to view the nationality as an historical personage. Sometimes the personification is symbolized by means of a flag or other emblem signifying the life or the spirit of a nationality. More often it is a mental image derived from the hearing of legends or the reading of tales in which scientific facts have been consciously or unconsciously subordinated to the purposes of art and romance. All such personification operates emotionally upon individuals, presenting them with a glorified picture of the spirit, the principle, the ideal of their group and thereby persuading them to a deeper loyalty to their common nationality. Not only this, but in the romantic history and in the idealized personification of one's nationality, one fancies to discover something eternal, the life of a group which existed without beginning long before any of its present members and which, by the same token, will exist without end long after its present members are gathered to their fathers' dust. Man's powerful longing for immortality receives aid and comfort from historic traditions which center in nationality.

The third distinguishing mark of nationality (after language and historic tradition) is the belief of its members that they compose a distinct, cultural society. It is but natural that a group which is cut off by difference of language from direct and general intercourse with other human beings and which has developed a peculiar attitude towards its past should feel that it is a unit distinct from others not only, but different. And as one surveys the history of nationality one is struck by the extent to which this feeling, this belief, is borne out by observable facts. Every nationality has a culture-pattern of its own, a distinctive complex of institutions, customs, and art, and the same is true even more strikingly of primitive tribes. Certain types of family relationship and social organization, certain modes of artistic expression, certain religious tenets and observances, certain habits of work and play, certain forms of clothing and shelter, are found among primitive peoples in all the continents, but no two tribes, speaking different languages, show the same combination of such habits, observances, modes, and types. The component elements may be identical, but the *tout ensemble*, in every instance, is distinctive.

Too much emphasis as well as too little, may, of course, be put upon cultural variations among tribes and nationalities. Certainly in modern times, improved means of travel and communication have given an impetus towards uniformity of culture throughout the world, and undoubtedly in all ages what has distinguished one nationality from another has been much less vital and valuable than what several nationalities have had in common. Yet it is true that each nationality still persistently regards itself as the tabernacle of a unique civilization. Perhaps what any group thinks itself to be is quite as significant as what it really is. It is assuredly so with a nationality.

Among elements of cultural differentiation, religion, at least in the past, has been prominent. It was in and about religion that the social customs of primitive tribesmen and of most ancient peoples were woven, so that with them religion was a peculiarly tribal or national affair. It provided a psychical content for their group-life and lent to nationality a grave dignity. In the historical case of the Hebrews it has always been very difficult to separate their religion from their nationality, and it is hardly less difficult to determine whether the Armenians, the Copts, and the Japanese owe their nationality to their religion or their religion to their nationality. Yet religion of itself cannot be deemed an invariable attitude of nationality, for the rise and propagation of "world religions," such as Graeco-Roman Paganism, Buddhism, Christianity, and Mohammedanism supplanted to a considerable degree tribal and national religions and, by creating cultural areas which overlapped—and still overlap—national borders, prove inimical rather than favorable to the principle of nationality. Besides, most modern nationalities manage to flourish without insisting upon uniformity of religious belief or practice.

Political institutions, like those of religion, may be an important factor in crystallizing a nationality. Among primitive men tribe differs from tribe not only in language and religion but in form of government. With the devolopment of civilization loyalty to a chieftain has been merged in loyalty to his law and this in turn has been merged in loyalty to the political institutions of the state. Frequently a dynasty has become the connecting link between the tribal chieftain and the abstract idea of the political state; and the prestige and all the supernaturalism contained in the notions of divine right and divine descent have been extended to the state and its government. In this way, the idea of the political state has commanded among historic peoples a very high degree of loyalty, and in many instances the expansion of a state by peaceful growth or violent conquest has served to unite various tribes in common allegiance to a common polity, to infuse all with a sentiment of solidarity, to promote the use of a uniform language, and thus to transform several small tribes into one large nationality. Such, at any rate, was the experience of the Hebrews, the Egyptians, the Latins, and many other ancient people; politics powerfully aided the transition from tribe to nationality. Such, too, was a fairly frequent occurrence in the middle ages; the growth of the French and English and Spanish nationalities was preceded by the expansion of the political sway respectively of the monarchs of France, England, and Spain.

Yet, as in the case of religion, political independence is not an indispensable condition of nationality. Many a nationality, in the long course of human history, has been engulfed by a "world-empire," such as the Egyptian, the Assyrian, Alexander the Great's, the Roman, the Turkish, the Russian, the Austrian, the British, and has thereby been deprived of its distinctive political institutions without losing its identity as a nationality. Many another nationality, such as the Phoenician, the Greek, the German, and the Polish, has continued obviously to be a nationality despite the fact that for centuries it was parcelled out among a number of states and possessed neither uniformity of political institutions nor unity of political allegiance.

5

We have now investigated at some length, though at no greater length than the subject requires, the bases and attributes of nationality; and we have satisfied ourselves that it is not dependent on an eternal "soul," that is, on constant and inherent mental variations, or on race (though a belief in community of blood may enhance it), or on geography (save in a very general way), or on human nature (except as all forms of human gregariousness depend ultimately upon the nature of man). Rather, we have confirmed our hypothesis that nationality rests upon cultural foundations, that a nationality is any group of persons who speak a common language, who cherish common historical traditions, and who constitute, or think they constitute, a distinct cultural society in which, among other factors, religion and politics may have played important though not necessarily continuous roles.

Thus defined, nationality has existed from the earliest times of which history and anthropology can treat. Most of the tribes described by anthropologists and most of the peoples whom we encounter in history, are nationalities. But this is not to say that a given nationality has always existed or always will. Nationalities wax and wane, rise and fall, appear and disappear. Most of the contemporary nationalities of Europe may be said, in relation to the enormous span of human life on this globe, to be of recent birth; and today, before our very eyes, numerous nationalities of American Indians are dying.

Besides, a nationality, as we have defined it, may embrace several sub-nationalities. For example, the English, the Scots, and the Welsh, in so far as they use the English language, cherish traditions of joint action against non-Britishers, and constitute, or think they constitute, a common, cultural society in contradistinction to that of Frenchmen or Germans, are one nationality, but the Scots and the Welsh in so far as they possess languages or dialects of their own, in addition to the King's English, and in so far as they retain peculiar historic traditions at variance with some of their English neighbours', are nationalities distinct from the English. Wherefore it may properly be maintained that the English, Scottish, and Welsh are sub-nationalities of a British nationality. Again, the Catalans and Provencals once formed a nationality with a distinctive language and literature, with distinctive historic traditions, and with a belief that they possessed a distinctive culture, but during centuries of French rule in Provence and of Spanish sway in Catalonia they have been so permeated by the language and traditions of other and dominant nationalities that the Catalans have been reduced to the position of a sub-nationality within the Spanish nationality whilst the Provencals, though still differing from the French in minor respects, are in major matters "good Frenchmen."

On the other hand, difference of historic traditions and emphasis upon cultural contrasts, real or fancied, especially when they are reenforced by political separation, may outweigh identity of language and thereby create a sub-nationality which becomes almost, if not quite, an absolutely independent nationality. The Portuguese who first went to Brazil, the Spaniards who first settled in Mexico and Peru, the English who first colonized Virginia and Massachusetts, were certainly of the Portuguese, Spanish, or British nationalities. Their descendants have used the same national languages, but adaptation to a new and different environment, economic quarrels with the mother-countries, and forceful political isolation have tended to create and exalt among these descendants peculiar historic traditions so powerful as to give rise to Brazilian, Mexican, Peruvian, and American nationalities. In one sense, these are now independent nationalities; in another sense, they are still sub-nationalities.

Nor can it be maintained that among historical peoples the consciousness and "drive" of nationality have always been of the same intensity. The facility with which "world-religions" and "world-empires" have been superimposed upon nationalities, the rapidity with which nationalities have been broken into sub-nationalities and dissolved into an urban or a feudal society, betoken that in many ages the claims of nationality upon man's allegiance have been slight. As a matter of fact, man's gregariousness has assumed many forms other than national, and similarly his sense of loyalty, which springs from his gregariousness, has not been limited to national objects; it has been displayed in a bewildering multiplicity of ways. Sometimes it has been loyalty to persons, as to tribal chieftains or to supposedly divine monarchs or to feudal lords or to fellow members of a caste, a clan, a guild, a trade-union, or a club. Sometimes it has been loyalty to places as to grove or stream, to thatched cottage or marble palace, to natal home or tomb of the ancestral dead, to pastoral hillside, fertile plain, or great busy city. Sometimes it has been loyalty to ideas, as to a religion, a political philosophy, a scheme of science, a programme of social reform, or an economic system. At all times man has simultaneously applied his sense of loyalty, quite naturally and without nice discrimination, to ideas, places, and persons. He has so applied it both within and without his nationality. He now applies it primarily to his nationality and his national state, but throughout a large part of his recorded history he has applied his sense of loyalty less to nationality than to other objects.

Patriotism, which nowadays we connect with nationality, has been historically more closely related to other loyalties of man. Patriotism means literally the love of one's *terra patria* or natal land. As such it must have been of slight significance to the member of an early nomadic tribe or nationality, who, as Professor J. H. Robinson has said, "can hardly have had any sweet and permanent associations with the tree or rock under which he was born." Patriotism did become a marked feature of ancient fixed and civilized life, but even then it was seldom a patriotism which reached throughout the length and breadth of the country where people of like speech had their homes; it was rarely a national patriotism. Usually the patriotism which existed was local: it was applied, for example, by the Greeks not indiscriminately to all Greek-speaking lands, but to a fragment of land such as Athens, Sparta, Corinth, or Smyrna; by the Phoenicians not generally to Phoenicia but specifically to Tyre, Sidon, or Carthage; by the Romans first and foremost not to the orbit of the Latin language but to the city of Rome.

This sort of patriotism is natural enough. Everybody who is born and reared where his ancestors have lived from time immemorial is almost certain to feel a sentimental attachment to that locality. It was easy for a mediaeval peasant to evince patriotism for the manor on which he was born and from which he derived his sustenance. It is easy for a modern French peasant to experience some patriotic emotion about the soil and scenery of his *pays*. It is less artificial for a native-born American to love a familiar little village in Massachusetts or Louisiana or California than to cherish impartially and equally all the United States.

Patriotism at an early date was extended in application from one's native locality to one's political country, from an immediate place to the person of a military or political leader, and thence to the idea of a state. But among ancient peoples, and mediaeval also, the sway of political and military chieftains infrequently coincided with any particular nationality, and consequently patriotism often changed from local sentiment into imperial pride without passing through an intermediate national stage. Perhaps it would be more accurate to say that on top of natural local patriotism was superimposed a more artificial imperial patriotism. At times in the history of certain ancient peoples, notably the Egyptians and the Hebrews, there was something resembling national patriotism, and doubtless, for the building and maintenance of many of the empires of the past, military conquerors and governors could rely on the special support and encouragement of the self-conscious nationality which constituted the core of an empire. But members of such a conquering self-conscious nationality could not experience quite the same emotion of patriotism about the extended empire as they felt about their own regions; and the conquered peoples, whilst they might come to regard the empire as a necessity, even as a blessing, and therefore as deserving of a kind of artificial patriotism, were certainly not inclined to bestow any particular affection upon the exclusively native land of their conquerors.

Imperial patriotism is necessarily much more artificial, more dependent on socially inherited knowledge and conscious effort, than is local patriotism. In order to realize this, we must, again and again, remind ourselves of the quantitative limitations of all the factors in the human type. We are apt to think of human societies as we think of equilateral triangles. We can imagine an equilateral triangle with sides either an inch long or a hundred miles long, and in either case its qualities as an equilateral triangle will be the same. But if we imagine a heap of sand composed of sand-grains, each grain being about a hundredth of an inch in diameter, we must remember that a change of size in the heap may change the relation between the grains, and therefore the character of the heap. A heap of twenty grains of sand will behave differently from a heap of twenty million grains. It will, for instance, have a different "angle of repose."

Ancient political philosophers, notably the greatest Greek minds, recognized this principle and argued from it that the ideal state (of which true patriotism should be an attribute) could not have an extensive territory or a numerous population; Plato in *The Laws* fixed the maximum number of free citizens at 5040. Hence, to them, a huge empire was a monstrosity and even the political union of a large nationality appeared undesirable and impractical. Whatever may have been the influence of the Greek philosophers, it is a fact that in ancient and middle ages strictly national states were rare and consequently national patriotism was unusual.

It is different in modern times. Nowadays there is preached and practised a twofold doctrine, (1) that each nationality should constitute a united independent sovereign state, and (2) that every national state should expect and require of its citizens not only unquestioning obedience and supreme loyalty, not only an exclusive patriotism, but also unshakable faith in its surpassing excellence over all other nationalities and lofty pride in its peculiarities and its destiny. This is nationalism and it is a modern phenomenon.

6

As we have seen, it has been a mark of nurture, if not of nature; for human beings since the dawn of history to possess some consciousness of nationality, some feeling that the linguistic, historical, and cultural peculiarities of a group make its members akin among themselves and alien from all other groups. But not until very modern times have whole peoples been systematically indoctrinated with the tenets that every human being owes his first and last duty to his nationality, that nationality is the ideal unit of political organization as well as the actual embodiment of cultural distinction, and that in the final analysis all other human loyalties must be subordinate to loyalty to the national state, that is, to national patriotism. These tenets, again, are the essence of modern nationalism.

Antiquity knew not nationalism as we know it. Ancient Egyptians were united in the bonds of a common loyalty to the sacred River Nile and to the sun-sprung Pharaoh, but the ordinary dwellers in Thebes and Memphis, though probably quite aware of common nationality, hardly felt that the claims of their nationality were superior to the claims of their Pharaoh and their priests; theirs was not exclusively a national state, and nationalism was not encouraged by the long line of Pharaohs, whose constant hieroglyph, chiselled on tomb and temple thousands of years ago, still reminds us that they aimed at a dominion on which the sun would never set. Phoenicians and Greeks alike were human in that they manifested the sense of loyalty in many ways, especially in worship of certain deities and in devotion to particular cities, but neither people was modern: they never constructed national states and their wars were chiefly interurban rather than international. The Romans had intense patriotism, but their patriotism was an expression of loyalty not to all persons who spoke the Latin language, but to the city of the seven hills with its legendary gods and heroes; and with the expansion of the city-state of Rome into an empire which encircled the Mediterranean and embraced Egyptian and Celt, Parthian and Moor, Teuton and Greek, the local patriotism of the Roman changed to pride in world-imperialism without passing through the intermediate state of nationalism, whilst among the subject provincials the assurance of the *Pax Romana* by Roman law and Roman legions became an object of general loyalty, which, however, was always supplementary to local loyalties rather than a substitute for them.

The Jews were no exception to the rule of antiquity, despite the perfervid rhapsodies of contemporary Zionists. A re-reading of the Hebrew scriptures should show that the "chosen people" did not think of themselves as singularly blest and set apart simply because they spoke Hebrew and lived in Palestine and constituted a national state. As a matter of fact, Palestine was not their original home; they had to conquer it and at a date when Egypt was already old; and even the semblance of a united national state survived with them an exceedingly brief time. The Jews were a "chosen people" because they believed in Yahweh and the law revealed by Him, and the foreigner who would proclaim in the words of Ruth to Naomi that "Thy God shall be my God" was admitted to full membership without embarrassing questions as to racial stock or linguistic accomplishment, or as to whether the quota of immigrants from the applicant's nation was full. Historically, both in ancient times and throughout the middle ages, and even down into modern times, the Jews have been not so much a nationality infused with nationalism as adherents to a religion.

During the thousand years which separate Luther and Machiavelli from Pope Gregory the Great and which we designate, for lack of a better term, the middle ages, there were few signs of nationalism anywhere in Europe. The Europeans during this long period had many loyalties—to Catholic Church, to bishop or abbot, to parish priest, to lay lord, to tribal chieftain, to duke or count or baron, to guild of merchants or of craftsmen, to manor or town, to realism or nominalism, to St. Francis or St. Dominic, to pope or emperor, to Christendom in arms against Islam. Nationalities surely persisted throughout the period and undoubtedly there was an acutely nascent consciousness of national differences towards the close of the middle ages, the result of the crusades, of the rise of vernacular literatures, and of the ambitious efforts of monarchs in western Europe, but if there was an object of popular loyalty superior to all others it was not the nation but Christendom. If a man whose native tongue was French encountered a fellow Christian whose native tongue was English, both men were fully aware of a difference, but they were quite as aware of a similarity; and it should be remembered that Joan of Arc, who is now hailed as a saint of French nationalism, appeared on battlefields of the Hundred Years' War, not in response to the appeals of a nationalist press or the pressure of a patriotic draft-board and not in conformity with the example of national heroes as set forth in hundred per cent French textbooks of history, but simply and solely in answer to "voices" which she heard from saints of God. It should be remembered, moreover, that Joan of Arc fought for one claimant to the throne of France against another, who, though simultaneously King of England and Prince of Wales, reigned over half of France and was supported by many French-speaking people. It should be remembered, too, that Joan of Arc was condemned to death, not by Englishmen but by Frenchmen, not for being a foreigner, a sort of forerunner of Edith Cavell, but for being an obstinate heretic and an advanced feminist; she dressed like a man and was, therefore, "possessed of the devil."

Nationality has always existed. Patriotism had long existed, either as applied to a locality or as extended to an empire. But the fusion of patriotism with nationality and the predominance of national patriotism over all other human loyalties—which is nationalism—is modern, very modern. How it has come about, we shall presently try to understand.

23

THE STRUGGLE FOR SPAIN: A. THE SPANISH REVOLUTION OF 1931 *

The Spanish Revolution of 1931 produced two blocs of parties, the Right and the Left, whose clashes became more violent and frequent each year, whose stands became more extreme, and who ultimately engaged in civil war in 1936. This Spanish civil war is sometimes called the "Little World War," because the USSR supported the Loyalists, whereas Italy and Germany supported the Insurgent forces.

American public opinion tended to oversimplify the Spanish issue and to back the Loyalist or the Insurgent forces according to the American's predisposition along religious and ideological lines. Generally speaking, the Insurgent forces of General Franco received the sympathy of Catholics, whereas the Loyalist cause was supported by Communists, Socialists, and those of liberal tendency. A few Catholics in Europe and America, such as Jacques Maritain and Waldemar Gurian, were sharply critical of Franco, but most Catholic papers in this country tended to overlook his faults and excuse his excesses because of the enemy he fought. Liberals in this country did the same with the Loyalists.

This tendency to see the Spanish civil war in simple black and white colors is naïve and unhistorical. Spaniards had no choice but to take sides, but Americans were free to see the faults and virtues on both sides and to get to the truth of the charges and countercharges made by Loyalists and Insurgents against each other. On both sides were good men and bad, those fighting for what they thought was right and those seeking selfish gain in a moment of national distress.

In the first of the two following selections, Father Peter M. Dunne tells the story of what happened in Spain from 1931 till 1936 as objec-

* Peter Masten Dunne, S.J., "The Spanish Revolution of 1931," *The Historical Bulletin,* XXIV (May, 1946), 77-78, 83-86. Reprinted by permission.

tively and as understandingly as it has been told anywhere. From this objective account the student can judge for himself the amount of right and wrong on each side. The second selection is by E. Allison Peers, an English observer in Spain, who probably knew more about the Spanish temperament and Spanish problems than anyone else writing in English. This selection contains Peer's conclusions in his work on The Spanish Tragedy.

THE 1931 revolution in Spain was long in the making. It sprang from dissatisfaction with the existing regime. The decline of the prestige of the Spanish monarchy had been going on steadily since the body blow it received during the Spanish-American war of 1898. Queen Mother Maria Christina was then ruling, Alfonso XIII was but a child. At the completeness and swiftness of Spain's defeat by the rising North American power of the United States, Spanish intellectuals (writers, university professors, professional men) began to reflect upon the helplessness and corruption of their government. As Spaniards they had enjoyed a proud tradition. But in the early part of the century (the nineteenth) Spain had lost most of her American colonies, and at the end of it she lost the rest of them: Cuba, Puerto Rico, and also the Philippines. She then sold her Pacific islands to Bismarck's Germany.

After the military and naval disasters of 1898 there arose a generation of writers who were disillusioned, humiliated, and wrathful concerning their government. They are known as "the generation of 1898." Many of them lived through the revolution of 1931. Pío Baroja who is an example of them writes in his *La Dama Errante,* (Madrid, 1916), a novel: "Spain is today a land of dreams for the decrepit, the Indians, for the broken down, for all who have no ambitions in life. . . ." He mentions the war with the Yankees and reflects: "Since our army is far inferior to what we thought, and the navy has been so weak that it was annihilated without effort, why then we have been deceived in these things; it is quite possible we have been deceived in everything." Baroja was anti-clerical, anti-Semitic, and against parliamentary government. Later he wrote, "I am opposed to parliamentary government and the power of the press because they are the means whereby cattle become masters." As Ricardo Leon said of this generation: "They knew only how to tear down and to curse; the majority of them did not believe in God, in their country, or in themselves." Baroja showed a trait peculiar to many Spaniards: "The theory and the practical results of anarchism have a powerful fascination for him." After the failure of the Republic he believed in a "White Dictatorship."

With Spanish authors and intellectuals writing and speaking thus during the early part of the twentieth century the future did not hold bright promise for the monarchy. Failures and inefficiency during the first three decades of the century further lowered its prestige and provoked an ominous degree of restlessness. Alfonso XIII took over the government in 1902. During the first four years, fourteen political crises occurred and eight prime ministers succeeded one another. In 1906 there was an attempt to murder the royal couple; in 1909 an anti-clerical and anarchical uprising in Barcelona took place, and in 1912 Canalejas was murdered in the streets of Madrid and Cánovas was assassinated. Both had been prime ministers of the constitutional monarchy. In 1917 Spain was paralyzed by a general strike to establish a republic on the Russian model, and in 1921 occurred the colonial disaster of Anual in Africa.

The African campaigns to keep Spanish Morocco and the Riff in order had for long been unpopular. They were a waste of money and of men, and there had been vast corruption. Now Spain suffered disgrace when the Moorish tribesmen routed her army at Anual and when General Silvester committed suicide. A tide of anarchy swept over the country. Its climax was reached in the murder of the Cardinal Archbishop of Saragossa—and there was revolution. Primo de Rivera, Captain General of Catalonia, rose in September, 1923, and issued a pronunciamento; and, at the same time, the ministers of state resigned. The King of Spain did what a year before (October, 1922) the King of Italy had done: Alfonso XIII called upon Primo de Rivera to organize a government, the "Military Directory" or a dictatorship.

Rivera introduced a strong regime. He made short shrift of the terrorizing gunmen, showed sympathy for the working classes, held the scales evenly in all industrial disputes, improved public services (4000 new schools were built), and in co-operation with the French achieved victory in Morocco (1926). Nevertheless, Rivera was not destined to enjoy the continuity of a Mussolini or Hitler. He had neglected to get his *coup d'état* ratified by the *Cortes* or parliament; he was ignorant and contemptuous of parliamentary government and of all it stood for; his brusk treatment of the politicians was highly impolitic; he was often at loggerheads with the king. Moreover, he had failed (unlike his Italian counterpart and later his German) to create a strong party behind him, nor did he care for the organization of public opinion. Given the proverbial restlessness of Spain these mistakes were fatal to his regime. During 1929 agitation ran strong against him, and he appealed by referendum to the army for the continuance of his power. This alienated the king. Primo de Rivera was forced to resign in January, 1930.

Things were quiet for a while, and many Spaniards doubtlessly looked forward to the return of constitutional government. It was not to be. The real revolution was in the offing, that of 1931; it was to lead to another Spanish republic, the first attempted since the disastrous republican failure of 1873. When Rivera went, the only organizations left intact were those of revolution. General Berenguer was appointed prime minister by the king, but he postponed elections to reconstitute parliamentary government partly because the politicians refused to co-operate with him. His regime was hardly less dictatorial than that of Primo de Rivera. The politicians, liberals and intellectuals for the most part wanted to rid Spain of what they considered the incubus of the monarchy (spirit of the generation of 1898); they desired a republic. So, during this year of 1930 they drew together and organized.

The Ateneo of Madrid, a literary club and focus of liberal opinion, was reopened without authorization at the fall of Rivera. Elected as president was Manuel Azaña, literary man, politician, and outspoken republican. Three of his school organized the "League for the Service of the Republic." These were Dr. Gregorio Marañon, medical specialist with wide clientele among royalty and the aristocracy; Ramón Pérez de Ayala, leading novelist; and José Ortega y Gasset, university professor and internationally known author of *The Revolt of the Masses.* These men demonstrated a typical Spanish idealism. Since the monarchy was in "the last stages of decomposition," they said in a manifesto, they would have a republic which would combine "dynamic force with discipline." They called upon all Spaniards "to join in the supreme enterprise of resuscitating the history of Spain." They appealed especially to the professional classes and invited the collaboration of the young. "The republic will be the symbol of the fact that Spaniards have at last resolved to act with vigor and to take into their own hands their own destiny." Such movements were accompanied by more stirring messages. In Madrid's most respected periodical Ortega y Gasset cried: "Spaniards, your state is no more. Reconstruct it! *Delenda est Monarchia.*" In the meantime a Revolutionary Committee was formed, while Alcalá Zamora became leader of the revolutionary intellectuals.

The movement was aided by the ineffectiveness of Prime Minister Berenguer's government. During the summer of 1930 the monetary exchange dropped steadily with resultant strikes in a dozen cities. When the universities reopened in October, a recurrance of student riots took place. December 15 was set for a general uprising of the military garrisons of Spain. The garrison of the little town of Jaca at the foot of the Pyrenees anticipated the date and caused the collapse of the plan. The eight hundred men were soon overpowered and two of their leaders were shot. These men, Galan and Garcia Hernandez, became now the "martyrs of the revolution," and their portraits were exhibited everywhere. The Revolutionary Committee at once issued a manifesto. It declared full consciousness of its "mission and responsibility" and called itself into the provisional government of the Spanish Republic. Twelve men signed the document. Some were arrested; the rest fled the country. One uprising of December 15 did materialize in Madrid. The commandant of the aerodrome, Ramón Franco, aided by General Queipo de Llano, took the aerodrome and flew over the capital dropping pamphlets which shouted from their pages: "Spaniards! The Republic has been proclaimed." This movement too was overpowered while martial law was proclaimed and censorship reimposed upon the press for a period of six weeks. The universities were closed. But all of this could not suppress the general strikes which especially in the north were plaguing the nation.

One hopeful note rose from the midst of the increasing chaos: the government began to speak of general elections, and these were finally promised. The date fixed was March, 1931. Nevertheless, the wave of national confusion continued to mount in a bewildering crescendo, until finally in the middle of February the Berenguer government resigned. After various maneuverings on the part of the now isolated king, the Conde de Ramonones formed a new government which made various important decisions, among them the fixing of the elections for Sunday, April 12. These would be municipal; they were to be followed by parliamentary elections which would select the Cortes for the framing of a new constitution. Meantime, leaders of the revolutionary manifesto—Alcalá Zamora, Fernando de los Ríos, Miguel Manura, Alvaro de Albornoz, Largo Cabellero, and Casares Quiroga—were tried and sentenced to imprisonment for six months and a day. But the popular manifestations against the sentence were so boisterous that these men were immediately released and became the idols of the people. This was less than three weeks before the municipal elections. It was the hope of the revolutionary leaders that the results of the elections would demonstrate an overwhelming majority in favor of the republic and that the monarchy might collapse by summer. The end came sooner than they expected.

Founding of the Second Republic

The elections went off quietly, more quietly than any election old timers could remember, and the returns in the two most important cities, Madrid and Barcelona, were overwhelmingly republican. In the latter the Republicans polled 90,000 to the Monarchists' 33,000, so that the prime minister was stunned at the "spectacle of a country which we believed to be monarchist turning republican within twenty-four hours." The later returns showed that all of the large towns had voted republican by large majorities. Count Romanones relayed this information to the king on Tuesday and advised his leaving the country. To this the king consented, for he said he wished no drop of blood to be shed. Romanones met with Alcalá Zamora, leader of the Revolutionary Committee. The latter insisted: "The King must hand over his authority to us and leave Spain immediately." By two in the afternoon (Tuesday, April 14) the arrangements were completed. Without formal abdication the king was to leave that night. He accepted with serenity and was soon on his way. Meanwhile the Republic had been proclaimed in Barcelona, while in Madrid by the middle of the afternoon the Republican tricolor of red, yellow, and purple, was hoisted over the Post Office building. The flag seemed suddenly to spring out from every home and shop, cabinet and shelf. Soon all Madrid was brilliant with the flashy colors. Before nightfall Alcalá Zamora and his group went to the Home Office, were admitted, and took over the government of Spain. Arrangements were completed that night, and by two in the morning Spain had her republican government. That day, Wednesday, April 15, was declared a national holiday, for it was the first day of the Second Republic.

This marked the end of the first phase of the revolution. Spaniards, Spanish leaders, had now a free and open field upon which to build that beautiful republic of their ideals and of their dreams. It was the second time they desired to fashion a republic. Events would demonstrate whether they would be able to succeed. Any obstacle would come from themselves, not from without.

Events had been thus far remarkably calm, an exceptional thing in Spain. Any excitement had been constructive enthusiasm for the Republic. Alas! The king's abdication was not yet a month old when trouble began, the trouble which recurred in successively greater waves which within five years would roar over and carry away the Republic.

The first stirring of division (that fatal malady of the Latin states) came from the famous monarchist newspaper, *A.B.C.,* whose editor had gone to London, obtained an interview with Alfonso XIII, featured it, and added expressions of loyalty to the "Parliamentary and Constitutional Monarchy." Within a few days the Cardinal-Archbishop of Toledo and Primate of all Spain, Monseñor Segura, uttered impolitic words, very disquieting to republican leaders: he praised the successful reign of Alfonso XIII, spoke of the present as a moment of terrible uncertainty, and of a road open to those who are attempting to destroy religion. As a result, the republican Minister of Justice condemned the pastoral as "bellicose"; the government petitioned the Holy See for his removal, and he was ultimately expelled from the country.

Conflict with the Monarchists

Spirits which harbor explosives cannot long be contained. On Sunday, May 10, within the first month of its career, what had been called the "immaculate republic" was going to be soiled in blood. This is what happened. Late Sunday morning a newly organized monarchist club was holding a meeting on the crowded Calle de Alcalá in Madrid. They offered some provocation in monarchist hymns or cries. A crowd collected; some began shouting "Long live the Republic!"; two monarchists arrived at the club and were paying their taxi fares. They shouted "Long live the Monarchy!" A riot ensued which spread all over the city. By nightfall monarchists had narrowly escaped lynching, the offices of the monarchist paper *A.B.C.* had been burned, while far into the night frenzied republicans wreaked their vengeance upon whatever house or building came under their suspicion. The blood of the Madrid mob was up. Next morning in broad daylight men set fire to the Jesuit church and crowds gathered, placidly watching it burn to the ground. When fireman came they were prevented from taking action. Then crowds with red flags marched to the new and magnificent house of the Carmelite fathers and dealt with it similarly. Before this second day of disorder was finished a dozen religious houses, colleges, or convents went up in smoke. An omnious sign for the new-born republic was this: the Government showed itself powerless to stop these destructive disorders; the thirteen-hour sitting of the cabinet was marked with inefficiency and division. Outside Madrid, a dozen other cities witnessed the same disorders. Málaga suffered conflagration for two days in which religious houses and churches, shops and public buildings were burned. Soon all was quiet again, except that revolutionary strikes began to break out and to increase in frequency as the weeks passed. The result was: death and the enactment of martial law.

The immediate task of the Government was to organize elections for the creation of a congress which should have full administrative and constituent powers. The elections held in June were gratifying to Republicans and to the left generally. Right wing republicans received only twenty-eight representatives, while those of the left wing polled 145 members. Moreover, Socialists won 114 seats, Radical Socialists, fifty-six. Conservatives or Monarchists numbered only twenty. The Congress met in Madrid early in July and proceded to create a constitution and to govern the country. But strikes organized by syndicalist and anarchist groups were increasing, and Seville all but passed completely under mob rule. On July 20 a general strike was declared. The result was: thirty killed and 200 wounded, martial law, armed aircraft over the capital, closing of syndicalist and communist headquarters. It was clear that many Spaniards, especially of the working classes, a long-abused and suffering mass of humanity, desired not a republic, but a thoroughgoing social revolution.

From July to December the Congress or *Cortes* worked on the constitution. By the end of the year (1931) the instrument was ready. There is no space to analyze it here. There were many admirable statements and provisions, liberal and generous, especially regarding the underprivileged. Among other economic provisions, it stipulated for more equitable distribution of the land, especially in the Southwest where a feudal *latifundia* effected extreme economic abuses. It was less liberal in its provisions concerning the religious orders, some of which the republican leaders (not without reason) considered potential enemies of the republic. Over this question the Congress split. The lead in this fight was taken by Manuel Azaña (himself product of education by a religious order) and by Fernando de los Ríos. Among other provisions were the following: that no member of an order be allowed to teach, and that the Jesuits be dissolved and expelled. Azaña admitted these were not "liberal" measures, but they were necessary for the well-being of the republic. In the midst of the controversy two cabinet members resigned, including the prime minister of the provisional government, Alcalá Zamora; and when the vote was taken, three other cabinet members were absent and half the assembly either remained away or did not vote.

This too was ominous for the future of the republic. There was going to be a split between clericals and anti-clericals even among the leaders, to say nothing of the people; and the passions thus aroused became furious and destructive. But the Left were for the nonce in the majority, and they were able to have their way. Historically, it has been a fault of Latins in their attempts at democracy to legislate not for the nation but for their own political party or group. Then action is followed by reaction, and the pendulum swings lustily.

This leftist regime continued from December, 1931, to November, 1933, with the mildly clerical Alcalá Zamora president of the republic and the passionately anti-clerical Manuel Azaña head of the cabinet! It was a troubled period. It began with the murder of four civil guards at Castilblanco in the Southwest by strikers. The murders were accompanied with the most revolting barbarities. The affair set strikes a-going all over Spain. Anarchists, communists, syndicalists, though fundamentally divided in their own incompatible ideas, united thus early to destroy the republic. The nationwide slogan was: "We have got our republic; now let us have our revolution." Bilbao in the north was for days a focal point of riots, shooting, and arson. Prime Minister Azaña, while he struck against the extremists of the Left, also moved against the Right. The Society of Jesus was declared officially dissolved in Spanish territory January 23, 1932. In August rightist revolts led by monarchists and army officers broke out both in Madrid and Seville. In January, 1933, rebels in the south proclaimed a communist regime. Thus early was the young republic torn from the Right and from the Left.

In the Northeast, Catalonia, having received its petitioned autonomy, remained quiet and content. The rest of Spain was in a mounting fever. In the midst of all of this the government (in too great haste, it would seem) took measures to apply the education laws. Seventeen thousand secondary pupils and the many more thousands of pupils of the elementary grades then taught by the religious orders were to be absorbed by the state in October, 1933. Seven thousand new schools had to be provided for, and 7,000 new teachers trained. Fernando de los Ríos said he could do it. But he was delayed and before anything happened this leftist government fell.

Rightist Reactions

The regime had endured for almost two years, but its unpopularity steadily increased. Among many other things, it was blamed for excessive cruelty in the suppression of the various revolts. Opposition in the *Cortes* itself became so great that the government resigned, and general elections were organized for November, 1933. They returned a government of the Right and Center as follows: Right parties, 207; center, 167; Left 99. The pendulum, constantly swinging in Spain, had swung again. The Right and Center would now have its day (November, 1933–January, 1936). Immediately there were revolts from the Left. In Barcelona,

Saragossa, Huesca, and Barbastro, anarcho-syndicalists organized attacks upon the civic guard which had to be repressed with bloodshed. The loyalty of the guards and of the army at this period saved the republic.

As time went on things quieted down and the influence of the Right was observable. The substitution of lay schools for religious was dropped; back salaries were paid to beneficed clergy; the Jesuits returned and began to teach again in the capital. Land reforms in the Southwest, in Estramadura and in Andalusia, hardly ever begun, were now entirely neglected. A new monarchist club appeared. Gil Robles united the Catholic parties under CEDA. For a brief term the internationally known scholar and thinker, Salvador de Madariaga, became Minister of Education.

But there was little stability: ministries rose and fell; the government could accomplish little of importance; Gil Robles could not attain the post of Prime Minister. In 1934 there was serious trouble. Regionalism now appeared in the two Basque provinces of Guipúzcoa and Vizcaya, and Catalonia assumed a practically independent position. There were peasant strikes owing to the slowness of the land reforms. Besides, Left leaders in the *Cortes* passed from abstentionism to obstruction and finally seemed not unwilling to stop short at open revolt. Manuel Azaña said he despaired of Spain. He could not serve a republic imbued with monarchism. "We do not want a republic such as that."

As the year waned trouble mounted: on October 5 an almost complete general strike paralyzed the whole of Spain; the following day Catalonia declared herself completely independent, and a rebellion in the Asturias almost knocked over Madrid's republican regime. Here the government found itself confronted with 6,000 rebels, chiefly miners, fully armed and provided with tanks, machine guns, armored cars, and dynamite. The rebels had possessed themselves by force of the important city of Oviedo which had to be stormed and retaken by General Lopez Ochoa. The toll was 1,335 killed, mostly civilians, and 2,951 wounded, also mostly civilians. Oviedo became a city of ruins; its principal streets and public buildings had been destroyed. "There has been war in Spain," said a Spanish reporter, "and the city devastated by it has been Oviedo."

The ravaging of the northern extremists strengthened the prestige of the Right and Center for a while, yet this government as it went into the months of 1935 became mired in divisions and changes, shifts and ineffectualities. Ministries rose and fell in a sort of kaleidoscopic rapidity. Some cabinets could last hardly more than a month, and then the country would be treated to a fresh batch of figure heads. Some said the condition was worse than the worse days of the monarchy. Many blamed this state of affairs on the passive resistance of President Alcalá Zamora who, because of personal reasons, would not appoint the leader of the strongest party, Gil Robles, to the premiership.

In the meantime a varied assortment of leftists and radicals—socialists, anarchists, syndicalists and communists—was organizing to overthrow the republic in a radical revolution. The Communist International (October,

1932) said: "Revolution is taking place in Spain, and at the present time the mass movement is seething and showing tendencies to develop into an armed revolt of the people." Andrés Nin, a Catalan, who had been in Moscow, said in January, 1933, to a correspondent of the London *Times:* "We began first with an educational campaign and now we are engaged in organizing Workers' Soviets in anticipation of the crucial moment when the workers must be the first to arrive on the scene and to seize power." Dolores Ibarruri, *"La Passionaria,"* addressed the Seventh Congress of the Communist International convened in 1935: "Comrades, I bring fraternal greetings to the Seventh World Congress of our Communist party, in the name of the revolutionary proletariat and peasantry, and particularly in the name of the heroic fighters of Asturias," (referring to the 1934 uprising). The intent of the 1935 revolutionaries is seen in a New Year's greeting to Moscow which was later sent by Largo Caballero, leader of the Socialists and former cabinet member: "The Proletariat of Iberia will try to follow the example of your great country." Finally, in the midst of this political welter Zamora's last cabinet passed a decree dissolving the *Cortes* and calling for reelections. After some hesitation the President on January 1, 1936, signed the decree of parliament and designated February 16 as the day for the elections.

These elections were to decide whether Spaniards were capable at that time of carrying on a democratic regime. Would the people return a clear mandate either of the Right or of the Left? Would a strong government be able to pilot through surging seas the republican ship of state? History has given the answer. It was negative.

Although the Right and Center had gained prestige in the suppression of the Asturias revolt, Manuel Azaña now showed remarkable ability in persuading the divided parties of the Left to coalesce into the famous "Popular Front." The elections of February 16 were duly held, and the pendulum again swung back to the Left. The figures of these elections have been variously reported. It was said that through chicanery and violence the Left increased its representation. Perhaps the most reliable figures for the makeup of the *Cortes* are the following: Left, 256 deputies; Center, 52; Right, 165. The Left, in any case, took over, and this was the beginning of a sanguinary chaos in the midst of which the republic came crashing down in civil war, while the radical social revolution was being enacted in many parts of Spain. "Spain was to be at peace no more. From the Capital of the Republic to the tiniest rural village, every town trembled with the spirit of extermination and was rocked by a mad storm of passion." Largo Caballero now cried out: "When the hour of revenge is at hand we shall not leave one stone upon another in this Spain which we shall destroy to rebuild our own."

Many prominent rightists, such as the industrial millionaire Juan March, fled over the frontier into France. Shooting matches took place in the streets of the large cities. Murders by the Left, retaliations by the Right or vice versa. Robberies, rapes, and confiscations. Seizures of landed property. Churches, religious houses, public buildings went up in smoke. And so Spain whirled dizzily and violently into the abyss. From June 16 to July 13, there were sixty-one dead and 224 wounded in and about Madrid. On July 4, rightist gunmen in passing cars fired point blank into a crowd emerging from a socialist meeting. Seven socialists were killed and a dozen wounded. July 12, José Castillo, lieutenant of the leftist shock troops, was assassinated while leaving his home in a small Madrid street. A companion swore to avenge the murder and the vengeance was swift; for at three the next morning, the thirteenth, a knock on the door of the home of rightist leader, Calvo Sotelo, summoned him out with a warrant for his arrest. He was put into a police van which drove in the direction of the East Cemetery. Sotelo was murdered in the van, and his body dumped against the cemetery wall. Both Left and Right were shaken by the crime. One deputy shouted: "This must be the end!"

Beginnings of Civil Strife

During these very days a plane was being procured in England presumably for a vacation flight to Africa. It put down at Las Palmas in the Canary Islands where General Francisco Franco, who had formerly supported the republic was stationed. On July 16, this English plane flew Franco to Africa. On July 17 a number of Moroccan regiments, including Moorish troops and the Foreign Legion, rose in Spanish Morocco. On July 18 in Spain itself, in the Carlist north and in the Monarchist southwest, garrisons were revolting and distinguished generals—Mola, Cabanellas, Queipo de Llano—were leading insurrections. On July 19 General Franco landed his first troops from Africa on the mainland. The cruel and sanguinary civil war had begun.

The republic, long tottering, was going to fall to the Right or to the Left. The communists, in collusion with other types of radicals, had matured specific and minute plans for an uprising against the leftist republican government, for they wanted their social revolution. A copy of these plans was discovered among the papers of Commandant Bayo of Majorca; another copy was found at Lora del Río, a third in a village near Badajoz, a fourth at La Línea, near Gibraltar. July 25 was the day they had set for the revolt. The rightist, however, had gone into action first. But when news of the revolt of the army ran over Spain, the radical revolution, with all its attendant horrors, actually took place in all parts of Spain not dominated by conservatives. There were horrors, too, among the latter. Neither side gave quarter. Spain for close to three years would be drenched in blood, while Josef Stalin would send aid to the one, and Hitler and Mossolini to the other. Not until March, 1939, would this agony end.

Final Judgement on the Second Republic

Thus was the Second Republic torn apart. Thus had it been with the First Republic, that of 1873. There is striking similarity. In 1873 leftist

General Castellar described Spain's plight: "Minds agitated, passions exalted, parties dissolved, administration disorganized, the treasury exhausted, the army distrusted, the civil war gaining way rapidly, and credit swiftly declining." The rightist Gil Robles described Spain's plight in 1933: "There now remains an army crushed, a navy in decline, wealth bled to death, workmen hungry and epileptic, the blood of many hundreds of victims, the orgy of some sterile sumptuary projects, justice torn to pieces, the rights of ownership totally disregarded." Professor W. C. Atkinson recently wrote: "It is a difficult lesson to the Spaniard that extremism is best countered by moderation; yet, until that lesson among others has been learnt, the nation will not have given proofs of its capacity for self-government." And, "All the tactical errors of half a century ago have been repeated. At every turn the Second Republic has walked into traps, often of its own contriving, with its eyes shut." "Impetuosity, personal and party passion, careerism, the intoxication of rhetoric, distrust of technical skill, doctrinaire idealism, impatience with the slowness of political processes, these are racial characteristics which no mere purity of initial purpose will conjure away, and their sum total is stultification." (*Dublin Review* [January, 1937], pp. 16ff.) The republican leader of 1873, Castellar, said: "We Republicans have many prophets, few politicians; we know much of the ideal, little of experience; we embrace the entire heaven of thought and stumble over the first hole in the road." The republican leader of 1936, President Manuel Azaña of the Popular Front Government, averred that democracy could never work smoothly in Spain until the country built up a middle class.

There was instability: the Second Republic had eleven premiers and eighty cabinet ministers in five years. There was division, the common fault of Latins: "The Right sees in each member of the Left a demagogue, and the Left sees in each member of the Right a traitor," said Castellar. In 1873 when a federal republic was proposed because "it had worked in the United States of America," the answer given was that until Spaniards change their nature they can never hope to succeed in organizing such a regime. The clergy had their special weaknesses. Cardinal Goma in the early years of the republic criticized his own clergy for their lack of cooperation, apathy, and the Spanish habit of "keeping yourself at home." "The great mass of the people," said Goma, successor to Segura and Primate of all Spain, "live at an unbridgable distance from the priest, sometimes with all the prejudices and hatred that the tenacious action of our enemies has inspired in the breast of the people. . . ." Hence the burning of churches. The Spanish clergy have been notorious for their uncompromising attitude (a common Spanish trait) and for their extreme or reactionary conservatism.

Practically all the initial leaders—Alcalá Zamora, Marañon, Lerroux, and the rest—bitterly regretted the part they had played in organizing the republic. President Zamora later said: "The Government gave reign to the mob, put tools in the hands of their leaders to establish a dictatorship of the streets. . . ." And Gregorio Marañon: "I wish to express my disillusionment in Republican Spain and my remorse for having taken part in creating it."

Perhaps the fortunes of the Second Republic and the above statements of Spanish republicans themselves (which could be multiplied tenfold) may give pause to many Americans who wished after World War II to see established in Spain a Third Republic. Wisdom can be learned from the facts of history; caution from past failures. The Spaniard, Alfred Mendizabel, declared in 1938: "One of the easiest things to do in Spain is to declare a republic, but one of the most difficult is to consolidate it."

B. THE SPANISH CIVIL WAR *

IN REFLECTING upon the war, and upon the tragedy of the Republic of 1931, one must at all costs resist the temptation to assign responsibilities. To reflect in that retaliatory spirit which was the bane of the Republic would tempt one to an excessive simplification of issues which have throughout been closely interdependent on each other and thus extremely involved.

It is a strange and a terrible paradox, for example, that the nation should have been plunged into bloodshed by the deliberate act of men fighting for the ideals of the party which had so recently gone to the country with the slogan of 'Law and Order', and that it should in fact be for this law and order—as they conceived it—that they fought. The politicians of the Right, no doubt, would say that the war was begun by an Army revolt in which they had no part, and of which many of them, if not all, were ignorant. However that may be, it soon resolved itself into a conflict, and a conflict to the death, between Left and Right. Men had to be on the one side or on the other: there was no longer any Centre.

Abroad, we have tended to think of the war as of one between Fascists and Communists, between the raised hand and the clenched fist, between Mussolini and Moscow. But in reality, though Fascism inspired the rebels and their followers, and it was largely the Communists who were responsible for rallying the forces of the Government, the opposing parties were by no means of such simple composition. On the one side were Generals of the Army dissatisfied with Republican rule and rebellious at having been struck by the latest swing-back of the pendulum. With them they carried the Foreign Legion in Morocco and large sections of the rank and file of the Army, not necessarily because these were Fascists, or even knew what Fascism was, but partly because their officers were distinguished soldiers in high positions and with fine army records, and their officers had told them that it was their duty to resist Bolshevism, and partly because many of them, like their leaders, were genuinely op-

* E. Allison Peers, *The Spanish Tragedy* (London: Methuen & Company, 1936), pp. 217-223. Reprinted by permission.

posed to a Government which had trampled underfoot so much that they and their fathers had held dear. On the other side was the Popular Front Government, followed by all who supported any one of the groups which made up so precarious a combination: the chief of these were Republican Union, Republican Left, Socialists, Syndicalists, Unified Marxists, Communists and Anarchists. This side was also supported by a great many law-abiding and democratically minded people, who had been on the side of the Centre-Right in October, 1934, but held that, whatever their political opinions might be, it was their clear duty to take the side of a Government constitutionally elected and therefore representing as nearly as possible the will of the people. Thus there were partisans of the Centre-Right who supported the Government, just as there were former allies of the Left who hoped, privately if not publicly, for the victory of the rebels, because, for all their dislike of military rule, they disliked it less than continued chaos or the rule of Anarchism or Communism. And here, it may be recalled how Sr. Largo Cabellero, advanced Socialist as he was, had declared his implacable opposition to Communism, and that Sr. Azana, only a few days before his election to the Presidency, had replied to a Conservative member, who had taunted him with Communistic sympathies: 'I have as much to lose from the possible advent of Communism as the honorable member has.' As a matter of fact, he very soon had a good deal more.

These will be sufficient indications of the very mixed nature of the forces on either side, inexactly labelled as Fascists versus Communists, chiefly because in this modern world every one has to be labelled as something. The rebels were fighting for one form or another of the *ancien régime:* for the Church, for the nobility, perhaps for the King. Some, no doubt, for a return to 1923 and a Fascist State in a Europe now riddled with Fascism. Others, undoubtedly, for a return to 1931 and a fresh start along the road to reform, but for a slow and moderate progress, not for a continuance of the pace at which Spain had rushed downhill to her own destruction. The loyal troops were fighting for rather more diverse aims: some merely for the inalienable right of the people to a government of its choice; some for the reforms on which the Left had already embarked—for 'that other Republic' to which Sr. Largo Cabellero had referred at his trial; some for the proletarian revolution, which at last, after five years of Republic, had been thoughtfully precipitated by capitalists and the Army; some for the destruction of hated institutions, for the destruction of anything, for destruction alone.

It is easy, and natural, to condemn the military leaders for rising against a lawfully constituted Government, but it must be remembered that less than two years had passed since a large section of the Left had done the same. They in their turn might have declared that General Sanjurjo's insurgents of 1932 had set them an example, and General Sanjurjo might have argued in his own favour from the influence exerted upon public opinion by the Republican rising at Jaca in 1930, even although this rising failed in its immediate objective. In the same way, precedents can be found for the brutality of which both sides in the conflict were undoubtedly guilty, as also for the earlier repression and the futile reprisals which stain the history of the Republic. Nor will it suffice to refer everything back to the Dictatorship of Primo de Rivera, for an examination of the condition of Spanish politics before its advent will convince one that there was ample cause for exasperation then as later.

A truly objective view of the Spanish arena will reveal patriotism and idealism on one side and on the other, and on both sides there are leaders whom we can admire for their ability and sympathize with for their defeat. No less deserving of condolence than Primo de Rivera and his royal master are the men who brought in the Second Republic. Moments there may have been in their short careers when the robe of their importance fell from them and left them standing all unconsciously in the garb of comedy, but it would be an intensification of the present tragedy if the Spanish state were to be permanently deprived of their usefulness. Some of them, at least, their sternest opponents will remember with honour and even with affection. They were men of high ideals, of amazing industry, of undoubted probity and of notable ability in administration. They failed in their main task for two reasons. First, like most of their race, they suffered from so intense an individualism that they were unable to maintain a coalition, such as that of April, 1931, which represented fairly accurately the different views of Spanish progressives, and, had it remained united, would unquestionably have made numerous converts. Secondly they were unable or unwilling to stop the pendulum, and the pendulum is the curse of Spain.

These views were powerfully expresed by one of the ablest of Republicans, Don Salvador de Madariaga, in a remarkable *Idearium for the Constitution of the Third Republic* which he published when the Second Republic was four years old. 'Those few of us,' he writes, 'who in 1931 dreamed that Spain had at last won her redemption and was about to take seriously in hand the fashioning of her new Constitution before setting herself to labour in earnest,

> have seen how the ambition of a few, the negligence of all, divisions in the ranks of the Centre and the intransigence of the extremists have dealt Spain a terrible blow both in her economy, her morale and her prestige abroad. We know that they will end by causing her ruin, unless we Spaniards can be inspired by passions of a generosity sufficient to raise us above our ambitions and prejudices, our impatiences and evil habits, and to fill us with a sense of our responsibility.

He was right. They could not or would not see—these idealists of the Left—that, by encouraging reaction instead of striving to check it, they were merely inviting extremists to use them as stepping-stones to their own desires. The extremists could afford to tolerate the Republic till the time was ripe for their long-desired revolution, after which they would be able to throw aside the Republic's founders as men who had served their purpose and for whom they had no further use.

Some of these founders would doubtless reply in all good faith that in the early days of the Republic severity was necessary for its consolidation and that malcontents with deeply implanted grievances against the old order would never have tolerated slow and gradual reforms. To discuss this reply would take us more deeply into the realm of hypothesis than it would here be practicable to enter. It must suffice to say that there are degrees of severity, as those who thought that Primo de Rivera had touched the maximum soon found, and that a great leader, had he arisen, could have kindled enthusiasm for reform based upon a ten or a twenty years' plan—the only road it would seem, to Spain's ultimate salvation.

The fundamental weakness of the Second Republic has been the lack of a great leader. It has produced no man powerful enough to rule yet capable of ruling with moderation and prudence, of rising above the recriminative aims of party politics and of persuading others to accept him and to believe that he holds the key to his country's prosperity. Such a man must of necessity arise before Spain can be saved. Government by the Left parties produced little but reaction. Government by the Right, had it been tried, would probably have produced no less. Centre government failed to do more than mark time and liquidate the results of reaction. But at some time, whether in the near or distant future, a Centre Government must come again, and this time it must come, not to compromise, but to rule.

The immediate outlook is almost indescribably dark. The hopefulness and buoyancy of five short years ago have given place to something like despair. 'Have proclaimed the Republic'; telegraphed the apocryphal *alcalde* of 1931 to the Home Office, 'what shall I do with the priest?' We laughed, for this was comedy—the priest was in little danger. 'Have slaughtered officers,' telegraphs the crew of a warship in 1936, 'what shall we do with the bodies?' We laughed no longer, for this is tragedy. Slaughter and counter-slaughter seem the only prospects. The rhythm of reaction has gathered speed till rhythm itself is lost in the whirl and clash of warfare. Men are at each other's throats. Civilization has given place to chaos. And there is one 'martyr' of the Republic above all others —Spain.

Yet I believe in Spain, as firmly as ever I have believed in her in the past, and I believe that the millions of her citizens who still place country above party will in due time, in a reunited and prosperous land, have their reward. There may be various opinions about kings, presidents, statesmen, demagogues and party politicians, but nobody who knows Spain, and to whom she is a second home, can have the smallest doubt as to the intrinsic greatness of her people. If Nature has endowed her with riches, history has crowned her again and again with enduring laurels. High above tyrannical rulers, capricious favourites and vacillating governments she has risen, and high she will yet rise above the fiercest party strife. For she still retains those essential virtues without which, in the old warlike Europe, she could never have enjoyed her splendid past; and those same virtues. in the new Europe, now struggling, like herself, in the throes of rebirth, will give her a still more splendid future.

24

CHRISTIANITY AND DEMOCRACY *

There is a tendency among Christians to identify their religion with the government and the society which allows their Church to flourish. In the seventeenth and eighteenth centuries, for example, most leaders of the various established churches (the Catholic Church in France and Spain, for example, the Lutheran Church in Scandinavian countries, and the Anglican Church in England) identified their religion with monarchical government and used religious arguments to support the king's authority. Should the monarchy fall, they felt, so too would their Church. In similar fashion, some Christians now believe that democracy is the only good form of government, that the Church cannot possibly accommodate itself to any other arrangement.

The last several popes, as well as the best Catholic thinkers, have stressed the fact that the Church looks favorably on a democracy that is not secularistic, but they warn that the Church is not to be identified with any form of government or with any society or culture. The Church approves any legitimate government which does not violate the rights of men or of God, which respects human dignity, and allows man so to live on this earth as to develop his natural and supernatural virtues.

This is not to say that individual Catholics are not free to argue that democracy is better than any other form of government—which many of us believe and, we think, can demonstrate. But demonstrating that democracy is better than other forms of government (other things, such as secular temper, being equal) is not to conclude that democracy is necessary for the Church, or that the latter cannot survive and even flourish under other forms of government. Most Catholic thinkers in the Western world distinguish the Anglo-American democratic tradition which limits

* J. V. Langmead Casserley, *The Bent World* (New York: Oxford University Press, 1955), pp. 65-101. Reprinted by permission.

the state from violating fundamental human rights, and the Rousseauvian democracy which gives unlimited power to majority rule.

The following selection delineates the various lines of relationship between organized Christian churches and democratic government in such fashion as to remove the confusion that frequently surrounds the subject.

FEW twentieth-century tendencies have been more surprising, disappointing, and shocking to the modern Western secular liberal mind—its convictions shaped by the eighteenth and nineteenth-century phases of our culture—than the marked disposition of peoples and nations during the last thirty years or so to withdraw from and go back upon the basic tenets of democracy. I can well remember the consternation and perplexity of my father during the twenties and thirties. For him the movement toward and into democracy was an example of irreversible progress. No people who had once made this journey could be prevailed upon or even tempted to retrace their steps. Anti-democratic trends and propagandas he could only interpret in terms of downright wickedness or pathetic insanity. Since his generous, optimistic humanism made it difficult for him to think in terms of human wickedness, he preferred on the whole the category of insanity, with occasional lapses into the category of wickedness whenever he felt more than usually angry and frustrated. His was a not uncommon state of mind. It is difficult indeed to react to and interpret the more horrific and demonic events of our time without some employment of the categories of wickedness and sin. We may say in theory that we do not believe in sin, but it is almost impossible in practice to deny the reality of sinners and sinful actions when we see them before our very eyes. It is wiser, perhaps, to take reality seriously and to search for the causes and reasons of the things of which we disapprove rather than merely to deplore and denounce them as irrational perversions.

What, then, are the most prevalent causes of the alienation of so much Western thought and energy from the democratic institutions and ideals? No doubt it is impossible for any one thinker to perceive and enumerate them all, but there are at least four tendencies at work which seem to me of the profoundest importance. I list them here not because they provide a complete account of the whole phenomenon but as my own contribution to the discussion.

(1) *The democratic movement has ceased to be a revolutionary movement.* In most of the great and leading countries of the Western world, democratic institutions, in one form or another, were more or less securely established by 1914. Germany was perhaps the only significant exception, and even she possessed at least a plausible façade of demo-

cratic institutions. The democratic struggle after 1918 was thus in most Western countries a struggle to preserve rather than to attain and establish democracy. Nowadays we talk about defending our democracy, not creating it. In other words, in countries like America, Britain, and France, enthusiasm for political democracy is an essentially conservative attitude.

There is nothing surprising about this. Every brand of revolutionism is transubstantiated into a form of conservatism once its goals have been attained. Nor is such a transition in itself a morally reprehensible one, for the conservative attitude has its proper place in a mature and balanced social outlook. Any community in which anything worth doing has been done and achieved is a community which embodies values worthy of preservation. A community in which nothing is worth conserving would be a very poor community indeed. What is worth doing in the first place is worth conserving in the second place. Nevertheless we must face the fact that a conservative emphasis finds it difficult to stimulate and sustain the zeal and devotion which revolutionary movements so easily arouse. A conservatism, however valid, is nearly always less exciting than a revolutionary propaganda, however mistimed and inappropriate. Ever since the French Revolution there has been abroad and at work in the world a certain mystique of revolution, and many of the most gifted and energetic of modern men and women feel intellectually, emotionally, and morally uncomfortable if they cannot tell themselves that they are on the revolutionary side. This is an undesirable social phenomenon, but it is a real phenomenon all the same. Revolution for revolution's sake is a poor and unconvincing kind of gospel when we put it in so many words, but people who live their lives on the basis of such a conviction very rarely put it into words. It is the excitement of it all, the sense of living dangerously, the conviction that they are on the side of the future against the past and the present, which warm their hearts and gladden their minds and give them a sense of purpose and validity in life which otherwise they could not find in our modern secular world. In short, the sort of people who once fought for democracy, precisely because it was not, tend now to react against it, precisely because it is.

The greatest handicap of democracy in the modern Western world is the fact it has arrived. It cannot be said that it has fulfilled all the hope and idealism of those who created it. In real history social and political programs never do that. Society is still confronted by grave problems; masses of men are still frustrated and unhappy; if many old wrongs have been righted, many new wrongs have been swift to take their place. The utopian dreamers are always disappointed in the event. If we would avoid disillusion at the last, it is better not to cherish any illusions at the first. Yet if democracy has not brought with it social and moral perfection and the dawning of a golden age, it has solid achievements to its credit and it is churlish and ungrateful not to acknowledge the achievements simply because men once hoped for too much. Still the disappointments and the disillusions are real factors which our strategy for the defense of democracy must take into serious account.

(2) *At least in our Western world democracy and nationalism have now parted company.* During the great period of the advance toward democracy in the nineteeenth and early twentieth centuries the cause of national independence and national unity often went hand in hand with the cause of democratic progress. To many thinkers and idealists they appeared to be but twin aspects of the same thing, for both were spontaneous uprisings of the people demanding at the same time democratic freedom for themselves and independence and unity for the nation to which they belonged. It is true that even in this period they did not always walk together. Thus, for example, Germany achieved its unity under the leadership of Bismarck's authoritarian Prussia, and the German liberals and democrats lost prestige precisely because they were not the party who succeeded in creating modern Germany. Normally, however, it was democracy which liberated dependent peoples and united divided people.

At a later stage, however, nationalism and democracy tend to come into conflict. For the genuinely democratic mind the achievement of democracy and the rule of law within nations is usually interpreted as the necessary prelude to the achievement of democracy and the rule of law among the nations; national order is thought of as the foundation of international order. But nationalism, which is quite distinct from patriotism, usually rejects this second movement of the democratic mind and becomes the enemy of democracy in this later phase of democratic development. Nationalism can take either of two forms. It can think in terms of conquest and domination or in terms of proud isolation and self-sufficiency. Sometimes the nationalist mind will oscillate bewilderingly between the two. Thus Nazi Germany tended to be isolationist and autarchic in its economic policy, and at the same time nationalistic and imperialistic in its military and political policy. Similarly we find not a few American nationalists alternating bewilderingly between a desire to cut themselves off from and take no responsibility for international situations—e.g. in the Far East—and a desire to dominate them. But whatever the form contemporary nationalism takes, its genius tends to be hostile to democracy. Nationalists regard the independence, security, and greatness of their nation as prior to and more important than its integrity as a democracy, and so they tend to become impatient with the strict observance of democratic forms, so essential to the survival and preservation of democracy, whenever they feel that higher and more important national aims are at stake.

(3) *Much of western democratic thought and policy has failed to preserve the essential foundations of human happiness.* In the most advanced Western democratic countries the most marked and characteristic failure of a rather superficial humanistic and individualistic secular democracy

has been its misinterpretation of the role of marriage and the family as one of the basic factors in human happiness. The two nations which most of all embody the democratic ideals and champion the democratic cause, America and Britain, are both of them areas of culture in which the unity and stability of the family are in greater danger than in any part of the civilized world, except perhaps Scandinavia. They must be described as societies given to the intemperate practice of divorce, with all the unhappiness, frustration, and neurosis which invariably accompany a gravely disordered sexuality. Few things are more essential to human happiness, and a rational and satisfying social order, than a cohesive, coherent, and secure family life, and this is one of the great blessings which the most advanced democratic societies have most singularly failed to confer upon their peoples. The weakness and failure of the family under democratic conditions is like a malignant cancer gnawing at the very vitals of democracy. We shall have to ask ourselves whether the so-called "democratic family" is really essential to democracy, or whether it is not, on the contrary, a tragic misinterpretation of democracy, rooted and grounded not in democracy itself but in the false understanding of democracy which has become widely current in its secular phase.

(4) *The prevailing secular tone of so much democratic thought, idealism, and policy has tended to estrange modern democracy from the religious motivations and impulses which lie at the heart of Western civilization.* When we find, as we do again and again in certain areas of Western civilization, Christian men dabbling and flirting with anti-democratic politics, this is almost always the root cause of the trouble. From their own point of view such men are rejecting not a democratic political order which represents and fulfills in political terms important elements in the Christian conception of man as a free person made in the image of God, and for the eternal service of God rather than the temporal service of the state, but, as they see it, a godless liberalism, a secular regime, which, although it may make a show of tolerating Christianity, is either fundamentally hostile to it or contemptuously writes it off as a second-class issue aside from the really serious business of life.

There is in fact a real conflict not between Christian faith and democracy but between Christian faith and the purely secular state, whether democratic or not. The widespread assumption that a democratic state must be secular, the tendency of not a few democratic thinkers and idealists to put forward democracy and what they call the "democratic way of life" as though it were in itself a kind of religious absolute standing over against Christianity, or possibly including a drastically reinterpreted and liberalized Christianity, or even as something higher or more valuable than Christianity, is clearly an assumption which no Christian can conceivably accept. When democracy presents itself to the world and seeks to justify itself as a merely humanistic secularism, it cannot expect to secure the allegiance and support of a Christianity worthy of the name, of a Christianity reawakened, as modern Christendom tends more and more to be, to a new consciousness of its own essential point of view and a renewed faith in the power and necessity of the Gospel. For such a Christianity nothing in life is really secular, and the doctrine of the secular state is something which it cannot accept. The re-emergence in the twentieth-century scene of a purged and disentangled Christianity, once more conscious of its Gospel and its own unique point of view about everything in God's creation, is one of those factors which we cannot conceivably exclude from our attention when we are discussing the whole question of the strategy to be adopted in the defense of democracy. Democracy must make its peace with the religious forces at work in the Western world if it is to succeed in uniting all its friends in its defense, and this means that the aggressively secular phase in democratic thought and policy must be brought to an end. It belongs to the eighteenth century, not the twentieth. It survives only as an outmoded anachronism.

The main concern here is with this last aspect of the contemporary predicament of democracy—its ambiguous relationship to Christianity. For me it is Christianity, not democracy, which is absolute, and democracy, not Christianity, which lies under the judgment. The question before us is not: how democratic is Christianity?, or, How can Christianity be so modified and interpreted as to make it compatible with the spirit of democracy?, but, How Christian is democracy? or, How can democracy be so conceived and formulated as to keep it in touch with the spirit of Christianity?

I am aware, of course, that there are some Christians, particularly in Britain and America, who can see no problem here. For them apparently Christianity is the religion of which democracy is the practice; Christianity is the cause of democracy and democracy the fulfillment of Christianity. I mean no disrespect to democracy when I say that I cannot accept such formulas of concord as these. I do not believe that any proposition of the form, "Christianity is the religion of which democracy—or whatever you will—is the practice," can ever be valid. Christianity is the religion of which Christianity is the practice. It may very well be that social forms and institutions desperately need and require the inspiration, counsel, and spiritual force of Christianity to give them the strength and the will to survive, but to Christianity nothing is absolutely essential but Christianity itself. We must find some other way of establishing the importance and validity of democracy, which does not commit the error of identifying it with Christianity.

On the other hand, we do not wish to separate democracy from Christianity altogether, for that would be to secularize democracy. Modern democracy has a Christian theological sanction, and to trace the history of modern democracy is to perceive its Christian origins. My contention will be that although we cannot properly say that Christianity needs democracy, we say that our Western democracy needs Christianity. We may also validly say that among the various alternative forms of political order between which we have to choose in a fallen world it is democracy which should be selected by the Christian mind as the best and most commendable type of political order here below, precisely because it has a theological sanction which no other set of political arrangements can claim to possess.

I propose to arrange my remarks under two heads: What can Christianity *not* say or do with or about democracy? and, What *can* Christianity say or do with or about democracy? I begin with two claims or affirmations concerning democracy which, in my view, Christianity ought not to make and cannot make.

(1) *Christianity cannot affirm democracy as higher than itself.* By this I mean that Christianity cannot conceivably accept the prevalent view that democracy has clearly grasped and put into practice truths and values to which Christianity was clumsily pointing throughout the predemocratic ages, without quite knowing precisely what it was doing. Some writers almost seem to suggest that Christianity is related to modern democracy rather as the Hebrew prophets were related to the coming of Christ. Christianity is much more than merely the prophecy which points toward a future fulfillment of its hopes in a democratic age.

We must remind ourselves again and again that democracy after all is no more than an important and valuable set of political arrangements. It is a way of carrying on the government of a group. Its greatness lies in the fact that if its forms and values are steadfastly respected, social change, even social changes of a very fundamental and revolutionary character, can take place without violence. In the same way the shifting of power from party to party and from group to group within the body politic, which, apart from democracy, usually involves a certain amount of fighting and bloodshed, can be achieved by democratic means without any violations of public peace. The advantages of such a system are manifest.

Unfortunately, however, many pepole are not satisfied with democracy merely as a desirable and advantageous type of political machinery. They want to turn it into a moral ideal, almost an absolute religion. They desire to get out of democracy more than democracy properly understood can possibly contain. Such an idealization of democracy is doomed to frustration. We cannot get a quart out of a pint pot. When we insist on using the adjective "democratic" to qualify social realities which lie deeper than the political level of human relationships we usually find that it does not fit this kind of reality at all well. Thus many enthusiasts have labored to describe what they call the "democratic family." But, in fact, it might be better to say that the "democratic family" is simply a name used to describe the inefficient family, the kind of family that is always breaking down and persistently failing to fulfill its functions both as the nursery of human character and as the architect of human happiness. The so-called "democratic family" means a matrimonial system in which divorce is almost as common as marriage, a family system in which children are continually and unjustly deprived of their human right to two parents; it means irresponsible parents and untrained children; it means the enthronement of insecurity and frustration in the very heart of the social life of the people. Such a radically unsuccessful way of conducting our domestic life does not merit such a high-sounding adjective as democratic. Our contemporary family system is just an inefficient and insecure one. It is much better to call a spade a spade.

The truth is that there is no "democratic way of life." Most of the basic ways of human life antedate democracy. The function of democracy is not to overturn and transform the basic types of human order which preceded democracy in time, but rather to defend and uphold them. Similarly it is a mistake to suppose that there are any characteristically democratic ethical virtues or moral values. Of course, we cannot maintain democracy or any other form of social order without the great ethical virtues and moral values, but there are no ethical virtues and moral values which are peculiar to democracy and which simply do not exist elsewhere. Thus some people, for example, regard tolerance as a democratic virtue. Many non-democratic governments and societies in the past have believed in and practiced tolerance, and some democratic societies, it must be confessed, have at times lapsed into intolerance. I would agree that a democratic society is more likely to be tolerant than any other, but it cannot be said that tolerance is impossible without democracy or that democracy automatically achieves tolerance. The great ethical virtues must be practiced and the great moral values must be reverenced whether our society is democratic or not. To appropriate some great universal virtue on behalf of some particular form of political order is as foolish and misleading as to appropriate some great virtue as though it were the peculiar possession of one particular nation. A phrase like democratic tolerance or democratic kindliness is quite as absurd as talking about British courage, Canadian honesty, or German self-discipline. The virtues and the values are not bounded and possessed in this exclusive way.

Democracy is primarily a political word, a word used to describe a particular technique for arriving at decisions which bind the group that makes them. Of course, the democratic group need not be a nation. It may, for example, be a church or a tennis club or a ladies' sewing guild. But whatever kind of group it is, it will be a democratic one if it believes in arriving at group decisions by way of open discussion, and perhaps by some technique which involves voting, the whole process being conducted in accordance with either a written constitution or some more flexible set of conventions and traditions which are accepted as binding by the whole group.

It should be noticed that no democratic group exists merely or primarily for the sake of behaving democratically. The primary purpose of a tennis club is playing tennis; the primary purpose of a ladies' sewing guild is presumably sewing in a ladylike manner. They are democratic insofar as they are doing what they have gathered together to do in a democratic way. Similarly, the primary purpose of a democratic nation is not to be a democracy but to be a nation. The democratic nation is democratic because it is convinced that the best and most successful way of being a nation is to be a nation in the democratic way. In a sense the primary purposes of democratic and non-democratic nations are the same. Contemporary Russia wants to be Russia, just as America is determined to be America. It is their political techniques, their ways of implementing their kindred purposes, which differentiate them so sharply from each other.

Democracy is thus essentially a method of group behavior. It does not usually dictate the primary purposes of the group although it may, indeed must, restrain it from pursuing purposes and objectives—for example, the domination of other nations by conquest and military power—which in the nature of the case cannot be pursued in a democratic way. But the positive purposes of a group stem from deeper levels of human existence than those on which we are politically organized together. It is this fact which makes it necessary to say that democracy cannot amount to, must not pretend to be, a complete system of social ethics and social purposes. There is no democratic way of life. There is only a way of common life which employs democratic techniques for regulating group relationships and arriving at group decisions. Democracy, even for the democratic man, indeed above all for the democratic man and the democratic society, is neither the highest nor the deepest thing in life. To absolutize and worship democracy, as some modern liberal thinkers would seem to do, is to absolutize and worship a technique, a process as ridiculous intellectually as it is unsatisfying existentially.

It is important that the reader should not misunderstand me at this point. In saying all this I am not decrying or criticizing democracy. I am only trying to ascertain what democracy really is, so that we can clearly understand wherein lies its real value and importance. Democratic philosophers who make false and inflated claims about democracy are not democracy's true friends. The false and inflated claims can be exposed, and those who expose them may easily be deluded into thinking that because they have refuted prevalent misinterpretations of democracy they have refuted democracy itself. So it is that I have set about the task of finding out what democracy is by saying in the first place as clearly as I can what democracy most certainly is not. It is not a complete ethic or a total way of life.

But a total way of life is precisely what Christianity is, and hence Christianity is both a higher thing and a deeper thing than democracy. What we really need in order to display to the world democracy at its best is a Christian society which practices and employs the techniques of democracy with sincerity and integrity. But to suppose that a society can survive and amount to anything in particular merely by concentrating on being a democracy and nothing else, would be like supposing that a man can become and be a real person and develop a rounded and balanced character simply by scrupulously observing all the ordinances of statute law, or that a teacher can become a good teacher simply by learning the best educational techniques and without having any idea of what it is that must be taught. (This second example is really not so fantastic as might be supposed, for not a few modern teachers do seem to have embarked on their life's vocation with a merely technical preparation of this kind. But the result has not tended to increase the efficiency or the health of the educational system!)

Thus the essential first step in what I might call a Christian reinterpretation of democracy is this salutary assertion that democracy is a good and useful social technique, and neither a rather feeble and unsatisfying humanistic religion without worship nor a cold and unconvincing social ethic without God. We shall value democracy more highly if we value it for what it is. To hymn the glories of democracy while ascribing to it heights and qualities that it does not in fact possess is not really to cherish democracy at all. It is simply a way of cherishing our own illusions.

(2) *Christianity cannot affirm democracy as essential to itself.* This is so obviously true that the point seems hardly worth laboring. Democracy cannot be essential to the profession of Christianity and the survival of the Christian Church for the very obvious reason that the Christian Church succeeded in existing and maintaining itself for many centuries before the first modern democratic state came into being. It is true, of course, that from the days of the Roman Empire onward the Christian Church found itself again and again at war with the kind of totalitarian state which is apt to demand that men should in some form or other worship the state itself and acknowledge their temporal, secular loyalty to the state as the highest and supreme obligation of their lives. The struggle between the prophetic religion of the living God and the doctrine of loyalty to the state as the highest of all loyalties, before which every other loyalty must give way, is clearly and unforgettably set out in the great myths that constitute the narrative portions of the Book of Daniel. The principle laid down in that book is clear: those who know that the supreme loyalty and moral obligation of man is to be found in the sphere of his relationship to the living God, and that to this loyalty every secular loyalty whatsoever must defer, cannot conceivably worship any emperor or state or temporal political reality. Loyalty to God in and through the life of the Church takes precedence of any possible loyalty to state and nation.

But we must not suppose that all non-democratic states, simply because they are non-democratic, necessarily come into conflict and oppress the conscience of the Christian man in this way. It is quite possible for a state not democratically constituted and ordered to respect and even share the conviction of its Christian citizens that their primary duty and loyalty is to God alone. It is equally possible, alas, for a democratic state so to mistake and misinterpret its own nature as to put loyalty to itself above the loyalty of the awakened religious consciousness to the God who makes Himself known to men in the Christian Gospel. Indeed, when democracy interprets itself in a purely secular way this is what tends to happen again and again. Sometimes loyalty to God in and through the life of the Church is even represented as incompatible with the duties of a democratic citizen. This seems to be the main point, for example, of the anti-Catholic writings of Mr. Paul Blanshard. By the adroit strategy of concentrating his fire on the Roman Church, Mr. Blanshard has succeeded in gaining for himself a fair measure of misguided Protestant sympathy, but in reality his point of view calls in question the legitimacy in a democracy of any church or supernatural loyalty whatsoever. He does not really believe that the democratic man ought to entertain and cherish any loyalty higher than his loyalty to the democratic state.

In fact it is precisely this doctrine that the highest loyalty of man is his loyalty to the state, however constituted, which is the real essence of totalitarianism, for the totalitarian conception of the state is really the view that the state holds unquestioned sway over the total area of human existence. We should avoid confusing the adjective "totalitarian" with the adjective "authoritarian." All states, even the most democratic ones, claim and exercise some measure of authority. It is essential to the very nature of the state that it must do so. A state is authoritarian in the bad sense when it exercises its authority in a totalitarian way. "Totalitarian" is thus a profounder and more significant word than "authoritarian." A totalitarian democracy, a democratically organized state which claims and proceeds on the assumption that the total life of man falls within the sphere of its responsibilities, is at least a possibility, but it is a paradoxical possibility, for such a claim would contradict something that lies at the very heart of democracy. Democracy is essentially a way of organizing the group life of a community which frankly acknowledges that there is much that is important and significant in the lives of the members of the community which does not fall within the scope of its authority.

"Man was not made for the state, but the state for man," we often say, boldly adapting a Gospel phrase for our own purposes. Do we pause as often as we should to consider what this means? If man was not made for the state, for what or for whom was he made? In what dimension of his existence does man transcend the sphere of the state's responsibility? Can we possibly say that man was made for himself? This, I suppose, is what a sheer individualistic humanism would have to say. But consider the enormity of such an utterance! It would mean that man transcends the sphere of the state in the dimension of his egocentricity, that his duty and loyalty to himself are somehow a higher thing than his duty and loyalty to the community in which he truly *finds* himself, which he needs in order to become and fulfill himself. It is surely impossible to hold that our selfhood is a reality prior to, independent of, and higher than the reality of the community in which we find ourselves. No, the various forms of collectivism, totalitarianism, and communalism seem to me at least nearer to the truth than sheer individualism. Surely we cannot say with any real conviction that man was not made for the state, but that on the contrary the state is made for the service of man, unless we first of all believe that God created man for Himself, that the human being is a being with an eternal destiny and an eternal significance, whereas the temporal state is no more than the servant of his destiny, a means in and through which he journeys onward through time toward his final and eternal end. Such a doctrine as this clearly rules all totalitarianism out of court as, and this is the important point, no other doctrine of man succeeds in doing.

We have already pointed out that individualism and totalitarianism go together. If men left to themselves are no more than a chaos of self-regarding, mutually independent individuals, then, since for the sake of their own peace men have got to be united and welded together for common action somehow or other, it seems plausible to suppose that the state is the best agency for bringing about this desirable result. The state from the point of view of sheer individualism thus becomes the creator and master instead of the servant of the community. All this was very clearly brought out by a great English political philosopher of the seventeenth century, Thomas Hobbes. Hobbes was at the same time a completely individualistic philosopher and a preacher and defender of political absolutism. I believe he was utterly wrong, but I cannot deny that he was rigidly logical. It is not in the dimension of his selfhood but in the dimension of his duty to God that man transcends the state and is clearly seen to be more important than the state.

And this great truth, to return to our original point, can conceivably be realized and recognized in a non-democratic order, just as it may unfortunately be forgotten in a democratic one. What makes a political and social order Christian in the last resort is the extent to which it knows and recognizes itself as a temporal order of being which is all the time transcended by the eternal destiny of each one of its members. It admits that it exists only to serve the temporal needs of the children. Thus, in certain favorable circumstances, a non-democratic social order may be a Christian one, just as, in unfavorable circumstances, a democracy may become a non-Christian, or even an anti-Christian, society.

But there is another and deeper reason why Christianity cannot conceivably concur in the view that democracy is essential to Christianity itself. The Church as we know it now in this world, the empirical Church which acts upon the stage of human history, "the Church Militant here on earth," as it describes itself in its liturgical phraseology, does not contain or make manifest the whole reality of the Church. The prevalent habit of using the word 'Church' in general conversation to mean simply the empirical Church as we know it on earth is a misleading one. The theologian, when he talks of the Church, refers to the death-transcending, time-transcending Body of Christ, of which the Church Militant here on earth is simply one phase or aspect, and not the most vital one at that. The full reality of the Church, its latent promise and inward yearning, will be achieved and made manifest only in the Kingdom of God. It is there that we shall see the Church as God intends it to be. The Church, in other words, is an *eschatological reality*.

Theological terms like this only cloud and mystify the issue so long as we are ignorant of their meaning; if and when we know what they mean, they clarify the discussion enormously. To say that a reality is eschatological means that it must be interpreted not in terms of what it is or has been but in terms of what it is becoming and what it is destined to be. Such a reality here and now only hints darkly at what it will be, and be seen to be, at the point of its ultimate consummation. So it is that the poet Wordsworth tells us that "the child is father of the man"; the young growing human being is not merely what he seems to be at the present moment but, more truly and profoundly understood, he *is* what he is to become. Even so the latent promise of the being of the Church, as yet unfulfilled, will only be realized in the Kingdom of God.

Now the Kingdom of God, and this is the important point, cannot conceivably be described as a democracy. It is indeed a *theocracy,* in which the kingdom, the power, and the glory belong to God alone. The best earthly analogy to employ when we attempt to grasp and illustrate the nature of the Kingdom of God in human images is not the democratic state but a serenely happy family, presided over and cared for by a loving and responsible father who is trusted and loved by his wife and children. No other consideration makes so clear to us the reason why Christianity, insofar as it appreciates and affirms the value and importance of democracy, is compelled by its own nature to interpret democracy, not as an absolute and ultimate value but as an essentially transitional, this-worldly phenomenon which is useful and perhaps even necessary in our present imperfect state of development, yet is at the same time an institution which must wither away and be no more seen when man is made perfect in the Kingdom of God.

But now, having briefly considered what Christianity cannot say about democracy, however much many enthusiastic devotees of democracy would like to have Christianity say it, let us turn to the more positive side of the picture. What claims can Christianity make for democracy in conformity with its own traditions and in complete loyalty to its own essential message?

(1) *Christianity can understand democracy and thus provide it with a really tenable philosophical foundation.* The great difference between the interpretation of democracy provided by secular humanists and the interpretation of democracy put forward by the Christian theologian is this: the secular humanist tends to understand and defend democracy in terms of a romantic belief in human perfectibility, whereas the Christian

theologian prefers to understand and defend democracy in terms of one of his basic dogmas, the doctrine of original sin.

The romantic belief in human perfectibility is usually closely associated with ideas, more or less clearly articulated, about a law of moral progress for mankind which became almost an article of faith in the secular humanism of the eighteenth and nineteenth centuries. In this twentieth century the notion has had to withstand many hard knocks but it is not quite dead yet. The notion is optimistic about man as he is; it supposes that he is already visibly better than he was in even the comparatively recent past, and that he will be better still very shortly. There are many different ways of formulating this doctrine, of which Marxism itself is perhaps the clearest and most cogent (that is why the secular humanist is often a poor defender of democracy against Marxism because he is already half a Marxist himself).

As a basis for the defense of the democratic idea, this optimistic doctrine of man has two serious defects. In the first place, as it seems to me and to most realistic interpreters of the human situation in the twentieth century, it is so plainly untrue. There never was very much to be said in its favor, and unless we are intellectual Bourbons, completely imprisoned behind the cozy walls of our optimism, incapable of either forgetting or learning anything, there is nothing to be said for it now. Man is not morally improved by the mere passage of time.

The second mistake of those who use a notion of this kind as the foundation of a democratic philosophy is that it does not really or necessarily point in the direction of democracy at all. If men really are perfectible, and in fact are moving rapidly toward perfection, is there any real reason why we should not trust administrative and technical experts to carry on the work of government on our behalf? An optimistic view of the moral potentialities of mankind in general should surely include an optimistic view of the moral potentials of statesmen, administrators, and technicians.

If we reject the view of human existence which teaches us that men are corruptible, and that above all men are corrupted again and again by power, then there is much to be said for interpreting government as a task for experts, for men of particular gifts heightened and concentrated by a specialized training, and for consigning the burden and responsibilities of government to them alone, just as we leave science to the scientists, art to the artists, and so on. Optimism about men in general surely implies and includes optimism about the experts. There is, indeed, more to be said for this point of view than most of us care to admit. If we are to take the notion of progress seriously, then plainly the most obvious form of progress is technical progress. It is often said, in a trite cliché, that the alleged moral progress of mankind has not kept pace with the alleged technical progress of mankind. This is an understatement. Technical progress is not only a reality, but has been carried very far indeed, whereas it is, to say the least, doubtful that there has been any moral progress at all. Civilized man is certainly as sinful, perhaps even more sinful, than the savage. Now one consequence of the technical progress of mankind—and this is one of the most acute problems which modern democracy has to face—is that more and more aspects of government have become highly technical matters. Whether we like it or not this is an age in which we are compelled increasingly to trust experts to do more and more of the things we want done because they alone understand the process by which they are done. Thus we are compelled to trust the physicist to create our military power, to turn to the economists for guidance in matters involving commercial and fiscal policy, to managerial experts to control and organize the vast bureaucracy that carries on the day-to-day business of the modern state. The plain fact is that we cannot exist without such men. Simple societies no doubt could get along without the assistance of such people but to a complex society like our own they are absolutely essential. The "apeheads" may furiously rage together and imagine many vain things, but they need the "eggheads" all the same. That is why it is foolish of the apeheads to devote so much of their time to the criticism of the eggheads, for what would happen to the apeheads if the eggheads suddenly sickened of serving them and decided to seek more sympathetic and understanding masters, or even to become the masters themselves? A democracy that cannot understand and respect its experts, and provide an honored place for them, is in mortal danger of being abandoned or even overthrown by its experts. The problem for democracy is the problem of retaining the service of the expert within a democratic framework. Part, at least, of the solution to the problem will be discovered by the democracy that learns to understand the expert and make him happy in its service. Yet although a modern democracy has learned to trust and respect the expert, it can never worship and trust itself completely to him without ceasing to be a democracy, and this is because the expert also is a fallen man. The uncommon man is a corruptible and corrupted sinner just as much as the common man. But the moment we see and say that this is true we are drawing attention to the fact of original sin.

The classical theological term "original sin" is a somewhat misleading one now that we have acquired the habit of using the word "original" to mean new, unusual or unique. Original sin certainly does not mean a new kind of sin that has never been sinned before. On the contrary, it refers to the spiritual sickness, the underlying sinfulness, which afflicts man from the very point of his origin, so that man is a sinner even when he is not sinning in any overt or particular fashion. We do not say that man is a sinner merely because he is observed to sin with regrettable frequency. That man is sinful is not an empirical observation based on a wide study of behaviouristic data, though no doubt such a generalization would be a valid and well-founded one. Man is not a sinner because he sins; on the contrary he sins because he is a sinner. The particular sins are facts which we observe; the doctrine of man's original sinfulness is a theological or philosophical category in terms of which we understand and account for what we observe. It answers for us the question, why is it that man is observed to sin again and again in this rather dull, repetitive fashion? Why is it that even when a man is not sinning in any overt, recognizable way we have always to bear in mind the possibility that he may begin sinning in some overt, recognizable way at the next moment? Why, in other words, is eternal vigilance the necessary price of freedom? Why is limiting and dividing earthly power and balancing the various forms of earthly power over against each other, and subjecting earthly power to the rule of law, the only way in the long run to avoid being overwhelmed by earthly power? The answer can only be in terms of the doctrine of original sin.

It is because men are everywhere corruptible and always corrupted that no single man or group of men can be trusted with too much power, indeed with any power at all that is not in some way balanced and checked by the power of other men. For the same reason a social situation which leaves any particular man without any power, influence, status, or rights whatsoever is one which leaves him at the mercy of the power of his neighbors. The wisdom of democracy is to divide and disperse, to limit and balance power, to reserve some tiny minimum of power for each citizen as his inalienable right, to create traditions, institutions, and written constitutional documents which insistently remind power of its responsibilities and its inherently limited character. But why is all this necessary and important? The answer is now clear: because this is a fallen world and because in a fallen world the problem of government and the consigning of power to particular persons and groups is the most hazardous problem of all. If men were morally perfect, or perfectible and rapidly approaching perfection, the case for democracy would not be so strong. But because this is not so the case for democracy is overwhelmingly strong.

To understand and interpret democracy in the light of the doctrine of original sin has the twofold advantage of reminding us at the same time of both the strength and limitations of democracy. To say that democracy consists of a series of socio-political arrangements and techniques designed to avoid unhealthy concentrations of power, which will certainly be abused in a fallen world, is to put it in its proper place and to see it in its correct perspective. The liberal humanist tendency toward an idolatrous absolutizing of democracy, which transforms it into an ultimate ethic or even a higher religion, is, of course, from such a point of view as this, a ridiculous illusion. I believe that Sir Winston Churchill once remarked, although I have not been able to check the reference, that a democracy is the least unsatisfactory way of arranging our political affairs that we poor mortals have yet stumbled upon in this sinful world. To say this is to make a very great and important claim for democracy, but it is at the same time to reject entirely any ethical or religious absolutizing of democracy. Now we can see clearly why it is that the Kingdom of God is not a democracy, and why Christianity cannot conceivably affirm democracy as something necessary to itself or higher than itself. Democracy is appropriate and valuable in the context of a fallen world. Outside such a context it cannot conceivably have any meaning or relevance. But it so happens that our world is a fallen world. This world of ours is the context in which democracy is appropriate and valuable. The Christian doctrine that defines the limitations of democracy at the same time perceives and diagnoses its essential value and strength. To perceive the limitations of democracy is to state the case for democracy within its limitations. We know of no alternative to democracy that has anything like the efficiency and validity of democracy here in this fallen world. It is the best and most effective way we have yet devised for ordering the process in and through which sinners govern each other and themselves.

Perhaps we should say just a little more about the notion of human perfectibility. Christianity does not necessarily deny that man is perfectible, although some forms of Christian theology do come very near to doing so. For them the great problem is not so much the elimination of sin, the setting free of men from the power of evil which holds them enthralled, but the problem of the forgiveness of sins, so that even in eternity and the Kingdom of God men will be a community of forgiven sinners rather than a community of unjust men made perfect. But the majority of Christian theologians, and this is certainly the biblical view, think in terms not merely of the forgiveness of sins but also of an ultimate conquest of sin. Sin is not merely forgiven by the loving Christ; its power is broken by the victory of the sinless Christ. For Christianity man is not merely perfectible; he will, in the kingdom of God, actually be perfected.

The real difference between Christianity and secular humanism is that the latter believes not merely in the perfectibility of man but in the *self-perfectibility* of man. According to secular humanism, man will be perfected either through his own efforts or by the mysterious semi-divine force called progress, which may be no more than the apathetic doctrine that man will be perfected by mere lapse of time, or which may more positively interpret man's own efforts to perfect himself as an essential part of the process. According to Christianity man will be perfected neither by mere lapse of time nor by his own efforts, but by the power of the grace of God. Of course, the Christian may say that man will not be perfected without some co-operative effort on his part, nor, since man is a temporal being, will the process be an all-at-once process without any temporal aspect. Nevertheless, for Christianity the primary and central agent of the process is God, and both human effort and the lapse of time will be utterly in vain apart from the grace of God. So long as this world order and the course of human history continue there can be no secure and abiding victory over the forces of evil, and we shall continue to be men struggling against the forces of evil in a fallen world. So long as this world-order and history continue, therefore, democracy will always be a valuable and effective device appropriate to man's sinful condition, and necessary to his temporal and political well-being.

To state the case for democracy in these terms is to state it realistically and effectively. We endanger the cause of democracy by claiming too much for it, because there is always the danger that men who have attached themselves to democracy because they have accepted the inflated claims of democracy put forward by undiscriminately democratic philosophers will react against it and reject it at last in a mood of disappointment and disillusion. When we expect too much of anything we are sometimes so frustrated when it fails to live up to our expectations that we fail to recognize its real though limited achievement. Democracy is not a recipe for the speedy production of the millennium; it is simply a way of securing a reasonable degree of decency and order in the conduct of human affairs in a fallen world. Man will not escape by way of democracy from his basic problems or his ultimate spiritual predicament. Even democracy will always be corruptible and sometimes corrupt, and it offers us no salvation from the sins that beset us. But a really democratic nation may hope to avoid the evils of tyranny and gross injustice, and a really democratic world order might even conceivably hope to avoid, or at least minimize, the evils of war. Surely to claim this for democracy is sufficient. It is quite unnecessary to try to present the kind of political arrangements and techniques that we call democratic as though they were an absolute ethic or an ultimate religion.

(2) *The Church can use democratic techniques in its own self-government and in the administration of its own affairs.* The Church itself is not and cannot be a democracy. It is, on the contrary, essentially a theocracy, the outlying earthly province of the Kingdom of God. Nevertheless the Church can employ democratic techniques in the carrying on of its earthly business and in fact it has done and does so. In our Western civilization the first parliamentary gatherings were in fact the councils of the Church, and during the Middle Ages the first parliamentary gatherings—the Cortes in Spain, for example, the States General in France, and the early parliaments convoked by Edward I and other monarchs in England—borrowed their rules of procedure, and their way of conducting their business, very largely from the much older experience of the Church in the conduct of its synods and councils. And still today the bulk of church business is conducted in this way. Thus we see in a church such as the Episcopal Church of the United States a large number of gatherings of elected representatives, parochial vestries, diocesan and national conventions, and so on, which carry on the day-to-day business of the Church despite the fact that the Church itself is not and cannot be a democracy.

The employment of democratic techniques in carrying on the business in what is fundamentally not a democratic society is quite a feasible and workable project. Thus a diocese may elect its bishop, yet the Church does not pretend that it is the election as such which makes a bishop a bishop. He becomes a bishop not when he is elected by the diocesan convention but at the moment when he is consecrated and raised to the rank and office of a bishop by other bishops. If all the other bishops refuse to consecrate him, then he could never become a bishop though he were elected ten times over. The process of electing a bishop is thus democratic, while the process of consecrating a bishop remains hierarchic. This is a very clear example of the way in which democratic techniques can be used effectively and wholesomely in what nevertheless remains a non-democratic society.

Nor is this really a departure from what we might call the norm of democracy, for the truth is that no society is democratic through and through. There is, as we have already seen, nothing which in fact corresponds to what is sometimes called the democratic way of life, nor is there any really democratic society. What we call a democratic society is only a human society resolved to employ democratic techniques as far as possible in the carrying on of its social business. But the business itself which a democratic society carries on in its democratic way would have to be carried on in some way or other whether the society was democratic or not. The fact is that our basic social arrangement and necessities are pre-democratic, and most of what makes up the common business of this life is in itself neither democratic nor undemocratic but simply human. For example, the family and the necessity of carrying on economic activities to support life are found in every form of human society. They are not in themselves democratic or undemocratic, though sometimes it may be possible to carry them on and protect them in a democratic manner. It is not necessary in a so-called democratic society that everything should be done democratically. Thus there is nothing peculiarly undemocratic in a father spanking his gravely disobedient son, nor is there any particularly democratic way of administering such a punishment. It may be important, indeed I think it is, that in a democracy fathers should occasionally chastise their sons, but the process itself is just a universally human one. It is equally necessary that fathers should chastise their sons even under a dictatorship. The family which does not discipline its children is neither democratic nor undemocratic; it is simply inefficient. Conversely it is a great mistake to suppose that everything which is done in a democracy must be democratic.

Even in a very democratic society most of the characteristic social customs are completely neutral so far as democracy is concerned. The clothes we wear, the code of manners we observe, our way of arranging our economical and matrimonial affairs will most certainly include certain customary elements that neither affirm democracy nor call it in question. There is a widespread idea that any characteristically British or American customs must necessarily be democratic social customs simply because Britain and America are democracies. This is a great illusion which may do harm, for it leads us to suppose that other peoples can only become democratic by adopting the whole round of our social customs, music, fashions, matrimonial and economic arrangements, and so on. Now quite possibly many peoples who would like to become democratic do not wish to adopt the entire cultural and social system of the English-speaking world. We have no right to insist that they should do so, and it may be unwise even to propose such a thing. The important thing to tell the swiftly developing peoples of Africa, Asia, and eastern Europe is that they can become democratic and remain themselves, that they can adopt democratic government and social techniques without aping the cultural conventions and habits of the English-speaking parts of the Western world. We must beware of turning the democratic philosophy into an ideology which cloaks and conceals what we may call a kind of cultural imperialism. The suspicion that when we talk about democratizing the world, we really mean Westernizing or even Americanizing the world does perhaps more harm than anything else to the cause of democracy. I repeat, not everything in a democracy need be democratic, nor is everything that is done in the existing democratic societies essential to the democratic idea.

The essential contention of this chapter has been that we can assert the case for democracy with greater effectiveness and more valid conviction if we are aware of its limitations. The best way of doing this in a democratic world is to rest the case for democracy fairly and squarely on a Christian philosophy of life. The Christian is unlikely to overstate the case for democracy because he can never forget that, "Behold a greater than democracy is here." But once he has observed the limitations of democracy he is in a position to perceive great strength within its limitations, for democracy has the priceless advantage among theories and methods of social organization of taking the doctrine of original sin seriously, and the doctrine of original sin, as has often been remarked, is the most obviously true of all Christian doctrines, perhaps the only one which can be verified and proved to the hilt beyond all question by a mere inspection and experience of the facts of life.

25

CHRISTIAN ETHICS AND THE WELFARE STATE *

One of the grounds on which Christians used to condemn Socialism was that it absorbed functions which properly belonged to private enterprise, and by doing so it led its citizens down the "road to serfdom" from

* V. A. Demant, "Christian Ethics and the Welfare State," *Cross Currents*, III (Fall, 1952), 6-13. Reprinted by permission of the editors of the review and the author.

which there would be no escape. But the Christian is faced with a dilemma. If millions of people in an industrial society cannot afford medical services, education for their children, healthful recreation, and other necessities of life, is the State to stand by while these people find the good life unattainable?

A principle stated clearly by Pope Pius XI in Quadragesimo Anno*—the principle of subsidiarity—maintains that the State should not interfere until lesser groups, such as the family, the local community, the local state or province, have clearly failed to handle the problem satisfactorily. This principle does not solve any single proposal for action by the national government, but it does suggest a line of reasoning which should help avoid either the trap of rushing into unnecessary state action or that of denying the state the right to act when it should.*

In the following selection the author discusses the problem, as it was faced in England in the years after the Second World War. He takes the historical point of view to argue that industrialization created such economic and social problems that the Welfare State, unwelcome as it is to the Christian conscience, was necessary at the time—much as a crutch is necessary to help a crippled man walk. The validity of any such argument comes from its proper assessment of the facts of the case in a given society at a given time. It cannot be transposed to another country unless the facts of the case in the new country are examined afresh. Nevertheless the possibility of the Welfare State must be faced in the other countries of the Western World, possible alternatives studied, and a conclusion in harmony with Christian principles arrived at when the problem presents itself.

SOCIETY is always sick, but it is not always structurally disordered. It is always sick because it is never free from division in human aims, discrepancies between central policies and personal goals; there are anglings for power and minor egoism—in short there is plain human sin. This is but to say that human society is not the Kingdom of God. But society has its own recuperative impulses and powers; there is a self-healing principle which tends to bend policies, theories and behaviour, to abate conflicts, in order to serve human existence. Therefore the state of society is not to be judged merely by looking at either forces of destruction or the forces of healing in it. We should consider the extent and rate of the two processes in comparison. Are the forces of growth or decline gaining the upper hand? A society is sound, as sound as any in a sinful world can be, when the positive social consciousness never lets the disruptive forces overpower it. And it is in decline, even with many aims of social health. when these are outrun by the forces of disintegration. In this case there is a structural disorder in addition to the dominion of sin and the counteracting impulses of social cohesion.

So when the Christian mind seeks to assess morally a social system or an experiment like the Welfare State, it must begin by distinguishing two different, though related, Christian callings. The first and primary one is to bring men into the state of grace, where the bond between them is *caritas* or *agape,* a replica of God's disinterested love for his creatures. The second is concern that, even among sinners and in the world outside the Church, there shall be that kind of balance of rights and duties among imperfect men by which they can live their secular lives to the fulfillment of their nature, without the supernatural heroism to be expected only of the saints. Suarez said,

> The concern of the State is the natural happiness of the perfect human community of which the civil legislature has the care, and the happiness of individuals as members of such a community, that they may live together peaceably and justly, and with so much rectitude as is necessary for the external peace and happiness of the community and the continued preservation of human life,

and T. S. Eliot defines a society acceptable to Christian judgment as "a society in which the natural end of man—virtue and well-being in community—is acknowledged for all, and the supernatural end—beatitude—for those who have eyes to see it." We are concerned here with this natural justice among sinful men. But Christians will not forget, even on this plane, that the recurring injustices in all societies and the repeated efforts of mankind to overcome them, represent man's alienation from God and his Kingdom and also a continual pull exercised by the reality of that kingdom, a pull which operates in man's being even when mostly he is not aware of its source of meaning.

I am insisting that both disruptive and constructive forces are at work in human society, apart from the ministry of grace which carries the supernatural and sacrificial love of God in Christ to the faithful believer. And therefore out of love for men, the Christian mind has the task of understanding these two natural forces in society; of fostering, where it can, those that make for healing, and of overcoming the destructive ones. How then does the Welfare State, as we know it under that name, look in the light of such a concern?

The Welfare State is one kind of State, and the State is a device of mankind to which the Biblical and Christian insight has rightly taken an ambiguous attitude. It is both bad and good. Read the accounts of the institution of the Kingship in the first book of Samuel. The Lord says, as it were, it were better if you did not have to have this; nevertheless, if you must, so be it, I give it my warrant, but you will regret it. Or, Jotham's parable in the book of Judges where the only tree that will accept rulership over the other trees is the bramble—the bush which has not only its fruit but also its thorns. That is why no people is ever satisfied with its government. A State as such can be an instrument of order and justice in general; it will always be felt by some to be unjust. We may say, speaking theologically, that the State exists because of sin, and itself often becomes infected with sin. It can not operate by love, for love is directed concretely to this or that particular person in his total nature, and that is beyond the capacity of an institution; those who have envisaged a state moved by love picture a utopia that ignores the tragedy of man. On the other hand, if there were no standard of love by which the rough justice of the State can be judged and in that light always be seen as imperfect justice, then we would never escape the ideologies and tyrannies that regard their imperfect or alleged justice as responsible to no higher court.

There is another aspect of the theology of the State which it is useful to recall. It is that the State does not belong to man by creation, as do the family, the race, the local community, the division of labour—as between Adam delving and Eve spinning. Again, the State does not belong to the order of redemption, as the totalitarians believe. It belongs to the order of history; it comes in when society transcends a merely tribal togetherness and makes a unity out of diverse peoples. Having no longer a merely tribal bond which is so close to nature, the larger society requires a central authority for its preservation from divisive forces. Therefore we may say that the State belongs to a man by divine providence at certain stages of his history, where the possibility of internal conflict is the price men pay for a wider and richer life than tribal organization allows. Its protective and preservative power in an imperfect world is thus under God—it represents the positive associative impulses of man counteracting the divisiveness of conflicting interests and wills. It stands for the link between man and God in the contradiction between man and God which Christians call sin. And the State is also liable to be captured by the sectional egoisms it exists to curb.

Theology distinguishes between the ultimate and the proximate will of God. For instance, physical health we may assume to be the ultimate will of God for man; so also the complete harmony of created wills. But for a sick or maimed human being there is his proximate will, that he should have medical help or a crutch. A crutch however is not the same as a good leg—nor is it necessarily a stage on the way to a live limb. But it represents the relative good in a defective condition. Medical treatment may or may not restore health; it aims when it is good at making itself unnecessary. The Divine will has both these forms. And what we should be asking about the Welfare State is whether the constrictions it imposes are the proximate will of God for us in our present situation—corresponding to the artificial leg which the maimed man must always use, or to the iron lung which will be discarded when health is restored.

With these preliminaries let us consider the fact of the Welfare State. What do we mean by it? It means a State which undertakes by its central government not only protection and order, but also to administer some of the requirements of the good life—especially men's physical and educational needs. As we know it in this country, it provides all its citizens with some amenities, apart from what they buy with their money wage—partly out of the common purse through taxes, and partly through insurance spending some of their incomes for them. I would point out that it is only in industrial society that the money income earned in employment was regarded as the sole valid source of livelihood. In previous ages men had many resources outside their employment and many perquisites within it besides their money wage. The Welfare State aims at a measure of security for all and at a partial re-allocation of the communal wealth. It should be noticed that this welfare provision now operates alongside of two other things—it could exist without them—which are often confused with it. One is the imposing of a comprehensive design upon society—planning and direction of activities; the second—also separable from social services—is a radical redistribution of economic power which tends to a certain rigidity, which varies the standards of living of different sections, controls rent and prices, and enforces rationing, subsidies, and so forth. One may validly approve or disapprove of these things, without prejudice to basic social services or to the supplementation of earned income by community benefits.

In order to estimate morally the fact of the Social Service State we must come to a view of how it has arrived. Here there are two influences at work, which should be distinguished. The first is an enlargement of social consciousness and conscience which, after the dislocations of the free-enterprise era, demanded that men's livelihood and some cultural benefits should not be dependent entirely upon competitive income earning. This impulse, where it was most genuine, was critical not of inequality in general, but of that particular kind of inequality which early industrialism brought about, vast concentration of economic power on the one hand, and a property-less status-less proletariat on the other. This impulse represents a positive moral attitude coming to expression in a period when the economic triumphs of the industrial age were won at the cost of colossal social dislocations, grave insecurity, and widespread hardship. We could put down this enlargement and deepening of social consciousness to a valiant attempt to atone for and remedy the particular form of human sinfulness which the economic age brought starkly to light. My own view is that the Christian mind must salute and approve of it. But this positive social impulse has often been misinterpreted. It is not a phase in social evolution by which mankind is growing out of primitive individualistic behaviour and recognizing an interdependence of which it was formerly ignorant, or which it had disregarded in the pursuit of private interests. No, it is rather that many saw, in the form which egoism took in developing industrialism, a dislocation of the natural social loyalties of previous ages. The welcome given to State responsibility was one sign that something had to take the place of the loyalties previously expressed in domestic cohesion, craft association, neighbourhood and a common religious culture. Whether State responsibility is or is not really a cure for the disintegration in these spheres, it represents a heave of the collective soul to find a substitute for them.

But that is only half the story. The other half tells of the Welfare State as a political device to prevent the complete disruption of an industrial society suffering from many internal disorders—disorders which no modern policy has seriously attempted to cope with. They are still with us under the Welfare State and many of them appear to be growing, so that some critics of the Welfare State imagine it to be the cause of what it does not cure. Here a commentator cannot avoid giving interpretations which still appear controversial. Let me then try to emulate Saint Paul and say: here it is I who speak, not the Lord, and my hearers must make their own judgment. I believe that there are forces of disruption inherent in a certain stage of industrial society, at which it begins to show diminishing returns and a self-defeating principle. I believe that this industrial society of ours could get along very well with a free enterprise philosophy and practice so long as there was underneath it a strong fabric of natural community, with land to feed its population, and a faith to live by that was not confined to economic progress. In the nineteenth century these foundations, which are partly spontaneous creations and, in our western civilization, partly due to the moral and social tradition of Christendom—all these were assumed to be permanent parts of man's natural life, and to be with him always. They tended to crumble under the highly sophisticated achievement of a predominantly industrial and commercial pattern of life. Centralization of initiative and loss of individual moral responsibility, which appear to be galloping in the Welfare State, are tendencies which began in the period of free enterprise and market economy. The family deprived of its agelong functions, the withering of all incentives but those of monetary gain, the weakening of a sense of vocation in one's job—all this is old history now, and has something to do with industrialism having grown apace in a secularized society without any doctrine of the valid ends of human activity. The Welfare State cannot be blamed for these defects; it inherited them. Its sponsors and defenders may however be upbraided for imagining that State enactment can cure what is really a disorder in society, and for thereby encouraging, reluctantly perhaps, an increase in these ills.

The Welfare State then is a necessary but defective political device to prevent society from crumbling under the chaos of productive relations, and of an atomized citizenship which has been deprived of all lesser loyalties and vital associations. It may be the wrong cure, but if so another must be found. On my analysis, just as Hobbes' Leviathan was a conception to overcome the ravages of the Civil War, so the Welfare State is a conception to overcome the disintegration of Industrial Society. And it could not well be denied that the Welfare State has given to the mass of the population a kind of security, as a substitute for the status of which the exclusively economic bonds of the last two centuries deprived them. We may think it hastens the insecurity of society as a whole—but that is a matter for consideration elsewhere. There are other dangers. In the first influence of which I spoke, the growth of social conscience, there was a real concern to restore the majority a basis for responsible living, a measure of economic security which is indispensable for initiative and a robust social initiative, and a concern to underpin the independence of the family. This was in line with what traditional Church teaching expressed as natural justice. Every man has a natural right to existence, to status and to a responsible function in society. The right to existence has been accorded by the Welfare State in provision of some of the family's physical necessities (though not in the matter of dwellings), while so much of our productive energy and material is given to such extravagances as civil aviation, television, and to a host of other expressions of our technical incontinence. The right to existence has been in a measure observed. But status—the condition of having roots somewhere, in a patch of earth and a community—that the Welfare State has not restored, except in the most abstract form of citizenship in an impersonal State. As to function—no modern society so far as I can see, free enterprise or socialist, has found the secret of giving to the mass of industrial workers what the original working-class movements stood for—a field of responsibility in the concrete setting of man's life—mainly in his work and his home.

In the pre-industrial age men expressed what social consciousness they had in the smaller areas of life—the family, the region, the work association, the Church. These bonds of craft, kinship, neighbourhood and creed were weakened and displaced by mainly economic relations—and the field of social responsibility then has to be narrowed and attenuated in the bare citizen-state relationship. This is too abstract a loyalty to move men. During the bombing of London anyone who could turn a hand to some sort of house building or repairs would patch up a dwelling for a neighbour without any thought of gain or prestige. The original community impulse came out on top in the crisis of war. The same men will not work all out when their occupation is part of the wages and hours contract; and when the good of the community as a whole—the only other incentive offered them—does not seem visually to them to have anything to do with the needs of their families or fellows in the concrete. I am saying that the Welfare State, intended as a basis of restored responsibility, is, in that respect, not a great success.

Now it is true that a Welfare State does become a moral State in the sense that by its allocation of resources it determines the ends of activities of its citizens, and this—what Professor Hayek has been so alarmed about—can easily become the "Road to Serfdom." But a non-moral State, existing merely for protection and order, like the liberal State of recent centuries—and a fine achievement it was—was possible only when it could count on a moral, cultural and social unity underneath it. When that foundation wears thin, then there is some inevitability about the State's assuming omnicompetent and directive functions—its claiming to know better than the people themselves what is good for them. This attitude was once attributed to parties of the right; it has now become the attitude of the left. Added to this tendency is of course the danger of the growth of a vested interest in the social administrator, a temptation to which many professional workers are liable—as the teacher to think of the young merely as the raw material of education, or the physician to consider the patient as a case, the parson to estimate his flock in terms merely of church fodder. This kind of professional bias is one which the Christian individual in his walk of life should be prepared to detect in himself and repent of.

I have tried so far to present the fact of the Welfare State in a double aspect partly as a deliberate answer to express a growing social conscience, and partly as a rather blind effort on the part of society and governments to preserve strength in an industrial situation with some serious contradictions. What then can the Christian man or woman do, accepting it as the *de facto* situation in which God has for the present set him or her?

There are two ways that Christians can take, one as possible participators in the social services, as public servants or as social service workers, and the other as Christian citizens. For the first, let us be quite clear that no organized state activity can cover and remedy all the tragedies and ills of human society. No government machine will ever be so perfect as to obviate the need for what used to be called, somewhat disparagingly, ambulance work. The need for personal help and guidance, felt by the wrecks of every human society, will always call for what has been offered by the voluntary social services, and this need will not disappear with any development of the Welfare State. Here is still a field for the living out of a Christian vocation—especially perhaps when it evokes a certain contempt from those who see salvation coming only by statutory measures. And then let no Christian man or woman think he or she has no way of expressing a love of man in the machinery of the statutory social organization itself. There is no sphere of life and work, however impersonal its machinery, in which an employee—if he has that intense concern for persons which the love of God in Christ gives him—cannot convey that personal attitude to his clients and his co-workers. Of course there will be strains—and often a feeling that one's human qualities are stifled by the equipment. Often a bewilderment as to how to find a cleft in the impersonal structure of administration, through which to minister the concern of one human being for another. But that is not a dilemma peculiar to the Welfare State; it confronts the intense personalism of Christianity as a challenge in all forms of large-scale organization. It is presented dramatically in Dorothy Sayers' *The Just Vengeance,* where the airman is in great moral bewilderment about the acceptability of his military and destructive duty before the throne of Christ. At the end of the play a number of personages appear with their offerings. The strong man offers his strength; the harlot offers her shame. The airman asks: What shall I bring? and Christ answers "You can bring the burden of perplexity, we shall meet each other in the darkest hour of all."

"The burden of perplexity"—that will confront every Christian, at times, who seeks to carry his Christian vocation into that rough and imperfect mechanism of justice which the natural man fashions by the device of legislation and administration. In one sense, wherever we are is where God wants us to be. There must be the acceptance of the situation as it is; then only can there also be protest in any constructive and healing form. Therefore, I say, there is a definite sphere of vocation for Christian workers in both voluntary and statutory social services. If it is undertaken with that mixture of acceptance and protest which the Christian has learned to live with in almost any human situation, he will not be crushed in his soul by the things against which he has to protest; nor will he slide into the apathy which deceives him into the attitude that all he can do in an unnatural situation is all he ought to be able to do in a more properly ordered society.

Lastly the Christian Community, in so far as it has a teaching mission for discriminating understanding of the true ends of human life and of the defects of every actual situation in relation thereto, has surely the task of interpreting the coming of the Welfare State and its dangers, in the way I have been suggesting. Christian moralists have been too liable to make an estimate of human nature from the ethos of the last two centuries, and to say that men are moved by only two impulses: either the pure self-regarding one which, in the social sphere, takes the form of gain—or else the supernatural and disinterested agape or love declared in the New Testament. But mankind has lived and survived by a great number of social motives in between these two: pride in doing a job, a sense of community, self-expression in serving one's fellows. These belong to the natural man along with the disruptive forces of bare egotism. It can then be part of the Christian's concern for the natural good of his fellows to want a social ordering which fosters these spontaneous social impulses—impulses which, though far short of love and the perfection of the saints, have led the human race over and over again to mend its own wreckage.

Our large-scale, technical and largely urbanized society has become so interlocked that its self-healing powers have become much weaker than in less tight and centralized civilizations. When Christians concerned for the liberty and small scale responsibility of persons and minor associations, are alarmed at the threat to these things by the onward march of State power, they should remember that no mere resistance and protest to that power is constructive. The only constructive attitude is to attend to the cultural and community weakness of society, under the level of the State; and then to see what can be done even through State enactment, to build up strength and responsibility in the smaller areas of life. Universities in receipt of state grants show that it is not impossible for the central government to pay the piper leaving the beneficiary to call its own tune.

We are called at this time, in the words of an important Church declaration:

to nurse ourselves back into a condition in which we can recognize social health for what it is, and learn how to enjoy it by a new obedience to its laws. The recovery of health involves not only a capacity to recognize the normal, but a readiness to prepare for it by such abnormal means as weakness imposes. It would perhaps help us to a better understanding of the significance of the apparatus of the Welfare State if we were to regard it in this light.

26

FREUD AND PSYCHOANALYSIS *

Sigmund Freud is one of the most controversial figures of the twentieth century. He replaced hypnosis with the technique of psychoanalysis to delve into the "unconscious" in an attempt to diagnose and cure neurotic disorders. Freud's clinical observations were an important addition to our knowledge of subconscious or unconscious motivation, but he is better known for the theories he developed to explain his observations. As Marx reduced all phenomena in life ultimately to production-relations, so Freud reduced all psychical disorders ultimately to sex difficulties. A group of young disciples took up Freudian doctrine and applied it to art and literature, to painting and fairy tales, to religion and to an explanation of all historical events.

Freud encouraged such use of his theories, but he refused to allow his disciples any doctrinal leeway whatsoever. As a result innumerable schisms developed within the Freudian school as Alfred Adler, for example, built a body of psychoanalytic thought around the idea of drive-for-power, and Carl Gustav Jung found that man is motivated by noble as well as animalistic drives. Freudian doctrine has been modified in many respects by contemporary psychoanalysts, but the fact remains that he broke with accepted psychological doctrine of the late nineteenth century to discover some new facts about man's behavior and to suggest others.

* Rudolf Allers, *The Successful Error* (New York: Sheed and Ward, Inc., 1940), pp. 247-261. Reprinted by permission.

This is what Dr. Allers has in mind when he refers to Freudianism as "the successful error" in the following selection. It is wrong and intellectually stubborn to reject everything Freud says because he lays undue stress on sex motivation. And it is just as wrong to accept everything he says simply because it is he who says it. Dr. Allers subjects Freudian thought to thorough analysis from the standpoint of a physician whose metaphysics is Thomistic. The object of his analysis is not only to reveal the mistakes in Freudian theory but also to indicate what can be learned from it and to show how it has helped us explore an aspect of man—the subconscious—which had till Freud's time been unduly neglected.

It is hardly necessary to repeat the principal objections which have to be raised against psychoanalysis in the name of sound reason, of philosophical truth, of psychological and ethnological fact. It is not that psychoanalysis flatly contradicts a philosophy we believe to be the true one; this argument will make no impression on anyone who either clings to another philosophy or sincerely believes he has none at all. To convince the man who holds a different philosophy it would be necessary to prove to him that the fundamentals of his own philosophy are mistaken. This is extremely difficult because philosophical attitudes are mixed up, very often, too often indeed, with emotional attitudes and also because too many people are not aware at all of the foundations of their philosophical ideas. To convince the man who despises philosophy and boasts of having none at all, it would be necessary to make him see that even the denial of philosophy is a particular philosophical position, worse in fact than any "fantastic" speculation, because it is ignorant of its own nature. This also is difficult because hatred of philosophy is an obstacle one can hardly expect to surmount. An appeal to sound reason or commonsense does not impress the average believer in science and scientific methods—be it real science or only the parody of science, masked in the dress of science and couching unscientific notions in the impressive terms of science—since commonsense lost its credit with the true scientist ages ago.

Even before Kant in a well known passage of his *Prolegomena* spoke so contemptuously of "commonsense," simple reason had come to be disregarded; reality was believed to be at bottom what physics showed it to be and no longer what the senses led man to believe. Neither an appeal to philosophy nor to reason is likely to shatter any of the convictions of the psychoanalysts. The only thing these admirers of science and despisers of reason and philosophy respect are facts and the self-consistency of a system. They all are likely to believe that a statement is true when it squares with all known facts, and that a system deserves to be called true when it is self-consistent and does not, even in its ultimate consequences, lead to any contradictions.

Though we, for our own part, are prepared to give more credit to philosophical principles and to trust reason more than the scientific mind today generally does, we shall not stress considerations either of philosophy or of reason. The incompatibility we have shown to exist between psychoanalysis and the principles of sound philosophy may serve as a warning to those who still believe that some synthesis may be brought about. As we have already pointed out, there are some who try to disengage the psychoanalytical method of investigation and treatment from the philosophy which is at the back of the whole Freudian system. We have endeavored to demonstrate that the bond between these is necessary and indestructible; the very moment the philosophy on which psychoanalysis rests is abandoned, the whole theory becomes impossible and self-contradictory. The psychoanalysts who will not allow that such a separation may be possible are right in this and show a better understanding of their ideas and their fundamental positions than do those critics who bow before the method and reject the philosophy.

We hope to have shown by conclusive arguments that Catholic philosophy and psychoanalysis exclude each other. The admirers of Freud and the advocates of "modern science" will, of course, conceive of this demonstration only as a new proof of the unmodernity of Scholastic philosophy. They cannot be expected to feel differently. They are, however, wrong. But it is not for these pages to point out the basic mistakes made by an ultramodern conception of science and of philosophy. Moreover, Scholasticism had for centuries grown accustomed to being considered obsolete and unmodern; for being so it has a remarkable vitality. But a person who has neither a sufficient knowledge of Scholastic philosophy nor the capacity or the inclination to become acquainted with it will be in no way impressed by being told of this incompatibility.

But, as we have tried to prove, there are facts with which psychoanalysis not only is incapable of coping, but which this theory simply disregards and which have to be taken at their full value. And there are in Freud's system contradictions and logical fallacies which an objective mind cannot put aside as unimportant. As long as psychoanalysis does not give a clear and satisfactory answer to the challenge of such facts and as long as it fails to justify itself against the reproach of logical inconsistency, its demand to be recognized as a true science, even as The Science of the human mind, remains unfounded, a mere pretension.

As a rule the psychoanalysts refuse to consider any criticism raised against their ideas. It was Freud's habit to disregard all criticism, and this procedure has been followed by his pupils. The father of psychoanalysis rarely and incidentally referred to any critical remarks; and his pupils have generally but one answer: the critic's statements are contrary to those of Freud. We remember being answered, many years ago, by one of Freud's most prominent pupils to the effect that, whenever asked why this or that statement is true, he would refer the critic to the works of Freud.

The psychoanalysts have, as we saw, another weapon of which they make extensive use. Inability to accept their ideas is not credited to objective reasons nor to rational arguments, but to the irrational forces which are at work, they say, in the minds of the critics. During the discussion referred to in the preceding paragraph we were told by another prominent representative of psychoanalysis that our unwillingness to accept the Freudian conception of "resistance" was due to—resistance and therefore a striking proof of this fact being real. Unless you have been analysed and unless analysis has taken from you the resistance against some general truths, a resistance conditioned by "unconscious" factors, you are incapable of evaluating psychoanalysis. For that reason the Psychoanalytical Association refuses to receive anyone who has not undergone complete analytical treatment.

This demand is unique in the history of science. It is true, of course, that a physicist will not take seriously the criticism of a person whom he knows to be ignorant of the principles of physics. The mere statement that this or that "cannot be true" has no weight with the scientist, if such an objection is not based on a full knowledge of the principles and the methods of science. But there are no principles and no method which permit and legitimatize the ignoring of facts or the sinning against the fundamental rules of logic.

We may concede to the psychoanalysts that many of the objections raised against their theory, especially in the first years when psychoanalysis began to be widely known, were based on prejudices or were urged with arguments which certainly lacked objectivity. Moral resentment, the feeling of being shocked by certain statements, and so forth, are not valid arguments in a discussion of scientific ideas. Psychoanalysis is indeed, as we have been at pains to demonstrate, contrary to morals; but it is not so because it lays such stress on sex or because it draws certain consequences, but simply because of its basic principles and because of the philosophy on which it rests and from which it cannot be separated. Earlier critics may have had some inkling of this, but they failed to penetrate sufficiently into the ideological background so as to become fully aware of it. We may hold them excused, because these fundamental ideas were not so visible in the first publications as they have become now. Today we are able to detect these basic principles in the early writings of Freud and of this school because we look after having been made aware of them by the study of later books and articles.

But let us, for one moment, suppose as true that this idea of "resistance" is the only cause of so many rejecting the teachings of Freud. Even if this supposition were really the case, the answer of the psychoanalysts would still be quite insufficient. We believe that the position taken by the Freudian school is another striking proof of their tendency to disregard objectivity and to seek reasons and causes exclusively in the subjectivity of the individual mind. But, assuming the position of the psychoanalysts to be justified, what would they have to do? Is it really enough to dismiss all criticism by referring it to subjective and individual factors? We do not think so.

Psychoanalysis boasts of being a thorough, all-comprising explanation of mental facts. Inability to accept the psychoanalytical theory is such a fact. It has therefore to be explained. The psychoanalyst says that he explains the fact by referring it to the working of resistance. But this explanation is merely a formal one. It takes no account of the particular reasons alleged against the propositions of psychoanalysis. To refer to resistance might be a sufficient explanation in those cases in which the critic without basing his judgment on any definite reasons simply declares psychoanalysis to be wrong and unacceptable. Mere resistance might have many ways of expressing itself. Why does it, when opposing psychoanalysis, take on just this form? By what peculiar trick does resistance condition the objections based on facts of psychology, of ethnology or on the logical fallacies contained in the Freudian system?

We have remarked that psychoanalysis shows an amazing disregard for the material contents of mental states and of their phenomenological peculiarities. The theory is really interested only in genesis. The only question it asks and desires to answer is where some mental fact had its origin. The particular nature of the mental state is of no importance. It is noteworthy that psychoanalysts, though they have collected probably a greater mass of material than any other psychologists on this matter, have not contributed anything essential to the descriptive psychology, for instance, of dreams.

This disregard makes the psychoanalysts an easy prey to rash generalizations. As soon as they form the idea of some attitude as being conditioned by certain of the factors they are accustomed to emphasize, they will have it that these conditions obtain in every case they observe. They do not think it possible that the deplorable resistance shown by their adversaries could have several reasons, least of all that there could be objective reasons, derived not from attitudes or complexes, but resulting from the objective structure of their own theory and its incompatibility with facts. They do not, therefore, even trouble to look at the arguments brought forth; these arguments are against psychoanalysis, *ergo* against the becoming conscious of repressed material, *ergo* due to resistance. Not worth while considering them. But that is no way of arguing. The only sensible reaction would be a carefully objective consideration of the arguments of their adversaries.

The way in which the psychoanalysts respond to criticism has to be abandoned. As long as they continue to answer by merely repeating that they are right and by referring to their own ideas, their defense is not worth anything, because it does not take account of the things of which they are accused. Logical fallacies are not eliminated by committing them a second and a third time. Nor have the psychoanalysts ever answered in a satisfactory manner the reproach of neglecting essential facts of ethnology and of relying on bad evidence. Asserting that these things have to be true because they fit in with Freud's ideas is not an acceptable answer.

Some authors have tried to prove that the statements of psychoanalysts might be confirmed by experimental research in psychology. They have referred to phenomena like retroactive inhibitions as being in accordance with Freud's conception of repression. Such and similar statements are based, however, more on analogies than on identities. S. Rosenzweig indeed predicts that the opposition against psychoanalysis will be overcome by experimental research. Until today little has been done to make his assertion probable. His thesis is indeed more of a program than of an achievement. There is one experiment, however, which ought to be made and which would, we feel sure, possibly shatter some of the psychoanalytic positions, because it has to be done with the very method of Freud. This decisive experiment has not been made, so far as we know, by any psychoanalyst.

It has sometimes been urged against the interpretation of dreams that a patient or some other person might, during analysis, tell the analyst a dream which was not dreamt at all but invented. The results of analysis, it was surmised, would then become misleading. To this the psychoanalysts answered, and they were quite right, that the fact of a dream having been invented does not matter since nobody can invent anything not belonging to and not expressive of his own mentality. But one might suggest this experiment: take a dream out of a book, for instance one of the prophetic dreams recorded in history or one of those told in some biography or even one of the experimenter himself. These dreams cannot contain any material belonging to the analyzed person. But the psychoanalysts might refer to the common knowledge of mankind, to ethnical symbols, to the persistence of prehistoric influences. It is therefore better to devise another experiment. Show a picture to the person to be analyzed. Let him look at it long enough to get a complete idea of it. Let him describe this picture while he still has it before his eyes. Thus even the selective influence of personal attitudes will be excluded. And proceed then as if this description were a dream of this person. Use the procedure of free association, starting from the various elements of the description the subject has given.

Many years ago I made some experiments of this kind. The analysis of this "dream" brings forth very much the same unconscious material as does the analysis of a real dream. The experiment is indeed not devised for disproving the statements on the unconscious material. But what it does definitely disprove is the idea of the causal relation between the mental fact or element which is made the starting-point of analysis, and the material which is brought forth. It destroys also the notion of symbolization. How could anything in the life of the analyzed person ever condition his having seen and reported the things he has been shown in a picture? This becomes especially impressive if one uses a picture which has nothing to do with the common situations of life, *e.g.*, a more or less schematical illustration of an apparatus for metabolism experiments.

It is up to the psychoanalysts to make such experiments and to discuss their bearing on Freudian psychology. Just as it is up to the psychoanalysts to answer the various criticisms many authors propose. And, to repeat this once more, the answer cannot be given by referring to the alleged results of psychoanalytical investigation, because it is the method itself whose reliability is doubted. Nor, as we endeavored to show, is practical success any proof of the truth of the theoretical statements.

The psychoanalysts must give a clear answer to the contention that their psychology rests on a materialistic basis. If they want their psychology to be what they believe and say it is, then its propositions ought to be independent of any philosophy. We are fully convinced that there is no psychology at all which could be independent of the philosophy which the psychologist consciously or unconsciously adopts. Accordingly, we do not feel that psychology ever can become a science molded on the ideal of physics or even of biology. But the psychoanalysts think such a psychology possible. Let them prove then that their psychology is truly independent of materialistic metaphysics and of hedonistic ethics, and that it is not necessarily subjectivistic and not incapable of incorporating in its system the idea of person.

To cope with these demands the psychoanalysts would have to become philosophers. It is to be hoped that, had they but acquired a little knowledge in philosophy and some capacity of perceiving the kind of logic they use, they would see a good deal of the truth regarding their psychology. But it is much more to be feared that not one of them will attempt to acquire the necessary knowledge in philosophy. They will not attempt it, first, because they are too sure of possessing the whole truth on human nature; secondly, because they despise philosophy—though without knowing much of it; and thirdly, because they believe they already know enough of this despised subject. It has been often the misfortune of philosophy that too many people believed themselves to be capable of passing judgment on metaphysical or other assertions without troubling to get reliable information and without bothering to learn how to deal with these problems. It is always much easier to deny the existence of a problem than to attempt to solve it. No wonder that there is a close friendship between psychoanalysis and positivism, since there is no "philosophy" so full of negations as positivism is.

Let us look again briefly at the criticism which we have seen to be demanded by the factual statements and the theoretical assumptions of psychoanalysis.

Psychoanalysis is a thoroughly materialistic conception. It stands and falls with its materialism. Whosoever feels incapable of accepting the philosophy of materialism cannot but reject psychoanalysis. Because of its materialism, the philosophy of Freud and his school is, in what regards ethics, a simple hedonism. It is addicted to an extreme subjectivism which even blinds the eyes of the psychoanalyst to obvious objective facts and truths. Because of its subjectivism it is impersonalistic and ignores the essence of the human person. Its philosophy, therefore, is based on ideas which not only a Catholic, but every man believing in a higher principle existing above matter and dominating it, cannot but reject.

As a theory, psychoanalysis rests on several serious logical fallacies. It is guilty of more than one *petitio principii*. It commits the same fault also in regard to facts, especially when applying its notions to ethnology or the study of religion. The alleged proofs to which the psychoanalysts refer their critics are no proofs at all, because they imply all the logical fallacies which invalidate the theory and the method.

The method is so closely linked to the theory and to its philosophy that no one rejecting these can adopt the method, unless it be that he understands by psychoanalytic method merely the production of free associations. But if a method is to bear the name of Freud, it must be more than the production of free associations—it must necessarily include certain interpretations which become meaningless outside of a purely naturalistic conception of man's nature.

The "axiomatic" propositions which pervade the theory and on which the latter is based imply several notions which are either self-contradictory or disproved by facts.

Psychoanalysis disregards the observations of experimental and otherwise empirical psychology, because it does not itself take account of obvious facts of introspective psychology. Thus it persists in identifying all kinds of pleasure with that arising from gratification of the instincts and it reaches accordingly mistaken ideas on the ends of strivings, conations and volitions. Its conceptions of the mental development of children are also characterized by a total disregard of the facts ascertained by immediate observation.

Nor is the contention that all mental phenomena ultimately derive from instincts and their representations without its serious drawbacks. Psychoanalysis can explain, at best, that at a given moment of a person's life some mental state arises and why; it can never give a satisfactory explanation of the existence of such mental states and of their peculiar qualities.

The ideas many psychoanalysts maintain in regard to facts of physiology are partly preposterous, partly, to say the least, arbitrary and lacking any reliable proof. Interpretation and fantastic speculation take the place of observation and experimental analysis. As a theory of neurosis the system of Freud is unsatisfactory, because many of its assertions rest exclusively on the interpretation suggested by this very same theory, illustrating thus the logical fallacy of which psychoanalysis becomes guilty. The successes obtained by this mode of treatment are no more convincing proof of its truth. Psychoanalysis, claiming to be the only reliable and truly scientific psychotherapy, fails to explain why results as good as its own may be achieved also by methods which retain no element of psychoanalysis, whether of the method or of the theory. There is no proof that psychoanalysis is necessary for the treatment of neurotic disturbances.

The applications to ethnology, of which the psychoanalysts are evidently rather proud and which they consider as one of Freud's greatest achievements, are absolutely erroneous, since the evidence to which they appeal is quite unreliable. Freud and his followers have neglected to make sure of the reliability of the authorities they quote and of the validity of the facts to which they allude. Their conceptions of primitive society, of the development of rituals, of totemism, and so forth, are contrary to the findings of ethnology and prehistoric research.

Neither Freud nor any of his followers has a true idea of what religion is or of the essential characteristics of the various religious forms. They are especially in the dark in regard to all facts referring to Christianity. Hasty generalization, arbitrary assertions, ignorance and imagination replace exactitude of analysis and critical appreciation of data in these vagaries.

The alleged confirmation of Freudist conceptions to be gained from the study of prehistory, of ethnology, of religion does not exist at all. It is the result not of two independent lines of research leading to the same conclusion—which alone would amount to a confirmation—but of a vicious circle in argumentation, the interpretation of ethnological and other facts presupposing already the truth of the psychoanalytical theory.

Psychoanalysis appears thus as an immense error. Its success in the modern world is caused by its being a compromise of divergent and even contradictory sets of ideas. Indeed psychoanalysis is a characteristic feature of the period of transition from the late nineteenth century to the present day or rather to the periods which are going to evolve out of the chaos of our days.

Psychoanalysis, as we see it, is indeed what I have called it in the title of this book: a "successful error." I have tried to show what Freud's error or errors were and why his system, in spite of its immanent falsity, came to achieve its success. But no system of ideas exists without containing some truth. There must be truth also in psychoanalysis.

We must be on our guard against the notion that the error of a gifted mind, let us say a genius, is better than the truth stated by an average personality. The error of a great mind does not become better by being associated with a remarkable effort of the intellect. An error is forever an error. It is measured by its relation to truth and is not altered, in its nature, by any factor of subjectivity. Freud may have been a genius; that makes things worse, not better. If we try now to state the merits of psychoanalysis and of its founder it is not because of any feeling of admiration for the person of Freud. I have said more than once, in the foregoing pages, that mine is not the biographer's attitude. We are studying the history of ideas and not of persons. Everyone of course is free to admire a man who for many years, in spite of great opposition, pursued what he believed to be the truth. But this admiration of a personal quality has nothing to do with our judgment on ideas and on their truth.

There may be more truths concealed in psychoanalysis than will be mentioned here. But these truths, if they exist, are hidden under such a mass of misconceptions, of mechanistic, materialistic imagery, and are so thoroughly disfigured by being clad in the vestments of a theory which disregards the essential features of human nature, that it would take a long time and much strenuous effort to clear away all the useless and utterly mistaken paraphernalia. Psychoanalysis has discovered this or that fact in psychology; but these discoveries would have been made anyhow because of the general tendencies in psychology, which we detect now as having been active in the past. All these things are of minor importance compared with Freud's two or three greater achievements.

Freud inaugurated the movement of medical psychology. Psychoanalysis was the first attempt at discovering the nature of neurosis and at devising means to help a group of sufferers who are more numerous than one might think at first and who are becoming steadily more numerous.

Freud's theory was the first to emphasize the enormous importance the experiences of the child have for the future development of personality. His views intensified the sense of responsibility of educators who have thus become conscious of their duty not only to impart knowledge and to teach morals but to observe with the utmost care the personality of the child and to avoid all influences which might threaten his further development. The vulnerability of the personality of children has thus been emphasized and brought to the attention of psychologists, physicians and educators.

One may call it a merit of psychoanalysis that, in an age of unduly exaggerated intellectualism, it has made visible the influence of non-intellectual factors within human personality. Though the relation of these factors to personality and to the faculties of the mind was misinterpreted by Freud, he nevertheless restored in a way the old and nearly forgotten knowledge that man is not pure reason or pure spirit, but a being composed of matter and soul.

Behind this, however, is hidden what is Freud's greatest and most unexpected achievement. He restored the knowledge of the leading rôle of the mind, the knowledge of the dominating place held by the soul in human nature. To do this was not his intention. He did not know that he was serving the rebirth of a truer conception of man's nature than he himself was ever capable of imagining. We do not here allude to his discoveries regarding the influence mental factors have on bodily phenomena, nor to his unveiling of the mental origin of so many troubles, nor to his having demonstrated the curative influence of mental attitudes. All this is but the peripheral manifestation of things much deeper and much more important. Freud's real achievement is: This discovery that mental treatment is capable of healing certain bodily troubles, that it may result in a total change of attitudes, has delivered mankind from the bondage of biologism. Not every thing is due to heredity, to bodily constitution, to an immutable set-up of personality, decreed by blind fate. The dominion of the mind is reestablished.

It is an irony of history that this was, we will not say achieved but started, by a man whose whole mentality and whose training made him a materialist. The rebirth of a better understanding of the dignity of the mind and of the place it holds in human nature has been partly the work of a scholar who endeavored more than many others to drag down the mind to the level of mere biological function. To have opened the road to such an understanding is not Freud's personal merit, nor can this be credited to psychoanalysis, the spirit of which is in fact contrary to a development which cannot end but by bringing back something of the truths of old to the general consciousness.

Freud and his school are, in regard to this fact, and to several others, but the exponents of a deeply hidden undercurrent which had started even before psychoanalysis came to exist and has gone on all these years, insensibly though steadily gaining in strength. But we may be grateful for a peripheral manifestation if by it we are led to become aware of some great truth, of some high value, of some enlivening.

Balaam *redivivus*. Freud, a discipline of materialism, a believer in science, a man to whom words like objective value or moral law had no meaning, a mind whose analyzing power tended towards the dissolution of human person, this very same man appears as a servant of higher plans and wider scopes. Ignorant of this fact himself, he prepared the way for views which are destined to overthrow his own, as falsehood will be always overthrown by truth.

Psychoanalysis lived and still lives by strength of the little truth it contains and of the greater truth of which it is the foreboding. Where it has sinned against truth lies its weakness and the germ of its end. Falsehood cannot survive forever. Truth lives eternally.

27

CATHOLICISM AND THE ECUMENICAL MOVEMENT *

The Protestant Revolt introduced the principle of individual interpretation of Holy Scripture, which served to divide and subdivide the various Protestant religions into innumerable sects. As long as the Western

* Dunstan Donovan, S.A., "True Religious Unity," *The Lamp* (November, 1944). Reprinted by permission.

world remained Christian, most Protestants looked upon this individuation as a good thing, for they believed that it gave variety within the essential unity of Christendom.

In the face of secularized opposition to Christianity, however, division within the Christian ranks seemed scandalous to many Protestant leaders. Many of them believed that the various Christian groups could unite in a loose federation to form a common front against forces inimical to religion, such as Communism or Nazism. Others thought it possible to effect true religious union by reducing the creed of each group to the least common denominator of them all, and by allowing considerable freedom of cult and ritual within the union. This drive toward unity among Christian religions is known in the twentieth century as the ecumenical movement.

Catholic participation in the ecumenical movement has been solicited by Protestant leaders from time to time. The pope has shown himself sympathetic to the movement, for he knows that there should be one flock and one shepherd, but he has consistently indicated that the ecumenical movement can be entertained by the Catholic Church only on its own terms. Union to the Church means a returning of the "lost brethren," not a compromise in creed, code, and cult, for such compromise says in effect that one religion is as good as another, that union is for political rather than metaphysical and theological reasons. The pope has, nevertheless, shown his willingness to make every concession possible to bring Protestants back to the Church, as has been indicated with German Lutherans and Anglicans.

In the following selection Father Donovan discusses the origin of the ecumenical movement among English Protestants and analyzes the position the Catholic Church must take on it—a sympathetic position, but a firm stand against compromising the deposit of truth with which she is entrusted or denying her unique position as the Church that was founded by Christ, Who is God.

THE GROWING popularity among bodies separated from the Catholic Church of the prayer period in January known as the Church Unity Octave can be readily understood by reason of the circumstances under which the Octave was inaugurated.

When the inspiration to set apart a week or more to be devoted to special prayer for the uniting of all Christian believers into one visible flock first came to Father Paul James Francis, S. A., late in 1907, his status was that of a superior of a group of religious men and women in the

Episcopal Church, known as the Society of the Atonement. When the idea crystallized and the eight days were chosen that extended from the Feast of St. Peter's Chair at Rome to the Feast of the Conversion of St. Paul, January 18 to 25, Father Paul's chief associate in promoting the observance of the Octave was the Rev. Spencer Jones, a clergyman of the Church of England. It is because of its Anglican origin that the Octave today still has the allegiance of many non-Catholics, particularly in England.

For the past four years, the eight-day period has also been recommended to the attention of the constituent bodies of the World Conference on Faith and Order as a time for special prayer for Christian Unity. As the churches represented in this world-wide association are for the most part of the Evangelical school, any general adoption of the Octave period on their part would seem a rather startling departure to Catholics. However, reports from various centers stress one important fact—that there are staunch Protestants in various places who are offering their prayerful supplications during the Church Unity Octave for Christian Unity.

It is consoling to note the general realization of the unfortunate divisions among Christians manifested so vividly in our day. Very few denominational conventions among Protestant bodies fail to go on record as deploring the existence of numerous sects and divisions among those who lay claim to the title of "Christian." Actual efforts to heal the breaches that divide one kind of Protestant from another are numerous in our time—witness the much-publicized overtures between the Presbyterian and Protestant Episcopal Churches in the United States which attracted so much attention in 1943, the final settlement of which was postponed by one of the interested parties.

For Catholics, it is significant that their separated brethren now realize, as never before, that the spectacle of disunited Christendom is of itself incompatible with Christ's Will for His followers—"that they be *one*," even as He and the Father are one. Time was when Protestant leaders as notable as Henry Ward Beecher looked to the multiplicity of Christian bodies as a sign of the wonderful variations possible on the original Christian ideal of belief. That day has passed, and Protestants in general are concerned today with efforts to merge and to eliminate the scandal of a disrupted Christian world. The change in outlook was well expressed by a world-famous exponent of prayer and work for Christian Unity, Dr. Leonard Hodgson, Regius Professor of Moral Theology at Oxford, in a sermon delivered in New York's Cathedral of Saint John the Divine in 1943: "For 400 years after the Reformation, the various denominations took no interest in each other but the past fifty years have brought us ever closer. I believe historians of the future will regard the Church Unity Movement as the most important aspect of present-day church history."

This same Canon Hodgson has been instrumental in bringing the

Church Unity Octave period to the attention of non-Catholics in Europe and America, as a time for revivifying prayer that the Holy Spirit will make all men conscious of the perils of division and draw them ever closer, so that one day there might be one Christian Church as Our Saviour intended. Though Canon Hodgson is an Anglican, his work on the Executive Committee of the World Conference on Faith and Order has won for him the respect and admiration of religious leaders of all the Reformed groups. Insofar as this zeal for the fulfillment of Christ's prayer has within a short time been rewarded by humble acknowledgment of their common short-comings on the part of Protestant Christians of all shades of belief, Dr. Hodgson deserves the respect and thanks of Catholics. Awarness of the essential wrongness of divisions among Christians was for many centuries the preoccupation of Catholics; now those outside the Fold of Peter are showing their deep concern.

Leaders of eminence among our separated brethern have put proper emphasis on prayer as the first and most important means of healing the divisions that now exist, in accordance with Canon Hodgson's eloquent pleas. Many of them have found the Octave period an ideal time for concentration on such prayer. As a consequence when, from January 18 to 25 each year, Catholics pray for the submission of all men to the authority of Christ's Vicar, there are many others who pray for true religious unity, expressing confidence that the Holy Spirit will point out for them the road that must be followed to attain it.

We who have been blessed by the fullness of the faith, resting our assurance in the teachings of an infallible Church founded by Jesus Christ on His Apostles, and in a special way upon Peter, whom He designated Head of the Church, must be charitable enough to concede that what our non-Catholic brethren appeal for in prayer is *true* unity, and not a federation of sects differing in belief but having a common purpose. Pan-Protestantism, or the fusion of various groups of non-Catholics no matter on how great a scale, would not be an answer to Our Savior's prayer. Even if the venerable Churches of the East, which retain so much of Catholic ritual and teachings, could be persuaded to amalgamate with the reformed bodies (and to many the possibility is as remote as that of the Catholic Church making concessions in matters of faith), the resultant product would be a body antagonistic to the Body of Christ. Unless Protestant leaders who ask for prayers for Christian Unity mean true unity, and not the formation of a mighty rival Christian Church, their efforts will be in vain. God is not going to bless movements that are intended to hamper the purpose of His One True Church.

In spite of the fact that they realized full well that Rome showed no tendency to compromise, the original founders of the World Conference did not neglect to invite Pope Pius X to its opening sessions in 1910, a gesture that indicated graphically the desire of its founders to work for true unity. The Pope, of course, could not accept, but indicated his willingness to provide the meeting with explanations of any of the

Church's teachings about which questions might come up. Behind the Pope's refusal lay his loyalty to the basic truth of Catholicism, that it alone is the Church of Christ and that it cannot consult with man-made churches on matters of faith, lest such a proceeding indicate a denial of her stand. Nevertheless, in 1927, the same group of non-Catholic leaders very courteously invited Pope Pius XI to Lausanne to attend a meeting of world-wide religious leaders, among them even representatives of the historic Orthodox churches. His Holiness issued an encyclical letter to the world to reassert the position of Catholics in reference to such conferences, lest some might be led astray in their happiness at seeing non-Catholics seriously concerned about the need for Christian Unity. As Vicar of Christ and spiritual Father of all Christians, the Pope spoke with authority. All Catholics, particularly those concerned with movements like the Church Unity Octave, attended to his voice.

After reviewing with sympathy and understanding both the aspirations and the methods which arouse non-Catholics enthusiasm regarding ways and means to achieve the desired unity among Christians, His Holiness set forth very clearly the reason why the Catholic Church cannot participate in such assemblies:

> The truth is that Christ founded His Church as a perfect Society, of its nature external and perceptible to the senses, which in the future should carry on the work of the salvation of mankind under one Head, with a living teaching authority, administering the sacraments which are the sources of heavenly grace. Wherefore He likened the Church to a kingdom (Matt. 13), to a house (cf. Matt. 16:18), to a sheepfold (John 10:16), and to a flock (John 21: 15-17). The Church thus wondrously united could not cease to exist with the death of its Founder and of the Apostles, the pioneers of its propagation; for its mission was to lead all men to salvation, without distinction of time or place: "Going therefore, teach ye all nations" (Matt. 28:19). Nor could the Church ever lack the effective strength necessary for the continued acomplishment of its task, since Christ Himself is perpetually present with it, according to His promise: "Behold I am with you all days, even to the consummation of the world" (Matt. 28: 20). Hence not only must the Church exist today and continue always to exist, but it must ever be exactly the same as it was in the days of the Apostles. Otherwise we must say—which God forbid—that Christ has failed in His purpose, or that He erred when He asserted of His Church that the gates of hell should never prevail against it (Matt. 16:18).

There being but one divinely-founded Church, that Church cannot even by silence give rise to the speculation that other bodies may be equal to her. For those who want true union, the Pope goes on to say:

> There is but one way in which the unity of Christians may be fostered, and that is by furthering the return to the One True Church of Christ of those who are separated from it; for from one true Church they have in the past fallen away. The One Church of Christ is visible to all, and will remain, according to the Will of its Author, exactly the same as He instituted it.

The Church Unity Octave began at Graymoor in 1908 on the firm dogmatic conviction that the Apostolic See of Peter was the only possible center to which Christians could look for any true unity. The founder of the Octave never swerved from emphasis on the dogmatic basis of the Octave prayer—belief in the authority of the Holy See as the guardian of the total deposit of Christian faith, even when other Catholic priests pleaded for a "liberalization" of the daily intentions of the Church Unity Octave that more and more non-Catholics might join in them without prejudice to their convictions.

Pope Benedict XV, when giving his apostolic blessing to the Church Unity Octave, prefaced his statement with these significant words: "In every age it has been the concern of the Roman Pontiffs, Our Predecessors, and likewise it concerns us very much, that Christians who have unfortunately withdrawn from the Catholic religion should be recalled to it as to a forsaken mother," indicating that the prayers of the Octave were specifically concerned with a return to Catholic obedience on the part of those outside the Church. Catholics who keep the Octave know that they pray for a return to the One True Church of those now outside its fold that all may be united in unity with Christ.

Non-Catholics pray during the Octave period for the Holy Spirit to manifest His Will as to how unity may be achieved. Bereft of that security that Catholics enjoy through God's grace, and beset by the many prejudices of long separation, they cannot clearly see the way. The very thought of submission to the Papacy is obnoxious to most of them, weighted down as are their notions of it with false fears and the cultural separation of centuries. But if they pray with hearts full of zeal for the coming of Christ's kingdom on earth, their prayers are going to be answered. Pope Pius XII, whose concern for men and women of every nation and every creed has won new respect for his office (witness the current non-Catholic indignation at the crude and violent attacks against his integrity), suggests in the encyclical, *Mystici Corporis,* that they look with objectivity on the fervent appeal of the Church for their early return:

> From a heart overflowing with love, We ask each and every one of them to be quick and ready to follow the interior grace, and to look to withdrawing from that state in which they cannot be sure of their salvation. For even though unsuspectingly they are related to the Mystical Body of the Redeemer in desire and resolution, they still remain deprived of so many precious gifts and helps from heaven, which one can enjoy only in the Catholic Church. May they then enter into Catholic unity, and united with us in the organic oneness of the Body of Jesus Christ may they hasten to the one Head in the society of glorious love. With persevering prayer to the Spirit of love and truth We wait for them with open arms to return not to a stranger's house, but to their Father's house.

In conformity with the plea of the Holy Father, Catholics should look forward to the coming Church Unity Octave with hearts full of confidence that God's gifts will be revealed in greater measure to those now outside the Fold. In all charity and brotherly affection, Catholics may well pray that those who pray for *true* Christian Unity will be blessed with the grace to see that such unity can only be achieved by submission, singly or in groups, to Christ's Vicar on earth. His is the only earthly center of an undivided Church, and He is in truth the Rock to whom Christ entrusted the Keys of His authority, to the end "that all might be one" in the fullness of Faith and Unity.

28

THE CHURCH OF SILENCE:
A. RELIGION BEHIND THE IRON CURTAIN *

The persecution of the Church behind the Iron Curtain surpasses any previous persecution in history. Behind the Iron Curtain, in the "Church of Silence," are an estimated 53 million Catholics. They are subjected to a new and more diabolical kind of persecution than that of Nero or Diocletian, for more insidious methods of torture have been devised in the twentieth century and means have been devised to break people in spirit as well as in body.

The persecution behind the Iron Curtain does not seek to destroy the Church as an institution. It tries, instead, to pervert it into an instrument to promote the cause of the Communist states under Soviet domination. Its methods are to break the wills of the bishops and priests and to dominate the minds of the laity through a subservient, broken clergy. How successful this psychological warfare has been is a disputed matter, but there is no doubt that it has succeeded in many individual cases.

The following two selections describe briefly the sufferings of the "Church of Silence" and explain what has been accomplished by the methodological persecution behind the Iron Curtain. In the first selection, Father Duff describes the general tactics employed against the Church in various countries under Soviet domination. In the second selection, an American reporter who was allowed to witness part of the trial of Cardinal Mindszenty tells the reader of his impressions and explains how an unusually strong man appeared broken in mind and in body by the tortures to which he had been subjected.

* Edward Duff, S.J., "Assault on God in Eastern Europe," *Catholic Mind* (January, 1950), pp. 33-37. Reprinted by permission.

THIS evening I am asked to describe to you in 15 minutes "the assault on God in Eastern Europe" so far as the regilious persecution in those unhappy lands affects Catholics. I am fully mindful, while attempting this summary, that Catholics have no exclusive franchise on the malevolent attention of the Soviet atheists. As a journalist, I am aware in pretty good detail of the facts Mr. Dulles and Mr. Rosenberg have presented to you regarding the persecution of Protestants and Jews. As an Associate Editor of *America*—and as a Catholic priest—it has been my business to report those facts and call for common action of religious-minded people so that the world community may be alerted to its peril and its obligations.

For the crucial struggle of our century is between two opposed explanations of the nature and destiny of man. In an encyclical letter, dated March 19, 1947, Pius XII declared that "for the first time in history we are witnessing a struggle, cold-blooded in purpose and mapped out to the last detail, between man and 'all that is called God.' Communism is by its nature anti-religious." It is no private feud, then, between some politicians in the Kremlin and some ecclesiastics in the Vatican that accounts for the essential antagonism between Communism and religion.

All assertions of human dignity derived from God, of goals for living not assigned by the state, are blasphemies that Communism must crush; for Marxism is a rampant religion of naked power demanding total subjection to its exclusively temporal ends. Baltic Lutheranism, Balkan Judaism, Turkistan Moslemism, Chinese Buddhism—as well as Eastern European Catholicism—are heresies that must be rooted out.

You will be disappointed tonight if you expect me to supply the lurid detail of Communist tortures of Catholics. I could tell of incidents like the bayoneting of Bishop Apor of Gyoer, who tried with arms outstretched to prevent soldiers from seizing the women of the town who had taken refuge in the cellar of his palace. Or of crucifixion of three Lithuanian priests, Fathers Petrika, Dabrila and Balsys, which was only an incident in the deportation of the Balts, 6,000 of whom died on the road between Minsk and Mohilov on a forced march that saved the Soviets the costs of rail transport. Crucifixion does, indeed, manifest a violent and specific hatred for Christianity.

But violence is not necessarily the preferred weapon of Communism. It is more important for us tonight to recognize the strategy behind the attack on religion than to spend our time counting corpses or listing the location of concentration camps.

The strategy calls for infiltration of religious organizations and the control of churches for the political purposes of Russia. Vishinsky makes no bones about it. Soviet courts, he blandly asserts, are instruments of the regime. If courts, so, too, the churches. Premier Peter Groza of Rumania is equally frank: "The (Orthodox) Church is a part of the state itself, keeping pace with the spirit of the times." To make religion serve the Party, with whatever means are necessary, is the end always in view.

In the Ukraine it will take the form of a persecution of Neronian proportions, anschlussing the Uniate Church of 5 million members into the docile Religious Cominform, that is, Kremlin-controlled Orthodoxy. Seven bishops and 2,700 priests of the Ukraine Uniate Church are in the hands of the Bolsheviks. Relief packages sent to the Metropolitan Josef Slipy in the concentration camp of Voluka, north of the Arctic Circle, were returned with the ominous notation "address unknown."

Just a year ago the same tactic was employed in Rumania. Police officials demanded that the Ruthenian Uniate priests petition for absorption into Anna Pauker's State Church. Thirty-eight out of a total of 2,645 priests agreed at a conference at Cluj on October 21 last year. It was enough. The merger was imposed, the five bishops were arrested and jailed, along with 600 of their priests (500 more are in the hills, we know), 1,726 churches and monasteries were seized by the government. "Religious freedom" is unctuously promised by the Rumanian Government—with these exceptions! A religious body requires state approval to exist and function. It requires state approval to have bishops allowed on a quota system. It requires state approval for congresses. The Minister of Religion may suspend any of its decisions, instructions or ordinances. It must not communicate with foreign bodies except through the Ministry of Foreign Affairs. It may not have any jurisdictional head outside Rumania.

Bulgaria's legislation on religion of February 17, 1949 is similarly cute. Article 32 reads: "All Church statutes, laws and regulations must be approved by the Minister of Cults who has the right to demand their amendment or withdrawal." Note the shrewdness of Article 22:

> No religious denomination or religious organization may maintain hospitals, welfare centers, kindergartens or similar institutions. Such institutions belonging to a Church when this law takes effect become State property.

Smothering the social role of religion is a universal strategy of the Communists. Welfare work—except the more unglamorous kind, like caring for the insane—is taken over by the state. That was done last spring in Czechoslovakia and is going on today in Poland.

On August 5, 1949, the Polish Government published an edict under the hypocritical title: "In defense of freedom of conscience and religion"—warning the clergy that they are legally liable to the death penalty if they implement the excommunication of Communists, if they teach that it is impossible to be a Catholic and a Communist, if they refuse to include Communists among those eligible for the sacraments of the Church. The regime sees to it that information is restricted. The last religious printing establishment in Poland was closed in June, on government orders, the presses dismantled and carried away. The publication of the

Warsaw Archdiocese—*Tygodnik Warszawski*—was closed down and its editor jailed. Arrests are multiplying for reading pastoral letters from the pulpit. Religious orders were told to register with the Government and apply for license to continue; for religious associations are now classed with political organizations as needing authorization for their existence as well as for meetings and processions.

Similarly in Czechoslovakia Alexei Cepicka, Minister of Justice, has declared illegal "all pastoral letters, circulars, instructions, orders and all other proclamations" unless cleared by the Ministry of Information. Also declared illegal are "all meetings and consultations of the clergy held without Government permit to be sought three days in advance." On November 1 a law went into effect in Czechoslovakia giving the Government control over the property, personnel, finances and administration of the Church. Appointments to any clerical position may be made only with the consent of the Government and from the list of those certified as "politically reliable." Seminary training is supervised according to the directive of Minister of Schools, Zdenek Nejedly, who declares that "every subject must follow the theory of Marx-Leninism and it must be the main subject taught in the schools." "Right," as Dr. Cepicka said at a lawyers' meeting in Prague last month, "is nothing but the will of the ruling class incorporated into law."

The "ruling class" in Yugoslavia is Communist. It is morally right, then, under the Cepicka definition, to contrive pretexts to close churches. The Jesuits in Ljubljana—the same kind of Jesuits who have run Georgetown University for 150 years—had their property taken from them as part of the sentence when five of them were tried for "political activity," which was legally defined as "collaboration with the Vatican." Priests are tolerated but must live where the Ministry of Interior gives permission. Children may receive religious instruction but only from Government-licensed, "politically-reliable" priests. Voluntary collections for the support of the clergy, without police permit, are forbidden.

The "ruling class" in Hungary is Matyas Rakosi and his fellow Moscow agents. It being their will, it is "right"—in Cepicka terms—to dissolve 4,000 Catholic organizations in Hungary, from old ladies' homes, schools and novitiates down to parish societies. It was financially profitable, too.

But the plan to poison minds is better illustrated by suppression of the religious press and the seizure, for instance, of the Stephaneum, the publishing house that had, in addition to its printing establishment, five book-stores. The printing board has decided against new impressions of traditional Catholic titles. Even a re-issue of the catechism was held up. A revised version offered by Bishop Hamas proved unsatisfactory. Economic pressure is used universally behind the iron curtain to force submission. The thousands of teaching nuns driven out of the nationalized schools in Hungary are forbidden to give private tutoring. The State Employment Agency refused to license them, even for work as domestics.

Their pathetic plight resembles that of the 1,400 Rumanian nuns ousted from their educational and charitable work a few months back.

The story of the "assault on God" is a story also of terror, as in Lithuania, where 2½ million Catholics had 1,600 priests serving under 11 bishops to minister to them. Ten of the 11 bishops and very nearly half of the priests have been killed or deported. It is a story of subversion, of the training of bogus priests in fake seminaries to send among the people to confuse them. It is a story of perverting of young minds. As an example, last summer little tots of five and six returned from Government-sponsored vacations at Lake Balaton in Hungary with a new grace before meals memorized:

> In the name of the Father and of the Son and of the Holy Ghost. The fly is a dangerous bug. It has many germs on its wings. If I don't kill flies and keep clean, I will get sick. In the name of the Father and of the Son and of the Holy Ghost.

It is the story of the "domestication" of the churches for political purposes. For the churches in Eastern Europe are not political enough to suit the Communist governments, which want compliant religious organizations ready to make public statements in support of government policy whenever the government needs them. It is a story that should have its interest for the people and the politicians of the free West. For as Cardinal Mindszenty declared to the St. Stephen Society of Budapest on November 15, 1946:

> The rights of men and of the Church are generally violated simultaneously. The Church has her own aims which are not part of the aims of the State. Neither the Church nor the State is directly subordinate to one another. The Church defends the rights and liberties of the State because the name of God and the moral order are the chief guarantees of the State.

If the political doctrine of a Catholic Cardinal is suspect, we might keep in mind that President Roosevelt declared in his Message to Congress on January 4, 1939, that religion is the source of democracy and international good faith. President Truman has said the same thing.

B. THE MINDSZENTY TRIAL *

A YEAR ago today, I saw brought to trial a brave man who acted like a coward. I saw a People's Court from which the people were barred. I saw an ex-Nazi sitting as a Communist chief judge. I saw a defense attorney out-prosecute a prosecutor.

On February 4, 1949, second day of the trial, I was admitted to a dimly-lit courtroom in Budapest, where Joseph Cardinal Mindszenty and six

* Gabriel Pressman, "The Mindszenty Trial," *New York World-Telegram and Sun*, (February 4, 1950). Reprinted by permission.

co-defendants sat before the bar of Communist justice. Edward Korry of the United Press and I were the only American correspondents representing American publications admitted to the trial.

There was one catch: I could not choose an interpreter, I was told by Ivan Boldizar, pudgy, nervous-eyed Government press chief. The Government would supply a bright, young Communist to translate for me.

The courtroom was two flights up—with six checkpoints of submachine gunners from the door of the dirty, red-brick courthouse on Marko St. to the door of the trial room itself.

It was a small, dark room. Not much light pierced the high windows. On the dais sat the People's Court President and four associate judges. On the first bench beneath were the seven defendants, charged with a Royalist conspiracy to overthrow the Government.

Their faces were drawn. Their attitudes ranged from indifference to resignation. Alongside each sat a militiaman. Throughout the courtroom, militiamen stood or sat among the carefully screened spectators. Only seven relatives of defendants were present.

Through an American's eyes, it was a trial of paradoxes. There was Vilmos Olti, before and during the war one of Hungary's foremost Nazis, now playing Communist chief judge.

Olti fired an endless stream of questions at the defendants, methodically building up the case against them with "yes" and "no" answers. He allowed seven prosecution witnesses, no defense witnesses. As he carried the case through in a lightning three days, the hard-faced prosecutor-juror seldom looked up from the papers he read.

The "trial" seemed a little academic. The defendants had confessed everything days before at the headquarters of the dread secret police, 60 Andrassy St. And the Government had the confessions bound neatly into a "yellow book" for the convenience of Red propagandists.

The defendants vied constantly to confess. Once it was even too much for the court. The Cardinal tried to read a repudiation of his pre-arrest warning against any future "confession," but Olti silenced him: "You don't want to read that now." So the Cardinal sat down and read it when directed.

Young Andreas Zakar, the Cardinal's secretary, was once his stubborn, good right arm. Now he stood, weak and timid, most pathetically trying to follow wherever Olti led. And the judge coached him benignly, like a teacher with a backward child.

Zakar used the word "democratic" in the Western sense. "Liberal, bourgeois democratic or people's democratic?" Olti demanded.

Zakar (searchingly): "Er . . . liberal."

Olti (with fatherly severity): "That means against progress."

Zakar: "Yes, sir."

The Cardinal, an excellent orator before his arrest, spoke monotonously, reading from prepared papers. Under prodding from the rasp-voiced director, the Cardinal said: "I'm very sorry" about everything—the book he had written, letters, money manipulations.

The script called for a Mindszenty of repudiation, confession and apology. And this, the Communists wanted the world to believe, was the same man who in a last interview said staunchly:

> I will never take back anything I have said against the Communist government. . . . Hungary has degenerated into a gigantic chamber of horrors, a den of robbers and thieves.

Crudest of the crudities was the attitude of the so-called defense attorneys. They spent most of the trial twiddling their mustaches or gazing into space. I didn't see them take a single note, or consult each other once.

Kalman Kiczko, a Communist of thirty years' standing, "defended" the Cardinal. Joseph Groh, prominent Catholic lawyer, had been jailed for offering to serve.

Kiczko pleaded well . . . for Kiczko. Most of his final speech told how much he, Kiczko, loved the People's Democracy.

Then, removing his spectacles, he denounced Western newspapers: "The foreign press has written numerous calumnies against Hungary." He disputed that the trial was unfair: "Nobody either at home or abroad can accuse us of restricting freedom." He cringingly thanked the prosecution for bringing up the charges against his client. And, when he sat down, even Olti smiled.

A year has passed and the world still wonders what made the defendants act as they did. Was the Cardinal tortured, drugged or hypnotized?

Pro-Communist correspondents reported the Cardinal seemed perfectly normal in every respect. It was hard to agree when you saw a man weak and cowardly whose actions for four years had spoken strength and courage.

Was he in his right mind when he offered to resign if the charges against him were dropped? Only the Pope could accept such a resignation. Before his arrest, he could deliver a perfect sermon from a few notes. At the trial he forgot frequently and—the interpreters did not hide it—had to be prodded by the court.

The key to what happened is, of course, the 38 days the Cardinal spent with the secret police before the trial. I did not speak to the Cardinal—the Government forbade it—but I have spoken to others educated to confess at 60 Andrassy St. The Communists have a standard curriculum: questioning for days on end under bright lights standing with arms overhead until faint, repeated blows with blunt instruments on the kidney, electric-shock treatments.

It is possible that all the standard methods and perhaps more were used on the defendants. Perhaps Zakar was tortured to arouse the

Cardinal's pity. Zakar's white face and trembling impatience to please marked him a likely graduate of the torture chamber.

Not all the clues were outside the court. In the Cardinal's final speech, he spoke with some feeling for the first time:

> I stand here with half a century of basic principles . . . principles that guide us as railway tracks guide trains. . . . I would not and am not an enemy of the Hungarian people . . . worker or peasant.

Perhaps the Cardinal here revealed his true thoughts—that he believed as he always did, that he still loved the people but not the Communist Government.

Significantly, the Hungarian press and radio did not carry the statement. For weeks before the trial, these Government-controlled media trumpeted the Cardinal's guilt. "A pitiable worm, a scared scoundrel, a blood-thirsty beast of prey," they called him.

Meanwhile, the Government had nightly press briefings to tell correspondents what to write. Boldizar, the press czar, said: "Tell your readers that the Cardinal is not a brave hero of freedom but a weakling and a coward." The second night Mr. Korry and I refused to sign a Communist-sponsored resolution, signed by the others, affirming there was no censorship and translations were accurate.

A Hungarian journalist secretly applauded our stand: "There are two kinds of censorship: one where the censor's pencil scratches out the words, the other where the fear in your heart scratches them out." He told me how every Hungarian-speaking person in that courtroom had been intimidated.

After my refusal to sign, the Government pretended I did not exist, withdrew even its slanted help. I had to scrape together at least the official version of what was happening—and that in itself was damning enough.

Time will never dim that last, sad scene of February 8. The defendants stood for more than an hour while Olti issued an anti-Western political tirade and their sentences.

The Cardinal's head was slightly bowed, his hands clasped before him. As he was sentenced to life imprisonment, his cheek twitched. Princess Esterhazy knelt reverently in prayer. A Government camera's flashbulb exploded.

There was a weird moment when Laszlo Toth, almost deaf Catholic editor, stepped forward to hear the unspeakable Olti shout his fate—ten years.

Then it was over. The heavily guarded defendants filed out. In the corridor I stopped gray-haired Hildegarde Zakar, the defendant's sister. Glancing nervously at detectives, her eyes moist, she said in French: "My brother is a good boy. He has always served God. If God wills it, then this must be."

The reaction of the people in the streets and coffee houses was bitter.

Through a Hungarian-speaking American, they told me: "They were afraid to give him the death penalty because they know his hold on the people is too great."

The Cardinal, says the Hungarian underground, languishes today in Gyujtofoghaz jail, ten miles north of Budapest.

Whatever happens, Cardinal Mindszenty's place in history is assured. A Hungarian student friend expressed it well that last night in Budapest as we strolled along the banks of the Danube. I had just come from a final press conference at which Boldizar said: "The trial is over, but the trial of you correspondents has just begun. You must tell the world the truth about this traitor."

My friend looked up at the sky. "You know, for once Boldizar is right," he said. "This was more than the trial of Cardinal Mindszenty. In the court of world public opinion, a Cardinal has convicted his judges and Communism stands condemned."

29

ARNOLD J. TOYNBEE'S *A STUDY OF HISTORY* *

Thinking people in the Western world have always been interested in the meaning of history or, as it is frequently called, the philosophy of history. To the ancients history had no meaning but that of endless repetition. But with the coming of Christ history took on a new meaning. Revelation showed the Christian that everything before Christ led to His coming, and since His time history is concerned with the extension of His redemption to all peoples. For the Christian, then, history has a beginning and an end. Its essence is the story of mankind's dialogue with God; its drama is man's relations with his Creator and with his fellow creatures, his meeting the challenges presented to him by his Creator, and his success or failure in realizing the goal set for him.

The Christian view of history persisted into modern times. Gradually it came to be secularized in modern history, as Providence was made subject to the "laws of history," as the beginning of history was placed in some vague, remote past, and the end of history was made a terrestial paradise reached through the laws of inevitable Progress. Such a view of history was deistic or agnostic in that it pushed God out of history and left man's destiny entirely up to man. This Progress view of history

* Thomas P. Neill, "The Complete Toynbee: A Modest Appraisal," *The Historical Bulletin, XXXIV* (March, 1956), 131-167. Reprinted by permission.

captured men's minds in the eighteenth century and held sway well into the nineteenth. Meanwhile, however, Karl Marx propounded a dialectical, materialistic view of history which resolved all human affairs ultimately into production-relations. And still a third view of history, propounded in this century, was a new version of an ancient cyclical view that history endlessly repeats itself in cyclical fashion and that human striving is all in vain.

To counteract these un-Christian views of history Arnold Toynbee wrote his ten-volume Study of History, *which brings God back into human history, sees man as possessed of free will, intelligence, and an immortal soul. Toynbee's is the first significant philosophy of history since Bishop Bossuet's in the seventeenth century to move back toward the Christian view of God and man's relation to Him. It cannot be called a truly Christian view of history without important qualifications, but it is impregnated with Christian elements and it is a healthy reaction to the Progress, the Marxian, and the Spenglerian philosophies of history.*

The last four volumes of Arnold J. Toynbee's *A Study of History* were published in October, 1954, and in the intervening eighteen months they have been submitted to the examination and appraisal of many capable critics. The reaction of these critics will some day constitute an interesting page in the book of Western historiography, for they agree but little among themselves in their praise and blame of Mr. Toynbee. On one thing they are agreed: Toynbee's ten-volume *Study* is a massive and impressive work. The publisher claims that it contains over three million words on 6,290 pages; it has about 19,000 footnotes; and the indexes total 332 pages with about 19,000 main entries. This is indeed a tremendous work for one man to accomplish, the most impressive work of our generation, and one which will take an important place in the history of English letters.

On this the critics agree. But they agree on little else. Mr. Toynbee has been accused of writing bad history, of not writing history at all, of seeking refuge in "religious mysticism," of trying to be a prophet, of writing theological poetry in prose, of imposing ill-conceived laws on the past, of being a positivist, a pseudo-scientist, a determinist, a poet relying on intuition—and of being and doing many other things. Obviously, even in ten volumes, Mr. Toynbee cannot be and do all these things; it is equally obvious that some of the criticisms negate others. But there is a significance in the fact that intelligent men—at least some of whom have read the ten volumes they criticize—can form such disparate estimates of Toynbee's intent and purpose, of his methodology, and of his success in accomplishing what he set out to do.

A Study of History is an important work. The first six volumes have already made an impact on historical thinking; certain "laws" educed in these volumes are now common coin among literate, thinking men, such as the "law" of challenge-and-response, and that of withdrawal-and-return. Whether one accepts them or not, he must understand what they mean. The last four volumes will have a similar importance, for in them Toynbee studies universal states and universal religions, as well as the contacts between civilizations and the prospects of the West. But the lasting importance of *A Study of History,* we believe, will lie in the impact it makes as a whole. For beneath the long excursions (sometimes of several hundred pages) into the curiosities of history, lies a plan and a scheme of development to which the author remains faithful from beginning to end. Examination of the complete Toynbee, in the light of his critics, therefore seems in order at this time.

A great deal of confusion is saved if we remember at the outset that Toynbee is not trying to write history. He is writing *about* history—and this is a very different thing. Since Toynbee's answer to two of his critics in the *Journal of the History of Ideas* last year, there can be no doubt about this point, made in the *Historical Bulletin* in 1948. Pieter Geyl, one of Toynbee's harshest and most consistent critics, and Edward Fiess reviewed the last four volumes under the respective titles of "Toynbee the Prophet" and "Toynbee as Poet." In a brief answer to these critics, Toynbee explained: "I am trying to use the knowledge of history as a telescope-lens for taking a look at the universe as a whole." He explained that a book about Shakespeare is not to be judged as a book by Shakespeare, and similarly "when one is studying history, one is examining history, not narrating it."

A Study of History is an inquiry into history with the purpose of throwing additional light on the meaning of man's existence and giving a fuller explanation of the purpose of his earthly sojourn with its trials and its fleeting pleasures. Put in another way, this is a "philosophy of history" that seeks to justify the ways of God to man. Since the development of modern critical history in the nineteenth century, practitioners of the craft have generally looked on "philosophies of history" with suspicion and hostility. Historians feel that such works attempt too much, are not subject to scientific verification, are highly subjective, and push historical data around to suit the investigator's purpose. Toynbee therefore had to launch his venture in the face of a traditional hostility on the part of historians. The professional journals did not bother reviewing his first three volumes when they appeared in 1934, nor was much attention paid to the next three when they were published in 1939. Somervell's condensation in 1947 appeared at a time, after the Second World War and two atom bombs, when literate people were ready to read anything that seemed to reveal the meaning of history and shed light on our future prospects. Everyone was talking about Toynbee, who was a professional historian and who had written *A Study of History,* so historians could not very well ignore him any longer. But by reason of their training they were predisposed to give Toynbee's ambitious *Study* hostile treatment.

Philosophers in the Christian tradition were ready to be tolerant of such a *Study,* but their tradition was long set against taking such a work seriously. It might be good reading, but it can hardly be a field of philosophy. Jacques Maritain expressed the traditional feeling toward any proposed "philosophy of history" in these words:

> The Angels who see all the happenings of the universe in the creative ideas, know the philosophy of history; philosophers cannot know it. . . . And as to detecting the causes and supreme laws working through the stream of incident, to do that we should need to share the counsel of the supreme Fashioner, or be directly enlightened by Him. That is why it is properly a prophetic work to deliver to men the philosophy of their history.

Historical events and the demands of men forced at least some philosophers to investigate again whether a philosophy of history is possible and—if it is—whether it is deserving of the time and effort one would have to give to it. At the risk of oversimplifying the difficulties involved in the problem, let us state the attitude of philosophers in the Christian tradition toward a philosophy of history when Toynbee's final volumes appeared in 1954: 1) the fact that we do not know all the happenings of the universe, past and future, does not preclude formulating a philosophy of history; 2) an adequate philosophy of history demands a certain knowledge of the end of history as well as the past, for without such knowledge it is impossible to arrive at any ultimate concepts about the meaning of history; 3) revelation is an historical fact, and in revelation man has learned a number of truths about the future; 4) a theology of history therefore seems a more proper and more feasible study than a philosophy of history; 5) history is concerned with free actions, and is therefore full of contingencies; 6) but these are not mutually exclusive subjects, and there is no essential reason why philosophers in the Christian tradition cannot follow their traditional practice of using the data of revelation to think philosophically about history. Put even more briefly, the *post Christum* philosopher can inquire philosophically into the meaning of history if he includes the data of revelation in his inquiry. It is an arduous and a delicate task, and whether it is deserving of cultivation as a field of philosophy remains an open question with most philosophers today.*

A third group of scholars were prepared to receive Toynbee's *Study* more favorably than historians or philosophers—*if* his methodology and

* Late in 1957, when this book was being typeset, Jacques Maritain's lectures on *The Philosophy of History* were published. In these lectures Maritain holds that the philosophy of history is properly a part of moral philosophy, that it is the last branch of philosophy to be worked out systematically, and that he hopes his work is an introduction to the task facing Thomists in working this subject into the corpus of their philosophy.

his assumptions conformed to their standards. These were the sociologists. From the time of its birth as an independent subject, sociology has been concerned with "patterns of human behavior," the comparative study of civilizations, and similar areas of investigation that are component parts of what is generally understood today as a "philosophy of history." Sociologists were therefore prepared to consider Toynbee's massive *Study* seriously and to accept or respect it accordingly as it conformed to their methodology and assumptions.

In this setting Toynbee's *Study of History* made its appearance in three installments (an important point to keep in mind): the first three volumes in 1934, the next three in 1939, and the final four in 1954. A final evaluation of the work must take into consideration its place in the genre to which it belongs, for Toynbee's *Study* is the latest in a notable series of similar studies that trace their ancestry back to St. Augustine's *City of God* and run through Orosius' *Seven Books Against the Pagans,* Otto of Freising's *The Two Cities,* down to Bossuet's *Discourse on Universal History*. Its more immediate predecessors are Vico's *New Science,* Turgot's, Condorcet's, and Comte's theories of Progress, Herder's *Philosophy of History,* and more immediate yet, Hegel's *Lectures on the Philosophy of History*. And it follows closely in the wake of Marx's dialectical materialism, found in his various writings, and Oswald Spengler's deterministic *Decline of the West.*

When Toynbee planned his *Study,* Marx and Spengler were in command of the field, except in certain restricted circles in which the Christian theory of history still prevailed. It is chiefly against Marx and Spengler, then, that Toynbee planned and wrote his *Study,* but like Marx and Spengler he is heir to the tradition created by Augustine, Bosquet, Voltaire, Vico, Hegel and others, and he cannot entirely escape their influence. There are passages in his *Study* that are almost perfect duplications of passages in Vico, or Turgot, or Comte—which is not a surprising thing in that all are examining the same subject for substantially the same purpose, and all are in the same general tradition. Most important, however, Toynbee tries to do what the others attempted: from historical data to justify the ways of God to man; from the evidence of history to work out empirically a philosophy of history that will give men satisfactory answers to the ultimate questions of whence?, why?, whither? He is interested in the historian's proper question of how? only insofar as it brings him closer to answering the three basic questions. A just appraisal of Toynbee's *Study* therefore requires for its setting a brief survey of the great standard philosophies of history in Western thought before his own.

To the Ancients history was a meaningless repetition of temporal events. Birth, youth, maturity, decline, and death were the lot of all living things and all human institutions. The universe also moved in eternal cycles of endless repetitions. From the observation of nature and of man in ancient times, then, came the classical theory that history moves in endless and meaningless cycles. One cannot speak of a beginning or an end of history, nor of a final purpose or ultimate meaning. Such a view of history gave a decisive role to Fate, before which man is helpless, and it wrote of human endeavor as ultimately futile.

The cyclical view of history could not very well be held by anyone who accepted the Incarnation and Redemption as historical facts, for God's personal intervention in the continuum of time was a unique event that could never be repeated. Jewish and Christian teaching implied a straight-line or progressive view of history instead of the classical cycle. History came with the Christians to have a beginning, a progress, and an end, a purpose and an ultimate meaning revealed by God to man. The beginning is God's creative act; the end is mankind's union with Him at the end of time. History leads from the Fall to the Redemption, the central point of all history, and after the Redemption to the Kingdom of God.

This is the historico-theological framework within which Christian philosophies of history have been formulated. The first such formulation to take on classical proportions was Augustine's *City of God,* an apologetic work in which the Bishop of Hippo seeks to refute the pagan charges that Christianity was to blame for Rome's decline. In the course of refuting these charges Augustine rejects the cyclical view of history explicitly and propounds his own formulation of the Christian view. He considers the cyclical view abhorrent because it destroys the meaning of life and of history. He then tells of the beginning of history in God's creative act, the unique event of the Redemption, and the end of history, which is the Kingdom of God.

God is given a sovereign place as creator and providential master of all things, including time and history. God remains distinct from history; he is the Lord of History, and He controls it. From history we can discern some fragments of truth which God has seen fit to manifest to us. Augustine handles the perennial problems facing the Christian philosopher of history more deftly and more philosophically than did his successors. The problem of particularism and universalism, for example (are the great masses of persons made to the image of God to be eliminated from "universal" history because they are not Jews or Christians?), and the problems of progress are handled respectively by his *logos* doctrine and by his distinction between the City of God and the Earthly City.

Orosius was a younger contemporary whom Augustine prevailed upon to do a supplementary work to his own *City of God.* Orosius follows Augustine in describing history as a drama in which God is more than a spectator; in His Providence He is an actor on the stage of history. Orosius pays more attention to historical data than Augustine had done, and he gives Rome a definite historic mission in making ready the world for Christ.

> Neither is there any doubt [he tells us] that it was by the will of our Lord Jesus Christ . . . that Rome was brought to such heights of power since to her, in preference to all others, He chose to belong when He came, thereby making it certain that He was entitled to be called a Roman citizen.

Orosius is considerably more optimistic about the future than Augustine, for, without glossing over the evil in the world, he finds that times kept getting better, and that the Christian can expect them to become progressively better in the future.

Augustine and Orosius were widely influential throughout the Middle Ages, and it was not until the twelfth century that a work of comparable magnitude was written. Between 1143 and 1147 Otto of Freising wrote his *Two Cities* in imitation of Augustine and Orosius. Otto is not the great theologian and philosopher that Augustine was, but he is a considerably better historian. For him, the function of the historian is to discover and tell the truth. Otto therefore rejected Augustine's apologetic aim in favor of relating the story of universal history, but he took a much narrower view of "universal" history than had Augustine.

> The faithless city of unbelieving Jews and Gentiles still remains [he tells us] but, since nobler kingdoms have been won by our people, while these unbelieving Jews and Gentiles are insignificant not only in the sight of God but even in that of the world, hardly anything done by these unbelievers is found to be worthy of record or to be handed on to posterity.

Otto's stand on this point is typical of the Christian "parochialism" which Toynbee so strongly condemns—and which so many of his critics so obviously manifest. (Whether Christian "parochialism" is justifiable is another matter; here we only make the observation that it has been an authentic part of the Western Christian tradition since the Middle Ages.)

Dante produced a more sophisticated Christian philosophy of history in the later Middle Ages. In it he includes the usual Christian teaching on Creation, the Fall, the Redemption, and the Kingdom of God, which gave history the unity peculiar to Christian thought. But Dante goes farther and adds another note of unity within history itself by assigning all humanity the common purpose of human perfectibility in time.

> Upon all men whom a common humanity has lifted to the love of truth, and who have been enriched by the labors of the past, there rests, surely, this responsibility of so toiling for the future that posterity may be enriched by them. . . . The peculiar task of the entire human race is to realize the potency of the passive intellect; first through speculation, and then through action.

To achieve this development human beings need an ordered society so that they can live in justice and peace. This is the purpose of social and political institutions, which must ultimately culminate in one church and one state. The first factor in Dante's philosophy of history, then, is progress toward political unity and human perfectibility. The second is Providence, which Dante believes is evident historically in such instances as the *Pax Romana* at Christ's birth, or the coming of a St. Francis or a St. Dominic at a certain point in history. The third factor is man's freedom, and the fourth is the Fall, which makes necessary political and ecclesiastical institutions.

The final major formulation of a Christian philosophy of history is Bossuet's *Discourse on Universal History*. Like Augustine, Bossuet is an apologist seeking to justify the ways of God to the skeptics of his age. "The freethinkers," he tells us, "declare war on divine providence and they find no better argument against it than the distribution of good and evil which seems unjust and irrational since it does not discriminate between the good and the wicked." Bossuet proposes to answer these freethinkers by showing how God shines forth so luminously in history that only the willfully blind can fail to find Him, and how the Christian religion has continually progressed while a succession of worldly empires have risen and fallen on the stage of history. Bossuet actually hurt the Christian interpretation of history by trying to prove too much, for although he did not eliminate secondary causes he assigned to Providence an unnecessarily willful, interfering role in human history. His God, it could be said, was made too much to the image and likeness of Louis XIV.

These Christian philosophies of history all accept on faith the fact and the content of revelation, and they seek to explain history within its context. They are more deserving of the label "theology of history" than philosophy of history because they think theologically rather than philosophically on the data available to them from history. They all give Providence a role in history, account for evil with man's free will and his sinfulness, and see the central fact of all history as the Redemption. They divide history into two parts: the first preparing for the Incarnation, the second preparing for the Kingdom of God by extending the effects of the Redemption to all mankind. The "universal" histories written in this Christian tradition concentrate on the Jews and the Christians; other peoples are included only insofar as they have been instruments of Providence in shaping the destiny of the Jews and the Christians.

The first notable departure from this standard Christian philosophy of history was made by Giambattista Vico early in the eighteenth century. Vico wrote in a transitional age between the older Christian thought and the Enlightenment. His view of history stands midway between the Christian theology of history and the modern secularized philosophies of history. Vico accepts revelation and believes that every word of the Bible is inspired truth, but in formulating his philosophy of history he neglects the Bible for such pagan sources as Homer and the early myths. The *New Science* was a terrifically ambitious project, for Vico thought that he had discovered the secret scheme that underlies apparent confusion in history and that he could therefore subsume all knowledge into one discipline which would enable him to set forth *a priori* the future or the past history of any people.

A Platonist, Vico thought that the history of each nation is an exemplification of the ideal eternal history. Each nation therefore follows the same pattern of development throughout its life. So identical are the patterns that Vico believes he can establish an accurate chronology of any nation simply from knowing the status of its present culture. What Vico was actually doing was using the history of the Graeco-Roman world as the arche-type to which he tried to make all nations conform. There can be no room for the providential God of the Christians in such a theory of history. But Vico does not deny Providence. Instead he secularized it by making it work in a way that is "natural," "simple," and "easy." "Once these orders were established by divine providence," he says, "the course of the affairs of the nations had to be, must now be and will have to be such as our Science demonstrates, even if infinite worlds were produced from time to time through eternity."

A reading of the *New Science* shows Vico trying to hold incompatibles together in his system. He seems to accept a thoroughly deterministic theory of history, and still he believes in free will; he does not deny the God of the Christians, but he makes Him conform to the rigid pattern of history He created for all nations and Vico has laid bare. Vico's ambiguous position is well summed up by Thomas Berry in this way:

In his treatise Vico has neither denied nor transcended the view of history presented in the Christian religious tradition. Indeed he passed to a lower realm of thought. The transcendent has given way to the imminent, the supernatural to the natural, and, in a most impressive way, simplicity has given way to multiplicity.

Little attention was paid to Vico until recent times. The prevailing view of history in the eighteenth and nineteenth centuries was the Progress theory, which was generally accepted by most thinkers in Western civilization until our own generation. The Progress view of history is basically a secularization of the Christian straight-line view. "Natural" laws of Progress replace Providence; all transcendent laws and agents are replaced by imminent laws and agents who realize the goal or purpose of history within historical time.

Progress is considered inevitable because knowledge is an accumulative matter: each generation knows everything known by previous generations, plus what it discovers itself and adds to the fund of human knowledge. In the eighteenth century it was felt that Western man could attain something approaching perfection if he rooted out tyranny and ignorance.

Nature has set no term to the perfection of human faculties [Condorcet wrote]; the perfectibility of man is truly indefinite: and the progress of this perfectibility, from now onwards independent of any power that might wish to halt it, has no other limit than the duration of the globe upon which nature has cast us. This progress will doubtless vary in speed, but it will never be reversed.

In the nineteenth century Progress had become as certain as the setting of the sun each evening.

This advancement [Spencer wrote in 1851] is due to the working of a universal law . . . and in virtue of that law it must continue until the state we call perfection is reached. . . . The advent of such a state is removed out of the region of probability into that of certainty. . . . As surely as the tree becomes bulky when it stands alone . . . as surely as a blacksmith's arm grows large . . . so surely must the things we call evil and immorality disappear; so surely must man become perfect.

Three different philosophies of history arose in the nineteenth and twentieth centuries to challenge the prevailing theory of Progress. The first of these was Hegel's interpretation of history as the self-realization of the Divine Idea in time. A philosophical idealist, Hegel looked on states—which are the intelligible units of history—as successive objective realizations of the Divine Idea on earth. The essence of history, he tells us, is the absolute spirit or Divine Idea realizing itself through its dialectical development. Put another way, history is the implicit becoming explicit, the abstract becoming concrete. Hegel discerns the big pattern of history as a movement from East to West through four stages of development, of which Germanic Europe is the final stage. In each stage, subjective freedom is realized by a greater number of pepole, from the one in the Oriental empires to the all in the German state. Hegel also formulates a smaller-scale pattern of development for all institutions, as well as for thought itself—the famous Hegelian dialectic whereby each state or institution evolves, through the inner necessity of its own nature, through the three stages of thesis, antithesis and synthesis. Hegel insists that this development is necessary, but he admits that external conditions modify the pattern considerably. The Hegelian dialectic, as applied to history, therefore does not turn out as rigid as it seems at first sight, and it is no less optimistic than the Progress theory about the realization of a perfect state in future time.

The second philosophy of history to challenge the Progress theory was the dialectical materialism of Marx and Engels. The basic factor in history, according to Marx and Engels, is the method of production dominant in a given society at any time. For the method of production determines class relations, and "the history of all hitherto existing society is the history of class struggles." The state, religion, literature, all social institutions, and the culture of a society are determined by the economic interests of the dominant class. The dialectic, as with Hegel, is the pattern whereby historical evolution takes place through the necessary conflict between the economic classes. Marx saw history as having taken place in four ages (primitive communism, ancient slavery, feudal society, bourgeois capitalism), each of which generated its own negation. These are progressive epochs moving toward the final state of industrial communism, the perfect society of the future, a secularized Kingdom of God in time. The pattern is deterministic; conflict is the means whereby progress is achieved, and the end of history, the perfect society, will inevitably be reached.

In 1917 Oswald Spengler published his *Decline of the West,* which challenged not only the Christian view of history but also every secularized version of the Christian view which held for progressive improvement of humanity's lot on earth. Spengler revived the pagan theory of cycles to show that each unit of history, a civilization, goes through the same birth-growth-decline-death cycle that the human organism undergoes. Spengler is thoroughly deterministic about the cycle, and his only advice to Westerners, whose civilization is supposed to be in the last stages of decline, is that they freely and courageously face their necessary fate—like the Roman soldier who stood at his post at Pompeii until the lava from Mt. Vesuvius destroyed him.

This survey has been sketched so that we may understand what had happened to Western man's philosophy of history by the time Toynbee planned his *Study* in 1927. The original Christian theory of history had God and man as the two free actors in the drama of history; geography economic institutions, and such were the conditioning factors or the setting for the drama. Moreover, the Christian theory of history admitted travail and evil in the world, but it was basically optimistic because it knew through faith that the purpose of history will be realized in good time, that God's will is done. This Christian view of history was secularized by denying Providence and excluding God from history (except for Hegel, of course, who makes God immanent within history), by substituting a perfect world state for the Kingdom of God as the goal of history, and by considering man a merely acquisitive, pleasure-seeking animal whose happiness consists in the elimination of pain and the surfeit of pleasure.

Within restricted Christian circles, of course, the older Christian view of history has been kept alive. But keeping alive the theory of an Augustine or a Bossuet is not enough today. Discoveries in biology, anthropology and the other sciences have added tremendously to our knowledge of man's past. Moreover, history has developed as a quasi-science rather than a literary genre within the last century. These developments seem to call for a reformulation of the Christian philosophy of history, which has been replaced by various secularized versions and by the revived pagan cyclical view. Any inquiry into history which incorporates all or most of Christianity's truths is therefore deserving of serious consideration, even if it prove wanting in some respects, for a step in the right direction from Marx and Spengler and the Progress enthusiasts should be welcomed by Christian historians.

A Study of History is the work of a specialist in Greek and Roman history, an important point for the reader to keep in mind as he goes through the ten volumes of this long work. Mr. Toynbee follows the political framework that is common to students of this period of history, but he is thoroughly at home with art, literature, philosophy, and other aspects of culture that enrich a merely political history and make it a treatment of a "civilization" instead of a political unit. There seems little doubt, from a close reading of these ten volumes, that Toynbee's creation follows the same sequence as Vico's: he arrived at his pattern from his study of the Graeco-Roman civilization, and then he studied another twenty civilizations to discover uniformity in them. The reader is beguiled by the author who continually describes his procedure and frequently reminds us that the study is empirical. But what is apparently an empirical study, or a comparative morphology of civilizations, turns out to be a search among these civilizations for evidence to support a pattern arrived at from a study of one of them, and the application of that theory *a priori* to the others.

Although Toynbee is a specialist on Graeco-Roman history, he does not write his *Study* as an historian. He writes rather as an eighteenth-century *philosophe*, the well-rounded man who is at home with modern science, with the literature of all ages and all cultures, who is intimately acquainted with the Bible (which is cited several thousand times), with classical literature, and with the classics of other cultures. Toynbee writes his *Study*, then, not as an historian or a philosopher or a theologian, but as a man—in the humanist sense—who lives in the Western Christian tradition but has read widely in the histories and the literatures of other cultures.

The work he has produced is therefore rich. But underneath it lies a skeletal pattern to which he faithfully adheres. It might be described briefly in this way: the intelligible unit of history is a civilization (through the first seven volumes), and the purpose of the inquiry is to discover the meaning of history through a comparative study of the world's civilizations. The first three volumes deal with the genesis and growth of various civilizations. In these volumes Toynbee arrives at suggestive "laws" of history, most important of which are the "laws" of challenge-and-response, and withdrawal-and-return. After examining the racialist and environmentalist explanations of the genesis of civilizations, Toynbee rejects them as explanations in physical-science terms of a problem that is really spiritual. He finds that the genesis of any civilization can best be explained in terms of response to a challenge presented by the physical or human environment. If the challenge is sufficiently strong, but not overwhelming, a society's response to it brings a civilization into being.

Civilizations grow, he tells us, by continuing to meet successfully the challenges which confront them, challenges which are internal rather than external, spiritual rather than material. In seeking to "prove" this "law" Toynbee examines a number of arrested civilizations (Polynesians,

Eskimos, and Nomads) to see why they failed to grow, and a number of fully developed civilizations to see how they grew. He finds that growth originates with creative individuals or creative minorities who generally pass their creative discoveries on to the masses through the process of "mimesis" or imitation. This proces takes place according to the law of withdrawal-and-return—the most strained of Toynbee's laws and the one which has evoked most derisive criticism from historians. The creative individual or minority is supposed to withdraw from society for personal enlightenment and then to return for the task of enlightening the rest of men. Toynbee uses the examples—among many others—of St. Paul, St. Benedict, Mohammed, Machiavelli, Italy, and England, and he suggests a similar role for contemporary Russia—which he could just as well have suggested for the United States withdrawing in isolation through the nineteenth century to return in the twentieth. This is the substance of the first three volumes.

The next three volumes, published as a unit in 1939, trace the pattern of breakdown and disintegration of civilizations. Here Toynbee enters on a more difficult field, but one of greater interest to our age because Western civilization is seen to be somewhere in the process of disintegration and we are anxious to know what Toynbee's prognosis—explicit or implicit—is for our future. He sums up breakdown under three main points: 1) a failure of creative power in the creative minority, which becomes a dominant rather than a creative group accepted by the rest of society; 2) a resulting withdrawal of allegiance and mimesis by the majority; 3) a consequent loss of social unity within the civilization.

Toynbee examines and rejects the deterministic explanations, such as Spengler's that the breakdown of a civilization is inevitable and is outside human control. He also rejects the explanation that it is due to aggression from outside. In each case he tries to show that decay of technical achievement and failure against outside aggressors are the result of breakdown that has already occurred rather than a cause of breakdown. This involves a readjustment of the time-table on the growth and decline of civilizations that has been challenged by most historians. To cite a single example: Toynbee sees the breakdown of Hellenic civilization beginning before the Roman Empire and analyzes the Antonine period as an "Indian Summer" rather than an apogee of that civilization. The Roman Empire is thus a "rally" in the rout-rally-rout-rally rhythm of disintegration. The section on breakdowns of civilizations involves Toynbee in some obvious difficulties as far as accepted interpretations of history are concerned, and his wealth of scholarship is not sufficient to convince most readers that his *Study* is not in need of basic revision in this section. But it does include several suggestive "laws" which become part of historical explanation for decades to come. The most important of these, in this writer's opinion, are three forms of the "nemesis of creativity": idolization of an ephemeral self, idolization of an ephemeral institution, and idolization of an ephemeral technique. The basic point in each case is that an institution or a technique that is once successful ensnares a people into using it when it becomes outmoded. Napoleon, for example, continued to rely on his original strategy and tactics even after they proved ineffective on the Iberian peninsula and on the Russian campaign. The bourgeoisie, again, were so successful with their production technique that they almost brought the roof of revolution down on their heads by failing to modify it—which, of course, they ultimately did with social legislation of various kinds and by working out a modified "partnership" relation with the proletariat.

Disintegration follows breakdown when the body social breaks into three fractions: the dominant minority, the internal proletariat, and the external proletariat. After discussing the characteristics and the role of each of these bodies, Toynbee devotes a 350-page chapter to a study of "schism in the soul" in disintegrating civilizations and in the behavior of individuals in such civilizatons. Alternative ways of behavior, feeling, and life are rather arbitarily set forth: abandon and self-control, truancy and martyrdom, the sense of drift and the sense of sin, the sense of promiscuity and the sense of unity, archaism and futurism, detachment and transfiguration. A considerable section is also devoted to the role of creative individuals who, in the disintegration stage, appear as saviors of one form or another (the military man, for example, the philosopher and the religious leader) to rescue the disintegrating society.

Two last points remain in the section on disintegration. One is that standardization is the mark of disintegration, as differentiation is a mark of growth. The second is that disintegration does not proceed by a straight-line process but rather by a series of "routs" and "rallies." In tracing out these routs and rallies Toynbee seems quite arbitrary, and most historians agree that he does considerable violence to history. At any rate, he concludes that the normal pattern is three-and-a-half beats: rout-rally-rout-rally-rout-rally-rout. The time of troubles which the West has been experiencing is an example of the "rout" beat, and the universal state is a "rally" beat.

Toynbee concludes his first six volumes by telling us that the genesis, growth, breakdown, and disintegration of civilizations is not a meaningless cycle, as with the pagans, but that it is creative process, the meaning of which can be understood only by an investigation of universal states, universal churches, and heroic ages in each disintegration; that is to be the subject of the remaining volumes. For these are something more than mere byproducts of social disintegration created by the dominant minority, the internal proletariat, and the external proletariat respectively. The "key to the meaning of the weaver's work" lies in understanding the destiny of the universal church in which every Higher Religion seeks to embody itself.

The first six volumes can therefore be summarized this way: First, as an inquiry into history, in the sense of Augustine's *City of God* or Vico's

New Science, Toynbee's *Study* has not yet solved the fundamental problem of the meaning of history. To borrow a simile Toynbee uses from time to time: at the end of the sixth volume he is like the mountain climber who has reached a ledge and can survey the slope and valley below, but he cannot see what lies above. Toynbee promises to continue the climb in the next installment with the hope of reaching the summit. Second, as a sociology of history or a comparative study of civilizations, Toynbee has formulated a number of laws that are deserving of serious consideration. They seem to provide for free will, for man's spiritual nature, and for a personal God Who is Creator, Final Cause, and Providential weaver of history. The author is careful to remind us throughout the study that there is nothing necessary in the working out of the laws he has discovered, that our civilization is not committed to the same process of disintegration as the twenty others he studies—but somehow the reader does not know whether these warnings against determinism are convincing. However, Toynbee does an effective job of dismissing such deterministic explanations for each phenomenon as that of Spengler and Marx, and he always insists that human history is a spiritual affair at bottom involving man's response to challenges confronting him.

The last four volumes of Toynbee's *Study of History* differ markedly from the first six. In them he treats universal states, universal churches, and heroic ages, as he announced he would, as well as the prospects of Western civilization, and the "inspirations of historians," all in the original prospectus drawn up in 1927. But the work appears, at first sight, to lose its unity and to become a number of book-length essays on loosely related subjects. The change in organization, however, is not as important as the change in point of view and in Toynbee's judgment on the role of various factors in history.

The first change is Toynbee's rejection of the notion that a civilization is an intelligible unit of history.

> We have found that a civilization can be studied intelligently in isolation so long as we are considering its genesis, its growth, or its breakdown . . .
>
> The history of a single civilization ceases to be intelligible in isolation when it enters its disintegration-phase; and this discovery that our initial working hypothesis is not valid for the study of all historical situations has been confirmed by our subsequent investigations into universal states, universal churches, and heroic ages; for each of these investigations has carried us beyond the limits, both in Space and Time, of the particular civilizations whose declines and falls have generated the institutions that we have been investigating.

The pattern changes also. Toynbee's first six volumes propose a pattern of history which, although not deterministic, is nevertheless cyclical rather than progressive. The twenty-one civilizations he treats are philosophically equivalent and apparently independent units of history. In the last four volumes Toynbee abandons this cyclical pattern in favor of a progressive pattern that introduces a qualitative principle to replace the philosophical equivalence between civilizations. The original pattern, which put all twenty-one civilizations side by side philosophically, is revised into these six stages:

1. The Primitive Societies, which are legion.
2. The Primary Civilizations, which are seven.
3. Eight Secondary Civilizations, which are derived from the primary ones.
4. The Higher Religions, which are apparently twelve.
5. Eight Tertiary Civilizations, of which Western Civilization is one.
6. The Secondary Higher Religions, which are eleven or so exotic religions, such as Kabirism, Baha'ism, Bedreddinism, the T'aip'ing, and Jodo Zen.

This chart is somewhat misleading in that Toynbee does not seem to expect any further development from the secondary higher religions. In the last four volumes he concludes that the purpose of a civilization is to give birth to a Higher Religion, and he concludes that the prospects of the future depend on four Higher Religions (Christianity, Mahayana Buddhism, Islamism, and Hinduism) cooperating harmoniously to concoct some sort of new religion acceptable to all, or, more properly, offering four variations of the worship of God. On the surface, Toynbee's *Study* seems to be approaching Augustine's *City of God*—without Toynbee committing himself unreservedly to a Christianity which he seems to understand and to appreciate as *one* of the ways in which God has revealed Himself to man. The Hellenism of the first six volumes wears thin in the last four as religion takes over. The first six volumes, indeed, can be considered profane history, and the last four sacred history. It is most important—and most difficult—to understand this fundamental change in the *Study* if one is to pass judgment on the work as a whole. Let us suggest, at the outset, that the change is due partly to the nature of the inquiry and partly to "challenging and transforming experiences" that the author underwent in the interval between the publication of the first six volumes and the writing of the last four.

A Study of History is an inquiry into the meaning of history, which if intelligently conducted by a man of good will, would inevitably transcend a comparative morphology of civilizations to arrive at religious history—for a search for the ultimate in history is bound by the nature of things to lead to God. That is why Toynbee qualifies earlier definitions as he proceeds, and rejects certain assumptions that were once helpful but are no longer valid. This has annoyed many reviewers who consider him inconsistent, but the procedure is quite legitimate and it should not annoy anyone who understands that the *Study* is an inquiry into history rather than history itself. This change makes additional demands on the reader who is already overburdened with Toynbee's vast erudition, but there is no way that he could have done otherwise and remain intellectually honest.

The fundamental change between the first six and last four volumes is also due to the world upheaval between 1939 and 1946, when Toynbee returned to work on the *Study*. It is understandable that the Second World War and the West's failure to win the peace could change a mature person's point of view considerably, but one cannot help wondering how seriously one should treat Toynbee's vision of millions of years of history if the vision is altered fundamentally by the events of a mere seven years. But the change was also due to Toynbee's personal affairs. "At the same time," he tells us after alluding to the Great War, "my inner world had been undergoing changes which, on the miniature scale of an individual life, were, for me, of proportionate magnitude." Toynbee seems to have wrestled with difficult religious and moral problems personally, which must be mentioned here because his *Study of History* becomes as personal in the last four volumes as an autobiography or a lyrical poem. During this interval Toynbee seems to have approached intellectually close to the Catholic Church and then to have withdrawn from it because of its hard exclusiveness, its jealous God, and its undeniable claim that it alone was founded by God. At any rate, Toynbee was divorced from his first wife, Rosalind Murray, who was herself a convert to the Catholic faith. These events undoubtedly influenced him to take the strange and almost inexplicable stand he takes toward Christianity in the last four volumes—to which we shall return later.

The last four volumes deal with the products of the three fractions of the body social during the period of disintegration: the universal state, created by the dominant minority; the universal religion created by the internal proletariat; and the pressures created by the external proletariat. Here Toynbee rightly says that the universal state is not an end in itself but that it serves as a means, primarily for the birth and progress of a universal religion. Here Toynbee leaves the reader—and the civilization under consideration—hanging in the air. For when a civilization has served its function of generating a new religion it is not going to wither quietly away. Moreover, a religion must take embodiment in a civilization. A religion cannot be indifferent to civilization, as Toynbee seems to think it should (for he condemns Christianity and Islamism for their exclusiveness), and Christians cannot subscribe to the theological equivalence of the Higher Religions that Toynbee substitutes in these volumes for the philosophic equivalence of civilization in the earlier volumes.

The greater part of Volume VIII is a study of the contacts between contemporary civilizations. Toynbee has been bitterly criticized by some reviewers for treating modern Western civilization too harshly in this section, but we are inclined to feel that many of these criticisms—as Douglas Jerrold's *The Lie About the West*—tend to prove Toynbee generally correct rather than to refute him. Contacts between civilizations of different times, *i.e.*, Renaissances, are treated in Volume IX. The rest of this volume and all of Volume X are a series of essays that contain some of the author's most valuable observations and some of his most annoying statements. These essays are "Law and Freedom in History," "The Prospects of the Western Civilization," and "The Inspirations of Historians."

The latter essay brings the original inquiry to an end with a section titled "The Quest for a Meaning Behind the Facts of History." In this essay Toynbee tells us:

> The meaning behind the facts of History towards which the poetry in the facts is leading us is a revelation of God and a hope of communion with Him . . . God is the source from which Man derives his significance as well as his consciousness and his life, and the purpose of God that is the reason for Man's existence is that the creature should re-enter into communion with its Creator.
>
> When the feeling for the poetry in the facts of History is thus transmuted into awe at the epiphany of God in History, the historian's inspiration is preparing him for an experience that has been described as 'the Beatific Vision' by souls to whom it has been vouchsafed. In this experience, God is seen face to face, and no longer through a glass darkly; and this means that the vision carries the Soul beyond the limits of History or of any other avenue of approach towards God through His revelation of His nature in His works. Yet, for every seeker after God, his own God-given glimpse of the marvels of the Created Universe—narrow-verged though his human horizon is bound to be—is a lamp unto his feet and a light unto his path; and the historian's path ascends from a feeling for the poetry in History through a sense of awe at God's action in History to a participation in Man's fellowship with Man which brings him to the threshold of the saint's communion with God.

What verdict is the reader to pass on this impressive work when he has finished the last essay? Can a simple verdict be passed? Toynbee tells us that for him history means "a vision—dim and partial, yet true to reality as far as it went—of God revealing Himself in action to souls that were sincerely seeking Him." The historian's is only one of many angles of vision from which one sees God partially, and its value lies in this:

> History's contribution is to give us a vision of God's creative activity on the move in a frame which, in our human experience of it, displays six dimensions. The historical angle of vision shows us the physical cosmos moving centrifugally in a four-dimensional frame of Space-Time; it shows us Life on our own planet moving evolutionarily in a five-dimensional frame of Life-Time-Space; and it shows us human souls, raised to a sixth dimension by the gift of the Spirit, moving, through a fateful exercise of their spiritual freedom, either towards their Creator or away from Him.

Toynbee confesses of himself that "the runner has not yet reached his goal." The average Christian historian would agree with Toynbee and tell him sympathetically that the goal cannot be reached in this life except by those who have been granted a mystical union with God for a moment in this life. The next question is whether Toynbee has provided us with as adequate a philosophy of history as man can formulate in this life. Again the average Christian historian must return a negative verdict. An adequate philosophy of history must take into consideration the beginning, the course, and the end of history, and it cannot be at variance with any provable facts of history. Toynbee fails (in our judgment) in his refusal to accept the traditional understanding of the uniqueness of Christian revelation. His judgment on past developments is thereby clouded and his vision of the future is out of focus.

A Study of History must be considered an impressive failure—an epic that failed, or an epic that almost succeeded, depending on how one wishes to describes this latest classic in the genre of "philosophies of history." For Toynbee's *Study* is a renewal of the great Christian tradition against the three "heretical" theories of history in the field today: the Progress theory, Marx's dialectical materialism, and Spengler's deterministic cycles of growth and decline. The fact that *A Study of History* is an impressive failure does not justify our dismissing it without further consideration, for there is great value in the *Study* and it can be used profitably by any Christian historian to enrich his knowledge of man's long life on earth and to obtain certain insights that had never occurred to him. Let us therefore see something more of these ten volumes.

(It should be remarked parenthetically that the author has promised an eleventh volume of maps and a gazatteer of place-names, and an even more potentially valuable volume of "reconsiderations" or *retractiones*, as Augustine used the word. This last volume will be written, the author tells us, after he has made a trip around the world this year (1956) and settled down to take a synoptic view of the criticisms that have been made of his *Study*. The work stands complete as it now is, then, except for the revisions that the author will make in his *retractiones*.)

Let us evaluate the worth and the usefulness of this *Study* under a number of observations:

1) *It is a large synthetic work.* Most historians condemn such a study *a priori* as attempting the impossible. The historian's task, they are convinced, is to work with minutiae carefully and "scientifically," to study a small section of the past with a microscope. This is good work, of course, but there is also need of the large synthetic work to give us an insight into the meaning of history and the pattern—if there be one—on which human history develops. In recent decades groups of mature historians have tried to give us the long view by producing cooperative works covering many centuries and many areas. But such works have generally been disappointing; the microscopic work of many specialists does not add up to a telescopic view simply by putting them under a single title. A study such as Toynbee's must be the work of a single author, a competent historian who can make critical use of the many microscopic studies of his fellows to arrive at sound generalizations. Such a man must be well read in the literatures of the world, understand the social and physical sciences, or at least the conclusions of scholars in these fields. He must be at once a humanist, a philosopher, and a theologian. The demands are heavy, and no single person can fully qualify in all respects. But Toynbee comes as close as anyone to having the knowledge

and the ability to produce the large synthetic work for which the times seem to cry out.

Toynbee's *Study* is extensive in two ways: vertically, he covers the entire time-scale of man's life on earth; horizontally, he takes into consideration every civilization about which mankind has knowledge today. It is good to have another twenty or twenty-two civilizations brought to Western man's attention, for there is no doubt that we of the Western tradition have developed a parochialism which is both intellectually bad and practically harmful. Toynbee sees the unity of mankind as, in a different way, Pope Pius XII has seen it and preached it since he issued his first encyclical. Toynbee's *Study* is the first "universal" history that can lay claim to universality. Although he has gone too far in this respect and at least through the first six volumes makes Western civilization merely one of twenty-one, nevertheless the over-all effect is good in that it calls attention to our parochialism and challenges it effectively. (We shall see later that in the last volumes he admits the possibility that Western Christian civilization has a unique significance in world history and that the earlier Christian philosophers of history were right in seeing other civilizations minister to the one in which God became man.)

2) *The style of the work makes heavy demands on any reader.* There are not likely a dozen men in the world qualified to read *A Study of History* without the aid of a good reference library. Toynbee's tremendous erudition has made his work too rich to digest easily. The man who can read a half-page Latin poem by Rutilius Namatianus, long quotations from Dante's early Italian, shorter verses from Goethe, and long passages of Greek verse, may still find himself troubled by casual references to the problem of Bedreddinism in the Ottoman Empire, the role of Ts'in She Hwang-ti, previously Cheng, king of Ts'in, the differences between Kabirism and Sikhism, or the "frustration of Evyenios Voulgharis." Much of the difficulty comes from the Western reader's parochialism, which Toynbee's *Study* does something to correct. At any rate, one who has carried the formidable task through will come to know something about such subjects as Siddhartha Gautama, the Hittite war bands, the Sikhs, the various forms of Islamism and Hinduism, and he will have at least a beginner's appreciation of non-Christian cultures.

When the nature of the work is remembered, Toynbee must be credited with having written well. Many historians have condemned him for not writing either journalese or in scientifically accurate phraseology. As for the first complaint, Toynbee writes as one educated on the classics, in long, complex setences—a style quite proper for the conveyance of complex thought. As for the second complaint, it reflects the inroads made on a literary form by natural science, for many historians would prefer to eliminate words in favor of signs that can have only one meaning and carry no connotation at all. Toynbee complains in a footnote that the resources of language are still inadequate for a work such as his, but that he has tried to employ traditional language whenever possible. His phrases are rich with connotations borrowed from myth and metaphor and from the classics of all tongues. At times, however, he seems unnecessarily stilted and desirous of parading his learning, especially in the use of foreign phrases when the English phraseology is obviously as good.

The most valid objection to Toynbee's phraseology is that he resorts to biological terminology in discussing states, empires, civilizations, and other societies. This is a typical passage to illustrate the danger involved:

> These divers endings of universal states bear concordant witness to the craving for life which these institutions are animated. So strong is this craving of theirs that they refuse to forego their claims to be brought into existence and to be allowed to live out their normal terms, and sometimes even refuse to pass out of existence after having duly realized their natural expectation of life.

Perhaps there is no other way to write about these institutions, but by using biological language in referring to them throughout ten long volumes Toynbee inadvertently creates the impression that they are supersized organisms with souls, bodies, and human faculties, that they breathe and live and die as we men do. Such is not his intention, for he labels such a view of the state or any other institution as blasphemous; nevertheless, his language breathes life into them. The reader must therefore keep on guard against the picture that this metaphorical language inches into his mind as he reads through one volume after another.

3) *The Study is marred by many inaccuracies of fact and obviously unsupportable interpretations.* No historian is competent to check Toynbee's accuracy in more than his own limited field of specialty. This author has found wrong dates and other misstatements of factual matter in the *Study*, but the cases are relatively few for so extensive a work. The factual data in Modern European history is reasonably accurate. Other historians have pointed out that inaccuracies abound in their respective fields, a professor of Greek history, for example, claiming that there are literally "thousands" of mistakes in his field of specialty, and a professor of Central European history saying there are "many" inaccuracies in the treatment of Central Europe.

This defect comes from Toynbee's frequently injudicious use of secondary sources. Anyone treating the history of mankind as a whole must use secondary sources for most of his work. But he should check these sources to see how they are accepted by the scholars in each field, and he should have strong reason to believe they are substantially without factual error if he is to take his "facts" from them—for obviously no one can check personally every "fact" in ten volumes delving into all of the world's history. Toynbee frequently uses second- or third-rate sources when first-rate treatments of the same subject are available. He is especially negligent in keeping up with the latest developments of scholarship in each field—an almost superhuman task, but one which his project imposes upon him.

The inaccuracies in the *Study* mar it, for each mistake is a defect detracting from the perfection of the finished work and scarring its beauty. Moreover, they make the reader feel that he cannot trust the author's accuracy in those areas which he must take on faith in Toynbee's accuracy. Nevertheless, the existence of a few hundred factual errors in these ten volumes—or even a few thousand—does not of itself invalidate *A Study of History*. The structure of the whole does not depend on factual data. They are rather the material with which the structure is dressed. An occasional defective brick mars the beauty of the building but it does not make it a defective structure.

4) *Toynbee's "laws of history" are deserving of serious consideration.* A study of these "laws" is a difficult and a delicate matter that is primarily the concern of the sociologist of history, for "law" is used here in the sense of regularity of pattern in the history of human affairs. Human affairs, of course, are not physical affairs of the human body, but man's action as man, as a rational, spiritual creature. Toynbee searches for such laws or regularities of history throughout his entire *Study*, but he faces the question directly in the book-length essay on "Law and Freedom in History" in the ninth volume. In this essay he attacks modern historians who, in reaction to Christians like Bossuet, have denied that there is any law of God discernible in history. He then proceeds 1) to show that there are laws or regularities to which human affairs are amenable without destruction of man's freedom; 2) that these laws are not inexorable, but are tendencies which work out within certain rather wide limits; 3) that sometimes human affairs prove recalcitrant to these laws, and they do not work at all; and 4) both the working and occasional non-working of these laws of history is explainable in terms of man's creative responses to challenges.

Finally, Toynbee moves from sociological considerations to a theology of history in seeking to reconcile law and freedom by means of the thesis "that Man does not live under one law only; he lives under two laws, and one of these two is a Law of God which is Freedom itself under another and more illuminating name." This is the "Law of Love."

The Law of Love is the one law that can never be served involuntarily. There is not, and cannot be, any externally applied coercion to obey this law, or any externally imposed punishment for disobeying it. The punishment for disobedience is inherent in the act of disobedience itself; for, in using his God-given freedom to reject the ideal in which the Law of Love consists, a human soul that has been created 'to glorify God and fully to enjoy Him for ever' is rejecting 'the true end of Man,' and is running, self-driven, into the disaster that overtakes Man through the inexorable working of the Law of Subconscious Human Nature, if he fails to respond to God's challenge to rise to the service of the Law of Love by using his God-given freedom to choose what is the will of God for him. Moreover, even this self-inflicted disaster is no final judgment and no irrevocable doom, since mundane disaster brings with it the opportunity of learning through suffering for any sinner who repents of his sin and is moved by his penitence to seek the aid of God's grace.

Such is Toynbee's statement on laws in history. Now let us see how he formulates various "laws," such as that of challenge-and-response or that of cycles of disintegration. We are given to believe, from his procedure, that he discovers these "laws" empirically. At the beginning of each step of the inquiry he proposes to proceed "along our customary empirical lines," or "have recourse to our well-tried empirical method of investigation." What Toynbee actually does is to discover his "law" by flashes of insight—some of them the work of genius, and some rather ludicrous—and then to "prove" them "empirically" by finding whatever evidence he can, sometimes by a considerable straining of the past. The reader is occasionally deceived by being offered two or three possible "laws" or explanations, but after two or three such experiences he knows at once which Toynbee has elected to accept. The procedure is legitimate in an inquiry, of course, because an inquiry is supposed to exhaust possible explanations and forestall possible objections. But the fact remains that Toynbee's laws are not arrived at empirically.

In respect to "laws" and patterns in history, Toynbee occupies a curious position among philosophers of history. The two general patterns, we have seen, are the pagan cyclical pattern and the Christian and Progress straight-line pattern of historical development. (There have been modifications of both basic patterns, of course, but the only basic modification before Toynbee is Vico's.) In the first six volumes Toynbee seems to accept the cyclical pattern, but with intimations that it is not simply cyclical. In the last four volumes he accepts a progress view of history without surrendering the cyclical pattern. The new pattern can perhaps best be described as spiral. This final position is summed up thus:

> The foregoing observations are all illustrations of our more general finding that cyclical movements in human history, like the physical revolutions of a cartwheel, have a way of forwarding, through their own monotonously repetitive circular motion, another movement with a longer rhythm which, by contrast, can be seen to be a cumulative progress in one direction, even if we cannot be equally sure that this course has ever been set for it deliberately in execution of a plan.

A smaller pattern Toynbee finds through all history is a two-beat rhythm, which replaces the usual straight-line view of most Western historians. This is found in all things: challenge-and-response, withdrawal-and-return, rout-and-rally, apparentation-and-affiliation, schism-and-palingenesia, all the way to the alternation between Yin and Yang. There is a certain validity to seeing human development in this fashion, as long as the pattern is not seen for more than it is worth. We are thirsty and we drink, we are hungry and we eat. But to draw up a thirst-drink or hunger-eat pattern tells us very little, and it suggests a regularity of eating and drinking which may not be true. It seems that Toynbee tends, in similar fashion, to get something too much of rhythmic regularity into history.

It is impossible to generalize about Toynbee's various "laws." Most critics ignore his qualifications that these laws do not work out inexorably and that a civilization is still free—to some extent—to follow a different course from that taken by other civilizations. He can be fairly criticized, this writer thinks, for setting cycles too arbitrarily and without sufficient evidence. It is easy to gather evidence for almost any kind of pattern or "law" that one wanst to hold, but it is not so easy to see these patterns and "laws" emerge from history and present themselves to one who does not already have them in mind. At any rate, Toynbee's "laws" are certainly a return to the Christian view of God and man when they are compared with the deterministic laws of the Progress historians, or with the alternatives proposed by Marx and Spengler.

5) *Toynbee's view of the prospects for Western civilization is an essential part of his Study.* This inquiry is needed, he tells us, because Western civilization is the only living civilization "that did not show indisputable signs of being already in disintegration," and because it has expanded to bring all other civilizations and primitive societies within its ambit. After taking the reader through the regular gamut of comparisons with other civilizations, Toynbee comes to the conclusion that it is still too early to make any sure prognosis about the future of the West, "because in A.D. 1952 the plot of this Occidental drama had not yet arrived at its denouement." He finds that in the West there are unmistakable signs of disintegration found in other disintegrating civilizations, such as idolization of the state, various forms of escapism, and standardization. But at the same time there are differences suggestive of hope, such as the persistent vitality of a Higher Religion, and the tendency of the social body to fight off hardening into castes.

Toynbee therefore concludes that it is an open question at this point whether Western civilizations will follow the course of disintegration relentlessly pursued by other civilizations or whether it will successfully meet the internal challenges which have developed within it. His grounds for optimism lie in the possibility that "a transfer of energy from Economics to Religion at the opening of a post-Modern Age might ultimately come to a self-stultified Western *Homo Economicus's* rescue." Toynbee argues that a civilization possesses only a certain amount of energy, and since the sixteenth century this energy has been transferred more and more to economic activity. By now, his argument continues, a great part of economic activity has become so mechanical that it no longer requires spiritual energy—much like a man, who had been taking thought to keep his heart and lungs working all the time, found that they worked automatically, and was now free to devote his thoughts to other things. If Western man devotes his thought and energy to seeking God, Toynbee concludes, Western civilization can have a different issue from the pattern of the other twenty civilizations. To put the matter more succinctly, Toynbee urges that the secularist drive of modern history be reversed into a religious movement.

This brings us to the last observation and the most difficult to make briefly.

6) *Toynbee's attitude toward religion, and particularly toward Christianity, is the crucial issue in adjudging the Study a failure or a success.* This subject is handled most directly in Volume VII in the unit on Universal Churches, but it remains the pivotal point around which Toynbee's whole philosophy of history crystallizes. At the outset let us observe that the *Study* is a religious work. It is a theological epic describing the creative work of God on earth and man's creative quest for Him in time. It is permeated by a driving hunger to find and to justify the Providence of God in history. Moreover, it is a Christian work in that it returns to Christian beliefs in refutation of the various mechanistic and deterministic statements on the meaning of history—but, as we shall see, it is a peculiar and unorthodox Christianity that Toynbee professes.

In the last four volumes, as we have already suggested, Higher Religions become an end in themselves to which civilizations minister. Toynbee examines and rejects the thesis of Rutilus, Celsus, Frazer, and Gibbon that the churches are cancers on the body social. He then examines the thesis that they are chrysalises, or the fixed points around which a new civilization forms as the old one disintegrates. Toynbee admits that churches have served this purpose—but he insists that a church is something more than a mere chrysalis. Churches take the place in Toynbee's final view of history as a species of higher society, ends in themselves, the promotion of which is the purpose of the universal state. Churches therefore push aside other societies in the divine plan, and in the future, if mankind meets the challenge, they will worship God in harmony in them.

Toynbee's attitude toward various religions is revealing. He is harsh, even unjust, in his treatment of Judaism. It is difficult to see how he can refuse to consider it one of the world's living Higher Religions, but he considers it instead a fossil of the Syriac civilization. Any religion, it seems to this writer, that commands the faith and devotion of men today is a living religion, no matter what its derivation might be. Toynbee finds Judaism abhorrent because its God is a jealous God and its adherents are intolerant of other religions. It is not a religion of Love but rather a religion of strict Justice. But Toynbee finds it especially abhorrent because it is a tribal religion identified with a people and taking the form of nationalism in modern times, which for Toynbee is the worst form of blasphemous idolatry.

The Catholic Church is treated understandingly and respectfully. Toynbee does not approve of the Church's claim to be the only true Church, nor does he like what he considers its harsh and intolerant treatment of heretics or dissenters throughout history He condemns it, therefore, for the Judaic elements which he believes are really foreign to it, for in his opinion Christ taught a message of Love which too few Catholics have taken to heart. (St. Francis Assisi, of course, is his ideal

Catholic.) The Catholic position on various controverted points is upheld faithfully by a certain Martin Wight who read the manuscript and commented on it in long passages put into the footnotes and the annexes of the *Study*. The only reason one can offer for the inclusion of Martin Wight's comments is that Toynbee respects the Catholic and orthodox Christian position sufficiently to present it when he diverges from it.

Toynbee's attitude toward Christ is equivocal and—to this writer—puzzling indeed. He compares Christ to the other saviors, but he considers Him unique among the god-saviors of civilizations. In one place he tells us:

> When we set out on this quest we found ourselves moving in the midst of a mighty host, but, as we have pressed forward, the marchers, company by company, have fallen out of the race. The first to fail were the swordsmen, the next the archaists and the futurists, until only gods were in the running. At the final ordeal of death, few, even of these would-be savior gods, have dared to put their title to the test. And now, as we stand and gaze, a single figure rises and straightway fills the whole horizon. There is the Savior.

And again:

> In the Person of Jesus Christ, Very God yet also Very Man, the divine society and the mundane society have a common member who in This World is born in the ranks of the proletariat and dies the death of a malefactor, while in the Other World He is King of God's Kingdom, a King who is God Himself.

These seem to be unequivocal assertions of Christ's divinity, and they are not explicitly made of Mohammed or Gautama or any other savior or founder of a religion. But Toynbee does not conclude from Christ's divinity that the religion which He founded has any objective claims over other religions. The prayer with which he concludes his *Study* "(London, June 15, 6:25 P.M., after looking once more, this afternoon, at Fra Angelico's picture of the Beatific Vision)" sets up a parallel among the four Higher Religions that at one reading seems reverent and at another blasphemous. It begins:

> *Christe, audi nos.*
> Christ Tammuz, Christ Adonis, Christ Osiris, Christ Balder, hear us, by whatever name we bless Thee for suffering death for our salvation.
> *Christe Jesu, exaudi nos.*
> Buddha Gautama, show us the path that will lead us out of our afflictions.

It is difficult and puzzling, then, to decide in what sense Toynbee accepts the divinity of Christ. He seems to want to be Christian—and something more, in a mystical Platonic sense of arriving at a Divine Idea of religion which denies no Higher Religion but transcends them all. Toynbee is convinced that modern Christianity is a "hybris," pure Christianity mixed with foreign elements, and he believes that original Christianity did not hold the exclusiveness nor the harshness as regards other religions that one finds in modern Christianity. Toynbee believes that he is a Christian in the original sense of the word.

We must conclude, then, that Toynbee is a different kind of Christian. He explains his position most clearly in answer to one of Martin Wight's comments. Mr. Wight is quoted as objecting to Toynbee's view that the four Higher Religions are "four variations on a single theme" and that they are not in discord but in harmony. Toynbee answers him by admitting that Wight's exposition of the relationship of Christianity to the other Higher Religions is a correct statement of the Christian position and goes to the heart of the matter. He therefore agrees with Wight that his own solution of the matter is not in traditional Christian terms, and that he considers any claim to the possession of a definitive revelation or a monopoly of Divine Light is both sinful and blasphemous. On these terms, Toynbee concludes, "I am not entitled to call myself a Christian."

Toynbee can best be qualified as a relativist in religion. He does not consider all religions of equal value by any means, but the four Higher Religions are four ways to the same Truth. They are the means God has adopted to evoke worship from four psychological types. This diversity shows the wisdom of God and is, indeed, "a hall-mark of God's creative work, [for] to enable human souls to receive the divine light is the purpose for which Religion exists, and it could not fulfil this purpose if it did not faithfully reflect the diversity of God's human worshippers." Why, then, one might ask, are there not as many religions as there are people? Are there four, and only four types of people? The answer apparently lies in one of Toynbee's flashes of insight. He finds the key in C. G. Jung's *Psychological Types,* wherein the latter describes four different psychological types into which human persons can be divided. Each of these is ministered to, Toynbee believes, by one of the Higher Religions.

This religious relativism leads Toynbee to the most lyrical but most untenable—both historically and theologically—conclusions. The real problem of the future, he is forced to conclude from his reasoning, is whether the four Higher Religions will unite mankind in a sort of spiritual quartet, or whether they will fail to respond to this challenge. There are grounds for hope, he assures us, that "the diversity of religions might resolve itself into a harmony in which the unity of Religion would be made manifest." But this, certainly, is impossible unless Christianity and Islamism change their very essence, for they are exclusive religions and they cannot readily become polytheistic or syncretistic. Toynbee is asking the Higher Religions to adopt the way of Mahayana Buddhism, which accepts the multiplicity and equality of the different roads to Spiritual Truth. And in his wishful conclusions that the four Higher Religions spread through the world to worship God in harmony, he personally seems to take the Buddhist step of departing from historical reality to take refuge in a dreamland of fantasy and metaphysical abstraction. History does not suggest that Toynbee's hoped-for eventuality shall come to pass, nor does theology suggest that it would be desirable. For while Toynbee is right in telling us that God is Love, he must not forget that He is also Truth. Although Toynbee does not see it this way, he is asking Christianity to abdicate its divinely appointed mission to make room for other religions, all of which have equally good claims. Thus, as we indicated earlier, his former philosophic equivalence of civilizations has been replaced by a theological equivalence of religions —and both are based upon a relativism that Toynbee accepts in order to transcend the parochialism of Western Christendom.

Let us summarize our appraisal of this massive and erudite work under the following points:

1) It is an effective repudiation of the mechanistic and deterministic theories of history which have occupied the field since the development of history as a "science." Moreover, it rescues history from the false position of being a social science in imitation of the physical sciences. It sees history rightly as a drama with God and Man the free actors, with the scenery and the drama created by God, and with Man free to play the role assigned to him—or, by refusing, to turn the drama into tragedy. It is a hopeful symptom of our age, we think, that such a work could be published by a respectable historian and could open with explosive force arguments that have been considered closed issues for some time. Toynbee does not have all the right answers, but he has asked the right questions—which "scientific" historians thought only children and primitives asked. And it is good to have right questions asked again.

2) Christians can be grateful to Toynbee for having reminded Westerners that our civilization has been corroded by secularism and that its healthy future depends first of all on a return to religion. Christopher Dawson has put this point well:

> However strongly we dissent from Dr. Toynbee's theological views, we can agree fully with him in his conclusions that the vital problem that confronts Western Civilization today is to prevent the modern secularized world empires from destroying one another, and humanity with them, and to bring back civilization to an awareness of its true function as a means to a higher end, as a bridge builder and a road maker, an interpreter and a peacemaker, preparing the way for spiritual unity.

3) As a corollary to the above conclusions, *A Study of History* is the first consequential step toward a Christian philosophy of history since Bossuet. It reintroduces Providence into history, treats man as a free spiritual being created by God to enjoy the Beatific Vision. Moreover, it is more truly a "universal" history than Bossuet's or any earlier Christian's "universal history," for it sees the unity of mankind in creation and in destiny, and it attempts to work out a theory of history to give all mankind a place. In this sense it is a richer and fuller inquiry into the meaning of history than any previous Christian study. One of its assets is that it transcends a

parochialism which historical circumstance thrust upon Western Christendom.

4) It contains many flashes of insight, legends, tales, short biographical sketches, essays on problems of history, and a tremendous store of information that the student of history and the teacher will find invaluable. Toynbee's *Study* can be rejected as an adequate theology of history and still be used as a storehouse of information with which one can increase his own knowledge, put the history of Christendom into something more like world focus, and broaden out Western man's parochialism.

5) As an inquiry into history, however, Toynbee arrives at an untenable theological position. In treating Christianity as a single religion he seems oblivious of the scandalous schisms and the vast theological chasms among the various Christian religions. Moreover, in advocating diversity of religion as necessary to serve the diversity of psychological types of humankind, Toynbee does not seem aware of the possibility of diversity within the one true religion. He praises Father Matteo Ricci for his adaptation of Catholic worship to Chinese customs, but he does not consider the possibility of a similar missionary effort in the future. To put it another way, in an even more literal sense than Belloc said "Europe is the Faith"—and Douglas Jerrold seems still to say—Toynbee implicitly accepts the identification of Christianity and Western culture —a point against which the Holy Father warned Catholics several times in 1955. Recent developments in the Catholic Church should have suggested to Toynbee that a true faith can serve all mankind and that there can be diversity within the unity of that faith. Failure of Catholics to understand that point is one of the unfortunate scandals in the history of the Church, but it is the failure of parochial-minded Catholics and not a failure of the Faith.

A Christian philosopher of history, it seems to this writer, can agree with much of Toynbee's inquiry. By accepting Christianity and Christian revelation as it has been traditionally expounded by the Church, however, he must part company with Toynbee on his theological relativism and on his resultant thin hope for the future. Toynbee is not convincing when he tries to exercise Christian optimism. A Christian philosopher of history, it seems to us, is likely to formulate some pattern whereby the one true religion can serve as the chrysalis of the civilization now aborning, as it once served as the chrysalis of our own Western civilization. Recent developments point in the direction of a unity of civilizations that seems in keeping with God's plan, insofar as we can apprehend it. And the universal religion in that civilization can well be the true religion. But the Christian philosopher of history hesitates to lay down the pattern of the future which is locked in God's mind and made known to us only fragmentarily and darkly through prophecy. "The wind breathes where it will," and "the kingdom of God comes unwatched by men's eyes."

A NOTE ON THE TYPE IN WHICH THIS BOOK IS SET

This book is set in Baskerville, a Linotype face, created from the original types used by John Baskerville, the eighteenth-century typefounder and printer. This type has long been considered one of the finest book types ever developed. The letters are wide and open and have a businesslike approach. The finer hairlines give exquisite delicacy. The heavier strokes give color and strength. The relation of the two in combination gives a brilliant effect and makes for easy reading. The book was composed, printed and bound by the Wickersham Printing Company of Lancaster, Pa. The typography and design are by Howard N. King.